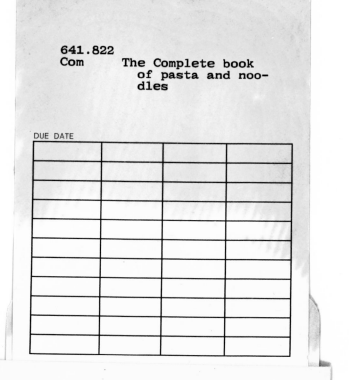

THE

COMPLETE

BOOK OF

PASTA

AND

NOODLES

Also by the Editors of *Cook's Illustrated*

The Cook's Illustrated Complete Book of Poultry

THE

COMPLETE

BOOK OF

PASTA

AND

NOODLES

By the Editors of *Cook's Illustrated*

PREFACE BY CHRISTOPHER KIMBALL

ILLUSTRATIONS BY JUDY LOVE

PHOTOGRAPHS BY DANIEL J. VAN ACKERE

Clarkson Potter/Publishers   New York

Copyright © 2000 by Boston Common Press, Inc.
Illustrations copyright © 2000 by Judy Love
Photographs copyright © 2000 by Daniel J. van Ackere

◆

All rights reserved. No part of this book may be reproduced
or transmitted in any form or by any means, electronic or mechanical,
including photocopying, recording, or by any information
storage and retrieval system, without permission in
writing from the publisher.

◆

Published by Clarkson Potter/Publishers,
New York, New York.
Member of the Crown Publishing Group.

Random House, Inc. New York, Toronto, London, Sydney, Auckland
www.randomhouse.com

CLARKSON N. POTTER is a trademark and POTTER
and colophon are registered trademarks of Random House, Inc.

◆

Printed in the United States of America

Design by JILL ARMUS

◆

Library of Congress Cataloging-in-Publication Data
The complete book of pasta and noodles / by the editors of *Cook's Illustrated*;
preface by Christopher Kimball; illustrations by Judy Love;
photography by Daniel J. van Ackere — 1st ed.
1. Cookery (Pasta)
TX809.M17 .C665   2000
641.8'22—dc21   99-040076

◆

ISBN 0-609-60064-8
10 9 8 7 6 5 4 3 2 1
First Edition

ACKNOWLEDGMENTS

ALL OF THE PROJECTS UNDERTAKEN BY *COOK'S ILLUSTRATED* ARE COLLECTIVE EFFORTS, THE COMBINED EXPERIENCE AND OPINIONS OF EDITORS, TEST COOKS, AND FOOD WRITERS, ALL JOINING IN THE SEARCH FOR THE BEST COOKING METHODS. *THE COOK'S ILLUSTRATED COMPLETE BOOK OF PASTA AND NOODLES* IS NO EXCEPTION.

The idea for a series of in-depth cookbooks on single subjects was initiated by our agents, Angela Miller and Coleen O'Shea. Our original executive editor, Mark Bittman, was very helpful in the planning stages of these books. The idea was further refined by our editor at Clarkson Potter, Roy Finamore, who has been demanding and thoughtful, in the best tradition of great book editors. Jack Bishop, *Cook's* Senior Writer, was then asked to spearhead the project, organizing and developing recipes as well as actually writing the book. Lauren Chattman was in charge of developing and testing many of the recipes in the pages that follow.

Dawn Yanagihara, Anne Yamanaka, Bridget Lancaster, and Kay Rentschler organized the step-by-step photography shoot that provided artwork for the illustrator. Photographer Daniel van Ackere captured hundreds of images on film during three long shoot days. Illustrator Judy Love turned these photos into the drawings you see throughout the book. The test kitchen team and Daniel van Ackere also produced the photographs of pasta types and shapes that appear in the first two chapters.

Many of the recipes and techniques in this book are based on work that has appeared in *Cook's Illustrated*. We would like to thank the following authors for their contributions: Pam Anderson, Jack Bishop, Mark Bittman, Stephana Bottom, John Clark, Julia della Croce, Eva Katz, Stephanie Lyness, Joni Miller, Gayle Pirie, Adam Ried, Franco Romagnoli, and Michele Scicolone.

CHRISTOPHER KIMBALL
Editor and Publisher

CONTENTS

/|\

PREFACE

/|\

AMERICANS HAVE ONLY RECENTLY WARMED TO THE TERM *PASTA*, HAVING MADE SPAGHETTI DINNERS, NOODLE CASSEROLES, AND MACARONI SALADS FOR GENERATIONS. PASTA IS A TERM THAT IS TRULY A BLANK CANVAS; HOME COOKS AND CHEFS CAN MAKE IT SIMPLE OR ELABORATE, PRACTICAL OR AS FOOLISH AS HIGH HEELS IN A HAY FIELD. HERE AT *COOK'S ILLUSTRATED* WE HAVE CHOSEN THE MORE PRACTICAL PATH, IGNORING THE MEDLEY OF MINIATURE RAVIOLIS OR THE DISH OF *TRICOLORE* SPAGHETTI WITH *FRUTTI DI MARE* IN FAVOR OF PASTA DISHES THAT CAN EASILY BE MADE AT HOME.

That being said, we recognize that America is home to the great revolution in pasta, from Asian noodles to sauces made from rabbit and rosemary, couscous to gnocchi and spätzle. We thought that it was time to turn our attention to this rich and varied category of dishes in order to make some sense of it from the perspective of the American home cook.

We started at the very beginning, with how to boil pasta. How much water and salt does one need for one pound of pasta? Should you add oil to the cooking water? How thoroughly should the pasta be drained? (Four quarts of water, one tablespoon of salt, never add oil, and the pasta should still be slightly wet.) We then moved on to testing pasta equipment (forget the expensive pasta machines) and taste-testing brands of pasta, finding that American spaghetti is as good as or better than the expensive imports. We determined the best brand and kind of tomatoes for making sauce (diced tomatoes packed in water, not puree, are best) and discovered that fresh supermarket pasta is not worth buying since it is flabby and tasteless.

Other tests revealed an unusual method

for making pesto (pound the leaves to release the oils, blanch the garlic, and toast the nuts), and we discovered the secret to making great pasta casseroles (use a shallow dish and high oven heat). We also set out to cover the whole range of pasta dishes, including thirteen different chapters on sauces, from simple cream sauces to those made with beans and lentils, seafood, poultry, and meat. We tested pasta soups, salads, and filled pasta dishes, as well as the basics of pasta making from fresh egg pasta to pasta without eggs.

Most of all, *The Cook's Illustrated Complete Book of Pasta and Noodles* is about the best methods for preparing pasta dishes. In the test kitchens of *Cook's Illustrated*, we assume we know nothing and then go into the kitchen to find the best methods of preparation. That may take five tests or fifty, or even one hundred, but through a series of blind tastings we make every effort to compare one ingredient or one cooking technique to another in the search for the best method. The result? A cookbook based on the combined experiences and tastes of many cooks with an eye to practical cooking so that every recipe can be prepared at home rather than in a restaurant.

Of course, cooking is a combination of objective technique and subjective taste and, over the years, we will surely make new discoveries and come across new pasta recipes. But *The Cook's Illustrated Complete Book of Pasta and Noodles* represents the best of our kitchen investigations, the state of the art of what we know today. We hope that you will enjoy the process of discovery as much as the recipes themselves.

All the best from everyone at *Cook's Illustrated*.

CHRISTOPHER KIMBALL
Editor and Publisher

THE
COMPLETE
BOOK OF
PASTA
AND
NOODLES

CHAPTER 1

A GUIDE TO

PASTA

AND NOODLES

/1\

THIS BOOK EXPLORES PASTA IN ALL THE VARIOUS

GUISES AMERICANS ARE LIKELY TO SEE IT, EVERYTHING

FROM FETTUCCINE TO SOBA NOODLES AND RAVIOLI

TO GNOCCHI. WE HAVE SPENT YEARS IN THE

TEST KITCHEN FIGURING OUT THE BEST WAYS TO

MAKE, COOK, AND SERVE EACH FORM OF PASTA. OUR

recommendations and favorite recipes are contained in the pages that follow.

What actually is pasta? It is flour—usually wheat flour if we are talking about pasta in this country or Europe, but rice flour or buckwheat flour in many parts of Asia—and water kneaded together to form a dough. Typically, this dough is rolled and then cut into a myriad of shapes—everything from thin strands to tubes.

A related category is dumplings, many of which are made with a similar dough. Some dumplings, such as gnocchi or spätzle, are simply bits of pastalike dough that are boiled and sauced. Other dumplings start with sheets of pasta that are used as wrappers. The wrappers are filled, sealed, and cooked to make ravioli and rice-paper spring rolls.

In this book, we have organized the recipes according to the type of pasta or noodles used. The first part of the book introduces pasta, both dried semolina pasta—the best-known in this country—and fresh pasta made with and without eggs. Rather than running all the possible recipes for dried semolina pasta in one chapter, we have divided the sauces based on the major ingredients—tomatoes, butter and cheese, meat, seafood, and so on.

The next part of the book covers fresh Italian pasta and the dishes that are usually made with this kind of pasta, such as lasagne, ravioli, and tortellini.

The third part of the book discusses miscellaneous Mediterranean pastas (couscous) and European dumplings (gnocchi and spätzle).

The fourth and final part of the book includes individual chapters on the major kinds of Asian noodles, including Chinese wheat noodles (both dried and fresh), Japanese wheat noodles (ramen, udon, and somen), rice noodles, cellophane noodles, and soba noodles.

Here's a brief overview of each kind of pasta covered in this book. Unless otherwise noted, all of these pastas and noodles are made from a wheat-based dough.

Dried Semolina Pasta

THIS COMMERCIAL PRODUCT was first widely produced in Italy during the nineteenth century. Dried semolina pasta is now manufactured around the globe. The ingredients could not be simpler: durum wheat flour and water. Durum wheat is a hard wheat variety that is especially high in protein, which makes it well suited to pasta making. When this wheat is ground into flour it may be called durum wheat flour or, more commonly, semolina. Golden semolina produces pasta with a springy texture and a modest amount of starch. Dried semolina pasta is admired for its versatility (it can be sauced with almost anything) and convenience (few pantry staples are more useful).

For day-to-day use, we prefer dried semolina pasta to fresh Italian egg pasta. Dried pasta has the texture to stand up to chunky sauces made with tomatoes, meat, fish, or vegetables. It is certainly the best choice with oil-based sauces.

DRIED SEMOLINA PASTA. From left to right, penne, linguine, and fusilli.

FINDING THE BEST EGG PASTA

CAN YOU ENJOY ALFREDO SAUCE ONLY IF YOU MAKE YOUR OWN PASTA? TO FIND OUT, WE TOSSED "FRESH" FETTUCCINE FROM THE SUPERMARKET REFRIGERATOR CASE, DRIED EGG FETTUCCINE, AND HOMEMADE FETTUCCINE WITH A BASIC CREAM SAUCE. THE "FRESH" FETTUCCINE FROM THE SUPERMARKET REFRIGERATOR CASE

cooked up gummy and flavorless and was rated far behind the other options. We had a hard time detecting any egg flavor. Most brands are made with whites, not whole eggs as is the custom, no doubt so they can be labeled "cholesterol-free." At $5 per pound, this pasta is widely overpriced.

Dried egg fettuccine cooked up springy yet tender in our test. It has a pleasant egg flavor that works well with the cream sauce. These noodles are more porous than dried pasta made without eggs so they do a better job of absorbing some of the sauce.

As we expected, homemade fettuccine was the clear favorite owing to its good egg flavor and ability to absorb some of the cream sauce.

Throughout the testing for this book, we purchased fresh pasta from various sources. We found that store-bought fettuccine can be quite good or quite horrible. The deciding factor is age. Pasta that sits in packages in the refrigerator case at your supermarket becomes gummy over time. It loses the suppleness and eggy flavor we demand from fresh pasta.

If the pasta has an expiration date that indicates weeks or months of possible shelf life, walk away. Go to a supermarket, gourmet store, or pasta shop that makes pasta fresh on a regular basis and discards the product after it is no longer fresh, no more than a couple of days. Of course, you can make your own or use dried pasta.

Fresh Egg Pasta (Italian)

FOR CENTURIES, ITALIANS have combined all-purpose flour and eggs to create soft, supple sheets of eggy pasta dough. These pasta sheets can be cut into long rectangles (to make lasagne), into thin strips (to make fettuccine), or into small squares or rounds and filled (to make ravioli or tortellini). As the name suggests, the best fresh pasta is truly fresh, made either at home or by a pasta store that prepares pasta daily, and served the same day. (For more details, see "Finding the Best Egg Pasta," page 3.)

We find that fresh egg pasta works best with cream- and butter-based sauces. The mild, eggy flavor of the pasta complements dairy sauces. In addition, fresh egg pasta does an excellent job of absorbing these liquidy sauces so that the cream or butter doesn't just pool at the bottom of the bowl, which can happen with dried pasta.

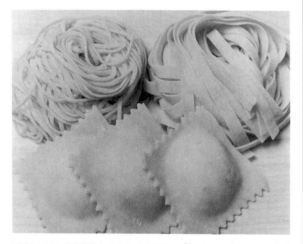

ITALIAN FRESH EGG PASTA. Clockwise from top left, taglierini, fettuccine, and ravioli.

Fresh Non-Egg Pasta (Italian)

IN SOME PARTS OF ITALY, especially in the rural South, fresh pasta is made with just flour and water. Semolina flour or whole wheat flour is generally used in combination with all-purpose flour to create a rugged, hearty pasta that can be cut and shaped by hand. While fresh egg pasta is often sauced with butter and cream, eggless fresh pasta responds best to hearty tomato- or oil-based sauces.

ITALIAN FRESH NON-EGG PASTA. From left to right, orecchiette and cavatelli.

Couscous

MANY COOKS THINK THAT couscous is a grain like barley or bulgur. In reality, it is a pasta made from semolina and water, just like spaghetti or linguine, which has been formed into tiny pellets. Couscous is precooked and dried so it does not need to be boiled. Simply add couscous to boiling water, cover, and wait about five minutes until the pasta is soft and fluffy. Couscous is commonly prepared in North Africa and parts of southern Italy. We serve couscous as a grain-like side dish, dress it with vinaigrette, and serve it at room temperature as a salad, or use it as a starch to accompany a juicy stew.

COUSCOUS. From left to right, Israeli couscous and regular couscous.

Gnocchi

THE TERM *GNOCCHI* IS used to describe a variety of Italian dumplings. Generally, gnocchi refers to small pieces of dough that are boiled, drained, and then sauced like pasta. The dough is most often made from potato and flour, although there are versions made with ricotta and flour. Unlike many other European dumplings, gnocchi should be light-textured, not heavy and dense.

Another type of gnocchi starts as a thick mixture of semolina, milk, butter, eggs, and Parmesan that is cooled and then cut into small rounds. These gnocchi are not sauced like boiled and sauced pasta, but are layered into a dish, sprinkled with butter and cheese, and baked.

GNOCCHI

Spätzle

THESE GERMAN DUMPLINGS ARE made from a flour, egg, and milk batter that is formed into thin, pastalike threads and boiled. Traditionally, the batter is poured through a graterlike device, called a spätzle machine, that breaks the batter into small bits. The name *spätzle* comes from the German word for "little sparrow" and is thought to refer to the round shape of the noodles, which look somewhat like the small worms birds eat. Once the dumplings have been boiled, they are drained and sauced, typically with butter, and served as a side dish.

SPATZLE (cooked)

Chinese Wheat Noodles

LONG CHINESE WHEAT NOODLES come in a variety of thicknesses and colors. They may be as thin as angel hair pasta or as thick and wide as fettuccine. These noodles are most commonly yellow, but white varieties also exist. Dried noodles are generally the same color and thickness as spaghetti and are typically boiled and then used in stir-fries. Fresh egg noodles, which are similar to Italian egg noodles, are usually bright yellow and are often round, not flat. They can be boiled and then stir-fried, browned to make noodle cakes, or chilled and used to make cold salads.

FRESH CHINESE WHEAT NOODLES. Clockwise from top left, flat noodles that are similar to fettuccine, thin noodles similar to spaghetti, and white noodles made without eggs.

DRIED CHINESE WHEAT NOODLES. From left, thin noodles that are similar to spaghetti, flat noodles similar to fettuccine, and white noodles made without eggs.

Udon

THESE LONG, WIDE NOODLES (similar to fettuccine in shape but white in color) come from Japan and are generally used in hearty soups. Their texture is slippery and starchy. The noodles are made with quite a bit of salt, so they are best boiled in unseasoned water. Although their texture and flavor are unique, Chinese wheat noodles (our first choice) or a fat dried semolina pasta, such as bucatini, may be used as a substitute.

UDON

Ramen

RAMEN ARE SIMILAR TO Chinese wheat noodles, but they originated in Japan. They may be fresh or dried, with eggs or without. In this country, we mostly see dried eggless ramen packaged in instant soup mixes. We like to use these golden noodles (which cook in just two minutes) and discard the instant soup packet in favor of homemade broth. When shopping for ramen, read labels carefully. Many contain a long list of additives to give them their characteristic yellow color. When possible, buy ramen with eggs and without artificial colors.

SOMEN

RAMEN

Somen

THE THIRD MAJOR TYPE of Japanese wheat noodle, somen are quite thin and delicate, akin to spaghettini in size but again white in color like udon. They may be used in brothy soups like ramen. In the summer, they also are served in ice water and accompanied by a dipping sauce. Thin Chinese wheat noodles, spaghettini, or even angel hair pasta may be used as a substitute.

Rice Noodles

IN SOUTHEAST ASIA AND southern regions of China, pasta is made from rice flour and water. White rice noodles may be thin and wiry; this product is often called rice vermicelli and is as thin as angel hair pasta. Thicker noodles (sometimes called rice sticks) may be similar to linguine or even fettuccine in size. Rice noodles may be used in stir-fries, salads, or soups. The same pasta dough is also shaped into sheer dried disks, called rice paper wrappers, that are used to make Vietnamese and Thai spring rolls.

RICE NOODLES. Top, thin rice noodles (sometimes called rice vermicelli). Bottom, thicker rice noodles.

Cellophane Noodles

CELLOPHANE NOODLES (or bean threads) look like rice noodles but are made from mung bean starch, not rice flour. (Mung beans are a legume; we generally see the sprouted form in our markets.) These dried noodles are white in the package but become transparent when cooked, hence the names cellophane or glass noodles. Cellophane noodles have almost no flavor of their own and are best used in highly seasoned cold salads and brothy soups. Their texture is quite chewy and starchy.

CELLOPHANE NOODLES

Soba Noodles

IN ADDITION TO WHEAT, the Japanese make noodles from buckwheat flour. These brown, earthy-tasting noodles are used in soups and salads. Soba noodles imported from Japan have a richer color and flavor than domestic versions. They cost more than American-made soba, but we find that the extra money is well spent.

SOBA NOODLES

DRIED
SEMOLINA
PASTA

/|\

DRIED PASTA IS NOTHING MORE THAN DURUM WHEAT

FLOUR (CALLED SEMOLINA IN ITALY) AND WATER.

DURUM WHEAT IS A HARD WHEAT VARIETY GROWN

IN TEMPERATE CLIMATES AROUND THE WORLD, IN-

CLUDING ITALY, THE UNITED STATES, AND CANADA.

When milled, it produces a high-protein flour, called durum wheat flour or semolina, that is used to make dried pasta. This flour is prized for its ability to make an elastic dough and springy, resilient noodles. These qualities, which are so appealing to commercial pasta manufacturers, make the flour poorly suited for home use. Lower-protein flours, such as all-purpose flour, are easier to knead into a dough with home equipment and produce pasta that is supple and delicate.

Once durum wheat flour arrives at a pasta factory, it is placed in huge commercial mixers with water and kneaded into a strong, elastic dough. After the dough has been kneaded, it is extruded through brass forms into one of fifty or more possible shapes. The extruded pasta is dried in an oven, packaged, and then shipped. Because most of the moisture has been removed from dried pasta, it is shelf-stable and should last for months if not years as long as it is kept in a dry, relatively cool place.

Semolina has more protein than other wheat flours and produces a pasta that is less starchy than dried pasta made from other wheat flours. In the past, some American companies used lower-protein wheat flours to make pasta. (This is no longer the case and all the major brands that we tested were deemed good. See "Tasting Dried Pasta" below for more details.) When pasta is made with lower-protein flour, the starch leaches into the cooking water (you can see the water become cloudy) and onto the surface of the noodles, which taste gummy and starchy. However, when pasta contains enough protein, those proteins are able to expand and encase the swelling starch molecules in the center of the noodle. The result is a firm pasta (the high protein content strengthens the structure of the noodle) that does not taste starchy.

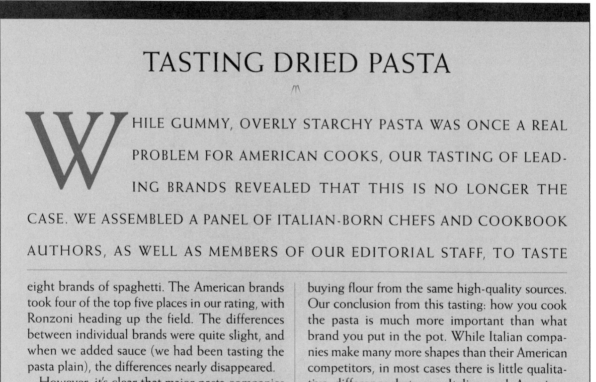

TASTING DRIED PASTA

WHILE GUMMY, OVERLY STARCHY PASTA WAS ONCE A REAL PROBLEM FOR AMERICAN COOKS, OUR TASTING OF LEADING BRANDS REVEALED THAT THIS IS NO LONGER THE CASE. WE ASSEMBLED A PANEL OF ITALIAN-BORN CHEFS AND COOKBOOK AUTHORS, AS WELL AS MEMBERS OF OUR EDITORIAL STAFF, TO TASTE

eight brands of spaghetti. The American brands took four of the top five places in our rating, with Ronzoni heading up the field. The differences between individual brands were quite slight, and when we added sauce (we had been tasting the pasta plain), the differences nearly disappeared.

However, it's clear that major pasta companies are all using the same high-tech equipment and buying flour from the same high-quality sources. Our conclusion from this tasting: how you cook the pasta is much more important than what brand you put in the pot. While Italian companies make many more shapes than their American competitors, in most cases there is little qualitative difference between Italian and American dried pasta.

While choosing a particular brand of pasta is not very important, cooking is another matter. Dried pasta is one of those things that is simple to cook but hard to cook exactly right. For perfect pasta, you must pay attention to everything from the water-to-pasta ratio to the time between draining and saucing.

Pasta needs to cook in a lot of boiling water—at least 4 quarts per pound of pasta—so that it has plenty of room to swell and rehydrate. When cooked in less water, we found that pasta has a tendency to stick together. If cooking pasta for a crowd, don't try to cook 2 pounds in one pot. It takes much too long for the water to come back to a boil once all that pasta has been added. It's better to cook each pound of pasta in its own pot.

As for the pot, we find that an 8-quart pot is best. When 4 quarts of water and 1 pound of pasta are placed in a smaller pot, you run the risk of boil-overs. (For this reason, we don't recommend so-called pasta pots that come with a strainer insert. These popular pots are too small to accommodate 4 quarts of water and 1 pound of pasta.) The material and weight of the pot are not terribly important since cooking pasta does not require sautéing or slow simmering. A cheap, lightweight pot is fine for cooking pasta.

Many cooks add oil to the cooking water. In our tests, we found that oil does lessen foaming and can reduce the chance of boil-overs. Unfortunately, oil in the water makes the pasta slick, which can prevent it from marrying properly with the sauce: the sauce literally slides off the pasta. We found most of the sauce at the bottom of the bowl when it was tossed with pasta cooked in oiled water.

After the water comes to a full rolling boil, add salt. We found that a full tablespoon of salt is required to flavor the pasta adequately. Most of this salt goes down the drain with the cooking water, but it is essential to season the pasta properly. Once the salt has been added, it's time to add the pasta to the pot. Stir several times to separate the pieces or strands.

The greatest danger for sticking occurs right after the pasta goes into the pot and before the water returns to a boil. If your stove is not very strong, you may want to throw the cover on the pot once the pasta goes into the pot to lessen the time necessary for

BEST DISH FOR PASTA

We like to serve pasta in wide soup bowls. The edge provides an easy place against which noodles can be twirled on a fork.

the water to return to a boil. Stay close to the stove so you can remove the lid when the water starts to boil. If you leave the lid on too long, the water will foam up and over the lid and onto your stove. As the pasta cooks, give it an occasional stir just to make sure the noodles are not sticking to the bottom of the pot or each other. However, we found that the agitation of the water should keep the pasta pieces from sticking together.

Once the pasta has cooked for several minutes, start tasting to see when it might be done. It's hard to be precise with the timing since each stove and brand and shape of pasta will be different. In general, thin-strand pasta like spaghetti will be done in seven or eight minutes. Thicker shapes, such as fusilli or far-falle, may require as much as twelve or thirteen minutes of cooking.

So how do you know when to drain the pasta? To some extent, personal taste comes into play here. The Italian term *al dente* literally means "to the tooth" and refers to pasta that is tender but not mushy, firm not hard, chewy not crunchy. However, this term means different things to different people. Even among Ital-

DRIED PASTA SHAPES

HERE ARE THE MOST COMMON DRIED PASTA SHAPES USED IN THIS BOOK. NOTE THAT THE SUFFIX *-INI* ADDED TO THE END OF ANY PASTA NAME SIGNIFIES A SMALLER OR THIN-NER VERSION, SUCH AS SPAGHETTINI. ALTERNATE NAMES ARE LISTED IN PARENTHESES.

BUCATINI (also called perciatelli)

CAPELLINI (also called angel hair)

CAVATELLI

DITALI

ELBOW MACARONI

FARFALLE (also called butterflies or bow ties)

FETTUCCINE

ORECCHIETTE

SHELLS

FUSILLI

ORZO

SPAGHETTI

LASAGNE

PENNE

VERMICELLI

LINGUINE

RIGATONI

ZITI

MATCHING PASTA SHAPES AND SAUCES

MANY PEOPLE ASK US HOW WE CHOOSE A PARTICULAR PASTA SHAPE FOR A PARTICULAR DISH. IN ITALY THERE IS A FINE ART TO MATCHING PASTA SHAPES AND SAUCES. SOME SNOBS WOULD RATHER FORGO A DISH THAN MAKE IT WITH SOMETHING OTHER THAN THE TRADITIONAL PASTA SHAPE. WE ARE MORE

loose in our matching of pasta shapes and sauces, following just one general rule—you should be able to eat the pasta and sauce easily in each mouthful. This means that the texture of the sauce should work with the pasta shape.

Long strands are best with smooth sauces or sauces with very small chunks. In general, wider long noodles, such as fettuccine, can more easily support slightly chunkier sauces than can very thin noodles like spaghetti.

Short tubular or molded pasta shapes do an excellent job of trapping chunkier sauces. Sauces with very large chunks are best with shells, riga-toni, or other large tubes. Sauces with small to medium chunks make more sense with fusilli or penne.

Italians have created dozens of shapes of dried pasta. (The most common shapes appear on pages 12–13.) No matter the shape of the pasta or the type of sauce, we adamantly believe that the pasta, not the sauce, should be the focal point. Italians eat pasta with sauce, not sauce "stretched" with some pasta, as is the case in many American restaurants. We heartily agree with the Italian philosophy, which is why it's so important to cook and handle pasta properly.

ians there is considerable controversy about how long pasta should be cooked. Regardless, pasta should never be so firm that it sticks to the back teeth when eaten. Nor should it be so tender that it falls apart.

Pasta continues to soften a bit owing to residual heat when drained and sauced, so drain pasta just *before* you think it is perfectly cooked. Our rule of thumb is simple: if we taste the pasta and think it will be perfectly done in thirty seconds, it is time to get the pot off the heat and the pasta into a colander.

Never shake pasta bone-dry in a colander. Instead, pour it into a colander, allowing the cooking water to flow out, and then jiggle the colander once or twice to remove excess liquid. The amount of cooking water that remains on the pasta helps spread the sauce. Slightly wet pasta will marry better with the sauce than absolutely dry pasta. In some recipes in this book, we suggest reserving some of the cooking water to moisten the pasta. This extra cooking water can help spread dry oil-based sauces.

Despite what your mother may have taught you, *never* rinse drained semolina pasta under running water. (Lasagna noodles, which must be shocked in ice water to prevent overcooking, are the one exception.) This only cools it down, makes it taste watery, and removes some of the starchy coating that helps the sauce adhere to the noodles.

Once the pasta has been drained, work quickly to sauce it so that the noodles don't stick together. If for some reason your sauce is not ready (we generally don't throw the pasta into the boiling water until the sauce is done or almost done), toss the pasta with a tablespoon or two of olive oil. Although this will make the pasta a tad greasy, at least the noodles won't stick together.

To keep pasta hot, we generally sauce it in the cooking pot or the pan used to make the sauce. After mixing the sauce and pasta, we immediately transfer it to individual soup dishes. If working with cream sauces (which cool down very quickly) or the temperature in your kitchen is cool, you may want to place the dishes in a 200-degree oven for five minutes. Just make sure to wear oven mitts when handling the dishes and warn everyone at the table about the hot plates.

We find that a wide soup dish (see page 11) is the best vessel for serving pasta. The edge provides a surface against which the noodles, especially long strands, can be twirled on a fork.

FRESH EGG
PASTA

/I\

FOR CERTAIN DISHES, ONLY FRESH PASTA WILL DO.

YOU CAN'T MAKE RAVIOLI OR TORTELLINI WITHOUT

FRESH PASTA (FOR MORE INFORMATION ON THESE

DISHES, SEE CHAPTER 23). ALSO, CREAM SAUCES ARE

MUCH BETTER WITH FLAVORFUL, ABSORBENT FRESH

PASTA. LASAGNE (SEE CHAPTER 21), TOO, IS ALWAYS

BETTER WITH FRESH PASTA. ◆ HOMEMADE PASTA IS

much better than anything you can buy, and making it should be a simple project. Many recipes call for just two ingredients (eggs and pasta) and no basic pasta recipe that we looked at had more than four. (Salt and oil are added by some cooks.) However, pasta dough is not very forgiving. Too dry and the dough won't roll out easily. Too wet and the dough is a sticky mess. The difference between a dough that is too wet and one that is too dry can be just a tablespoon or two of liquid.

We wanted to develop a foolproof recipe for basic fresh egg pasta. We wanted to figure out the proper ratio of eggs to flour as well as the role of salt and olive oil in the dough. Most recipes start with all-purpose flour, but we figured it was worth testing various kinds of flour. Perhaps most important, we wanted to devise a kneading method that was quick and easy.

Before beginning to develop our pasta dough recipe, we figured we should settle on a basic technique. Pasta dough can be made in one of three ways. Traditionally, the dough is made by hand on a clean counter. The flour is formed into a ring, the eggs are cracked into the center, and the flour is slowly worked into the eggs with a fork. When the eggs are no longer runny, you must start kneading by hand. The whole process takes at least twenty minutes and requires a lot of hand strength.

Another option is an electric pasta maker (see "Are Electric Pasta Machines Worth the Money?" on page 20) that kneads the dough and cuts it into various shapes. Although these machines have some limited appeal, they are quite expensive. We find that a food processor makes pasta dough much more quickly than the old-fashioned hand method. Since most cooks already own a food processor, we recommend it for making fresh pasta dough.

Most recipes for fresh egg pasta start with three eggs and then add various amounts of flour. A three-egg dough will produce about 1 pound of fresh pasta, so this seemed like a good place to start our working recipe. We saw recipes that called for as little as ½ cup of flour per egg. Other recipes called for as much as ¾ cup of flour per egg. After several tests, we settled on ⅔ cup of flour per egg, or an even 2 cups of all-purpose flour for three eggs.

In most tests, this ratio produced perfect pasta

dough, without adjustments. However, on a few occasions the dough was a bit dry. This seemed to happen most often on dry days, but it also could be that slight variations in egg size were throwing things off. It was easy enough to add a little water to bring the dough together. Thankfully, the dough was almost never too wet, which is a good thing. It's much harder to add flour to a sticky dough than it is to add a little bit of water to a dry, crumbly dough.

If after thirty seconds of processing the dough does not come together, start adding water ½ teaspoon at a time until you can get the dough into a rough ball. Once the dough comes together, we found it beneficial to knead the dough by hand for a minute or two. The motor on our food processor started to labor before the dough was really smooth enough. Taking the dough out as soon as it came together prevented our food processor from overheating.

At this point, we had a recipe and method for making pasta dough that we liked quite a lot. It seemed time to start testing additional flavorings. We found no benefit from adding salt to the dough. If the pasta is cooked in salted water, it will taste well seasoned. Adding olive oil makes fresh pasta a bit slick and the olive oil flavor seems out of place, especially since egg pasta is often sauced with butter.

We had been using unbleached all-purpose flour in our tests. We then tested several brands of bleached all-purpose flour and found only minimal differences in the way each flour absorbed the egg. We could not detect any significant differences in flavor, either.

However, using low-protein cake flour or high-protein bread flour was a disaster when we used it to make pasta dough. Bread flour produced a very tough dough that was hard to handle. Pasta dough should be supple and elastic, not stiff and difficult to stretch. At the opposite end of the spectrum, pasta made with cake flour was too soft and crumbly; the dough did not have enough structure. Cake flour also has a sour chemical flavor, which is obscured by sugar and butter in cake but comes through loud and clear in pasta.

With our dough made, it was time to test rolling techniques. Many Italian sources tout the superiority of hand-rolled pasta. However, every time we rolled pasta dough with a pin, it was very thick. Although

DRIED VERSUS FRESH PASTA

D RIED PASTA IS NOT A SUBSTITUTE FOR FRESH. EACH HAS DIFFERENT PROPERTIES AND QUALITIES. DRIED PASTA COOKS UP SPRINGY AND AL DENTE. ITS FIRM TEXTURE STANDS UP TO A WIDE ARRAY OF SAUCES. ITS NEUTRAL WHEATY FLAVOR ALSO WORKS WITH ALMOST EVERY INGREDIENT IMAGINABLE.

Fresh egg pasta is delicate. The texture is soft but not mushy. The wheat is complemented by a strong egg flavor. Fresh pasta tends to absorb sauces. (In contrast, sauces cling to dried pasta.) For all these reasons, fresh pasta is especially good with dairy-based sauces. The flavors of the pasta and sauce are in harmony. Also, cream sauces have more liquid available, some of which can be absorbed by the pasta.

Dried egg noodles are very different from fresh fettuccine. Likewise, dried lasagna noodles are not the same as fresh. Although there are recipes for which either fresh or dried pasta is appropriate, in most cases we call for one or the other throughout this book.

These recipes each make about 1 pound of fresh pasta. When cut as fettuccine, the recipes will serve four; when turned into a filled pasta, they are enough for six to eight.

---

thick fettuccine is not an abomination, pasta for lasagne and filled pastas (which have double-thick edges) must be thin or the dishes will suffer. Perhaps after years of practice we could roll pasta thin enough, but for now we prefer hand-cranked manual pasta machines.

Two hand-cranked pasta machines are widely available in this country, one made by Atlas, the other by Imperia. The design for both models is similar. The exterior is stainless steel and the machine clamps onto the edge of the counter. The machines have a set of rollers as well as cutting blades. The width between the rollers is controlled by an adjustable dial. To turn the dough into sheets of pasta, simply lop off a chunk and start rolling it through the machine. To get the

pasta thinner, turn the dial that narrows the space between the rollers.

Once all the pasta has been rolled out, insert one of the two cutters. One cutter turns sheets of pasta into fettuccine, the other cranks out spaghetti. We tested both the Atlas and Imperia with a variety of pasta doughs and shapes. We liked both machines quite a lot. Since they can be hard to find (cookware stores stock one or the other, but not both), we recommend that you pick up whichever model you can find. They both cost about $40 and will last a lifetime as long as you clean them properly. Don't wash any parts, especially the cutters, which can rust. Just let any pieces of dough dry thoroughly and then use a clean pastry brush to sweep them off the machine.

ARE ELECTRIC PASTA MACHINES WORTH THE MONEY?

THE APPEAL OF AN ELECTRIC PASTA MACHINE IS CLEAR. LIKE BREAD MACHINES, THESE HIGH-TECH WONDERS TAKE RAW INGREDIENTS AND TURN THEM INTO A FINISHED PRODUCT— IN THIS CASE, RIBBONS OF FETTUCCINE OR THIN STRANDS OF SPAGHETTI. THE DESIGN IS STRAIGHTFORWARD. DUMP FLOUR AND

eggs into the mixing compartment. When the dough seems sufficiently kneaded, you must flip a switch to extrude the dough through a die. Different dies make different shapes, everything from lasagne to ziti.

The attraction is clear, but the performance of the nine models we tested fell far short of our expectations. One machine was decent (the Italian-made Simac), but the rest were not worth the bother. Even the Simac had its problems (wider fettuccine noodles were fine, but thin spaghetti tended to stick together as it was extruded) and we preferred our trusty hand-crank pasta maker. Since the Simac costs more than $200 (even on sale), we have a hard time recommending it.

If you decide you must own a pasta machine, here are a few things to keep in mind. We found that brass dies are essential. Plastic dies turn out pasta that is way too thick. Only the Simac and a model made by Cuisinart come with brass dies.

Even with a brass die, don't expect to make tubular pasta like ziti. The Simac model we tested made great fettuccine and spaghetti, but ziti and rigatoni were a disaster. You must stand at the machine and cut off pieces of ziti or rigatoni by hand. Invariably the pressure from the knife causes the ends of the tubes to close up. You can pry apart the ends with a toothpick, but this process is incredibly tedious.

One final word of caution. Electric pasta machines require the active participation of the cook. Unlike bread machines, which judge when the dough has been kneaded enough or when it has risen sufficiently and is ready to be baked, the cook must decide when the pasta dough is properly kneaded and ready to be extruded. These machines are not for dummies. If you are willing to learn how these machines work, you can turn out some great pasta. But we think the time is better spent learning how to knead dough in a food processor and then roll it out with a manual pasta machine. And as for the money, we don't have to tell you what an extra $150 is worth.

Fresh Egg Pasta

MAKES ABOUT 1 POUND; ENOUGH
FETTUCCINE FOR 4 TO 6;
ENOUGH FILLED PASTA FOR 6 TO 8

LTHOUGH THE FOOD processor does most of the work, you must finish kneading the dough by hand. Keep pressing and folding the dough until it is extremely smooth (see illustration 4, page 23). See illustrations 1–5 on page 24 for more information about rolling out the dough.

2 cups all-purpose flour
3 large eggs, beaten

1. Pulse the flour in the work bowl of a food processor fitted with the metal blade to evenly distribute and aerate. Add the eggs; process until the dough forms a rough ball, about 30 seconds. (If the dough resembles small pebbles, add water, ½ teaspoon at a time; if the dough sticks to the side of the work bowl, add flour, 1 tablespoon at a time, and process until the dough forms a rough ball. See illustrations 1–3, page 23, for tips on judging moisture level in the dough.)

2. Turn the dough ball and small bits out onto a dry work surface; knead until the dough is smooth, 1 to 2 minutes. Cover with plastic wrap and set aside for at least 15 minutes and up to 2 hours to relax.

3. Cut about one-sixth of the dough from the ball and flatten into a disk; rewrap the remaining dough. Run the dough through the widest setting of a manual pasta machine. Bring the ends of the dough toward the middle and press down to seal. Run the dough, open side first, through the widest setting again. Fold, seal, and roll again. Without folding, run the pasta through the widest setting about 2 more times, until the dough is smooth. If at any point the dough is sticky, lightly dust with flour. Continue to run the dough through the machine; narrow the setting each time, until you use the last setting on the machine, and the outline of your hand is visible through the dough sheet. Lay the sheet of pasta on a clean kitchen towel and cover it with a damp cloth to keep the pasta from drying out. Repeat the process with the remaining pieces of dough.

4. Leave the pasta sheets as is for use in lasagne or filled pastas. Or, cut the pasta sheets, following the appropriate steps on page 29, to make noodles.

Spinach Pasta

FRESH SPINACH DOES NOT ADD MUCH FLAVOR TO PASTA DOUGH AND IT'S MUCH MORE CONVENIENT TO USE FROZEN. BUT EVEN FROZEN CHOPPED SPINACH MUST BE CHOPPED FURTHER TO BE DISTRIBUTED EVENLY THROUGH THE PASTA DOUGH. MAKE SURE THE COOKED SPINACH IS SQUEEZED AS DRY AS POSSIBLE BEFORE IT IS ADDED TO THE FLOUR. MAKES ABOUT 1 POUND.

> 1/2 10-ounce package frozen chopped
>   spinach, thawed
> 3 large eggs, beaten
> 2 1/2 cups all-purpose flour

1. Bring 1 cup of water to a boil in a small saucepan. Add the spinach and cook until tender, 2 to 3 minutes. Drain in a colander, pressing on it with the back of a large spoon to remove as much water from it as possible. Place the spinach on a cutting board and finely chop. Press the spinach with your hands, tilting the board over the sink to drain off any remaining liquid (see illustration). Beat the spinach with the eggs and set aside.

2. Pulse the flour in the work bowl of a food processor fitted with the metal blade to evenly distribute and aerate. Add the spinach and eggs; process until the dough forms a rough ball, about 30 seconds. (If the dough resembles small pebbles, add water, 1/2 teaspoon at a time; if the dough sticks to the side of the work bowl, add flour, 1 tablespoon at a time, and process until the dough forms a rough ball.)

3. Turn the dough ball and small bits out onto a dry work surface; knead until the dough is smooth, 1 to 2 minutes. Cover with plastic wrap and set aside for at least 15 minutes and up to 2 hours to relax.

4. Follow the method on page 24 to roll the pasta.

STEP-BY-STEP

SQUEEZING SPINACH DRY

Press the cooked, chopped spinach with your hands, tilting the board over a large bowl or the sink to drain off any remaining liquid. It is imperative that the spinach be as dry as possible.

Fresh Herb Pasta

FINELY MINCED HERBS ADD FRESH GREEN COLOR AS WELL AS SUBTLE FLAVOR TO EGG PASTA. FRESH HERB PASTA CAN BE USED INTERCHANGEABLY WITH SPINACH PASTA IN RECIPES. MATCH THE FLAVOR OF YOUR HERBS WITH THE FLAVORS OF YOUR SAUCE. BASIL AND PARSLEY PASTA WORK WELL WITH MOST SIMPLE TOMATO SAUCES. USE CILANTRO FETTUCCINE IN PLACE OF THE FUSILLI IN RAW TOMATO SAUCE AND AVOCADO (PAGE 107). SAGE PASTA COMPLEMENTS SAUCES WITH HAM AND MUSHROOMS. MAKES ABOUT 1 POUND.

> 2 cups all-purpose flour
> 3 large eggs, beaten
> 2 tablespoons minced fresh parsley, basil,
>   mint, cilantro, sage, thyme, oregano, or
>   marjoram

MAKING PASTA DOUGH IN A FOOD PROCESSOR

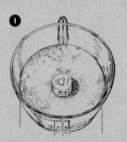

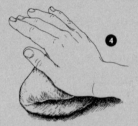

1. If after 30 seconds the dough resembles small pebbles, it is too dry. With the motor running, add ½ teaspoon water. Repeat one more time if necessary.

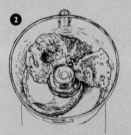

2. If the dough sticks to the sides of the work bowl, it is too wet. Add 1 tablespoon flour at a time until the dough is no longer tacky.

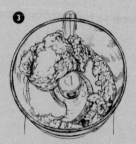

3. Dough that is of proper moistness will come together in one large mass. If there are some small bits that remain unincorporated, turn the contents of the work bowl onto a board and knead together.

4. Press the dough against the counter with the heel of your palm to flatten it. Fold the dough over onto itself. You won't be able to fold it entirely in half, but you should be able to get one edge of the dough into the center. Keep pressing and folding the dough until it is extremely smooth.

1. Pulse the flour in the work bowl of a food processor fitted with the metal blade to evenly distribute and aerate. Add the eggs and herbs; process until the dough forms a rough ball, about 30 seconds. (If the dough resembles small pebbles, add water, ½ teaspoon at a time; if the dough sticks to the side of the work bowl, add flour, 1 tablespoon at a time, and process until the dough forms a rough ball.)

2. Turn the dough ball and small bits out onto a dry work surface; knead until the dough is smooth, 1 to 2 minutes. Cover with plastic wrap and set aside for at least 15 minutes and up to 2 hours to relax.

3. Follow the method on page 24 to roll the pasta.

ROLLING OUT PASTA DOUGH

1. Cut about one-sixth of the dough from the ball and flatten into a disk. Run the disk through the rollers set to the widest position.

2. Bring the ends of the dough toward the middle and press down to seal.

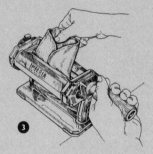

3. Feed the open side of the pasta through the rollers. Repeat steps 1 and 2.

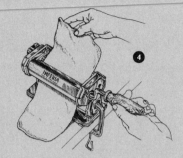

4. Without folding again, run the pasta through the widest setting twice or until the dough is smooth. If the dough is at all sticky, lightly dust it with flour.

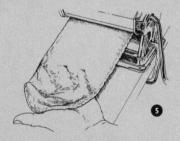

5. Begin to roll the pasta thinner by putting it through the machine repeatedly, narrowing the setting each time. Roll until the dough is thin and satiny (setting 6 on the Imperia pasta machine and setting 6 or 7 on the Atlas machine), dusting with flour if sticky. You should be able to see the outline of your hand through the pasta. Lay the sheet of pasta on a clean kitchen towel and cover it with a damp cloth to keep the pasta from drying out. Repeat with other pieces of dough.

Buckwheat Pasta

BUCKWHEAT PASTA, A SPECIALTY OF THE LOMBARDY REGION OF ITALY, IS TRADITIONALLY SERVED WITH HEARTY SAUCES MADE WITH LEAFY GREENS, CABBAGE, AND POTATOES (SEE BUCKWHEAT PASTA WITH SPINACH, POTATO, AND TALEGGIO, PAGE 338). IT HAS A WHOLE-SOME, NUTTY FLAVOR AND CHEWY TEXTURE. BUCK-WHEAT FLOUR IS NOT ACTUALLY MADE FROM GRAIN; IT IS MADE FROM THE SEED OF A PLANT IN THE RHU-BARB FAMILY. BECAUSE IT CONTAINS NO GLUTEN, IT MUST BE COMBINED WITH A LOT OF ALL-PURPOSE FLOUR TO MAKE PASTA. BUCKWHEAT FLOUR IS AVAIL-ABLE THROUGH BAKING CATALOGS AND AT NATURAL FOODS STORES. **MAKES ABOUT 1 POUND.**

> 1 ½ cups all-purpose flour
> ½ cup buckwheat flour
> 3 large eggs, beaten

1. Pulse the flours in the work bowl of a food proces-sor fitted with the metal blade to evenly distribute and aerate. Add the eggs; process until the dough forms a rough ball, about 30 seconds. (If the dough resembles small pebbles, add water, ½ teaspoon at a time; if the dough sticks to the side of the work bowl, add flour, 1 tablespoon at a time, and process until the dough forms a rough ball.)

2. Turn the dough ball and small bits out onto a dry work surface; knead until the dough is smooth, 1 to 2 minutes. Cover with plastic wrap and set aside for at least 15 minutes and up to 2 hours to relax.

3. Follow the method opposite to roll the pasta.

Whole Wheat Pasta

IN OUR TESTING, WE FOUND IT POSSIBLE TO REPLACE MOST BUT NOT ALL OF THE ALL-PURPOSE FLOUR WITH WHOLE WHEAT FLOUR. A LITTLE WHITE FLOUR IS NEEDED TO KEEP THE DOUGH SUPPLE. WHOLE WHEAT PASTA DOUGH TAKES A MINUTE OR TWO LONGER TO KNEAD TOGETHER. SAVE DELICATE CREAM, BUTTER, AND CHEESE SAUCES FOR EGG PASTA MADE WITH WHITE FLOUR. WHOLE WHEAT FLOUR PRODUCES A HEARTY PASTA SUITABLE FOR CHUNKY MEAT AND VEGETABLE SAUCES MADE WITH OLIVE OIL RATHER THAN BUTTER. TRY FRESH WHOLE WHEAT FETTUCCINE IN PLACE OF PENNE IN WHOLE WHEAT PENNE WITH CAULIFLOWER AND PROSCIUTTO (PAGE 147) OR USE IN FETTUCCINE WITH DUCK AND OLIVES (PAGE 227). **MAKES ABOUT 1 POUND.**

> 1 ½ cups whole wheat flour
> ½ cup all-purpose flour
> 3 large eggs, beaten

1. Pulse the flours in the work bowl of a food proces-sor fitted with the metal blade to evenly distribute and aerate. Add the eggs; process until the dough forms a rough ball, about 30 seconds. (If the dough resembles small pebbles, add water, ½ teaspoon at a time; if the dough sticks to the side of the work bowl, add flour, 1 tablespoon at a time, and process until the dough forms a rough ball.)

2. Turn the dough ball and small bits out onto a dry work surface; knead until the dough is smooth, 3 to 4 minutes. Cover with plastic wrap and set aside for at least 15 minutes and up to 2 hours to relax.

3. Follow the method opposite to roll the pasta.

Corn Pasta

CORNMEAL GIVES THIS FRESH PASTA A MILD CORN FLAVOR AND BEAUTIFUL PALE YELLOW COLOR. USE CORN PASTA WITH ANY SAUCE YOU MIGHT USE WITH POLENTA. HEARTY SAUCES WITH GREENS AND SAUSAGES WORK IN THE WINTER; IN THE SUMMER, TRY CORNMEAL FETTUCCINE IN PLACE OF THE FUSILLI IN FUSILLI WITH RAW TOMATO SAUCE AND CORN (PAGE 103). AS WITH BUCKWHEAT, CORNMEAL DOES NOT CONTAIN ANY GLUTEN AND MUST BE USED IN SMALL QUANTITIES AND IN COMBINATION WITH ALL-PURPOSE FLOUR. MAKES ABOUT 1 POUND.

> 1 1/2 cups all-purpose flour
> 1/2 cup yellow cornmeal
> 3 large eggs, beaten

1. Pulse the flour and cornmeal in the work bowl of a food processor fitted with the metal blade to evenly distribute and aerate. Add the eggs; process until the dough forms a rough ball, about 30 seconds. (If the dough resembles small pebbles, add water, 1/2 teaspoon at a time; if the dough sticks to the side of the work bowl, add flour, 1 tablespoon at a time, and process until the dough forms a rough ball.)

2. Turn the dough ball and small bits out onto a dry work surface; knead until the dough is smooth, 1 to 2 minutes. Cover with plastic wrap and set aside for at least 15 minutes and up to 2 hours to relax.

3. Follow the method on page 24 to roll the pasta.

Beet Pasta

AS WITH SPINACH IN FRESH PASTA, EXCESS WATER MUST BE PRESSED FROM THE COOKED BEETS SO THAT THEY ARE AS DRY AS POSSIBLE BEFORE THEY ARE COMBINED WITH THE FLOUR AND EGGS. THE ROSY PINK COLOR OF THIS PASTA CONTRASTS NICELY WITH THE GREENS OF SPRING VEGETABLES—LEEKS, PEAS, ASPARAGUS. TRY BEET FETTUCCINE IN FETTUCCINE WITH LEEKS, PEAS, AND CREAM (PAGE 166). BEET PASTA IS ALSO GOOD WITH SIMPLE CHEESE SAUCES SUCH AS PENNE WITH RICOTTA AND LEMON (PAGE 75). MAKES ABOUT 1 POUND.

> 1 small beet, all but last inch of stem
>   trimmed (see illustration 1)
> 2 1/4 cups all-purpose flour
> 3 large eggs, beaten

1. Place the beet in a medium saucepan and cover with water. Boil until tender, about 1 hour. Drain and cool the beet. Slip off the skin (see illustration 2). To puree, put the beet through a food mill or potato ricer (see illustration 3). Place the beet puree in a fine sieve over a bowl or sink, pressing down occasionally with the back of a large spoon, until most of the water has drained off (see illustration 4). Reserve 1 tablespoon of the beet puree for the pasta; discard the remaining puree or save for another use.

2. Pulse the flour in the work bowl of a food processor fitted with the metal blade to evenly distribute and aerate. Add the eggs and beet puree; process until the dough forms a rough ball, about 30 seconds. (If the dough resembles small pebbles, add water, 1/2 teaspoon at a time; if the dough sticks to the side of the work bowl, add flour, 1 tablespoon at a time, and process until the dough forms a rough ball.)

3. Turn the dough ball and small bits out onto a dry work surface; knead until the dough is smooth, 1 to 2 minutes. Cover with plastic wrap and set aside for at least 15 minutes and up to 2 hours to relax.

4. Follow the method on page 24 to roll the pasta.

HANDLING BEETS

1. Beets can be messy. To reduce the possibility of staining, cook beets with the skin on. Also, keep the last inch or so of the stem attached to the beet as it cooks. Do remove any dangling roots before cooking.

2. When the beet is tender (a skewer should glide through the beet easily), drain and cool. Use a paper towel to rub off the skin.

3. Puree the peeled beet in a food mill or potato ricer fitted with the finest disk. Don't use a food processor. It will make the puree too smooth and the liquid won't drain out properly.

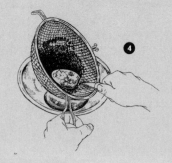

4. To remove moisture, place the puree in a fine sieve and press on the beet puree with the back of a large spoon.

Saffron Pasta

SAFFRON PASTA ADDS FLAVOR AS WELL AS COLOR TO A DISH. USE WITH ANY SAUCE THAT WOULD BE COMPLEMENTED BY SAFFRON, ESPECIALLY SAUCES WITH SEAFOOD AND TOMATOES. **MAKES ABOUT 1 POUND.**

> 2 cups all-purpose flour
> ¼ teaspoon saffron threads
> 3 large eggs, beaten

1. Pulse the flour in the work bowl of a food processor fitted with the metal blade to evenly distribute and aerate. Crumble the saffron into the eggs and stir to dissolve; add the mixture to the flour and process until the dough forms a rough ball, about 30 seconds. (If the dough resembles small pebbles, add water, ½ teaspoon at a time; if the dough sticks to the side of the work bowl, add flour, 1 tablespoon at a time, and process until the dough forms a rough ball.)

2. Turn the dough ball and small bits out onto a dry work surface; knead until the dough is smooth, 1 to 2 minutes. Cover with plastic wrap and set aside for at least 15 minutes and up to 2 hours to relax.

3. Follow the method on page 24 to roll the pasta.

Tomato Pasta

WE WANTED THE MOST TOMATO FLAVOR AND COLOR WITH THE LEAST AMOUNT OF LIQUID. TOMATO PASTE WAS THE OBVIOUS CHOICE. PALE ORANGE TOMATO PASTA GIVES DISHES MADE WITH CREAM SAUCE SOME COLOR; TRY IT WITH FETTUCCINE WITH FRESH HERBS AND CREAM (PAGE 82) OR FETTUCCINE WITH PROSCIUTTO AND CREAM (PAGE 82). GREEN VEGETABLE SAUCES AND SEAFOOD SAUCES ARE GOOD CHOICES, TOO. AVOID TOMATO SAUCES—THIS WOULD BE TOO MUCH OF A GOOD THING. **MAKES ABOUT 1 POUND.**

> 2¼ cups all-purpose flour
> 2 tablespoons tomato paste
> 3 large eggs, beaten

1. Pulse the flour in the work bowl of a food processor fitted with the metal blade to evenly distribute and aerate. Stir the tomato paste into the eggs and add to the processor; process until the dough forms a rough ball, about 30 seconds. (If the dough resembles small pebbles, add water, ½ teaspoon at a time; if the dough sticks to the side of the work bowl, add flour, 1 tablespoon at a time, and process until the dough forms a rough ball.)

2. Turn the dough ball and small bits out onto a dry work surface; knead until the dough is smooth, 1 to 2 minutes. Cover with plastic wrap and set aside for at least 15 minutes and up to 2 hours to relax.

3. Follow the method on page 24 to roll the pasta.

Black Pepper Pasta

COARSELY GROUND BLACK PEPPER GIVES EGG PASTA A MILD SPICINESS AND PLEASANT SPECKLED APPEARANCE. IN ORDER TO TASTE THE BLACK PEPPER, USE THIS PASTA IN SIMPLE DISHES WITH BUTTER AND CHEESE, SUCH AS FETTUCCINE WITH BUTTER AND PARMESAN (PAGE 67). FOR THE BEST FLAVOR, GRIND THE PEPPER YOURSELF. **MAKES ABOUT 1 POUND.**

> 2 cups all-purpose flour
> 1½ teaspoons coarsely ground black pepper
> 3 large eggs, beaten

1. Pulse the flour and pepper in the work bowl of a food processor fitted with the metal blade to evenly distribute and aerate. Add the eggs; process until the dough forms a rough ball, about 30 seconds. (If the dough resembles small pebbles, add water, ½ teaspoon at a time; if the dough sticks to the side of the work bowl, add flour, 1 tablespoon at a time, and process until the dough forms a rough ball.)

2. Turn the dough ball and small bits out onto a dry work surface; knead until the dough is smooth, 1 to 2 minutes. Cover with plastic wrap and set aside for at least 15 minutes and up to 2 hours to relax.

3. Follow the method on page 24 to roll the pasta.

MAKING VARIOUS PASTA SHAPES

/|\

THE FOLLOWING SHAPES ARE THE MOST USEFUL. THE FIRST THREE CAN BE CUT USING A MANUAL PASTA MACHINE; THE OTHERS MUST BE CUT BY HAND. ONCE A PASTA SHEET HAS BEEN CUT, LAY THE INDIVIDUAL NOODLES OUT ON PAPER TOWELS OR CLEAN KITCHEN TOWELS. SEPARATE THE NOODLES SO THEY DON'T stick to one another. (We found that as long as the noodles are separated at this stage, there is no need to flour or dust them with cornmeal, both of which can make the noodles gummy when they are cooked.) It's best to let the noodles firm up for at least 15 minutes before cooking. The noodles can be left out for up to 2 hours. For longer storage, let the noodles firm up for 15 minutes and then transfer them to a large sealable plastic bag and freeze for up to 1 month. Add frozen noodles directly to boiling water and increase the cooking time by a minute or so.

Don't refrigerate noodles, even for just a few hours—they will become tacky and stick together.

FOR FETTUCCINE, run each sheet through the wide cutter of a pasta machine. Each noodle should measure 1/8 to 1/4 inch across. These noodles are sometimes called tagliatelle or trenette, especially when cut by hand into slightly wider strips.

FOR TAGLIERINI, run each sheet through the narrow cutter of a pasta machine. Each noodle should measure about 1/16 inch across.

FOR SPAGHETTI, only run the pasta sheets through the machine to next-to-last setting, and then run through the narrow center of a pasta machine. The noodles will be as narrow as taglierini but thicker.

FOR PAPPARDELLE, use a paring knife to cut each long pasta sheet into pieces that are 12 to 15 inches long. Then use a scalloped pastry cutter to cut the sheets lengthwise into 3/4- to 1-inch-wide strips.

FOR PIZZOCCHERI, cut buckwheat pasta sheets with a pastry cutter into 2 1/2-by-3/4-inch pieces. Traditionally, pizzoccheri have straight edges, but we like this shape with scalloped edges.

FOR FAZZOLETTI ("silk handkerchiefs"), cut each pasta sheet at 4-inch intervals to make large squares. Fazzoletti are traditionally sauced with pesto. To serve fazzoletti, drop 4 or 5 pieces of the cooked pasta on each serving plate so that they resemble fallen handkerchiefs. Top with 2 tablespoons pesto and a sprinkling of grated cheese.

FRESH PASTA

WITHOUT

EGGS

/|\

FOR MOST AMERICANS (AND FOR THAT MATTER MOST

ITALIANS), HOMEMADE PASTA MEANS LONG SHEETS

OF EGGY DOUGH THAT HAVE BEEN CRANKED OUT OF

A PASTA MACHINE. HOWEVER, IN SOME PARTS OF

SOUTHERN ITALY, FRESH PASTA OFTEN CONTAINS JUST

flour and water. These home-style pastas are hand-molded into shell shapes called cavatelli and ear shapes known as orecchiette.

While fresh egg pasta must be made with all-purpose flour for proper suppleness, a dough made from just all-purpose flour and water is quite gummy and the resulting pasta tastes like boiled dough. In southern Italy, eggless fresh pasta is usually made from a blend of semolina flour (the same hard wheat flour used to make commercial dried pasta) and all-purpose flour.

We began our tests by making an all-semolina dough. This hard flour produced a dough that was hard to manipulate and cooked up too tough. We started blending in some all-purpose flour to make the dough more malleable until we reached the correct ratio, which was just slightly more than two parts all-purpose flour to one part semolina flour.

While most eggless fresh pastas are made with this blend of semolina and all-purpose flours, there is a second type of dough made with whole wheat flour. Again, when we tested a recipe made with 100 percent whole wheat flour, we did not like the results—the dough was too rustic and hard to handle. As with

USING FRESH PASTA WITHOUT EGGS

HOMEMADE CAVATELLI AND ORECCHIETTE ARE BEST WITH RUGGED VEGETABLE, MEAT, BEAN, OR SEAFOOD SAUCES. IN GENERAL, THEY WORK BEST WITH CHUNKY SAUCES, WITH BITS THAT WILL CLING TO THE CREVICES OR NESTLE IN THE INDENTATIONS. WHILE FRESH EGG PASTA SCREAMS OUT FOR CREAM,

cheese, and butter, these hearty pastas work best with sauces that are based on tomatoes and/or olive oil.

Here are some specific ideas for matching up these shapes and sauces throughout this book. Use either the semolina or whole wheat dough with any of these sauces, remembering that the whole wheat dough works best with strongly fla-vored sauces.

ORECCHIETTE
Orecchiette with Broccoli Rabe (page 142)

Orecchiette with White Beans and Broccoli Rabe (page 190)
Orecchiette with Fava Beans, Pancetta, and Tomatoes (page 152)
Orecchiette with Lentils (page 196)

CAVATELLI
Fusilli with Chopped Arugula and Raw Tomatoes (page 135)
Ziti with Broccoli-Anchovy Sauce (page 141)
Cavatelli with White Beans and Clams (page 235)

the semolina, blending in some softer all-purpose flour made the dough easier to work with and it cooked up better. A ratio of three parts whole wheat flour to two parts all-purpose flour delivers the right combination of wheaty flavor and proper texture.

Since these doughs are rather stiff, they are best kneaded in a food processor rather than by hand. A final hand-kneading on a lightly floured surface gives the dough a smooth, elastic finish.

Unlike fresh egg pasta—which must rest before being stretched—semolina and whole wheat pasta doughs are shaped, not stretched, so there's no need for the dough to relax. It is simply cut into pieces, rolled into long thin ropes, and then cut into small pieces that can be shaped with a knife and your fingers. We found that shaping the pasta on a wooden cutting board or a plastic board with a slightly rough surface gave the pasta rougher surface texture, an advantage in that sauce will adhere to the noodles more easily.

Semolina pasta is creamy white and smooth. Whole wheat pasta has a rougher texture and more robust flavor. Both pastas are chewy and substantial, a good match for hearty vegetables, meat, and seafood sauces. (For specific ideas, see page 32.)

The pasta is best used within a few hours or frozen. Since the dough does not contain egg, it can be fully dried. However, we found that fully dried pasta took an extremely long time to cook and never tasted the same—this is fresh pasta, after all. For storage, turn to the freezer, which does a better job of retaining the special character of this unusual homemade pasta.

As with egg pasta, it's best to cook fresh cavatelli and orecchiette in an abundant amount of salted water to prevent sticking. We found that 1 pound of these pastas needs 6 quarts of water.

SHAPING NON-EGG PASTA DOUGH

1. Once the dough has been kneaded, it is ready to cut into individual pieces. Unlike egg pasta, which must be rolled into thin sheets, this pasta is cut with a knife into small pieces and then hand-formed. Start by cutting the dough into 8 pieces. Roll one piece into a ½-inch-thick rope, keeping the remaining dough covered with plastic wrap so it does not dry out. Once the first rope is completely shaped, start the process over with the next piece of dough.

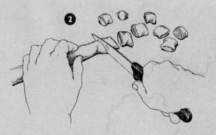

2. Cut the dough rope into ½-inch lengths. Shape each piece into orecchiette or cavatelli (see pages 34–35.

SHAPING CAVATELLI

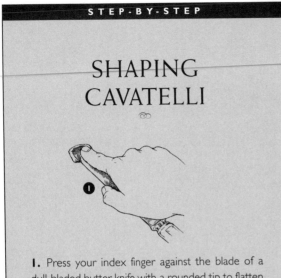

1. Press your index finger against the blade of a dull-bladed butter knife with a rounded tip to flatten each piece of dough until fairly thin.

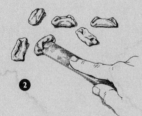

2. Pull the knife toward you, keeping it pressed against the dough so the dough drags across the work surface and curls itself around the tip of the knife to form a shell shape.

Fresh Semolina Pasta

MAKES ABOUT 1 POUND

MAKE SURE TO BUY finely ground semolina flour (available at Italian markets as well as some gourmet stores and natural foods shops), not regular semolina, which will be much too coarse for this recipe. Semolina flour is sometimes labeled "pasta flour."

1¾ cups unbleached all-purpose flour
¾ cup semolina flour
About ¾ cup hot water
1 tablespoon salt

1. Place the flours in the work bowl of a food processor fitted with a metal blade to evenly blend. With the machine running, add just enough hot water to form a stiff dough that forms a ball. It's fine if a few bits of dough remain unincorporated—you can knead them into the dough ball by hand. Make sure to add the water slowly (over at least 30 seconds) to ensure that you don't add too much water. The dough should not be tacky or sticky.

2. Remove the dough from the food processor and knead it on a lightly floured work surface until smooth and elastic, about 1 minute. (The dough can be tightly wrapped in plastic wrap for several hours.)

SHAPING ORECCHIETTE

1. Press your index finger against the blade of a dull-bladed butter knife with a rounded tip to flatten each piece of dough; drag the dough across the work surface just enough to form a shallow concave disk.

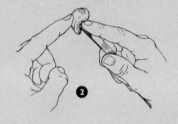

2. With the dough still on the end of the knife, place the index finger of the other hand against the convex side of the disk.

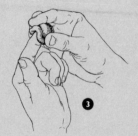

3. Put the knife down and then use the fingers on your free hand to push the disk down over the tip of your finger, turning it inside out.

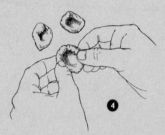

4. Take the pasta off your finger. The finished orecchiette should be deeply concave in shape.

3. Line 2 large jelly-roll pans with kitchen towels that have been lightly dusted with flour. Transfer the pieces to the pans as you shape them, and do not let the pieces of pasta touch each other or they may stick. Following the illustrations on pages 33–34 and above, cut and shape dough into the desired shape. Use pasta within a few hours or place pans in the freezer; transfer frozen pieces to an airtight container, and freeze for up to 1 month.

4. Bring 6 quarts of water to a boil in a large pot. Add the salt and pasta to the boiling water. Cook until al dente, 6 to 8 minutes. (Add a minute or two if the pasta was frozen.) Drain, reserving some cooking water (eggless pasta absorbs sauces quite readily and may dry out). Toss the pasta with the desired sauce, adding the reserved cooking water if necessary. Serve immediately.

Fresh Whole Wheat Pasta

MAKES ABOUT 1 POUND

T HIS PASTA IS A medium brown color and has a rough texture. The flavor is pleasantly wheaty. Some all-purpose flour is blended with the whole wheat flour to make the pasta tender and more pliable.

> 1 ½ cups whole wheat flour
> 1 cup unbleached all-purpose flour
> About ¾ cup hot water
> 1 tablespoon salt

1. Place the flours in the work bowl of a food processor fitted with a metal blade to blend. With the machine running, add just enough hot water to form a stiff dough that forms a ball. It's fine if a few bits of dough remain unincorporated—you can knead them into the dough ball by hand. Make sure to add the water slowly (over at least 30 seconds) to ensure that you don't add too much water. The dough should not be tacky or sticky.

2. Remove the dough from the food processor and knead it on a lightly floured work surface until smooth and elastic, about 1 minute. (The dough can be tightly wrapped in plastic wrap for several hours.)

3. Line 2 large jelly-roll pans with kitchen towels that have been lightly dusted with flour. Transfer the pieces to the pan as you shape them, and do not let the pieces of pasta touch each other, or they may stick. Following the illustrations on pages 33–35, cut and shape dough into the desired shape. Use pasta within a few hours or place pans in the freezer; transfer frozen pieces to an airtight container, and freeze for up to 1 month.

4. Bring 6 quarts of water to a boil in a large pot. Add the salt and pasta to the boiling water. Cook until al dente, 6 to 8 minutes. (Add a minute or two if the pasta was frozen.) Drain, reserving some cooking water (eggless pasta absorbs sauces quite readily and may dry out). Toss the pasta with the desired sauce, adding the reserved cooking water if necessary. Serve immediately.

OLIVE
OIL–BASED
SAUCES

/‖\

THESE RECIPES ARE AMONG THE SIMPLEST TO PREPARE

IN THIS BOOK. COMBINE OLIVE OIL AND SEASONINGS

WHILE THE PASTA IS COOKING AND THEN SIMPLY

DRESS THE PASTA WITH THE FLAVORED OIL AND SERVE.

◆ THERE ARE TWO CATEGORIES OF OIL-BASED SAUCES:

those that are heated and those that are not. Uncooked oil sauces contain small amounts of garlic (no more than a clove) and generally derive much of their flavor from the oil itself and the other seasonings, such as fresh herbs, citrus zest, and hot red pepper flakes. Since the olive oil is not heated, it is imperative to use the highest quality here. We tested these sauces with pure olive oil and found that the pastas were bland and uninspired.

Even when oil-based sauces are heated, you must use extra-virgin olive oil. Again, pure olive oil was disappointing in our tests. There are so few ingredients and oil is such a major component in these sauces that this is no place to skimp.

The most famous heated-oil sauce is called *aglio e olio* in Italian, or "garlic and oil." Recipes for this simple sauce call for as much as eight cloves of garlic or as few as two. Some recipes rely on ⅔ cup of oil, others call for as little as ¼ cup. After several tests, we found that ⅓ cup of oil was enough to sauce a pound of spaghetti. (Oil-based sauces are best with long, thin pasta shapes. They coat long strands from end to end and the sauce does not pool up on the noodles and become greasy, as can happen with stubby pasta shapes.) More oil made the spaghetti greasy, less oil and the pasta was too dry. As for the garlic, four medium cloves delivered the best flavor without overwhelming the pasta.

Besides finding the right ratio of ingredients, we also wanted to devise a surefire method for keeping the garlic from burning and becoming bitter. To tame its sharpness, the garlic must be fully cooked, but the garlic often goes from golden to dark brown in seconds in the hot oil.

We tried preparing the garlic several ways, including slicing, crushing, mincing, pressing, and pureeing. We found that the larger the pieces of garlic, the more likely they are to burn and become acrid. Putting peeled cloves through a press is the best way to get the pieces very small. If you don't own a press, you can mince the garlic by hand, sprinkle it with salt, and continue mincing and pressing on the garlic until it forms a smooth puree (see page 45).

As an added precaution against burning, we dilute the pressed or pureed garlic with a little bit of water, a tip we discovered when cooking spices to make curry.

We also found it imperative to heat the oil and garlic together, rather than heating the oil and adding the garlic. Letting the garlic gradually heat up ensures even cooking, as does the use of low heat. Pressing the garlic, diluting it with water, and heating it with the oil over low heat guarantees sweet garlic flavor every time.

Cheese is generally not a component in oil-based sauces. It usually does not mesh with the other strongly flavored ingredients, such as olives, anchovies, capers, and hot red pepper flakes, which dominate these sauces. That said, we do like grated pecorino cheese with the simplest garlic and oil sauces. Pecorino has a sharp flavor that works well with these ingredients. We prefer to save Parmesan for sauces with butter or tomatoes. There's one exception: a mellow combination of garlic, oil, and balsamic vinegar.

Although there is enough oil to moisten the pasta, it helps to combine the drained pasta with the oil when it is still dripping wet. Diluting these dishes with reserved pasta cooking water—a trick used elsewhere in this book—does not really work well and tends to make the pasta watery. There simply is not enough bulk in the sauce to withstand the addition of water. It's better to keep the extra water dripping from the noodles (where it needs to be anyway) rather than adding a lot of water to the sauce.

Since there is so little sauce and that sauce may be uncooked or just barely warm, these pastas tend to cool off very quickly. We think it's always a good idea to heat pasta bowls to help keep the pasta warm, right down to the last noodle. Heating the bowls is merely recommended elsewhere in the book—piping hot tomato sauce will keep the pasta much warmer than a few tablespoons of oil—but it is essential when serving the recipes in this chapter.

Spaghetti with Olive Oil, Lemon, and Parsley Sauce

SERVES 4

THIS IS THE SIMPLEST of all olive oil–based sauces. The sauce is uncooked—hot pasta is simply dressed with a mixture of oil, lemon zest, garlic, and parsley. You may vary the herb as you like, adjusting the amount to reflect the intensity of the herb.

⅓ cup extra-virgin olive oil
1 teaspoon grated lemon zest
  (see illustration, page 42)
1 medium garlic clove, minced
¼ cup minced fresh flat-leaf parsley leaves
Salt
1 pound spaghetti or other long, thin
  pasta
Ground black pepper

1. Bring 4 quarts of water to a boil in a large pot for cooking the pasta.

2. Place the oil, zest, garlic, parsley, and 1 teaspoon salt in a small bowl.

3. When the water comes to a boil, add 1 tablespoon salt and the pasta. Cook until al dente. Drain, allowing some of the cooking water to cling to the noodles. Return the dripping noodles to the pot and toss with the oil mixture. Season with salt and pepper to taste. Divide among 4 warmed pasta bowls and serve immediately.

PEELING GARLIC

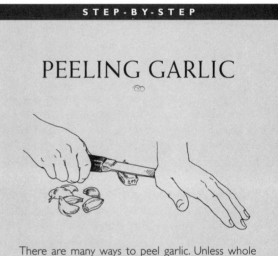

There are many ways to peel garlic. Unless whole cloves are needed, we crush the cloves with the side of a large chef's knife or a cleaver to loosen their skins and then pull the skins off with our fingers.

BUYING AND USING OLIVE OIL
FOR PASTA SAUCES

OLIVE OIL IS A KEY INGREDIENT IN NUMEROUS PASTA SAUCES, ESPECIALLY THOSE IN THIS CHAPTER. NATURALLY, WE WONDERED IF IT MATTERS WHAT KIND OR BRAND OF OLIVE OIL IS USED. FOR INSTANCE, CAN YOU TASTE A DIFFERENCE BETWEEN PURE AND EXTRA-VIRGIN OILS IN PASTA SAUCES?

Also, is there a difference between mass-market and boutique extra-virgin oils?

To answer the first question, we tested two widely available pure olive oils and two widely available supermarket extra-virgin olive oils in three different pasta sauces. We made a simple olive oil–based sauce with just garlic and salt. We then made a basic tomato sauce with oil, garlic, basil, salt, and canned tomatoes. Finally, we made a pesto with basil, parsley, toasted pine nuts, garlic, cheese, and salt. All three sauces were tossed with linguine.

In all three applications, tasters preferred the sauces made with the extra-virgin oils. The oil and garlic sauces made with pure olive oil were bland and received low marks from our tasters. The tomato and pesto sauces made with the pure oils were not bad, they just were not as flavorful or complex. Extra-virgin olive oil is essential when it is a main flavoring agent in a pasta sauce. However, even in a sauce with many flavorful ingredients, good oil can still make a difference. For this reason, we recommend using extra-virgin oil in all pasta sauces that call for olive oil.

A little research into how pure and extra-virgin oils are processed explained the results of our tasting and confirmed our feeling that extra-virgin oils are in fact worth the extra money.

The oil from a ripe olive can be rendered simply by pressing on the olive. When you squeeze an olive, you get a mixture of oil and water. Skim off the water and you've got oil. This cannot be done with corn, flax, or almost any other seed or vegetable, all of which must be refined either to extract the oil or to remove any poisonous substances accompanying it.

There are two methods that producers use to extract the oil from olives. Today, a relatively small percentage of olive oil is made by the traditional method. After picking and sorting, the olives are quickly moved to the pressing area. (Fermentation can begin within hours, so there is some urgency.) The olives are crushed, using a stone or steel mill. The paste is spread on round straw mats, which are in turn layered high on the press, with a steel plate every few mats. The press is usually turned by machine, or sometimes by whatever beast of burden is available, and the water is siphoned off from the resultant extract.

The modern method is similar, but uses extrusion devices and centrifuges, mimicking the old style but doing it more efficiently and obtaining a higher yield from each olive.

To qualify as extra-virgin, the oil must contain less than 1 percent acidity. It also must meet a list of subjective measures regarding flavor and smell. Most oils fail the acidity test and even more are weeded out because of defects in flavor. Extra-virgin oil may be filtered, but otherwise it cannot be further treated.

Most oil fails to meet the threshold necessary to earn the extra-virgin grade. The olives were not in ideal shape at pressing time and the oil is too acidic. Or, some off flavor is present that must be removed. In either case, refining makes the oil palatable, but also strips away any flavor. A little extra-virgin oil may be added back for flavor, but otherwise pure olive oil is not especially flavorful. Some companies are now labeling pure olive oil simply as olive oil. Unless you see the words "extra-virgin" on the label, assume that the oil is of middling quality.

So extra-virgin oil makes better pasta sauces and the reasons are fairly clear—flavor has not been stripped from the oil during processing. But there are thousands of extra-virgin olive oils on the market, so how do you choose a brand? Some supermarket extra-virgin oils cost $10 a liter, while boutique extra-virgin oils at gourmet stores sometimes cost as much as $100 a liter. Are these expensive oils worth the premium?

To answer this question, we tasted eleven extra-virgin olive oils from a variety of sources. We included all three major supermarket brands (Colavita, Bertolli, and Berio), as well as boutique oils from Italy, Spain, and California. We tasted the oils as professionals do. Each oil was poured into a small cup. Tasters were instructed to cover the cup with their hand to warm the oil slightly and trap aromas. The oil was smelled and then tasters poured a few drops on their tongues and drew air into their mouths to spray the droplets over the palate. As a second test, we also tossed cooked linguine with each oil and served the pasta plain.

When tasted plain, tasters were able to identify specific flavor characteristics about each oil. One oil was "peppery," another "floral" or "reminiscent of almonds." However, once the oil was poured over hot pasta, it was hard to detect these subtle nuances. The heat from the pasta causes many of the volatile compounds that make each oil so distinctive to go up in steam.

In the end, all eleven extra-virgin oils were liked by our panel, testament to the rigors of the grading of olive oil. But it was hard to draw any firm conclusions about the merits of a particular oil. (If you are not cooking olive oil—for instance, in a salad dressing—this is not necessarily true.) When making pasta sauces (and for other cooking), we recommend that you use an inexpensive supermarket extra-virgin olive oil. It has much more flavor than pure olive oil and is indistinguishable from more expensive oils.

When you get the olive oil home, make sure to store it in a cool pantry away from the light. (Heat and light will cause olive oil to degrade.) Check labels for "use by" dates. Even properly stored oils will start to turn rancid about eighteen months after processing. Some high-end oils rely on vintage or harvest dates instead of "use by" dates. If a label says 1999, you can assume that the oil was produced in the fall of 1999 (the olive harvest runs from September to December in most regions) and that the oil will be at the peak of its flavor until the spring of 2001.

Spaghetti with Oil, Lime, and Mint

LIME ZEST AND MINT MAKE FOR A BRACING VARIATION ON THE MASTER RECIPE. CILANTRO MAY BE SUBSTITUTED FOR MINT IF YOU LIKE. **SERVES 4.**

⅓ cup extra-virgin olive oil
1 teaspoon grated lime zest (see illustration)
1 medium garlic clove, minced
¼ cup minced fresh mint leaves
Salt
1 pound spaghetti or other long, thin pasta
Ground black pepper

1. Bring 4 quarts of water to a boil in a large pot for cooking the pasta.

2. Place the oil, zest, garlic, mint, and 1 teaspoon salt in a small bowl.

3. When the water comes to a boil, add 1 tablespoon salt and the pasta. Cook until al dente. Drain, allowing some of the cooking water to cling to the noodles. Return the dripping noodles to the pot and toss with the oil mixture. Season with salt and pepper to taste. Divide among 4 warmed pasta bowls and serve immediately.

◆

Spicy Spaghetti with Oil, Orange, and Ginger

ORANGE AND GINGER GIVE THIS PASTA A VAGUELY ASIAN FLAVOR. FOR A SOUTHERN ITALIAN VERSION, OMIT THE GINGER AND ADD ½ CUP COARSELY CHOPPED BLACK OLIVES INSTEAD. **SERVES 4.**

⅓ cup extra-virgin olive oil
2 teaspoons grated orange zest (see illustration)
1 medium garlic clove, minced
½-inch-long piece fresh gingerroot, peeled and minced (see illustrations 1–3, page 43)
2 tablespoons minced fresh cilantro leaves
½ teaspoon hot red pepper flakes, or to taste
Salt
1 pound spaghetti or other long, thin pasta

1. Bring 4 quarts of water to a boil in a large pot for cooking the pasta.

2. Place the oil, zest, garlic, ginger, cilantro, red pepper flakes, and 1 teaspoon salt in a small bowl.

3. When the water comes to a boil, add 1 tablespoon salt and the pasta. Cook until al dente. Drain, allowing some of the cooking water to cling to the noodles. Return the dripping noodles to the pot and toss with the oil mixture. Season with salt to taste. Divide among 4 warmed pasta bowls and serve immediately.

STEP-BY-STEP

GRATING CITRUS ZEST

The fine teeth on a box grater produce very thin, nearly transparent zest, almost like a puree, that will melt into whatever it is added to. To use the box grater, hold it down against the counter for support. Grate only the colored part of the skin; most of the zest should fall to the counter, but you can remove any that remains with a clean toothbrush or other small brush.

PEELING AND MINCING GINGER

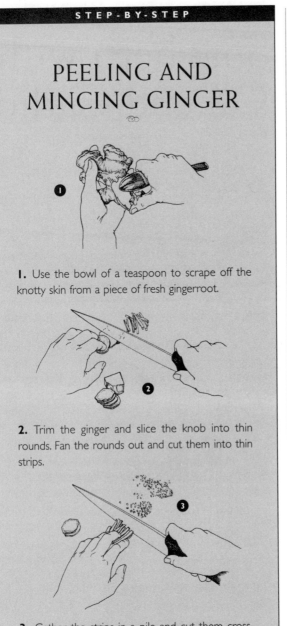

1. Use the bowl of a teaspoon to scrape off the knotty skin from a piece of fresh gingerroot.

2. Trim the ginger and slice the knob into thin rounds. Fan the rounds out and cut them into thin strips.

3. Gather the strips in a pile and cut them crosswise into very small pieces.

Spaghetti with Lemon and Olives

BLACK OLIVES AND THYME ARE AN ESPECIALLY GOOD MATCH AND GIVE THIS UNCOOKED SAUCE A DISTINCTIVE FLAVOR. FOR VARIETY, OTHER HERBS—PARSLEY, BASIL, OREGANO, MINT, MARJORAM—MAY BE SUBSTITUTED. SERVES 4.

> ⅓ cup extra-virgin olive oil
> 1 teaspoon grated lemon zest (see illustration, page 42)
> 1 medium garlic clove, minced
> ½ cup black olives, such as Kalamata, pitted and coarsely chopped (see illustrations 1–2, page 62)
> 2 tablespoons minced fresh thyme leaves
> Salt
> 1 pound spaghetti or other long, thin pasta
> Ground black pepper

1. Bring 4 quarts of water to a boil in a large pot for cooking the pasta.

2. Place the oil, zest, garlic, olives, thyme, and 1 teaspoon salt in a small bowl.

3. When the water comes to a boil, add 1 tablespoon salt and the pasta. Cook until al dente. Drain, allowing some of the cooking water to cling to the noodles. Return the dripping noodles to the pot and toss with the oil mixture. Season with salt and pepper to taste. Divide among 4 warmed pasta bowls and serve immediately.

Spaghetti with Fried Capers

CAPERS CRISP-FRIED IN OLIVE OIL PROVIDE A CRUNCHY
GARNISH FOR THIS UNCOOKED SAUCE. BE CAREFUL TO
DRY THE CAPERS WELL BEFORE FRYING; IF THEY ARE
WET, THEY WILL SPLATTER THE STOVETOP WITH HOT
OIL AND POSSIBLY CAUSE A GREASE FIRE. SERVES 4.

⅔ cup extra-virgin olive oil
½ cup drained capers, rinsed and patted
    dry with paper towels
1 teaspoon grated lemon zest (see
    illustration, page 42)
2 tablespoons lemon juice
6 anchovy fillets, rinsed and minced
1 medium garlic clove, minced
¼ cup minced fresh flat-leaf parsley leaves
Salt
1 pound spaghetti or other long, thin
    pasta
Ground black pepper

1. Bring 4 quarts of water to a boil in a large pot for
cooking the pasta.

2. Heat ⅓ cup oil in a small skillet over medium-high
until shimmering. Add the capers and cook, stirring
occasionally, until brown, 3 to 4 minutes. Remove
with a slotted spoon and drain on paper towels. Discard the oil.

3. Combine the remaining ⅓ cup oil, the zest, juice,
anchovies, garlic, and parsley in a small bowl.

4. When the water comes to a boil, add 1 tablespoon
salt and the pasta. Cook until al dente. Drain, allowing some of the cooking water to cling to the noodles.
Return the dripping noodles to the pot and toss with
the oil mixture and capers. Season with salt and pepper to taste. Divide among 4 warmed pasta bowls and
serve immediately.

Spaghetti with Oil and Garlic

SERVES 4

SPAGHETTI WITH GARLIC and olive oil
is a favorite late-night supper dish all
over Italy. For our version, we puree garlic and dilute it with a little bit of water
before sautéing it in olive oil; this gives the pasta a
mild, even garlic flavor while greatly reducing the
possibility of overcooking the garlic. Refer to the
illustrations.

4 medium garlic cloves, peeled (see
    illustration, page 39)
⅓ cup extra-virgin olive oil
Salt
1 pound spaghetti or other long, thin
    pasta
¼ cup minced fresh flat-leaf parsley leaves
Ground black pepper

1. Bring 4 quarts of water to a boil in a large pot for
cooking the pasta.

2. Process the garlic through a garlic press into a
small bowl; stir in 1 teaspoon water (see illustrations
1–3, page 45). Place the oil, diluted garlic, and 1 teaspoon salt in a small skillet and turn the heat to low.
Cook very slowly until the garlic turns golden, about
3 minutes. Be careful not to brown the garlic or your
sauce will be bitter. Remove from heat.

3. When the water comes to a boil, add 1 tablespoon salt and the pasta. Cook until al dente. Drain, allowing some of the cooking water to cling to the noodles. Return the dripping noodles to the pot and toss with the oil mixture and parsley. Season with salt and pepper to taste. Divide among 4 warmed pasta bowls and serve immediately.

◆

Spaghetti with Oil, Garlic, and Herbs

ABUNDANT FRESH HERBS—USE WHATEVER YOU HAVE ON HAND—GIVE PANTRY STAPLES LIKE GARLIC AND OLIVE OIL A FRESH TASTE. USE STRONGER HERBS LIKE ROSEMARY, OREGANO, TARRAGON, THYME, AND SAGE IF YOU LIKE, BUT CUT THE QUANTITY TO 2 TABLESPOONS PER POUND OF PASTA. SERVES 4.

> 4 medium garlic cloves, peeled (see illustration, page 39)
> 1/3 cup extra-virgin olive oil
> Salt
> 1 pound spaghetti or other long, thin pasta
> 1/2 cup minced fresh flat-leaf parsley, basil, mint, and/or cilantro leaves
> Ground black pepper

1. Bring 4 quarts of water to a boil in a large pot for cooking the pasta.

2. Process the garlic through a garlic press into a small bowl; stir in 1 teaspoon water (see illustrations 1–3). Heat the oil, diluted garlic, and 1 teaspoon salt in a small skillet and turn the heat to low. Cook very slowly until the garlic turns golden, about 3 minutes. Be careful not to brown the garlic or your sauce will be bitter. Remove from heat.

3. When the water comes to a boil, add 1 tablespoon salt and the pasta. Cook until al dente. Drain, allowing some of the cooking water to cling to the noodles. Return the dripping noodles to the pot and toss with the oil mixture and herbs. Season with salt and pepper to taste. Divide among 4 warmed pasta bowls and serve immediately.

CUTTING GARLIC VERY FINE

1. In cooked garlic and oil sauces, it's especially important to keep the garlic from burning while still giving it time to become fragrant. Our solution is to cut the garlic as small and evenly as possible. A heavy-duty garlic press with sturdy handles (don't buy a cheap, flimsy one) does this best. Mix the pressed garlic into a bowl and stir in 1 teaspoon water to form a wet puree.

2. If you don't own a garlic press, mince it on a cutting board, sprinkling the garlic with a little salt. The coarse crystals of kosher salt do the best job of breaking down the garlic; regular table salt will work, but more slowly.

3. Drag the flat side of a chef's knife over the garlic-salt mixture, then mince, continuing both steps to form a fairly smooth puree. Dilute the pureed garlic with 1 teaspoon water to form a wet puree. If you like, you can prepare garlic for all pasta sauces in this manner; it is essential when the sauce contains just tomatoes, oil, garlic, herbs, and salt.

Spaghetti with Oil, Garlic, and Hot Red Pepper

HOT RED PEPPER FLAKES ARE OFTEN ADDED TO A SIM-PLE OLIVE OIL AND GARLIC SAUCE. MAKE SURE THAT YOUR PEPPER FLAKES ARE RELATIVELY FRESH; LIKE OTHER SPICES, PEPPER FLAKES THAT HAVE BEEN SITTING IN YOUR CUPBOARD OR ON A SUPERMARKET SHELF FOR SEVERAL MONTHS LOSE MUCH OF THEIR HEAT. **SERVES** 4.

> 4 medium garlic cloves, peeled (see illustration, page 39)
> ⅓ cup extra-virgin olive oil
> ½ teaspoon hot red pepper flakes, or to taste
> Salt
> 1 pound spaghetti or other long, thin pasta
> ¼ cup minced fresh flat-leaf parsley leaves

1. Bring 4 quarts of water to a boil in a large pot for cooking the pasta.

2. Process the garlic through a garlic press into a small bowl; stir in 1 teaspoon water (see illustrations 1–3, page 45). Heat the oil, diluted garlic, red pepper flakes, and 1 teaspoon salt in a small skillet and turn the heat to low. Cook very slowly until the garlic turns golden, about 3 minutes. Be careful not to brown the garlic or your sauce will be bitter. Remove from heat.

3. When the water comes to a boil, add 1 tablespoon salt and the pasta. Cook until al dente. Drain, allowing some of the cooking water to cling to the noodles. Return the dripping noodles to the pot and toss with the oil mixture and parsley. Season with salt and red pepper flakes to taste. Divide among 4 warmed pasta bowls and serve immediately.

Spaghetti with Oil, Garlic, and Ginger

ALTHOUGH WE USUALLY THINK OF GINGER AS AN ASIAN INGREDIENT, ITALIANS SOMETIMES USE IT IN GARLIC AND OIL SAUCES IN PLACE OF HOT RED PEPPER FLAKES. GINGER GIVES THE SAUCE A DIFFERENT, BUT EQUALLY DELICIOUS, KIND OF SPICINESS. **SERVES** 4.

> 4 medium garlic cloves, peeled (see illustration, page 39)
> ⅓ cup extra-virgin olive oil
> ½-inch-long piece fresh gingerroot, peeled and finely chopped (see illustrations 1–3, page 43)
> Salt
> 1 pound spaghetti or other long, thin pasta
> 2 tablespoons minced fresh flat-leaf parsley or cilantro leaves

1. Bring 4 quarts of water to a boil in a large pot for cooking the pasta.

2. Process the garlic through a garlic press into a small bowl; stir in 1 teaspoon water (see illustrations 1–3, page 45). Heat the oil, diluted garlic, ginger, and 1 teaspoon salt in a small skillet and turn the heat to low. Cook very slowly until the garlic turns golden, about 3 minutes. Be careful not to brown the garlic or your sauce will be bitter. Remove from heat.

3. When the water comes to a boil, add 1 tablespoon salt and the pasta. Cook until al dente. Drain, allowing some of the cooking water to cling to the noodles. Return the dripping noodles to the pot and toss with the oil mixture and parsley. Season with salt to taste. Divide among 4 warmed pasta bowls and serve immediately.

Spaghetti with Oil, Garlic, and Arugula

HERE, A BUNCH OF CHOPPED ARUGULA IS USED IN PLACE OF FRESH HERBS FOR A MORE PEPPERY FLAVOR. THE ARUGULA WILTS ON CONTACT WITH THE HOT PASTA. STEMMED WATERCRESS MAY BE SUBSTITUTED FOR THE ARUGULA IF YOU LIKE. **SERVES 4.**

> 4 medium garlic cloves, peeled (see illustration, page 39)
> 1/3 cup extra-virgin olive oil
> Salt
> 1 pound spaghetti or other long, thin pasta
> 1 small bunch arugula, washed, stemmed, and coarsely chopped
> Ground black pepper

1. Bring 4 quarts of water to a boil in a large pot for cooking the pasta.

2. Process the garlic through a garlic press into a small bowl; stir in 1 teaspoon water (see illustrations 1–3, page 45). Heat the oil, diluted garlic, and 1 teaspoon salt in a small skillet and turn the heat to low. Cook very slowly until the garlic turns golden, about 3 minutes. Be careful not to brown the garlic or your sauce will be bitter. Remove from heat.

3. When the water comes to a boil, add 1 tablespoon salt and the pasta. Cook until al dente. Drain, allowing some of the cooking water to cling to the noodles. Return the dripping noodles to the pot and toss with the oil mixture and arugula. Season with salt and pepper to taste. Divide among 4 warmed pasta bowls and serve immediately.

Spaghetti with Oil, Garlic, and Pecorino

IN GENERAL, PASTA DRESSED IN OLIVE OIL IS NOT SPRINKLED WITH CHEESE. THE EXCEPTION ARE SAUCES INCORPORATING PECORINO, A SHARP GRATING CHEESE WELL SUITED TO THE STRONG FLAVORS OF GARLIC AND OLIVE OIL. *SPAGHETTI ALLA CARRETTIERA* ("COACHMAN STYLE") IS THE MOST BASIC OF THESE. PECORINO CAN BE QUITE SALTY, SO LESS SALT IS ADDED TO THE OIL AND GARLIC. **SERVES 4.**

> 2 medium garlic cloves, peeled (see illustration, page 39)
> 1/3 cup extra-virgin olive oil
> Salt
> 1 pound spaghetti or other long, thin pasta
> 1/4 cup minced fresh flat-leaf parsley or basil leaves
> 1/2 cup grated pecorino cheese
> Ground black pepper

1. Bring 4 quarts of water to a boil in a large pot for cooking the pasta.

2. Process the garlic through a garlic press into a small bowl; stir in 1 teaspoon water (see illustrations 1–3, page 45). Heat the oil, diluted garlic, and 1/2 teaspoon salt in a small skillet and turn the heat to low. Cook very slowly until the garlic turns golden, about 3 minutes. Be careful not to brown the garlic or your sauce will be bitter. Remove from heat.

3. When the water comes to a boil, add 1 tablespoon salt and the pasta. Cook until al dente. Drain, allowing some of the cooking water to cling to the noodles. Return the dripping noodles to the pot and toss with the oil mixture, parsley, and cheese. Season with salt and pepper to taste. Divide among 4 warmed pasta bowls and serve immediately.

SEPARATING A HEAD OF GARLIC INTO CLOVES

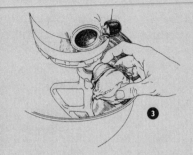

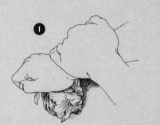

1. When a recipe calls for a lot of garlic, separating the individual cloves from the head and then peeling them can be a time-consuming chore. To make this task faster and easier, press down on the garlic head with the heel of your hand to loosen the cloves.

3. Place the head of garlic in a very lightly oiled mixing bowl of an electric mixer and fit the mixer with the paddle attachment.

4. Mix slowly until the cloves are separate and the peels are removed.

2. Remove as much of the papery skin from the outside of the head as possible.

Linguine with Oil, Walnuts, and Garlic

THE ADDITION OF WALNUTS GIVES THIS VERSION OF *CARRETIERRA* A SOUTHERN ITALIAN FLAVOR. BE CAREFUL TO BROWN, NOT BURN, THE NUTS. SERVES 4.

  2 medium garlic cloves, peeled (see
     illustration, page 39)
  1/3 cup extra-virgin olive oil
  Salt
  3/4 cup finely chopped walnuts
  1 pound linguine or other long, thin pasta
  1/4 cup minced fresh flat-leaf parsley or
     basil leaves
  1/4 cup grated pecorino cheese
  Ground black pepper

1. Bring 4 quarts of water to a boil in a large pot for cooking the pasta.

2. Process the garlic through a garlic press into a small bowl; stir in 1 teaspoon water (see illustrations 1–3, page 45). Combine the oil, diluted garlic, 1 teaspoon salt, and walnuts in a small skillet and turn the heat to low. Cook very slowly until the nuts are toasted and fragrant, 3 to 4 minutes. Remove from heat.

3. When the water comes to a boil, add 1 tablespoon salt and the pasta. Cook until al dente. Drain, allowing some of the cooking water to cling to the noodles. Return the dripping noodles to the pot and toss with the oil mixture, parsley, and cheese. Season with salt and pepper to taste. Divide among 4 warmed pasta bowls and serve immediately.

Spaghetti with Oil, Garlic, Parmesan, and Balsamic Vinegar

MILDER PARMESAN, RATHER THAN PECORINO, IS USED HERE BECAUSE IT COMPLEMENTS RATHER THAN COMPETES WITH THE MILDLY ACIDIC, SWEET BALSAMIC VINEGAR. SERVES 4.

  4 medium garlic cloves, peeled (see
     illustration, page 39)
  1/3 cup extra-virgin olive oil
  Salt
  1 pound spaghetti or other long, thin
     pasta
  1 cup grated Parmesan cheese
  2 tablespoons balsamic vinegar
  Ground black pepper

1. Bring 4 quarts of water to a boil in a large pot for cooking the pasta.

2. Process the garlic through a garlic press into a small bowl; stir in 1 teaspoon water (see illustrations 1–3, page 45). Heat the oil, diluted garlic, and 1 teaspoon salt in a small skillet and turn the heat to low. Cook very slowly until the garlic turns golden, about 3 minutes. Be careful not to brown the garlic or your sauce will be bitter. Remove from heat.

3. When the water comes to a boil, add 1 tablespoon salt and the pasta. Cook until al dente. Drain, allowing some of the cooking water to cling to the noodles. Return the dripping noodles to the pot and toss with the oil mixture, cheese, and vinegar. Season with salt and pepper to taste. Divide among 4 warmed pasta bowls and serve immediately.

Spaghetti with Oil, Garlic, and Tomato Paste

THIS IS NOT A TOMATO SAUCE, BUT A VERSION OF OIL AND GARLIC SAUCE FLAVORED WITH A SMALL QUANTITY OF TOMATO PASTE. THE TOMATO PASTE TENDS TO ABSORB OIL, SO A LITTLE MORE OIL IS NEEDED TO MOISTEN THE PASTA. SERVES 4.

> 4 medium garlic cloves, peeled (see illustration, page 39)
> 1/2 cup extra-virgin olive oil
> 1/4 cup canned tomato paste
> Salt
> 1 pound spaghetti or other long, thin pasta
> 1/4 cup finely chopped fresh basil leaves
> Ground black pepper

1. Bring 4 quarts of water to a boil in a large pot for cooking the pasta.

2. Process the garlic through a garlic press into a small bowl; stir in 1 teaspoon water (see illustrations 1–3, page 45). Heat the oil, diluted garlic, tomato paste, and 1 teaspoon salt in a small skillet and turn the heat to low. Cook very slowly until the garlic loses its raw flavor, about 3 minutes. Be careful not to brown the garlic or your sauce will be bitter. Remove from heat.

3. When the water comes to a boil, add 1 tablespoon salt and the pasta. Cook until al dente. Drain, allowing some of the cooking water to cling to the noodles. Return the dripping noodles to the pot and toss with the oil mixture and basil. Season with salt and pepper to taste. Divide among 4 warmed pasta bowls and serve immediately.

Spaghetti with Lemon and Pine Nuts

TOASTED PINE NUTS ADD A SURPRISINGLY RICH AND LUXURIOUS NOTE TO THE USUALLY SPARE OIL AND GARLIC SAUCE. KEEP A CAREFUL WATCH ON THE NUTS AS THEY TOAST BECAUSE THEY QUICKLY TURN FROM GOLDEN BROWN TO BURNT. SERVES 4.

> 1/4 cup pine nuts
> 4 medium garlic cloves, peeled (see illustration, page 39)
> 1/3 cup extra-virgin olive oil
> Salt
> 1 pound spaghetti or other long, thin pasta
> 1 teaspoon grated lemon zest
> 1/4 cup minced fresh flat-leaf parsley leaves
> Ground black pepper

1. Bring 4 quarts of water to a boil in a large pot for cooking the pasta.

2. Toast the nuts in a small skillet over medium heat, stirring frequently, until just golden and fragrant, 4 to 5 minutes. Set the nuts aside on a plate.

3. Process the garlic through a garlic press into a small bowl; stir in 1 teaspoon water (see illustrations 1–3, page 45). Heat the oil, diluted garlic, and 1 teaspoon salt in the empty skillet and turn the heat to low. Cook very slowly until the garlic turns golden, about 3 minutes. Be careful not to brown the garlic or your sauce will be bitter. Remove from heat.

4. When the water comes to a boil, add 1 tablespoon salt and the pasta. Cook until al dente. Drain, allowing some of the cooking water to cling to the noodles. Return the dripping noodles to the pot and toss with the toasted nuts, oil mixture, zest, and parsley. Season with salt and pepper to taste. Divide among 4 warmed pasta bowls and serve immediately.

Spaghetti with Anchovies, Capers, and Olives

OLIVES, ANCHOVIES, AND CAPERS ARE CLASSIC ADDI-
TIONS TO THE BASIC OLIVE OIL SAUCE FOR PASTA. OF
COURSE, THEY ARE ALL QUITE SALTY, SO ADD LITTLE
OR NO SALT TO THE SAUCE. IF YOU LIKE, ADD HOT RED
PEPPER FLAKES TO TASTE (UP TO 1 TEASPOON) ALONG
WITH THE ANCHOVIES, CAPERS, AND OLIVES. SERVES 4.

> 2 medium garlic cloves, peeled (see
>   illustration, page 39)
> 1/3 cup extra-virgin olive oil
> 2 anchovy fillets, minced
> 2 tablespoons capers, rinsed
> 10 large green olives, pitted and coarsely
>   chopped (see illustrations 1–2, page
>   62)
> Salt
> 1 pound spaghetti or other long, thin
>   pasta
> 1/4 cup minced fresh flat-leaf parsley leaves
> Ground black pepper

1. Bring 4 quarts of water to a boil in a large pot for
cooking the pasta.

2. Process the garlic through a garlic press into a
small bowl; stir in 1 teaspoon water (see illustrations
1–3, page 45). Heat the oil and diluted garlic in a
small skillet and turn the heat to low. Cook very
slowly until the garlic turns golden, about 3 minutes.
Be careful not to brown the garlic or your sauce will be
bitter. Stir in the anchovies, capers, and olives and
cook until the anchovies begin to dissolve, about 1
minute. Remove from heat.

3. When the water comes to a boil, add 1 tablespoon
salt and the pasta. Cook until al dente. Drain, allowing some of the cooking water to cling to the noodles.
Return the dripping noodles to the pot and toss with
the oil mixture and parsley. Season with salt and pepper to taste. Divide among 4 warmed pasta bowls and
serve immediately.

Linguine with Walnuts and Anchovies

WALNUTS AND ANCHOVIES ARE A TRADITIONAL COMBI-
NATION IN THIS MEATLESS PASTA SERVED ON CHRIST-
MAS EVE IN SOUTHERN ITALY. SIX ANCHOVIES GIVE THE
SAUCE QUITE A STRONG FLAVOR; IF YOU LIKE A SUB-
TLER TASTE, CUT BACK TO FOUR. SINCE THIS SAUCE
HAS SO MANY ANCHOVIES, WE RECOMMEND THAT YOU
RINSE THEM TO WASH AWAY SOME OF THEIR SALTINESS.
SERVES 4.

> 4 medium garlic cloves, peeled (see
>   illustration, page 39)
> 1/3 cup extra-virgin olive oil
> 3/4 cup walnuts, finely chopped
> 6 anchovy fillets, rinsed and minced
> Salt
> 1 pound linguine or other long, thin pasta
> 1/4 cup minced fresh flat-leaf parsley or
>   basil leaves
> Ground black pepper

1. Bring 4 quarts of water to a boil in a large pot for
cooking the pasta.

2. Process the garlic through a garlic press into a
small bowl; stir in 1 teaspoon water (see illustrations
1–3, page 45). Combine the oil, diluted garlic, walnuts, and anchovies in a small skillet and turn the heat
to low. Cook very slowly until the nuts are toasted and
fragrant, 3 to 4 minutes. Remove from heat.

3. When the water comes to a boil, add 1 tablespoon
salt and the pasta. Cook until al dente. Drain, allowing some of the cooking water to cling to the noodles.
Return the dripping noodles to the pot and toss with
the oil mixture and parsley. Season with salt and pepper to taste. Divide among 4 warmed pasta bowls and
serve immediately.

Spaghetti with Garlic, Onions, and Pancetta

LESS OLIVE OIL IS NEEDED HERE SINCE THE PASTA IS MOISTENED BY THE FAT RENDERED FROM THE PANCETTA (UNSMOKED ITALIAN BACON). YOU CAN SUBSTITUTE REGULAR AMERICAN BACON. IN EITHER CASE, ADD LITTLE OR NO SALT TO THE SAUCE. SERVES 4.

2 medium garlic cloves, peeled (see illustration, page 39)
¼ cup extra-virgin olive oil
4 ounces pancetta, finely chopped
1 small onion, minced
Salt
1 pound spaghetti or other long, thin pasta
¼ cup minced fresh flat-leaf parsley leaves
½ cup grated pecorino cheese
Ground black pepper

1. Bring 4 quarts of water to a boil in a large pot for cooking the pasta.

2. Process the garlic through a garlic press into a small bowl; stir in 1 teaspoon water (see illustrations 1–3, page 45). Heat the oil over low in a small skillet and add the pancetta and onion. Cook until the pancetta and onion begin to soften and color slightly, 3 to 5 minutes. Add the diluted garlic and cook until fragrant, another 1 to 2 minutes. Remove from heat.

3. When the water comes to a boil, add 1 tablespoon salt and the pasta. Cook until al dente. Drain, allowing some of the cooking water to cling to the noodles. Return the dripping noodles to the pot and toss with the oil mixture, parsley, and cheese. Season with salt and pepper to taste. Divide among 4 warmed pasta bowls and serve immediately.

Spaghetti with Roasted Garlic

IF YOU LOVE MELLOW, CREAMY ROASTED GARLIC, TRY THIS VERSION OF OLIVE AND GARLIC SAUCE, IN WHICH PEELED AND HALVED CLOVES ARE BAKED IN A SMALL DISH OF OIL AND THEN TOSSED WITH PASTA AND PARSLEY. THE ROASTED GARLIC CLOVES FLAVOR THE OIL THAT THEY ARE BAKED IN; THE CREAMY CLOVES MAKE THIS MORE OF A VEGETABLE SAUCE THAN A SIMPLE OIL-BASED SAUCE. SERVES 4.

50 garlic cloves (about 2 heads), peeled and halved (see illustrations 1–4, page 48)
⅓ cup extra-virgin olive oil
Salt
1 pound spaghetti or other long, thin pasta
¼ cup minced fresh flat-leaf parsley leaves
Ground black pepper

1. Preheat the oven to 375 degrees. Combine the garlic, oil, and 1 teaspoon salt in a small baking dish. Cover tightly with aluminum foil and bake until the cloves are soft when pierced with a fork, 30 to 35 minutes. Remove from the oven and keep covered.

2. Meanwhile, bring 4 quarts of water to a boil in a large pot. Add 1 tablespoon salt and the pasta. Cook until al dente. Drain, allowing some of the cooking water to cling to the noodles. Return the dripping noodles to the pot and toss with the roasted garlic mixture and parsley. Season with salt and pepper to taste. Divide among 4 warmed pasta bowls and serve immediately.

PESTO AND

OTHER PUREED

SAUCES

/I\

PESTO IS A POUNDED BASIL SAUCE THAT COMES FROM

LIGURIA, A COASTAL AREA IN NORTHWESTERN ITALY.

TRADITIONALLY, THE SAUCE IS MADE IN A MORTAR

AND PESTLE FROM BASIL LEAVES, RAW GARLIC, EXTRA-

VIRGIN OLIVE OIL, PINE NUTS, GRATED CHEESE, AND

SALT. HOWEVER, EVEN WITHIN ITALY, THIS RECIPE

is open to countless variations. Pesto's incredible popularity in this country has spawned numerous non-Italian variations made with other herbs and cheeses.

For the sake of convenience, we use the term *pesto* when talking about any uncooked, pureed, oil-based sauce. Most of these other sauces contain herbs or at least are green from spinach or arugula. But some pestos rely on black olives or sun-dried tomatoes and look and taste quite different from Ligurian pesto. However, all of these pureed sauces are uncooked and all of them contain olive oil.

We had several questions about making the original basil pesto. Once we settled these issues, we figured the answers would apply to other variations as well.

In our experience, the bright herbal fragrance of basil always hinted at more flavor than it really delivered. Also, the raw garlic can sometimes have a sharp, acrid taste that bites through the other flavors in the sauce. We also wondered about the nuts. Some sources suggest that only pine nuts are appropriate, while others mention walnuts as an alternative. Our goals when testing pestos were simple: heighten the flavor of the basil, mellow the punch of the garlic, and figure out how to handle the nuts.

We started our tests by using a mortar and pestle to make pesto. The advantage of this method was that it produced a silky paste with an unusually full basil flavor. The disadvantage was that it required fifteen minutes of constant pounding and a piece of equipment not found in many modern kitchens. The blender and food processor are more practical for making pesto. Of the two, we found that the food processor makes a sauce with a finer, more consistent texture. In the blender, the ingredients tended to bunch up beneath the blade, which prevented them from being chopped and mixed uniformly. To keep the solids moving, we found it necessary to add more oil to the blender. Also, we found it more difficult to remove the finished pesto from a blender.

We decided to use the food processor for our recipe, but we wondered how to get the full basil flavor of pesto made in a mortar and pestle. Because the basil was broken down totally in the mortar and pestle, it released its full range of herbal and anise flavors in a way that the chopping action of a food processor

alone did not accomplish. Attempting to approximate that fuller flavor in a food processor, we tried separate tests of chopping, tearing, and bruising the leaves (packed in a sealable plastic bag) with a meat pounder before processing. Bruising released the most flavor from the basil leaves and is recommended.

Garlic is a star player in pesto, but we often find that this star shines a little too brightly. Wondering how to cut the raw garlic edge, we tried roasting it, sautéing it, and even infusing its flavors into olive oil, but none of these methods was ideal. Blanching whole garlic cloves in boiling water turned out to be the best solution for several reasons: it's quick (the garlic needs less than a minute in boiling water), it loosens the papery skin from cloves for easy peeling, and it eliminates the raw garlic sting. Whole cloves don't break down all that well in the food processor and we found it worthwhile then to mince them by hand.

With the basil flavor boosted and the garlic toned down, we began to experiment with nuts. We often toast nuts when using them in recipes and found that toasting the nuts in a dry skillet until fragrant brings out their flavor in pesto. We found that pine nuts, walnuts, and almonds all work well in pesto. Almonds are relatively sweet, which works beautifully with the basil, but they are also hard, so they give pesto a coarse, granular texture. Walnuts break down a little more, but they still remain distinctly meaty in flavor and texture. Pine nuts were the favorite nut for the vast majority of our tasters. They become very creamy when processed and give pesto an especially smooth, luxurious texture.

Cheese is the last important component of pesto. We found that it should be finely grated so it becomes powdery enough to blend smoothly into the sauce. (For more information, see page 72.) All of our tasters preferred the combination of Parmesan and sharper pecorino Romano than either cheese alone. However, the pesto made with all Parmesan was a close second, and as a nod to convenience, we have made the pecorino optional.

Basil pesto usually discolors quite quickly. Adding a little parsley helps keep the color green without distracting from the basil flavor. Pesto can be used immediately or refrigerated for up to five days. To keep discoloration to a minimum, place plastic wrap directly on the surface of the pesto or pour a thin film of olive oil over the sauce.

When using pesto to sauce pasta, it is imperative to use some of the cooking liquid to thin out the consistency. Thinning the pesto with ¼ cup of pasta cooking water allows good distribution of the sauce over noodles, softens and blends the flavors a bit, and highlights the creaminess of the cheese and nuts. If the pesto and pasta still seem dry when tossed together, stir in a few more tablespoons of reserved cooking water.

When making nonbasil pestos, the same principles apply. Tame the garlic flavor by blanching, bruise herbs to release their flavors, make sure the cheese is finely grated, and use the food processor to bring the ingredients together.

Pasta with pesto makes an excellent main course for four. It also can be served as a side dish; figure at least eight servings per pound of pasta. When serving pasta with pesto as a main course, try warming the bowls in a 200-degree oven for ten minutes. Room-temperature pesto sauce can cool down hot drained pasta fairly quickly. Warm bowls can slow down this process. Wear oven mitts when handling bowls and warn everyone at the table that the bowls are hot.

MASTER RECIPE

Linguine with Pesto

SERVES 4

BASIL USUALLY DARKENS in homemade pesto, but you can boost the green color by adding the optional parsley. For sharper flavor, substitute 1 tablespoon finely grated pecorino cheese for 1 tablespoon of the Parmesan. Linguine, a long, thin pasta, is traditional, but a curly shape, like fusilli, can trap bits of the pesto.

> ¼ cup pine nuts, walnuts, or almonds
> 3 medium garlic cloves, threaded on a skewer
> 2 cups packed fresh basil leaves
> 2 tablespoons fresh flat-leaf parsley leaves (optional)
> 7 tablespoons extra-virgin olive oil
> Salt
> ¼ cup finely grated Parmesan cheese
> 1 pound linguine or other long, thin pasta

1. Toast the nuts in a small, heavy skillet over medium heat, stirring frequently, until just golden and fragrant, 4 to 5 minutes.

2. Meanwhile, bring 4 quarts of water to a boil in a large pot. Lower the skewered garlic into the water (see illustration 1, page 56); boil for 45 seconds. Immediately run the garlic under cold water. Remove from the skewer; peel and mince.

3. Place the basil and parsley (if using) in a heavy-duty, quart-size, sealable plastic bag; pound with the flat side of a meat pounder until all the leaves are bruised (see illustration 2, page 56).

4. Place the nuts, garlic, basil, oil, and ½ teaspoon salt to taste in the work bowl of a food processor; process until smooth, stopping as necessary to scrape down the sides of the bowl. Transfer the mixture to a small bowl, stir in the cheese, and adjust the salt. (The surface of the pesto can be covered with a sheet of plastic wrap or a thin film of oil and refrigerated for up to 5 days.)

5. Add 1 tablespoon salt and the pasta to the boiling water. Cook until al dente. Reserve ½ cup of the cooking water; drain the pasta and transfer it back to the cooking pot. Mix in ¼ cup of the reserved cooking water and the pesto; use the additional ¼ cup cooking water as needed to moisten the sauce. Divide among 4 warmed pasta bowls and serve immediately.

TWO ESSENTIAL STEPS WHEN MAKING PESTO

1. Briefly blanching whole unpeeled cloves of garlic tames their flavor and prevents the garlic from over-powering the other ingredients in pesto. Skewer whole unpeeled cloves and then lower them into a pot of boiling water (use the boiling water for cooking pasta unless making the pesto in advance) for 45 seconds. Immediately run the garlic under cold water to stop the cooking process.

If making pesto in advance, you won't have a large pot of water on the stove to cook the pasta. In this case, blanch the garlic in a small saucepan filled with boiling water.

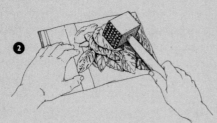

2. Bruising herb leaves in a sealable plastic bag with the flat side of a meat pounder (or rolling pin) is a quick but effective substitute for hand-pounding with a mortar and pestle and helps to release their flavor.

Fusilli with Creamy Basil Pesto

THE ADDITION OF RICOTTA CHEESE MAKES PASTA WITH PESTO MILD AND CREAMY. THIS SAUCE IS FAIRLY THICK AND CLINGS NICELY TO THE CURVES ON FUSILLI PASTA. SERVES 4.

> ¼ cup pine nuts, walnuts, or almonds
> 3 medium garlic cloves, threaded on a skewer
> 2 cups packed fresh basil leaves
> 2 tablespoons fresh flat-leaf parsley leaves (optional)
> 7 tablespoons extra-virgin olive oil
> Salt
> ¼ cup finely grated Parmesan cheese
> ¼ cup ricotta cheese
> 1 pound fusilli or other curly pasta

1. Toast the nuts in a small, heavy skillet over medium heat, stirring frequently, until just golden and fragrant, 4 to 5 minutes.

2. Meanwhile, bring 4 quarts of water to a boil in a large pot. Lower the skewered garlic into the water (see illustration 1); boil for 45 seconds. Immediately run the garlic under cold water. Remove from the skewer; peel and mince.

3. Place the basil and parsley (if using) in a heavy-duty, quart-size, sealable plastic bag; pound with the flat side of a meat pounder until all the leaves are bruised (see illustration 2).

4. Place the nuts, garlic, basil, oil, and ½ teaspoon salt in the work bowl of a food processor; process until smooth, stopping as necessary to scrape down the sides of the bowl. Transfer the mixture to a small bowl, stir in the cheeses, and adjust the salt. (The surface of the pesto can be covered with a sheet of plastic wrap or a thin film of oil and refrigerated for up to 5 days.)

5. Add 1 tablespoon salt and the pasta to the boiling water. Cook until al dente. Reserve ½ cup of the cooking water; drain the pasta and transfer it back to the cooking pot. Mix in ¼ cup of the reserved cooking water and the pesto; use the additional ¼ cup cooking water as needed to moisten the sauce. Divide among 4 warmed pasta bowls and serve immediately.

Spaghetti with Basil–Red Onion Pesto

THIS SICILIAN VERSION OF PESTO SUBSTITUTES RED ONION AND FRESH HOT PEPPER FOR GARLIC. CHEESE IS TRADITIONALLY NOT ADDED TO THIS SAUCE, BUT YOU CAN ADD ¼ CUP FINELY GRATED PARMESAN OR PECORINO CHEESE IF YOU LIKE. **SERVES 4.**

> ¼ cup pine nuts, walnuts, or almonds
> 2 cups packed fresh basil leaves
> 2 tablespoons fresh flat-leaf parsley leaves (optional)
> 7 tablespoons extra-virgin olive oil
> Salt
> 2 tablespoons minced red onion
> ½ jalapeño chile, or to taste, stemmed, halved, and seeded
> 1 pound spaghetti or other long, thin pasta

1. Toast the nuts in a small, heavy skillet over medium heat, stirring frequently, until just golden and fragrant, 4 to 5 minutes.

2. Meanwhile, bring 4 quarts of water to a boil in a large pot for cooking the pasta.

3. Place the basil and parsley (if using) in a heavy-duty, quart-size, sealable plastic bag; pound with the flat side of a meat pounder until all the leaves are bruised (see illustration 2, page 56).

4. Place the nuts, basil, oil, ½ teaspoon salt, the onion, and chile in the work bowl of a food processor; process until smooth, stopping as necessary to scrape down the sides of the bowl. Transfer the mixture to a small bowl and adjust the salt. (The surface of the pesto can be covered with a sheet of plastic wrap or a thin film of oil and refrigerated for up to 5 days.)

5. When the water comes to a boil, add 1 tablespoon salt and the pasta. Cook until al dente. Reserve ½ cup of the cooking water; drain the pasta and transfer it back to the cooking pot. Mix in ¼ cup of the reserved cooking water and the pesto; use the additional ¼ cup cooking water as needed to moisten the sauce. Divide among 4 warmed pasta bowls and serve immediately.

Linguine with Mint Pesto

MINT PESTO HAS A STRONGER FLAVOR THAN CLASSIC BASIL PESTO. SERVE THIS DISH ON THE SIDE WITH BROILED OR GRILLED SALMON, SQUID, LAMB CHOPS, OR OTHER EQUALLY ASSERTIVE SEAFOOD OR MEAT. **SERVES 8 AS A SIDE DISH.**

> ¼ cup pine nuts, walnuts, or almonds
> 3 medium garlic cloves, threaded on a skewer
> 2 cups packed fresh mint leaves
> 7 tablespoons extra-virgin olive oil
> Salt
> ¼ cup finely grated Parmesan cheese
> 1 pound linguine or other long, thin pasta

1. Toast the nuts in a small, heavy skillet over medium heat, stirring frequently, until just golden and fragrant, 4 to 5 minutes.

2. Meanwhile, bring 4 quarts of water to a boil in a large pot. Lower the skewered garlic into the water (see illustration 1, page 56); boil for 45 seconds. Immediately run the garlic under cold water. Remove from the skewer; peel and mince.

3. Place the mint in a heavy-duty, quart-size, sealable plastic bag; pound with the flat side of a meat pounder until all the leaves are bruised (see illustration 2, page 56).

4. Place the nuts, garlic, mint, oil, and ½ teaspoon salt in the work bowl of a food processor; process until smooth, stopping as necessary to scrape down the sides of the bowl. Transfer the mixture to a small bowl, stir in the cheese, and adjust the salt. (The surface of the pesto can be covered with a sheet of plastic wrap or a thin film of oil and refrigerated for up to 5 days.)

5. Add 1 tablespoon salt and the pasta to the boiling water. Cook until al dente. Reserve ½ cup of the cooking water; drain the pasta and transfer it back to the cooking pot. Mix in ¼ cup of the reserved cooking water and the pesto; use the additional ¼ cup cooking water as needed to moisten the sauce. Place in a warmed serving bowl and serve immediately.

Linguine with Cilantro Pesto

THE STRONG FLAVOR OF WALNUTS PAIRS WELL WITH
CILANTRO. LIKEWISE, IN PLACE OF PARMESAN, WE LIKE
THE MORE ASSERTIVE PECORINO ROMANO IN THIS
PESTO. FOR EXTRA KICK, ADD THE OPTIONAL LIME
ZEST. SERVES 4.

¼ cup walnuts
3 medium garlic cloves, threaded on a
   skewer
2 cups packed fresh cilantro leaves
7 tablespoons extra-virgin olive oil
½ teaspoon grated lime zest (optional;
   see illustration, page 42)
Salt
¼ cup finely grated pecorino cheese
1 pound linguine or other long, thin pasta

1. Toast the nuts in a small, heavy skillet over
medium heat, stirring frequently, until just golden and
fragrant, 4 to 5 minutes.

2. Meanwhile, bring 4 quarts of water to a boil in a
large pot. Lower the skewered garlic into the water
(see illustration 1, page 56); boil for 45 seconds.
Immediately run the garlic under cold water. Remove
from the skewer; peel and mince.

3. Place the nuts, garlic, cilantro, oil, zest if using,
and ½ teaspoon salt in the work bowl of a food
processor; process until smooth, stopping as necessary
to scrape down the sides of the bowl. Transfer the
mixture to a small bowl, stir in the cheese, and adjust
the salt. (The surface of the pesto can be covered with
a sheet of plastic wrap or a thin film of oil and refrigerated for up to 5 days.)

4. Add 1 tablespoon salt and the pasta to the boiling
water. Cook until al dente. Reserve ½ cup of the
cooking water; drain the pasta and transfer it back to
the cooking pot. Mix in ¼ cup of the reserved cooking water and the pesto; use the additional ¼ cup
cooking water as needed to moisten the sauce. Divide
among 4 warmed pasta bowls and serve immediately.

Linguine with Lemon-Dill Pesto

PASTA FLAVORED WITH LEMON AND DILL MAKES A
GOOD SIDE DISH FOR SPRING CLASSICS LIKE ROAST LEG
OF LAMB OR POACHED SALMON. FEATHERY DILL LEAVES
ARE TOO SMALL TO BENEFIT FROM BRUISING IN A PLAS-
TIC BAG. SERVES 8 AS A SIDE DISH.

¼ cup pine nuts, walnuts, or almonds
3 medium garlic cloves, threaded on a
   skewer
1½ cups packed fresh dill leaves
7 tablespoons extra-virgin olive oil
1 teaspoon grated lemon zest (see
   illustration, page 42)
Salt
¼ cup finely grated Parmesan cheese
1 pound linguine or other long, thin pasta

1. Toast the nuts in a small, heavy skillet over
medium heat, stirring frequently, until just golden and
fragrant, 4 to 5 minutes.

2. Meanwhile, bring 4 quarts of water to a boil in a
large pot. Lower the skewered garlic into the water
(see illustration 1, page 56); boil for 45 seconds.
Immediately run the garlic under cold water. Remove
from the skewer; peel and mince.

3. Place the nuts, garlic, dill, oil, zest, and ½ teaspoon salt in the work bowl of a food processor;
process until smooth, stopping as necessary to scrape
down the sides of the bowl. Transfer the mixture to a
small bowl, stir in the cheese, and adjust the salt. (The
surface of the pesto can be covered with a sheet of
plastic wrap or a thin film of oil and refrigerated for up
to 5 days.)

4. Add 1 tablespoon salt and the pasta to the boiling
water. Cook until al dente. Reserve ½ cup of the
cooking water; drain the pasta and transfer it back to
the cooking pot. Mix in ¼ cup of the reserved cooking water and the pesto; use the additional ¼ cup
cooking water as needed to moisten the sauce. Place
in a warmed serving dish and serve immediately.

Penne with Fusion Pesto

WHEN ASIAN AND MEDITERRANEAN FLAVORS ARE COM-
BINED, THE RESULT IS A SURPRISINGLY VERSATILE
PESTO. THIS DISH COULD BE SERVED WITH EITHER A
LEMONY ROAST CHICKEN OR HOISIN-BARBECUED RIBS.
SERVES 8 AS A SIDE DISH.

> ¼ cup pine nuts, walnuts, or almonds
> 3 medium garlic cloves, threaded on a
>   skewer
> 1 cup packed fresh basil leaves
> ½ cup packed fresh mint leaves
> ½ cup packed fresh cilantro leaves
> ½-inch-long piece fresh gingerroot,
>   peeled and sliced (see illustrations 1–3,
>   page 43)
> ½ teaspoon hot red pepper flakes, or to
>   taste
> 7 tablespoons extra-virgin olive oil
> Salt
> 1 pound penne or other short, tubular
>   pasta

1. Toast the nuts in a small, heavy skillet over medium heat, stirring frequently, until just golden and fragrant, 4 to 5 minutes.

2. Meanwhile, bring 4 quarts of water to a boil in a large pot. Lower the skewered garlic into the water (see illustration 1, page 56); boil for 45 seconds. Immediately run the garlic under cold water. Remove from the skewer; peel and mince.

3. Place the basil, mint, and cilantro in a heavy-duty, quart-size, sealable plastic bag; pound with the flat side of a meat pounder until all the leaves are bruised (see illustration 2, page 56).

4. Place the nuts, garlic, herbs, ginger, red pepper flakes, oil, and ½ teaspoon salt in the work bowl of a food processor; process until smooth, stopping as necessary to scrape down the sides of the bowl. Transfer the mixture to a small bowl and adjust the salt. (The surface of the pesto can be covered with a sheet of plastic wrap or a thin film of oil and refrigerated for up to 5 days.)

5. Add 1 tablespoon salt and the pasta to the boiling water. Cook until al dente. Reserve ½ cup of the cooking water; drain the pasta and transfer it back to the cooking pot. Mix in ¼ cup of the reserved cooking water and the pesto; use the additional ¼ cup cooking water as needed to moisten the sauce. Place in a warmed serving dish and serve immediately.

◆

Spaghetti with Mixed Herb Pesto

DEPENDING ON WHAT YOU HAVE IN YOUR REFRIGERA-
TOR OR HERB GARDEN, ANY ASSORTMENT OF HERBS MAY
BE USED TO MAKE PESTO; JUST REMEMBER TO USE ONLY
MILDER HERBS—PARSLEY, BASIL, MINT, CILANTRO—IN
LARGE QUANTITIES, UP TO 1 CUP. ADD ONLY A TABLE-
SPOON OR SO EACH OF STRONGER HERBS LIKE THYME,
OREGANO, SAGE, TARRAGON, AND ROSEMARY, OR YOUR
PESTO WILL BE OVERWHELMINGLY STRONG. SERVES 4.

> ¼ cup pine nuts, walnuts, or almonds
> 3 medium garlic cloves, threaded on a
>   skewer
> 1 cup packed fresh flat-leaf parsley leaves
> ¾ cup packed fresh basil leaves
> 1 tablespoon fresh thyme leaves
> 1 tablespoon fresh oregano leaves
> 1 tablespoon fresh tarragon leaves
> 1 tablespoon fresh sage leaves
> 7 tablespoons extra-virgin olive oil
> 1 tablespoon lemon juice
> Salt
> ¼ cup finely grated Parmesan cheese
> 1 pound spaghetti or other long, thin
>   pasta

1. Toast the nuts in a small, heavy skillet over medium heat, stirring frequently, until just golden and fragrant, 4 to 5 minutes.

2. Meanwhile, bring 4 quarts of water to a boil in a large pot. Lower the skewered garlic into the water (see illustration 1, page 56); boil for 45 seconds. Immediately run the garlic under cold water. Remove from the skewer; peel and mince.

(continued on next page)

3. Place the herbs in a heavy-duty, quart-size, sealable plastic bag; pound with the flat side of a meat pounder until all the leaves are bruised (see illustration 2, page 56).

4. Place the nuts, garlic, herbs, oil, juice, and ½ teaspoon salt in the work bowl of a food processor; process until smooth, stopping as necessary to scrape down the sides of the bowl. Transfer the mixture to a small bowl, stir in the cheese, and adjust the salt. (The surface of the pesto can be covered with a sheet of plastic wrap or a thin film of oil and refrigerated for up to 5 days.)

5. Add 1 tablespoon salt and the pasta to the boiling water. Cook until al dente. Reserve ½ cup of the cooking water; drain the pasta and transfer it back to the cooking pot. Mix in ¼ cup of the reserved cooking water and the pesto; use the additional ¼ cup cooking water as needed to moisten the sauce. Divide among 4 warmed pasta bowls and serve immediately.

◆

Linguine with Arugula Pesto

ARUGULA MAKES A PEPPERY PESTO. USED ALONE, THE FLAVOR IS TOO STRONG. PARSLEY REINFORCES THE GREEN COLOR OF THE ARUGULA, TAMING WITHOUT COMPETING WITH ITS FLAVOR. A LITTLE RICOTTA CHEESE TEMPERS THE ARUGULA'S FLAVOR EVEN FURTHER. SERVES 4.

> ¼ cup pine nuts, walnuts, or almonds
> 3 medium garlic cloves, threaded on a
>   skewer
> 1 cup packed fresh stemmed arugula
>   leaves
> 1 cup packed fresh flat-leaf parsley leaves
> 7 tablespoons extra-virgin olive oil
> Salt
> ⅓ cup ricotta cheese
> 2 tablespoons finely grated Parmesan
>   cheese
> 1 pound linguine or other long, thin pasta

1. Toast the nuts in a small, heavy skillet over medium heat, stirring frequently, until just golden and fragrant, 4 to 5 minutes.

2. Meanwhile, bring 4 quarts of water to a boil in a large pot. Lower the skewered garlic into the water (see illustration 1, page 56); boil for 45 seconds. Immediately run the garlic under cold water. Remove from the skewer; peel and mince.

3. Place the arugula and parsley in a heavy-duty, quart-size, sealable plastic bag; pound with the flat side of a meat pounder until all the leaves are bruised (see illustration 2, page 56).

4. Place the nuts, garlic, arugula, parsley, oil, and ½ teaspoon salt in the work bowl of a food processor; process until smooth, stopping as necessary to scrape down the sides of the bowl. Transfer the mixture to a small bowl, stir in the cheeses, and adjust the salt. (The surface of the pesto can be covered with a sheet of plastic wrap or a thin film of oil and refrigerated for up to 5 days.)

5. Add 1 tablespoon salt and the pasta to the boiling water. Cook until al dente. Reserve ½ cup of the cooking water; drain the pasta and transfer it back to the cooking pot. Mix in ¼ cup of the reserved cooking water and the pesto; use the additional ¼ cup cooking water as needed to moisten the sauce. Divide among 4 warmed pasta bowls and serve immediately.

Fusilli with Spinach and Ricotta Pesto

SPINACH FUNCTIONS AS A FLAVORFUL HERB RATHER THAN A LEAFY VEGETABLE WHEN IT REPLACES BASIL IN PESTO. THE ADDITION OF RICOTTA CHEESE GIVES THIS PESTO DISH A HINT OF CREAMED-SPINACH FLAVOR. SERVES 4.

> 1/4 cup pine nuts, walnuts, or almonds
> 3 medium garlic cloves, threaded on a skewer
> 2 cups packed fresh spinach, stemmed and washed
> 7 tablespoons extra-virgin olive oil
> Salt
> 1/2 cup ricotta cheese
> 1/4 cup finely grated Parmesan cheese
> 1 pound fusilli or other curly pasta

1. Toast the nuts in a small, heavy skillet over medium heat, stirring frequently, until just golden and fragrant, 4 to 5 minutes.

2. Meanwhile, bring 4 quarts of water to a boil in a large pot. Lower the skewered garlic into the water (see illustration 1, page 56); boil for 45 seconds. Immediately run the garlic under cold water. Remove from the skewer; peel and mince.

3. Place the nuts, garlic, spinach, oil, and 1/2 teaspoon salt in the work bowl of a food processor; process until smooth, stopping as necessary to scrape down the sides of the bowl. Transfer the mixture to a small bowl, stir in the cheeses, and adjust the salt. (The surface of the pesto can be covered with a sheet of plastic wrap or a thin film of oil and refrigerated for up to 5 days.)

4. Add 1 tablespoon salt and the pasta to the boiling water. Cook until al dente. Reserve 1/2 cup of the cooking water; drain the pasta and transfer it back to the cooking pot. Mix in 1/4 cup of the reserved cooking water and the pesto; use the additional 1/4 cup cooking water as needed to moisten the sauce. Divide among 4 warmed pasta bowls and serve immediately.

Linguine with Sun-Dried Tomato and Goat Cheese Pesto

USE SUN-DRIED TOMATOES PACKED IN OIL, BUT BLOT THEM WELL WITH PAPER TOWELS TO REMOVE EXCESS OIL. WE FIND THAT USING FRESH OLIVE OIL IN THE PESTO, RATHER THAN THE TOMATO OIL, GIVES THE PESTO A CLEANER FLAVOR. SERVES 4.

> 1/4 cup pine nuts, walnuts, or almonds
> 3 medium garlic cloves, threaded on a skewer
> 16 sun-dried tomatoes packed in olive oil, drained
> 2 tablespoons fresh flat-leaf parsley leaves
> 7 tablespoons extra-virgin olive oil
> Salt
> 1/4 cup fresh goat cheese (about 2 ounces)
> 1 pound linguine or other long, thin pasta

1. Toast the nuts in a small, heavy skillet over medium heat, stirring frequently, until just golden and fragrant, 4 to 5 minutes.

2. Meanwhile, bring 4 quarts of water to a boil in a large pot. Lower the skewered garlic into the water (see illustration 1, page 56); boil for 45 seconds. Immediately run the garlic under cold water. Remove from the skewer; peel and mince.

3. Place the nuts, garlic, tomatoes, parsley, oil, and 1/2 teaspoon salt in the work bowl of a food processor; process until smooth, stopping as necessary to scrape down the sides of the bowl. Transfer the mixture to a small bowl, stir in the cheese, and adjust the salt. (The surface of the pesto can be covered with a sheet of plastic wrap or a thin film of oil and refrigerated for up to 5 days.)

4. Add 1 tablespoon salt and the pasta to the boiling water. Cook until al dente. Reserve 1/2 cup of the cooking water; drain the pasta and transfer it back to the cooking pot. Mix in 1/4 cup of the reserved cooking water and the pesto; use the additional 1/4 cup cooking water as needed to moisten the sauce. Divide among 4 warmed pasta bowls and serve immediately.

Spaghetti with Olivada

OLIVADA CAN BE AS SIMPLE AS PUREEING BLACK OLIVES WITH OLIVE OIL. WE LIKE TO ADD BASIL, THYME, SHALLOT, AND LEMON JUICE TO BALANCE THE INTENSITY OF THE OLIVE FLAVOR. SUBSTITUTE BLANCHED GARLIC FOR THE SHALLOT IF YOU LIKE. MEATY BLACK OLIVES, SUCH AS KALAMATAS, WILL BE EASIER TO PIT. DEPENDING ON THEIR SALTINESS, YOU MAY NEED VERY LITTLE, IF ANY, SALT IN THE PESTO. **SERVES 4.**

> 1½ cups black olives, pitted (see
>   illustrations 1–2)
> 1 medium shallot, coarsely chopped
> 6 large fresh basil leaves
> 2 teaspoons fresh thyme leaves
> 2 tablespoons extra-virgin olive oil
> 1 tablespoon lemon juice
> Salt
> 1 pound spaghetti or other long, thin
>   pasta

1. Place the olives, shallot, herbs, oil, and juice in the work bowl of a food processor; process until smooth, stopping as necessary to scrape down the sides of the bowl. Transfer the mixture to a small bowl and add salt to taste. (The surface of the pesto can be covered with a sheet of plastic wrap or a thin film of oil and refrigerated for up to 5 days.)

2. Meanwhile, bring 4 quarts of water to a boil in a large pot. Add 1 tablespoon salt and the pasta to the boiling water. Cook until al dente. Reserve ½ cup of the cooking water; drain the pasta and transfer it back to the cooking pot. Mix in ¼ cup of the reserved cooking water and the pesto; use the additional ¼ cup cooking water as needed to moisten the sauce. Divide among 4 warmed pasta bowls and serve immediately.

PITTING OLIVES

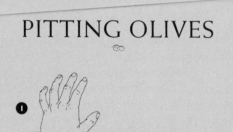

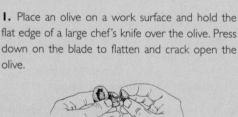

1. Place an olive on a work surface and hold the flat edge of a large chef's knife over the olive. Press down on the blade to flatten and crack open the olive.

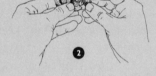

2. Separate the pit from the olive meat with your fingers.

Fusilli with Parsley, Green Olive, and Caper Pesto

THE PARSLEY, OLIVES, AND CAPERS GIVE THIS SAUCE AN ATTRACTIVE BRIGHT GREEN COLOR. THE OPTIONAL ANCHOVY FILLETS MAKE THE FINISHED DISH A GOOD STARTER OR SIDE FOR EIGHT TO A MEAL OF PAN-SEARED OR GRILLED TUNA STEAKS OR SHRIMP. **SERVES 4.**

> 3 medium garlic cloves, threaded on a
> skewer
> ½ cup packed fresh flat-leaf parsley
> leaves
> 1½ cups green olives, pitted (see
> illustrations 1–2, page 62)
> 1 tablespoon capers, rinsed
> 2 anchovy fillets (optional)
> 2 tablespoons extra-virgin olive oil
> 2 tablespoons lemon juice
> Salt
> 1 pound fusilli or other curly pasta

1. Bring 4 quarts of water to a boil in a large pot. Lower the skewered garlic into the water (see illustration 1, page 56); boil for 45 seconds. Immediately run the garlic under cold water. Remove from the skewer; peel and mince.

2. Place the garlic, parsley, olives, capers, anchovies if using, oil, and juice in the work bowl of a food processor; process until smooth, stopping as necessary to scrape down the sides of the bowl. Transfer the mixture to a small bowl and add salt to taste. (The surface of the pesto can be covered with a sheet of plastic wrap or a thin film of oil and refrigerated for up to 5 days.)

3. Add 1 tablespoon salt and the pasta to the boiling water. Cook until al dente. Reserve ½ cup of the cooking water; drain the pasta and transfer it back to the cooking pot. Mix in ¼ cup of the reserved cooking water and the pesto; use the additional ¼ cup cooking water as needed to moisten the sauce. Divide among 4 warmed pasta bowls and serve immediately.

Linguine with Tuna Pesto

IN ITALY, CHEESE AND SEAFOOD ARE RARELY USED TOGETHER IN THE SAME DISH. WE AGREE THAT THE FLAVOR AND RICHNESS OF THE CHEESE USUALLY OVERWHELMS THE SEAFOOD. THIS PESTO, MADE FROM PUREED CANNED TUNA, GETS ITS CREAMINESS FROM OLIVE OIL ALONE. **SERVES 4.**

> 3 medium garlic cloves, threaded on a
> skewer
> 2 cups packed fresh flat-leaf parsley leaves
> 1 6-ounce can tuna packed in olive oil,
> drained
> 3 anchovy fillets
> 4 tablespoons extra-virgin olive oil
> 2 tablespoons lemon juice
> Salt
> 1 pound linguine or other long, thin pasta

1. Bring 4 quarts of water to a boil in a large pot. Lower the skewered garlic into the water (see illustration 1, page 56); boil for 45 seconds. Immediately run the garlic under cold water. Remove from the skewer; peel and mince.

2. Place the garlic, parsley, tuna, anchovies, oil, and juice in the work bowl of a food processor; process until smooth, stopping as necessary to scrape down the sides of the bowl. Transfer the mixture to a small bowl and add salt to taste. (The surface of the pesto can be covered with a sheet of plastic wrap or a thin film of oil and refrigerated for up to 5 days.)

3. Add 1 tablespoon salt and the pasta to the boiling water. Cook until al dente. Reserve ½ cup of the cooking water; drain the pasta and transfer it back to the cooking pot. Mix in ¼ cup of the reserved cooking water and the pesto; use the additional ¼ cup cooking water as needed to moisten the sauce. Divide among 4 warmed pasta bowls and serve immediately.

Fusilli with Nut Pesto

GROUND NUTS MAKE A RICH PESTO. YOU CAN USE ANY
VARIETY OF NUTS—IF YOU DON'T HAVE HAZELNUTS ON
HAND, JUST ADD ¼ CUP EXTRA OF ANY OF THE OTHERS
THAT YOU DO HAVE. PECANS AND/OR PISTACHIOS MAY
ALSO STAND IN FOR ANY OF THE NUTS HERE. JUST
MAINTAIN THE PROPORTIONS GIVEN IN THE RECIPE.
BUY SKINNED HAZELNUTS IF YOU CAN OR TOAST THEM
IN A 350-DEGREE OVEN FOR 10 MINUTES, WRAP THE
HOT NUTS IN A CLEAN KITCHEN TOWEL, AND RUB OFF
AS MUCH OF THE SKINS AS POSSIBLE. SERVES 4.

> ¼ cup skinned hazelnuts
> ¼ cup whole almonds
> ¼ cup walnuts
> ¼ cup pine nuts
> 3 medium garlic cloves, threaded on a
>   skewer
> ¼ cup packed fresh flat-leaf parsley leaves
> 7 tablespoons extra-virgin olive oil
> Salt
> ¼ cup finely grated Parmesan cheese
> 1 pound fusilli or other short, curly pasta

1. Toast the nuts in a medium, heavy skillet over
medium heat, stirring frequently, until just golden and
fragrant, 4 to 5 minutes.

2. Meanwhile, bring 4 quarts of water to a boil in a
large pot. Lower the skewered garlic into the water
(see illustration 1, page 56); boil for 45 seconds.
Immediately run the garlic under cold water. Remove
from the skewer; peel and mince.

3. Place the nuts, garlic, parsley, oil, and ½ teaspoon
salt in the work bowl of a food processor; process until
smooth, stopping as necessary to scrape down the
sides of the bowl. Transfer the mixture to a small bowl,
stir in the cheese, and adjust the salt. (The surface of
the pesto can be covered with a sheet of plastic wrap
and refrigerated for up to 5 days.)

4. Add 1 tablespoon salt and the pasta to the boiling
water. Cook until al dente. Reserve ½ cup of the
cooking water; drain the pasta and transfer it back to
the cooking pot. Mix in ¼ cup of the reserved cooking water and the pesto; use the additional ¼ cup
cooking water as needed to moisten the sauce. Divide
among 4 warmed pasta bowls and serve immediately.

◆

Fusilli with White Pesto

LIKE THE PREVIOUS RECIPE, THIS TRADITIONAL SOUTH-
ERN ITALIAN PASTA SAUCE DEPENDS ON NUTS RATHER
THAN HERBS FOR FLAVOR. THE ADDITION OF RICOTTA
CHEESE MAKES THIS PESTO SMOOTHER AND CREAMIER.
SERVES 4.

> ¾ cup walnuts
> 3 medium garlic cloves, threaded on a
>   skewer
> 2 tablespoons extra-virgin olive oil
> Salt
> 1 cup ricotta cheese
> ¼ cup finely grated Parmesan cheese
> 1 pound fusilli or other short, curly pasta

1. Toast the nuts in a small, heavy skillet over
medium heat, stirring frequently, until just golden and
fragrant, 4 to 5 minutes.

2. Meanwhile, bring 4 quarts of water to a boil in a
large pot. Lower the skewered garlic into the water
(see illustration 1, page 56); boil for 45 seconds.
Immediately run the garlic under cold water. Remove
from the skewer; peel and mince.

3. Place the nuts, garlic, oil, and ½ teaspoon salt in
the work bowl of a food processor; process until
smooth, stopping as necessary to scrape down the
sides of the bowl. Transfer the mixture to a small bowl,
stir in the cheeses, and adjust the salt. (The surface of
the pesto can be covered with a sheet of plastic wrap
and refrigerated for up to 5 days.)

4. Add 1 tablespoon salt and the pasta to the boiling
water. Cook until al dente. Reserve ½ cup of the
cooking water; drain the pasta and transfer it back to
the cooking pot. Mix in ¼ cup of the reserved cooking water and the pesto; use the additional ¼ cup
cooking water as needed to moisten the sauce. Divide
among 4 warmed pasta bowls and serve immediately.

BUTTER AND CHEESE SAUCES

/|\

SAUCES THAT DERIVE THEIR FLAVOR FROM BUTTER

AND CHEESE ARE AMONG THE SIMPLEST IN THIS BOOK.

LIKE OIL-BASED SAUCES, THEY REQUIRE MINIMAL

WORK AND CAN BE PREPARED IN THE TIME IT TAKES

TO BRING WATER TO A BOIL AND COOK THE PASTA.

Some butter and cheese sauces are not cooked. The butter or cheese (as well as flavorings) is simply tossed with hot pasta and served. In other cases, the butter and cheese may be melted to make a quick sauce. In both cases, we find it necessary to reserve some of the pasta cooking water to thin out these sauces. In addition, these sauces add little bulk or heat to pasta (in fact, some of the unheated sauces actually cool the pasta down), so we always warm serving bowls to keep these pastas hot as they are eaten.

Butter is an important ingredient in many of the sauces in this chapter. (For more information on cheeses, see pages 68–70.) We recommend using unsalted butter in pasta dishes and all your cooking. Salted butter does not have the same fresh dairy flavor as sweet butter. Also, manufacturers add varying amounts of salt, which makes it difficult to judge how much more salt a dish might require. We prefer to add salt directly to a dish, not through the butter.

So what is butter? Simply put, butter is over-whipped or churned cream. In cream, globules of fat protected by a phospholipid membrane float about in a suspension of water. When cream is agitated or churned, the fat globules collide with one another, causing the membranes to break. The freed fat globules then begin to clump together, trapping little pockets of water along with the broken membrane pieces and some intact fat crystals. After the cream is churned into a semisolid mass of butter, any remaining liquid is drawn off as buttermilk. So what begins as an oil-in-water emulsion (cream) is reversed into a water-in-oil emulsion (butter).

All butter must consist of at least 80 percent milk fat, according to U.S. government standards. Most domestic commercial butters do not exceed this standard. A few European butters are exceptions, containing as much as 88 percent milk fat. All butters contain about 2 percent milk solids and the remainder is water.

Butter is extremely perishable. Exposure to light and air is particularly harmful, which is why some brands of butter are wrapped in foil rather than paper. The fats in butter are vulnerable not only to oxidation but also to picking up odors, especially at warmer temperatures. For this reason, we do not recommend storing butter in the refrigerator's butter compartment,

which tends to be warmer than the main part of the refrigerator. To find out how much of a difference this made, we stored one stick of butter in its original wrapper in the butter compartment and one in the center of the refrigerator. After one week, the butter in the compartment had begun to pick up off flavors, while the one stored in the center tasted fresh.

To see how different brands perform, we tasted eight leading brands in a variety of dishes, including a yellow cake with frosting, pie pastry, and melted on bread. With the exception of the buttercream test where higher-fat butters (Plugrá and Celles Sur Belle) excelled, we found few differences among various brands. We did notice in our testing that freshness matters, with fresher samples clearly outperforming older samples from the same company. We recommend that you pay more attention to the condition in which you buy the butter, and the conditions under which you store it, than to a particular brand. Purchase butter from a reliable store with a high turnover of products. The best way to store butter is sealed in an airtight plastic bag in the freezer, pulling out sticks as you need them. Butter will keep in the freezer for several months, and in the refrigerator for no more than two or three weeks.

Many butter and cheese sauces are traditionally served over fresh pasta. We wanted to understand the logic behind the recommendation, so we tested every recipe in this chapter with both fresh and dried pasta. With several very simple butter sauces, we felt that fresh pasta was far superior to dried pasta and it is the only recommendation given in these recipes. Fresh noodles absorbed some of these sauces (simple butter sauces tended to slide off dried noodles). Also, the egg flavor of good fresh pasta melded better with many of these sauces, making for more complex dishes.

In other cases, we preferred the results when we used fresh pasta, but we found the versions made with dried pasta to be quite good. In these instances, we have indicated that you may use either fresh or dried pasta.

Lastly, some sauces, especially those with ricotta cheese, tasted best with dried pasta. These sauces are more rugged and we felt that they overwhelmed the delicate texture and flavor of fresh pasta.

Fettuccine with Butter and Parmesan

SERVES 4

NE OF THE SIMPLEST and best pasta dishes, this should be made with fresh egg noodles. When we tested this dish with dried pasta, we were quite disappointed. The sauce slid off the dried noodles and pooled in the bottom of each serving bowl. In contrast, the fresh noodles absorbed some sauce (and thus tasted better) and the remaining sauce clung to these noodles much better. Toss the drained pasta and "sauce" over low heat to give the noodles a chance to absorb the butter and cheese.

Salt
1 pound Fresh Egg Pasta (page 21) cut
   into fettuccine
5 tablespoons unsalted butter, softened
1/2 cup grated Parmesan cheese

Bring 4 quarts of water to a boil in a large pot. Add 1 tablespoon salt and the pasta to the boiling water. Cook just until al dente. Drain the pasta and return it to the cooking pot. Add the butter and cheese, and cook over low heat, tossing to combine ingredients, for 1 minute. Adjust the seasonings. Divide among 4 warmed pasta bowls and serve immediately.

◆

Fettuccine with Rosemary Butter

THIS SIMPLE HERB-INFUSED BUTTER SAUCE IS BEST ON FRESH PASTA—THE ABSORBENT, SOFT EGG PASTA COMPLEMENTS THE LUXURIOUS FLAVOR OF THE ROSEMARY BUTTER. OTHER FRESH, HIGHLY AROMATIC HERBS, SUCH AS SAGE OR THYME, MAY BE USED SIMILARLY. WE FOUND IT BEST TO LET THE HERBS STEEP IN THE MELTED BUTTER FOR 5 MINUTES, ENOUGH TIME FOR THE BUTTER TO BE PERFUMED WITH—BUT NOT OVERWHELMED BY—THE FLAVOR OF THE ROSEMARY. SERVES 4.

5 tablespoons unsalted butter
2 tablespoons minced fresh rosemary
   leaves
Salt
1 pound Fresh Egg Pasta (page 21) cut
   into fettuccine
1/2 cup grated Parmesan cheese

1. Bring 4 quarts of water to a boil in a large pot for cooking the pasta.

2. Place the butter and rosemary in a sauté pan large enough to accommodate the cooked pasta. Heat over low until the butter is melted. Turn off the heat and set aside for 5 minutes to allow the rosemary to flavor the butter.

3. Add 1 tablespoon salt and the pasta to the boiling water. Cook just until al dente. Drain the pasta and add it to the sauté pan. Add the cheese and cook over low heat, tossing to combine ingredients and flavors, 1 to 2 minutes. Adjust the salt. Divide among 4 warmed pasta bowls and serve immediately.

A GUIDE TO POPULAR CHEESES

THERE ARE DOZENS OF CHEESES THAT MAY BE USED IN PASTA DISHES. HERE'S A SHOPPING GUIDE TO THE CHEESES THAT ARE USED MOST FREQUENTLY IN THIS CHAPTER AND THROUGHOUT THE BOOK. ◆ FOR LONG-TERM STORAGE IN THE REFRIGERATOR, WE FIND THAT CHEESES ARE BEST WRAPPED IN

parchment paper and then in aluminum foil. The paper allows the cheese to breathe a bit while the foil keeps out off flavors from the refrigerator and prevents the cheese from drying out. Simply placing the cheese in a plastic bag, pressing out all the air, and then sealing the bag tight is our second choice. We find that pressing plastic wrap directly against the surface of most cheeses will cause a slight sour flavor to develop over time and we do not recommend this storage method.

CHEDDAR. American classics, such as macaroni and cheese (see chapter 20), often call for this cheese. In general, we don't use very sharp Cheddar cheese in cooking. For pasta dishes, choose a mild Cheddar cheese, either white or orange as you prefer. In general, we find that Wisconsin Cheddars are milder than cheeses from Vermont and New York.

FONTINA. Real Italian Fontina comes from the Valle d'Aosta area in the far northern reaches of the country. It has a creamy, semi-soft texture and nutty, buttery flavor. Fontina is also made in Denmark, Sweden, and the United States. These cheeses tend to be much firmer (almost like Cheddar) and sometimes rubbery. We find that

these versions also lack the full flavor of the Italian cheese and are often quite bland.

GOAT. Because of its creamy texture, fresh goat cheese has become a popular addition to pasta dishes in recent years, especially among American chefs. In many ways it functions like mascarpone cheese by adding creaminess and richness to pasta dishes. However, goat cheese brings a distinct tang as well. American goat cheese is every bit as good as imported chèvre from France. It is also generally much less expensive. When shopping, make sure to buy creamy fresh goat cheese unless otherwise directed. Aged goat cheese, which generally has a firm, edible rind, will not melt as easily.

GORGONZOLA. Gorgonzola is Italy's most famous blue cheese. It can be aged and quite crumbly or rather young and creamy. Aged Gorgonzola has a much more potent blue cheese flavor, similar to Roquefort. In general, we like young Gorgonzola in pasta dishes; its flavor is not so overwhelming, and the cheese yields a luxurious, creamy sauce when melted. When shopping, look for Gorgonzola dolce (sweet Gorgonzola), or simply shop by texture. If the cheese looks creamy enough to spread on bread, it should have a pleasant but not overpowering blue cheese flavor. Note that other creamy blue cheeses, such as Saga Blue, may be used in place of Gorgonzola, but the flavor may be somewhat different.

GRUYÈRE. This Swiss cheese has a rich, assertive flavor that comes from long aging. The texture is firm but not at all crumbly. When melted, Gruyère is creamy and smooth, which no doubt accounts for its appeal in pasta dishes. Because Gruyère has such a strong flavor, it is generally used in small quantities in pasta dishes and may be balanced by milder cheeses. Emmenthal is a similar Swiss cheese, although the flavor is not as complex.

MASCARPONE. This creamy Italian cheese is now made on both sides of the Atlantic. It is generally sold in tubs and has a consistency similar to cream cheese beaten with a little heavy cream. Unlike American cream cheese, mascarpone is not tangy and, in fact, it has a quite buttery, creamy flavor. Although there is no substitute for mascarpone, we find that American versions of this cheese are admirable and work as well as Italian mascarpone in recipes.

MONTEREY JACK. Like Cheddar, Monterey Jack is popular in some American pasta casseroles, such as macaroni and cheese. Good Jack cheese is semi-soft (not rubbery) and has a mild, acidic tang. Beware of mass-market Jack cheese that can be rubbery and as bland as American cheese.

MOZZARELLA. There are two types of mozzarella and they taste and perform quite differently in the kitchen. Shrink-wrapped mozzarella is fine for pizzas. It melts beautifully and no one notices how bland this cheese is when covered with pepperoni and tomato sauce. However, in simple pasta dishes, we prefer fresh mozzarella packed in water. This cheese has a milky, some-

times floral flavor that stands out in simple pasta dishes. Its moist texture also works well with pasta since there is no concern about soggy crusts. Mozzarella, especially water-packed versions, can be quite hard to shred by hand. Use a food processor if at all possible. Never buy pre-shredded mozzarella, which is dry and tasteless.

PARMESAN. Parmesan is the most popular cheese for pasta in the world. The finest Parmesan comes from Italy and is called Parmigiano-Reggiano. This cheese is aged longer than Parmesan made elsewhere and has a rich, nutty flavor. When shopping, look for the words "Parmigiano-Reggiano" stenciled on the rind. Expect to pay at least $12 a pound for this cheese. If the price is less, you are not buying the real thing; if Parmigiano-Reggiano is just too expensive for your budget (note that a pound of this cheese lasts for weeks when wrapped tightly and refrigerated and it will flavor many pasta dishes), there are alternatives. Grana Padano is made in the same part of Italy as Parmigiano-Reggiano, but it is not aged nearly as long. It has a good flavor but is not as piquant or nutty as Parmigiano-Reggiano. In either case, try to get pieces that have been freshly cut from a large wheel of cheese. And make sure to buy pieces with only a small amount of rind, which can be thrown into a pot of minestrone to flavor the broth (see page 270) but otherwise has no culinary use. We find that Parmesan cheese made outside Italy is not nearly as flavorful and tends to be very salty.

PECORINO ROMANO. Pecorino Romano is bone-white cheese with an intense peppery flavor and strong sheepy quality. Pecorino is best in dishes with assertive ingredients like capers, olives, or hot red pepper flakes. Pecorino is traditionally made from sheep's milk, although some manufacturers add some cow's milk to reduce the

(continued on next page)

pungency or save money. In Italy, pecorino is often sold fresh or lightly aged and served as an eating cheese. (These young pecorinos are not widely known elsewhere.) Most of the pecorino that is exported has been aged much longer. Like Parmesan, it is designed for grating, but it has a much saltier and more pungent flavor.

Most of the exported pecorino is from the Rome area, hence the name Pecorino Romano. (Pecorino cheeses are also made in Sardinia, Sicily, and Tuscany.) Like Parmigiano-Reggiano, the words "Pecorino Romano" are stenciled on the rind to make shopping for the authentic product easy. Many American-made pecorinos taste of salt and nothing else and should be avoided.

RICOTTA. Good ricotta should be creamy and thick, not watery and curdish like so many supermarket brands sold in plastic containers. In Italy, local cheese makers produce fresh ricotta with a dry, firm consistency (akin to goat cheese). The flavor is sweet and milky. This cheese is so perishable it is rarely exported. In the United States, however, locally made fresh ricotta is available in and near urban centers with large Italian-American populations. This cheese shares many qualities with the Italian versions. You can use supermarket ricotta cheese, but it tastes bland by comparison.

RICOTTA SALATA. Fresh ricotta cheese is salted and pressed to make this firm but crumbly cheese with a texture that is similar to feta but a flavor that is milder and far less salty. Ricotta salata is pleasingly piquant, although it is milder than pecorino. This cheese is generally shredded and used like mozzarella in baked pasta dishes or tossed with hot pasta when a sharper, saltier cheese flavor is desired.

Fettuccine with Brown Butter, Prosciutto, and Pine Nuts

BROWN BUTTER IMPARTS AN INTENSE, NUTTY FLAVOR TO PASTA AND ENHANCES THE FLAVORS OF THE PROSCIUTTO AND PINE NUTS. THIS IS A RICH DISH AND MIGHT SERVE 6 TO 8 AS AN APPETIZER BEFORE A MAIN COURSE OF CHICKEN, PORK, OR VEAL. SERVES 4.

2 tablespoons pine nuts
Salt
1 pound Fresh Egg Pasta (page 21) cut into fettuccine *or* dried fettuccine
5 tablespoons unsalted butter
2 ounces thinly sliced prosciutto, chopped
2 tablespoons minced fresh flat-leaf parsley leaves
1/4 cup grated Parmesan cheese
Ground black pepper

1. Bring 4 quarts of water to a boil in a large pot for cooking the pasta.

2. Toast the nuts in a small skillet over medium heat, stirring frequently, until just golden and fragrant, 4 to 5 minutes. Set the nuts aside on a plate.

3. Add 1 tablespoon salt and the pasta to the boiling water. Cook until al dente.

4. While the pasta is cooking, heat the butter in the empty skillet over medium heat, swirling occasionally until it is light brown, 3 to 4 minutes. Stir in the prosciutto and remove from the heat.

5. Reserve 1/2 cup of the pasta cooking water; drain the pasta and transfer it back to the cooking pot. Mix in the butter and prosciutto, toasted nuts, parsley, cheese, salt and pepper to taste, and enough reserved water to keep the mixture moist. Adjust the seasonings. Divide among 4 warmed pasta bowls and serve immediately.

Spaghetti with Pecorino and Black Pepper

HOT RED PEPPER FLAKES MAY BE SUBSTITUTED FOR THE BLACK PEPPER. THE STRONG FLAVOR OF THE CHEESE STANDS UP WELL TO EITHER KIND OF PEPPER. NOTE THAT THIS DISH CONTAINS QUITE A BIT OF CHEESE, WHICH MELTS ON CONTACT WITH THE PASTA TO FORM A CREAMY SAUCE THAT COATS THE SPAGHETTI FROM END TO END. SERVES 4.

Salt
1 pound spaghetti or other long, thin pasta
¼ cup extra-virgin olive oil
2 cups grated pecorino cheese
1 teaspoon ground black pepper or to taste

Bring 4 quarts of water to a boil in a large pot. Add 1 tablespoon salt and the pasta to the boiling water. Cook until al dente. Reserve ½ cup of the cooking water; drain the pasta and transfer it back to the cooking pot. Mix in the oil, cheese, and pepper and enough reserved water to keep the mixture moist. Adjust the seasonings. Divide among 4 warmed pasta bowls and serve immediately.

◆

Spaghetti alla Carbonara

MOST ITALIAN COOKS PREFER MILD PANCETTA IN THIS CLASSIC DISH. WE LIKE PANCETTA AS WELL AS THE SMOKIER FLAVOR AMERICAN BACON GIVES. IF USING BACON, WHICH IS FATTIER THAN PANCETTA, REDUCE THE AMOUNT OF OLIVE OIL TO 2 TABLESPOONS. WE LIKE THE FLAVOR OF GARLIC IN THIS DISH, BUT PREFER TO SAUTE CRUSHED CLOVES IN OIL AND THEN DISCARD THEM RATHER THAN MINCING THE GARLIC AND KEEPING IT IN THE SAUCE. THIS METHOD PROVIDES A HINT OF GARLIC BUT ALLOWS THE FLAVORS OF THE PANCETTA, EGGS, AND CHEESE TO DOMINATE. NOTE THAT WE RECOMMEND PECORINO IN THIS DISH; WE FOUND THAT THE FLAVOR OF THE BACON AND EGGS OVERWHELMS MORE DELICATE PARMESAN. SERVES 4.

Salt
1 pound spaghetti or other long, thin pasta
¼ cup extra-virgin olive oil
4 medium garlic cloves, peeled and crushed
¼ pound pancetta or bacon, sliced ¼ inch thick and then cut into ¼-inch dice
¼ cup dry white wine
3 large eggs
1 cup grated pecorino cheese
2 tablespoons minced fresh flat-leaf parsley leaves
Ground black pepper

1. Bring 4 quarts of water to a boil in a large pot for cooking the pasta. Add 1 tablespoon salt and the pasta to the boiling water. Cook until al dente.

2. While the pasta is cooking, heat the oil and garlic in a skillet over medium heat. Cook the garlic until golden, 2 to 3 minutes, and discard. Add the pancetta and cook until just beginning to crisp, 2 to 3 minutes. Add the wine and simmer until the alcohol aroma has cooked off, 2 to 3 minutes. Remove from the heat, cover, and keep warm.

3. Lightly beat the eggs with the cheese and parsley in a large bowl.

4. Drain the pasta, leaving it slightly wet, and transfer it to the bowl with the egg mixture. Immediately toss the pasta with the egg mixture to coat evenly. Stir in the pancetta mixture. Season with salt and pepper to taste. Divide among 4 warmed pasta bowls and serve immediately.

CAUTION: This recipe contains raw egg. Because of the threat of salmonella, food safety experts advise against serving raw eggs to the very young, the elderly, and those whose immune systems are compromised. The rest of us eat them at our own risk.

HOW TO GRATE AND SHRED CHEESE

/\

MANY PASTA RECIPES, INCLUDING ALL THE RECIPES IN THIS CHAPTER, CALL FOR GRATED OR SHREDDED CHEESE OF SOME KIND. HARD CHEESES, SUCH AS PARMESAN AND PECORINO, SHOULD BE GRATED INTO VERY FINE THREADS, ALMOST A POWDER. SOFTER CHEESES, SUCH AS MOZZARELLA AND FONTINA,

should be cut into long, thin shreds. We decided to test various methods for grating and shredding, including various hand graters as well as the food processor, to determine the best tool for these jobs.

A good grater should have sharp teeth, a comfortable handle or grip, and good leverage for pressing the cheese onto the grater. We found that The Cheese Grater (yes, that's its name; see illustration 1) was by far the best tool for grating hard cheeses. Essentially the shape and size of a standard ruler (about 12 inches long and 1 inch wide), The Cheese Grater is modeled after a woodworking tool called a rasp. Rasps have lots and lots of tiny, sharp, raised teeth that remove wood smoothly and efficiently. The rasplike Cheese Grater was both the fastest and most controlled grater we tested, turning out mounds of grated Parmesan in seconds. The black plastic handle, which was the most comfortable we tested, also earned high marks.

Our second choice is a rotary grater (see illustration 2), which has a stainless steel drum and a plastic or metal body and crank. It grates Parmesan and pecorino, even large amounts, with minimal effort and no danger of scraped knuckles. Simply place a small piece of cheese in the drum, press down on the clamp, and turn the handle to

rotate the drum and grate the cheese. This gadget can also be used to grate chocolate or grind nuts.

Many cooks own a small flat grater similar to the one seen in illustration 3. These graters are fine for grating small amounts (less than ½ cup) of hard cheese. A better common option is a standard box grater (illustration 4), which grates hard cheeses and also shreds soft cheeses, such as mozzarella. This grater is not ideal when working with small pieces of cheese (you tend to scrape your knuckles against the grater), but it functions adequately on large blocks of cheese.

Many cooks use the food processor to grate hard cheeses, especially when they need large amounts. However, our tests revealed that the food processor is the worst tool for this task. The sharp metal blade cuts Parmesan into small round bits, but the cheese is not as fine or as powdery as cheese that is grated by hand. These larger bits of Parmesan don't melt nearly as well as powdery hand-grated cheese. When cheese that has been grated in a food processor is sprinkled over pasta dishes, the result is never as fine or as delicate.

Many cooks also make the mistake of buying pregrated cheese. Grated Parmesan cheese loses freshness rather quickly. Cheese that was grated several weeks ago in the store will never be as moist or as flavorful as cheese you grate yourself just before using. That said, we have found that extra cheese you grate at home can be refrigerated in an airtight container for up to one week with minimal loss in flavor or texture. It seems that the real problem with store-bought grated cheese is that it is often quite old (and you have no way of telling when it was grated) and it may be from lesser grades of cheese. Grating cheese yourself lets you choose the highest quality cheese and track how long it has been since the cheese was grated.

Hard cheeses are grated, but soft cheeses are shredded on the large holes of a box grater. While these holes will turn a block of mozzarella or Fontina into a mound of long, thin shreds, we find that the shredding disk on a food processor does this job quicker, more efficiently, and safer. When working with a box grater, medium-sized bits of cheese tend to fall off into the pile of shredded cheese. These chunks are really too small to shred, unless of course you are willing to scrape your knuckles against the holes. The result is a mass of shredded cheese with some very large chunks that may not melt well when tossed with hot pasta.

The shredding disk on a food processor turns even the smallest hunk of soft cheese into long, thin shreds. Simply cut the block of cheese into pieces small enough to fit into the feed tube. Place the pieces of cheese into the feed tube and use the food pusher to run them through the whirling shredding disk.

Shredded soft cheese may be refrigerated in an airtight bag for a day or two, but it will start to dry out and will not be as moist and creamy if stored for longer periods of time. We suggest avoiding packages of shredded cheese sold in the dairy aisle of the supermarket. In our tests, we found that low-grade cheeses are usually packaged this way and that it is possible to buy better quality cheeses in blocks or wedges.

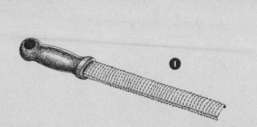

THIS RASPLIKE GRATER has very sharp teeth and a long, solid handle. It is our favorite tool for grating Parmesan and other hard cheeses.

THE ROTARY GRATER is an efficient tool for grating hard cheeses, especially in large amounts.

A FLAT GRATER does a decent job of grating small amounts of Parmesan and other hard cheeses.

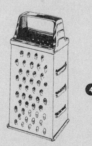

A RECTANGULAR BOX GRATER can grate hard cheese and shred soft cheeses, although we prefer the food processor for the latter task.

Bucatini with Pancetta, Pecorino, and Black Pepper

BUCATINI (OR PERCIATELLI) IS A LONG, TUBULAR PASTA, THICKER AND MORE SUBSTANTIAL THAN SPAGHETTI. IT IS PARTICULARLY WELL SUITED TO A STURDY SAUCE OF GRATED PECORINO AND SALTY PANCETTA, ALTHOUGH SPAGHETTI MAY BE SUBSTITUTED. BUY A THICK SLICE OF PANCETTA; CHUNKS OF HAM CONTRIBUTE TO THE RUSTIC CHARACTER OF THE DISH. SERVES 4.

> Salt
> 1 pound bucatini or other long, thick
>   pasta
> ¼ cup extra-virgin olive oil
> 2 ounces pancetta, sliced ¼ inch thick
>   and then cut into ¼-inch dice
> 1 cup grated pecorino cheese
> 1 teaspoon ground black pepper or to
>   taste

1. Bring 4 quarts of water to a boil in a large pot. Add 1 tablespoon salt and the pasta to the boiling water. Cook until al dente.

2. While the pasta is cooking, heat the oil in a small skillet over medium heat. Add the pancetta and cook until just beginning to crisp, 2 to 3 minutes.

3. Reserve ½ cup of the cooking water; drain the pasta and transfer it back to the cooking pot. Mix in the oil and pancetta, cheese, pepper, and enough reserved water to keep the mixture moist. Adjust the seasonings. Divide among 4 warmed pasta bowls and serve immediately.

Fusilli with Ricotta and Pecorino

RICOTTA CHEESE, EITHER WHOLE-MILK OR PART-SKIM, PROVIDES A CREAMY BASE FOR SHARP PECORINO CHEESE. FOR A MILDER FLAVOR, SUBSTITUTE PARMESAN FOR THE PECORINO. YOU MAY USE ANOTHER FRESH HERB, SUCH AS BASIL OR EVEN MINT, IN PLACE OF THE PARSLEY. GOOD RICOTTA CHEESE CAN BE QUITE STIFF SO BE PREPARED TO USE THE ENTIRE ½ CUP OF RESERVED PASTA COOKING WATER TO THIN OUT THE SAUCE. SERVES 4.

> Salt
> 1 pound fusilli or short, tubular pasta
> 1 cup ricotta cheese
> 2 tablespoons unsalted butter, softened
> ½ cup grated pecorino cheese
> 2 tablespoons minced fresh flat-leaf
>   parsley leaves
> Ground black pepper

Bring 4 quarts of water to a boil in a large pot. Add 1 tablespoon salt and the pasta to the boiling water. Cook until al dente. Reserve ½ cup of the cooking water; drain the pasta and transfer it back to the cooking pot. Mix in the ricotta, butter, pecorino, parsley, salt and pepper to taste, and enough reserved water to keep the mixture moist. Divide among 4 warmed pasta bowls and serve immediately.

Penne with Ricotta and Lemon

THIS CREAMY DISH, ENLIVENED BY LEMON ZEST, IS A GOOD MATCH FOR A MAIN DISH OF CHICKEN, FISH, OR VEAL. SERVES 8 AS A SIDE DISH.

Salt
1 pound penne or other short, tubular pasta
1 cup ricotta cheese
2 tablespoons unsalted butter, softened
½ cup grated Parmesan cheese
1 teaspoon grated lemon zest (see illustration, page 42)
2 tablespoons minced fresh basil leaves
Ground black pepper

Bring 4 quarts of water to a boil in a large pot. Add 1 tablespoon salt and the pasta to the boiling water. Cook until al dente. Reserve ½ cup of the cooking water; drain the pasta and transfer it back to the cooking pot. Mix in the ricotta, butter, Parmesan, lemon zest, basil, salt and pepper to taste, and enough reserved water to keep the mixture moist. Place in a warmed serving dish and serve immediately.

Penne with Ricotta and Bacon

RICOTTA CHEESE PROVIDES A SMOOTH, NEUTRAL BACK-GROUND FOR MANY FLAVORS. HERE, SAUTEED BACON AND ONION TURN PLAIN CHEESE INTO A HEARTY, SAT-ISFYING PASTA DISH. SERVES 4.

2 ounces sliced bacon, cut into ½-inch dice
2 tablespoons extra-virgin olive oil
1 medium onion, minced
Salt
1 pound penne or other short, tubular pasta
1 cup ricotta cheese
1 cup grated Parmesan cheese
2 tablespoons minced fresh flat-leaf parsley leaves
Ground black pepper

1. Bring 4 quarts of water to a boil in a large pot for cooking the pasta.

2. Heat the bacon in a medium skillet. Cook until the fat is rendered and the bacon is lightly browned, 3 to 4 minutes. Add the oil and onion and cook until the onion is softened, 6 to 7 minutes. Remove from the heat and set aside.

3. Add 1 tablespoon salt and the pasta to the boiling water. Cook until al dente. Reserve ½ cup of the cooking water; drain the pasta and transfer it back to the cooking pot. Mix in the bacon and onion, ricotta, Parmesan, parsley, salt and pepper to taste, and enough reserved water to keep the mixture moist. Divide among 4 warmed pasta bowls and serve immediately.

Rigatoni with Ricotta Salata

RICOTTA SALATA IS RELATIVELY DRY AND LOW IN FAT. TO ENSURE EVEN DISTRIBUTION, IT NEEDS TO BE GRATED BEFORE BEING STIRRED INTO HOT PASTA. HOT RED PEPPER FLAKES AND HALF A DOZEN FINELY CHOPPED OIL-PACKED SUN-DRIED TOMATOES MAY BE STIRRED INTO THIS DISH FOR COLOR AND A LITTLE BRIGHT TOMATO FLAVOR, IF YOU LIKE. SERVES 4.

> Salt
> 1 pound rigatoni or other large tubular
>   pasta
> ¼ cup extra-virgin olive oil
> ½ pound ricotta salata, grated
> ¼ cup grated pecorino cheese
> Ground black pepper

Bring 4 quarts of water to a boil in a large pot. Add 1 tablespoon salt and the pasta to the boiling water. Cook until al dente. Reserve ½ cup of the cooking water; drain the pasta and transfer it back to the cooking pot. Mix in the oil, ricotta salata, pecorino, salt and pepper to taste, and enough reserved water to keep the mixture moist. Divide among 4 warmed pasta bowls and serve immediately.

Penne with Ricotta Salata and Black Olives

THIS IS A GOOD EXAMPLE OF A SIMPLE, HIGHLY SEASONED PASTA SAUCE THAT REQUIRES ABSOLUTELY NO COOKING. GARLIC, CHEESE, OLIVES, A HOT PEPPER, AND SOME PARSLEY GIVE THE PASTA FLAVOR WITHOUT ANY FUSS. THE CHEESE AND OLIVES ARE SALTY, SO TASTE BEFORE ADDING ADDITIONAL SALT TO THE FINISHED DISH. THIS WOULD MAKE A GOOD FIRST COURSE OR ACCOMPANIMENT TO A SIMPLE MEAL OF GRILLED CHICKEN OR FISH, OR IT CAN BE SERVED AS A MAIN COURSE. SERVES 4.

> Salt
> 1 pound penne or other short, tubular
>   pasta
> ¼ cup extra-virgin olive oil
> 4 ounces ricotta salata, grated
> ½ cup black olives (such as Kalamata),
>   pitted and coarsely chopped (see
>   illustrations 1–2, page 62)
> 1 small fresh red hot pepper, seeded and
>   finely chopped, or ½ teaspoon hot red
>   pepper flakes
> 1 medium garlic clove, minced
> 2 tablespoons minced fresh flat-leaf
>   parsley leaves

Bring 4 quarts of water to a boil in a large pot. Add 1 tablespoon salt and the pasta to the boiling water. Cook until al dente. Reserve ½ cup of the cooking water; drain the pasta and transfer it back to the cooking pot. Mix in the oil, cheese, olives, chile, garlic, parsley, and enough reserved water to keep the mixture moist. Adjust the salt. Divide among 4 warmed pasta bowls and serve immediately.

Fettuccine with Mascarpone and Walnuts

MASCARPONE STIRRED INTO PASTA DISAPPEARS LIKE BUTTER BUT GIVES IT BODY AND MILD CREAMINESS. TOASTED WALNUTS ADD ANOTHER LAYER OF FLAVOR—CHOP THEM FINE FOR A DISH THAT IS CREAMY BUT WITH A BIT OF TEXTURE. SERVES 4.

> 1 cup walnuts
> Salt
> 1 pound Fresh Egg Pasta (page 21) cut
>   into fettuccine *or* dried fettuccine
> 2 tablespoons unsalted butter, softened
> ¼ pound mascarpone cheese
> ¼ cup grated Parmesan cheese
> 2 tablespoons minced fresh flat-leaf
>   parsley leaves
> Ground black pepper

1. Bring 4 quarts of water to a boil in a large pot for cooking the pasta.

2. Toast the nuts in a small skillet over medium heat, stirring frequently, until just golden and fragrant, 4 to 5 minutes. Chop the nuts quite fine and set them aside.

3. Add 1 tablespoon salt and the pasta to the boiling water. Cook until al dente. Reserve ½ cup of the cooking water; drain the pasta and transfer it back to the cooking pot. Mix in the butter, mascarpone, Parmesan, toasted nuts, parsley, salt and pepper to taste, and enough reserved water to keep the mixture moist. Divide among 4 warmed pasta bowls and serve immediately.

Fettuccine with Mascarpone and Prosciutto

RICH EGG PASTA IS A GOOD MATCH FOR MASCARPONE AND SILKY PROSCIUTTO, BUT DRIED EGG NOODLES WORK WELL ALSO. THINLY SLICED PROSCIUTTO CONTRIBUTES TO THE SAUCE'S SILKY QUALITY. IT SEEMS TO MELT INTO THE MASCARPONE AND PASTA, FLAVORING THE DISH WITHOUT MAKING THE SAUCE THE LEAST BIT CHUNKY. SERVES 4.

> Salt
> 1 pound Fresh Egg Pasta (page 21) cut
>   into fettuccine *or* dried fettuccine
> 2 tablespoons unsalted butter, softened
> ¼ pound mascarpone cheese
> ¼ cup grated Parmesan cheese
> 2 ounces thinly sliced prosciutto, chopped
> 2 tablespoons minced fresh basil leaves
> Ground black pepper

Bring 4 quarts of water to a boil in a large pot. Add 1 tablespoon salt and the pasta to the boiling water. Cook until al dente. Reserve ½ cup of the cooking water; drain the pasta and transfer it back to the cooking pot. Mix in the butter, mascarpone, Parmesan, prosciutto, basil, pepper to taste, and enough reserved water to keep the mixture moist. Adjust the seasonings. Divide among 4 warmed pasta bowls and serve immediately.

Penne with Four Cheeses

THIS RICH DISH—CALLED *PENNE AI QUATTRO FORMAGGI*, OR PENNE WITH FOUR CHEESES—SHOWCASES THE CHEESES OF ITALY—MELLOW FONTINA, PIQUANT GORGONZOLA, BUTTERY MASCARPONE, AND NUTTY PARMESAN. HEAT THE CHEESES JUST UNTIL THEY ARE MELTED, AND THEN REMOVE FROM THE HEAT TO PREVENT SCORCHING. THE CREAM AND SMALL PAT OF BUTTER HELP SMOOTH OUT THE CONSISTENCY OF THE SAUCE AND KEEP THE CHEESES FROM STICKING TO THE PAN AS THEY MELT. SERVES 4.

Salt
1 pound penne or other short, tubular pasta
1 tablespoon unsalted butter
1/2 cup heavy cream
4 ounces Italian Fontina cheese, shredded
4 ounces Gorgonzola cheese, crumbled
2 ounces mascarpone cheese
1/2 cup grated Parmesan cheese
Ground black pepper

1. Bring 4 quarts of water to a boil in a large pot. Add 1 tablespoon salt and the pasta to the boiling water. Cook until al dente.

2. Meanwhile, heat the butter and cream in a small saucepan over low heat. Add the cheeses and stir until melted and well combined, 2 to 3 minutes.

3. Drain the pasta and return it to the cooking pot. Stir in the cheese sauce. Season with salt and pepper to taste. Divide among 4 warmed pasta bowls and serve immediately.

Orzo with Mozzarella and Basil

CREAMY MOZZARELLA MELTS INTO THIN STRANDS THAT BIND THE RICE-SHAPED PASTA TOGETHER. THIS DISH MAKES A GOOD ACCOMPANIMENT TO CHICKEN, BEEF, OR PORK IN PLACE OF THE USUAL RICE OR POTATOES. OTHER PASTA SHAPES MAY BE SUBSTITUTED TO TURN THIS INTO A MAIN COURSE FOR 4; TRY SHELLS OR FUSILLI. SERVES 6 TO 8 AS A SIDE DISH.

Salt
1 pound orzo
6 ounces mozzarella cheese, shredded
1/2 cup grated Parmesan cheese
1 tablespoon unsalted butter
1/4 cup minced fresh basil leaves
Ground black pepper

Bring 4 quarts of water to a boil in a large pot. Add 1 tablespoon salt and the pasta to the boiling water. Cook until al dente. Reserve 1/2 cup of the cooking water; drain the pasta and transfer it back to the cooking pot. Mix in the mozzarella, Parmesan, butter, basil, salt and pepper to taste, and enough reserved water to keep the mixture moist. Place in a warmed serving dish and serve immediately.

CREAM SAUCES

WHEN CREAM SAUCES ARE GOOD, THEY ARE WORTH

EVERY CALORIE. BUT CREAM SAUCES ARE OFTEN THICK

AND GLOPPY; AT OTHER TIMES, THE SAUCE IS TOO

RUNNY AND JUST SITS AT THE BOTTOM OF THE BOWL.

WE WANTED TO DEVELOP A FOOLPROOF CREAM SAUCE

THAT WAS THICK ENOUGH TO COAT PASTA FROM

END TO END WITHOUT BECOMING DRY OR GLOPPY.

The most famous cream sauce for pasta comes from Italy and is commonly called "Alfredo." This rich sauce of cream, butter, and Parmesan cheese is named for a restaurant in Rome that popularized this dish at the 1939 World's Fair in New York. We had a number of questions about this sauce. First, what is the right ratio of ingredients? Does the type of cream matter? Should the cream be reduced? Must this sauce be used with fresh pasta only?

We started out with a composite recipe and decided to test cooking methods first. Some sources suggest reducing the cream to thicken its texture. Others merely heat the cream. Some just pour room-temperature cream over drained pasta. We found problems with all three methods.

If all the cream is reduced, the sauce becomes too thick and does not easily coat the noodles. However, if the cream is just warmed (or left unheated), it remains too liquidy and pools up around the pasta. We decided to test reducing part of the cream to give the sauce enough body to cling to the pasta and then adding the remaining cream to the sauce along with the cooked pasta. This worked beautifully. After several tests, we settled on using a total of 1⅔ cups cream for one pound of pasta and bringing most of the cream (1⅓ cups) to a simmer to reduce it slightly. Once the cream comes to a bare simmer, remove the pan from the heat to prevent the cream from cooking down too much.

In the spirit of trying weird suggestions, we had seen a few recipes that called for whipping the cream lightly instead of reducing it to give the cream body. As might be expected, this did not work. The sauce was fluffy and odd on pasta. Save whipped cream for dessert.

Since the butter must be melted for this sauce, we decided to add the butter directly to the cream. We tested as little as 2 tablespoons and as much as two sticks. Five tablespoons was just right, providing the right amount of lubrication to the pasta and good buttery flavor. To round out the sauce, we settled on a cup of grated Parmesan cheese and some salt, pepper, and nutmeg.

We tested our working recipe with ultrapasteurized as well as pasteurized cream. Ultrapasteurized cream is the standard in most markets. It is subjected to high temperatures during pasteurization to promote longer shelf life. This process gives the cream a slightly cooked flavor, which we could taste in a blind test against a sauce made with pasteurized cream.

Pasteurized cream is heated during processing, but to a lower temperature that will kill bacteria but won't prolong shelf life. In our tests, it had a fresher, sweeter cream flavor and we think it is worth searching out this product when making cream sauces. (It also makes great whipped cream.) Many organic creams are pasteurized, so check out the organic dairy section in your supermarket or visit a natural foods store.

Cream sauces do an excellent job of coating wide, long noodles like fettuccine. Many sources indicate that cream sauces meld better with fresh pasta, and until this point we had been using our own homemade fettuccine in tests. We decided to test store-bought fresh fettuccine as well as dried fettuccine with our cream sauce.

Dried fettuccine was a disappointment. When cooked, dried pasta is much less porous than fresh and the cream sauce did not adhere very well to the noodles. When we finished our bowls of dried pasta with cream sauce, there still was sauce in the bottom of the bowls.

The package of mass-market fresh fettuccine from the supermarket refrigerator case cooked up gummy (a common problem with these products) and the cream sauce slid right off the noodles. Store-bought fettuccine that had been freshly made at a local gourmet shop was quite good, holding onto every drop of sauce as did our homemade fresh pasta.

Some sources suggest cooking the fresh pasta a bit less to leave it a little firmer than usual and then finishing the cooking process right in the cream sauce. We tested this method against pasta that was fully cooked and sauced, and much preferred cooking the pasta in the sauce. The sauce really penetrates into the noodles and the combination of creamy sauce and fresh egg pasta is unbeatable.

Some final observations. The pasta may look a bit soupy as you divide it among individual serving bowls. However, the pasta will continue to absorb sauce as it sits in bowls. In fact, pasta that looks perfect going into bowls will be too dry by the time you start eating. Lukewarm cream sauces are not very appetizing, so heating the pasta bowls is a must. Lastly, pasta with cream sauce is quite rich. We prefer to serve it in small portions as an appetizer. A few bites more than satisfies any longing for creamy richness.

Fettuccine with Cream, Butter, and Parmesan (Fettuccine Alfredo)

SERVES 6 AS AN APPETIZER

THE GOLD STANDARD by which all cream sauces are judged, this classic combination of cream, butter, and Parmesan is quite simple to prepare. Do not cook the sauce over too high a heat or for too long, or it will be gluey instead of creamy. Fresh egg pasta is a must here; dried pasta can't stand up to the richness of the Alfredo ingredients. Make sure to cook your pasta extra-firm, since it will cook some more (and absorb some of the butter and cream) when added to the sauce.

1²/₃ cups heavy cream, preferably not ultrapasteurized
5 tablespoons unsalted butter
Salt
1 pound Fresh Egg Pasta (page 21) cut into fettuccine
1 cup grated Parmesan cheese
Ground black pepper
Pinch ground nutmeg

1. Bring 4 quarts of water to a boil in a large pot for cooking the pasta.

2. Combine 1⅓ cups cream and the butter in a sauté pan large enough to accommodate the cooked pasta. Heat over low until the butter is melted and the cream comes to a bare simmer. Turn off the heat and set aside.

3. When the water comes to a boil, add 1 tablespoon salt and the pasta. Cook until almost al dente. Drain the pasta and add it to the sauté pan. Add the remaining ⅓ cup cream, cheese, ½ teaspoon salt, pepper to taste, and nutmeg. Cook over very low heat, tossing to combine ingredients, until the sauce is slightly thickened, 1 to 2 minutes. Divide among 6 warmed pasta bowls and serve immediately.

Fettuccine with Fresh Herbs and Cream

HERBS OF SIMILAR STRENGTH MAY BE SUBSTITUTED FOR EACH OTHER (PARSLEY FOR BASIL, MARJORAM FOR OREGANO OR SAGE, TARRAGON FOR THYME OR ROSE-MARY), DEPENDING ON WHAT'S AVAILABLE AT YOUR MARKET OR FROM YOUR GARDEN. PARMESAN WOULD COMPETE WITH THE DELICATE FLAVOR OF THE HERBS, SO IT IS LEFT OUT HERE. **SERVES 6 AS AN APPETIZER.**

1⅔ cups heavy cream, preferably not ultrapasteurized
5 tablespoons unsalted butter
Salt
1 pound Fresh Egg Pasta (page 21) cut into fettuccine
¼ cup minced fresh basil leaves
2 tablespoons minced fresh mint leaves
2 tablespoons minced fresh oregano leaves
2 tablespoons minced fresh sage leaves
1 teaspoon minced fresh thyme leaves
1 teaspoon minced fresh rosemary leaves
Ground black pepper

1. Bring 4 quarts of water to a boil in a large pot for cooking the pasta.

2. Combine 1⅓ cups cream and the butter in a sauté pan large enough to accommodate the cooked pasta. Heat over low until the butter is melted and the cream comes to a bare simmer. Turn off the heat and set aside.

3. When the water comes to a boil, add 1 tablespoon salt and the pasta. Cook until almost al dente. Drain the pasta and add it to the sauté pan. Add the herbs, remaining ⅓ cup cream, ½ teaspoon salt, and pepper to taste. Cook over very low heat, tossing to combine ingredients, until the sauce is slightly thickened, 1 to 2 minutes. Divide among 6 warmed pasta bowls and serve immediately.

Fettuccine with Prosciutto and Cream

FOR THIS RECIPE, WE LIKE PROSCIUTTO CUT IN THICK SLICES AND THEN DICED; PROSCIUTTO SLICED PAPER-THIN SEEMS TO DISAPPEAR AMID THE SAUCE AND NOO-DLES. **SERVES 6 AS AN APPETIZER.**

5 tablespoons unsalted butter
¼ pound prosciutto, sliced ¼ inch thick and then cut into ¼-inch dice
1⅔ cups heavy cream, preferably not ultrapasteurized
Salt
1 pound Fresh Egg Pasta (page 21) cut into fettuccine
1 cup grated Parmesan cheese
Ground black pepper

1. Bring 4 quarts of water to a boil in a large pot for cooking the pasta.

2. Combine the butter and prosciutto in a sauté pan large enough to accommodate the cooked pasta. Heat over low until the butter is melted and the prosciutto softened, 2 to 3 minutes. Add 1⅓ cups cream and heat until it comes to a bare simmer. Turn off the heat and set aside.

3. When the water comes to a boil, add 1 tablespoon salt and the pasta. Cook until almost al dente. Drain the pasta and add it to the sauté pan. Add the remaining ⅓ cup cream, cheese, ½ teaspoon salt, and pepper to taste. Cook over very low heat, tossing to combine ingredients, until the sauce is slightly thickened, 1 to 2 minutes. Divide among 6 warmed pasta bowls and serve immediately.

White and Green Fettuccine with Peas, Prosciutto, and Cream

IN ITALY, THIS DISH IS CALLED *PAGLIA E FIENO*, WHICH TRANSLATES AS "STRAW AND HAY" AND REFERS TO THE MIXTURE OF EGG AND SPINACH NOODLES. THE NOODLES ARE MOISTENED WITH A CREAM SAUCE AND TOSSED WITH A VARIETY OF INGREDIENTS. IN OUR VERSION, ONIONS, PROSCIUTTO, AND PEAS PROVIDE FLAVOR, COLOR, AND TEXTURAL CONTRAST. SAUTEED MUSHROOMS ALSO MAKE A NICE ADDITION. COOK 2 CUPS OF SLICED BUTTON OR CREMINI MUSHROOMS IN A SEPARATE PAN AND ADD THEM WITH THE CHEESE. THE MUSHROOMS ARE AN ESPECIALLY GOOD ADDITION IF YOU WOULD RATHER OMIT THE MEAT FROM THIS SAUCE. IF YOU LIKE, YOU USE THIS SAUCE ON 1 POUND OF EGG FETTUCCINE INSTEAD OF THE MIXTURE OF HALF EGG AND HALF SPINACH NOODLES. **SERVES 6 AS AN APPETIZER.**

> 5 tablespoons unsalted butter
> ¼ cup minced onion
> ¼ pound prosciutto, sliced ¼ inch thick and then cut into ¼-inch dice
> 1 cup frozen peas, thawed
> 1⅔ cups heavy cream, preferably not ultrapasteurized
> Salt
> ½ pound Fresh Egg Pasta (page 21) cut into fettuccine
> ½ pound Spinach Pasta (page 22) cut into fettuccine
> 1 cup grated Parmesan cheese
> Ground black pepper

1. Bring 4 quarts of water to a boil in a large pot for cooking the pasta.

2. Combine the butter, onion, and prosciutto in a sauté pan large enough to accommodate the cooked pasta. Heat over low until the butter is melted and the prosciutto softened, 2 to 3 minutes. Add the peas and 1⅓ cups cream and heat until it comes to a bare simmer. Turn off the heat and set aside.

3. When the water comes to a boil, add 1 tablespoon salt and the pasta. Cook until almost al dente. Drain the pasta and add it to the sauté pan. Add the remaining ⅓ cup cream, cheese, ½ teaspoon salt, and pepper to taste. Cook over very low heat, tossing to combine ingredients, until the sauce is slightly thickened, 1 to 2 minutes. Divide among 6 warmed pasta bowls and serve immediately.

◆

Fettuccine with Lemon and Cream

LEMON JUICE AND ZEST MAKE FOR A SURPRISINGLY LIGHT-TASTING (BUT CERTAINLY NOT LOW-CALORIE) CREAM SAUCE. **SERVES 6 AS AN APPETIZER.**

> 1⅔ cups heavy cream, preferably not ultrapasteurized
> 5 tablespoons unsalted butter
> ¼ cup lemon juice
> Salt
> 1 pound Fresh Egg Pasta (page 21) cut into fettuccine
> 2 teaspoons grated lemon zest (see illustration, page 42)
> 1 cup grated Parmesan cheese
> Ground black pepper

1. Bring 4 quarts of water to a boil in a large pot for cooking the pasta.

2. Combine 1⅓ cups cream, the butter, and juice in a sauté pan large enough to accommodate the cooked pasta. Heat over low until the butter is melted and the cream comes to a bare simmer. Turn off the heat and set aside.

3. When the water comes to a boil, add 1 tablespoon salt and the pasta. Cook until almost al dente. Drain the pasta and add it to the sauté pan. Add the zest, remaining ⅓ cup cream, cheese, ½ teaspoon salt, and pepper to taste. Cook over very low heat, tossing to combine ingredients, until the sauce is slightly thickened, 1 to 2 minutes. Divide among 6 warmed pasta bowls and serve immediately.

Fettuccine with Gorgonzola and Cream

SWEET GORGONZOLA, SOMETIMES LABELED GOR-GONZOLA DOLCE, IS MILDER THAN THE HARDER, DRIER AGED GORGONZOLA, AND MAKES FOR A SLIGHTLY PIQUANT BUT STILL CREAMY VARIATION ON ALFREDO SAUCE. IT IS AVAILABLE AT CHEESE SHOPS, ITALIAN DELIS, AND MANY SUPERMARKETS. SERVES 6 AS AN APPETIZER.

1²⁄₃ cups heavy cream, preferably not
    ultrapasteurized
5 tablespoons unsalted butter
4 ounces sweet Gorgonzola, crumbled
Salt
1 pound Fresh Egg Pasta (page 21) cut
    into fettuccine
Ground black pepper

1. Bring 4 quarts of water to a boil in a large pot for cooking the pasta.

2. Combine 1¹⁄₃ cups cream and the butter in a sauté pan large enough to accommodate the cooked pasta. Heat over low until the butter is melted and the cream comes to a bare simmer. Stir in the cheese. Turn off the heat and set aside.

3. When the water comes to a boil, add 1 tablespoon salt and the pasta. Cook until almost al dente. Drain the pasta and add it to the sauté pan. Add the remaining ¹⁄₃ cup cream, ¹⁄₂ teaspoon salt, and pepper to taste. Cook over very low heat, tossing to combine ingredients, until the sauce is slightly thickened, 1 to 2 minutes. Divide among 6 warmed pasta bowls and serve immediately.

Fettuccine with Smoked Salmon and Cream

SILKY SMOKED SALMON MARRIES VERY WELL WITH SMOOTH CREAM SAUCE. SINCE MOST SALMON IS QUITE SALTY, ADD JUST ¹⁄₄ TEASPOON OF SALT AND TASTE TO SEE IF THE SAUCE NEEDS MORE. THE SPLASH OF SCOTCH WHISKEY ADDS ANOTHER SMOKY NOTE TO THE DISH BUT IS NOT ESSENTIAL. SERVES 6 AS AN APPETIZER.

5 tablespoons unsalted butter
1 shallot, minced
1²⁄₃ cups heavy cream, preferably not
    ultrapasteurized
Salt
1 pound Fresh Egg Pasta (page 21) cut
    into fettuccine
1 cup grated Parmesan cheese
3 ounces smoked salmon, finely chopped
2 tablespoons Scotch whiskey (optional)
Ground black pepper

1. Bring 4 quarts of water to a boil in a large pot for cooking the pasta.

2. Melt the butter over very low heat in a sauté pan large enough to accommodate the cooked pasta and add the shallot. Cook until slightly softened, 2 to 3 minutes. Add 1¹⁄₃ cups cream and heat until the cream comes to a bare simmer. Turn off the heat and set aside.

3. When the water comes to a boil, add 1 tablespoon salt and the pasta. Cook until almost al dente. Drain the pasta and add it to the sauté pan. Add the remaining ¹⁄₃ cup cream, cheese, salmon, Scotch if using, ¹⁄₄ teaspoon salt, and pepper to taste. Cook over very low heat, tossing to combine ingredients, until the sauce is slightly thickened, 1 to 2 minutes. Divide among 6 warmed pasta bowls and serve immediately.

Fettuccine with Saffron and Cream

SAFFRON THREADS ARE STEEPED IN CREAM AS THE PASTA WATER BOILS, ENSURING A HIGHLY FLAVORED, BRILLIANT YELLOW CREAM SAUCE. **SERVES 6 AS AN APPETIZER.**

1²⁄₃ cups heavy cream, preferably not ultrapasteurized
5 tablespoons unsalted butter
¼ teaspoon saffron threads, crumbled
Salt
1 pound Fresh Egg Pasta (page 21) cut into fettuccine
1 cup grated Parmesan cheese
2 tablespoons minced fresh flat-leaf parsley leaves
Ground black pepper

1. Bring 4 quarts of water to a boil in a large pot for cooking the pasta.

2. Combine 1⅓ cups cream, the butter, and saffron in a sauté pan large enough to accommodate the cooked pasta. Heat over low until the butter is melted and the cream comes to a bare simmer. Turn off the heat and set aside.

3. When the water comes to a boil, add 1 tablespoon salt and the pasta. Cook until almost al dente. Drain the pasta and add it to the sauté pan. Add the remaining ⅓ cup cream, cheese, parsley, ½ teaspoon salt, and pepper to taste. Cook over very low heat, tossing to combine ingredients, until the sauce is slightly thickened, 1 to 2 minutes. Divide among 6 warmed pasta bowls and serve immediately.

SAUCES WITH

BREAD

CRUMBS

IN SOME ITALIAN RECIPES, BREAD CRUMBS ARE USED

IN PLACE OF GRATED CHEESE TO ADD FLAVOR AND

TEXTURE TO PASTA DISHES. THE SAUCES ARE GENER-

ALLY MADE WITH OIL AND A FEW FLAVORFUL INGRE-

DIENTS, SUCH AS GARLIC, OLIVES, OR ANCHOVIES.

For this chapter, we wanted to discover the best way to make bread crumbs. Ideally, bread crumbs will be crunchy and neither so small that they are powdery nor so large that they won't combine well with the pasta. They should have a rich toasted flavor, but they should not be at all burnt. We also wanted to figure out how to flavor toasted bread crumbs. This would include determining whether fat was part of the equation and, if so, what kind.

After testing fifteen types of bread, we found that supermarket wheat, white, multigrain, nut, and rye breads are not suitable for making crumbs. The biggest problem with these sandwich breads is that they are highly refined; in addition to having a "processed" taste, they have a high sugar content. The added sugar is considered a virtue by marketers, since it retards the development of gluten, keeping the bread soft and tender for days. But it is a vice when making bread crumbs. By the time the loaves get stale enough to make into crumbs, all you can really make from them is a fine powder that dissolves quickly on your tongue, the opposite effect of what you want.

We found that the best crumb is made from a good-quality bread that has no strong flavor. Leftover sweet or sourdough French baguettes from your local bakery will give you the best-tasting, crispest bread crumbs. Italian bread or a loaf of country or peasant white bread will also work well.

Bread that is two to three days old is ideal for making bread crumbs because it has become quite firm but still retains some moisture, which is important in controlling the size of the crumbs. Bread that is four days old or older will be so dry that it will be pulverized by the cutting blades, yielding an unusable powder instead of individual crumbs. Bread that is one day old or less, on the other hand, will probably need to be dried in an oven before it can be made into crumbs. To do so, simply cut fresh bread into thick slices and heat in a 225-degree oven until the slices have dried out a bit, ten to twenty minutes depending on the freshness of the bread.

When you make crumbs at home, you want them irregular and coarse, roughly the size of dried black beans, so they contribute texture as well as richness to your food. Crumbs that are too fine, including store-bought dry bread crumbs, have a texture like sawdust and don't add much to pasta dishes.

We found that there are several ways to create crumbs. When using a food processor, the fastest and easiest way, it is important to monitor crumb size closely. Coarse crumbs, the size of dried black beans, are made in twenty to forty-five seconds, depending on the type and age of the bread. Generally, the older the bread, the longer it takes to turn it into crumbs. But again, be careful; crumbs that are overprocessed will be too fine.

Crumbs can also be made by hand with a bread knife or using a box grater. Grated crumbs, even when cut on the largest holes, are a bit finer than crumbs made in a food processor or cut with a knife but still fine for use in pasta sauces.

Toasted crumbs have a richer flavor than plain crumbs. After testing various cooking methods, we found using an oven was the clear winner for ease and consistency. Microwaving is absolutely out of the question because the crumbs never brown; they simply dry out. Crumbs can be sautéed, but this requires more attention than using an oven and is more likely to result in burned crumbs.

For oven browning, we tested various temperatures and cooking times. We found that baking in a standard 325-degree oven for twelve minutes proved the most successful method. At 275 degrees, the crumbs took twice as long to bake and were desiccated and hard, as opposed to baked and crisp; they were also pale and visually unappealing. In a 350-degree oven, the crumbs cooked quickly but very unevenly—the smaller crumbs burned despite our cautious stirring while baking.

We prepared bread crumbs with olive oil, butter, margarine, vegetable oil, and safflower oil to see which fat worked best. Margarine and vegetable and safflower oils resulted in heavy, greasy crumbs. Extra-virgin olive oil and butter gave us the best results.

Flavoring bread crumbs is easy as long as you add the seasonings at the right time. Herbs and other ingredients that tend to burn should be stirred into the crumbs after they have been toasted. Spices, such as black pepper, can be added with the oil and salt before the crumbs go into the oven.

The last key to perfect bread crumbs is not to bake them too far ahead of time. They are best right out of the oven but can be held for an hour or so in a 200-degree oven until you're ready to sprinkle them over pasta. Just don't try to store them on the shelf in a plastic bag. Remember this method is for making crumbs as condiments, not as an ingredient for meatloaf.

Economical cooks can cut stale bread into crumbs and store the crumbs in a sealable bag in the freezer. Take the crumbs right from the freezer, season as desired, and then toast, increasing the baking time by a minute or two.

The following recipes derive most of their flavor from bread crumbs. Other recipes using bread crumbs appear throughout the book, especially in the vegetable, seafood, and baked pasta chapters. When using so much bread crumbs (we found that one cup

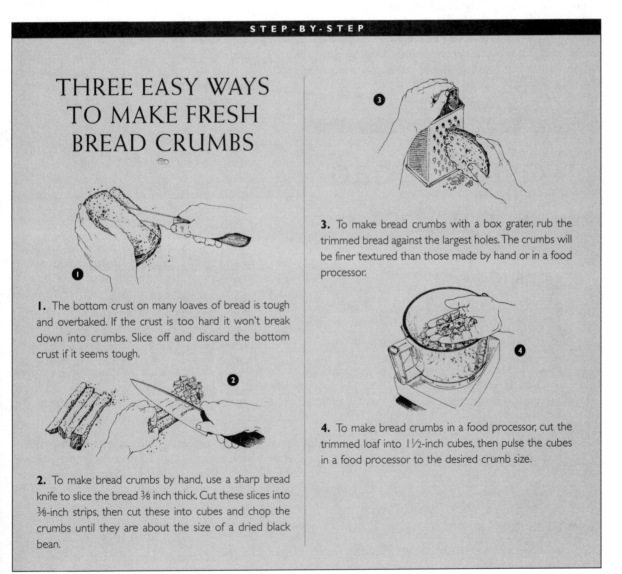

THREE EASY WAYS TO MAKE FRESH BREAD CRUMBS

1. The bottom crust on many loaves of bread is tough and overbaked. If the crust is too hard it won't break down into crumbs. Slice off and discard the bottom crust if it seems tough.

2. To make bread crumbs by hand, use a sharp bread knife to slice the bread ⅜ inch thick. Cut these slices into ⅜-inch strips, then cut these into cubes and chop the crumbs until they are about the size of a dried black bean.

3. To make bread crumbs with a box grater, rub the trimmed bread against the largest holes. The crumbs will be finer textured than those made by hand or in a food processor.

4. To make bread crumbs in a food processor, cut the trimmed loaf into 1½-inch cubes, then pulse the cubes in a food processor to the desired crumb size.

of crumbs is the right amount of flavor for one pound of pasta), we like to add all the crumbs to the drained pasta and toss well with the sauce. Some sources suggest sprinkling the crumbs over the sauced pasta, but we found that the crumbs were too hard and did not meld properly with the pasta.

In some cases, bread crumbs can make the pasta a bit dry. The crumbs soak up the sauce (in most cases a flavored oil) and the pasta ends up too dry. Reserve some of the pasta cooking water and use it to moisten any pasta that seems to dry when tossed with the oil and crumbs. A caution: Don't add the cooking water haphazardly. If the pasta seems moist enough, leave out the water; the crumbs will become soggy if water is added when it is not needed.

Toasted Bread Crumbs

MAKES 1 CUP

THIS IS THE BASIC recipe to use for garnishing pastas with vegetable-based sauces or baked pasta gratins. These bread crumbs are best used immediately, but they can be held in a 200-degree oven for an hour or so. If you like, freeze fresh bread crumbs and then season and toast as needed, increasing the baking time by a minute or two.

1 cup fresh bread crumbs (see illustrations 1–4, page 89)
1 ½ tablespoons extra-virgin olive oil or melted butter
¼ teaspoon salt

1. Adjust the oven rack to the center-low position and heat the oven to 325 degrees. Mix the bread crumbs with the oil and salt to coat evenly. Spread in a single layer on a small baking sheet.

2. Bake the crumbs, stirring once after 5 minutes, until golden brown, about 12 minutes.

◆

Toasted Bread Crumbs with Herbs and Lemon Zest

MARJORAM, THYME, AND LEMON ZEST SEASON FRESH BREAD CRUMBS. OTHER STRONG HERBS, SUCH AS OREGANO, CILANTRO, TARRAGON, AND MINT, CAN ALSO BE USED TO FLAVOR BREAD CRUMBS. **MAKES 1 CUP.**

1 cup fresh bread crumbs (see illustrations 1–4, page 89)
1 ½ tablespoons extra-virgin olive oil
¼ teaspoon salt
½ teaspoon minced lemon zest (see illustrations 1–4, page 91)
½ teaspoon minced fresh thyme leaves
¼ teaspoon minced fresh marjoram leaves

1. Adjust the oven rack to the center-low position and heat the oven to 325 degrees. Mix the bread crumbs with the oil and salt to coat evenly. Spread in a single layer on a small baking sheet.

2. Bake the crumbs, stirring once after 5 minutes, until golden brown, about 12 minutes. Stir in the zest, thyme, and marjoram. Use immediately or keep warm in a 200-degree oven for up to 1 hour.

Toasted Bread Crumbs with Orange and Sage

IF YOU PREFER, USE OREGANO OR THYME INSTEAD OF SAGE. MAKES 1 CUP.

- 1 cup fresh bread crumbs (see illustrations 1–4, page 89)
- 1 ½ tablespoons extra-virgin olive oil
- ¼ teaspoon salt
- 1 teaspoon minced orange zest (see illustrations 1–4)
- 2 teaspoons minced fresh sage leaves

1. Adjust the oven rack to the center-low position and heat the oven to 325 degrees. Mix the bread crumbs with the oil and salt to coat evenly. Spread in a single layer on a small baking sheet.

2. Bake the crumbs, stirring once after 5 minutes, until golden brown, about 12 minutes. Stir in the zest and sage. Use immediately or keep warm in a 200-degree oven for up to 1 hour.

STEP-BY-STEP

MINCING CITRUS ZEST

1. Minced citrus zest is more noticeable than grated zest, something that is desirable in simple recipes with bread crumbs and little else in the way of flavorings. To mince lemon, lime, or orange zest, use a vegetable peeler to remove strips of the peel of roughly the same size, which are easy to stack and julienne. Hold the citrus so one full side is exposed. Grasping the peeler horizontally, use a downward motion to remove strips of citrus rind from the top of the fruit to the bottom.

2. If you have included much of the bitter white pith with the zest, you can remove it by sliding a paring knife along the inside of the zest. Be careful not to cut into the colored peel itself.

3. Stack several pieces of peel on top of one another and use a chef's knife to slice them into very thin strips.

4. Cut the strips crosswise into fine mince.

Toasted Bread Crumbs with White Wine and Butter

WINE-FLAVORED BREAD CRUMBS ARE MADE WITH BUT-
TER TO CREATE ESPECIALLY RICH-TASTING CRUMBS.
MAKES 1 CUP.

> 1 cup fresh bread crumbs (see illustrations
> 1–4, page 89)
> 1 1/2 tablespoons unsalted butter, melted
> 2 tablespoons white wine
> 1/4 teaspoon salt

1. Adjust the oven rack to the center-low position
and heat the oven to 325 degrees. Mix the bread
crumbs with the melted butter, wine, and salt to coat
evenly. Spread in a single layer on a small baking
sheet.

2. Bake the crumbs, stirring once after 5 minutes,
until golden brown, about 12 minutes. Use immediately or keep warm in a 200-degree oven for up to 1
hour.

◆

Toasted Bread Crumbs with Cracked Black Pepper

ALTHOUGH THESE BREAD CRUMBS CONTAIN A LOT OF
BLACK PEPPER, BAKING SOFTENS THE HEAT AND ACTU-
ALLY DEEPENS THE PEPPERCORN FLAVOR. MAKES 1 CUP.

> 1 cup fresh bread crumbs (see illustrations
> 1–4, page 89)
> 1 1/2 tablespoons extra-virgin olive oil
> 1/2 teaspoon coarsely ground black pepper
> 1/4 teaspoon salt

1. Adjust the oven rack to the center-low position
and heat the oven to 325 degrees. Mix the bread
crumbs with the oil, pepper, and salt to coat evenly.
Spread in a single layer on a small baking sheet.

2. Bake the crumbs, stirring once after 5 minutes,
until golden brown, about 12 minutes. Use immediately or keep warm in a 200-degree oven for up to
1 hour.

Spaghetti with Toasted Bread Crumbs, Oil, and Garlic

SERVES 4

BREAD CRUMBS TAKE a basic garlic and
oil sauce to the next level, adding crunch
and flavor. This dish is very plain, but
still delicious. The recipes that follow
add herbs, citrus zest, and other flavors and are more
complex.

> 4 medium garlic cloves, peeled (see
> illustration, page 39)
> 6 tablespoons extra-virgin olive oil
> Salt
> 1 pound spaghetti or other long, thin
> pasta
> 1 recipe Toasted Bread Crumbs (page 90)
> Ground black pepper

1. Process the garlic through a garlic press into a small
bowl; stir in 1 teaspoon water (see illustrations 1–3,
page 45). Heat the oil, diluted garlic, and 1 teaspoon
salt in a small skillet and turn the heat to low. Cook
very slowly until the garlic turns golden, about 3 minutes. Be careful not to brown the garlic or your sauce
will be bitter. Remove from heat.

2. Meanwhile, bring 4 quarts of water to a boil in a large pot. Add 1 tablespoon salt and the pasta to the boiling water. Cook until al dente. Reserve ½ cup of the cooking water; drain the pasta and transfer it back to the cooking pot. Mix in the garlic oil, bread crumbs, and enough reserved water to keep the mixture moist. Adjust the salt and pepper. Divide among 4 warmed pasta bowls and serve immediately.

◆

Spaghetti with Toasted Bread Crumbs, Herbs, and Lemon Zest

PASTA WITH OLIVE OIL AND GARLIC CAN ALSO BE EM-
BELLISHED WITH FLAVORED BREAD CRUMBS. SERVES 4.

> 4 medium garlic cloves, peeled (see illustration, page 39)
> 6 tablespoons extra-virgin olive oil
> Salt
> 1 pound spaghetti or other long, thin pasta
> 1 recipe Toasted Bread Crumbs with Herbs and Lemon Zest (page 90)
> Ground black pepper

1. Process the garlic through a garlic press into a small bowl; stir in 1 teaspoon water (see illustrations 1–3, page 45). Heat the oil, diluted garlic, and 1 teaspoon salt in a small skillet and turn the heat to low. Cook very slowly until the garlic turns golden, about 3 minutes. Be careful not to brown the garlic or your sauce will be bitter. Remove from heat.

2. Meanwhile, bring 4 quarts of water to a boil in a large pot. Add 1 tablespoon salt and the pasta to the boiling water. Cook until al dente. Reserve ½ cup of the cooking water; drain the pasta and transfer it back to the cooking pot. Mix in the garlic oil, bread crumbs, and enough reserved water to keep the mixture moist. Adjust the salt and pepper. Divide among 4 warmed pasta bowls and serve immediately.

Spaghetti with Toasted Bread Crumbs, White Wine, and Butter

THIS PASTA IS GOOD AS A MAIN COURSE OR AS A SIDE
DISH WITH ANYTHING THAT IS COMPLEMENTED BY
WINE AND BUTTER—MILD FISH FILLETS, SAUTÉED
CHICKEN BREASTS, OR STEAMED LOBSTERS, FOR EXAM-
PLE. SERVES 4.

> 4 medium garlic cloves, peeled (see illustration, page 39)
> 4½ tablespoons unsalted butter
> Salt
> ½ cup white wine
> 1 pound spaghetti or other long, thin pasta
> 1 recipe Toasted Bread Crumbs with White Wine and Butter (page 92)
> ¼ cup minced fresh flat-leaf parsley leaves
> ½ cup grated Parmesan cheese
> Ground black pepper

1. Process the garlic through a garlic press into a small bowl; stir in 1 teaspoon water (see illustrations 1–3, page 45). Heat the butter, diluted garlic, and 1 teaspoon salt in a small skillet and turn the heat to low. Cook very slowly until the garlic turns golden, about 3 minutes. Be careful not to brown the garlic or your sauce will be bitter. Stir in the wine and simmer another 2 minutes. Remove from heat.

2. Meanwhile, bring 4 quarts of water to a boil in a large pot. Add 1 tablespoon salt and the pasta to the boiling water. Cook until al dente. Reserve ½ cup of the cooking water; drain the pasta and transfer it back to the cooking pot. Mix in the garlic butter, bread crumbs, parsley, cheese, and enough reserved water to keep the mixture moist. Adjust the salt and pepper. Divide among 4 warmed pasta bowls and serve immediately.

Spaghetti with Toasted Bread Crumbs and Cracked Black Pepper

PECORINO CHEESE WORKS ESPECIALLY WELL WITH PEP-PERY BREAD CRUMBS. **SERVES 4.**

> 4 medium garlic cloves, peeled (see illustration, page 39)
> 6 tablespoons extra-virgin olive oil
> Salt
> 1 pound spaghetti or other long, thin pasta
> 1 recipe Toasted Bread Crumbs with Cracked Black Pepper (page 92)
> ½ cup grated pecorino cheese

1. Process the garlic through a garlic press into a small bowl; stir in 1 teaspoon water (see illustrations 1–3, page 45). Heat the oil, diluted garlic, and 1 teaspoon salt in a small skillet and turn the heat to low. Cook very slowly until the garlic turns golden, about 3 minutes. Be careful not to brown the garlic or your sauce will be bitter. Remove from heat.

2. Meanwhile, bring 4 quarts of water to a boil in a large pot. Add 1 tablespoon salt and the pasta to the boiling water. Cook until al dente. Reserve ½ cup of the cooking water; drain the pasta and transfer it back to the cooking pot. Mix in the garlic oil, bread crumbs, cheese, and enough reserved water to keep the mixture moist. Adjust the salt. Divide among 4 warmed pasta bowls and serve immediately.

Spaghetti with Toasted Bread Crumbs, Capers, Olives, and Anchovies

THE SALTY COMBINATION OF CAPERS, OLIVES, AND ANCHOVIES IS OFFSET BY A CRUNCHY GARNISH OF HOMEMADE BREAD CRUMBS. **SERVES 4.**

> 4 medium garlic cloves, peeled (see illustration, page 39)
> 6 tablespoons extra-virgin olive oil
> Salt
> ½ cup black olives (such as Kalamata), pitted and coarsely chopped (see illustrations 1–2, page 62)
> 2 tablespoons capers, rinsed
> 4 anchovy fillets, rinsed and minced
> 1 pound spaghetti or other long, thin pasta
> 1 recipe Toasted Bread Crumbs (page 90)
> ¼ cup minced fresh flat-leaf parsley leaves
> Ground black pepper

1. Process the garlic through a garlic press into a small bowl; stir in 1 teaspoon water (see illustrations 1–3, page 45). Heat the oil, diluted garlic, and 1 teaspoon salt in a small skillet and turn the heat to low. Cook very slowly until the garlic turns golden, about 3 minutes. Be careful not to brown the garlic or your sauce will be bitter. Stir in the olives, capers, and anchovies. Remove from heat.

2. Meanwhile, bring 4 quarts of water to a boil in a large pot. Add 1 tablespoon salt and the pasta to the boiling water. Cook until al dente. Reserve ½ cup of the cooking water; drain the pasta and transfer it back to the cooking pot. Mix in the garlic oil mixture, bread crumbs, parsley, and enough reserved water to keep the mixture moist. Adjust the salt and pepper. Divide among 4 warmed pasta bowls and serve immediately.

Spaghetti with Toasted Bread Crumbs and Golden Raisins

HERE IS ANOTHER TYPICALLY SOUTHERN ITALIAN COM-BINATION—LIGHTLY OILED PASTA, BREAD CRUMBS, AND A HANDFUL OF PLUMP RAISINS. SERVES 4.

½ cup golden raisins or currants
6 tablespoons extra-virgin olive oil
1 medium onion, minced
Salt
2 medium garlic cloves, minced
1 pound spaghetti or other long, thin pasta
1 recipe Toasted Bread Crumbs (page 90)
1 teaspoon minced fresh thyme leaves
Ground black pepper

1. Place the raisins or currants in a small bowl and cover with hot tap water. Let stand until softened, 10 to 15 minutes. Drain and set aside.

2. Place the oil, onion, and 1 teaspoon salt in a small skillet and turn the heat to low. Cook until the onion begins to soften, 2 to 3 minutes. Add the garlic and cook very slowly until the garlic turns golden, about 3 minutes. Be careful not to brown the garlic or your sauce will be bitter. Remove from heat.

3. Meanwhile, bring 4 quarts of water to a boil in a large pot. Add 1 tablespoon salt and the pasta to the boiling water. Cook until al dente. Reserve ½ cup of the cooking water; drain the pasta and transfer it back to the cooking pot. Mix in the onion mixture, bread crumbs, thyme, raisins, and enough reserved water to keep the mixture moist. Adjust the salt and pepper. Divide among 4 warmed pasta bowls and serve immediately.

Fusilli with Dried Figs, Toasted Bread Crumbs, Orange, and Sage

FUSILLI OR ANY OTHER CURLY PASTA SHAPE WORKS WELL HERE, TO CATCH AND HOLD BITS OF DRIED FIG AND BREAD CRUMB. ORANGE ZEST AND SAGE COMPLE-MENT THE FLAVOR OF THE FIGS NICELY. WE ESPECIALLY LIKE CALMYRNA FIGS IN THIS RECIPE. SERVES 4.

6 dried figs, stemmed
4 medium garlic cloves, peeled (see illustration, page 39)
6 tablespoons extra-virgin olive oil
Salt
1 pound fusilli or other short, curly pasta
1 recipe Toasted Bread Crumbs with Orange and Sage (page 91)
Ground black pepper

1. Place the figs in a small bowl and cover with hot tap water. Let stand until softened, 10 to 15 minutes. Drain, finely chop, and set aside.

2. Process the garlic through a garlic press into a small bowl; stir in 1 teaspoon water (see illustrations 1–3, page 45). Heat the oil, diluted garlic, and 1 tea-spoon salt in a small skillet and turn the heat to low. Cook very slowly until the garlic turns golden, about 3 minutes. Be careful not to brown the garlic or your sauce will be bitter. Remove from heat.

3. Meanwhile, bring 4 quarts of water to a boil in a large pot. Add 1 tablespoon salt and the pasta to the boiling water. Cook until al dente. Reserve ½ cup of the cooking water; drain the pasta and transfer it back to the cooking pot. Mix in the garlic oil, bread crumbs, figs, and enough reserved water to keep the mixture moist. Adjust the salt and pepper. Divide among 4 warmed pasta bowls and serve immediately.

Fusilli with Sun-Dried Tomatoes and Toasted Bread Crumbs

THIS DISH MAY BE SERVED AT ROOM TEMPERATURE AS A PASTA SALAD; JUST WAIT UNTIL IMMEDIATELY BEFORE SERVING TO STIR IN THE BREAD CRUMBS. **SERVES 4**.

4 medium garlic cloves, peeled (see illustration, page 39)
6 tablespoons extra-virgin olive oil
Salt
1 pound spaghetti or other long, thin pasta
1 recipe Toasted Bread Crumbs with Herbs and Lemon Zest (page 90)
12 sun-dried tomatoes packed in oil, drained, patted dry, and finely chopped
1 tablespoon red wine vinegar
Ground black pepper

1. Process the garlic through a garlic press into a small bowl; stir in 1 teaspoon water (see illustrations 1–3, page 45). Heat the oil, diluted garlic, and 1 teaspoon salt in a small skillet and turn the heat to low. Cook very slowly until the garlic turns golden, about 3 minutes. Be careful not to brown the garlic or your sauce will be bitter. Remove from heat.

2. Meanwhile, bring 4 quarts of water to a boil in a large pot. Add 1 tablespoon salt and the pasta to the boiling water. Cook until al dente. Reserve ½ cup of the cooking water; drain the pasta and transfer it back to the cooking pot. Mix in the garlic oil, bread crumbs, tomatoes, vinegar, and enough reserved water to keep the mixture moist. Adjust the salt and pepper. Divide among 4 warmed pasta bowls and serve immediately.

CHAPTER 10

RAW TOMATO
SAUCES

/I\

AT THE HEIGHT OF SUMMER, RAW TOMATO SAUCES

ARE OUR FAVORITE CHOICE. DICED TOMATOES CAN BE

THE BASIS FOR LITERALLY DOZENS OF DIFFERENT PASTA

SAUCES. OF COURSE, THE QUALITY OF THESE SAUCES

DEPENDS ON REALLY RIPE, REALLY GOOD TOMATOES.

DON'T BOTHER WITH ANY OF THE RECIPES IN THIS

CHAPTER IF YOU HAVE LESS THAN STELLAR TOMA-

TOES. ◆ THAT SAID, HOW SHOULD THE TOMATOES

be handled? Must they be peeled and seeded? What kind of tomatoes work best in a raw pasta sauce? Also, will the tomatoes be moist enough to sauce the pasta, or do they need some oil, and if so, how much? Also, what herbs and other seasonings are best in this kind of sauce?

We tested a basic recipe using chopped tomatoes as well as seeded and chopped tomatoes and peeled, seeded, and chopped tomatoes. Peeling is a lot of work, and in this case we did not feel that the work justified the effort. When fresh tomatoes are cooked, the skins tend to separate from the flesh and shrivel up into tiny, not very appealing bits. However, in this dish, the heat of the pasta is not sufficient to separate the peel from the flesh. We don't mind tomato peel as long as it stays attached to some flesh, and so opted not to peel tomatoes for this dish.

Seeding is another matter. The pasta tossed with chopped (but not seeded) tomatoes was very watery. The pasta tossed with seeded tomatoes was much better, with no watery juices pooling up in the bottom of the bowl. Seeding is quick (just core, cut the tomatoes in half through their equator, and squeeze out the seeds) and the benefits are worth the minimal effort.

We had been conducting our tests with round (or beefsteak) tomatoes. We wondered how other tomatoes would fare in this dish. We went to a local farmer's market and tried a half dozen kinds of tomatoes in various shapes and sizes. Our results are easily summarized—any tomato that tastes good raw works well in a raw pasta sauce. In general, plum or Roma tomatoes are a bit firmer than ripe round tomatoes; they don't soften quite as nicely when tossed with hot pasta, and given the choice we recommend using round tomatoes. We liked yellow tomatoes in this dish, although they lack some of the pleasing acidity of red tomatoes. If you want yellow tomatoes, we recommend using half red tomatoes and half yellow tomatoes for the best flavor. (This combination also happens to look very good.)

As we suspected, olive oil is a must, both for moistening the pasta and for flavoring the sauce. Because the oil is not cooked, extra-virgin oil is essential. In addition to tomatoes, oil, salt, and pepper, we like to add a little garlic to our raw tomato sauce. The heat of the pasta will slightly tame the raw garlic flavor. How-

SEEDING RIPE TOMATOES

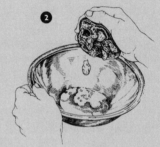

1. Cut the cored tomatoes in half crosswise, at the equator of the tomato, not through the stem end.

2. Gently squeeze each tomato half over the sink or a bowl to push out the seeds.

3. Use your finger to push out any seeds that remain in the tomatoes. The seeded tomatoes are now ready to be chopped.

ever, don't use more than a clove of garlic or the flavor will be too intense. Some minced fresh basil completes our master recipe.

We recommend preparing raw tomato sauce in the time it takes to bring 4 quarts of water to a boil and cook the pasta. The salt in the sauce will cause the tomatoes to give up some of their flavorful juices and the garlic flavor can become too harsh if this sauce is left to marinate for more than a half hour or so.

Chunks of raw tomato work best with tubular shapes, like penne, or short, curly pasta shapes, such as fusilli. These shapes, along with small shells and orecchiette, will trap bits of tomato better than long strand pasta.

The recipes in this chapter are not meant to be served piping hot. The raw sauce cools down the drained pasta, making it a palatable temperature even on the hottest summer day. We suggest serving these dishes immediately (when warm but not hot), although they can be allowed to cool for ten minutes or so and eaten when tepid if the weather is especially warm. The recipes in this chapter should not be served with grated cheese at the table. There's not enough heat to melt it properly. Save grated cheese for dishes with cooked tomato sauce, or add the cheese directly to the pot with the hot pasta and sauce so it will melt.

Penne with Raw Tomato Sauce

SERVES 4

CALLED *SALSA CRUDA* in Italy, this raw sauce depends on absolutely ripe summer tomatoes. The tomatoes are seeded (but not peeled), and tossed with the finest olive oil and seasonings.

If you prefer, omit the garlic.

1 ½ pounds ripe tomatoes, halved and
   seeded (see illustrations 1–3, page 98)
¼ cup extra-virgin olive oil
1 medium garlic clove, minced
2 tablespoons minced fresh basil leaves
Salt and ground black pepper
1 pound penne or other short, tubular
   pasta

1. Bring 4 quarts of water to a boil in a large pot for cooking the pasta.

2. Cut the seeded tomatoes into ¼-inch dice and place them in a medium bowl. Add the oil, garlic, basil, and salt and pepper to taste, and mix well.

3. Add 1 tablespoon salt and the pasta to the boiling water. Cook until al dente. Drain the pasta and transfer it back to the cooking pot. Mix in the sauce. Divide among 4 pasta bowls and serve immediately.

Penne with
Spicy Raw Tomato Sauce

HOT RED PEPPER FLAKES ARE CONVENIENT, BUT A FRESH
CHILE THAT HAS BEEN STEMMED, SEEDED, AND MINCED
MAY ALSO BE USED TO SPICE UP A RAW TOMATO SAUCE.
SERVES 4.

> 1½ pounds ripe tomatoes, halved and
>   seeded (see illustrations 1–3, page 98)
> ¼ cup extra-virgin olive oil
> 1 medium garlic clove, minced
> 2 tablespoons minced fresh basil leaves
> ½ teaspoon hot red pepper flakes, or to
>   taste
> Salt and ground black pepper
> 1 pound penne or other short, tubular
>   pasta

1. Bring 4 quarts of water to a boil in a large pot for
cooking the pasta.

2. Cut the seeded tomatoes into ¼-inch dice and
place in a medium bowl. Add the oil, garlic, basil, red
pepper flakes, and salt and pepper to taste, and mix
well.

3. Add 1 tablespoon salt and the pasta to the boiling
water. Cook until al dente. Drain the pasta and transfer it back to the cooking pot. Mix in the sauce.
Divide among 4 pasta bowls and serve immediately.

KEEPING HERBS FRESH

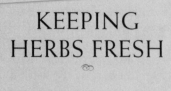

1. Parsley and other fresh herbs with long stems
can be kept fresh for at least a week, if not longer,
by washing and drying the herbs, and then trimming
the stem ends.

2. Place the herbs in a tall, airtight container with a
tight-fitting lid. Add water up to the top of the
stems, but don't cover the leaves. Seal the container
tightly and refrigerate. In our tests, the combination
of water and relatively little air kept the herbs much
fresher than other storage methods.

Penne with Raw Tomato Sauce and Mixed Herbs

WE LIKE THE COMBINATION OF MILDER AND STRONGER HERBS SUGGESTED IN THIS RECIPE. HOWEVER, YOU MAY SUBSTITUTE CILANTRO OR TARRAGON FOR THE MINT AND OREGANO OR MARJORAM FOR THE THYME IF DESIRED. SERVES 4.

1 ½ pounds ripe tomatoes, halved and
    seeded (see illustrations 1–3, page 98)
¼ cup extra-virgin olive oil
1 medium garlic clove, minced
3 tablespoons minced fresh basil leaves
3 tablespoons minced fresh flat-leaf
    parsley leaves
1 tablespoon minced fresh mint leaves
1 tablespoon minced fresh thyme leaves
Salt and ground black pepper
1 pound penne or other short, tubular
    pasta

1. Bring 4 quarts of water to a boil in a large pot for cooking the pasta.

2. Cut the seeded tomatoes into ¼-inch dice and place in a medium bowl. Add the oil, garlic, basil, parsley, mint, thyme, and salt and pepper to taste, and mix well.

3. Add 1 tablespoon salt and the pasta to the boiling water. Cook until al dente. Drain the pasta and transfer it back to the cooking pot. Mix in the sauce. Divide among 4 pasta bowls and serve immediately.

Penne with Raw Tomato Sauce, Olives, and Capers

CONSIDER THIS DISH A SUMMER VERSION OF THE FAMED PUTTANESCA SAUCE (SEE PAGE 122), MADE WITH FRESH TOMATOES RATHER THAN CANNED. GO EASY ON THE ADDED SALT, AS THE OLIVES AND CAPERS ALREADY SEASON THE DISH. SERVES 4.

1 ½ pounds ripe tomatoes, halved and
    seeded (see illustrations 1–3, page 98)
⅓ cup Kalamata olives, pitted and
    coarsely chopped (see illustrations 1–2,
    page 62)
2 tablespoons capers, rinsed
¼ cup extra-virgin olive oil
1 medium garlic clove, minced
2 tablespoons minced fresh basil leaves
Salt and ground black pepper
1 pound penne or other short, tubular
    pasta

1. Bring 4 quarts of water to a boil in a large pot for cooking the pasta.

2. Cut the seeded tomatoes into ¼-inch dice and place in a medium bowl. Add the olives, capers, oil, garlic, basil, and salt and pepper to taste, and mix well.

3. Add 1 tablespoon salt and the pasta to the boiling water. Cook until al dente. Drain the pasta and transfer it back to the cooking pot. Mix in the sauce. Divide among 4 pasta bowls and serve immediately.

Fusilli with Raw Tomato Sauce and Pesto

A LITTLE PESTO COMPLEMENTS THE FLAVORS OF RIPE SUMMER TOMATOES. ADD PARSLEY TO THE PESTO TO KEEP ITS COLOR FROM DULLING ON CONTACT WITH THE HOT PASTA. SEE CHAPTER 6 FOR MORE INFORMATION ON MAKING PESTO. SERVES 4.

- 2 tablespoons pine nuts, walnuts, or almonds
- 2 small garlic cloves, threaded on a skewer
- 1 cup packed fresh basil leaves
- 2 tablespoons fresh flat-leaf parsley leaves (optional)
- 4 tablespoons extra-virgin olive oil
- Salt and ground black pepper
- 2 tablespoons finely grated Parmesan cheese
- 1 1/2 pounds ripe tomatoes, halved and seeded (see illustrations 1–3, page 98)
- 1 pound fusilli or short, tubular pasta

1. Toast the nuts in a small, heavy skillet over medium heat, stirring frequently, until just golden and fragrant, 4 to 5 minutes.

2. Meanwhile, bring 4 quarts of water to a boil in a large pot. Lower the skewered garlic into the water (see illustration 1, page 56); boil for 45 seconds. Immediately run the garlic under cold water. (Do not discard the water.) Remove from the skewer; peel and mince.

3. Place the basil and parsley (if using) in a heavy-duty, quart-size, sealable plastic bag; pound with the flat side of a meat pounder until all the leaves are bruised (see illustration 2, page 56).

4. Place the nuts, garlic, basil, parsley, oil, and salt and pepper in the work bowl of a food processor; process until smooth, stopping as necessary to scrape down the sides of the bowl. Transfer the mixture to a medium bowl, stir in the cheese, and adjust the salt.

5. Cut the seeded tomatoes into 1/4-inch dice and place in the bowl with the pesto. Toss to combine.

6. Add 1 tablespoon salt and the pasta to the boiling water. Cook until al dente. Drain the pasta and transfer it back to the cooking pot. Mix in the sauce. Divide among 4 pasta bowls and serve immediately.

◆

Fusilli with Raw Tomato Sauce and Olivada

OLIVADA IS A FRAGRANT PUREE MADE FROM PITTED BLACK OLIVES, SHALLOT, HERBS, LEMON JUICE, AND OLIVE OIL. IT COMBINES BEAUTIFULLY WITH RAW TOMATOES. SERVES 4.

- 3/4 cup black olives (such as Kalamata), pitted (see illustrations 1–2, page 62)
- 1 small shallot, coarsely chopped
- 3 large fresh basil leaves
- 1 teaspoon fresh thyme leaves
- 1 tablespoon extra-virgin olive oil
- 1 1/2 teaspoons lemon juice
- 1 1/2 pounds ripe tomatoes, halved and seeded (see illustrations 1–3, page 98)
- Salt
- 1 pound fusilli or short, tubular pasta

1. Bring 4 quarts of water to a boil in a large pot for cooking the pasta.

2. Place the olives, shallot, basil, thyme, oil, and juice in the work bowl of a food processor; process until smooth, stopping as necessary to scrape down the sides of the bowl. Transfer the mixture to a bowl.

3. Cut the seeded tomatoes into 1/4-inch dice and place in the bowl with the olive puree. Toss to combine.

4. Add 1 tablespoon salt and the pasta to the boiling water. Cook until al dente. Drain the pasta and transfer it back to the cooking pot. Mix in the sauce. Divide among 4 pasta bowls and serve immediately.

Fusilli with Raw Tomato Sauce and Corn

THIS DISH IS AN AMERICAN INVENTION, TAKING ADVANTAGE OF FINE SUMMER CORN AND TOMATOES. MAKE SURE NOT TO OVERCOOK THE CORN. YOU WANT IT TO HAVE SOME TEXTURE IN THE PASTA SAUCE. SHOCKING THE COOKED CORN UNDER COLD RUNNING WATER STOPS THE EARS FROM SOFTENING FURTHER AS THEY COOL. SERVES 4.

> 2 medium ears of corn, husked
> 1½ pounds ripe tomatoes, halved and seeded (see illustrations 1–3, page 98)
> ¼ cup extra-virgin olive oil
> 1 medium garlic clove, minced
> 2 scallions, white and light green parts, finely chopped
> Salt and ground black pepper
> 1 pound fusilli or other short, tubular pasta

1. Bring 4 quarts of water to a boil in a large pot. Add the corn and boil until just cooked, 3 to 5 minutes. Remove with tongs and immediately cool under cold, running water. (Do not discard the water.) Stand the ears on end and remove the kernels with a sharp knife (see illustration). Place the corn kernels in a medium bowl.

2. Cut the seeded tomatoes into ¼-inch dice and place in the bowl with the corn. Add the oil, garlic, scallions, and salt and pepper to taste, and mix well.

3. Return the water to a boil. Add 1 tablespoon salt and the pasta. Cook until al dente. Drain the pasta and transfer it back to the cooking pot. Mix in the sauce. Divide among 4 pasta bowls and serve immediately.

REMOVING KERNELS FROM AN EAR OF CORN

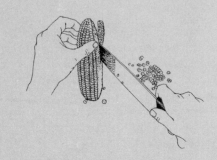

Stand a cooked (or raw) ear of corn on one end and carefully cut down along one side to remove the kernels. Rotate the ear slightly and cut again. Repeat until all the kernels have been removed.

Shells with Raw Tomato Sauce, Prosciutto, and Black Olives

A SPLASH OF SWEET BALSAMIC VINEGAR BALANCES THE SALTINESS OF PROSCIUTTO AND OLIVES IN THIS QUICK PASTA DISH. ADDING THE PROSCIUTTO DIRECTLY TO THE HOT PASTA (RATHER THAN TO THE TOMATO SAUCE) HELPS THE PROSCIUTTO MAINTAIN ITS CHARACTER BETTER. **SERVES 4.**

> 1 ½ pounds ripe tomatoes, halved and
>   seeded (see illustrations 1–3, page 98)
> ⅓ cup Kalamata olives, pitted and
>   coarsely chopped (see illustrations 1–2,
>   page 62)
> ¼ cup extra-virgin olive oil
> 1 tablespoon balsamic vinegar
> 1 medium garlic clove, minced
> 1 tablespoon minced fresh thyme leaves
> Salt and ground black pepper
> 1 pound small shells or orecchiette
> ¼ pound thinly sliced prosciutto, finely
>   chopped

1. Bring 4 quarts of water to a boil in a large pot for cooking the pasta.

2. Cut the seeded tomatoes into ¼-inch dice and place in a medium bowl. Add the olives, oil, vinegar, garlic, thyme, and salt and pepper to taste, and mix well.

3. Add 1 tablespoon salt and the pasta to the boiling water. Cook until al dente. Drain the pasta and transfer it back to the cooking pot. Mix in the sauce and prosciutto. Divide among 4 pasta bowls and serve immediately.

Spaghetti with Raw Tomato Sauce and Almonds

IN THIS SICILIAN PREPARATION, THE INGREDIENTS ARE PUREED FOR A SMOOTHER RAW TOMATO SAUCE, WHICH NICELY COATS SPAGHETTI OR OTHER STRAND PASTA FROM END TO END. A MORTAR AND PESTLE IS TRADITIONALLY USED TO PREPARE THIS SAUCE, BUT A FOOD PROCESSOR IS QUICK AND CONVENIENT. **SERVES 4.**

> ½ cup blanched almonds
> 1 ½ pounds ripe tomatoes, halved and
>   seeded (see illustrations 1–3, page 98)
> ¼ cup extra-virgin olive oil
> 1 medium garlic clove, minced
> 2 tablespoons minced fresh basil leaves
> ¼ teaspoon hot red pepper flakes, or to
>   taste
> Salt
> 1 pound spaghetti or other long, thin
>   pasta

1. Bring 4 quarts of water to a boil in a large pot for cooking the pasta.

2. Toast the nuts in a small, heavy skillet over medium heat, stirring frequently, until just golden and fragrant, 4 to 5 minutes. Set aside and cool completely.

3. Coarsely chop the tomatoes and place in the work bowl of a food processor. Add the almonds, oil, garlic, basil, red pepper flakes, and salt to taste, and process until smooth, scraping down the sides of the bowl as necessary.

4. Add 1 tablespoon salt and the pasta to the boiling water. Cook until al dente. Drain the pasta and transfer it back to the cooking pot. Mix in the sauce. Divide among 4 pasta bowls and serve immediately.

Penne with Raw Tomato Sauce, Fennel, and Red Onion

FENNEL ADDS A CRISP, SWEET FLAVOR TO A RAW TOMATO SAUCE. MAKE SURE TO MINCE THE FENNEL QUITE FINE SO THAT THE HEAT OF THE PASTA CAN SOFTEN IT A BIT. LARGER CHUNKS OF FENNEL WILL SEEM TOO CRUNCHY. SERVES 4.

- 1½ pounds ripe tomatoes, halved and seeded (see illustrations 1–3, page 98)
- 1 small fennel bulb (about ¾ pound), stems, fronds, and base trimmed; bulb cored and minced fine (see illustrations 1–5, page 154)
- 2 tablespoons minced red onion
- ¼ cup extra-virgin olive oil
- 2 tablespoons lemon juice
- 1 medium garlic clove, minced
- 2 tablespoons minced fresh mint leaves
- Salt and ground black pepper
- 1 pound penne or other short, tubular pasta

1. Bring 4 quarts of water to a boil in a large pot for cooking the pasta.

2. Cut the seeded tomatoes into ¼-inch dice and place in a medium bowl. Add the fennel, onion, oil, juice, garlic, mint, and salt and pepper to taste, and mix well.

3. Add 1 tablespoon salt and the pasta to the boiling water. Cook until al dente. Drain the pasta and transfer it back to the cooking pot. Mix in the sauce. Divide among 4 pasta bowls and serve immediately.

Shells with Raw Tomato Sauce, Tuna, and Anchovies

ADDING TUNA PACKED IN OIL GIVES A LIGHT RAW TOMATO SAUCE SOME HEFT. DON'T USE TUNA PACKED IN WATER, WHICH WILL BE TOO DRY IN THIS DISH. TUNA PACKED IN OIL, ESPECIALLY ITALIAN TUNA PACKED IN OLIVE OIL, IS MUCH CREAMIER AND BLENDS BETTER WITH PASTA. SERVES 4.

- 1½ pounds ripe tomatoes, halved and seeded (see illustrations 1–3, page 98)
- 1 6½-ounce can tuna packed in oil, drained and flaked with a fork
- 2 anchovy fillets, minced
- ¼ cup Kalamata olives, pitted and coarsely chopped (see illustrations 1–2, page 62)
- ¼ cup extra-virgin olive oil
- 1 medium garlic clove, minced
- 2 tablespoons minced fresh basil leaves
- Salt and ground black pepper
- 1 pound small shells or fusilli

1. Bring 4 quarts of water to a boil in a large pot for cooking the pasta.

2. Cut the seeded tomatoes into ¼-inch dice and place in a medium bowl. Add the tuna, anchovies, olives, oil, garlic, basil, and salt and pepper to taste, and mix well.

3. Add 1 tablespoon salt and the pasta to the boiling water. Cook until al dente. Drain the pasta and transfer it back to the cooking pot. Mix in the sauce. Divide among 4 pasta bowls and serve immediately.

REMOVING THE FLESH
FROM AN AVOCADO

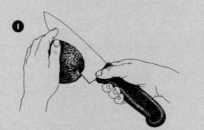

1. Slice around the pit by cutting around both ends of the avocado with a sharp knife.

2. Twist to separate the avocado halves. Holding an avocado half with a kitchen towel, stick the blade of a large chef's knife sharply into the pit.

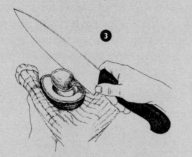

3. Lift the blade, twisting if necessary to loosen and remove the pit. To remove the pit, push it from the blade with a wooden spatula or spoon, not your hand.

4. Slice through the flesh but not the skin with a paring knife.

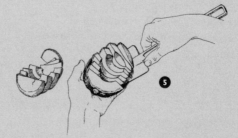

5. Run a rubber spatula around the circumference, just inside the skin, to loosen the flesh, then twist the spatula to pop the flesh out. Dice the avocado as needed.

Fusilli with Raw Tomato Sauce and Avocado

AVOCADO WILL TURN BROWN IF STIRRED INTO THE TOMATOES AHEAD OF TIME, SO WAIT UNTIL THE PASTA IS ALMOST COOKED TO PEEL, PIT, AND CHOP THE AVOCADO. A SPRINKLING OF LEMON JUICE (OR LIME JUICE IF YOU PREFER) SHOULD KEEP IT A FRESH GREEN COLOR UNTIL THE DISH IS EATEN. THE MINCED FRESH OREGANO GIVES THIS DISH A MEXICAN ACCENT. SERVES 4.

1 1/2 pounds ripe tomatoes, halved and
    seeded (see illustrations 1–3, page 98)
1/4 cup extra-virgin olive oil
2 tablespoons capers, rinsed
1 medium garlic clove, minced
1 tablespoon minced fresh oregano leaves
Salt and ground black pepper
1 pound fusilli or short, tubular pasta
1 medium avocado
2 tablespoons lemon juice

1. Bring 4 quarts of water to a boil in a large pot for cooking the pasta.

2. Cut the seeded tomatoes into 1/4-inch dice and place in a medium bowl. Add the oil, capers, garlic, oregano, and salt and pepper to taste, and mix well.

3. Add 1 tablespoon salt and the pasta to the boiling water. Cook until al dente.

4. While the pasta is cooking, halve, pit, peel, and cut the avocado into 1/4-inch dice (see illustrations 1–5, opposite). Place in a small bowl and toss with the lemon juice.

5. Drain the pasta and transfer it back to the cooking pot. Mix in the sauce. Divide among 4 pasta bowls, top with the avocado mixture, and serve immediately.

Spaghetti with Raw Tomato Sauce and Lemon

ALTHOUGH TOMATO AND LEMON ARE BOTH ACIDIC, THEIR COMBINATION ISN'T OVERLY TART. RATHER, THIS SAUCE IS SURPRISINGLY SWEET AND REFRESHING, PERFECT WITH SPICY GRILLED OR BROILED CHICKEN OR SEAFOOD. SERVES 4, OR 8 AS A SIDE DISH.

1 1/2 pounds ripe tomatoes, halved and
    seeded (see illustrations 1–3, page 98)
1/4 cup extra-virgin olive oil
2 tablespoons lemon juice
1 teaspoon grated lemon zest (see
    illustration, page 42)
1 medium garlic clove, minced
2 tablespoons minced fresh basil leaves
Salt and ground black pepper
1 pound penne or other short, tubular
    pasta

1. Bring 4 quarts of water to a boil in a large pot for cooking the pasta.

2. Cut the seeded tomatoes into 1/4-inch dice and place in a medium bowl. Add the oil, juice, zest, garlic, basil, and salt and pepper to taste, and mix well.

3. Add 1 tablespoon salt and the pasta to the boiling water. Cook until al dente. Drain the pasta and transfer it back to the cooking pot. Mix in the sauce. Divide among 4 pasta bowls and serve immediately.

Fusilli with Raw Tomato Sauce and Ricotta

THE RICOTTA CHEESE MAKES THIS DISH ESPECIALLY CREAMY, WITH CHEESE COATING THE NOODLES QUITE THOROUGHLY. THE PARMESAN MELTS INTO THE RICOTTA AND ADDS ITS DISTINCTIVE NUTTY, BUTTERY FLAVOR. SERVES 4.

1 1/2 pounds ripe tomatoes, halved and
    seeded (see illustrations 1–3, page 98)
1/4 cup extra-virgin olive oil
1 medium garlic clove, minced
2 tablespoons minced fresh basil leaves
Salt and ground black pepper
1 pound fusilli or other short, curly pasta
3/4 cup ricotta cheese
1/2 cup grated Parmesan cheese

1. Bring 4 quarts of water to a boil in a large pot for cooking the pasta.

2. Cut the seeded tomatoes into 1/4-inch dice and place in a medium bowl. Add the oil, garlic, basil, and salt and pepper to taste, and mix well.

3. Add 1 tablespoon salt and the pasta to the boiling water. Cook until al dente. Drain the pasta and transfer it back to the cooking pot. Mix in the tomato sauce, ricotta, and Parmesan. Divide among 4 pasta bowls and serve immediately.

Fusilli with Raw Tomato Sauce and Mozzarella

USE FRESH MOZZARELLA CHEESE PACKED IN WATER FOR THIS RECIPE. IT'S CREAMIER AND HAS MORE MOISTURE THAN THE SHRINK-WRAPPED VERSION. SERVES 4.

1 1/2 pounds ripe tomatoes, halved and
    seeded (see illustrations 1–3, page 98)
1/4 cup extra-virgin olive oil
1 medium garlic clove, minced
2 tablespoons minced fresh basil leaves
6 ounces fresh mozzarella cheese,
    shredded (about 1 1/2 cups)
Salt and ground black pepper
1 pound fusilli or other short, curly pasta

1. Bring 4 quarts of water to a boil in a large pot for cooking the pasta.

2. Cut the seeded tomatoes into 1/4-inch dice and place in a medium bowl. Add the oil, garlic, basil, cheese, and salt and pepper to taste, and mix well.

3. Add 1 tablespoon salt and the pasta to the boiling water. Cook until al dente. Drain the pasta and transfer it back to the cooking pot. Mix in the tomato sauce. Divide among 4 pasta bowls and serve immediately.

COOKED FRESH

TOMATO

SAUCES

/|\

GIVEN THE STATE OF THE AMERICAN TOMATO, WE

GENERALLY PREFER PASTA SAUCES MADE WITH

CANNED TOMATOES. IT'S A SAD ADMISSION, BUT IT

REFLECTS THE LOW QUALITY OF FRESH TOMATOES

DURING MOST OF THE YEAR. SO WHEN QUALITY IS AT

ITS PEAK—AT THE HEIGHT OF TOMATO SEASON—WE

PEELING AND SEEDING TOMATOES

T O PEEL MORE THAN ONE OR TWO TOMATOES AT A TIME, WE RECOMMEND THAT YOU BRING A QUART OR TWO OF WATER TO A BOIL AND THEN DIP THE TOMATOES INTO THE BOILING WATER FOR ABOUT 30 SECONDS TO LOOSEN THEIR SKIN. (IF PEELING JUST ONE OR TWO TOMATOES, YOU MAY ROAST THEM

over a burner to loosen the skin; see page 111.) Many sources suggest cutting an X in the bottom of each tomato before simmering in water to help make peeling easier. We found that the flesh near the X tends to overcook and become mushy.

Many sources suggest shocking the tomatoes in a bowl of ice water to stop the cooking process. However, we found that tomatoes don't overcook after just thirty seconds in boiling water. They will be cooked further in the sauce, too. Ice water does cool down the tomatoes so they can be handled right away, but we are happy to wait five minutes or so and skip the ice water bath.

Before removing the skin, use a paring knife to cut out the core. Removing the core exposes some of the skin, which can then be easily peeled away with a paring knife or your fingers. As with raw tomato sauces, it's imperative to seed the tomatoes as well. Removing the seeds ensures that the sauce is thick and meaty.

often don't bother cooking fresh tomatoes at all. We simply seed, chop, season, and toss them with hot pasta for a light, refreshing dish that captures the flavor of the tomatoes with minimal changes. (For more information on raw tomato sauces, see chapter 10.)

However, there are times when you might want to turn fresh tomatoes into a cooked sauce. Perhaps your garden has produced an abundance of fresh tomatoes and you need to find ways to turn your windfall into something other than tomato salad. Or maybe the weather has turned cool (tomato season can last in many parts of the country into early fall) and the idea of pasta sauces with raw tomatoes isn't appealing.

For those occasions, we wanted to develop a formula for turning fresh tomatoes into a delicious sauce.

Our goals were simple: to preserve the flavor and character of ripe tomatoes while making a sauce that would be meaty and dense, which certainly would require some cooking.

Our first question was what kind of tomatoes. We simmered four kinds of tomatoes in some garlic and oil. We purchased ripe, yielding plum (also called Roma) tomatoes from a local farmer's market as well as very ripe round tomatoes. We then went to the supermarket and purchased firm but red plum tomatoes and some hard and fairly anemic-looking round tomatoes.

The local round tomatoes made the best-tasting tomato sauce, with a complex balance between sweet and acidic flavors that the other sauces lacked. The sauce made with local, ripe Romas was good, but not quite as complex or flavorful. The plum tomatoes from the supermarket made a decent sauce but without the rich, complex flavor of one made from really ripe round or plum tomatoes. However, these are rarely mealy and will produce a fairly meaty-textured sauce. The rock-hard round tomatoes that we tested (the kind shipped thousands of miles to market and available even in the summer in most supermarkets) produced a bland, mushy sauce and are not recommended.

With the tomato issue settled, we moved on to preparation. We wondered if it is really necessary to

ROUND TOMATOES

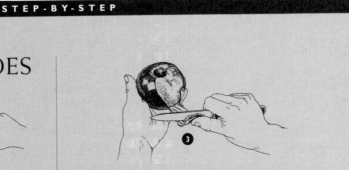

1. To remove the skins from fresh tomatoes, drop the tomatoes into a pan of simmering water. Use a slotted spoon to turn the tomatoes (you want all sides to touch the water). After 30 seconds, use the spoon to remove the tomatoes from the water.

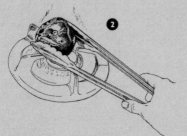

2. If you prefer, hold a tomato with long-handled tongs over a burner set to high. Turn the tomato often until the skin blisters and starts to separate, about 30 seconds. This method makes sense when peeling just one or two tomatoes, but for a whole batch you will save time by simmering them in water.

3. With either method, wait until the tomatoes are cool enough to handle and then cut out the core. Removing the core makes it easy to grab hold of the skin and peel it off with a knife.

4. Halve each cored and peeled tomato crosswise and then squeeze the seeds out over a bowl or into the sink. Use your finger to push out any remaining seeds. Cut the seeded tomatoes into ½-inch dice and reserve for the sauce.

peel tomatoes for a cooked sauce. Unfortunately, the answer is yes. We tried making a fresh tomato sauce with seeded and diced tomatoes, and the skin loosened from the tomato cubes and shriveled up into hard, bitter bits that detracted from both the flavor and texture of the sauce. Peeled tomatoes make a far superior sauce and we think the result is worth the effort.

The next issue was how long to simmer the tomato sauce. We tested simmering the tomato in garlic and oil for five, ten, twenty, and thirty minutes, and for one and two hours. We found that fresh tomatoes require about twenty minutes to break down into a nice, thick sauce. However, cooking them further drives off any remaining fresh tomato flavor. Your grandmother may have simmered fresh tomato sauce for hours, but we found that long cooking produces a dull, flat sauce with little contrast between the sweet and acidic flavors.

Since our sauce is a little chunky, it works best with penne, fusilli, farfalle, shells, or other small pasta shapes that will trap bits of tomato. If you prefer a smoother texture (which will work best with long strand pasta like spaghetti and linguine), puree it in a blender or food processor.

Many old-fashioned recipes suggest putting the tomatoes through a food mill either before or after cooking. We find it easier to peel and seed the tomatoes before cooking by hand. A food mill can be very messy, and you lose a lot of tomato flesh if raw tomatoes are peeled and seeded in this fashion. As for using the food mill after cooking, a blender or food processor is much easier and neater.

As with sauces made from canned tomatoes, we like to reserve a tablespoon of oil for tossing with the pasta. It adds fresh olive oil flavor and helps the sauce coat the noodles. Reserving some of the cooking water and adding it to the drained pasta also helps the sauce coat the noodles evenly.

PLUM TOMATOES

1. Plum tomatoes are usually firmer than round tomatoes and can be peeled without dipping the tomatoes in boiling water. Start by cutting around the stem end with a paring knife and remove the core.

2. Starting where the skin has been cut at the core end, slide the vegetable peeler down to remove the skin in wide strips. Repeat until the tomato has been peeled.

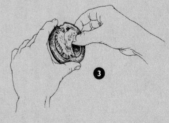

3. Halve the peeled tomato lengthwise and use your fingers to push out the seeds. Cut the seeded tomatoes into 1/2-inch dice and reserve for the sauce.

Penne with Fresh Tomato Sauce

SERVES 4

Whek ROUND TOMATOES are in season, use them in this recipe. Otherwise, stick with oblong plum tomatoes. We prefer to peel the tomatoes (the sauce is silkier without the skin), but you may skip this step if you like. For a smooth version, puree the sauce in a blender or food processor. The tablespoon of olive oil tossed with the pasta and sauce adds another level of flavor.

2 medium garlic cloves, peeled (see
   illustration, page 39)
3 tablespoons extra-virgin olive oil
2 pounds ripe tomatoes, cored, peeled,
   seeded, and cut into ½-inch dice (see
   illustrations, pages 111, 112)
2 tablespoons coarsely chopped fresh
   basil leaves
Salt
1 pound penne or other short, tubular
   pasta

1. Process the garlic through a garlic press into a small bowl; stir in 1 teaspoon water. Heat 2 tablespoons oil and the garlic in a medium sauté pan over medium heat until fragrant but not brown, about 2 minutes. Stir in the tomatoes; simmer until somewhat thickened, about 20 minutes. (If desired, puree the sauce in a blender or food processor. Return the sauce to the pan and heat through.) Stir in the basil and salt to taste.

2. Meanwhile, bring 4 quarts of water to a boil in a large pot. Add 1 tablespoon salt and the pasta. Cook until al dente. Reserve ¼ cup of the cooking water; drain the pasta and transfer it back to the cooking pot. Mix in the reserved cooking water, sauce, and remaining tablespoon of oil. Divide among 4 pasta bowls and serve immediately.

◆

Penne with Fresh Tomato Sauce and Mint

A SIMPLE SWITCH FROM BASIL TO MINT RESULTS IN AN ENTIRELY DIFFERENT FRESH TOMATO SAUCE. THE MINT GIVES THE SAUCE A LIVELY, FLORAL AROMA AND FLAVOR. SERVES 4.

2 medium garlic cloves, peeled (see
   illustration, page 39)
3 tablespoons extra-virgin olive oil
2 pounds ripe tomatoes, cored, peeled,
   seeded, and cut into ½-inch dice (see
   illustrations, pages 111, 112)
2 tablespoons coarsely chopped fresh
   mint leaves
Salt
1 pound penne or other short, tubular
   pasta

1. Process the garlic through a garlic press into a small bowl; stir in 1 teaspoon water. Heat 2 tablespoons oil and the garlic in a medium sauté pan over medium heat until fragrant but not brown, about 2 minutes. Stir in the tomatoes; simmer until somewhat thickened, about 20 minutes. Stir in the mint and salt to taste.

(continued on next page)

2. Meanwhile, bring 4 quarts of water to a boil in a large pot. Add 1 tablespoon salt and the pasta. Cook until al dente. Reserve ¼ cup of the cooking water; drain the pasta and transfer it back to the cooking pot. Mix in the reserved cooking water, sauce, and remaining tablespoon of oil. Divide among 4 pasta bowls and serve immediately.

◆

Fusilli with Fresh Tomato Sauce, Butter, and Onions

THIS SWEET, DELICATE SAUCE, A CLASSIC IN NORTHERN ITALY, IS WELL SUITED TO FILLED PASTAS OR GNOCCHI. THE BUTTER AND SAUTEED ONIONS (RATHER THAN GARLIC) COMPLEMENT THE DELICATE FLAVORS IN FRESH PASTA. THIS SAUCE IS ALSO DELICIOUS WITH DRIED PASTA. SERVES 4.

  3 tablespoons unsalted butter
  1 small onion, minced
  2 pounds ripe tomatoes, cored, peeled, seeded, and cut into ½-inch dice (see illustrations, pages 111, 112)
  Salt
  1 pound fusilli or other short, curly pasta

1. Heat 2 tablespoons butter and the onion in a medium sauté pan over medium heat until translucent, about 5 minutes. Stir in the tomatoes; simmer until somewhat thickened, about 20 minutes. Stir in salt to taste.

2. Meanwhile, bring 4 quarts of water to a boil in a large pot. Add 1 tablespoon salt and the pasta. Cook until al dente. Reserve ¼ cup of the cooking water; drain the pasta and transfer it back to the cooking pot. Mix in the reserved cooking water, sauce, and remaining tablespoon of butter. Divide among 4 pasta bowls and serve immediately.

Farfalle with Fresh Tomato Sauce and Aromatic Vegetables

THIS IS A HEARTY SAUCE WITH STRONG VEGETABLE FLA-VORS. WE LIKE FARFALLE, WHICH CATCH THE BITS OF ONION, CARROT, AND CELERY. MAKE SURE TO MINCE THE VEGETABLES QUITE FINE SO THAT THEY WILL MELT INTO THE TOMATO SAUCE. SERVES 4.

  3 tablespoons extra-virgin olive oil
  1 medium onion, minced
  2 medium carrots, peeled and minced
  2 medium celery stalks, trimmed and minced
  2 pounds ripe tomatoes, cored, peeled, seeded, and cut into ½-inch dice (see illustrations, pages 111, 112)
  2 tablespoons coarsely chopped fresh basil leaves
  Salt
  1 pound farfalle or other short pasta

1. Heat 2 tablespoons oil and the onion, carrots, and celery in a medium sauté pan over medium heat until softened, 8 to 10 minutes. Stir in the tomatoes; simmer until somewhat thickened, about 20 minutes. Stir in the basil and salt to taste.

2. Meanwhile, bring 4 quarts of water to a boil in a large pot. Add 1 tablespoon salt and the pasta. Cook until al dente. Reserve ¼ cup of the cooking water; drain the pasta and transfer it back to the cooking pot. Mix in the reserved cooking water, sauce, and remaining tablespoon of oil. Divide among 4 pasta bowls and serve immediately.

Fusilli with Fresh Tomato Sauce and Cream

THE CREAM MAKES THIS SAUCE ESPECIALLY SWEET AND RICH, PERFECT OVER FRESH PASTA OR WITH DRIED PASTA. FOR AN ESPECIALLY SMOOTH, REFINED SAUCE, PUREE THE SAUCE IN A BLENDER OR FOOD PROCESSOR AND RETURN IT TO THE PAN BEFORE ADDING THE HEAVY CREAM. SERVES 4.

3 tablespoons extra-virgin olive oil
1 medium onion, minced
2 medium carrots, peeled and minced
2 medium celery stalks, trimmed and minced
2 pounds ripe tomatoes, cored, peeled, seeded, and cut into ½-inch dice (see illustrations, pages 111, 112)
½ cup heavy cream
2 tablespoons coarsely chopped fresh basil leaves
Salt
1 pound fusilli or short, tubular pasta

1. Heat 2 tablespoons oil and the onion, carrots, and celery in a medium sauté pan over medium heat until softened, 8 to 10 minutes. Stir in the tomatoes; simmer until somewhat thickened, about 20 minutes. (If desired, puree the sauce in a blender or food processor. Return the sauce to the pan.) Add the cream and simmer until slightly thickened, 2 to 3 minutes. Stir in the basil and salt to taste.

2. Meanwhile, bring 4 quarts of water to a boil in a large pot. Add 1 tablespoon salt and the pasta. Cook until al dente. Reserve ¼ cup of the cooking water; drain the pasta and transfer it back to the cooking pot. Mix in the reserved cooking water, sauce, and remaining tablespoon of oil. Divide among 4 pasta bowls and serve immediately.

Penne with Fresh Tomato Sauce and Pancetta

THE PANCETTA CAN MAKE THIS SAUCE A BIT SALTY, SO ADD SALT LIGHTLY. THIS SAUCE IS HEARTY ENOUGH TO STAND UP TO SOME GRATED PECORINO CHEESE. SERVES 4.

3 tablespoons extra-virgin olive oil
4 ounces pancetta, finely chopped
1 medium onion, minced
2 pounds ripe tomatoes, cored, peeled, seeded, and cut into ½-inch dice (see illustrations, pages 111, 112)
2 tablespoons fresh basil leaves, coarsely chopped
Salt
1 pound penne or other short, tubular pasta
½ cup grated pecorino cheese

1. Heat 2 tablespoons oil, the pancetta, and the onion in a medium sauté pan over medium heat until the onion is softened and the pancetta is crisp, 8 to 10 minutes. Stir in the tomatoes; simmer until somewhat thickened, about 20 minutes. Stir in the basil and salt to taste.

2. Meanwhile, bring 4 quarts of water to a boil in a large pot. Add 1 tablespoon salt and the pasta. Cook until al dente. Reserve ¼ cup of the cooking water; drain the pasta and transfer it back to the cooking pot. Mix in the reserved cooking water, sauce, remaining tablespoon of oil, and cheese. Divide among 4 pasta bowls and serve immediately.

Fusilli with Fresh Tomato Sauce and Fontina

SHREDDED ITALIAN FONTINA AND FRESH TOMATO SAUCE MAKE AN ESPECIALLY RICH DISH. THE BUTTERY, NUTTY FLAVOR OF THE CHEESE WORKS SURPRISINGLY WELL WITH THE BRIGHT ACIDITY OF THE TOMATOES. SERVES 4.

    2 medium garlic cloves, peeled (see
      illustration, page 39)
    3 tablespoons extra-virgin olive oil
    2 pounds ripe tomatoes, cored, peeled,
      seeded, and cut into ½-inch dice (see
      illustrations, pages 111, 112)
    2 tablespoons coarsely chopped fresh
      basil leaves
    Salt
    1 pound fusilli or other short, curly pasta
    ¼ pound Italian Fontina cheese, shredded

1. Process the garlic through a garlic press into a small bowl; stir in 1 teaspoon water. Heat 2 tablespoons oil and the garlic in a medium sauté pan over medium heat until fragrant but not brown, about 2 minutes. Stir in the tomatoes; simmer until somewhat thickened, about 20 minutes. Stir in the basil and salt to taste.

2. Meanwhile, bring 4 quarts of water to a boil in a large pot. Add 1 tablespoon salt and the pasta. Cook until al dente. Reserve ¼ cup of the cooking water; drain the pasta and transfer it back to the cooking pot. Mix in the reserved cooking water, sauce, Fontina, and remaining tablespoon of oil. Divide among 4 pasta bowls and serve immediately.

Fusilli with Fresh Tomato Sauce and Bell Pepper

WE PREFER THE WAY THE FLAVORS OF THE TOMATO AND PEPPER MELD WHEN PUREED, BUT YOU CAN SKIP THIS STEP IF YOU LIKE A CHUNKIER SAUCE. SERVES 4.

    2 medium garlic cloves, peeled (see
      illustration, page 39)
    3 tablespoons extra-virgin olive oil
    1 red or yellow bell pepper, stemmed,
      seeded, and cut into ¼-inch dice
    2 pounds ripe tomatoes, cored, peeled,
      seeded, and cut into ½-inch dice (see
      illustrations, pages 111, 112)
    2 tablespoons coarsely chopped fresh
      basil leaves
    Salt
    1 pound fusilli or short, tubular pasta
    ½ cup grated Parmesan cheese

1. Process the garlic through a garlic press into a small bowl; stir in 1 teaspoon water. Heat 2 tablespoons oil and the garlic in a medium sauté pan over medium heat until fragrant but not brown, about 2 minutes. Add the pepper and sauté until slightly softened, another 5 minutes. Stir in the tomatoes; simmer until somewhat thickened, about 20 minutes. (If desired, puree the sauce in a blender or food processor. Return the sauce to the pan and heat through.) Stir in the basil and salt to taste.

2. Meanwhile, bring 4 quarts of water to a boil in a large pot. Add 1 tablespoon salt and the pasta. Cook until al dente. Reserve ¼ cup of the cooking water; drain the pasta and transfer it back to the cooking pot. Mix in the reserved cooking water, sauce, Parmesan, and remaining tablespoon of oil. Divide among 4 pasta bowls and serve immediately.

CANNED TOMATO SAUCES

/|\

TRYING TO DEFINE THE "BEST" QUICK TOMATO SAUCE

IS ALMOST AS SILLY AS TRYING TO SETTLE ON THE

BEST TYPE OF CORN. AND ASKING FAMOUS ITALIAN

COOKBOOK AUTHORS AND CHEFS TO CHOOSE THE

BEST ALL-PURPOSE TOMATO SAUCE IS AKIN TO ASKING

them which of their children they prefer. On the face of it, it seems like an exercise in culinary hairsplitting.

After some thought, however, we managed to define a style of sauce that would be particularly useful to an American home cook: a quick year-round sauce that would be best served over fresh-boiled pasta. In narrowing our definition, we decided that canned tomatoes were in and the fresh variety was out, given that good, fresh tomatoes are a rare commodity most of the year. We wanted to use the fewest ingredients possible, so we selected the key players—tomatoes, oil, garlic, and salt—and eliminated nonessentials such as carrots, meat, wine, and so forth. This immediately eliminated a whole category of longer-cooked, full-bodied Italian sauces. The sauce we were looking for had to be quick to make, twenty minutes or less from pantry to table. Finally, it had to taste first and foremost of tomatoes, with a nice hint of acidity and a light, fresh flavor.

With this fairly limited mission statement, a number of fundamental issues came to mind. What sort of canned tomatoes are best: whole, chopped, or crushed, packed in puree or juice? How do you get a nice hint of garlic without overpowering the sauce? How does cooking time affect flavor? Do you need sugar to boost tomato flavor? And what about tomato paste?

To get a better sense of the possibilities, we went into the kitchen and cooked a batch of different sauces from our favorite Italian cooks. For this test, we just tasted our results with a spoon. To our surprise, there was considerable agreement among the staff as to what worked and what didn't. Butter tended to dull the bright, slightly acidic flavor of the tomatoes. Although this was fine in a few sauces with cream, as a general rule we preferred oil in a basic tomato sauce. Nobody was enthusiastic about the rather one-dimensional flavor of tomato paste. More than two cloves of garlic and three tablespoons of olive oil for one 28-ounce can of tomatoes was too much. In general, shorter cooking times of ten to fifteen minutes produced a fresher, brighter tomato flavor. A large sauté pan was preferred to a saucepan because it sped up the cooking.

We also came to some conclusions about overall flavor. The sauces we preferred tasted like tomatoes—not garlic, basil, or any other ingredient. The better recipes also had a nice balance between sweetness and acidity to give the sauce some depth. This layering of flavors in fact became the Holy Grail of this testing. The proper balances between sweet and tart, smoothness and bite, tomato and garlic, basil and olive oil, were crucial to achieving an exciting, multidimensional sauce.

With these decisions made, we compiled a master recipe using 1 teaspoon of minced garlic, 3 tablespoons of olive oil, one 28-ounce can of diced tomatoes, eight chopped basil leaves, ¼ teaspoon of sugar, and salt to taste. This would make enough to sauce 1 pound of pasta.

The first test was aimed at finding the best method of preparing the garlic. Early on we discovered that recipes that browned the garlic often resulted in a bitter sauce. When developing recipes for olive oil–based sauces (see chapter 5), we discovered that using a garlic puree that was diluted with water and sautéed briefly in olive oil provided a mild, even garlic flavor while greatly reducing the possibility of over-cooking the garlic. When we tried this method with tomato sauces, it turned out to be superior to any of the others we tested—mincing and sautéing, simply crushing the cloves, using slices, adding minced garlic just before serving without cooking it, or cooking minced garlic along with the tomatoes without sautéing it. The puree method resulted in a sweeter, less bitter garlic flavor, which helped the sauce achieve a nice balance between sweet and tart.

Next we tried making sauces with no sweetener, with ¼ teaspoon of sugar (we ended up testing higher and lower amounts as well), and with carrots instead of sugar. (Although we had initially decided to forgo additional ingredients such as carrots, we thought they were worth testing as a sweetener.) The results were as follows:

♦ The no-sugar sauce had a slightly reduced tomato flavor.
♦ The ¼ teaspoon was judged to be just right.
♦ The carrot method added too much cooking time.

We evaluated the quantity of olive oil and judged it to be ideal at 3 tablespoons. We also tested whether all of the olive oil should be added at the beginning of cooking or some withheld and added at the end to provide a nice burst of fresh flavor. As we suspected, it

THE MARRIAGE OF SWEET AND TART

/\\

THE SURPRISING, ALMOST SHOCKING, SUBTEXT TO OUR TESTING FOR THIS CHAPTER IS THE DELICATE BUT CRUCIAL BALANCE BETWEEN SWEET AND TART. SOME SAUCES TASTED FLAT AND DULL, WHILE OTHERS SPARKLED WITH AN UNDERLYING TANG OF ACIDITY, FRESH TOMATO FLAVOR, AND A NICE UP-FRONT

boost of sweetness. We first noticed this disparity when using tomatoes packed in puree. In this simple tomato sauce, they were lackluster. That's because puree is cooked for a long time to create its characteristic thick texture. During the cooking process, the fresh, bright flavor of the tomato diminishes, losing acidity and bite. Tomatoes packed in juice are a must for a quick-cooking tomato sauce.

The role of sugar is more complex, and in the end far less important than the tomatoes. In the simplest tomato sauce (just tomatoes, oil, garlic, and basil), there was a preference for sauces made with a little sugar. The sugar not only boosted flavor but also made the overall taste of the sauce

more complex and improved the balance between sweetness and acidity. When sugar is added to a plain tomato sauce, you taste a burst of sweetness, followed by the acidity, followed by a subtle interplay of both.

However, once you add other flavors to a simple tomato sauce, especially assertive ingredients like bacon, olives, or capers, the role of the sugar is less important. There's no harm in adding the sugar, but its impact is hard to detect in sauces with many contrasting flavors and textures. While sugar is a key ingredient in the plainest of all tomato sauces, we have omitted the sugar from other tomato sauces since its effect was so minimal.

was best to use 2 tablespoons of olive oil for cooking and 1 tablespoon at the end to finish the sauce. Not surprisingly, we preferred a high-quality extra-virgin oil because it delivered a pleasant hint of fresh olives.

As we continued testing variant after variant of our simple sauce, a key issue began to emerge: What is the best type of tomato to use? We had already established that among canned crushed tomatoes, we preferred Progresso, Muir Glen, and Redpack, in that order.

For our current testing, we started with crushed tomatoes but were disappointed with the lackluster

flavor they showed in this particular recipe. We then moved on to whole tomatoes, with mixed results. Fortunately, we then stumbled on to what was to be our clear favorite, Muir Glen Diced Tomatoes. To begin with, they were convenient because the entire contents of the can could be used; with whole tomatoes, using all of the packing liquid resulted in a substantially thinner sauce. Even better, the flavor was fresh and bright with a good balance of sweet and acid. (Incidentally, Muir Glen also sells ground tomatoes, which we did not like as much, in that they had a flatter, duller flavor. This supported our finding that overly processed tomatoes tend to have less flavor.)

However, because Muir Glen Diced Tomatoes may not be available in your supermarket, we retested crushed versus whole tomatoes and decided that the latter was the clear winner. Our favorite brand was Muir Glen once again, followed closely by Progresso. The thick puree used in the Redpack brand we found unappealing for this particular recipe, although the tomatoes themselves are high quality. While we were at it, we tested the claim of many cooks that seeding the tomatoes is important to remove bitterness and found that seedless sauce tasted no different from the version with seeds.

We also decided that, when using whole tomatoes, it is important to drain the tomatoes first, reserving the liquid, to prevent the tendency of the quick-cooked sauce to be too thin.

Now we were ready to taste the sauce on pasta. Much to our surprise, we found that it did not properly cling to the pasta, and the flavor was unexpectedly bland. Our complex, well-balanced sauce, it turned out, was too delicate for the texture and flavor of the pasta. Our first fix was to add back ¼ cup of pasta cooking water to the drained pasta once it had been returned to its original pot. This dramatically improved the consistency of the sauce and, to our great surprise, also improved the flavor.

As a final note, we found that adding the tomato sauce, stirring to coat the pasta, and then heating everything for one minute was the most effective saucing method, giving the sauce better distribution and overall consistency.

Pasta and Simple Tomato Sauce

SERVES 4

IF USING WHOLE TOMATOES, avoid those packed in sauce or puree—which produces a dull, relatively flavorless sauce without the interplay of sweetness and acidity—and choose a brand packed in juice. You will need to drain the contents of a 28-ounce can and then start dicing and measuring. Depending on the brand, you may need several tablespoons of juice to yield the amount specified below. If you choose Muir Glen Diced Tomatoes instead, use the entire contents of a single 28-ounce can, without discarding any liquid. If you do not have a garlic press, mince the garlic very fine with a little salt (see illustration 2, page 45) and sauté it for 1 minute rather than 2. Serve with any pasta shape.

1 28-ounce can diced tomatoes or whole tomatoes packed in juice
2 medium garlic cloves, peeled (see illustration, page 39)

3 tablespoons extra-virgin olive oil
2 tablespoons coarsely chopped fresh
  basil leaves (about 8 leaves)
¼ teaspoon sugar
Salt
1 pound pasta, any shape

1. If using diced tomatoes, go to step 2. If using whole tomatoes, drain and reserve the liquid. Dice the tomatoes by hand or in the work bowl of a food processor (use three or four ½-second pulses). The tomatoes should be coarse, with ¼-inch pieces visible. If necessary, add enough reserved liquid to the tomatoes to total 2⅔ cups.

2. Process the garlic through a garlic press into a small bowl; stir in 1 teaspoon water. Heat 2 tablespoons oil and the garlic in a medium sauté pan over medium heat until fragrant but not brown, about 2 minutes. Stir in the tomatoes; simmer until thickened slightly, about 10 minutes. Stir in the basil, sugar, and ½ teaspoon salt. Adjust the seasonings.

3. Meanwhile, bring 4 quarts of water to a boil in a large pot. Add 1 tablespoon salt and the pasta. Cook until just al dente. Reserve ¼ cup of the cooking water; drain the pasta and transfer it back to the cooking pot. Mix in the reserved cooking water, sauce, and remaining 1 tablespoon oil. Cook together over medium heat for 1 minute, stirring constantly. Divide among 4 pasta bowls and serve immediately.

◆

Penne with Tomatoes and Mozzarella

BUY FRESH MOZZARELLA PACKED IN WATER, IF YOU CAN; DRAIN WELL AND PAT DRY BEFORE DICING IT. SERVE WITH HOT AND SWEET ITALIAN SAUSAGES AND A GREEN SALAD. **SERVES 4**.

Follow the Master Recipe for Pasta and Simple Tomato Sauce (above), omitting the sugar and stirring 8 ounces mozzarella, cut into ¼-inch dice, into the pasta with the sauce.

Fusilli with Spicy Tomato Sauce and Ricotta Salata

RICOTTA SALATA RESEMBLES FETA CHEESE BUT IS MILDER AND LESS SALTY. IT IS AVAILABLE IN ITALIAN DELIS AND MANY SUPERMARKETS. WE LIKE TO SEASON THIS SAUCE WITH ABUNDANT RED PEPPER FLAKES TO BALANCE THE STRONG FLAVOR OF THE CHEESE, BUT USE LESS IF YOU LIKE. THE CHEESE IS QUITE CRUMBLY AND HARD TO GRATE BY HAND. USE THE SHREDDING DISK ON A FOOD PROCESSOR FOR THE BEST TEXTURE. **SERVES 4**.

Follow the Master Recipe for Pasta and Simple Tomato Sauce (page 120), cooking 1 teaspoon hot red pepper flakes with the garlic and oil. Omit the basil and sugar. Stir 6 ounces shredded ricotta salata cheese into the pasta with the sauce.

◆

Penne with Spicy Tomato Sauce

THE ADDITION OF HOT RED PEPPER FLAKES TURNS SIMPLE TOMATO SAUCE INTO *ARRABBIATA*, OR "ANGRY" SAUCE IN ITALIAN. YOU MAY SUBSTITUTE MINCED DRIED CHILES OF YOUR CHOICE FOR THE RED PEPPER FLAKES. **SERVES 4**.

Follow the Master Recipe for Pasta and Simple Tomato Sauce (page 120), cooking ¾ teaspoon hot red pepper flakes with the garlic and oil. Replace basil with ¼ cup minced fresh flat-leaf parsley leaves and omit sugar.

Fusilli with Tomato Sauce, Bacon, and Parsley

CRISP-COOKED BACON MAKES THIS PASTA A HEARTY WINTER MAIN COURSE. SERVE WITH SAUTEED SPINACH OR BROCCOLI RABE FOR A COMPLETE MEAL. **SERVES 4.**

> 6 ounces (about 6 slices) bacon, cut into
>   ½-inch pieces
> 1 28-ounce can diced tomatoes or whole
>   tomatoes packed in juice
> 2 medium garlic cloves, peeled (see
>   illustration, page 39)
> 2 tablespoons minced fresh flat-leaf
>   parsley leaves
> Salt
> 1 pound fusilli or other short, curly pasta
> 1 tablespoon extra-virgin olive oil

1. Fry the bacon in a medium sauté pan over medium-high heat until crisp and brown, about 5 minutes. Transfer with a slotted spoon to a paper towel–lined plate; pour all but 2 tablespoons fat from the pan.

2. If using diced tomatoes, go to step 3. If using whole tomatoes, drain and reserve the liquid. Dice the tomatoes by hand or in the work bowl of a food processor (use three or four ½-second pulses). The tomatoes should be coarse, with ¼-inch pieces visible. If necessary, add enough reserved liquid to the tomatoes to total 2⅔ cups.

3. Process the garlic through a garlic press into a small bowl; stir in 1 teaspoon water. Heat the bacon fat and garlic in the sauté pan over medium heat until fragrant but not brown, about 2 minutes. Stir in the tomatoes; simmer until thickened slightly, about 10 minutes. Stir in the bacon, parsley, and ¼ teaspoon salt. Adjust the seasonings.

4. Meanwhile, bring 4 quarts of water to a boil in a large pot. Add 1 tablespoon salt and the pasta. Cook until just al dente. Reserve ¼ cup of the cooking water; drain the pasta and transfer it back to the cooking pot. Mix in the reserved cooking water, sauce, and oil. Cook together over medium heat for 1 minute, stirring constantly. Divide among 4 pasta bowls and serve immediately.

◆

Spaghetti with Tomato Sauce, Anchovies, and Olives

OUR VERSION OF THE CLASSIC PUTTANESCA SAUCE. ANCHOVIES AND OLIVES GIVE THIS PASTA A BRINY FLAVOR, MAKING IT A GOOD SIDE DISH WITH GRILLED OR BROILED FISH OR SHRIMP. IT MAY NOT BE NECESSARY TO ADD SALT TO THE SAUCE, SINCE THE ANCHOVIES, OLIVES, AND CAPERS ARE QUITE SALTY. **SERVES 4, OR 8 AS A SIDE DISH.**

> 1 28-ounce can diced tomatoes or whole
>   tomatoes packed in juice
> 3 medium garlic cloves, peeled (see
>   illustration, page 39)
> 3 tablespoons extra-virgin olive oil
> ½ teaspoon hot red pepper flakes
> 3 anchovy fillets, minced
> ¼ cup minced fresh flat-leaf parsley leaves
> ¼ cup pitted, sliced black olives, such as
>   Kalamata (see illustrations 1–2, page
>   62)
> 2 tablespoons capers, rinsed
> Salt
> 1 pound spaghetti or other long, thin
>   pasta

1. If using diced tomatoes, go to step 2. If using whole tomatoes, drain and reserve the liquid. Dice the tomatoes by hand or in the work bowl of a food processor (use three or four ½-second pulses). The tomatoes should be coarse, with ¼-inch pieces visible. If necessary, add enough reserved liquid to the tomatoes to total 2⅔ cups.

2. Process the garlic through a garlic press into a small bowl; stir in 1 teaspoon water. Heat 2 tablespoons oil, the garlic, red pepper flakes, and anchovies in a medium sauté pan over medium heat until fragrant but not brown, about 2 minutes. Stir in the tomatoes; simmer until thickened slightly, about 10 minutes. Stir in the parsley, olives, and capers. Adjust the seasonings, adding salt if necessary.

3. Meanwhile, bring 4 quarts of water to a boil in a large pot. Add 1 tablespoon salt and the pasta. Cook until just al dente. Reserve ¼ cup of the cooking water; drain the pasta and transfer it back to the cooking pot. Mix in the reserved cooking water, sauce, and remaining 1 tablespoon oil. Cook together over medium heat for 1 minute, stirring constantly. Serve immediately.

◆

Penne with Tomato Sauce with Vodka and Cream

THIS LUXURIOUS PASTA IS A GOOD PRELUDE TO AN EQUALLY LUXURIOUS MEAL OF THICK BROILED VEAL CHOPS OR STEAMED LOBSTERS. SERVES 4, OR 8 AS A FIRST COURSE.

> 1 28-ounce can diced tomatoes or whole tomatoes packed in juice
> 2 medium garlic cloves, peeled (see illustration, page 39)
> 2 tablespoons extra-virgin olive oil
> ¼ teaspoon hot red pepper flakes
> ½ cup vodka
> 1 cup heavy cream
> 2 tablespoons coarsely chopped fresh basil leaves (about 8 leaves)
> Salt
> Ground black pepper
> 1 pound penne or other small tubular pasta

1. If using diced tomatoes, go to step 2. If using whole tomatoes, drain and reserve the liquid. Dice the tomatoes by hand or in the work bowl of a food processor (use three or four ½-second pulses). The tomatoes should be coarse, with ¼-inch pieces visible. If necessary, add enough reserved liquid to the tomatoes to total 2⅔ cups.

2. Process the garlic through a garlic press into a small bowl; stir in 1 teaspoon water. Heat the oil, garlic, and red pepper flakes in a medium sauté pan over medium heat until fragrant but not brown, about 2 minutes. Stir in the tomatoes; simmer 5 minutes. Stir in the vodka and simmer until the alcohol evaporates and the sauce has thickened, another 5 to 7 minutes. Stir in the cream, basil, ½ teaspoon salt, and pepper to taste. Transfer the sauce to the work bowl of a food processor; pulse to a coarse puree. Return the sauce to the pan; simmer over medium heat to thicken, 2 to 3 minutes.

3. Meanwhile, bring 4 quarts of water to a boil in a large pot. Add 1 tablespoon salt and the pasta. Cook until just al dente. Reserve ¼ cup of the cooking water; drain the pasta and transfer it back to the cooking pot. Mix in the reserved cooking water and sauce. Cook together over medium heat for 1 minute, stirring constantly. Divide among 4 pasta bowls and serve immediately.

TYPES OF CANNED TOMATO PRODUCTS

FRESH TOMATOES ARE PROCESSED AND CANNED IN VARIOUS WAYS. HERE ARE THE MOST COMMON TOMATO PRODUCTS USED IN PASTA SAUCES.

WHOLE TOMATOES. This product is the closest to fresh tomatoes. Whole tomatoes, either plum or round, are steamed to removed their skins and then packed in tomato juice or puree. We prefer tomatoes packed in juice; they generally have a fresher, more lively flavor. In a test of eleven leading supermarket brands, we preferred Muir Glen and Progresso.

DICED TOMATOES. Whole tomatoes that are peeled, diced, and packed in juice. Some companies add seasonings and call this product "recipe-ready" tomatoes. We prefer them plain—with just salt; no garlic, no herbs. Muir Glen is our favorite brand.

CRUSHED TOMATOES. Whole tomatoes that have been put through a crushing device and turned into tiny solid bits and liquid. (Although a few seeds and bits of skin are fine, there should not be an abundance of either in good crushed tomatoes.) Straight from the machine, crushed tomatoes are very thin and are supplemented with some puree to give them body and viscosity.

In our testing of seven leading brands, we preferred brands with more tomatoes than puree. (Read labels and check to see that tomatoes, not puree, is listed first.) Too much puree gives the tomatoes a cooked flavor. We found that Pro-gresso and Muir Glen had the freshest tomato flavor. Note though that crushed tomatoes are never as fresh tasting as whole tomatoes packed in juice. However, when you want a smooth, thick tomato presence in a particular recipe, crushed tomatoes are an excellent choice.

STEWED TOMATOES. Diced tomatoes are cooked (or stewed) with seasonings. We prefer to add our own seasonings, so we do not use this product.

TOMATO PUREE. A smooth, cooked-down tomato product without seeds or visible bits of skin. It generally has the texture of tomato sauce, but it lacks fresh tomato flavor. We don't use tomato puree.

TOMATO PASTE. A super-concentrated tomato product, similar to puree only cooked down much further. Paste is made from juice that has been seasoned with salt, spices, and often sugar and then reduced to a thick, smooth consistency. Paste can add tomato color and flavor when liquid is not wanted. Paste is sold in small cans in supermarkets. Also look for tubes of double-concentrated tomato paste from Italy, which have a particularly strong tomato flavor.

Fettuccine with Tomato Sauce with Butter

BUTTER SMOOTHS THE ACIDITY OF THE TOMATOES, MAKING THIS SAUCE MORE MUTED THAN SAUCE MADE WITH OLIVE OIL. TOMATO SAUCE WITH BUTTER IS ESPECIALLY GOOD WHEN YOU WANT TO HIGHLIGHT THE FLAVOR AND TEXTURE OF FRESH EGG PASTA. **SERVES 4.**

1 28-ounce can diced tomatoes or whole
    tomatoes packed in juice
2 medium garlic cloves, peeled (see
    illustration, page 39)
4 tablespoons unsalted butter
2 tablespoons coarsely chopped fresh
    basil leaves (about 8 leaves)
Salt
1 pound Fresh Egg Pasta (page 21) cut
    into fettuccine *or* dried fettuccine
Grated Parmesan cheese for serving

1. If using diced tomatoes, go to step 2. If using whole tomatoes, drain and reserve the liquid. Dice the tomatoes by hand or in the work bowl of a food processor (use three or four 1/2-second pulses). The tomatoes should be coarse, with 1/4-inch pieces visible. If necessary, add enough reserved liquid to the tomatoes to total 2 2/3 cups.

2. Process the garlic through a garlic press into a small bowl; stir in 1 teaspoon water. Heat 2 tablespoons butter and the garlic in a medium sauté pan over medium heat until fragrant but not brown, about 2 minutes. Stir in the tomatoes; simmer until thickened slightly, about 10 minutes. Stir in the basil and 1/2 teaspoon salt. Adjust the seasonings.

3. Meanwhile, bring 4 quarts of water to a boil in a large pot. Add 1 tablespoon salt and the pasta. Cook until just al dente. Reserve 1/4 cup of the cooking water; drain the pasta and transfer it back to the cooking pot. Mix in the reserved cooking water, sauce, and remaining 2 tablespoons butter. Cook together over medium heat for 1 minute, stirring constantly. Divide among 4 pasta bowls and serve immediately, with cheese passed at the table.

Fettuccine with Tomato-Cream Sauce

HERE IS ANOTHER RICH SAUCE SUITABLE FOR SERVING WITH HOMEMADE EGG PASTA. PUREE THE SAUCE IN A FOOD PROCESSOR FOR EXTRA REFINEMENT. TOMATO-CREAM SAUCE IS ALSO GOOD WITH HOMEMADE FILLED PASTAS (SEE CHAPTER 23). **SERVES 4.**

1 28-ounce can diced tomatoes or whole
    tomatoes packed in juice
2 medium garlic cloves, peeled (see
    illustration, page 39)
3 tablespoons unsalted butter
2 tablespoons coarsely chopped fresh
    basil leaves (about 8 leaves)
Salt
1 cup heavy cream
1 pound Fresh Egg Pasta (page 21) cut
    into fettuccine *or* dried fettuccine

1. If using diced tomatoes, go to step 2. If using whole tomatoes, drain and reserve the liquid. Dice the tomatoes by hand or in the work bowl of a food processor (use three or four 1/2-second pulses). The tomatoes should be coarse, with 1/4-inch pieces visible. If necessary, add enough reserved liquid to the tomatoes to total 2 2/3 cups.

2. Process the garlic through a garlic press into a small bowl; stir in 1 teaspoon water. Heat 2 tablespoons butter and the garlic in a medium sauté pan over medium heat until fragrant but not brown, about 2 minutes. Stir in the tomatoes; simmer until thickened slightly, about 10 minutes. Stir in the basil, 1/2 teaspoon salt, and cream. Simmer until the sauce thickens slightly, 2 to 3 minutes. Adjust the seasonings.

3. Meanwhile, bring 4 quarts of water to a boil in a large pot. Add 1 tablespoon salt and the pasta. Cook until just al dente. Reserve 1/4 cup of the cooking water; drain the pasta and transfer it back to the cooking pot. Mix in the reserved cooking water, sauce, and remaining 1 tablespoon butter. Cook together over medium heat for 1 minute, stirring constantly. Divide among 4 pasta bowls and serve immediately.

Fusilli with Saffron-Tomato Sauce

SAFFRON TINTS THE PASTA BRIGHT ORANGE AND TRANSFORMS PLAIN TOMATOES INTO AN UNUSUAL AND EXOTIC SAUCE. SERVE AS A FIRST COURSE OR SIDE DISH WITH STRONG-FLAVORED MEATS LIKE PORK OR LAMB. SERVES 8 AS A SIDE DISH.

1 28-ounce can diced tomatoes or whole
    tomatoes packed in juice
2 medium garlic cloves, peeled (see
    illustration, page 39)
3 tablespoons extra-virgin olive oil
¼ cup dry vermouth
Pinch saffron threads, crumbled
2 tablespoons coarsely chopped fresh
    basil leaves (about 8 leaves)
Salt
1 pound fusilli or other short, curly pasta

1. If using diced tomatoes, go to step 2. If using whole tomatoes, drain and reserve the liquid. Dice the tomatoes by hand or in the work bowl of a food processor (use three or four ½-second pulses). The tomatoes should be coarse, with ¼-inch pieces visible. If necessary, add enough reserved liquid to the tomatoes to total 2⅔ cups.

2. Process the garlic through a garlic press into a small bowl; stir in 1 teaspoon water. Heat 2 tablespoons oil and the garlic in a medium sauté pan over medium heat until fragrant but not brown, about 2 minutes. Stir in the tomatoes; simmer until thickened slightly, about 10 minutes. Add the vermouth and saffron and simmer just until the alcohol evaporates and the saffron softens, about 2 minutes. Stir in the basil and ½ teaspoon salt. Adjust the seasonings.

3. Meanwhile, bring 4 quarts of water to a boil in a large pot. Add 1 tablespoon salt and the pasta. Cook until just al dente. Reserve ¼ cup of the cooking water; drain the pasta and transfer it back to the cooking pot. Mix in the reserved cooking water, sauce, and remaining 1 tablespoon oil. Cook together over medium heat for 1 minute, stirring constantly. Divide among 4 pasta bowls and serve immediately.

Penne with Tomatoes and Balsamic Vinegar

BALSAMIC VINEGAR, LESS ACIDIC THAN RED WINE VINEGAR, BRINGS OUT THE SWEETNESS IN THE TOMATOES. ROSEMARY ADDS A FRAGRANT, WOODSY NOTE, ALTHOUGH OTHER HERBS, LIKE BASIL OR PARSLEY, MIGHT BE USED HERE INSTEAD, BUT INCREASE THE AMOUNT TO AT LEAST 1 TABLESPOON. SERVES 4.

1 28-ounce can diced tomatoes or whole
    tomatoes packed in juice
2 medium garlic cloves, peeled (see
    illustration, page 39)
3 tablespoons extra-virgin olive oil
1 teaspoon minced fresh rosemary leaves
Salt
2 teaspoons balsamic vinegar
1 pound penne or other short, tubular
    pasta

1. If using diced tomatoes, go to step 2. If using whole tomatoes, drain and reserve the liquid. Dice the tomatoes by hand or in the work bowl of a food processor (use three or four ½-second pulses). The tomatoes should be coarse, with ¼-inch pieces visible. If necessary, add enough reserved liquid to the tomatoes to total 2⅔ cups.

2. Process the garlic through a garlic press into a small bowl; stir in 1 teaspoon water. Heat 2 tablespoons oil and the garlic in a medium sauté pan over medium heat until fragrant but not brown, about 2 minutes. Stir in the tomatoes and rosemary; simmer until thickened slightly, about 10 minutes. Stir in ½ teaspoon salt and the balsamic vinegar. Adjust the seasonings.

3. Meanwhile, bring 4 quarts of water to a boil in a large pot. Add 1 tablespoon salt and the pasta. Cook until al dente. Reserve ¼ cup of the cooking water; drain the pasta and transfer it back to the cooking pot. Mix in the reserved cooking water, sauce, and remaining 1 tablespoon oil. Cook together over medium heat for 1 minute, stirring constantly. Divide among 4 pasta bowls and serve immediately.

Spaghetti with Sicilian Tomato Sauce

ANCHOVIES, RAISINS, AND PINE NUTS ARE TYPICAL ADDITIONS TO A TOMATO SAUCE IN SICILY. BREAD CRUMBS ARE OFTEN USED AS A GARNISH FOR PASTA IN PLACE OF CHEESE, ESPECIALLY WHEN THE SAUCE CONTAINS FISH. FOR MAXIMUM FLAVOR, TOAST THE NUTS IN A DRY SKILLET OVER MEDIUM HEAT UNTIL GOLDEN BROWN. SERVES 4.

1 28-ounce can diced tomatoes or whole tomatoes packed in juice
2 medium garlic cloves, peeled (see illustration, page 39)
3 tablespoons extra-virgin olive oil
6 anchovy fillets, rinsed and minced
2 tablespoons golden raisins
2 tablespoons pine nuts, toasted
¼ cup minced fresh flat-leaf parsley leaves
Salt
1 pound spaghetti or other long, thin pasta
¼ cup Toasted Bread Crumbs (page 90; optional)

1. If using diced tomatoes, go to step 2. If using whole tomatoes, drain and reserve the liquid. Dice the tomatoes by hand or in the work bowl of a food processor (use three or four ½-second pulses). The tomatoes should be coarse, with ¼-inch pieces visible. If necessary, add enough reserved liquid to the tomatoes to total 2⅔ cups.

2. Process the garlic through a garlic press into a small bowl; stir in 1 teaspoon water. Heat 2 tablespoons oil and the garlic in a medium sauté pan over medium heat until fragrant but not brown, about 2 minutes. Stir in the tomatoes; simmer until thickened slightly, about 10 minutes. Stir in the anchovies, raisins, pine nuts, parsley, and ½ teaspoon salt. Adjust the seasonings.

3. Meanwhile, bring 4 quarts of water to a boil in a large pot. Add 1 tablespoon salt and the pasta. Cook until just al dente. Reserve ¼ cup of the cooking water; drain the pasta and transfer it back to the cooking pot. Mix in the reserved cooking water, sauce, and remaining 1 tablespoon oil. Cook together over medium heat for 1 minute, stirring constantly. Toss with the bread crumbs if desired. Divide among 4 pasta bowls and serve immediately.

◆

Penne with Tomatoes and Mint

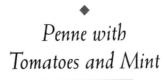

A HEALTHY ADDITION OF MINT TO SIMPLE TOMATO SAUCE GIVES THIS PASTA A STRONG HERBAL FLAVOR. THE PASTA COMPLEMENTS HIGHLY SEASONED MEAT AND POULTRY; SERVE WITH CHILI-RUBBED FLANK STEAK OR CURRY-RUBBED GRILLED CHICKEN BREASTS. SERVES 6 TO 8 AS A SIDE DISH.

1 28-ounce can diced tomatoes or whole tomatoes packed in juice
2 medium garlic cloves, peeled (see illustration, page 39)
3 tablespoons extra-virgin olive oil
½ cup minced fresh mint leaves
Salt
1 pound penne or other short, tubular pasta

1. If using diced tomatoes, go to step 2. If using whole tomatoes, drain and reserve the liquid. Dice the tomatoes by hand or into the work bowl of a food processor (use three or four ½-second pulses). The tomatoes should be coarse, with ¼-inch pieces visible. If necessary, add enough reserved liquid to the tomatoes to total 2⅔ cups.

2. Process the garlic through a garlic press into a small bowl; stir in 1 teaspoon water. Heat 2 tablespoons oil and the garlic in a medium sauté pan over medium heat until fragrant but not brown, about 2 minutes. Stir in the tomatoes; simmer until thickened slightly, about 10 minutes. Stir in the mint and ½ teaspoon salt. Adjust the seasonings.

3. Meanwhile, bring 4 quarts of water to a boil in a large pot. Add 1 tablespoon salt and the pasta. Cook until just al dente. Reserve ¼ cup of the cooking water; drain the pasta and transfer it back to the cooking pot. Mix in the reserved cooking water, sauce, and remaining 1 tablespoon oil. Cook together over medium heat for 1 minute, stirring constantly. Serve immediately.

Bucatini with Spicy Tomato Sauce and Pancetta

THIS POPULAR ITALIAN DISH IS CALLED *BUCATINI ALL' AMATRICIANA*. PANCETTA, ITALIAN-STYLE BACON, IS AVAILABLE IN ITALIAN DELIS AND MANY SUPERMARKETS. IT IS SALTY, SO TASTE BEFORE YOU ADD ADDITIONAL SALT TO THE SAUCE. YOU MAY USE REGULAR AMERICAN BACON. UNLIKE PANCETTA, AMERICAN BACON IS SMOKED AND HAS A DIFFERENT FLAVOR. AMERICAN BACON ALSO TENDS TO BE FATTIER, SO REDUCE THE AMOUNT OF OIL IN STEP 2 TO JUST 1 TABLESPOON. SERVES 4.

> 1 28-ounce can diced tomatoes or whole tomatoes packed in juice
> 2 medium garlic cloves, peeled (see illustration, page 39)
> 3 tablespoons extra-virgin olive oil
> 4 ounces pancetta, finely chopped
> 1/2 teaspoon hot red pepper flakes, or to taste
> 1 tablespoon minced fresh sage leaves
> Salt
> 1 pound bucatini or linguine
> 1/2 cup grated Parmesan or pecorino cheese

1. If using diced tomatoes, go to step 2. If using whole tomatoes, drain and reserve the liquid. Dice the tomatoes by hand or in the work bowl of a food processor (use three or four 1/2-second pulses). The tomatoes should be coarse, with 1/4-inch pieces visible. If necessary, add enough reserved liquid to the tomatoes to total 2 2/3 cups.

2. Process the garlic through a garlic press into a small bowl; stir in 1 teaspoon water. Heat 2 tablespoons oil, the garlic, pancetta, and red pepper flakes in a medium sauté pan over medium heat until fragrant but not brown, about 4 minutes. Stir in the tomatoes and sage; simmer until thickened slightly, about 10 minutes. Adjust the seasonings, adding salt if necessary.

3. Meanwhile, bring 4 quarts of water to a boil in a large pot. Add 1 tablespoon salt and the pasta. Cook until just al dente. Reserve 1/4 cup of the cooking water; drain the pasta and transfer it back to the cooking pot. Mix in the reserved cooking water, sauce, and remaining 1 tablespoon oil. Cook together over medium heat for 1 minute, stirring constantly. Toss with the cheese. Divide among 4 pasta bowls and serve immediately.

◆

Perciatelli with Tomato-Walnut Sauce

THE PASTA IS GARNISHED WITH TOASTED BREAD CRUMBS RATHER THAN CHEESE, AS IS OFTEN THE CUSTOM IN SOUTHERN ITALY. BREAD CRUMBS ABSORB LIQUID, SO SAVE A LITTLE EXTRA COOKING LIQUID IN CASE YOUR PASTA NEEDS MORE MOISTURE. SERVES 4.

> 1 28-ounce can diced tomatoes or whole tomatoes packed in juice
> 2 medium garlic cloves, peeled (see illustration, page 39)
> 3 tablespoons extra-virgin olive oil
> 1/4 cup minced fresh flat-leaf parsley leaves
> 1/4 cup finely chopped walnuts, toasted
> Salt
> 1 pound perciatelli, bucatini, or other long, thick pasta
> 1/4 cup Toasted Bread Crumbs (page 90)

1. If using diced tomatoes, go to step 2. If using whole tomatoes, drain and reserve the liquid. Dice the tomatoes by hand or in the work bowl of a food processor (use three or four 1/2-second pulses). The tomatoes should be coarse, with 1/4-inch pieces visible. If necessary, add enough reserved liquid to the tomatoes to total 2 2/3 cups.

2. Process the garlic through a garlic press into a small bowl; stir in 1 teaspoon water. Heat 2 tablespoons oil and the garlic in a medium sauté pan over medium heat until fragrant but not brown, about 2 minutes. Stir in the tomatoes; simmer until thickened slightly, about 10 minutes. Stir in the parsley, nuts, and ½ teaspoon salt. Adjust the seasonings.

3. Meanwhile, bring 4 quarts of water to a boil in a large pot. Add 1 tablespoon salt and the pasta. Cook until just al dente. Reserve ½ cup of the cooking water; drain the pasta and transfer it back to the cooking pot. Mix in ¼ cup of the reserved cooking water, sauce, and remaining 1 tablespoon oil. Cook together over medium heat for 1 minute, stirring constantly. Stir in the bread crumbs, adding more cooking liquid if the pasta seems dry. Divide among 4 pasta bowls and serve immediately.

◆

Spaghetti with Jalapeño-Tomato Sauce

JALAPENOS AND CILANTRO GIVE THIS PASTA A SOUTH-WESTERN FLAVOR. THE DISH WOULD NOT BE OUT OF PLACE ON THE TABLE WITH GRILLED CHORIZO AND AN AVOCADO SALAD DRESSED WITH LIME JUICE. SERVES 4, OR 6 TO 8 AS A SIDE DISH.

> 1 28-ounce can diced tomatoes or whole tomatoes packed in juice
> 2 medium garlic cloves, peeled (see illustration, page 39)
> 3 tablespoons extra-virgin olive oil
> 1 jalapeño chile, stemmed, seeded, and finely chopped
> ¼ cup minced fresh cilantro leaves
> Salt
> 1 pound spaghetti or long, thin pasta

1. If using diced tomatoes, go to step 2. If using whole tomatoes, drain and reserve the liquid. Dice the tomatoes by hand or in the work bowl of a food processor (use three or four ½-second pulses). The tomatoes should be coarse, with ¼-inch pieces visible. If necessary, add enough reserved liquid to the tomatoes to total 2⅔ cups.

2. Process the garlic through a garlic press into a small bowl; stir in 1 teaspoon water. Heat 2 tablespoons oil, the garlic, and chile in a medium sauté pan over medium heat until fragrant but not brown, about 2 minutes. Stir in the tomatoes; simmer until thickened slightly, about 10 minutes. Stir in the cilantro and ½ teaspoon salt. Adjust the seasonings.

3. Meanwhile, bring 4 quarts of water to a boil in a large pot. Add 1 tablespoon salt and the pasta. Cook until just al dente. Reserve ¼ cup of the cooking water; drain the pasta and transfer it back to the cooking pot. Mix in the reserved cooking water, sauce, and remaining 1 tablespoon oil. Cook together over medium heat for 1 minute, stirring constantly. Divide among 4 pasta bowls and serve immediately.

SAUCES WITH VEGE-TABLES

/I\

IN THIS CHAPTER WE WILL EXPLAIN HOW TO TURN

EVERYTHING FROM ASPARAGUS TO ZUCCHINI INTO

SAUCES FOR PASTA. EACH VEGETABLE PRESENTS

ITS OWN SET OF CHALLENGES, IN TERMS OF BOTH

PREPARATION AND COOKING. HOWEVER, HERE ARE

a few general thoughts to keep in mind as you cook.

Most vegetable-based pasta sauces don't have a lot of liquid. (Sauces with canned tomatoes and cream are the exception.) In many cases, it is necessary to reserve some of the pasta cooking water to moisten the pasta and sauce. Don't omit this step or your pasta may be too dry.

Unlike meat sauces, which generally freeze quite well, vegetable sauces don't hold up all that well. The color and texture of the vegetables really suffer. The recipes in this chapter are meant to be prepared and used straight off. Since most vegetables require brief cooking, most of the recipes in this chapter are quick to prepare, perfect for weeknight cooking.

Sauces with Artichokes

UNLIKE MOST VEGETABLES, artichokes require tedious preparation and a long cooking time to make them palatable. However, don't be put off by these factors. The meaty texture and complex flavor of artichokes are an excellent match for pasta. Just don't think of artichokes when you are in a hurry to get dinner on the table.

Artichokes come in a variety of sizes, weighing as much as 12 ounces or as little as 1. "Baby" artichokes grow on the same plants as large artichokes. The artichoke growing on the center stalk is the largest; those growing where the leaves meet the stem grow in the shade of the leaves and are smaller. They are not younger than the larger artichokes, just smaller. Cooking times vary depending on size.

Since medium-size artichokes (about 8 ounces each) are most widely available, we have developed recipes with this in mind. Avoid jumbo artichokes, which can be quite woody. You may substitute baby artichokes if you like. Use at least three "babies" for each medium artichoke. Babies may not have chokes, but otherwise they must be prepared in the same fashion. Baby artichokes are generally more tender and will require less cooking time.

No matter the size, make sure to buy artichokes with compact leaves. An artichoke is a flower and the leaves should be tightly closed, not wide open. When shopping, break off a leaf to judge freshness; it should snap, not tear.

When you eat steamed artichokes as a vegetable, you can scrape off the edible part with your teeth at the table. This is not possible when turning artichokes into a pasta sauce. All inedible parts must be removed before cooking (see illustrations 1 through 8, page 134). When trimming the artichoke, it is necessary to rub all cut surfaces with a lemon half to keep them from discoloring too much. Like apples that turn brown, artichokes will discolor when cut and exposed to air. Acids, such as lemon juice, partially inactivate the enzymes that are responsible for the unattractive color change. Don't expect artichokes to retain their green color, even with the lemon juice. However, the lemon will keep them from becoming completely brown, something that will happen in minutes if the cut artichokes are not protected.

For pasta sauces, artichokes are best braised in a covered pan with wine, water, stock, or tomatoes. The artichokes become silky smooth and impart their complex flavor to the sauce, while also taking on the flavors of the braising liquid. In our testing, we found that it is far worse to undercook the artichokes than to overcook them. Tough, chewy artichoke wedges can ruin a perfectly good bowl of pasta. Make sure all the artichoke pieces are completely tender before the pasta is cooked.

◆

Spaghetti with Braised Artichokes and Tomatoes

WHOLE CANNED TOMATOES, WHICH HAVE BEEN HALVED AND SEEDED (SEE ILLUSTRATION , PAGE 136), ARE CALLED FOR IN THIS RECIPE. SEEDING THE TOMATOES REMOVES EXCESS MOISTURE AND KEEPS THE TOMATOES FROM OVERWHELMING THE ARTICHOKES. THE TOMATO PIECES REMAIN QUITE CHUNKY, RATHER THAN FORMING A SMOOTH SAUCE. SERVES 4.

1 lemon, halved
4 medium artichokes (about 2 pounds), rinsed
2 tablespoons extra-virgin olive oil

3 medium garlic cloves, minced

½ small onion, minced

⅓ cup dry white wine

¼ cup water

1 can (15 ounces) plum tomatoes, drained, halved, and seeded (see illustration, page 136)

¼ teaspoon dried thyme leaves

Salt

1 pound spaghetti or other long, thin pasta

1 tablespoon minced fresh flat-leaf parsley leaves

1. Squeeze the juice from 1 lemon half into a large bowl filled with cold water; drop in the lemon half. Trim and slice the artichokes according to the instructions on page 134, using the other lemon half to rub cut surfaces as you prepare them.

2. Heat the oil in a large sauté pan. Add the drained artichokes and sauté over medium heat, stirring frequently, until light brown, about 7 minutes.

3. Add the garlic and onion; sauté until softened, about 4 minutes. Stir in the wine; simmer until reduced by half, 2 to 3 minutes. Add the water, tomatoes, thyme, and salt to taste. Cover and cook over low heat until the artichokes are tender, about 25 minutes.

4. Uncover and simmer until the juices thicken, about 5 minutes.

5. Meanwhile, bring 4 quarts of water to a boil in a large pot. Add 1 tablespoon salt and the pasta to the boiling water. Cook until al dente. Drain the pasta and transfer it back to the cooking pot. Stir in the sauce and parsley. Divide among 4 pasta bowls and serve immediately.

Linguine with Braised Artichoke Sauce

THIS RECIPE DELIVERS THE PUREST ARTICHOKE FLAVOR. THE SLICED ARTICHOKE HEARTS ARE BRAISED IN WHITE WINE AND FLAVORED WITH GARLIC, LEMON, AND PARSLEY. THE TOTAL COOKING TIME IS FAIRLY LONG FOR THIS DISH, BUT YOU CAN BE FINISHED WITH THE HANDS-ON WORK IN ABOUT 20 MINUTES. SERVES 4.

1 lemon, 1 teaspoon zest, grated and reserved (see illustration, page 42); lemon halved

4 medium artichokes (about 2 pounds), rinsed

6 medium garlic cloves, cut into thin slivers

¼ cup extra-virgin olive oil

2 cups dry white wine

Salt

¼ cup minced fresh flat-leaf parsley leaves

1 pound linguine or other long, thin pasta

1. Squeeze the juice from 1 lemon half into a large bowl filled with cold water; drop in the lemon half. Trim and slice the artichokes according to the instructions on page 134, using the other lemon half to rub cut surfaces as you prepare them.

2. Heat the garlic with the oil in a large sauté pan. When the garlic starts to sizzle and color, stir in the lemon zest, drained artichokes, and wine; bring to a simmer; season to taste with salt. Cover the pan and simmer until the artichokes are tender when pierced with a fork, about 40 minutes. Stir in the parsley and adjust the seasonings.

3. Bring 4 quarts of water to a boil in a large pot. Add 1 tablespoon salt and the pasta to the boiling water. Cook until al dente. Drain the pasta and transfer it back to the cooking pot. Stir in the sauce. Divide among 4 pasta bowls and serve immediately.

TRIMMING ARTICHOKES

Always use stainless steel knives when preparing artichokes. Carbon steel will discolor them.

1. Use a chef's knife to cut off the stem just below the leaves. Discard the stem.

2. Bend back and snap off the outer leaves, leaving the thick bottom portion attached to the base. Continue snapping off the leaves until you reach the light yellow cone at the center.

3. With a small knife, carefully peel the dark green outer layer from the bottom of the artichoke.

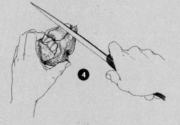

4. Cut off the dark green section from the top of the artichoke.

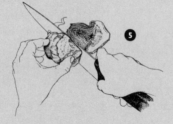

5. Halve the trimmed heart in half through the base.

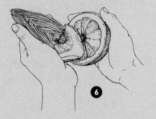

6. Rub all cut surfaces with a lemon half as you work.

7. Remove the purple leaves and fuzzy choke with a sharp-edged spoon. A grapefruit spoon is ideal for this job.

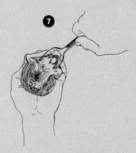

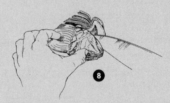

8. Place the cleaned artichoke halves cut side down on a work surface and slice them into ¼-inch-wide wedges. Drop the artichoke pieces into a bowl of acidulated cold water. (To make acidulated cold water, squeeze half a lemon in a bowl of cold water and then drop the lemon half into the water.)

Fusilli with Artichokes, Olives, and Feta

STRONG, SALTY FETA CHEESE STANDS UP WELL TO ARTI-CHOKES AND BLACK OLIVES. IF YOU LIKE A LESS ASSERTIVELY FLAVORED CHEESE, SUBSTITUTE CRUM-BLED RICOTTA SALATA FOR THE FETA. **SERVES 4.**

1 lemon, halved
4 medium artichokes (about 2 pounds), rinsed
2 tablespoons extra-virgin olive oil
3 medium garlic cloves, minced
¼ teaspoon hot red pepper flakes
1 cup white wine
Salt
1 pound fusilli or other short, curly pasta
4 ounces feta cheese, crumbled
½ cup grated pecorino cheese
½ cup Kalamata or other large black olives, pitted and coarsely chopped (see illustrations 1–2, page 62)
2 teaspoons minced fresh oregano leaves

1. Squeeze the juice from 1 lemon half into a large bowl filled with cold water; drop in the lemon half. Trim and slice the artichokes according to the instructions opposite, using the other lemon half to rub cut surfaces as you prepare them.

2. Heat the oil in a large sauté pan. Add the artichokes and sauté over medium heat, stirring frequently, until light brown, about 7 minutes.

3. Add the garlic and red pepper flakes and sauté until the garlic has softened, about 2 minutes. Add the wine. Cover and cook over low heat until the artichokes are tender, about 25 minutes.

4. Meanwhile, bring 4 quarts of water to a boil in a large pot. Add 1 tablespoon salt and the pasta to the boiling water. Cook until al dente. Drain the pasta and transfer it back to the cooking pot. Stir in the artichoke sauce, feta, pecorino, olives, and oregano. Adjust the seasonings; you may not need to add salt, since the cheese and olives are very salty. Divide among 4 pasta bowls and serve immediately.

Sauces with Arugula

AMONG LEAFY GREENS, arugula is the easiest to add to pasta sauces. In our testing, we found that arugula does not even need to be cooked; the heat of the drained pasta will wilt the leaves on contact. In fact, when we cooked arugula, even just for a few minutes, it lost all its texture and shape.

Make sure to remove the tough stems and wash the leaves thoroughly. When the pasta is drained, add the arugula and other sauce ingredients and stir well until the arugula wilts, about 30 seconds. Arugula adds a bracing peppery flavor that works especially well with the sweetness and acidity of tomatoes.

◆

Fusilli with Chopped Arugula and Raw Tomatoes

THIS FRESH-TASTING DISH IS REALLY A SIMPLY DRESSED SALAD OF ARUGULA AND TOMATOES TOSSED WITH HOT PASTA. **SERVES 4.**

Salt
1 pound fusilli or other short, curly pasta
1 large bunch arugula (⅓ pound), stemmed, washed, and coarsely chopped
1 medium ripe tomato, cored and cut into ¼-inch dice
4 tablespoons extra-virgin olive oil
1 tablespoon lemon juice
1 medium garlic clove, minced
Ground black pepper
½ cup grated Parmesan cheese

1. Bring 4 quarts of water to a boil in a large pot. Add 1 tablespoon salt and the pasta to the boiling water. Cook until al dente.

2. Meanwhile, combine the arugula, tomato, oil, juice, garlic, and salt and pepper to taste in a large bowl.

3. Drain the pasta and transfer it back to the cooking pot. Stir in the arugula mixture and cheese. Mix until the arugula wilts. Divide among 4 pasta bowls and serve immediately.

SEEDING A CANNED TOMATO

Halve a canned tomato lengthwise and then use your fingers to push out the seeds.

Fusilli with Arugula and Black Olives

FOR A VARIATION ON THIS SIMPLE SAUCE, LEAVE OUT THE OLIVES AND STIR IN 1 CUP CRUMBLED RICOTTA SALATA WITH THE ARUGULA. SERVES 4.

- 1 28-ounce can diced tomatoes or whole tomatoes packed in juice
- 2 medium garlic cloves, minced
- 1/2 teaspoon hot red pepper flakes, or to taste
- 3 tablespoons extra-virgin olive oil
- 20 oil-cured black olives, pitted and chopped (see illustrations 1–2, page 62)
- Salt
- 1 pound fusilli or other short, curly pasta
- 1 large bunch arugula (1/3 pound), stemmed, washed, and finely chopped

1. If using diced tomatoes, go to step 2. If using whole tomatoes, drain and reserve the liquid. Dice the tomatoes by hand or in the work bowl of a food processor (use three or four 1/2-second pulses). The tomatoes should be coarse, with 1/4-inch pieces visible. If necessary, add enough reserved liquid to the tomatoes to total 2 2/3 cups.

2. Heat the garlic and red pepper flakes with 2 tablespoons oil in a medium sauté pan over medium heat. When the garlic starts to color, stir in the tomatoes and olives; simmer over medium heat until the sauce thickens a bit, about 10 minutes. Season to taste with salt, if necessary.

3. Bring 4 quarts of water to a boil in a large pot. Add 1 tablespoon salt and the pasta to the boiling water. Cook until al dente. Drain the pasta and transfer it back to the cooking pot. Stir in the tomato sauce, arugula, and remaining 1 tablespoon oil. Mix until the arugula wilts. Divide among 4 pasta bowls and serve immediately.

Sauces with Asparagus

ASPARAGUS IS GENERALLY cooked separately and then added to pasta sauces. We wanted to develop an all-purpose cooking method for asparagus that would work with a variety of pasta sauces and investigated boiling, steaming, and microwaving. (Broiling, roasting, and grilling are fine for pasta salads—see chapter 18—but the flavor of browned asparagus clashes with many other ingredients and we don't consider these methods to be all-purpose.)

We cooked asparagus spears of varying thicknesses by all three water-based methods. Microwaving caused the spears to shrivel up and dry out in places and was quickly rejected. Boiling and steaming were comparable, but the boiled asparagus tasted a bit more watery and mushy. Steaming was also much quicker since less water must be brought to a boil. For these reasons, we prefer steaming.

Up until this point, we had been testing whole spears and then chopping them into bite-size pieces. However, it can be difficult to cut cooked asparagus into neat pieces. We wondered what would happen if we cut the asparagus first. The results of this second round of testing were slightly more dramatic. Cut asparagus becomes more watery when boiled and is prone to overcooking.

In order to incorporate asparagus pieces into a pasta sauce, we found it best to cut medium-thick spears in half lengthwise, then into bite-size pieces (about 1 inch long). You can skip the splitting lengthwise step when working with very thin asparagus. If your asparagus are especially thick, quarter them lengthwise before cutting the spears into bite-size pieces.

◆

Linguine with Asparagus, Mushrooms, and Caramelized Shallots

SOME OF THE WATER USED TO STEAM THE ASPARAGUS IS RESERVED AND ADDED TO THE SAUCE. IT HAS A SLIGHT ASPARAGUS FLAVOR AND IS PREFERABLE TO ADDING PLAIN WATER. YOU COULD ADD ¼ CUP PARMESAN CHEESE WHEN YOU TOSS THE SAUCE WITH THE PASTA, AND THEN OFFER EXTRA PARMESAN AT THE TABLE. SERVES 4.

1 pound medium asparagus, tough ends snapped off; spears halved lengthwise, then cut diagonally into 1-inch pieces (see illustrations 1–3, page 138)
¼ cup extra-virgin olive oil
4 large shallots, thinly sliced
½ pound button or cremini mushrooms, wiped clean and thinly sliced
Salt and ground black pepper
1 pound linguine or other long, thin pasta

1. Bring 1 inch of water to a boil in a large pot. Put the asparagus in a steamer basket, then carefully place the steamer basket in a pot. Cover and steam over medium-high heat until the asparagus is just tender, about 2 minutes. Remove the asparagus and set aside. Reserve ¾ cup of the asparagus steaming liquid.

2. Heat the oil in a large skillet over medium heat. Add the shallots; sauté, stirring occasionally to separate the rings, until crisp and light brown, about 10 minutes. Add the mushrooms, increase the heat to medium-high, and sauté until they soften and release their juices, about 5 minutes longer. Season with salt and pepper to taste.

3. Add the asparagus and reserved cooking liquid. Simmer until the asparagus is heated through and the sauce has reduced a bit, about 2 minutes longer. Adjust the seasonings.

4. Meanwhile, bring 4 quarts of water to a boil in a large pot. Add 1 tablespoon salt and the pasta to the boiling water. Cook until al dente. Drain the pasta and transfer it back to the cooking pot. Stir in the sauce. Divide among 4 pasta bowls and serve immediately.

PREPARING ASPARAGUS

∽

1. Hold the spear in one hand and break off the tough end with the other hand. The spear will break in just the right place.

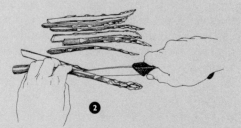

2. Medium-thick spears should be halved lengthwise. Jumbo asparagus should be cut into quarters lengthwise.

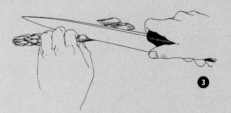

3. Cut halved asparagus spears on the diagonal into 1-inch pieces that will be easily incorporated into a pasta sauce.

Linguine with Asparagus and Tomatoes

WITH REGULAR LINGUINE, THIS SAUCE MAKES A FINE WEEKNIGHT MEAL; SERVE WITH HOMEMADE SAFFRON FETTUCCINE FOR SPECIAL OCCASIONS. **SERVES 4.**

> 1 pound medium asparagus, tough ends snapped off; spears halved lengthwise, then cut diagonally into 1-inch pieces (see illustrations 1–3)
> ¼ cup extra-virgin olive oil
> 3 medium garlic cloves, minced
> 1½ pounds plum tomatoes, cored, seeded, and diced (see illustrations 1–3, page 112)
> 1 tablespoon lemon juice
> **Salt and ground black pepper**
> 1 pound linguine or Saffron Pasta (page 28) cut into fettuccine
> **Grated Parmesan cheese**

1. Bring 1 inch of water to a boil in a large pot. Put the asparagus in a steamer basket, then carefully place the steamer basket in a pot. Cover and steam over medium-high heat until the asparagus is just tender, about 2 minutes. Remove the asparagus and set aside.

2. Heat the oil over medium heat in a large skillet. Add the garlic and cook until golden, about 2 minutes. Stir in the tomatoes and cook until slightly softened, 2 to 3 minutes. Add the asparagus and lemon juice. Season with salt and pepper to taste.

3. Meanwhile, bring 4 quarts of water to a boil in a large pot. Add 1 tablespoon salt and the pasta to the boiling water. Cook until al dente. Reserve ½ cup of the cooking water; drain the pasta and transfer it back to the cooking pot. Stir in the asparagus mixture and moisten with some of the cooking liquid if necessary. Divide among 4 pasta bowls and serve immediately with cheese passed at the table.

Penne with Asparagus and Fresh Goat Cheese

A LITTLE BIT OF CREAM ADDS SMOOTHNESS TO A SAUCE OF TANGY CRUMBLED GOAT CHEESE, CHOPPED MINT, AND STEAMED ASPARAGUS. PENNE ARE THE PERFECT SHAPE FOR THIS DISH, SINCE THEY ARE SO SIMILAR IN SIZE TO THE COOKED ASPARAGUS. **SERVES 4.**

1 pound medium asparagus, tough ends snapped off; spears halved lengthwise, then cut diagonally into 1-inch pieces (see illustrations 1–3, page 138).
3 ounces fresh goat cheese, crumbled
¼ cup heavy cream
1 small garlic clove, minced
Salt
1 pound penne or other short, tubular pasta
2 tablespoons finely chopped fresh mint leaves
Ground black pepper

1. Bring 1 inch of water to a boil in a large pot. Put the asparagus in a steamer basket, then carefully place the steamer basket in a pot. Cover and steam over medium-high heat until the asparagus is just tender, about 2 minutes. Remove the asparagus and set aside.

2. Place the goat cheese, cream, and garlic in a small bowl and stir with a fork to combine.

3. Meanwhile, bring 4 quarts of water to a boil in a large pot. Add 1 tablespoon salt and the pasta to the boiling water. Cook until al dente. Reserve ½ cup of the cooking water; drain the pasta and transfer it back to the cooking pot. Stir in the asparagus, goat cheese mixture, and mint; moisten with some of the cooking liquid if necessary. Season with salt and pepper to taste. Divide among 4 pasta bowls and serve immediately.

Spaghetti with Asparagus and Toasted Bread Crumbs

MANY COOKED VEGETABLES CAN BE ADDED TO A BASIC BREAD CRUMB SAUCE. TRY ARTICHOKES, BROCCOLI, CAULIFLOWER, FENNEL, PEPPERS, OR ZUCCHINI IN PLACE OF THE ASPARAGUS. **SERVES 4.**

1 pound medium asparagus, tough ends snapped off; spears halved lengthwise, then cut diagonally into 1-inch pieces (see illustrations 1–3, page 138)
2 medium garlic cloves, peeled (see illustration, page 39)
6 tablespoons extra-virgin olive oil
Salt
½ teaspoon grated lemon zest (see illustration, page 42)
1 pound spaghetti or other long, thin pasta
1 recipe Toasted Bread Crumbs (page 90)

1. Bring 1 inch of water to a boil in a large pot. Put the asparagus in a steamer basket, then carefully place the steamer basket in a pot. Cover and steam over medium-high heat until the asparagus is just tender, about 2 minutes. Remove the asparagus and set aside.

2. Process the garlic through a garlic press into a small bowl; stir in 1 teaspoon water. Place the oil, diluted garlic, and 1 teaspoon salt in a small sauté pan and turn the heat to low. Cook very slowly until the garlic turns golden, about 3 minutes. Be careful not to brown the garlic or your sauce will be bitter. Stir in the zest. Remove from heat.

3. Meanwhile, bring 4 quarts of water to a boil in a large pot. Add 1 tablespoon salt and the pasta to the boiling water. Cook until al dente. Reserve ½ cup of the cooking water; drain the pasta and transfer it back to the cooking pot. Mix in the asparagus, garlic oil, bread crumbs, and enough reserved water to keep the mixture moist. Adjust the seasonings. Divide among 4 pasta bowls and serve immediately.

Sauces with Broccoli

WE TESTED BROCCOLI by boiling, steaming, sautéing, and stir-frying. For pasta sauces, boiling and steaming make the most sense. Steaming allows the broccoli to retain more color and texture than boiling and is our preferred method. Steam heat is more gentle than boiling, so it's not as easy to overcook the broccoli. However, boiling is appropriate in several cases. If the broccoli is going to be pureed, texture is not an important factor. Also, cooking broccoli with the pasta is so convenient (no need to dirty two pots) that we have included a recipe with this method.

In our tests, we have found that broccoli has an internal clock, one that starts ticking at almost exactly seven minutes. At this point, chemical changes begin to occur that cause an initial undesirable loss of color and texture. By nine minutes, the stems have become quite discolored and mushy.

The deterioration is due to two distinct actions: heat and acid. As broccoli is heated during cooking, the chlorophyll begins to break down, resulting in a change in color and texture. In addition, all vegetables contain acids, which leach out in cooking. These acids further contribute to the breakdown of the broccoli.

Luckily, we find that broccoli needs only five minutes of cooking time. Just pay attention to the clock and your broccoli will be perfectly cooked every time.

Many cooks discard the stalks. However, we think the stalks are quite delicious. If they are peeled and cut into bite-size pieces, they will cook at the same rate as the florets. Don't try to use a vegetable peeler on the stalks; it won't remove enough of the tough skin. Use a knife to trim away at least ⅛ inch of woody cellulose from all sides of the stalk.

◆

STEP-BY-STEP

PREPARING BROCCOLI

1. Place the head of broccoli upside down on a cutting board and trim off the florets very close to their heads with a large knife.

2. The stalks may also be trimmed and cooked. Stand each stalk up on the cutting board and square it off with a large knife. This will remove the tough green skin and reveal the whitish green core underneath. Cut the stalk lengthwise into quarters and then into bite-size pieces.

Spaghetti with Broccoli and Caramelized Onions

SWEET CARAMELIZED ONIONS TAKE THE EDGE OFF THE SOMEWHAT BITTER FLAVOR OF STEAMED BROCCOLI. TO BE SURE THAT THE MIXTURE IS MOIST ENOUGH, DON'T SHAKE THE PASTA COMPLETELY DRY BEFORE ADDING THE SAUCE. SERVES 4.

2 medium onions, sliced thin
¼ cup extra-virgin olive oil
1 teaspoon chopped fresh thyme leaves
1 large bunch broccoli (about 1½ pounds), prepared according to the instructions (see illustrations 1–2)
Salt and ground black pepper
1 pound spaghetti or other long, thin pasta

1. Heat the onions and oil in a large skillet over medium heat. Cook, stirring frequently, until the onions are deep golden, 10 to 12 minutes. Stir in the thyme.

2. Bring about 1 inch of water to a boil in a large pot. Put the broccoli in a steamer basket. Lower the basket into the pot so it rests above the water; cover and steam until just tender, 4½ to 5 minutes. Add to the onions and season with salt and pepper to taste.

3. Meanwhile, bring 4 quarts of water to a boil in a large pot. Add 1 tablespoon salt and the pasta to the boiling water. Cook until al dente. Drain the pasta and transfer it back to the cooking pot. Toss with the sauce. Divide among 4 pasta bowls and serve immediately.

◆

Ziti with Broccoli-Anchovy Sauce

AN ESPECIALLY QUICK WAY TO PREPARE BROCCOLI FOR A PASTA SAUCE IS TO BOIL IT IN THE SAME POT AS THE PASTA. THIS DISH IS A SPECIALTY OF APULIA, AN AREA IN SOUTHERN ITALY. DON'T BE PUT OFF BY THE ANCHOVIES IN THE SAUCE. THEY DISSOLVE COMPLETELY IN THE HOT OLIVE OIL. SERVES 4.

> 1 can (2 ounces) anchovy fillets, drained, rinsed, and minced
> ½ cup extra-virgin olive oil
> Salt
> 1 pound ziti or other short, tubular pasta
> 1 large bunch broccoli (about 1½ pounds), prepared according to the instructions on page 140

1. Heat the anchovies and oil in a small skillet over medium until the anchovies dissolve, about 3 minutes. Set aside.

2. Meanwhile, bring 4 quarts of water to a boil in a large pot. Add 1 tablespoon salt and the pasta to the boiling water. After 5 minutes, add the broccoli; cook until the pasta is al dente, 4 to 5 minutes longer. Drain, leaving some of the cooking water clinging to the pasta. Return the pasta and broccoli to the cooking pot. Toss with the anchovy oil. Divide among 4 pasta bowls and serve immediately.

Fusilli with Broccoli-Ricotta Sauce

THIS SIMPLE SAUCE DERIVES ITS FLAVOR FROM THE BROCCOLI, AND IS MADE CREAMY BY THE ADDITION OF RICOTTA AND PARMESAN. WHOLE-MILK RICOTTA MAKES A DELICIOUS SAUCE, BUT PART-SKIM RICOTTA CAN BE USED IF FAT AND CALORIES ARE CONSIDERATIONS IN YOUR DIET. SINCE THE BROCCOLI WILL BE PUREED, WE BOIL IT IN THIS RECIPE (IT DOESN'T MATTER IF THE BROCCOLI OVERCOOKS SLIGHTLY) AND THEN USE THE SAME WATER TO COOK THE PASTA. SERVES 4.

> Salt
> 1 large bunch broccoli (about 1½ pounds), prepared according to the instructions on page 140
> 1 medium garlic clove, minced
> 1 cup ricotta cheese
> ½ cup grated Parmesan cheese
> 1 pound fusilli or other short, curly pasta

1. Bring 4 quarts of water to a boil in a large pot. Add 1 tablespoon salt and the broccoli and cook until tender, about 5 minutes. Retrieve the broccoli with a slotted spoon and transfer to the work bowl of a food processor. Leave the water at a boil.

2. Add the garlic to the food processor and pulse several times to coarsely chop. Do not overprocess; the broccoli should still be a little chunky. Scrape into a bowl and stir in the ricotta and Parmesan. Season with salt to taste.

3. Add the pasta to the boiling water and cook until al dente. Reserve ½ cup of the cooking liquid and drain. Return the pasta to the cooking pot. Stir in the broccoli sauce. If the pasta looks too dry, add the cooking liquid 1 tablespoon at a time. Divide among 4 pasta bowls and serve immediately.

Fusilli with Lemony Broccoli and Sun-Dried Tomatoes

LEMON ZEST GIVES BROCCOLI A BRIGHT LEMON FLAVOR WITHOUT TURNING IT BROWN THE WAY JUICE DOES. THE SUN-DRIED TOMATOES ADD SOME COLOR AND SWEETNESS. ABUNDANT GARLIC BALANCES OUT THE ACIDIC ELEMENTS. SERVES 4.

> 1 large bunch broccoli (about 1½ pounds), prepared according to the instructions on page 140
> ¼ cup extra-virgin olive oil
> 4 medium garlic cloves, minced
> 1 teaspoon grated lemon zest (see illustration, page 42)
> 12 sun-dried tomatoes packed in oil, drained and coarsely chopped
> Salt and ground black pepper
> 1 pound spaghetti or other long, thin pasta

1. Bring about 1 inch of water to a boil in a large pot. Put the broccoli in a steamer basket. Lower the basket into the pot so it rests above the water; cover and steam until just tender, 4½ to 5 minutes.

2. Heat the oil and garlic over medium heat in a large skillet. Cook, until the garlic is golden, 1 to 2 minutes. Add the zest and tomatoes and stir to heat through. Add the steamed broccoli and toss to coat. Season with salt and pepper to taste.

3. Meanwhile, bring 4 quarts of water to a boil in a large pot. Add 1 tablespoon salt and the pasta to the boiling water. Cook until al dente. Drain the pasta and transfer it back to the cooking pot. Toss with the sauce. Divide among 4 pasta bowls and serve immediately.

Sauces with Broccoli Rabe

BROCCOLI RABE MAY TASTE like other tough greens, but it requires a different cooking method. The stems and thick stalks are trimmed from collards and such before cooking. All that is left is the leaves, which cook at an even rate.

Broccoli rabe contains thick stalks, tender leaves, and small florets. If all the stalks were removed, there would be little left to this plant. We had to devise a cooking method that would soften the stalks but keep the florets and leaves from becoming mushy.

We tested boiling and steaming and found that steaming cooks this tough green unevenly. By the time the thick stalks soften up, the tender florets were mushy. Boiling did a better job of cooking the various parts of this plant evenly, if only because it is faster and there is less time for the florets to become mushy. Since the florets still tend to overcook, we drain and refresh broccoli rabe in a bowl of cold water to stop the cooking process. It's also a good idea to pull broccoli rabe off the heat before it is completely tender, especially since it will be cooked again in the pasta sauce.

The thick ends of each stalk never soften properly, even when boiled, and so should be removed before cooking. The remaining portion of the stalks and the florets should be cut into bite-size pieces (about 1 inch long) for use in pasta sauces.

◆

Orecchiette with Broccoli Rabe

TRY THIS SIMPLE SAUCE WITH HOMEMADE SEMOLINA ORECCHIETTE (PAGE 34). YOU MAY SUBSTITUTE BROCCOLI FLORETS, OR ANY WINTER GREEN, SUCH AS KALE OR COLLARDS, FOR THE BROCCOLI RABE. SERVES 4.

> Salt
> 1 pound broccoli rabe, washed, trimmed, and cut into 1-inch pieces (see illustrations 1–2, page 143)
> ⅓ cup extra-virgin olive oil
> 4 medium garlic cloves, minced
> ½ teaspoon hot red pepper flakes
> 1 pound orecchiette or other shell-shaped pasta
> ½ cup grated Parmesan cheese

1. Bring 1 quart of water to a boil in a large pot. Add salt to taste and the broccoli rabe. Return to a boil and cook until the broccoli rabe is bright green and almost tender, 2 to 3 minutes. Drain the broccoli rabe and plunge into cold water to stop the cooking process; drain the broccoli rabe and set aside.

2. Heat the oil with the garlic in a large skillet until the garlic is golden, 1 to 2 minutes; add the red pepper flakes and broccoli rabe. Sauté over medium-high heat until heated through, 3 to 4 minutes.

3. Meanwhile, bring 4 quarts of water to a boil in a large pot. Add 1 tablespoon salt and the pasta to the boiling water. Cook until al dente. Reserve ½ cup of the cooking liquid and drain. Return the pasta to the cooking pot and toss with the sauce. Stir in the cooking liquid, 1 tablespoon at a time, if the sauce seems dry. Stir in the cheese, divide among 4 pasta bowls, and serve immediately.

PREPARING BROCCOLI RABE

1. The thick stalk ends on broccoli rabe should be trimmed and discarded. Use a sharp knife to cut off the thickest part (usually the bottom 2 inches) of each stalk.

2. Cut the remaining stalks, leaves, and florets into bite-size pieces, about 1 inch long.

Fusilli with Broccoli Rabe and Kielbasa

STRONGLY FLAVORED BROCCOLI RABE IS WELL MATCHED WITH SMOKY, SALTY KIELBASA IN THIS HEARTY MAIN DISH. OTHER MILD OR SPICY SMOKED SAUSAGES SUCH AS CHORIZO OR ANDOUILLE MAY BE SUBSTITUTED. SERVES 4.

> Salt
> 1 pound broccoli rabe, washed, trimmed, and cut into 1-inch pieces (see illustrations 1–2)
> ¾ pound kielbasa, quartered lengthwise and cut into ½-inch pieces
> 2 tablespoons extra-virgin olive oil
> 4 medium garlic cloves, minced
> 1 pound fusilli or other shell-shaped pasta

1. Bring 1 quart of water to a boil in a large pot. Add salt to taste and the broccoli rabe. Return to a boil and cook until the broccoli rabe is bright green and almost tender, 2 to 3 minutes. Drain the broccoli rabe and plunge into cold water to stop the cooking process; set aside.

2. Place the kielbasa in a heavy skillet and brown over medium heat, stirring occasionally, about 5 minutes. Transfer to paper towels with a slotted spoon and drain off all but 2 tablespoons of the fat. Add the oil and garlic and cook until the garlic is golden, 1 to 2 minutes; add the broccoli rabe. Sauté over medium-high heat until heated through, 3 to 4 minutes.

3. Meanwhile, bring 4 quarts of water to a boil in a large pot. Add 1 tablespoon salt and the pasta to the boiling water. Cook until al dente. Reserve ½ cup of the cooking liquid and drain. Return the pasta to the cooking pot and toss with the broccoli rabe sauce and kielbasa. Stir in the cooking liquid, 1 tablespoon at a time, if the sauce seems dry. Divide among 4 pasta bowls and serve immediately.

Sauces with Cabbage

CABBAGE MAKES AN especially hearty pasta sauce, perfect for cold winter nights. The first step is to cut the cabbage into thin shreds. Cabbage cooks down quite a bit so it's fine if the shreds are long, but don't cut them too thick—you don't want the pieces of cabbage to overwhelm the pasta. Ideally, the cooked shredded cabbage will wrap around noodles.

We tested various cooking methods for cabbage, including blanching, steaming, sautéing, and braising. Blanching and steaming make the cabbage watery and do nothing to counter the strong mustardy flavor. Sautéing causes the cabbage to brown and become sweeter, but the cabbage pieces scorch rather quickly, long before they are tender.

For pasta sauces, shredded cabbage must become totally pliant. We found that braising was the preferred cooking method. Cooking flavorful ingredients, such as bacon, onions, and garlic, in the pan before adding the cabbage helps balance its strong flavor. So does a flavorful braising liquid. We like the mild acidity and flavor of wine, although stock ran a close second in our tests.

We added just enough wine to cook the cabbage and, in fact, let the cabbage continue cooking a bit after the wine had evaporated. At this point, the cabbage starts to brown and gains some of the sweetness we liked from sautéing. However, because the cabbage is fully cooked and moist, it won't scorch as easily. Once the cabbage has browned a bit, take it off the heat and toss with pasta.

Fusilli with Cabbage and Bacon

CABBAGE BRAISED WITH SOME BACON AND DICED ONION BECOMES SOFT AND ALMOST CREAMY-TASTING. TOSSED WITH PASTA, IT MAKES A FILLING WINTER MEAL. THE CREVICES IN FUSILLI HOLD STRANDS OF THE CABBAGE, BUT PENNE AND OTHER SHORT SHAPES WORK WELL, TOO. SERVES 4.

> 2 tablespoons extra-virgin olive oil
> 1 medium onion, minced
> 4 ounces bacon, cut into 1/4-inch dice
> 1/2 small cabbage (about 1 pound), cored
>   and shredded (see illustrations 1–3,
>   page 145)
> 1/2 cup dry white wine
> Salt
> 1 pound fusilli or other short, curly pasta
> 1/2 cup grated Parmesan cheese

1. Heat the oil in a large sauté pan over medium-high heat. Add the onion and bacon; sauté, stirring occasionally, until the onion softens and the bacon begins to brown, 3 to 5 minutes. Add the cabbage and wine. Cover the pan and cook over medium heat, stirring occasionally, until the wine has evaporated and the cabbage is very soft, limp, and beginning to brown, 18 to 20 minutes.

2. Meanwhile, bring 4 quarts of water to a boil in a large pot. Add 1 tablespoon salt and the pasta to the boiling water. Cook until al dente. Drain the pasta and transfer it back to the cooking pot. Toss with the sauce and cheese. Divide among 4 pasta bowls and serve immediately.

Fusilli with Red Cabbage and Red Wine

ABUNDANT PECORINO CHEESE, WITH ITS SLIGHTLY SHARP FLAVOR, OFFSETS THE SWEETNESS OF RED CABBAGE BRAISED IN RED WINE. SERVE THIS SUBSTANTIAL PASTA AS A FIRST COURSE OR AS A SIDE DISH TO ROASTED OR PAN-FRIED CHICKEN. **SERVES 6 TO 8 AS A SIDE DISH.**

> ¼ cup extra-virgin olive oil
> 2 medium onions, thinly sliced
> 4 medium garlic cloves, minced
> ½ small red cabbage (about 1 pound), cored and shredded (see illustrations 1–3)
> ½ cup red wine
> Salt
> 1 pound fusilli or other short, curly pasta
> ½ cup grated pecorino cheese

1. Heat the oil in a large sauté pan over medium heat. Add the onions; sauté, stirring occasionally, until the onions are golden, 8 to 10 minutes. Add the garlic and cook for another minute. Add the cabbage and wine. Cover the pan and cook over medium heat, stirring occasionally, until the wine has evaporated and the cabbage is very soft, limp, and beginning to brown, 18 to 20 minutes.

2. Meanwhile, bring 4 quarts of water to a boil in a large pot. Add 1 tablespoon salt and the pasta to the boiling water. Cook just until al dente. Drain the pasta and transfer it back to the cooking pot. Toss with the sauce and cheese. Divide among 4 pasta bowls and serve immediately.

SHREDDING CABBAGE

1. Cut the cabbage into quarters through the stem end. Remove the piece of the core attached to each quarter.

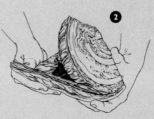

2. Pull off several cabbage leaves at a time and press them flat against a cutting board.

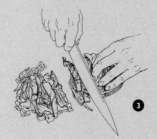

3. Use a chef's knife to cut each stack of cabbage leaves into thin shreds.

PREPARING CAULIFLOWER

1. Pull off all the outer leaves and trim off the stem near the base of the head.

2. Turn the cauliflower upside down, stem up. Using a sharp knife, cut around the core to remove it.

3. Separate the individual florets from the inner stem using the tip of a chef's knife.

4. Cut the florets in half or quarters if necessary so that individual pieces are about 1 inch long.

Sauces with Cauliflower

WHEN WE PREPARE CAULIFLOWER as a side dish, we either steam it and dress it, or we brown the cauliflower and then braise it. We thought the same two methods could be applied to pasta sauces.

Browning cauliflower and then adding juicy ingredients, such as tomatoes, works beautifully. The cauliflower becomes golden brown and develops a rich, nutty flavor. Use a heavy-bottomed pan over medium heat, so it will become golden without burning. The liquid is added for flavor and moisture, but the cauliflower is mostly cooked when it is added to the pan.

Steaming the cauliflower worked fine in our tests with pasta, but we wondered if we really needed two pots—one for the cauliflower and another for the pasta. Boiled cauliflower can be a bit watery tasting when served as a side dish, but in a pasta sauce we could not detect any wateriness. In fact, the extra moisture (boiled cauliflower gains an additional 10 percent of its original weight, while steamed cauliflower does not pick up any water weight when cooked) helps moisten the sauce.

Steam cauliflower florets destined for a pasta sauce if you like, but we find no advantage to this cooking method. Besides, cooking the cauliflower and then the pasta in the same water is so much more efficient.

Whole Wheat Penne with Cauliflower and Prosciutto

NUTTY, TOOTHSOME WHOLE WHEAT PENNE IS WONDERFUL WITH THIS CHUNKY, SUBSTANTIAL SAUCE, ALTHOUGH PLAIN PENNE IS FINE, TOO. HAVE THE PROSCIUTTO SLICED THICK AT THE DELI COUNTER; PAPER-THIN PIECES WILL JUST DISAPPEAR. **SERVES 4.**

> Salt
> 1 medium head cauliflower, trimmed and
>   cut into 1-inch florets (see illustrations
>   1–4, page 146)
> 3 tablespoons extra-virgin olive oil
> 1 medium onion, minced
> ¼ pound prosciutto, sliced ¼ inch thick
>   and cut into ¼-inch dice
> Ground black pepper
> 1 pound whole wheat or plain penne
> 2 tablespoons minced fresh flat-leaf
>   parsley leaves
> ½ cup grated pecorino cheese

1. Bring 4 quarts of water to a boil in a large pot. Add 1 tablespoon salt and the cauliflower to the boiling water. Cook until tender, 3 to 5 minutes. Remove the cauliflower with a slotted spoon and set aside. Leave the water at a boil.

2. Heat the oil in a large skillet over medium heat. Add the onion and cook until golden, 5 to 7 minutes. Add the prosciutto and cook until softened, 2 to 3 minutes. Stir in the cauliflower. Season with salt and pepper to taste.

3. Add the pasta to the boiling water and cook until al dente. Reserve ½ cup of the cooking water; drain the pasta and return it to the cooking pot. Stir in the cauliflower mixture, parsley, and cheese. If the pasta is too dry, add cooking water, 1 tablespoon at a time, until you reach the desired consistency. Divide among 4 pasta bowls and serve immediately.

Penne with Cauliflower, Raisins, and Pine Nuts

CAULIFLOWER, RAISINS, AND PINE NUTS ARE ALL STAPLE INGREDIENTS OF SOUTHERN ITALIAN COOKING. TO MAINTAIN THE SOUTHERN ITALIAN SPIRIT OF THE DISH, DON'T ADD CHEESE, BUT ADD TOASTED BREAD CRUMBS IF YOU LIKE. **SERVES 4.**

> Salt
> 1 medium head cauliflower, trimmed and
>   cut into 1-inch florets (see illustrations
>   1–4, page 146)
> ¼ cup pine nuts
> ¼ cup extra-virgin olive oil
> 4 medium garlic cloves, minced
> ½ cup raisins
> 2 tablespoons minced fresh flat-leaf
>   parsley leaves
> Ground black pepper
> 1 pound penne
> ½ cup Toasted Bread Crumbs (page 90;
>   optional)

1. Bring 4 quarts of water to a boil in a large pot. Add 1 tablespoon salt and the cauliflower to the boiling water. Cook until tender, 3 to 5 minutes. Remove the cauliflower with a slotted spoon and set aside. Leave the water at a boil.

2. Toast the nuts in a skillet over medium heat, stirring frequently, until just golden and fragrant, 4 to 5 minutes. Remove them from the pan and set aside.

3. Add the oil and garlic to the empty skillet. Cook over medium heat until the garlic is golden, 1 to 2 minutes. Stir in the cauliflower, pine nuts, raisins, and parsley. Cook to heat through, 1 to 2 minutes. Season with salt and pepper to taste.

4. Add the pasta to the boiling water and cook until al dente. Reserve ½ cup of the cooking water; drain the pasta and return it to the cooking pot. Stir in the cauliflower mixture and the bread crumbs if using. If the pasta is too dry, add cooking water, 1 tablespoon at a time, until you reach the desired consistency. Divide among 4 pasta bowls and serve immediately.

Spaghetti with Spicy Cauliflower Sauce

CAULIFLOWER IS SAUTEED RATHER THAN BLANCHED IN THIS RECIPE, GIVING IT A GOLDEN COLOR AND SWEET FLAVOR. SUBTLE GARLIC FLAVOR COMES FROM CRUSHED CLOVES, WHICH ARE COOKED WITH THE CAULIFLOWER AND THEN DISCARDED. SERVES 4.

- ¼ cup extra-virgin olive oil
- 1 medium head cauliflower, trimmed and cut into 1-inch florets (see illustrations 1–4, page 146)
- 4 medium garlic cloves, peeled and crushed (see illustration, page 39)
- 1 medium onion, sliced thin
- 1½ cups canned crushed tomatoes
- ½ teaspoon hot red pepper flakes, or to taste
- 2 tablespoons minced fresh flat-leaf parsley leaves
- Salt and ground black pepper
- 1 pound spaghetti or other long, thin pasta
- ½ cup grated pecorino cheese

1. Heat 3 tablespoons oil over medium heat in a large, heavy-bottomed skillet. Add the cauliflower and garlic. Sauté, stirring occasionally, until the cauliflower is golden, 15 to 20 minutes. Remove the cauliflower from the pan and set aside.

2. Add the remaining tablespoon oil and the onion to the pan and cook until golden brown, 7 to 10 minutes. Meanwhile, pick through the cauliflower and discard the garlic cloves.

3. Add the tomatoes and red pepper flakes to the onion and cook until slightly thickened, 2 to 3 minutes. Return the cauliflower to the pan and heat through, 2 to 3 minutes. Stir in the parsley. Season with salt and pepper to taste.

4. Meanwhile, bring 4 quarts of water to a boil in a large pot. Add 1 tablespoon salt and the pasta to the boiling water and cook until al dente. Drain the pasta

and return it to the cooking pot. Stir in the sauce and cheese. Divide among 4 pasta bowls and serve immediately.

Sauces with Eggplant

MANY PEOPLE COMPLAIN that their eggplant dishes are either tough, pithy, and astringently bitter, or oil-soaked, slimy, and tasteless. This is not inevitable. Eggplant can—and should—be firm and meaty, with a rich, sweet, nutty flavor.

The biggest challenge that confronts the cook preparing eggplant is excess moisture. While the grill will evaporate this liquid and allow the eggplant to brown nicely, this won't happen in a skillet, no matter how hot it is. The eggplant will steam in its own juices and the result is insipid flavor and mushy texture.

Salting is the classic technique for drawing some moisture out of the eggplant before cooking. We experimented with both regular table salt and kosher salt and prefer kosher salt because the crystals are large enough to wipe away after the salt has done its job. Finer table salt crystals dissolve into the eggplant flesh and must be flushed out with water. The eggplant must then be thoroughly dried, which adds more prep time, especially if the eggplant has been diced for use in a pasta sauce.

If you don't have the time to salt eggplant, you may choose a cooking method other than sautéing. We found that roasting or grilling eggplant are both alternatives. The intense heat of the grill drives off the excess liquid from eggplant slices and eggplant needs only a light brushing of oil to keep it from sticking to the rack. Grilled eggplant is meaty and delicious, much like eggplant that has been salted, pressed, and sautéed.

Roasting a whole eggplant creates something different. The skin holds in the moisture and the pulp steams. When the eggplant is totally soft and collapsed, it is ready. Simply remove the skin and then chop or pulse the flesh in the food processor. Eggplant cooked this way is meaty, but not as sweet as eggplant that has been browned in a pan or on the grill.

Pasta alla Norma

ADD CRUSHED TOMATOES TO SAUTEED EGGPLANT, TOSS WITH RIGATONI, AND YOU HAVE PASTA ALLA NORMA. GRATED RICOTTA SALATA IS OPTIONAL. IF YOU DO USE IT, HOLD OFF ON ADDING SALT TO THE SAUCE; BETWEEN THE EGGPLANT AND THE CHEESE, THERE WILL PROBABLY BE ADEQUATE SALT FOR THE FINISHED DISH. SERVES 4.

- 2 medium eggplants (about 2 pounds), ends trimmed and cut into ¾-inch cubes
- Kosher salt
- 3 tablespoons extra-virgin olive oil
- 1 tablespoon minced garlic
- ¼ teaspoon hot red pepper flakes, or to taste
- 1¼ cups canned crushed tomatoes
- Ground black pepper
- 1 pound rigatoni or other short, tubular pasta
- 1 cup shredded ricotta salata cheese
- ¼ cup minced fresh flat-leaf parsley or basil leaves

1. Place the eggplant in a large colander and sprinkle with 1 tablespoon salt. Let stand 30 minutes. Using paper towels or a large kitchen towel, wipe the salt off and pat the excess moisture from the eggplant.

2. Heat the oil in a large, heavy-bottomed skillet over medium-high heat until it shimmers and becomes fragrant. Add the eggplant; sauté until it begins to brown, about 4 minutes. Reduce the heat to medium-low and cook, stirring occasionally, until the eggplant is fully tender and lightly browned, 10 to 15 minutes. Stir in the garlic and red pepper flakes; cook to blend flavors, about 2 minutes. Add the tomatoes, bring to a simmer, and cook until slightly thickened, 2 to 3 minutes. Season with salt and pepper to taste.

3. Meanwhile, bring 4 quarts of water to a boil in a large pot. Add 1 tablespoon salt and the pasta to the boiling water. Cook until al dente. Reserve ½ cup of the cooking liquid and drain. Return the pasta to the cooking pot and toss with the eggplant, cheese, herbs, and ¼ cup cooking liquid. Stir in more cooking liquid, 1 tablespoon at a time, if the sauce seems dry. Divide among 4 pasta bowls and serve immediately.

◆

Fusilli with Sautéed Eggplant

EGGPLANT SOAKS UP AS MUCH OIL AS IS ADDED TO THE PAN; TO AVOID GREASY EGGPLANT, SAUTE IN JUST A LITTLE OIL AND RESERVE SOME FOR DRIZZLING OVER THE FINISHED DISH AT THE END. SERVES 4.

- 2 medium eggplants (about 2 pounds), ends trimmed and cut into ¾-inch cubes
- Kosher salt
- 5 tablespoons extra-virgin olive oil
- 4 medium garlic cloves, minced
- Ground black pepper
- 1 pound fusilli or other short, curly pasta
- ¼ cup minced fresh flat-leaf parsley or basil leaves

1. Place the eggplant in a large colander and sprinkle with 1 tablespoon salt. Let stand 30 minutes. Using paper towels or a large kitchen towel, wipe the salt off and pat the excess moisture from the eggplant.

2. Heat 3 tablespoons oil in a large heavy-bottomed skillet over medium-high until it shimmers and becomes fragrant. Add the eggplant; sauté until it begins to brown, about 4 minutes. Reduce the heat to medium-low and cook, stirring occasionally, until the eggplant is fully tender and lightly browned, 10 to 15 minutes. Stir in the garlic; cook to blend flavors, about 2 minutes. Season with salt and pepper to taste.

3. Meanwhile, bring 4 quarts of water to a boil in a large pot. Add 1 tablespoon salt and the pasta to the boiling water. Cook just until al dente. Reserve ½ cup of the cooking liquid and drain. Return the pasta to the cooking pot and toss with the eggplant, remaining 2 tablespoons oil, parsley, and ¼ cup cooking liquid. Stir in more cooking liquid, 1 tablespoon at a time, if the sauce seems dry. Divide among 4 pasta bowls and serve immediately.

Ziti with Roasted Eggplant and Ricotta

IF YOU DON'T WANT TO SALT AND SAUTE THE EGG-
PLANT, ROASTING IS A GOOD ALTERNATIVE. FOR THE
LEAST BITTER END PRODUCT, TRY TO BUY FRESH FARM-
STAND EGGPLANTS RATHER THAN EGGPLANTS THAT
HAVE BEEN SITTING ON A TRUCK AND IN A SUPERMAR-
KET FOR DAYS. RICOTTA CHEESE MAKES THE SAUCE
CREAMY; SUBSTITUTE ½ CUP GRATED PARMESAN OR
PECORINO IF YOU LIKE. **SERVES 4.**

1 medium eggplant (about 1 pound)
3 tablespoons extra-virgin olive oil
2 medium garlic cloves, minced
1¼ cups canned crushed tomatoes
Salt and ground black pepper
1 pound ziti or other short, tubular pasta
1 cup ricotta cheese
¼ cup minced fresh basil leaves

1. Preheat the oven to 400 degrees. Place the eggplant on a baking sheet and brush with 1 tablespoon
oil. Roast, turning 2 or 3 times, until the eggplant is
soft, 35 to 40 minutes. Let the eggplant cool until it is
just warm to the touch.

2. Place the remaining 2 tablespoons oil and the garlic in a medium skillet. Sauté over medium heat until
the garlic is golden, 1 to 2 minutes. Add the tomatoes,
bring to a simmer, and cook until slightly thickened, 2
to 3 minutes.

3. Trim the stem of the eggplant and peel away the
skin with your fingers. Chop the flesh coarsely.

4. Add the eggplant to the tomato sauce and heat
through. Season with salt and pepper to taste.

5. Meanwhile, bring 4 quarts of water to a boil in a
large pot. Add 1 tablespoon salt and the pasta to the
boiling water. Cook until al dente. Return the pasta
to the cooking pot and toss with the sauce, cheese,
and basil. Divide among 4 pasta bowls and serve
immediately.

Linguine with Grilled Eggplant and Pesto

GRILLING IS ANOTHER EGGPLANT OPTION IF YOU'RE IN
A RUSH. THE HEAT OF THE GRILL WILL QUICKLY COOK
OFF MUCH OF THEIR MOISTURE. GRILLED EGGPLANT
MARRIES WELL WITH PUNGENT BASIL PESTO. ANOTHER
PESTO OF YOUR CHOICE MAY BE SUBSTITUTED FOR
CLASSIC BASIL PESTO (SEE CHAPTER 6 FOR RECIPES).
SERVE WITH A SALAD OF FRESH MOZZARELLA AND RIPE
TOMATOES. **SERVES 4.**

1 medium or 2 small eggplants (about 1
  pound), ends trimmed and cut
  lengthwise into ½-inch-thick slices
Salt and ground black pepper
¼ cup pine nuts, walnuts, or almonds
3 medium garlic cloves, threaded on a
  skewer
2 cups packed fresh basil leaves
2 tablespoons fresh flat-leaf parsley leaves
  (optional)
7 tablespoons extra-virgin olive oil
¼ cup finely grated Parmesan cheese
1 pound linguine or other long, thin pasta

1. Light the grill or make a charcoal fire. Bring 4
quarts of water to a boil in a large pot. Sprinkle both
sides of the eggplant slices with salt and pepper to
taste and set aside while you make the pesto.

2. Toast the nuts in a small, heavy skillet over
medium heat, stirring frequently, until just golden and
fragrant, 4 to 5 minutes.

3. Lower the skewered garlic into the water; boil for
45 seconds (see illustration 1, page 56). Immediately
run the garlic under cold water. Remove from the
skewer; peel and mince. Leave the pot with the water
on the stove.

4. Place the basil and parsley (if using) in a heavy-
duty, quart-size, sealable plastic bag; pound with the
flat side of a meat pounder until all the leaves are
bruised (see illustration 2, page 56).

5. Place the nuts, garlic, basil, parsley, oil, and a pinch of salt in the work bowl of a food processor; process until smooth, stopping as necessary to scrape down the sides of the bowl. Transfer the mixture to a small bowl, stir in the cheese, and adjust the salt.

6. Grill the eggplant slices, turning once, until both sides are marked with dark stripes, about 7 minutes. Cool slightly and cut into bite-size pieces.

7. Return the water to a boil. Add 1 tablespoon salt and the pasta and cook until al dente. Reserve ½ cup of the cooking water; drain the pasta and return it to the cooking pot. Mix in the eggplant, ¼ cup of the reserved cooking water, and the pesto; use the additional ¼ cup cooking water as needed to moisten the sauce. Divide among 4 pasta bowls and serve immediately.

Sauces with Fava Beans

FAVA BEANS HAVE A rich bittersweet flavor and firm, creamy texture that makes them a welcome addition to pasta sauces. There's no denying that fava beans require a lot of preparation, but the result is well worth the effort. The beans are enclosed in a furry pod. Like fresh peas, the pods must be opened and the beans removed. Then the tough outer skin of each fava bean must be removed. This light green skin is tightly attached to the dark green bean inside, so in order to loosen the skin the beans must be blanched. We tested various cooking times and found that three minutes is sufficient to loosen the skin. The beans should be drained, refreshed in cold water to stop the cooking process and cool off the beans, and then peeled. To remove the skin, pinch open at one end of the bean. Once the skin has been split open, simply pop out the dark green bean and discard the skin. The two halves of the bean will separate.

Peeled fava beans are fully cooked at this stage. They may be heated through with other ingredients to make a pasta sauce, but they should not be cooked further. The amounts of favas called for in these recipes may seem quite a bit, but remember that most of the weight will be in the pods and skins, which are discarded.

◆

Fettuccine with Fava Bean Pesto

IN THIS RECIPE, ABOUT HALF THE FAVA BEANS ARE USED TO MAKE A PESTO. THE OTHER HALF ARE STIRRED INTO THE COOKED DISH FOR TEXTURE. ALTHOUGH GOOD WITH DRIED PASTA, IT IS ESPECIALLY NICE WITH FRESH EGG FETTUCCINE. SERVES 4.

> 4 pounds fresh fava beans
> 1 medium garlic clove, coarsely chopped
> 7 tablespoons extra-virgin olive oil
> 2 tablespoons lemon juice
> ½ cup finely grated pecorino cheese
> Salt
> 1 pound Fresh Egg Pasta (page 21) cut into fettuccine *or* dried fettuccine

1. Bring several quarts of water to a boil in a pot. Remove the fava beans from their pods. Add the favas to the boiling water and cook for 3 minutes. Drain and rinse with cold water. Slip the beans from their outer skins (see illustrations 1–2, page 153).

2. Combine half the beans with the garlic, oil, and juice in the work bowl of a food processor. Process until smooth, stopping as necessary to scrape down the sides of the bowl. Transfer the mixture to a small bowl, stir in the cheese, and adjust the salt.

3. Meanwhile, bring 4 quarts of water to a boil in a large pot. Add 1 tablespoon salt and the pasta to the boiling water and cook until al dente. Reserve ½ cup of the cooking water; drain the pasta and return it to the cooking pot. Mix in ¼ cup of the reserved cooking water, the pesto, and the remaining whole beans; use the additional ¼ cup cooking water as needed to moisten the sauce. Divide among 4 pasta bowls and serve immediately.

Orecchiette with Fava Beans, Pancetta, and Tomatoes

FRESH FAVA BEANS BENEFIT FROM THE PRESENCE OF OTHER FRESH INGREDIENTS LIKE PLUM TOMATOES (WITH JUICE AND SEEDS) AND CHOPPED CHIVES. FRESH MINT OR BASIL MAY BE SUBSTITUTED IF YOU LIKE. SERVES 4.

- 4 pounds fresh fava beans
- 2 tablespoons extra-virgin olive oil
- 1 medium onion, minced
- ¼ pound pancetta, sliced ¼ inch thick and then cut into ¼-inch dice
- 3 medium plum tomatoes, cut into ¼-inch dice
- Salt
- ¾ pound orecchiette
- ½ cup grated Parmesan cheese
- 1 tablespoon chopped fresh chives

1. Bring several quarts of water to a boil in a pot. Remove the fava beans from their pods. Add the favas to the boiling water and cook for 3 minutes. Drain and rinse with cold water. Slip the beans from their outer skins (see illustrations 1–2, page 153).

2. Heat the oil and onion in a large skillet over medium heat. Cook until the onion begins to soften, 3 to 4 minutes. Add the pancetta and cook, stirring occasionally, until the fat is rendered, 3 to 4 minutes. Add the tomatoes and beans and heat through, 1 to 2 minutes. Taste for salt.

3. Meanwhile, bring 4 quarts of water to a boil in a large pot. Add 1 tablespoon salt and the pasta to the boiling water and cook until al dente. Drain the pasta and transfer it back to the cooking pot. Stir in the bean sauce, cheese, and chives. Divide among 4 pasta bowls and serve immediately.

Penne with Fava Beans, Asparagus, and Ricotta

RICOTTA CHEESE PROVIDES A CREAMY, BUT NOT OVERLY RICH, BACKGROUND FOR SPRING VEGETABLES IN THIS LIGHT DISH. EITHER WHOLE-MILK OR PART-SKIM CHEESE MAY BE USED, ALTHOUGH WHOLE-MILK RICOTTA WILL TASTE A BIT CREAMIER. SERVES 4.

- 1 pound medium asparagus, tough ends snapped off; spears halved lengthwise, then cut diagonally into 1-inch pieces (see illustrations 1–3, page 138)
- 4 pounds fresh fava beans
- ¾ pound penne or other short, tubular pasta
- Salt
- 1 cup ricotta cheese
- ½ cup grated Parmesan cheese
- 2 scallions, white and light green parts, chopped
- Ground black pepper

1. Bring several quarts of water to a boil in a pot. Add the asparagus and cook until tender, 2 to 3 minutes. Remove with a slotted spoon and set aside. Leave the water at a boil.

2. Remove the fava beans from their pods. Add the favas to the boiling water and cook for 3 minutes. Drain and rinse with cold water. Slip the beans from their outer skins (see illustrations 1–2, page 153).

3. Meanwhile, bring 4 quarts of water to a boil in a large pot. Add 1 tablespoon salt and the pasta to the boiling water and cook until al dente. Reserve ½ cup cooking liquid and drain the pasta. Return to the cooking pot and add the asparagus, fava beans, ricotta, Parmesan, scallions, ¼ cup cooking liquid, and salt and pepper to taste. If the pasta looks too dry, add more cooking liquid, 1 tablespoon at a time. Divide among 4 pasta bowls and serve immediately.

PEELING FAVA BEANS

1. After fava beans are shelled, their tough outer skins must also be removed. Blanch the beans, rinse with cold water, and drain. Working with one bean at a time, pinch open the skin at one end.

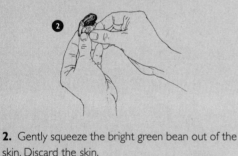

2. Gently squeeze the bright green bean out of the skin. Discard the skin.

Sauces with Fennel

ALTHOUGH FENNEL IS ALMOST always available in larger supermarkets, most Americans have little idea what to do with this anise-flavored vegetable. Maybe it's the funny Italian name, *finocchio*, or the odd appearance: a white, squat bulb erupting into several light green stems, which are topped with feathery dark green fronds. Each portion—the bulb, stems, and fronds—has a different culinary use.

For most recipes, only the white bulb is used. The stems can be reserved for making stock, while the fronds can be minced and used as a garnish for dishes made with the bulb.

Raw fennel is crisp and has a fairly strong anise flavor. Cooking softens the fennel and mellows the licorice flavor to fade, but no matter how it is cooked fennel will be slightly sweet.

Our first goal was to devise an easy method for preparing the oddly shaped bulb. Most fennel bulbs, especially larger ones, have an outer layer of dried or blemished flesh. At the market, pick firm bulbs with a bright white color and as little blemishing as possible. But even on the freshest fennel, the outer layer should be removed, much as you might peel away the outer layer on a large onion.

We find it best to start out by trimming a thin slice from the bottom of the bulb. Invariably this flesh is discolored and needs to be removed. This cut usually loosens the outer layer on the bulb sufficiently so that it can be peeled away with your fingers. If the outer layer will not yield to your fingers, make a shallow vertical cut through this layer and then slide your fingers into the cut to pry off this first layer of the bulb.

Fennel must be cut into fairly small pieces for the sauces we developed. Start by cutting the bulb in half through the base. Each half will contain a small portion of the core at its base. Use a small, sharp knife to remove this triangular piece. This is a small refinement that helps promote even cooking since the core can remain tough long after the rest of the bulb has softened.

The next step is to lay each fennel half on a work surface with the flat side down. We cut each half crosswise to yield three or four slices. These slices can be cut lengthwise to yield long strips that are about 1/2 inch thick.

We tested five cooking methods. Boiling, steaming, and microwaving did not add much flavor and boiling had the additional problem of causing mushy texture. Sautéing caused the natural sugars in the fennel to caramelize and enhanced its flavor. Braised fennel absorbed flavors from the cooking liquid (usually stock or wine). We recommend either sautéing or braising fennel for pasta sauces.

The common thread in all our testing was to

PREPARING FENNEL

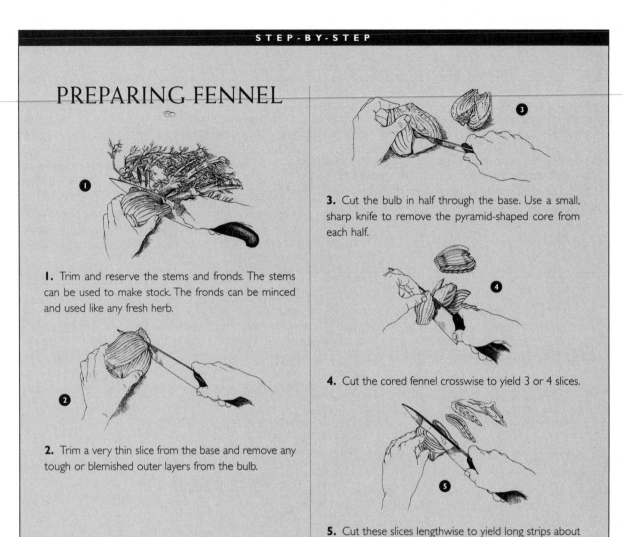

1. Trim and reserve the stems and fronds. The stems can be used to make stock. The fronds can be minced and used like any fresh herb.

2. Trim a very thin slice from the base and remove any tough or blemished outer layers from the bulb.

3. Cut the bulb in half through the base. Use a small, sharp knife to remove the pyramid-shaped core from each half.

4. Cut the cored fennel crosswise to yield 3 or 4 slices.

5. Cut these slices lengthwise to yield long strips about 3 inches long and ½ inch thick.

achieve tenderness throughout the fennel pieces. It's easy enough to cook fennel until mushy, but we prefer that it offer some resistance. However, fennel that is soft on the exterior and crunchy on the inside is not to our taste, either. Fairly slow cooking turned out to be the key. Both sautéing over medium heat for a considerable period (about 15 minutes) and braising for 25 minutes work beautifully.

Attempts to hurry fennel along did not succeed. However, braised fennel can be sautéed first to cut cooking time if you like. Sautéed fennel is sweeter because of all the caramelization and the texture is a bit firmer. Braised fennel is creamier and moister.

Spaghetti with Fennel Braised in White Wine

HERE, FENNEL COOKS SLOWLY IN BUTTER AND WHITE WINE UNTIL TENDER. THEN IT'S TOSSED WITH PASTA AND A LITTLE PARMESAN CHEESE. SIMPLE AND TASTY. SERVES 4.

> 3 tablespoons unsalted butter
> 2 medium or 3 small fennel bulbs (about 2¼ pounds), prepared according to the instructions on page 154
> Salt and ground black pepper
> ⅓ cup dry white wine
> 1 pound spaghetti or other long, thin pasta
> ½ cup grated Parmesan cheese

1. Melt the butter in a sauté pan large enough to hold the fennel in almost a single layer. Add the fennel and sprinkle with salt and pepper to taste. Add the wine and cover the pan. Simmer over medium heat 15 minutes. Turn the slices and continue to simmer, covered, until the fennel is quite tender, has absorbed most of the pan liquid, and starts to turn golden, about 10 minutes longer. Turn the fennel again and continue cooking until the fennel starts to color on the other side, about 4 minutes longer.

2. Meanwhile, bring 4 quarts of water to a boil in a large pot. Add 1 tablespoon salt and the pasta. Cook until al dente. Reserve ½ cup of the cooking water; drain the pasta and return it to the cooking pot. Mix in ¼ cup of the reserved cooking water, the fennel mixture, and the cheese. Toss, adding more cooking water as needed to moisten the pasta. Divide among 4 pasta bowls and serve immediately.

Spaghetti with Braised Fennel and Bitter Greens

FENNEL'S NATURAL SWEETNESS MAKES IT A GOOD PARTNER FOR BITTER GREENS LIKE KALE, MUSTARD, TURNIP, OR BEET. SERVES 4.

> ¼ cup extra-virgin olive oil
> 1 medium onion, minced
> 1 medium fennel bulb (about 1 pound), prepared according to the instructions on page 154; fronds reserved and minced
> Salt and ground black pepper
> 2 tablespoons balsamic vinegar
> 1 pound spaghetti
> ¾ pound kale or other bitter green, washed thoroughly and coarsely chopped
> ¼ cup grated Parmesan cheese

1. Heat the oil in a large sauté pan. Add the onion and sauté over medium heat until softened, about 5 minutes. Stir in the fennel and sauté until golden, about 10 minutes. Add ½ cup water and season to taste with salt and pepper. Cover and simmer over medium-low heat until the fennel is tender, about 8 minutes longer. Stir in the vinegar; simmer to blend the flavors, 1 minute longer. Adjust the seasonings.

2. Meanwhile, bring 4 quarts of water to a boil in a large pot. Add 1 tablespoon salt and the pasta; return to a boil. Add the kale to the pot; continue to cook until the pasta is al dente.

3. Drain the pasta and greens and return them to the cooking pot. Toss with the fennel mixture and cheese. Divide portions among 4 pasta bowls. Garnish with the reserved minced fennel fronds and serve immediately.

Penne with Sautéed Fennel

SAUTEING IS AN ALTERNATIVE TO BRAISING. THE ANISE FLAVOR OF FENNEL WILL FADE BUT THE NATURAL SUG-ARS IN THE VEGETABLE CONCENTRATE. **SERVES 4.**

    4 tablespoons extra-virgin olive oil
    2 medium fennel bulbs (about 2 pounds), prepared according to the instructions on page 154; fronds reserved and minced
    4 medium garlic cloves, minced
    Salt and ground black pepper
    1 pound penne or other short, tubular pasta
    1/2 cup grated Parmesan cheese
    2 tablespoons minced fresh flat-leaf parsley leaves

1. Heat 3 tablespoons oil in a large skillet over medium heat. Add the fennel strips; toss to coat with oil. Cook, stirring often, until the fennel has softened considerably but still offers some resistance, about 15 minutes. Add the garlic and sauté until lightly colored, about 1 minute. Season generously with salt and pepper to taste.

2. Meanwhile, bring 4 quarts of water to a boil in a large pot. Add 1 tablespoon salt and the pasta. Cook until al dente. Reserve 1/2 cup of the cooking water; drain the pasta and return it to the cooking pot. Mix in 1/4 cup of the reserved cooking water, the fennel mixture, the remaining 1 tablespoon oil, reserved fronds, cheese, and parsley. Toss, adding more cooking water as needed to moisten the pasta. Divide among 4 pasta bowls and serve immediately.

Sauces with Green Beans

GREEN BEANS ARE EASILY incorporated into pasta sauces. They are quick to prepare. Simply snap off both ends with your fingertips and cut the beans into bite-size pieces—about 1/2 inch long is ideal. Green beans are also easy to cook.

We tested boiling and steaming and preferred boiling. Steam heat does not cook the beans as evenly. We found that steamed beans were often tender on the outside but too crunchy inside. Boiling cooks the beans more evenly. It's also more convenient: the beans can be added to the pot with the pasta, when the noodles are almost al dente. Or, the beans and pasta can be cooked one after the other in the same pot of water. Boiling has one last advantage over steaming: the beans can be seasoned with salt, something they badly need as they cook.

Yellow wax beans may be substituted in any of the recipes that follow, as may tiny haricots verts. If using the latter, leave the beans whole and cook for about 2 minutes, so that they are tender but still fresh-tasting.

◆

Penne with Green Beans, Potatoes, and Pesto

IN THIS TRADITIONAL GENOVESE COMBINATION, PASTA AND BEANS ARE COOKED TOGETHER, THE POTATOES ARE BOILED SEPARATELY, AND ALL ARE COMBINED WITH BASIL PESTO MADE WITHOUT CHEESE. **SERVES 4.**

    1/4 cup pine nuts, walnuts, or almonds
    3 medium garlic cloves, threaded on a skewer
    1 pound small red potatoes
    2 cups packed fresh basil leaves
    2 tablespoons fresh flat-leaf parsley leaves (optional)
    7 tablespoons extra-virgin olive oil
    Salt
    1 pound penne or other short, tubular pasta
    1 pound green beans, ends snapped off and cut into 1/2-inch lengths

1. Toast the nuts in a small, heavy skillet over medium heat, stirring frequently, until just golden and fragrant, 4 to 5 minutes.

2. Meanwhile, bring 2½ quarts of water to a boil in a large saucepan. Lower the skewered garlic into the water; boil for 45 seconds (see illustration 1, page 56). Immediately run the garlic under cold water. Remove from the skewer; peel and mince.

3. Add the potatoes to the boiling water and cook until tender when pierced with a sharp paring knife, 15 to 25 minutes, depending on size. Drain, cool slightly, and cut into quarters or eighths, depending on size. Set aside.

4. Meanwhile, place the basil and parsley (if using) in a heavy-duty, quart-size, sealable plastic bag; pound with the flat side of a meat pounder until all the leaves are bruised (see illustration 2, page 56).

5. Place the nuts, garlic, basil, parsley, oil, and a pinch of salt in the work bowl of a food processor; process until smooth, stopping as necessary to scrape down the sides of the bowl. Transfer the mixture to a small bowl and adjust the salt.

6. Meanwhile, bring 4 quarts of water to a boil in a large pot. Add 1 tablespoon salt and the pasta. Cook until the pasta is about 3 minutes from being done (see the timing on the pasta box and use your instincts). Add the beans and cook until the pasta is al dente and the beans are tender. Reserve ½ cup of the cooking water; drain the pasta and beans and return them to the cooking pot. Mix in ¼ cup of the reserved cooking water, the pesto, and the potatoes. Toss, adding more water as needed to moisten the pasta. Divide among 4 pasta bowls and serve immediately.

Spaghetti with Green Beans, Walnuts, and Tarragon

IN THIS SIMPLE PASTA SAUCE, GREEN BEANS ARE BOILED AND THEN TOSSED WITH TOASTED WALNUTS, TAR-RAGON, AND OLIVE OIL. FOR A STRONGER WALNUT FLA-VOR, SUBSTITUTE 2 TABLESPOONS WALNUT OIL FOR SOME OF THE OLIVE OIL. USE TENDER, YOUNG BEANS THAT DO NOT NEED A LOT OF COOKING TO SOFTEN AND WILL RETAIN THEIR FRESH FLAVOR AFTER A QUICK DUNK IN BOILING WATER. SERVES 4.

> ¼ cup chopped walnuts
> 4 small plum tomatoes (about ¾ pound), cut into ¼-inch dice
> 1½ tablespoons minced fresh tarragon leaves
> ¼ cup extra-virgin olive oil
> Salt
> 1 pound spaghetti or other long, thin pasta
> 1 pound green beans, ends snapped off and cut into ½-inch lengths
> Ground black pepper

1. Toast the nuts in a small, heavy skillet over medium heat, stirring frequently, until just golden and fragrant, 4 to 5 minutes. Set the nuts aside in a large bowl. Add the tomatoes, tarragon, and oil to the bowl and mix to combine.

2. Meanwhile, bring 4 quarts of water to a boil in a large pot. Add 1 tablespoon salt and the pasta to the boiling water. Cook until the pasta is about 3 minutes from being done (see the timing on the pasta box and use your instincts). Add the beans and cook until the pasta is al dente and the beans are tender. Drain the pasta and beans and return them to the pot. Stir in the tomato mixture. Season with salt and pepper. Divide among 4 pasta bowls and serve immediately.

Fusilli with Green Beans and Black Olives

AFTER THEY ARE BOILED, BEANS MAY BE SAUTEED BRIEFLY TO HEIGHTEN THEIR FLAVOR. **SERVES 4.**

> 1 pound green beans, ends snapped off and cut into ½-inch lengths
> Salt
> ¼ cup extra-virgin olive oil
> ½ medium onion, minced
> 1 medium garlic clove, minced
> ½ cup black olives, such as Kalamata, pitted and coarsely chopped (see illustrations 1–2, page 62)
> 1 teaspoon minced fresh thyme leaves
> Ground black pepper
> 1 pound fusilli or other short, curly pasta
> ¼ cup grated pecorino cheese

1. Bring 4 quarts of water to a boil in a large pot. Add the beans and 1 tablespoon salt and cook until tender, about 3 minutes. Remove with a slotted spoon and set aside. Leave the water at a boil.

2. Heat the oil in a large sauté pan over medium heat. Add the onion and cook until softened, 3 to 4 minutes. Add the garlic and cook another minute. Stir in the beans, olives, and thyme and cook until the beans have absorbed some of the flavors and are heated through, 2 to 3 minutes. Adjust the seasonings with salt and pepper to taste.

3. Add the pasta to the boiling water. Cook until the pasta is al dente. Drain the pasta and return it to the cooking pot. Add the bean mixture and cheese and toss to combine. Divide among 4 pasta bowls and serve immediately.

Sauces with Greens

TOO OFTEN, GREENS ARE lumped together in one big pile. Cooks use the same set of instructions for stemming, cutting, and cooking this odd mix, even though some of them are delicate enough for salads, while others seem tough as shoe leather.

After cleaning, stemming, and cooking over 100 pounds of Swiss chard, spinach, beet greens, turnip greens, mustard greens, kale, and collards, we realized that about all they had in common was their color. All of these greens couldn't be cooked the same way—they couldn't even be stemmed the same way.

As we reviewed our notes, we saw that leafy greens could be divided into two categories—tender and tough. The former category includes spinach, Swiss chard, and beet greens. All are tender and mild enough to use in salads and all can be cooked in the same fashion. Tougher greens such as kale, collards, mustard, and turnip greens require a different cooking technique because they are drier and their flavor is more assertive.

All greens must be washed thoroughly, but it is more difficult to get tender greens to give up their grit. We tried washing them before stemming, but found it hard to work with cold, messy greens. Instead, we recommend stemming the greens and dropping them into a bowl of cold water. Swish the leaves around and lift them out with your hands. Discard the water and then rinse away any grit at the bottom of the bowl. Add more cold water to the bowl along with the leaves. Repeat this swishing and draining process until there is no grit at the bottom of the bowl. (Tough greens can be cleaned the same way, but they are generally less sandy. One or two rinses should be enough.)

As for stemming, we found that spinach and beet greens were best stemmed by holding each leaf between the thumb and index finger and pulling. Much like an asparagus stalk, the tough stems break off naturally at just the point where they are tender enough to eat.

Swiss chard has a thick stem that runs through the middle of the leaf. We prefer to hold each leaf by the end of the stalk and then cut off the leafy portion on

STEMMING GREENS

1. Spinach and beet greens should be stemmed by pinching just below where the leaf starts.

2. For Swiss chard, collard, kale, and mustard greens, hold each leaf at the base of the stem over a bowl filled with water, then tear the leafy portions from each side of the thick stem. Discard the stem. Roughly tear each piece in half so that the pieces don't overwhelm the pasta.

3. Turnip greens are most easily stemmed by grasping the leaf between your thumb and index finger at the base of the stem and stripping it off by hand.

4. When using this method with turnip greens, the very tip of the stem will break off along with the leaves. It is tender enough to cook along with the leaves.

either side of the central vein. As it turned out, the same stemming method works for collards, kale, and mustard greens. Turnip greens should be handled differently (see illustrations 3 and 4 above).

We tested three cooking methods with full-grown (not baby) tender greens: boiling, steaming, and wilting. Although boiling produced the most brilliant color, it compromised the flavor of the greens and made them mushy. Steaming was cumbersome (it's hard to fit two pounds of greens in a steamer basket) and not worth the effort. Wilting the damp leaves in a covered pot was the easiest and best method. The steam that rises from the water clinging to the greens will cook them.

When combined with sautéing, wilting was the clear favorite because it added flavor as well. We start our pasta sauce by cooking onion, garlic, bacon, and/or spices in fat; we then added the damp greens, covered the pot, and cooked until the greens are tender. If the greens are soupy, simply remove the lid and let simmer until the greens are moist but not swimming in liquid.

Tougher greens, such as kale and collards, cannot be cooked this way. They will scorch long before they are tender. We started testing other cooking methods, also looking for a technique that might lessen the assertive flavor of these greens. We did not want to neutralize their peppery flavor, but we did want to tame it a bit so it would not overpower the pasta and other ingredients in the sauce.

Steaming these greens kept them from burning but did nothing to affect their flavor. Clearly, we would have to cook them in water. Greens boiled in a large quantity of water had a lot going for them. They were tender, brilliantly colored, and less bitter. The salt in the water rounded out their flavor. However, this method also left the greens rather pallid and generic. The water was washing away much of the individual character of each green.

We tried cooking each green in less water. After several attempts, we settled on cooking one pound of greens in one quart of water for seven minutes. This was enough water and time to mellow out the flavor a bit, without making the greens insipid. Shallow-blanched greens should be shocked in cold water, lightly squeezed, and then roughly cut. We found it much easier to cut the greens after cooking, when they were a fraction of their original volume.

◆

Spaghetti with Tender Greens and Garlic

TENDER GREENS—SPINACH, SWISS CHARD, BEET GREENS —DON'T NEED TO BE PARBOILED, MAKING THEM ESPE-CIALLY EASY AND QUICK TO PREPARE FOR PASTA. NUTTY, CHEWY WHOLE WHEAT PASTA IS A GOOD MATCH FOR THESE GREENS, ALTHOUGH PLAIN PASTA IS DELICIOUS, TOO. SERVES 4.

> 3 tablespoons extra-virgin olive oil
> 2 medium garlic cloves, minced
> 2 pounds tender greens such as spinach, beet greens, or Swiss chard, stemmed, washed, and chopped (see illustrations 1–2, page 159)
> Salt and ground black pepper
> 1 pound whole wheat or regular spaghetti
> 2 tablespoons lemon juice

1. Heat the oil with the garlic in a large sauté pan or Dutch oven over medium heat. When the garlic sizzles and starts to turn golden, add the wet greens. Cover and cook over medium-high heat, stirring occasionally, until the greens completely wilt but are still bright green, about 5 minutes. Uncover and season to taste with salt and pepper. Cook over high heat until most of the liquid evaporates, 2 to 3 minutes longer.

2. Meanwhile, bring 4 quarts of water to a boil in a large pot. Add 1 tablespoon salt and the pasta to the boiling water and cook until al dente. Drain the pasta and return it to the cooking pot. Stir in the greens and lemon juice. Divide among 4 pasta bowls and serve immediately.

◆

Spaghetti with Tender Greens and Gorgonzola

CRUMBLED GORGONZOLA GIVES THIS DISH CREAMINESS AS WELL AS A LITTLE BITE, WITHOUT MOST OF THE FAT OF A REAL CREAM SAUCE. SERVES 4.

> ¼ cup extra-virgin olive oil
> 4 medium garlic cloves, minced
> 2 pounds tender greens such as spinach, beet greens, or Swiss chard, stemmed, washed, and chopped (see illustrations 1–2, page 159)
> Salt and ground black pepper
> 1 pound spaghetti
> 4 ounces gorgonzola or other blue cheese, crumbled

1. Heat the oil with the garlic in a large sauté pan or Dutch oven over medium heat. When the garlic sizzles and starts to turn golden, add the wet greens. Cover and cook over medium-high heat, stirring occasionally, until the greens completely wilt but are still bright green, about 5 minutes. Uncover and season to taste with salt and pepper. Cook over high heat until most of the liquid evaporates, 2 to 3 minutes longer.

2. Meanwhile, bring 4 quarts of water to a boil in a large pot. Add 1 tablespoon salt and the pasta to the boiling water and cook until al dente. Reserve ½ cup cooking liquid and drain the pasta. Return it to the cooking pot. Stir in the greens and cheese. If the pasta seems too dry, add the cooking liquid 1 tablespoon at a time until you reach the desired consistency. Divide among 4 pasta bowls and serve immediately.

◆

Penne with Tender Greens and Shiitake Mushrooms

SHIITAKE MUSHROOMS ARE ESPECIALLY FLAVORFUL, BUT CREMINIS OR EVEN PLAIN BUTTON MUSHROOMS ALSO PAIR WELL WITH GREENS IN THIS SIMPLE SAUCE. SERVES 4.

¼ cup extra-virgin olive oil
4 medium garlic cloves, minced
1 pound fresh shiitake mushrooms, stemmed and coarsely chopped
2 pounds tender greens such as spinach, beet greens, or Swiss chard, stemmed, washed, and chopped (see illustrations 1–2, page 159)
Salt and ground black pepper
1 pound penne
½ cup grated Parmesan cheese

1. Heat the oil and garlic in a large sauté pan or Dutch oven over medium heat. When the garlic sizzles and starts to turn golden, add the mushrooms and sauté until they have begun to give off their juices, about 4 minutes. Add the wet greens. Cover and cook over medium-high heat, stirring occasionally, until the greens completely wilt but are still bright green, about 5 minutes. Uncover and season to taste with salt and pepper. Cook over high heat until most of the liquid evaporates, 2 to 3 minutes longer.

2. Meanwhile, bring 4 quarts of water to a boil in a large pot. Add 1 tablespoon salt and the pasta to the boiling water and cook until al dente. Reserve ½ cup cooking liquid and drain the pasta. Return it to the cooking pot. Stir in the mushrooms, greens, and cheese. If the pasta seems too dry, add the cooking liquid 1 tablespoon at a time until you reach the desired consistency. Divide among 4 pasta bowls and serve immediately.

Spaghetti with Tender Greens, Cumin, Tomatoes, and Cilantro

CUMIN AND CILANTRO GIVE THIS PASTA A SLIGHTLY EXOTIC INDIAN FLAVOR. ADD ¼ TEASPOON CAYENNE PEPPER TO GIVE THE SAUCE SOME HEAT, IF YOU LIKE. SERVES 4.

3 tablespoons extra-virgin olive oil
1 small onion, minced
2 medium garlic cloves, minced
½ medium jalapeño chile, stemmed, seeded if desired, and minced
1½ teaspoons ground cumin
2 large plum tomatoes, cored, seeded, and chopped (see illustrations 1–3, page 112)
2 pounds tender greens such as spinach, beet greens, or Swiss chard, stemmed, washed, and chopped (see illustrations 1–2, page 159)
Salt and ground black pepper
1 pound spaghetti or other long, thin pasta
2 tablespoons minced fresh cilantro
1 tablespoon lime juice

1. Heat the oil with the onion in a large sauté pan or Dutch oven over medium heat. Sauté until partially softened, about 1 minute. Add the garlic, jalapeño, and cumin; sauté until the onion softens, about 2 minutes longer. Add the tomatoes; cook until their juices release, about 1 minute. Add the wet greens. Cover and cook over medium-high heat, stirring occasionally, until the greens completely wilt, but are still bright green, about 5 minutes. Uncover and season to taste with salt and pepper. Cook over high heat until most of the liquid evaporates, 2 to 3 minutes longer.

2. Meanwhile, bring 4 quarts of water to a boil in a large pot. Add 1 tablespoon salt and the pasta to the boiling water and cook until al dente. Drain the pasta and return it to the cooking pot. Stir in the greens, cilantro, and lime juice. Divide among 4 pasta bowls and serve immediately.

Spaghetti with Tender Greens, Raisins, and Almonds

ALMONDS LEND THEIR PARTICULAR SWEETNESS TO THIS SICILIAN-STYLE DISH; PINE NUTS OR WALNUTS MAY BE SUBSTITUTED. **SERVES 4.**

1/3 cup slivered almonds

3 tablespoons extra-virgin olive oil

2 medium garlic cloves, minced

1/4 teaspoon hot red pepper flakes

1/3 cup golden raisins

2 pounds tender greens such as spinach, beet greens, or Swiss chard, stemmed, washed, and chopped (see illustrations 1–2, page 159)

1/2 teaspoon minced lemon zest (see illustrations 1–4, page 91)

Salt and ground black pepper

1 pound spaghetti or other long, thin pasta

1. Toast the nuts in a small, heavy skillet over medium heat, stirring frequently, until just golden and fragrant, 4 to 5 minutes.

2. Heat the oil with the garlic and red pepper flakes in a large sauté pan or Dutch oven over medium heat. When the garlic sizzles and starts to turn golden, add the raisins and wet greens. Cover and cook over medium-high heat, stirring occasionally, until the greens completely wilt, but are still bright green, about 5 minutes. Uncover, stir in the zest, and season to taste with salt and pepper. Cook over high heat until most of the liquid evaporates, 2 to 3 minutes longer.

3. Meanwhile, bring 4 quarts of water to a boil in a large pot. Add 1 tablespoon salt and the pasta to the boiling water and cook until al dente. Drain the pasta and return it to the cooking pot. Stir in the greens and almonds. Divide among 4 pasta bowls and serve immediately.

Penne with Blanched Greens and Prosciutto

THIS PASTA IS PERFECT WHEN YOU WANT TO EAT SOMETHING HEALTHY BUT CRAVE JUST A LITTLE BIT OF MEAT FLAVOR. THE SMALL QUANTITY OF THINLY SLICED PROSCIUTTO ALMOST MELTS INTO THE OTHER INGREDIENTS HERE, GIVING THE DISH A MEATY FLAVOR. **SERVES 4.**

Salt

2 pounds assertive greens, such as kale, collards, mustard, or turnip greens, stemmed and washed (see illustrations 2–4, page 159)

2 large garlic cloves, sliced thin

1/4 teaspoon hot red pepper flakes

3 tablespoons extra-virgin olive oil

1 ounce thinly sliced prosciutto, cut crosswise into thin strips

1/3–1/2 cup chicken stock or low-sodium chicken broth

1 pound penne or other short, tubular pasta

1/4 teaspoon minced lemon zest (see illustrations 1–4, page 91)

1/3 cup grated Parmesan cheese

1. Bring 2 quarts of water to a boil in a soup kettle or large, deep sauté pan. Add 1 1/2 teaspoons salt and the greens; stir until wilted. Cover and cool until the greens are just tender, about 7 minutes; drain in a colander. Rinse the kettle or pan with cold water to cool, then refill with cold water. Dump the greens into the cold water to stop the cooking process. Gather a handful of greens, lift out of the water, and squeeze until only droplets fall from them. Repeat with the remaining greens. Roughly cut each bunch of greens.

2. In a large sauté pan, heat the garlic and red pepper flakes with the oil over medium heat until the garlic starts to sizzle. Stir in the prosciutto. Add the greens; stir to coat with oil. Add 1/3 cup stock; cover and cook over medium-high heat, adding more stock during cooking if necessary, until the greens are tender and juicy and most of the stock has been absorbed, about 5 minutes.

3. Meanwhile, bring 4 quarts of water to a boil in a large pot. Add 1 tablespoon salt and the pasta to the boiling water and cook until al dente. Drain the pasta and return it to the cooking pot. Stir in the greens, zest, and cheese. Divide among 4 pasta bowls and serve immediately.

◆

Penne with Blanched Greens and Red Bell Pepper

SLIVERS OF RED BELL PEPPER ADD COLOR AND SWEET FLAVOR TO QUICK-COOKED GREENS IN THIS DISH. SERVE WITH BROILED OR GRILLED SAUSAGES FOR A SIMPLE WEEKNIGHT MEAL. **SERVES 4.**

> Salt
> 2 pounds assertive greens, such as kale, collards, mustard, or turnip greens, stemmed and washed (see illustrations 2–4, page 159)
> 3 tablespoons extra-virgin olive oil
> ½ red bell pepper, cored, seeded, and sliced thin
> 2 large garlic cloves, sliced thin
> ¼ teaspoon hot red pepper flakes
> ⅓–½ cup chicken stock or low-sodium chicken broth
> 1 pound penne or other short, tubular pasta
> ⅓ cup grated Parmesan cheese

1. Bring 2 quarts of water to a boil in a soup kettle or large, deep sauté pan. Add 1½ teaspoons salt and the greens; stir until wilted. Cover and cool until the greens are just tender, about 7 minutes; drain in a colander. Rinse the kettle or pan with cold water to cool, then refill with cold water. Dump the greens into the cold water to stop the cooking process. Gather a handful of greens, lift out of the water, and squeeze until only droplets fall from them. Repeat with the remaining greens. Roughly cut each bunch of greens.

2. In a large sauté pan, heat the oil over medium heat and sauté the pepper until softened, about 4 minutes. Add the garlic and red pepper flakes and sauté until the garlic starts to sizzle. Add the greens; stir to coat with oil. Add ⅓ cup stock; cover and cook over medium-high heat, adding more stock during cooking if necessary, until the greens are tender and juicy and most of the stock has been absorbed, about 5 minutes.

3. Meanwhile, bring 4 quarts of water to a boil in a large pot. Add 1 tablespoon salt and the pasta to the boiling water and cook until al dente. Drain the pasta and return it to the cooking pot. Stir in the greens and cheese. Divide among 4 pasta bowls and serve immediately.

◆

Penne with Blanched Greens and Black Olives

ANY HIGH-QUALITY BLACK OLIVES MAY BE USED HERE, DEPENDING ON TASTE AND WHAT YOU HAVE ON HAND. OIL-CURED OLIVES ARE SALTIER AND TOUGHER IN TEXTURE; BRINED VARIETIES SUCH AS KALAMATA ARE MELLOWER AND MEATIER. **SERVES 4.**

> Salt
> 2 pounds assertive greens, such as kale, collards, mustard, or turnip greens, stemmed and washed (see illustrations 2–4, page 159)
> 2 large garlic cloves, sliced thin
> ¼ teaspoon hot red pepper flakes
> 3 tablespoons extra-virgin olive oil
> ⅓ cup pitted, coarse-chopped black olives (see illustrations 1–2, page 62)
> ⅓–½ cup chicken stock or low-sodium chicken broth
> 1 pound penne or other short, tubular pasta
> ¼ teaspoon minced lemon zest (see illustrations 1–4, page 91)
> ⅓ cup grated Parmesan cheese

(continued on next page)

1. Bring 2 quarts of water to a boil in a soup kettle or large, deep sauté pan. Add 1½ teaspoons salt and the greens; stir until wilted. Cover and cool until the greens are just tender, about 7 minutes; drain in a colander. Rinse the kettle or pan with cold water to cool, then refill with cold water. Dump the greens into the cold water to stop the cooking process. Gather a handful of greens, lift out of the water, and squeeze until only droplets fall from them. Repeat with the remaining greens. Roughly cut each bunch of greens.

2. In a large sauté pan, heat the garlic and red pepper flakes with the oil over medium heat until the garlic starts to sizzle. Stir in the olives. Add the greens; stir to coat with oil. Add ⅓ cup stock; cover and cook over medium-high heat, adding more stock during cooking if necessary, until the greens are tender and juicy and most of the stock has been absorbed, about 5 minutes.

3. Meanwhile, bring 4 quarts of water to a boil in a large pot. Add 1 tablespoon salt and the pasta to the boiling water and cook until al dente. Drain the pasta and return it to the cooking pot. Stir in the greens, zest, and cheese. Divide among 4 pasta bowls and serve immediately.

Sauces with Leeks

LIKE A SWEETER VERSION of onions, leeks can be used in any number of pasta sauces as part of the flavoring base. However, they also can be the focal point of a dish if used in sufficient quantity.

For pasta sauces, leeks must be cut into thin strips and sautéed. No other cooking method makes much sense. The real issue with leeks is getting them clean. Leeks collect dirt between their layers as they grow. They must be scrupulously cleaned or the pasta sauce will be ruined.

Before cleaning, leeks should be trimmed. Many recipes suggest slicing the leeks at the point where the outer layer darkens. We found that you could trim the leeks about 2 inches above the point, saving much of the light green part of the leek. Next, trim off the roots and slit the leek in half lengthwise. You can use a

pair of scissors to trim away any remaining dark green portions that seem thick or tough.

We tested swishing trimmed leeks in a bowl of cold water as well as rinsing them under cold, running water. Neither method was 100 percent reliable. We found that soaking the leeks in cold water for several minutes gets rid of most of the sand. As an added precaution, we then spread the leek layers apart and swished the leek in the water to flush out any remaining grit.

◆

Linguine with Leeks and Tomato-Cream Sauce

THIS LUXURIOUS LEEK SAUCE CALLS FOR THE LEEKS TO BE SAUTEED IN A LITTLE BUTTER, WITH A SMALL AMOUNT OF CREAM TO TINT THE TOMATO SAUCE PINK. FOR A MORE AUSTERE TREATMENT, USE OLIVE OIL INSTEAD OF BUTTER AND OMIT THE CREAM. **SERVES 4.**

> **2 tablespoons unsalted butter**
> **2 large leeks, trimmed, washed, and sliced
>   thin (see illustrations 1–6, page 165)**
> **½ cup dry sherry**
> **1 28-ounce can whole tomatoes packed in
>   juice, drained, halved, seeded, and
>   chopped (see illustration, page 136)**
> **¼ cup heavy cream**
> **1 teaspoon minced fresh tarragon leaves**
> **Salt and ground black pepper**
> **1 pound linguine or other long, thin pasta**

1. Melt the butter over medium heat in a medium skillet. Add the leeks and sauté until softened, 5 to 7 minutes. Add the sherry and tomatoes and simmer until the alcohol aroma has dissipated and the sauce has thickened slightly, about 5 minutes. Add the cream and cook another 2 minutes. Stir in the tarragon and season with salt and pepper to taste.

2. Meanwhile, bring 4 quarts of water to a boil in a large pot. Add 1 tablespoon salt and the pasta to the boiling water. Cook until al dente. Drain the pasta and return it to the cooking pot. Toss with the sauce. Divide among 4 pasta bowls and serve immediately.

TRIMMING AND CLEANING LEEKS

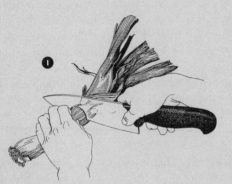

1. Trim the leeks about 2 inches beyond the point where the leaves start to darken.

2. Trim the root end, keeping the base intact.

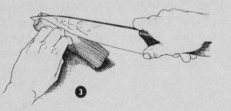

3. Slit the leek lengthwise in half, cutting through the base and toward the green portion.

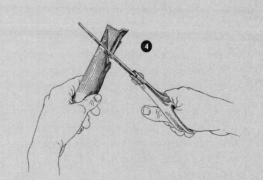

4. By trimming only the dark green parts of each half with a pair of scissors, more of the leek can be saved.

5. Soak the trimmed leeks in a bowl of cold water to loosen excess dirt, then swish the leeks in water, pulling apart the layers with your fingers to expose any clinging dirt.

6. Place the leek halves cut side down on a cutting board and slice them crosswise to the desired thickness.

Fettuccine with Leeks, Peas, and Cream

THIS RICH SAUCE WITH LEEKS AND PEAS IS ACTUALLY A VARIATION ON CLASSIC ALFREDO. PALE PINK BEET PASTA MAKES A BEAUTIFUL PRESENTATION, BUT PLAIN EGG PASTA TASTES EQUALLY GOOD. SERVES 4.

4 tablespoons unsalted butter
2 large leeks, trimmed, washed, and sliced
   thin (see illustrations 1–6, page 165)
1 medium onion, minced
2 shallots, minced
½ cup frozen peas, thawed
1½ cups heavy cream, preferably not
   ultrapasteurized
Salt
1 pound Beet Pasta (page 26) or Fresh
   Egg Pasta (page 21) cut into fettuccine
1 cup grated Parmesan cheese
Ground black pepper

1. Melt the butter over medium-low heat in a sauté pan large enough to accommodate the cooked pasta. Add the leeks and onion and sauté until softened, 5 to 7 minutes. Add the shallots and cook another 2 minutes. Add the peas and cook 1 minute. Add 1 cup cream and heat over low until the cream comes to a bare simmer. Turn off the heat and set aside.

2. Meanwhile, bring 4 quarts of water to a boil in a large pot. Add 1 tablespoon salt and the pasta to the boiling water. Cook until just al dente. Drain the pasta and add it to the sauté pan. Add the remaining ½ cup cream, the cheese, ½ teaspoon salt, and pepper to taste. Cook over very low heat, tossing to combine ingredients, until the sauce is slightly thickened, 1 to 2 minutes. Divide among 4 warmed pasta bowls and serve immediately.

Sauces with Mushrooms

SAUTEED MUSHROOMS ARE the basis for countless pasta sauces. Buy wild mushrooms if you can, but domesticated varieties are fine as long as they are well seasoned. The most common variety is the white button. You may see light brown cremini mushrooms. They can be prepared in the same fashion but have a slightly stronger, earthier flavor. You may also see oversized portobello mushrooms, which are simply large cremini. Portobello stems are usually quite tough and should be removed and discarded before cooking. Any of these fresh mushrooms can be used in the recipes below.

Dried porcini mushrooms are also an excellent addition to pasta sauces. After a number of tests, we concluded that hot tap water is the best medium for softening them. Boiling water can result in a listless texture and lukewarm water takes too long. Soak dried mushrooms in hot water for about 20 minutes and then strain.

The straining technique is actually more important than the soaking method. Dried porcini are packaged with foreign matter. Lifting the mushrooms from the soaking liquid with a fork helps keep the grit in the bowl. Inspect the mushrooms and remove any twigs. Strain the liquid through a coffee filter or paper towel set in a mesh strainer.

When shopping, look for dried porcini that are large, thick, and tan or brown in color rather than black. Avoid bags with lots of brittle or crumbled pieces or dust. If porcini are sold loose, smell them; the aroma should be earthy, not musty or stale.

Fusilli with Simple Sautéed Mushroom Sauce

THE ANCHOVIES ARE UNDETECTABLE AS SUCH IN THIS SAUCE, YET THEY GIVE PLAIN BUTTON MUSHROOMS CHARACTER THAT THEY DON'T HAVE ON THEIR OWN. SERVES 4.

> 4 tablespoons extra-virgin olive oil
> 1 medium onion, minced
> 2 medium garlic cloves, minced
> 2 anchovy fillets, minced
> 1½ pounds fresh mushrooms, trimmed and thinly sliced
> 2 tablespoons lemon juice
> Salt and ground black pepper
> 1 pound fusilli or other short, curly pasta
> 2 tablespoons minced fresh flat-leaf parsley leaves

1. Heat the oil in a large sauté pan. Add the onion and cook until softened, 3 to 4 minutes. Add the garlic and cook until fragrant, another minute. Add the anchovies and mushrooms and cook, stirring occasionally, until the mushrooms release their juices, 5 to 7 minutes. Stir in the lemon juice. Season with salt and pepper to taste.

2. Meanwhile, bring 4 quarts of water to a boil in a large pot. Add 1 tablespoon salt and the pasta to the boiling water. Cook until al dente. Drain the pasta and return it to the cooking pot. Toss with the sauce and parsley. Divide among 4 pasta bowls and serve immediately.

Orzo with Mushrooms and Fontina

SERVE THIS CREAMY PASTA AS A MAIN DISH, OR SERVE IT AS YOU WOULD SERVE A RISOTTO—AS A FIRST COURSE OR SIDE DISH. BUY ONLY FONTINA IMPORTED FROM ITALY; DOMESTIC AND DUTCH VERSIONS ARE CHARACTERLESS IMITATIONS. SERVES 6 TO 8 AS A SIDE DISH.

> 2 tablespoons extra-virgin olive oil
> 1 small onion, minced
> 1 medium garlic clove, minced
> 1 pound fresh mushrooms, trimmed and sliced thin
> 3 canned whole tomatoes, finely chopped
> 2 teaspoons finely chopped fresh sage leaves
> Salt and ground black pepper
> 1 pound orzo or other tiny pasta
> 4 ounces Italian Fontina cheese, shredded
> ½ cup grated Parmesan cheese

1. Heat the oil in a large sauté pan. Add the onion and cook until softened, 3 to 4 minutes. Add the garlic and cook until fragrant, another minute. Add the mushrooms and cook, stirring occasionally, until they release their juices, 5 to 7 minutes. Add the tomatoes and sage and cook until the sauce is slightly thickened, 3 to 4 minutes. Season with salt and pepper to taste.

2. Meanwhile, bring 4 quarts of water to a boil in a large pot. Add 1 tablespoon salt and the pasta to the boiling water. Cook until al dente. Drain the pasta and return it to the cooking pot. Toss with the sauce, Fontina, and Parmesan. Serve immediately.

Fettuccine with Porcini Mushroom–Cream Sauce

DRIED FETTUCCINE WORKS WELL WITH THIS RICH SAUCE, BUT HOMEMADE EGG FETTUCCINE WILL ABSORB THE SAUCE BETTER. PASS EXTRA CHEESE AT THE TABLE. SERVES 4.

- 3 tablespoons unsalted butter
- 1 medium onion, minced
- 2 ounces dried porcini mushrooms, rehydrated in 2 cups hot water, strained, and chopped coarse; soaking liquid reserved (see illustrations 1–2, page 169)
- Salt and ground black pepper
- 6 tablespoons heavy cream
- 3 tablespoons minced fresh flat-leaf parsley leaves
- 1 pound Fresh Egg Pasta (page 21) cut into fettuccine *or* dried fettuccine

1. Heat the butter in a large sauté pan over medium heat. Add the onion; sauté until the edges begin to brown, about 7 minutes. Add the porcini and salt and pepper to taste; sauté to release the flavors, 1 to 2 minutes.

2. Increase the heat to medium-high. Add the soaking liquid; simmer briskly until the liquid has reduced by half, about 10 minutes. Stir the cream into the sauce; simmer until the sauce just starts to thicken, about 2 minutes. Stir in the parsley and adjust the seasonings.

3. Meanwhile, bring 4 quarts of water to a boil in a large pot. Add 1 tablespoon salt and the pasta to the boiling water. Cook until al dente. Drain the pasta and return it to the cooking pot. Toss with the sauce. Divide among 4 pasta bowls and serve immediately.

Fusilli with Porcini Mushroom–Tomato Sauce

PORCINI GIVE THIS TOMATO SAUCE AN ALMOST MEATY FLAVOR AND CONSISTENCY, EVEN THOUGH IT IS VEGETARIAN. SERVES 4.

- 3 tablespoons extra-virgin olive oil
- 1 medium onion, minced
- 1 celery stalk, minced
- 1 small carrot, peeled and minced
- 1 ounce dried porcini mushrooms, rehydrated, strained, and chopped coarse; soaking liquid reserved (see illustrations 1–2, page 169)
- Salt
- 1 28-ounce can whole tomatoes packed in juice, drained, seeded, and chopped (see illustrations, page 136)
- 3 tablespoons minced fresh flat-leaf parsley leaves
- 1 pound fusilli or other short, curly pasta

1. Heat the oil in a large sauté pan over medium heat. Add the onion, celery, and carrot; sauté until the vegetables soften, 8 to 10 minutes. Add the porcini and salt and cook for 1 to 2 minutes to release flavors.

2. Increase the heat to medium-high; add the tomatoes and soaking liquid. Bring the sauce to a boil, lower the heat, then simmer until the sauce thickens, about 15 minutes. Stir in the parsley and taste for salt.

3. Meanwhile, bring 4 quarts of water to a boil in a large pot. Add 1 tablespoon salt and the pasta to the boiling water. Cook until al dente. Drain the pasta and return it to the cooking pot. Toss with the sauce. Divide among 4 pasta bowls and serve immediately.

HOW TO REHYDRATE DRIED PORCINI MUSHROOMS

Place 1 ounce dried porcini mushrooms in a small bowl and cover with 1 cup hot water. Soak for 20 minutes. Carefully lift the mushrooms from the liquid with a fork and pick through to remove any foreign debris (see illustration 1). Wash the mushrooms under cold water if they feel gritty, then chop. Strain the soaking liquid through a sieve lined with a coffee filter or paper towel (see illustration 2). Reserve the mushrooms and strained soaking liquid separately.

To rehydrate more mushrooms, simply increase the liquid, keeping the ratio at 1 cup of hot water for every ounce of mushrooms.

2. The best way to remove the grit at the bottom of the bowl is to pour the soaking liquid through a small mesh strainer lined with a coffee filter or single paper towel and set in a large measuring cup. The filter or towel traps the dirt and absorbs a minimum of the liquid.

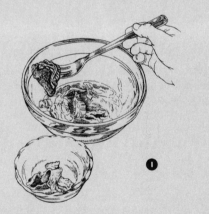

1. Rather than draining the softened mushrooms into a sieve, lift the mushrooms from the liquid with a fork so that the grit stays at the bottom of the bowl.

Orecchiette with Two Mushroom Sauce

BUTTON MUSHROOMS GET A TREMENDOUS BOOST FROM A HANDFUL OF DRIED PORCINI. FOR ADDED CREAMINESS, STIR IN 1/3 CUP GRATED PARMESAN CHEESE WITH SAUCE AND PASTA. SERVES 4.

 2 tablespoons unsalted butter
 1 tablespoon extra-virgin olive oil
 1 medium onion, minced
 2 medium garlic cloves, minced
 1 teaspoon minced fresh rosemary leaves
 1 pound white button mushrooms, stems trimmed and sliced thin
 1 ounce dried porcini mushrooms, rehydrated, strained, and chopped coarse; soaking liquid reserved (see illustrations 1–2, page 169)
Salt and ground black pepper
 2 tablespoons minced fresh flat-leaf parsley leaves
 1 pound orecchiette or other small, shell-shaped pasta

1. Heat the butter and oil over medium heat in a large sauté pan. Add the onion; sauté until translucent, about 5 minutes. Add the garlic and rosemary; sauté until the garlic is golden, about 1 minute.

2. Add the button mushrooms; sauté until golden and the liquid evaporates, about 8 minutes. Add the chopped porcini; sauté to release the flavors, 1 to 2 minutes. Season with salt and pepper to taste. Add the soaking liquid; bring to a simmer. Stir in the parsley and adjust the seasonings.

3. Meanwhile, bring 4 quarts of water to a boil in a large pot. Add 1 tablespoon salt and the pasta to the boiling water. Cook until al dente. Drain the pasta and return it to the cooking pot. Toss with the sauce. Divide among 4 pasta bowls and serve immediately.

Fettuccine with Morels

MORELS ARE AMONG THE RICHEST-TASTING (AND MOST EXPENSIVE) MUSHROOMS. WE LIKE TO SHOWCASE THEM IN A LUXURIOUS ALFREDO-TYPE SAUCE. TRY THIS SAUCE IN THE SPRING, WHEN FRESH MORELS ARE AVAILABLE; OR USE DRIED MORELS THAT HAVE BEEN REHYDRATED IN WARM WATER UNTIL TENDER (15 TO 25 MINUTES) AND PATTED DRY WITH PAPER TOWELS. SERVES 4.

 1 2/3 cups heavy cream, preferably not ultrapasteurized
 5 tablespoons unsalted butter
 2 tablespoons brandy
 4 ounces fresh morels, rinsed, drained, and patted dry, or 1 ounce dried morels, soaked, drained, and patted dry (see illustrations 1–2, page 169)
Salt
 1 pound Fresh Egg Pasta (page 21) cut into fettuccine
 1 cup grated Parmesan cheese
Ground black pepper

1. Combine 1 1/3 cups cream, butter, brandy, and morels in a sauté pan large enough to accommodate the cooked pasta. Heat over low until the butter is melted and the cream comes to a bare simmer. Cover and cook at a bare simmer for 2 minutes to combine flavors. Turn off the heat and set aside.

2. Bring 4 quarts of water to a boil in a large pot. Add 1 tablespoon salt and the pasta to the boiling water. Cook until almost al dente. Drain the pasta and add it to the sauté pan. Add the remaining 1/3 cup cream, cheese, 1/2 teaspoon salt, and pepper to taste. Cook over very low heat, tossing to combine ingredients, until the sauce is slightly thickened, 1 to 2 minutes. Divide among 4 warmed pasta bowls and serve immediately.

Sauces with Onions

ONIONS ARE USED AS part of the base for hundreds of pasta sauces. On a few occasions, onions can be the dominant ingredient, and for these recipes the onions are usually not minced. Slicing or chopping keeps the onions from melting into the sauce. When onions are the focal point, they should be sautéed until golden to bring out their full flavor. This means keeping the heating at a moderate level (you don't want the onions to scorch before they cook through) and cooking them for at least ten minutes.

We like regular yellow onions in the recipes that follow, but they can be made with sweet onions (such as Vidalias) or even red onions with slightly different results.

◆

Fusilli with Onions, Black Olives, and Capers

THIS INTENSELY FLAVORED DISH IS A GOOD PRELUDE TO OR SIDE DISH FOR A MEAL OF EQUALLY RICH-TASTING FISH SUCH AS BLUEFISH OR TUNA. SERVES 4.

¼ cup extra-virgin olive oil
2 medium onions, sliced thin
6 garlic cloves, sliced thin
½ cup Kalamata or other large black olives, pitted and coarsely chopped (see illustrations 1–2, page 62)
2 anchovy fillets, minced
1 tablespoon balsamic vinegar
1 teaspoon minced fresh marjoram or ½ teaspoon dried
2 tablespoons minced fresh flat-leaf parsley leaves
Salt and ground black pepper
1 pound fusilli or other short, curly pasta

1. Heat the oil in a large sauté pan. Add the onions and sauté over medium heat until golden, about 10 minutes. Add the garlic; sauté until fragrant, about 1 minute. Stir in the olives, anchovies, vinegar, marjoram, parsley, and salt and pepper to taste.

2. Meanwhile, bring 4 quarts of water to a boil in a large pot. Add 1 tablespoon salt and the pasta to the boiling water. Cook until al dente. Drain the pasta and return it to the cooking pot. Toss with the sauce. Divide among 4 pasta bowls and serve immediately.

◆

Fettuccine with Caramelized Onions, White Wine, and Cream

SAUTEED ONIONS BECOME CREAMY AND SWEET; WITH THE ADDITION OF WHITE WINE AND HEAVY CREAM, THEY MAKE A RICH-TASTING AND SOPHISTICATED PASTA SAUCE. FOR VARIETY, TRY REPLACING THE PARSLEY WITH A HANDFUL OF MIXED CHOPPED HERBS FROM THE GARDEN. SERVES 4.

¼ cup extra-virgin olive oil
4 medium onions, chopped
½ cup white wine
¼ cup heavy cream
2 tablespoons minced fresh flat-leaf parsley leaves
Salt and ground black pepper
1 pound Fresh Egg Pasta (page 21) cut into fettuccine or dried fettuccine
½ cup grated Parmesan cheese

1. Heat the oil in a large sauté pan. Add the onions and sauté over medium-low heat until deep golden, 15 to 18 minutes. Raise the heat to medium, and add the wine. Simmer, scraping the bottom of the pan to loosen any brown bits, until the aroma of alcohol fades, about 3 minutes. Stir in the cream and parsley, cook until slightly thickened, about 1 minute, and remove from the heat. Season with salt and pepper to taste.

2. Meanwhile, bring 4 quarts of water to a boil in a large pot. Add 1 tablespoon salt and the pasta to the boiling water. Cook until al dente. Drain the pasta and return it to the cooking pot. Toss with the sauce and cheese. Divide among 4 pasta bowls and serve immediately.

Sauces with Peas

IF YOU HAVE GROWN peas yourself, you know how good they can be. However, fresh peas bought at the supermarket are always a disappointment. After all the work that shelling entails, fresh peas are usually bland and mealy. (Unless you grow your own, we suggest avoiding fresh shell peas.) Frozen peas are fine in a simple side dish made with orzo, lemon, and garlic, but when we want to make a main-course pasta with peas, we choose sugar snap peas.

Sugar snaps first came to market in the 1970s. They are a cross between the snow pea and the green garden pea. The entire pea, pod and all, is edible. Good sugar snaps look like compact fresh garden peas in the shell. They are firm and lustrous with barely discernible bumps along the pods.

Raw sugar snaps taste chalky and flat, but they can turn to mush if overcooked. They taste best crisptender. We tested several cooking methods to see which would deliver the best results. Sautéing was problematic because the peas did not soften quickly enough. By the time they were tender enough to eat, they had lost their bright green color.

Steaming yielded tender peas that tasted flat. Peas benefit from being cooked with some salt, so blanching seemed like the obvious best choice. Although boiling in salted water yielded peas with excellent flavor and texture, the peas tended to shrivel or pucker a bit as they cooled. We solved this problem by plunging the cooked peas into ice water as soon as they were drained. This also helped set their bright color and prevent further softening from residual heat.

Penne with Sugar Snap Peas, Ham, and Mint

SUGAR SNAP PEAS SHOULD BE EATEN COOKED, BUT JUST BARELY. THEY TASTE BEST WHEN THEY ARE STILL QUITE CRISP. ADD THEM TO THE PASTA A MERE MINUTE OR TWO BEFORE IT IS READY. TWO CUPS FRESH OR FROZEN SHELLED PEAS MAY BE SUBSTITUTED. DO NOT USE SLICED BOILED HAM FOR THIS RECIPE. RATHER, BUY A SMALL HUNK OF COUNTRY OR SMOKED HAM AND CUT IT INTO QUARTER-INCH DICE. SERVES 4.

2 tablespoons unsalted butter
2 tablespoons extra-virgin olive oil
¼ pound country or smoked ham, cut into ¼-inch dice
1 tablespoon chopped fresh chives
Salt
¾ pound sugar snap peas, stems snipped off
1 pound penne or other short, tubular pasta
2 tablespoons chopped fresh mint leaves
½ cup grated Parmesan cheese
Ground black pepper

1. Heat the butter and olive oil in a small skillet. Add the ham and chives; sauté until fragrant, 1 to 2 minutes. Set aside.

2. Meanwhile, bring 4 quarts of water to a boil in a large pot. Add 1 tablespoon salt and the peas to the boiling water. Cook until crisp-tender, 1½ to 2 minutes. Remove the peas from the pot with a slotted spoon and transfer them to a bowl of ice water. Drain and pat dry.

3. Add the pasta to the boiling water. Cook until al dente. Drain the pasta and return it to the cooking pot. Toss with the peas, ham mixture, mint, and cheese. Adjust the seasonings. Divide among 4 pasta bowls and serve immediately.

Orzo with Peas, Lemon, and Garlic

TINY, RICE-SHAPED ORZO IS A GOOD PAIR WITH PEAS. THE ORZO MAKES AN EXCELLENT ACCOMPANIMENT TO FISH, CHICKEN, OR VEAL. UNLESS YOU GROW YOUR OWN PEAS, FROZEN PEAS ARE LIKELY TO BE BETTER THAN FRESH. **SERVES 6 TO 8 AS A SIDE DISH.**

- 4 tablespoons unsalted butter
- 4 medium garlic cloves, minced
- 1 teaspoon grated lemon zest (see illustration, page 42)
- 1 tablespoon lemon juice
- Salt
- 1 pound orzo
- 2 1/2 cups fresh or frozen green peas
- 2 tablespoons minced fresh basil leaves
- 1/2 cup grated Parmesan cheese

1. Heat 2 tablespoons butter in a small skillet. Add the garlic and sauté until golden, 1 to 2 minutes. Stir in the zest and juice. Set aside.

2. Meanwhile, bring 4 quarts of water to a boil in a large pot. Add 1 tablespoon salt and the pasta to the boiling water. Cook until almost al dente. Add the peas and cook until just tender, 30 seconds to 1 minute. Drain the pasta and peas and return them to the cooking pot. Toss with the garlic mixture, remaining 2 tablespoons butter, basil, and cheese. Serve immediately.

Sauces with Peppers

ROASTING BELL PEPPERS is our preferred way to use this vegetable in pasta sauces. Their crisp flesh is rendered soft and silky, making it a much better match with pasta. The flavor is improved as well, becoming sweeter, smokier, and altogether more complex. Sometimes, however, the flesh becomes too soft, even mushy. Ideally, peppers should be cooked just long enough to loosen their skins and bring out the desirable flavors. The flesh should soften but not fall apart.

So what's the best way to roast a pepper? We roasted a lot to find out. We first roasted peppers over a stovetop gas burner. We knew this method had limited appeal, but wondered if it should be first choice of cooks with gas stoves. The one benefit to this method is that the peppers are roasted whole and keep all their juices. The peppers should be held in place with tongs, not a long-handled fork, which pierces the skin and causes the pepper to drip everywhere. We found several disadvantages to this method. The peppers require constant tending and they tend to cook unevenly, no matter how diligently they are turned. Worst of all, you can only roast one pepper at a time.

Our second approach was high-heat roasting in a 550-degree oven. Whether the peppers are kept whole or split open and flattened, this method takes at least fifteen minutes. By this time, the peppers are soggy and overcooked. Lower oven temperatures take even longer and also overcook the peppers.

Broiling whole peppers has problems as well. The broiler element in most ovens is about 3 inches away from the upper rack, which means that whole peppers usually touch the element. When placed on a lower rack, the cooking time is too long and the flesh becomes mushy.

We finally stumbled upon the answer when we cut up the peppers before broiling. The skin is easier to lift off the roasted peppers when they have been cut into wedges before cooking. It's also much easier to remove those pesky seeds from raw peppers.

We found that steaming the roasted peppers is helpful but not essential. The skin lifts off fairly easily once the roasted pepper wedges have been cooled. To make the process even quicker, you can put the peppers in a glass bowl and cover the bowl with plastic wrap for fifteen minutes. The choice is yours.

Roasted peppers can be drizzled with olive oil and refrigerated in an airtight container for up to one week. We found that they don't freeze very well, so don't try roasting dozens of peppers at once, unless of course you are planning to use them all quickly.

When you don't have the time to roast peppers, you can cut them into thin strips and sauté. Their texture is not nearly as silky (in fact, they will remain a bit crunchy) and the flavor is not as sweet. However, sautéed peppers are still a good addition to pasta sauces and are certainly much less work to prepare.

Farfalle with Roasted Red and Yellow Pepper Sauce

THIS SAUCE IS COMPATIBLE WITH ALMOST ANY STRING OR RIBBON-TYPE PASTA EXCEPT ANGEL HAIR, AND IS PARTICULARLY NICE WITH FARFALLE. MOST MACARONI-TYPE PASTAS ARE ALSO SUITABLE EXCEPT FOR SMALL PASTINE OR THE LARGE TUBULAR VARIETIES. CHOP THE PEPPERS WITH A KNIFE. DO NOT USE A FOOD PROCESSOR BECAUSE IT WILL PUREE THE PEPPERS, CAUSING THEM TO BLEND RATHER THAN TO RETAIN THEIR BRILLIANT RED AND YELLOW COLORS. TOSS THIS AT ROOM TEMPERATURE WITH HOT PASTA, USING SOME OF THE PASTA WATER TO THIN THE SAUCE. SERVES 4.

2 medium yellow bell peppers and 2 medium red bell peppers, roasted and peeled (see illustrations 1–7, page 175)
6 tablespoons extra-virgin olive oil
1 large garlic clove, minced
Salt and ground black pepper
1 pound farfalle, fettuccine, or other thick ribbon pasta

1. Finely chop the peppers and mix with the oil and garlic in a large bowl. Season with salt and pepper to taste. Cover and set aside to let the flavors meld, at least 30 minutes.

2. Bring 4 quarts of water to a boil in a large pot. Add 1 tablespoon salt and the pasta to the boiling water. Cook until al dente. Drain, reserving ¼ cup of the cooking water. Return the pasta to the cooking pot and toss with the sauce, adding the reserved cooking water as needed to moisten the pasta. Divide among 4 pasta bowls and serve immediately.

Fettuccine with Roasted Red Pepper–Cream Sauce

FRESH EGG PASTA ABSORBS THIS ROASTED PEPPER SAUCE WONDERFULLY, BUT DRIED PASTA ALSO WORKS WELL. CANNED CHIPOTLE CHILES GIVE THE SAUCE AN EXTRA-SMOKY FLAVOR; THEY ARE AVAILABLE IN LATIN MARKETS AND MANY SUPERMARKETS. SUBSTITUTE CAYENNE PEPPER TO TASTE, IF YOU LIKE; IT WILL ADD HEAT WITHOUT THE SMOKINESS. SERVES 4.

2 tablespoons extra-virgin olive oil
1 medium onion, minced
2 medium garlic cloves, minced
2 medium red bell peppers, roasted and peeled (see illustrations 1–7, page 175), then diced
1 cup chicken stock or low-sodium canned broth
½ cup heavy cream
½ canned chipotle chile in adobo, minced, or ¼ teaspoon cayenne pepper, or to taste
Salt
1 pound Fresh Egg Pasta (page 21) cut into fettuccine or dried fettuccine

1. Heat the oil in a large sauté pan over medium heat. Add the onion and cook until softened, 3 to 4 minutes. Add the garlic and cook until fragrant, 1 to 2 minutes. Add the peppers, stock, cream, and chile. Simmer over low heat until slightly thickened, about 5 minutes. Puree the sauce in a food processor or blender. Return the sauce to the skillet and season with salt to taste.

2. Meanwhile, bring 4 quarts of water to a boil in a large pot. Add 1 tablespoon salt and the pasta to the boiling water. Cook until al dente. Drain the pasta and return it to the cooking pot. Toss with the sauce. Divide among 4 pasta bowls and serve immediately.

ROASTING BELL PEPPERS

1. Slice ¼ inch from the top and bottom of the pepper.

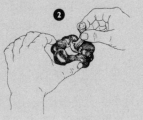

2. Gently remove the stem from the top lobe.

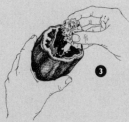

3. Pull the core out of the pepper.

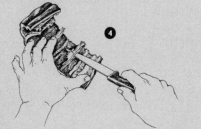

4. Slit down one side of the pepper, then lay it flat, skin side down, in one long strip. Use a sharp knife to slide

along the inside of the pepper, removing all white ribs and any remaining seeds.

5. Arrange the strips of peppers and the top and bottom lobes on a foil-lined baking sheet, skin side up. Flatten the strips with your hands.

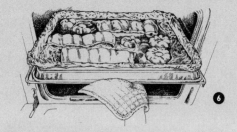

6. Adjust the oven rack to its top position. If the rack is more than 3½ inches from the heating element, set a jelly-roll pan, bottom up, on the rack under the baking sheet to raise it.

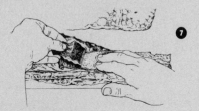

7. Roast until the skin of the peppers is charred and puffed up like a balloon but the flesh is still firm. You may steam the peppers in a covered bowl at this point or not, as you wish. Start peeling where the skin has charred and bubbled the most. The skin will come off in large strips.

Fusilli with Bell Peppers and Balsamic Vinegar

SAUTEING PEPPERS IS QUICKER THAN ROASTING AND RESULTS IN A SAUCE WITH MORE CRUNCH. RED PEPPERS GIVE THIS DISH SWEETNESS; GREEN PEPPERS GIVE IT COLOR. SERVES 4.

> 2 tablespoons extra-virgin olive oil
> 1 medium garlic clove, minced
> 1/2 medium red bell pepper, stemmed, cored, and sliced thin
> 1/2 medium green bell pepper, stemmed, cored, and sliced thin
> 1 1/2 cups diced canned tomatoes
> 1 tablespoon balsamic or red wine vinegar
> Salt and ground black pepper
> 1 pound fusilli or other short, curly pasta

1. Heat the oil over medium heat in a medium saucepan; add the garlic and bell peppers. Cover and cook until the vegetables soften, about 5 minutes. Add the tomatoes; simmer, uncovered, until thickened, about 15 minutes. Stir in the vinegar and season to taste with salt and pepper.

2. Meanwhile, bring 4 quarts of water to a boil in a large pot. Add 1 tablespoon salt and the pasta to the boiling water. Cook just until al dente. Drain the pasta and return it to the pot. Toss with the sauce. Divide among 4 pasta bowls and serve immediately.

Sauces with Radicchio

RADICCHIO MAKES A DELICIOUS if somewhat unusual addition to pasta sauces. The leaves can be shredded like cabbage and then sautéed until tender and lightly browned. Sautéing adds some sweetness to the radicchio and helps balance the inherent bitter flavor of this red chicory. Radicchio is quite dry and needs some liquid before it can be tossed with pasta. We also found that sautéed radicchio, even when the cooking time was ten minutes or more, was still fairly crunchy. Simmering wilted radicchio in some liquid makes it especially tender and helps it to combine with pasta better.

As for the choice of liquid, we used chicken stock successfully in our kitchen tests. However, we found that the sweetness of heavy cream is a better foil for the strong flavor of radicchio. Cream tames some of the remaining bitterness and, of course, adds richness.

◆

Fettuccine with Radicchio and Cream

THIS UNUSUAL DISH IS A GOOD PRELUDE TO A MEAL OF ROASTED VEAL OR PORK. SERVES 4, OR 6 TO 8 AS A FIRST COURSE.

> 2 tablespoons unsalted butter
> 1 medium onion, minced
> 1 small head radicchio (about 1/2 pound), wilted outer leaves and core removed; remaining leaves shredded
> 1/2 cup heavy cream
> Salt and ground black pepper
> 1 pound fettuccine or other long, wide pasta
> 1/2 cup grated Parmesan cheese
> 2 tablespoons minced fresh flat-leaf parsley leaves

1. Heat the butter over medium heat in a skillet large enough to hold the cooked pasta. Add the onion and cook until softened, 3 to 4 minutes. Add the radicchio and cook, stirring occasionally, until tender, 5 to 7 minutes. Stir in the cream and cook until slightly thickened, 1 to 2 minutes. Season with salt and pepper to taste.

2. Meanwhile, bring 4 quarts of water to a boil in a large pot. Add 1 tablespoon salt and the pasta to the boiling water and cook until al dente. Drain the pasta and transfer it to the skillet. Stir in the cheese and parsley. Divide among 4 pasta bowls and serve immediately.

Sauces with Zucchini

GIVEN ZUCCHINI'S ABILITY to take over a garden, it's no surprise that cooks have devised dozens of ways to use this vegetable in pasta sauces. But what are the best ways to cook zucchini?

The main problem that confronts the cook when preparing zucchini is its wateriness. Zucchini is 95 percent water (among vegetables, only lettuce contains more water) and will become soupy if it is just thrown into a hot pan.

If zucchini cooks in its own juices it will not brown. Since browning gives zucchini (as well as other foods) a rich, sweet flavor, we wanted to figure out a way to rid zucchini of some its water before cooking. We also suspected that water was responsible for another problem we often encountered when cooking zucchini. We sometimes find that thick slices of zucchini are soft on the outside but firm and crunchy in the middle after cooking. We wanted to devise a method to ensure that the zucchini was evenly cooked throughout.

The first precautions against wateriness must take place in the supermarket. Size and firmness are the most important factors when purchasing zucchini. Smaller zucchini are more flavorful and less watery than larger specimens. Smaller zucchini also have fewer seeds. We look for zucchini that weigh less than 8 ounces, and ideally less than 6 ounces. Mammoth zucchini may be fine as boats for a vegetable stuffing, but they are not good for much else.

The second issue is preparation. Many cookbooks recommend salting zucchini in order to draw out some of the moisture before cooking. The chemistry behind this reaction is quite simple. Water inside the zucchini is attracted to areas of higher ion concentration on the salted surface.

After conducting about a dozen tests with salting, we found this step was sometimes but not always necessary—it depended on the cooking method. Given the intense heat of the grill, we found that the high moisture content in the zucchini actually helps prevent the vegetable from scorching over hot coals. In effect, the water allows the zucchini to cook through without becoming incinerated. Also, since the cooking surface on a grill is open, water simply drops down onto the coals rather than sitting in a skillet. So much evaporation occurs during grilling over a hot fire that salting is not an issue.

Sautéing, however, is another matter. Even in a blazing hot pan, the zucchini will soon start to steam in its own juices. We found two methods for eliminating some of the water from zucchini before cooking. Sliced zucchini that was tossed with 1½ teaspoons of kosher salt per pound shed about 20 percent of its weight after sitting for thirty minutes. Almost 3 tablespoons of water was thrown off by the zucchini, further confirmation that the salt was in fact drawing out water. Although salting is not worth the effort unless you have thirty minutes, we found that longer periods (we tried up to three hours) did not increase the amount of moisture that was extracted.

As you might expect, varying amounts of salt were more or less effective. However, even with rinsing we thought zucchini sprinkled with more than 1½ teaspoons of kosher salt per pound was too salty after cooking. The 1½ teaspoons of salt delivered the maximum results while not adversely affecting flavor if the zucchini was rinsed and thoroughly dried just before cooking.

If you don't have the time to salt the zucchini before sautéing, there is another option. Moisture from grated zucchini can be extracted manually by simply wrapping shredded zucchini between several layers of paper towels or a large kitchen towel and squeezing. In fact, we were able to reduce the weight of shredded zucchini by 25 percent (more than salting ever achieved) by firmly squeezing it in paper towels. Since sliced zucchini has so much less surface area, this manual method for water extraction does not work.

In addition to salting, there is some controversy about soaking zucchini before cooking. Many Italian cookbooks claim that soaking zucchini "freshens" their flavor. In our tests, we found no difference between whole zucchini soaked in a bowl of cold water for thirty minutes before slicing or shredding and zucchini that was simply washed. Although we had expected soaked zucchini to become even more waterlogged, they showed no weight gain at all—no doubt a testament to their thick skins.

Our recommendation is to skip soaking unless the zucchini is particularly dirty. Because zucchini grows close to the ground, small particles of sand or dirt sometimes become embedded in the skin. A quick washing under cold water is usually sufficient to remove any dirt. However, if you feel any grit when you run your hand over washed zucchini, soaking for five minutes in a bowl of cold water is advised, as is thorough scrubbing.

Zucchini benefits from dry-heat cooking methods like grilling, since liquid in the vegetable evaporates, concentrating the delicate flavor. Zucchini can also be sautéed over medium-high heat until golden brown, a process that also concentrates flavor as the vegetable sheds water.

◆

Penne with Sautéed Zucchini and Goat Cheese

SALTING ZUCCHINI AND DRAINING IT BEFORE SAUTE-ING RESULTS IN LESS WATERY SLICES THAT ARE NICELY BROWNED. QUARTER-INCH SLICES ARE THE PERFECT THICKNESS. THINNER SLICES FALL APART DURING COOKING; THICKER SLICES REQUIRE A LONGER SALTING TIME. WE LIKE SMALL QUANTITIES OF STRONGER HERBS —OREGANO, THYME, MARJORAM—IN THIS RECIPE. IF YOU'D LIKE TO USE MILDER BASIL, PARSLEY, OR MINT, DOUBLE THE TOTAL QUANTITY OF HERBS. SERVES 4.

4 small zucchini (about 1 pound), rinsed, trimmed, and sliced crosswise into rounds about ¼ inch thick (see illustration 1, page 179)

Kosher salt

¼ cup extra-virgin olive oil

2 large garlic cloves, minced

1 teaspoon finely chopped fresh oregano leaves

1 teaspoon finely chopped fresh thyme leaves

1 teaspoon finely chopped fresh marjoram leaves

1 pound penne or other short, tubular pasta

4 ounces fresh goat cheese, crumbled

1. Place the zucchini slices in a colander and sprinkle with 1½ teaspoons salt. Set the colander over a bowl until about 3 tablespoons water drains from the zucchini, about 30 minutes. Rinse and thoroughly dry the zucchini.

2. Heat the oil in a large skillet over medium-high heat. Add the zucchini and sauté, stirring frequently, until golden and tender, 8 to 10 minutes. Add the garlic and herbs and cook until fragrant, another minute.

3. Meanwhile, bring 4 quarts of water to a boil in a large pot. Add 1 tablespoon salt and the pasta to the boiling water. Cook until al dente. Reserve ½ cup cooking liquid and drain the pasta. Return the pasta to the cooking pot. Toss with the sauce and cheese. If the pasta seems too dry, add the cooking liquid 1 tablespoon at a time until you reach the desired consistency. Divide the pasta among 4 bowls and serve immediately.

◆

Fettuccine with Zucchini, Red Pepper, and Tomato Sauce

SERVE THIS RATATOUILLE-LIKE SAUCE WITH WHOLE WHEAT PASTA IF POSSIBLE. THE GRAINY, NUTTY FLAVOR OF THIS PASTA CONTRASTS BEAUTIFULLY WITH THE SOFT, SWEET VEGETABLES. THE SAUCE ALSO WORKS WELL WITH PLAIN PASTA. SERVES 4.

4 small zucchini (about 1 pound), rinsed, trimmed, and sliced crosswise into rounds about ¼ inch thick (see illustration 1, page 179)

Kosher salt

5 tablespoons extra-virgin olive oil

2 large shallots, minced

2 large garlic cloves, minced

1 medium red bell pepper, stemmed, seeded, and cut into medium dice

2 tablespoons minced fresh mint leaves

2 teaspoons minced fresh thyme leaves

2 medium tomatoes (about ¾ pound), peeled, seeded, and diced (see illustrations 1–4, page 111)

1 pound fettuccine

1. Place the zucchini slices in a colander and sprinkle with 1½ teaspoons salt. Set the colander over a bowl until about 3 tablespoons water drains from the zucchini, about 30 minutes. Rinse and thoroughly dry the zucchini.

2. Heat 3 tablespoons oil in a large skillet over medium-high heat. Add the zucchini and sauté, stirring frequently, until golden and tender, 8 to 10 minutes. Add the shallots, garlic, and pepper and sauté to soften slightly, 2 to 3 minutes. Stir in the mint, thyme, and salt to taste. Add the tomatoes; cook until the tomatoes release their juices and thicken slightly, 2 to 3 minutes. Remove from the heat and stir in the remaining 2 tablespoons oil. Adjust the seasonings.

3. Meanwhile, bring 4 quarts of water to a boil in a large pot. Add 1 tablespoon salt and the pasta to the boiling water. Cook until al dente. Drain the pasta and return it to the cooking pot. Toss with the sauce. Divide among 4 pasta bowls and serve immediately.

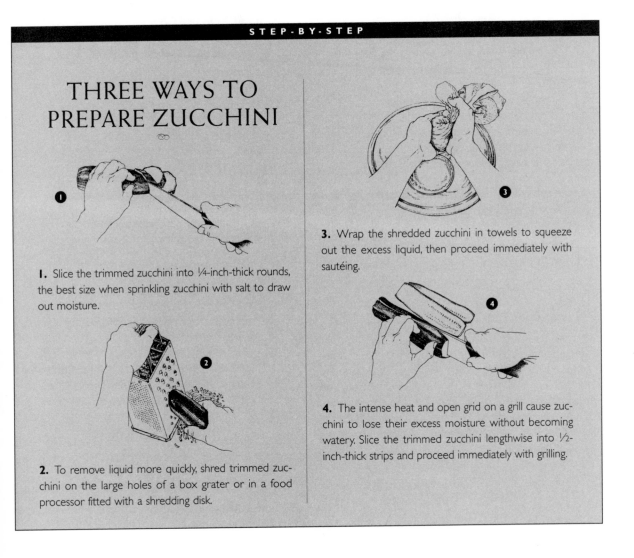

THREE WAYS TO PREPARE ZUCCHINI

1. Slice the trimmed zucchini into ¼-inch-thick rounds, the best size when sprinkling zucchini with salt to draw out moisture.

2. To remove liquid more quickly, shred trimmed zucchini on the large holes of a box grater or in a food processor fitted with a shredding disk.

3. Wrap the shredded zucchini in towels to squeeze out the excess liquid, then proceed immediately with sautéing.

4. The intense heat and open grid on a grill cause zucchini to lose their excess moisture without becoming watery. Slice the trimmed zucchini lengthwise into ½-inch-thick strips and proceed immediately with grilling.

Spaghetti with Shredded Zucchini and Carrots

THIS SHREDDING AND DRYING TECHNIQUE IS THE BEST CHOICE WHEN YOU ARE PRESSED FOR TIME AND WANT TO COOK ZUCCHINI INDOORS. USE ANY FRESH HERB ON HAND, VARYING THE AMOUNT DEPENDING ON ITS INTENSITY. FOR INSTANCE, USE 2 TABLESPOONS OF BASIL, PARSLEY, OR CHIVES, BUT JUST 1 TABLESPOON OF OREGANO, THYME, OR TARRAGON. SERVES 4.

- ¼ cup extra-virgin olive oil
- 4 small zucchini (about 1 pound), rinsed, trimmed, shredded, and squeezed dry (see illustrations 2–3, page 179)
- 2 carrots, peeled and shredded
- 2 medium garlic cloves, minced
- 1–2 tablespoons minced fresh herbs such as parsley, basil, tarragon, or mint
- Salt and ground black pepper
- 1 pound spaghetti or other long, thin shape
- 2 tablespoons unsalted butter, softened
- ½ cup grated Parmesan cheese

1. Heat the oil in a large skillet over medium-high heat. Add the zucchini, carrots, and garlic; cook, stirring occasionally, until the vegetables are tender, about 7 minutes. Stir in the herbs and salt and pepper to taste.

2. Meanwhile, bring 4 quarts of water to a boil in a large pot. Add 1 tablespoon salt and the pasta to the boiling water. Cook until al dente. Reserve ½ cup cooking liquid and drain the pasta. Return the pasta to the cooking pot. Toss with the sauce, butter, and cheese. If the pasta seems too dry, add the cooking liquid 1 tablespoon at a time until you reach the desired consistency. Divide among 4 pasta bowls and serve immediately.

Farfalle with Grilled Zucchini and Tomato

IT IS NOT NECESSARY TO SALT ZUCCHINI BEFORE GRILLING, SINCE THE HEAT FROM THE FIRE CAUSES THE LIQUID IN THE VEGETABLE TO EVAPORATE. FOR EASY TURNING ON THE GRILL, SLICE ZUCCHINI INTO THIN STRIPS RATHER THAN ROUNDS. WE USE BALSAMIC VINEGAR IN THE DRESSING, BUT RED WINE VINEGAR MAY BE SUBSTITUTED. SERVES 4.

- 4 small zucchini (about 1 pound), rinsed, trimmed, and sliced lengthwise into ½-inch-thick strips (see illustration 4, page 179)
- 6 tablespoons extra-virgin olive oil
- Salt and ground black pepper
- 1 pound farfalle or shell-shaped pasta
- 2 tablespoons balsamic vinegar
- 2 large ripe tomatoes, cored and cut into ¼-inch dice
- 2 tablespoons minced fresh basil leaves

1. Heat the grill. Lay the zucchini on a large baking sheet and brush both sides with 2 tablespoons of the oil. Sprinkle generously with salt and pepper to taste.

2. When the grill rack is hot, use a stiff wire brush to scrape the surface clean. Grill the zucchini until dark grill marks are visible on one side, 4 to 5 minutes. Turn and continue to grill until the other side is marked, about 4 minutes. Remove from the grill and cool briefly. Cut into ½-inch pieces.

3. Meanwhile, bring 4 quarts of water to a boil in a large pot. Add 1 tablespoon salt and the pasta to the boiling water. Cook until al dente.

4. While the pasta is cooking, whisk together the remaining 4 tablespoons oil with the balsamic vinegar, ½ teaspoon salt, and ¼ teaspoon pepper. Toss the tomatoes and basil with the dressing in a large bowl. Add the zucchini and toss. Adjust the seasonings.

5. Drain the pasta and toss with the zucchini mixture. Divide among 4 pasta bowls and serve immediately.

Pasta Primavera

PASTA PRIMAVERA IS THE best-known mixed vegetable pasta dish in the United States. Unlike most dishes, pasta primavera has a clear pedigree. The first version was created at Le Cirque, New York's famed French restaurant, in the 1970s. Patrons told restaurateur Sirio Maccioni that they wanted healthier, lighter dishes, so he created a pasta dish loaded with fresh vegetables. He dubbed his invention spaghetti primavera—*primavera* is the Italian word for spring—and it quickly became a New York sensation. Within a few short years, pasta primavera (as the dish was renamed by most restaurants) became as common as roast chicken or grilled steak on American menus.

We used to make the Le Cirque recipe. We loved the flavors and it was always a winner with company. But eventually we decided that Le Cirque's spaghetti primavera was just too much work. The recipe calls for blanching each green vegetable in a separate pot to retain its individual character. We reused the same pot to cook the six green vegetables (broccoli, green beans, peas, snow peas, zucchini, and asparagus), so this first step took almost an hour.

If that wasn't enough of a bother, once the vegetables were blanched, we still need *five* more pots to make this dish—one to cook the vegetables in garlicky olive oil; one to sauté mushrooms; one to make a fresh tomato sauce flavored with basil; one to make a cream sauce with butter and Parmesan; and one to cook the pasta.

No single task was difficult, but the timing was complicated and better suited to a professional kitchen where different cooks could handle different jobs. And the total prep time of the original recipe is nearly two hours. We wanted to make this appealing dish a lot simpler to execute, but still keep the fresh vegetable flavors that attracted us to this dish in the first place.

The first issue was to decide which vegetables were a must for primavera sauce, and which could be dropped. Despite its name, this dish as originally conceived contains many non-spring vegetables, including broccoli, green beans, and zucchini. Only the peas, snow peas, and asparagus are truly spring vegetables.

We began testing other spring vegetables and soon realized why they were not included. Artichokes were way too much work to prepare, adding another half hour to the prep time. We liked the flavor of leeks but found they tasted better when sautéed rather than blanched, which meant an extra pan and more work. We usually like fennel, but its sweet anise flavor overwhelmed the other vegetables.

We decided to jettison the broccoli (tasters liked this vegetable the least in this sauce) and snow peas (the pea family was already represented by shelled peas). That left four spring-summer vegetables—asparagus, peas, zucchini, and green beans. You could eliminate one or even two of these vegetables and increase the quantity of the remaining vegetables. However, this compromise did not save any time and tasters felt that the name *primavera* connotes a variety of vegetables, not just two or three.

With the vegetables chosen, we had to figure out how to cook them. We rejected the notion of blanching each in a separate pot of water. We found we could blanch all the green vegetables together in a single pot. To make sure each was properly cooked, we had to add them at different times—but after some trial and error we devised a cooking regimen: green beans first, followed by the asparagus, then the zucchini, and ending with the peas.

We tried adding the cooked vegetables directly to the drained pasta. They were watery and bland. Clearly, they needed to be sautéed to build flavor. A couple of minutes in a hot skillet with some garlicky butter is essential.

In the original recipe, the mushrooms are sautéed and then added to the green vegetables and then sautéed again. We wondered if we could just keep the mushrooms in the pan and build the tomato sauce on top of them. This worked fine. We tried cooking the mushroom-tomato sauce (as well as the green vegetables) in butter and in olive oil. Tasters preferred the sweet, rich flavor of the butter, which worked better with the cream.

Next, we focused on the tomatoes. We concluded that this dish needs fresh tomatoes for flavor and juiciness. Plum tomatoes are not as watery as fresh round tomatoes and are best in this dish.

Finally, we found that a separate pot for the cream sauce (with butter, cheese, and cream) was unnecessary. We reduced some cream in the mushroom-tomato mixture and discovered that this worked fine. There was plenty of butter in the sauce already, and we found that cheese could just as well be sprinkled on at the table. So instead of three pans—one for mushrooms, one for tomato sauce, and one for cream sauce, we had cooked them together in one pan.

Our recipe was just as delicious as the original and we were down to just three pans. We had also reduced total preparation and cooking time by more than half. Pasta primavera may not be Tuesday night supper, but when you want a fancier pasta dish, there's no reason to run screaming when someone suggests primavera sauce.

Pasta Primavera

SERVES 6 AS A MAIN COURSE,
10 AS A FIRST COURSE

THE RIGHT PASTA WILL greatly improve this dish. We tested six nationally available brands and found that dried egg noodles from DeCecco and Delverde were far superior to the competition. They cooked up springy yet tender and have a pleasant egg flavor that works well with the cream and butter in the sauce. These noodles are more porous than pasta made without eggs so they do a better job of absorbing some of the sauce. We found that fresh egg fettuccine actually becomes a bit overwhelmed by all the vegetables in this dish and we don't think it's worth the effort in this case.

Salt
6 ounces green beans, cut into ¾-inch pieces
12 medium asparagus spears, tough ends snapped off, halved lengthwise, and cut diagonally into ¾-inch pieces (see illustrations 1–3, page 138)
1 medium zucchini, cut into ½-inch dice
1 cup frozen peas, thawed
6 tablespoons unsalted butter
8 ounces white button mushrooms, ends trimmed and sliced thin
4 large plum tomatoes (about 1 pound), cored, peeled, and diced (see illustrations 1–3, page 112)
½ teaspoon hot red pepper flakes (optional)
⅓ cup heavy cream
1 pound dried egg fettuccine
2 medium garlic cloves, minced
¼ cup shredded fresh basil leaves
1½ tablespoons lemon juice
Grated Parmesan cheese for the table

1. Bring 6 quarts of water to a boil in a large stockpot for cooking the pasta. Bring 3 quarts of water to a boil in a large saucepan for cooking the green vegetables. Fill a large bowl with ice water and set it aside.

2. Add salt to taste and the green beans to the boiling water in the saucepan. Cook for 1½ minutes. Add the asparagus and cook for 30 seconds. Add the zucchini and cook for 30 seconds. Add the peas and cook for 30 seconds. Drain the vegetables and immediately plunge them into the bowl filled with ice water. When chilled, drain and set aside.

3. Heat 3 tablespoons butter over medium-high heat in the now-empty saucepan. Add the mushrooms and sauté over medium-high heat until golden brown, about 8 minutes. Add the tomatoes and red pepper flakes (if using), reduce the heat to medium, and simmer until the tomatoes begin to lose their shape, about 7 minutes. Add the cream and simmer until slightly thickened, about 4 minutes. Add salt to taste; cover to keep warm and set aside.

4. Add 1 tablespoon salt and the pasta to the boiling water in the stockpot and cook until just al dente.

5. While the pasta is cooking, heat the remaining 3 tablespoons butter in a large skillet over medium heat until foamy. Add the garlic and sauté over medium heat until lightly colored, about 1 minute. Add the green vegetables and sauté until heated through and nicely flavored, about 2 minutes. Season with salt to taste, cover, and set aside. Meanwhile, bring the mushroom-tomato sauce back to a simmer over medium heat.

6. Drain the pasta and return it back to the now-empty stockpot. Add the mushroom-tomato sauce and toss to coat over low heat. Add the vegetables, basil, and lemon juice; season to taste with salt and toss well. Divide portions among individual bowls. Serve immediately with cheese passed separately at the table.

Lighter Pasta Primavera

WHILE NOT AS DELECTABLY RICH AS THE MASTER RECIPE, THIS VERSION HAS CONSIDERABLY LESS SATURATED FAT AND IS STILL DELICIOUS. SERVES 6 AS A MAIN COURSE, 10 AS A FIRST COURSE.

Salt

6 ounces green beans, cut into ¾-inch pieces

12 medium asparagus spears, tough ends snapped off, halved lengthwise, and cut diagonally into ¾-inch pieces (see illustrations 1–3, page 138)

1 medium zucchini, cut into ½-inch dice

1 cup frozen peas, thawed

4 tablespoons extra-virgin olive oil

8 ounces white button mushrooms, ends trimmed and sliced thin

4 large plum tomatoes (about 1 pound), cored, peeled, and diced (see illustrations 1–3, page 112)

½ teaspoon hot red pepper flakes (optional)

⅓ cup chicken stock or low-sodium canned broth

1 pound dried egg fettuccine

2 medium garlic cloves, minced

2 tablespoons unsalted butter, softened

¼ cup shredded fresh basil leaves

1½ tablespoons lemon juice

Grated Parmesan cheese for the table

1. Bring 6 quarts of water to a boil in a large stockpot for cooking the pasta. Bring 3 quarts of water to a boil in a large saucepan for cooking the green vegetables. Fill a large bowl with ice water and set it aside.

2. Add salt to taste and the green beans to the boiling water in the saucepan. Cook for 1½ minutes. Add the asparagus and cook for 30 seconds. Add the zucchini and cook for 30 seconds. Add the peas and cook for 30 seconds. Drain the vegetables and immediately plunge them into the bowl filled with ice water. When chilled, drain and set aside.

(continued on next page)

3. Heat 2 tablespoons oil over medium-high heat in the now-empty saucepan. Add the mushrooms and sauté over medium-high heat until golden brown, about 8 minutes. Add the tomatoes and red pepper flakes (if using), reduce the heat to medium, and simmer until the tomatoes begin to lose their shape, about 7 minutes. Add the stock and simmer until slightly thickened, about 4 minutes. Add salt to taste; cover to keep warm and set aside.

4. Add 1 tablespoon salt and the pasta to the boiling water in the stockpot and cook until just al dente.

5. While the pasta is cooking, heat the remaining 2 tablespoons oil in a large skillet over medium heat until foamy. Add the garlic and sauté over medium heat until lightly colored, about 1 minute. Add the green vegetables and sauté until heated through and nicely flavored, about 2 minutes. Season with salt to taste, cover, and set aside. Meanwhile, bring the mushroom-tomato sauce back to a simmer over medium heat. Swirl in the butter to thicken the sauce.

6. Drain the pasta and add it back to the now-empty stockpot. Add the mushroom-tomato sauce and toss to coat over low heat. Add the vegetables, basil, and lemon juice; season to taste with salt and toss well. Divide portions among individual bowls. Serve immediately with cheese passed separately at the table.

SAUCES

WITH BEANS

AND LENTILS

/|\

DRIED LEGUMES—CANNELLINI BEANS, CHICKPEAS,

LENTILS, AND MORE—MAKE ESPECIALLY HEARTY PASTA

SAUCES. MANY OF THESE DISHES ARE BEST IN THE

WINTER—NONE IS VERY LIGHT—AND ARE IDEAL FOR A

VEGETARIAN MAIN COURSE. ◆ OUR MAIN QUESTION

WHEN MAKING PASTA AND BEANS IS HOW TO COOK

the beans. At the outset, we decided to divide our work into two parts—dried beans and lentils. The latter are never soaked before cooking and are considered separately (see page 193).

We set out to discover the best way to cook beans. We assumed that the method for various dried beans would be the same but that the cooking times would vary. Besides developing flavor, we wanted a cooking process that would produce beans that were tender but not mushy. Beans, especially those that will be used in a pasta sauce, should have some tooth.

Our first discovery was the importance of using plenty of water. When we cooked beans in just enough water to cover, the beans on the top of the pot cooked more slowly. We ended up extending the cooking time and the result was that some of the beans overcooked and became too soft. You need a full 7 cups of water for every cup of beans.

We next tested soaking overnight, no soaking, and the "quick-soak" method—bringing the beans to a boil for two minutes, turning off the heat, covering the pot, and soaking for an hour. The quick-soak method caused a large percentage of beans to burst during cooking. Overnight soaking reduced the cooking time by ten or fifteen minutes, but did not improve the texture. Since most cooks are rarely organized enough to soak beans, we have omitted this step from our final recipe.

To examine the theory that salt toughens the skins of the beans and lengthens the cooking time, we

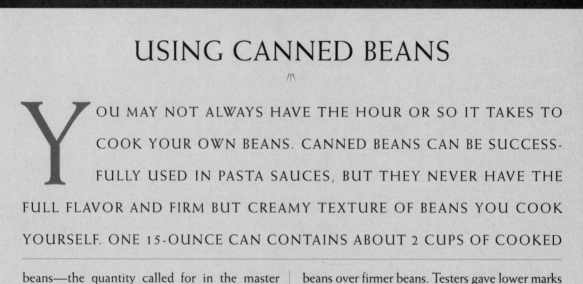

USING CANNED BEANS

YOU MAY NOT ALWAYS HAVE THE HOUR OR SO IT TAKES TO COOK YOUR OWN BEANS. CANNED BEANS CAN BE SUCCESSFULLY USED IN PASTA SAUCES, BUT THEY NEVER HAVE THE FULL FLAVOR AND FIRM BUT CREAMY TEXTURE OF BEANS YOU COOK YOURSELF. ONE 15-OUNCE CAN CONTAINS ABOUT 2 CUPS OF COOKED

beans—the quantity called for in the master recipe. Don't use the bean packing liquid in pasta sauces—it's usually very salty and has an unpleasant viscous texture. Drain and rinse beans thoroughly, and if you need liquid for the pasta sauce, use chicken stock or even plain water.

We tested six brands of white beans and red kidney beans straight from the can and in a pasta and bean soup to see how they would hold up to some further cooking.

In all tests, testers preferred creamier, softer beans over firmer beans. Testers gave lower marks to beans that were not well seasoned. Green Giant beans came out on top in both tastings and Goya was a distant second. Tasters put the two organic brands at the bottom of the rankings. The organic beans were far less salty and most tasters thought they were bland. Tasters also complained about their chalky, dry texture when tasted straight from the can. When simmered in soup, their texture improved but tasters still felt that they were too bland.

tested beans salted at the end of the cooking time, beans salted halfway through the cooking time, and beans salted at the start of the cooking time. In a blind tasting, we could not tell any difference in texture, but only those beans salted at the beginning tasted right, with the salt flavor penetrating deep in each bean. Now we always add salt at the start when cooking beans.

One nagging problem remained. We had been cooking most beans for about an hour, and we noticed that some beans were losing their shape near the end of the cooking time. We then tested cooking the beans until almost tender, then turning off the heat and allowing the beans to sit in the covered pot. The beans continue to cook, but without the agitation of the boiling water. After fifteen minutes of covered "cooking," the beans were fully cooked but there was less splitting of skins.

Each bean did require a different cooking time, based on size (larger beans generally take longer to cook) and age. Since there is no way to judge the age of the bean, it's impossible to come up with definitive cooking times for various types of beans. In general, smaller beans will take less time, but not always. Our advice is to start tasting the beans after thirty minutes of simmering. If they seem almost done, cover the pot and turn off the heat. Most beans won't be all that close after thirty minutes and will need another ten minutes or so.

In addition to salt, we tested various flavoring agents in the water. We found that bay leaves and peeled garlic cloves do the best job of lending beans some additional flavor. Other herbs are simply not strong enough, so it makes more sense to add them directly to the pasta sauce.

When turning beans into a pasta sauce, we often use some of the bean cooking liquid to provide moisture. Even if the liquid is not used in a pasta sauce, it's a good idea to store the cooked beans in their liquid, which keeps them moist for up to five days in the refrigerator. We found that beans add so much bulk to pasta sauces that the usual 1 pound of pasta is too much for four servings. Consequently, recipes in this chapter call for 12 ounces of pasta for four people.

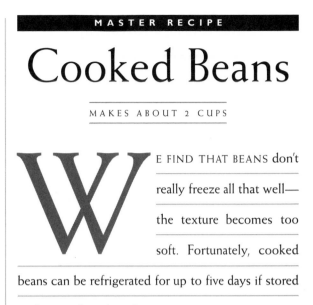

MASTER RECIPE

Cooked Beans

MAKES ABOUT 2 CUPS

WE FIND THAT BEANS don't really freeze all that well— the texture becomes too soft. Fortunately, cooked beans can be refrigerated for up to five days if stored in their cooking liquid.

> 1 cup (about 6 ounces) **dried beans**
> 1 **bay leaf**
> 4 **garlic cloves**, peeled (see illustration, page 39)
> 1 ¹/₂ teaspoons **salt**

Bring the beans, bay leaf, garlic, salt, and 7 cups water to boil in a large saucepan. Simmer, partially covered, until the beans are just tender, 30 to 45 minutes (timing will depend on the type of bean and its age). Remove from the heat, cover, and let the beans stand until completely tender, about 15 minutes. Discard the bay leaf and garlic. (The beans in liquid can be cooled, covered, and refrigerated up to 5 days.) Reserve 1 cup of cooking liquid and drain the beans when you are ready to use them.

Ditali with Escarole and White Beans

USE LARGE DITALI ("THIMBLES"), NOT THE SMALL SOUP-SIZE VERSION OF THIS PASTA. SUBSTITUTE ORECCHIETTE IF DITALI ARE UNAVAILABLE. EITHER GREEN FROM THE CHICORY FAMILY CAN BE USED IN THIS RECIPE; ESCAROLE IS SWEETER, CURLY ENDIVE MORE BITTER. SERVES 4.

6 tablespoons extra-virgin olive oil
6 medium garlic cloves, minced
1 large head escarole or curly endive (about 1 pound), wilted outer leaves removed and core discarded, remaining leaves cut crosswise into $1/2$-inch strips and rinsed thoroughly
2 teaspoons minced fresh oregano leaves *or* 1 teaspoon dried oregano
Salt and ground black pepper
2 cups cooked cannellini or other small white beans and 1 cup reserved cooking liquid *or* 1 15-ounce can beans, drained and rinsed, plus 1 cup chicken stock or low-sodium canned broth
$3/4$ pound ditali or other short, tubular pasta

1. Heat the oil with the garlic over low heat in a large sauté pan. Add the greens, increase the heat to medium-high, and sauté until completely wilted, 4 to 5 minutes. Add the oregano, salt and pepper to taste, and the bean cooking liquid or stock; cover and simmer to cook completely, about 5 minutes. Add the beans; cover and simmer to blend the flavors, 3 to 4 minutes longer.

2. Meanwhile, bring 4 quarts of water to a boil in a large pot. Add 1 tablespoon salt and the pasta to the boiling water. Cook until al dente. Drain the pasta and return it to the cooking pot. Stir in the beans and greens. Divide among 4 pasta bowls and serve immediately.

Penne with Greens, White Beans, and Rosemary

GREENS, WHITE BEANS, AND ROSEMARY ARE A CLASSIC ITALIAN FLAVOR COMBINATION. WHEN ADDED TO PASTA THEY COMBINE TO MAKE A COMPLETE MEAL. ASSERTIVE GREENS LIKE KALE, COLLARDS, MUSTARD, AND TURNIP NEED TO BE BLANCHED BEFORE THEY ARE SAUTEED AND TOSSED WITH PASTA. SEE PAGE 159 FOR TIPS ON PREPARING THESE GREENS FOR COOKING. SERVES 4.

Salt
2 pounds assertive greens, such as kale, collards, mustard, or turnip greens, stemmed and washed in 2 or 3 changes of clean water (see illustrations 2–4, page 159)
3 tablespoons extra-virgin olive oil
2 large garlic cloves, sliced thin
$1/4$ teaspoon hot red pepper flakes
1 teaspoon minced fresh rosemary leaves
2 cups cooked great northern or other large white beans and 1 cup reserved cooking liquid *or* 1 15-ounce can beans, drained and rinsed, plus 1 cup chicken stock or low-sodium canned broth
$3/4$ pound penne or other short, tubular pasta
$1/4$ teaspoon minced lemon zest (see illustrations 1–4, page 91)

1. Bring 2 quarts of water to a boil in a soup kettle or large, deep sauté pan. Add $1 1/2$ teaspoons salt and the greens; stir until wilted. Cover and cook until the greens are just tender, about 7 minutes; drain in a colander. Rinse the kettle or pan with cold water to cool, then refill with cold water. Dump the greens into the cold water to stop the cooking process. Gather a handful of greens, lift out of the water, and squeeze until only droplets fall from them. Repeat with the remaining greens. Roughly cut the greens.

2. In a large sauté pan, heat the oil with the garlic, red pepper flakes, and rosemary over medium heat until the garlic starts to sizzle. Add the greens; sauté to coat with oil. Add $1/2$ cup bean cooking liquid or stock;

cover and cook over medium-high heat, adding more stock during cooking if necessary, until the greens are tender and juicy and most of the stock has been absorbed, about 5 minutes. Stir in the beans and the remaining cooking liquid or stock. Bring to a simmer; cover and simmer to blend flavors, about 5 minutes. Adjust the seasonings.

3. Meanwhile, bring 4 quarts of water to a boil in a large pot. Add 1 tablespoon salt and the pasta to the boiling water and cook until al dente. Drain the pasta and return it to the cooking pot. Stir in the beans, greens, and zest. Divide among 4 pasta bowls and serve immediately.

◆

Penne with White Beans, Tomatoes, and Potatoes

PASTA, BEANS, AND POTATOES MIGHT SOUND LIKE A STARCH OVERLOAD, BUT THIS COMBINATION IS ACTU-ALLY A GOOD MIXTURE OF FLAVORS AND TEXTURES—AL DENTE PASTA, CREAMY BEANS, AND SLIGHTLY CRISPY BROWNED POTATOES LIGHTENED BY TOMATOES. TO PREVENT STICKING, DRY THE POTATOES WELL BEFORE ADDING THEM TO THE PAN AND STIR THEM OFTEN DURING COOKING. SERVES 4.

1/4 cup extra-virgin olive oil
1 medium Yukon Gold potato, peeled and cut into 1/4-inch dice
2 medium garlic cloves, minced
1 1/2 cups diced canned tomatoes
2 cups cooked great northern or other large white beans *or* 1 15-ounce can beans, drained and rinsed
2 tablespoons finely chopped fresh basil leaves
Salt
3/4 pound penne or other short, tubular pasta

1. Heat the oil over medium-high heat in a large skil-let. Add the potato and cook until tender and golden, stirring frequently, about 5 minutes. Add the garlic and cook until fragrant, 1 minute. Add the tomatoes

and simmer until slightly thickened, 5 to 7 minutes. Stir in the beans and simmer until warmed through, 2 to 3 minutes. Stir in the basil and season with salt to taste.

2. Meanwhile, bring 4 quarts of water to a boil in a large pot. Add 1 tablespoon salt and the pasta to the boiling water and cook until al dente. Drain the pasta and return it to the cooking pot. Stir in the sauce. Divide among 4 pasta bowls and serve immediately.

◆

Penne with White Beans and Radicchio

WHEN SAUTEED, RADICCHIO LOSES ITS BITTERNESS AND BECOMES MELTINGLY TENDER. WE LIKE THE SLIGHTLY SWEET FLAVOR OF BALSAMIC VINEGAR HERE, BUT SHARPER RED WINE VINEGAR MAY BE SUBSTITUTED IF YOU LIKE. SERVES 4.

1/4 cup extra-virgin olive oil
1 medium onion, minced
1 small head radicchio (about 1/2 pound), wilted outer leaves removed, remaining leaves shredded
2 cups cooked great northern or other large white beans *or* 1 15-ounce can beans, drained and rinsed
2 tablespoons balsamic vinegar
Salt
12 ounces penne or other short, tubular pasta
2 tablespoons minced fresh basil leaves

1. Heat the oil over medium heat in a large skillet. Add the onion and cook until softened, 3 to 4 min-utes. Add the radicchio and cook, stirring occasion-ally, until tender, 5 to 7 minutes. Stir in the beans and vinegar. Season with salt.

2. Meanwhile, bring 4 quarts of water to a boil in a large pot. Add 1 tablespoon salt and the pasta to the boiling water and cook until al dente. Drain the pasta and return it to the cooking pot. Stir in the sauce and the basil. Divide among 4 pasta bowls and serve immediately.

Orecchiette with White Beans and Broccoli Rabe

BROCCOLI RABE HAS A RATHER STRONG FLAVOR THAT IS BALANCED IN THIS DISH BY HOT RED PEPPER FLAKES AND A GENEROUS SPRINKLING OF PECORINO, A MORE ASSERTIVE GRATING CHEESE THAN PARMESAN. **SERVES 4.**

- ¼ cup extra-virgin olive oil
- 4 medium garlic cloves, minced
- ¼ teaspoon hot red pepper flakes, or to taste
- 1 bunch broccoli rabe (about 1 pound), washed, trimmed, and coarsely chopped (see illustrations 1–2, page 143)
- 1½ cups diced canned tomatoes
- 2 cups cooked great northern or other large white beans *or* 1 15-ounce can beans, drained and rinsed
- Salt
- ¾ pound orecchiette or other short, shell-shaped pasta
- ½ cup grated pecorino cheese

1. Heat the oil, garlic, and red pepper flakes in a large skillet over medium heat. Cook until fragrant, 1 to 2 minutes. Add the broccoli rabe and cook, stirring occasionally, until wilted, 3 to 5 minutes. Add the tomatoes and cook until slightly thickened, 5 to 7 minutes. Stir in the beans. Season with salt to taste.

2. Meanwhile, bring 4 quarts of water to a boil in a large pot. Add 1 tablespoon salt and the pasta to the boiling water and cook until al dente. Drain the pasta and return it to the cooking pot. Stir in the sauce and cheese. Divide among 4 pasta bowls and serve immediately.

Elbow Macaroni with Greens, Bacon, and Black-Eyed Peas

THE STRONG, SMOKY FLAVOR OF BACON STANDS UP WELL TO ASSERTIVE GREENS LIKE KALE, COLLARDS, MUSTARD, OR TURNIP. BLACK-EYED PEAS GIVE THIS RECIPE AN ESPECIALLY SOUTHERN FLAVOR, BUT WHITE BEANS MAY BE SUBSTITUTED. **SERVES 4.**

- Salt
- 2 pounds assertive greens, such as kale, collards, mustard, or turnip greens, stemmed (see illustrations 2–4, page 159) and washed in 2 or 3 changes of clean water
- 2 slices bacon (about 2 ounces), cut crosswise into thin strips
- ½ medium onion, minced
- 2 medium garlic cloves, sliced thin
- 2 cups cooked black-eyed peas and 1 cup reserved cooking liquid *or* 1 15-ounce can black-eyed peas, drained and rinsed, plus 1 cup chicken stock or low-sodium canned broth
- ¾ pound elbow macaroni or other short, tubular pasta

1. Bring 2 quarts of water to a boil in a soup kettle or large, deep sauté pan. Add 1½ teaspoons salt and the greens; stir until wilted. Cover and cool until the greens are just tender, about 7 minutes; drain in a colander. Rinse the kettle or pan with cold water to cool, then refill with cold water. Dump the greens into the cold water to stop the cooking process. Gather a handful of greens, lift out of the water, and squeeze until only droplets fall from them. Repeat with the remaining greens. Roughly cut the greens.

2. Fry the bacon in a large sauté pan over medium-low heat until crisp, 4 to 5 minutes. Remove bacon with a slotted spoon and set aside. If necessary, add oil to bacon drippings to bring up to 2 tablespoons. Add the onion and sauté until softened, about 4 minutes. Add the garlic and sauté until fragrant, about 1 minute.

3. Add the greens; sauté to coat with oil. Add ½ cup bean cooking liquid or stock; cover and cook over medium-high heat, adding more stock during cooking if necessary, until the greens are tender and juicy and most of the stock has been absorbed, about 5 minutes. Stir in the beans and the remaining reserved cooking liquid or stock. Bring to a simmer; cover and simmer to blend flavors, about 5 minutes. Adjust the seasonings.

4. Meanwhile, bring 4 quarts of water to a boil in a large pot. Add 1 tablespoon salt and the pasta to the boiling water and cook until al dente. Drain the pasta and return it to the cooking pot. Stir in the beans and greens. Divide among 4 pasta bowls and serve immediately.

◆

Penne with Red Beans and Sausage

THIS HEARTY, STEWLIKE DISH IS EQUAL PARTS PASTA, BEANS, AND SAUSAGE. SERVE WITH A CRISP SPINACH SALAD FOR A COMPLETE MEAL. BORLOTTI ARE RUST-COLORED BEANS POPULAR IN ITALY. THEY HAVE A RICH, EARTHY FLAVOR—LOOK FOR THEM IN NATURAL FOODS STORES. RED KIDNEY BEANS ARE A BIT SWEETER BUT MAY BE USED SUCCESSFULLY IN THIS DISH. SERVES 4.

> 2 tablespoons extra-virgin olive oil
> 1 medium onion, minced
> 2 medium garlic cloves, minced
> 1 pound Italian sausage, casings removed
>   and crumbled
> 1 14.5-ounce can diced tomatoes
> 2 cups cooked borlotti or red kidney
>   beans *or* 1 15-ounce can beans, drained
>   and rinsed
> Salt
> ¾ pound penne or other short, tubular
>   pasta
> 2 tablespoons minced fresh basil leaves
> ½ cup grated pecorino or Parmesan
>   cheese

1. Heat the oil and onion over medium heat in a large skillet. Cook until softened, 3 to 4 minutes. Add the garlic and cook another minute. Add the sausage and cook, stirring occasionally to break up, until it loses its pink color, 5 to 7 minutes. Add the tomatoes and cook until slightly thickened, 5 to 7 minutes. Stir in the beans. Season with salt to taste.

2. Meanwhile, bring 4 quarts of water to a boil in a large pot. Add 1 tablespoon salt and the pasta to the boiling water and cook until al dente. Drain the pasta and return it to the cooking pot. Stir in the bean sauce, basil, and cheese. Divide among 4 pasta bowls and serve immediately.

◆

Spaghetti with Chickpeas and Swiss Chard

SWISS CHARD IS A RELATIVELY MILD AND TENDER GREEN THAT DOESN'T NEED TO BE BLANCHED BEFORE IT IS SAUTEED. IN THIS RECIPE, IT IS COMBINED WITH GARLIC AND COOKED CHICKPEAS. SERVES 4.

> 3 tablespoons extra-virgin olive oil
> 2 medium garlic cloves, minced
> 2 pounds Swiss chard, cleaned, stemmed,
>   and coarsely chopped (see illustration
>   2, page 159)
> Salt and ground black pepper
> 2 cups cooked chickpeas *or* 1 15-ounce
>   can chickpeas, drained and rinsed
> ¾ pound spaghetti or other long, thin
>   pasta

1. Heat the oil with the garlic in a large sauté pan or Dutch oven. When the garlic sizzles and starts to turn golden, add the wet greens. Cover and cook over medium high heat, stirring occasionally, until the greens completely wilt, but are still bright green, about 5 minutes. Uncover and season to taste with salt and pepper. Add the chickpeas and cook over high heat until the liquid evaporates and the chickpeas are heated through, 2 to 3 minutes longer.

2. Meanwhile, bring 4 quarts of water to a boil in a large pot. Add 1 tablespoon salt and the pasta to the boiling water and cook until al dente. Drain the pasta and return it to the cooking pot. Stir in the greens and chickpeas. Divide among 4 pasta bowls and serve immediately.

Pasta with Pureed Chickpeas

CHICKPEAS ARE PUREED AND THINNED WITH A LITTLE OF THEIR COOKING LIQUID TO MAKE A LIGHT YET NUTRITIOUS SAUCE. THE FLAVORS MAY BE VARIED BY SUBSTITUTING LIME JUICE FOR THE LEMON AND MINT OR BASIL FOR THE PARSLEY. SERVES 4.

- 7 tablespoons extra-virgin olive oil
- 2 medium garlic cloves, minced
- 2 cups cooked chickpeas and ¾ cup reserved cooking liquid *or* 1 15-ounce can chickpeas, drained and rinsed, plus ¾ cup chicken stock or low-sodium canned broth
- ½ cup tightly packed fresh flat-leaf parsley leaves
- 2 tablespoons lemon juice
- Salt and ground black pepper
- ¾ pound fettuccine or other long, flat pasta

1. Heat the oil and garlic in a large skillet and cook until the garlic is fragrant, 1 to 2 minutes. Add the chickpeas and cook to heat through, 1 to 2 minutes. Transfer the chickpeas to the work bowl of a food processor. Add the parsley, juice, and ¼ cup of the cooking liquid or stock and process until smooth, stopping as necessary to scrape down the sides of the bowl. Season with salt and pepper to taste.

2. Meanwhile, bring 4 quarts of water to a boil in a large pot. Add 1 tablespoon salt and the pasta to the boiling water and cook until al dente. Drain the pasta and return it to the cooking pot. Mix in ¼ cup of the bean cooking liquid or stock and the pureed chickpeas; use the additional liquid as needed to moisten the sauce. Divide among 4 pasta bowls and serve immediately.

Penne with Black Beans and Chipotle-Tomato Sauce

THIS MEXICAN-INSPIRED SAUCE GETS SOME HEAT FROM SMOKY CANNED CHIPOTLE CHILES, AVAILABLE AT LATIN MARKETS AND MANY SUPERMARKETS. LIKE MOZZA-RELLA, REGULAR JACK CHEESE WILL GIVE THE DISH A CREAMY FINISH; DRY, AGED JACK (MORE LIKE PARME-SAN) ADDS A SHARPER NOTE. SERVES 4.

- 2 tablespoons extra-virgin olive oil
- 1 medium onion, minced
- 2 medium garlic cloves, minced
- 1 canned chipotle chile in adobo, finely chopped
- 1½ cups diced canned tomatoes
- 2 cups cooked black beans *or* 1 15-ounce can beans, drained and rinsed
- Salt
- ¾ pound penne or other short, tubular pasta
- 2 tablespoons minced fresh cilantro leaves
- 1 cup grated Monterey Jack or mozzarella, or ½ cup grated aged jack cheese

1. Heat the oil and onion over medium heat in a large skillet. Cook until softened, 3 to 4 minutes. Add the garlic and chile and cook another minute. Add the tomatoes and cook until slightly thickened, 5 to 7 minutes. Stir in the beans. Season with salt to taste.

2. Meanwhile, bring 4 quarts of water to a boil in a large pot. Add 1 tablespoon salt and the pasta to the boiling water and cook until al dente. Drain the pasta and return it to the cooking pot. Stir in the sauce, cilantro, and cheese. Divide among 4 pasta bowls and serve immediately.

Cooked Lentils

MAKES ABOUT 2 CUPS

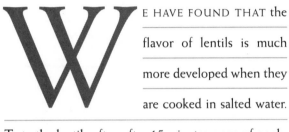E HAVE FOUND THAT the flavor of lentils is much more developed when they are cooked in salted water.

Taste the lentils often after 15 minutes or so of cooking because cooking times can vary greatly from batch to batch, and lentils can very quickly turn to mush if overcooked just a few minutes. If you can find French green lentils (often labeled lentils du Puy), buy them. They have a richer flavor and firmer texture than common brown lentils. To cook green lentils, follow this recipe, increasing the simmering time to about 25 minutes.

> ¾ cup (about 5 ounces) brown lentils
> 1 teaspoon salt

Bring the lentils, salt, and 7 cups water to a boil in a large saucepan. Boil for 5 minutes. Turn down the heat and simmer, partially covered, until the lentils are tender but not mushy, 10 to 20 minutes. Drain the lentils and refrigerate for up to 1 day.

Fusilli with Lentils and Spinach

THE ACID FROM THE TOMATOES WOULD PREVENT RAW LENTILS FROM SOFTENING, BUT COOKED LENTILS WILL COMBINE BEAUTIFULLY WITH THE SAUCE. **SERVES 4**.

> 2 tablespoons extra-virgin olive oil
> 1 medium onion, minced
> 1 medium garlic clove, minced
> 1 ½ cups diced canned tomatoes
> 1 teaspoon minced fresh tarragon leaves
>   *or* ¼ teaspoon dried tarragon
> 1 pound fresh spinach, washed, stemmed, and coarsely chopped (see illustration 1, page 159)
> 2 cups cooked lentils
> Salt
> ¾ pound fusilli or other short, curly pasta

1. Heat the oil and onion over medium heat in a large skillet. Cook until the onion begins to soften, 3 to 4 minutes. Add the garlic and cook another minute. Add the tomatoes and tarragon and simmer until slightly thickened, 8 to 10 minutes. Stir in the spinach and cook until wilted, about 2 minutes. Stir in the lentils. Season with salt to taste.

2. Meanwhile, bring 4 quarts of water to a boil in a large pot. Add 1 tablespoon salt and the pasta to the boiling water and cook until al dente. Drain the pasta and return it to the cooking pot. Stir in the lentil sauce. Divide among 4 pasta bowls and serve immediately.

HOW TO COOK LENTILS

T HE CONVENTIONAL PRACTICE WHEN COOKING DRIED LEGUMES IS TO SOAK THEM BEFORE COOKING, AND TO AVOID SALT OR ACIDIC INGREDIENTS DURING COOKING, WHICH ARE SAID TO PREVENT PROPER SOFTENING DURING COOKING. ONE OF THE CHARMS OF LENTILS IS THAT THEY DON'T NEED TO BE

soaked. We wondered if this nonconformist status would also apply to the restrictions on salt and acid. We set out to test these factors and cooking times for common brown lentils and French green lentils du Puy.

Before cooking, all lentils must be inspected for stones, seeds, and other foreign objects. After sorting, lentils should be rinsed in water to remove any residual dirt.

To determine how long it takes the lentils to cook without any graininess, we cooked ¾ cup of each kind of cleaned lentils in 7 cups of plain water. Common brown lentils became tender in about twenty minutes, cooked all the way through and in fact starting to lose their shape. (While salads might require firm, intact lentils, it's fine if some of the lentils have split during cooking. However, you don't want the lentils to turn to mush.) The flavor of the brown lentils was a bit dull.

The green lentils took twenty-five minutes to soften and held their shape extremely well. Their flavor was more robust and earthy.

Our next test was to add 1 teaspoon of salt to the cooking water. Common brown lentils cooked up with a fuller flavor. The salt was a definite improvement. Green lentils tasted better, too, but their cooking time stretched to thirty minutes.

Next, we cooked each lentil in the same amount of water, substituting 1 tablespoon of vinegar for the salt. The vinegar had a striking effect on the lentils, doubling their cooking time and giving them a grainy texture. Subsequent tests with wine and tomato yielded similar results. Several experts told us that acids interfere with the ability of the lentils to bind with water. This causes them to take longer to soften and to have a rather dry taste. Our conclusion—for best flavor cook lentils in salted water but avoid acids until the lentils have softened properly.

As a final test, we cooked lentils with a variety of seasonings, including herbs, onions, and garlic. Unlike dried beans, which benefit from cooking with garlic and bay leaves, we found that lentils don't spend enough time in the pot to pick up any real flavor from other ingredients.

So what's the best way to use lentils in a pasta sauce? Unlike beans, lentils should be used rather quickly after cooking. If possible, cook and drain lentils, then add them directly to the pasta sauce. In a pinch, the lentils can be drained and refrigerated for a day. However, they will continue to soften and eventually fall apart in their cooking liquid, so don't store them as you would other dried legumes.

Penne with Lentils, Tomatoes, and Carrots

LENTILS AND GRATED PARMESAN BALANCE THE SWEET-NESS OF TOMATOES AND CARROTS IN THIS RUSTIC SAUCE. SERVE AS A VEGETARIAN MAIN COURSE, OR AS A FIRST COURSE TO A MORE ELABORATE MEAL OF ITALIAN-STYLE BOILED BRISKET OR PORK ROAST. SERVES 4, OR 6 TO 8 AS A FIRST COURSE.

> 2 tablespoons extra-virgin olive oil
> 1 medium onion, minced
> 3 medium carrots, peeled and cut into
>   ¼-inch dice
> 1½ cups diced canned tomatoes
> 2 cups cooked lentils
> Salt and ground black pepper
> ¾ pound penne or other short, tubular
>   pasta
> ½ cup grated Parmesan cheese

1. Heat the oil and onion over medium heat in a large skillet. Cook until the onion begins to soften, 3 to 4 minutes. Add the carrots and cook until softened, 8 to 10 minutes. Add the tomatoes and simmer until slightly thickened, 8 to 10 minutes. Stir in the lentils. Season with salt and pepper to taste.

2. Meanwhile, bring 4 quarts of water to a boil in a large pot. Add 1 tablespoon salt and the pasta to the boiling water and cook until al dente. Drain the pasta and return it to the cooking pot. Stir in the lentil sauce and cheese. Divide among 4 pasta bowls and serve immediately.

Spaghetti with Lentils and Prosciutto

LENTILS HAVE AN AFFINITY FOR SALTY PROSCIUTTO AND SAGE. PANCETTA OR EVEN BACON CAN BE SUBSTI-TUTED; BOTH OF THESE WILL BE SALTIER THAN THE PROSCIUTTO, SO ADJUST THE SEASONINGS ACCORD-INGLY. SERVES 4.

> ½ cup extra-virgin olive oil
> 1 medium onion, minced
> 2 medium garlic cloves, minced
> ¼ pound prosciutto, sliced ¼ inch thick
>   and then cut into ¼-inch dice
> 2 cups cooked lentils
> 1 tablespoon minced fresh sage leaves
> Salt and ground black pepper
> ¾ pound spaghetti or other long, thin
>   pasta
> ½ cup grated Parmesan cheese

1. Heat ¼ cup oil and the onion over medium heat in a large skillet. Cook until the onion begins to soften, 3 to 4 minutes. Add the garlic and prosciutto and cook, stirring occasionally, until the fat from the prosciutto has rendered, 3 to 4 minutes. Add the lentils and sage and stir to mix. Season with salt and pepper to taste.

2. Meanwhile, bring 4 quarts of water to a boil in a large pot. Add 1 tablespoon salt and the pasta to the boiling water and cook until al dente. Drain the pasta and return it to the cooking pot. Stir in the lentil sauce and cheese. Divide among 4 pasta bowls, drizzle each bowl with 1 tablespoon oil, and serve immediately.

Penne with Lentils and Fennel

FENNEL, ONIONS, AND CARROTS ALL BENEFIT FROM REL-
ATIVELY SLOW COOKING TOGETHER. COMBINED WITH
EARTHY LENTILS, THESE MELTINGLY SOFT VEGETABLES
MAKE A SATISFYING WINTER SAUCE. SERVES 4.

> ¼ cup extra-virgin olive oil
> 1 fennel bulb, stems, fronds, and base
>   trimmed; bulb cored and cut into
>   ½-inch-thick strips (see illustrations
>   1–5, page 154)
> 1 medium onion, minced
> 2 medium carrots, peeled and cut into
>   ¼-inch dice
> 2 cups cooked lentils
> 1½ teaspoons sweet paprika
> Salt and ground black pepper
> ¾ pound penne or other short, tubular
>   pasta

1. Heat the oil over medium heat in a large skillet.
Add the fennel, onion, and carrots and cook, stirring
frequently, until the vegetables soften, 12 to 15 minutes. Stir in the lentils and paprika. Season with salt
and pepper to taste.

2. Meanwhile, bring 4 quarts of water to a boil in a
large pot. Add 1 tablespoon salt and the pasta to the
boiling water and cook until al dente. Reserve ½ cup
of the cooking liquid; drain the pasta and return it to
the cooking pot. Add the lentil sauce, stir, and moisten
with the cooking liquid, 1 tablespoon at a time, if
necessary. Divide among 4 pasta bowls and serve
immediately.

Orecchiette with Lentils

ORECCHIETTE ("LITTLE EARS") ARE THE IDEAL SHAPE
FOR CATCHING TINY LENTILS. OREGANO IS WONDER-
FULLY AROMATIC IN THIS SIMPLE PASTA DISH, BUT
OTHER HERBS—INCLUDING PARSLEY, SAGE, OR THYME—
MAY BE SUBSTITUTED. USE A VERY FRUITY EXTRA-
VIRGIN OLIVE OIL FOR DRIZZLING TO ADD AN EXTRA
FLAVOR DIMENSION. SERVES 4.

> ½ cup extra-virgin olive oil
> 2 medium garlic cloves, minced
> ½ teaspoon hot red pepper flakes, or to
>   taste
> 2 cups cooked lentils
> 1 tablespoon minced fresh oregano leaves
> ¾ pound orecchiette or shells

1. Heat ¼ cup oil, garlic, and red pepper flakes over
medium heat in a large skillet. Cook until the garlic
begins to color, 2 to 3 minutes. Add the lentils and stir
to coat with the oil. Add the oregano and adjust the
seasonings.

2. Meanwhile, bring 4 quarts of water to a boil in a
large pot. Add 1 tablespoon salt and the pasta to the
boiling water and cook until al dente. Drain the pasta
and return it to the cooking pot. Stir in the lentil
sauce. Divide among 4 pasta bowls, drizzle 1 tablespoon oil over each bowl, and serve immediately.

CHAPTER

1 5

SAUCES

WITH MEAT

/|\

TRADITIONALLY, MEAT SAUCES RELY ON INEXPENSIVE

CUTS SUCH AS GROUND MEAT, RIBS, AND CHOPS TO

MAKE RICH-TASTING SAUCES FOR PASTA. THE NOTION

IS THAT EXPENSIVE CUTS OF MEAT ARE BEST ROASTED

OR GRILLED. WE HEARTILY AGREE. IN OUR TESTING,

WE FOUND THAT INEXPENSIVE CUTS WITH SOME FAT

ARE THE BEST CANDIDATES FOR PASTA SAUCES. THIS

means ground chuck instead of ground sirloin, spareribs instead of pork chops, and so on. Lean cuts tend to dry out and don't soften properly when simmered in a tomato sauce.

In addition to choosing meats with some fat, it's important to choose the right cooking technique. Although it's possible to make relatively quick sauces from ground meats and sausage, slow-simmering produces better results and is essential when starting with a larger cut of meat, such as a rib. The meat becomes especially tender and soft after slow-simmering, a texture that is especially appealing over pasta.

On many stoves, a flame tamer will help maintain the laziest simmer without scorching. We use a chrome-plated flame tamer in our test kitchen that measures about 8 inches in diameter and rests just above the burner on our electric stove. You may also shape aluminum foil into a ring and use that as a flame tamer (see illustration 2, page 199). Of course, make sure to use a heavy-bottomed pot to prevent scorching as the sauce simmers.

The recipes in this chapter are divided into five categories: slow-simmering sauces with ground meat, quick sauces with ground meat, sauces with sausage, spaghetti and meatballs, and sauces with ribs and chops.

Slow-Simmering Sauces with Ground Meat

BOLOGNESE IS A dense, rich meat sauce that is spooned over fresh fettuccine or cheese ravioli or used to make lasagne. Unlike other meat sauces where tomatoes dominate (think jars of spaghetti sauce with flecks of meat in a sea of tomato puree), bolognese sauce is about meat, with the tomatoes in a supporting role. Bolognese also differs from many tomato-based meat sauces because it contains dairy—butter, milk, and cream—which gives the meat an especially sweet, appealing flavor.

Bolognese is not hard to prepare (the hands-on work is less than thirty minutes), but it does require hours of slow simmering. For the sauce to be worth the effort, it must have a good balance of meaty, sweet, salty, and acidic flavors.

All bolognese recipes can be broken down into three steps. First, vegetables are sautéed in fat. Second, ground meat is browned in the pan. The final step is the addition of liquids and long, slow simmering.

After an initial round of testing, we found that we preferred just onions, carrots, and celery as our vegetables. Other items tested, including garlic and mushrooms, proved distracting from the meat flavor. We found that sautéing the vegetables in butter (rather than oil) gave the finished sauce a desirable extra richness. We also discovered that a combination of ground beef, veal, and pork made the sauce especially complex and rich tasting. The veal adds finesse and delicacy to the sauce, while the pork makes it sweet. Beef alone can be used with slightly less interesting results.

Our vegetables and ground meats chosen, we focused on liquid. The secret to great bolognese sauce is the sequential reduction of various liquids over the sautéed meat and vegetables. The idea is to build flavor and tenderize the meat, which will have toughened during the browning phase. Many recipes insist on a particular order to adding these liquids. The most common choices include milk, cream, stock, wine (both red and white), and tomatoes (fresh, canned whole, crushed, or paste).

We tested all possible choices and found that liquids are best treated in two ways. In the early part of the process (right after the meat has been browned), the liquids are added to the pan and simmered briskly until fully evaporated, the point being to add flavor. Wine is always treated this way; if the wine is not evaporated the sauce will be too alcoholic. Milk and cream are usually treated this way. Later, either stock or tomatoes are added in greater quantity to cook off very slowly. These liquids add flavor and also serve as the "cooking medium" for the sauce during the slow-simmering phase.

We found that meat cooked in milk first (rather than wine) was sweeter and softer. As the bits of meat cook, they develop a hard crust that makes it more difficult for them to absorb liquid. Adding the milk first, when the meat is not as crusty, allows it to penetrate and tenderize the meat.

We tested cream as well as milk and felt that cream was too rich. As for the wine, white wine is more delicate and is preferred. However, red wine adds a robust flavor that works well when pancetta is added to the sauce.

Next we moved on to the final element, the cooking liquid. When testing with stock, we found that canned products gave the sauce an odd chemical flavor when reduced the necessary amount. Homemade chicken or beef stock was not worth the considerable effort. Tomatoes have the acidity and complexity that this sauce needed. We found that canned whole tomatoes have the best flavor and were preferred by our tasters over fresh tomatoes, tomato paste, or crushed tomatoes.

Our recipe was pretty much in shape but we had a few remaining questions. Some sources suggest that deep browning builds flavor, a theory that makes some sense. Other sources caution against overcooking the meat and suggest adding the first liquid to the pan as soon as the meat loses its raw color. We found this latter warning to be true. Sauces made with fully browned meat had a pleasant browned meat flavor, but the meat itself was not especially tender and the sauce was not as smooth. When the milk was added to the pan as soon as the meat was no longer rosy, the sauce was more delicate and tender.

Our last avenue of inquiry involved timing. After two hours on low heat, the sauce was too soupy and the meat was still pretty firm. At three hours, the meat was much softer, with a melt-in-your-mouth consistency. The sauce was dense and smooth as well. We tried simmering the sauce for four hours but found no benefit. In fact, some batches cooked this long reduced too much and scorched a bit.

MAKING BOLOGNESE SAUCE

1. To achieve the very fine, smooth texture of bolognese, crumble the ground meats with the edge of a wooden spoon as they cook so no clumps remain.

2. If your burners run too hot for very low simmering and you don't have a commercial flame tamer, you can fashion a flame tamer by making a thick, slightly flattened ring of aluminum foil and placing it on top of the burner.

Fettuccine with Classic Bolognese Sauce

SERVES 4

ON'T DRAIN THE PASTA of its cooking water too meticulously when using this sauce; a little water left clinging to the noodles will help distribute the very thick sauce evenly into the noodles, as will adding 2 tablespoons of butter along with the sauce. Pass grated Parmesan cheese at the table. If doubling this recipe, increase the simmering times for the milk and the wine to 30 minutes each, and the simmering time once the tomatoes are added to 4 hours.

5 tablespoons unsalted butter
2 tablespoons minced onion
2 tablespoons minced carrot
2 tablespoons minced celery

¾ pound meatloaf mix *or* ¼ pound each ground beef chuck, ground veal, and ground pork
Salt
1 cup whole milk
1 cup dry white wine
1 28-ounce can whole tomatoes packed in juice, finely chopped, with juice reserved
1 pound Fresh Egg Pasta (page 21) cut into fettuccine *or* dried fettuccine
Grated Parmesan cheese

1. Heat 3 tablespoons butter in a large, heavy-bottomed Dutch oven over medium heat; add the onion, carrot, and celery and sauté until softened but not browned, about 6 minutes. Add the ground meat and ½ teaspoon salt; following illustration 1 on page 199, crumble the meat with the edge of a wooden spoon to break it apart into tiny pieces. Cook, continuing to crumble the meat, just until it loses its raw color but has not yet browned, about 3 minutes.

2. Add the milk and bring to a simmer; continue to simmer until the milk evaporates and only clear fat remains, 10 to 13 minutes. Add the wine and bring to a simmer; continue to simmer until the wine evaporates, 10 to 13 minutes longer. Add the tomatoes and their juice and bring to a simmer; reduce the heat to low so that the sauce continues to just barely simmer, with an occasional bubble or two at the surface, until the liquid has evaporated, about 3 hours (if the lowest burner setting is too high to allow such a low simmer, use a flame tamer or, following illustration 2 on page 199, a foil ring to elevate the pan). Adjust the seasonings with extra salt to taste. (Can be refrigerated in an airtight container for several days or frozen for several months. Warm over low heat before serving.)

3. Bring 4 quarts of water to a boil in a large pot. Add 1 tablespoon salt and the pasta. Cook until al dente. Reserve ¼ cup of the cooking water; drain the pasta and return it to the cooking pot. Mix in the sauce, remaining 2 tablespoons butter, and the reserved cooking water if necessary. Serve immediately with cheese passed separately at the table.

Fettuccine with Bolognese Sauce with Beef, Pancetta, and Red Wine

USING ALL GROUND BEEF WORKS BEST WITH THE PANCETTA WITH THIS SAUCE. IF YOU CAN'T FIND PANCETTA, SUBSTITUTE PROSCIUTTO, BUT DON'T USE AMERICAN BACON, WHICH IS SMOKED AND WILL OVERWHELM THE BEEF. WE FOUND THAT RED WINE STANDS UP TO THE MORE ROBUST FLAVORS IN THIS SAUCE BETTER THAN THE WHITE WINE IN THE MASTER RECIPE. SERVES 4.

    5 tablespoons unsalted butter
    2 tablespoons minced onion
    2 tablespoons minced carrot
    2 tablespoons minced celery
    2 ounces pancetta, minced
    ¾ pound beef chuck
    Salt
    1 cup whole milk
    1 cup dry red wine
    1 28-ounce can whole tomatoes packed in
      juice, finely chopped, with juice
      reserved
    1 pound Fresh Egg Pasta (page 21) cut
      into fettuccine or dried fettuccine
    Grated Parmesan cheese

1. Heat 3 tablespoons butter in a large, heavy-bottomed Dutch oven over medium heat; add the onion, carrot, celery, and pancetta and sauté until softened but not browned, about 6 minutes. Add the ground meat and ½ teaspoon salt; crumble the meat with the edge of a wooden spoon to break it apart into tiny pieces (see illustration 1, page 199). Cook, continuing to crumble the meat, just until it loses its raw color but has not yet browned, about 3 minutes.

2. Add the milk and bring to a simmer; continue to simmer until the milk evaporates and only clear fat remains, 10 to 13 minutes. Add the wine and bring to a simmer; continue to simmer until the wine evaporates, 10 to 13 minutes longer. Add the tomatoes and their juice and bring to a simmer; reduce the heat to low so that the sauce continues to just barely simmer, with an occasional bubble or two at the surface, until

the liquid has evaporated, about 3 hours (if the lowest burner setting is too high to allow such a low simmer, use a flame tamer or a foil ring to elevate the pan; see illustration 2, page 199). Adjust the seasonings with extra salt to taste. (Can be refrigerated in an airtight container for several days or frozen for several months. Warm over low heat before serving.)

3. Bring 4 quarts of water to a boil in a large pot. Add 1 tablespoon salt and the pasta. Cook until al dente. Reserve ¼ cup of the cooking water; drain the pasta and return it to the cooking pot. Mix in the sauce, remaining 2 tablespoons butter, and the reserved cooking water if necessary. Serve immediately with cheese passed separately at the table.

◆

Fettuccine with Beef Bolognese Sauce

THERE IS SOMETHING VERY APPEALING ABOUT THE SIMPLICITY OF AN ALL-BEEF SAUCE. WHILE IT MAY LACK SOME OF THE FINESSE AND SWEETNESS OF THE MASTER RECIPE, ITS PURE BEEF FLAVOR IS UNIQUELY SATISFYING. SERVES 4.

    5 tablespoons unsalted butter
    2 tablespoons minced onion
    2 tablespoons minced carrot
    2 tablespoons minced celery
    ¾ pound ground beef chuck
    Salt
    1 cup whole milk
    1 cup dry white wine
    1 28-ounce can whole tomatoes packed in
      juice, finely chopped, with juice
      reserved
    1 pound Fresh Egg Pasta (page 21) cut
      into fettuccine or dried fettuccine
    Grated Parmesan cheese

1. Heat 3 tablespoons butter in a large, heavy-bottomed Dutch oven over medium heat; add the onion, carrot, and celery and sauté until softened but not browned, about 6 minutes. Add the ground meat

(continued on next page)

and ½ teaspoon salt; crumble the meat with the edge of a wooden spoon to break it apart into tiny pieces (see illustration 1, page 199). Cook, continuing to crumble the meat, just until it loses its raw color but has not yet browned, about 3 minutes.

2. Add the milk and bring to a simmer; continue to simmer until the milk evaporates and only clear fat remains, 10 to 13 minutes. Add the wine and bring to a simmer; continue to simmer until the wine evaporates, 10 to 13 minutes longer. Add the tomatoes and their juice and bring to a simmer; reduce the heat to low so that the sauce continues to just barely simmer, with an occasional bubble or two at the surface, until the liquid has evaporated, about 3 hours (if the lowest burner setting is too high to allow such a low simmer, use a flame tamer or a foil ring to elevate the pan; see illustration 2, page 199). Adjust the seasonings with extra salt to taste. (Can be refrigerated in an airtight container for several days or frozen for several months. Warm over low heat before serving.)

3. Bring 4 quarts of water to a boil in a large pot. Add 1 tablespoon salt and the pasta. Cook until al dente. Reserve ¼ cup of the cooking water; drain the pasta and return it to the cooking pot. Mix in the sauce, the remaining 2 tablespoons butter, and the reserved cooking water if necessary. Serve immediately with cheese passed separately at the table.

◆

Fettuccine with Ground Lamb Ragù

GROUND LAMB INSTEAD OF BEEF, VEAL, AND PORK PRODUCES AN EARTHIER, MORE PUNGENT VERSION OF CLASSIC BOLOGNESE. **SERVES 4**.

    5 tablespoons unsalted butter
    ¼ cup minced onion
    2 ounces pancetta, minced
    1 teaspoon minced fresh rosemary leaves
    ¾ pound ground lamb
    Salt
    1 cup whole milk
    1 cup dry white wine

    1 28-ounce can whole tomatoes packed in juice, finely chopped, with juice reserved
    1 pound Fresh Egg Pasta (page 21) cut into fettuccine *or* dried fettuccine
    Grated pecorino cheese

1. Heat 3 tablespoons butter in a large, heavy-bottomed Dutch oven over medium heat; add the onion, pancetta, and rosemary and sauté until softened but not browned, about 6 minutes. Add the ground meat and ½ teaspoon salt; crumble the meat with the edge of a wooden spoon to break it apart into tiny pieces (see illustration 1, page 199). Cook, continuing to crumble the meat, just until it loses its raw color but has not yet browned, about 3 minutes.

2. Add the milk and bring to a simmer; continue to simmer until the milk evaporates and only clear fat remains, 10 to 13 minutes. Add the wine and bring to a simmer; continue to simmer until the wine evaporates, 10 to 13 minutes longer. Add the tomatoes and their juice and bring to a simmer; reduce the heat to low so that the sauce continues to just barely simmer, with an occasional bubble or two at the surface, until the liquid has evaporated, about 3 hours (if the lowest burner setting is too high to allow such a low simmer, use a flame tamer or a foil ring to elevate the pan; see illustration 2, page 199). Adjust the seasonings with extra salt to taste. (Can be refrigerated in an airtight container for several days or frozen for several months. Warm over low heat before serving.)

3. Bring 4 quarts of water to a boil in a large pot. Add 1 tablespoon salt and the pasta. Cook until al dente. Reserve ¼ cup of the cooking water; drain the pasta and return it to the cooking pot. Mix in the sauce, the remaining 2 tablespoons butter, and the reserved cooking water if necessary. Serve immediately with cheese passed separately at the table.

Quick Sauces with Ground Meat

A QUICK MEAT SAUCE is best made simply. After all, the emphasis is on speed of preparation. After some initial testing, we realized that delicacy and finesse (two goals when developing our recipe of bolognese sauce) were impossible if total preparation and cooking time were going to be limited to a half hour or so. Instead, we preferred the rugged, robust sauces that were prepared in our initial testing for this kind of sauce.

Olive oil seemed like a better cooking medium than butter in a sauce made without milk. Likewise, the rough flavor of garlic worked better than the sweetness of sautéed aromatics like onions, carrots, and celery. Again, we found that the freshness and bright acidity of canned whole tomatoes was preferable to either crushed tomatoes or tomato puree.

As with bolognese sauce, we found that the meat remained more supple when it was not fully browned. Just cook it long enough to lose the raw color and then add the tomatoes. While rich bolognese sauce is best with fresh egg pasta, this rustic sauce is best with rigatoni, ziti, or another sturdy tubular shape.

Rigatoni with Quick Meat Sauce

SERVES 4

I F THERE'S NO TIME TO simmer Classic Bolognese, a satisfying, rustic meat sauce can be made in under 30 minutes with ground chuck and canned tomatoes. This sauce lacks the finesse of one that has been slow-simmered but the flavors are quite good. See page 221 for a variation on this recipe using ground chicken.

2 tablespoons extra-virgin olive oil
1 medium garlic clove, minced
¼ cup minced fresh flat-leaf parsley leaves
½ pound ground beef chuck
½ teaspoon dried oregano
Salt
1 28-ounce can whole tomatoes packed in juice, finely chopped, with juice reserved
1 pound rigatoni or other tubular pasta
Grated Parmesan cheese

1. Heat the oil in a large, heavy-bottomed Dutch oven over medium heat; add the garlic and parsley and sauté until fragrant, about 1 minute. Add the ground meat, oregano, and ½ teaspoon salt; crumble the meat

(continued on next page)

with the edge of a wooden spoon to break it apart into tiny pieces (see illustration 1, page 199). Cook, continuing to crumble the meat, just until it loses its raw color but has not yet browned, about 3 minutes.

2. Add the tomatoes and their juice and bring to a simmer; simmer gently until the sauce begins to thicken, about 20 minutes. Adjust the seasonings with extra salt to taste.

3. Bring 4 quarts of water to a boil in a large pot. Add 1 tablespoon salt and the pasta. Cook until al dente. Reserve ¼ cup of the cooking water; drain the pasta and return it to the cooking pot. Mix in the sauce and the reserved cooking water if necessary. Serve immediately with cheese passed separately at the table.

◆

Rigatoni with Quick Meat and Celery Sauce

ABUNDANT CELERY GIVES THIS QUICK SAUCE AN INTER-ESTING FLAVOR WITH LITTLE EXTRA EFFORT. SERVES 4.

> 2 tablespoons extra-virgin olive oil
> 1 small onion, minced
> 1 cup minced celery (2 large or 3 small stalks)
> ¼ cup minced fresh flat-leaf parsley leaves
> ½ pound ground beef chuck
> Salt
> 1 28-ounce can whole tomatoes packed in juice, finely chopped, with juice reserved
> 1 pound rigatoni or other tubular pasta
> Grated Parmesan cheese

1. Heat the oil in a large, heavy-bottomed Dutch oven over medium heat; add the onion, celery, and parsley and sauté until softened but not browned, about 6 minutes. Add the ground meat and ½ teaspoon salt; crumble the meat with the edge of a wooden spoon to break it apart into tiny pieces (see illustration 1, page 199). Cook, continuing to crumble the meat, just until it loses its raw color but has not yet browned, about 3 minutes.

2. Add the tomatoes and their juice and bring to a simmer; simmer gently until the sauce begins to thicken, about 20 minutes. Adjust the seasonings with extra salt to taste.

3. Bring 4 quarts of water to a boil in a large pot. Add 1 tablespoon salt and the pasta. Cook until al dente. Reserve ¼ cup of the cooking water; drain the pasta and return it to the cooking pot. Mix in the sauce and the reserved cooking water if necessary. Serve immediately with cheese passed separately at the table.

◆

Rigatoni with Spicy Meat and Mushroom Sauce

MEAT SAUCE CAN BE LIGHTENED BY ADDING SLICED MUSHROOMS TO THE MIX. FOR ADDED INTEREST, WE FLAVOR THIS VERSION WITH RED PEPPER FLAKES. SERVES 4.

> 2 tablespoons extra-virgin olive oil
> 10 ounces white button mushrooms, cleaned and thinly sliced
> 2 medium garlic cloves, minced
> ½ teaspoon hot red pepper flakes or to taste
> ¼ cup minced fresh flat-leaf parsley leaves
> ½ pound ground beef chuck
> Salt
> 1 28-ounce can whole tomatoes packed in juice, finely chopped, with juice reserved
> 1 pound rigatoni or other tubular pasta
> Grated Parmesan cheese

1. Heat the oil in a large, heavy-bottomed Dutch oven over medium heat; add mushrooms and sauté until they begin to give off their juices, about 5 minutes. Add the garlic, red pepper flakes, and parsley and cook until fragrant, 1 to 2 minutes. Add the ground meat and ½ teaspoon salt; crumble the meat with the edge of a wooden spoon to break it apart into tiny pieces (see illustration 1, page 199). Cook, continuing to crumble the meat, just until it loses its raw color but has not yet browned, about 3 minutes.

2. Add the tomatoes and their juice and bring to a simmer; simmer gently until the sauce begins to thicken, about 20 minutes. Adjust the seasonings with extra salt to taste.

3. Bring 4 quarts of water to a boil in a large pot. Add 1 tablespoon salt and the pasta. Cook until al dente. Reserve ¼ cup of the cooking water; drain the pasta and return it to the cooking pot. Mix in the sauce and the reserved cooking water if necessary. Serve immediately with cheese passed separately at the table.

◆

Rigatoni with Meat, Tomato, and Cream Sauce

ENRICHING OUR QUICK MEAT SAUCE WITH HEAVY CREAM MAKES IT A BIT MORE LIKE BOLOGNESE SAUCE. SERVES 4.

2 tablespoons extra-virgin olive oil
1 medium garlic clove, minced
¼ cup minced fresh flat-leaf parsley leaves
½ pound ground beef chuck
½ teaspoon dried oregano
Salt
1 28-ounce can whole tomatoes packed in juice, finely chopped, with juice reserved
½ cup heavy cream
1 pound rigatoni or other tubular pasta
Grated Parmesan cheese

1. Heat the oil in a large, heavy-bottomed Dutch oven over medium heat; add the garlic and parsley and sauté until fragrant, about 1 minute. Add the ground meat, oregano, and ½ teaspoon salt; crumble the meat with the edge of a wooden spoon to break it apart into tiny pieces (see illustration 1, page 199). Cook, continuing to crumble the meat, just until it loses its raw color but has not yet browned, about 3 minutes.

2. Add the tomatoes and their juice and bring to a simmer; simmer gently until the sauce begins to thicken, about 20 minutes. Stir in the cream, bring to a simmer, and cook until thickened, 2 to 3 minutes. Adjust the seasonings with extra salt to taste.

3. Bring 4 quarts of water to a boil in a large pot. Add 1 tablespoon salt and the pasta. Cook until al dente. Reserve ¼ cup of the cooking water; drain the pasta and return it to the cooking pot. Mix in the sauce and the reserved cooking water if necessary. Serve immediately with cheese passed separately at the table.

◆

Penne with Quick Veal Sauce

GROUND VEAL MAKES A QUICK BUT REFINED PASTA SAUCE. TO COMPENSATE FOR THE RELATIVE LEANNESS OF THE MEAT, BUTTER ADDS RICHNESS AND FLAVOR TO THE SAUCE. SERVES 4.

3 tablespoons unsalted butter
1 tablespoon extra-virgin olive oil
1 small onion, minced
½ pound ground veal
Salt
1 28-ounce can whole tomatoes packed in juice, finely chopped, with juice reserved
1 pound penne or other small tubular pasta
Grated Parmesan cheese

1. Heat 2 tablespoons butter and the oil in a large, heavy-bottomed Dutch oven over medium heat; add the onion and sauté until softened but not browned, about 6 minutes. Add the ground meat and ½ teaspoon salt; crumble the meat with the edge of a wooden spoon to break it apart into tiny pieces (see illustration 1, page 199). Cook, continuing to crumble the meat, just until it loses its raw color but has not yet browned, about 3 minutes.

2. Add the tomatoes and their juice and bring to a simmer; simmer gently until the sauce begins to thicken, about 20 minutes. Adjust the seasonings with extra salt to taste.

3. Bring 4 quarts of water to a boil in a large pot. Add 1 tablespoon salt and the pasta. Cook until al dente. Reserve ¼ cup of the cooking water; drain the pasta and return it to the cooking pot. Mix in the sauce, the remaining tablespoon butter, and the reserved cooking water if necessary. Serve immediately with cheese passed separately at the table.

Sauces with Sausage

SAUSAGE MAY BE USED in place of ground beef to make quick pasta sauces. Almost all sausage has more than enough fat to make a good sauce, so focus on flavor rather than fat content when shopping. (In fact, some brands may be a bit too fatty.) Flavor is another matter. When we tested recipes with relatively bland sausage from the supermarket, we were consistently underwhelmed. However, when we used good Italian sausage from a local butcher, the quality of the sauce improved dramatically.

This is no surprise. Supermarket sausage often skimps on flavor enhancers like garlic, herbs, and spices. Handmade Italian sausage is likely to be brimming with flavor. When good sausage (either sweet or hot) is used, everything falls into place and the sausage needs little embellishment. A bit more garlic, some dried oregano, and some canned whole tomatoes, and you have a quick, rustic sauce for pasta.

We prefer to use Italian sausage in the recipes that follow. The flavor of the sausage, redolent with garlic, herbs, and anise, works best with the other sauce ingredients. However, you may use other flavorful kinds of sausage—andouille, chorizo, or even kielbasa—with different but still delicious results.

Fusilli with Quick Sausage Sauce

SERVES 4

SAUSAGE CAN BE substituted for ground beef in the Master Recipe for Rigatoni with Quick Meat Sauce (page 203). Seek out an Italian market that makes its own sausage, since the flavor and quality of the mixture will affect the outcome of the recipe. Since some sausage is very salty, we recommend waiting until the sauce is almost finished before adjusting the seasonings.

2 tablespoons extra-virgin olive oil
1 medium garlic clove, minced
½ pound Italian sausage, casings removed
½ teaspoon dried oregano
1 28-ounce can whole tomatoes packed in juice, finely chopped, with juice reserved
Salt
1 pound fusilli or short, tubular pasta
Grated Parmesan cheese

1. Heat the oil in a large, heavy-bottomed Dutch oven over medium heat; add the garlic and sauté until fragrant, about 1 minute. Add the sausage and oregano; crumble the meat with the edge of a wooden spoon to break it apart into tiny pieces (see illustration 1, page 199). Cook, continuing to crumble the meat, just until it loses its raw color but has not yet browned, about 3 minutes.

2. Add the tomatoes and their juice and bring to a simmer; simmer gently until the sauce begins to thicken, about 20 minutes. Adjust the seasonings with salt to taste.

3. Bring 4 quarts of water to a boil in a large pot. Add 1 tablespoon salt and the pasta. Cook until al dente. Reserve ¼ cup of the cooking water; drain the pasta and return it to the cooking pot. Mix in the sauce and the reserved cooking water if necessary. Serve immediately with cheese passed separately at the table.

◆

Fusilli with Sausage, Tomatoes, and Cream

CREAM CAN BE ADDED TO A SAUSAGE SAUCE FOR EXTRA RICHNESS. SERVES 4.

2 tablespoons extra-virgin olive oil
1 medium garlic clove, minced
½ pound Italian sausage, casings removed
1 28-ounce can whole tomatoes packed in juice, finely chopped, with juice reserved
½ cup heavy cream
2 tablespoons minced fresh flat-leaf parsley leaves
Salt
1 pound fusilli or short, tubular pasta
Grated Parmesan cheese

1. Heat the oil in a large, heavy-bottomed Dutch oven over medium heat; add the garlic and sauté until fragrant, about 1 minute. Add the sausage; crumble the meat with the edge of a wooden spoon to break it apart into tiny pieces (see illustration 1, page 199). Cook, continuing to crumble the meat, just until it loses its raw color but has not yet browned, about 3 minutes.

2. Add the tomatoes and their juice and bring to a simmer; simmer gently until the sauce begins to thicken, about 20 minutes. Stir in the cream, bring to a simmer, and cook until thickened, 2 to 3 minutes. Stir in the parsley. Adjust the seasonings with salt to taste.

3. Bring 4 quarts of water to a boil in a large pot. Add 1 tablespoon salt and the pasta. Cook until al dente. Reserve ¼ cup of the cooking water; drain the pasta and return it to the cooking pot. Mix in the sauce and the reserved cooking water if necessary. Serve immediately with cheese passed separately at the table.

◆

Penne with Sausage and Spicy Paprika–Cream Sauce

PAPRIKA AND CAYENNE PEPPER ARE ADDED TO A SAUSAGE-CREAM SAUCE FOR THIS SIMPLE BUT UNUSUAL VARIATION. SERVES 4.

2 tablespoons extra-virgin olive oil
1 medium shallot, minced
½ pound Italian sausage, casings removed
3 tablespoons sweet paprika
¼ teaspoon cayenne or to taste
1 28-ounce can whole tomatoes packed in juice, finely chopped, with juice reserved
½ cup heavy cream
2 tablespoons minced fresh flat-leaf parsley leaves
Salt
1 pound penne or other short, tubular pasta
Grated Parmesan cheese

1. Heat the oil in a large, heavy-bottomed Dutch oven over medium heat; add the shallot and sauté until fragrant, about 1 minute. Add the sausage, paprika, and cayenne; crumble the meat with the edge of a wooden spoon to break it apart into tiny pieces (see illustration 1, page 199). Cook, continuing to crumble the meat, just until it loses its raw color but has not yet browned, about 3 minutes.

(continued on next page)

2. Add the tomatoes and their juice and bring to a simmer; simmer gently until the sauce begins to thicken, about 20 minutes. Stir in the cream, bring to a simmer, and cook until thickened, 2 to 3 minutes. Stir in the parsley. Adjust the seasonings with salt to taste.

3. Bring 4 quarts of water to a boil in a large pot. Add 1 tablespoon salt and the pasta. Cook until al dente. Reserve ¼ cup of the cooking water; drain the pasta and return it to the cooking pot. Mix in the sauce and the reserved cooking water if necessary. Serve immediately with cheese passed separately at the table.

◆

Fusilli with Sausage and Ricotta

RICOTTA CHEESE IS A GOOD ALTERNATIVE TO HEAVY CREAM WHEN YOU WANT A CREAMY SAUSAGE SAUCE THAT'S NOT QUITE SO RICH. SERVES 4.

2 tablespoons extra-virgin olive oil
1 small onion, minced
½ pound Italian sausage, casings removed
1 28-ounce can whole tomatoes packed in juice, finely chopped, with juice reserved
Salt
1 pound fusilli or short, tubular pasta
½ cup ricotta cheese
2 tablespoons minced fresh basil leaves
Grated Parmesan cheese

1. Heat the oil in a large, heavy-bottomed Dutch oven over medium heat; add the onion and sauté until softened but not brown, about 6 minutes. Add the sausage; crumble the meat with the edge of a wooden spoon to break it apart into tiny pieces (see illustration 1, page 199). Cook, continuing to crumble the meat, just until it loses its raw color but has not yet browned, about 3 minutes.

2. Add the tomatoes and their juice and bring to a simmer; simmer gently until the sauce begins to thicken, about 20 minutes. Adjust the seasonings with salt to taste.

3. Bring 4 quarts of water to a boil in a large pot. Add 1 tablespoon salt and the pasta. Cook until al dente. Reserve ¼ cup of the cooking water; drain the pasta

and return it to the cooking pot. Mix in the sauce, ricotta, basil, and the reserved cooking water if necessary. Serve immediately with grated cheese passed separately.

◆

Spaghetti with Sausage and Egg

SPAGHETTI ALLA CARBONARA CAN BE MADE MEATIER BY SUBSTITUTING ITALIAN SAUSAGE FOR THE TRADITIONAL PANCETTA OR BACON. SEE THE CAUTION ON PAGE 71. SERVES 4.

2 tablespoons extra-virgin olive oil
4 medium garlic cloves, peeled and crushed
½ pound Italian sausage, casings removed
¼ cup dry white wine
3 large eggs
1 cup grated pecorino cheese
2 tablespoons minced fresh flat-leaf parsley leaves
Salt
1 pound spaghetti or other long, thin pasta
Ground black pepper

1. Bring 4 quarts of water to a boil in a large pot for cooking the pasta.

2. Heat the oil and garlic in a skillet over medium heat. Cook the garlic until golden, 2 to 3 minutes. Discard the garlic and add the sausage; crumble the meat with the edge of a wooden spoon to break it apart into tiny pieces (see illustration 1, page 199). Cook, continuing to crumble the meat, just until it loses its raw color but has not yet browned, about 3 minutes. Add the wine and simmer until the alcohol aroma has cooked off, 2 to 3 minutes. Remove from heat, cover, and keep warm.

3. Lightly beat the eggs with the cheese and parsley in a large bowl.

4. Add 1 tablespoon salt and the pasta to the boiling water. Cook until al dente. Drain the pasta, leaving it slightly wet, and transfer it to the bowl with the egg mixture. Immediately toss the pasta with the egg mixture to coat evenly. Stir in the sausage mixture. Season with salt and pepper to taste. Divide among 4 warmed pasta bowls and serve immediately.

Spaghetti and Meatballs

THE PROBLEM WITH MOST meatballs is that they are too dense and heavy. Serving meatballs over thin, long noodles is already a bit awkward. But if the meatballs are compact, overcooked little hamburgers, the dish can be so leaden that Alka-Seltzer is the only dessert that makes sense.

Many cooks think of meatballs as hamburgers with seasonings (cheese, herbs, garlic, etc.) and a round shape. This is partly true. Unlike hamburgers, which are best cooked rare or medium-rare, meatballs are cooked through until well done. At this point, a simple combination of ground beef and seasonings will form dry, tough hockey pucks. Meatballs require additional ingredients to keep them moist and lighten their texture. Our testing first focused on ingredients that would give meatballs a moister, softer consistency.

We started out with a simple recipe (ground beef, grated cheese, parsley, salt, and pepper) and tested the most common binders—eggs, dried bread crumbs, fresh bread crumbs, ground crackers, and bread soaked in milk. We found that meatballs made with an egg yolk were lighter and moister than those without egg and added the yolk to our working recipe.

As for bread or cracker crumbs, all were disappointing except for the white bread soaked in milk. Dry crumbs soaked up any available moisture and compounded the problems caused by cooking meatballs to the well-done stage. Meatballs made with soaked bread were moister, creamier, and richer.

We tested soaking the bread in regular milk, buttermilk, and yogurt thinned with milk and preferred the rich flavor and tang provided by the buttermilk or thinned yogurt. To make sure that the bread dissolves into the meat mixture, we found it necessary to mash the crustless bread cubes and milk with a fork to form a thick paste.

We next tested various meats. Veal was too bland in meatballs, but pork added another flavor dimension and is worth adding if possible to ground chuck. As for cooking the meatballs, pan-frying is the obvious choice and we found that it worked better than roasting or broiling. To save cleanup time and flavor, we

MAKING MEATBALLS

1. Mash the bread cubes and buttermilk together with a fork. Let stand, mashing occasionally, until a smooth paste forms, about 10 minutes.

2. Once all the ingredients for the meatballs are in the bowl, mix with a fork to roughly combine. At this point, use your hands to make sure that the flavorings are evenly distributed throughout the mixture.

3. Meatballs must be browned well on all sides. This may involve standing meatballs on their sides near the end of the cooking process. If necessary, lean them up against each other to get the final sides browned.

found it possible to build the tomato sauce in the pan used to fry the meatballs. Simply drain off the grease, leaving behind any browned (and flavorful) bits. Add fresh oil (use vegetable oil for pan-frying the meatballs, but add olive oil for flavoring the tomato sauce), followed by garlic, tomatoes, and basil.

Meatballs need a thick, smooth sauce—the kind produced by canned crushed tomatoes. Once the sauce thickens, add the meatballs for several minutes to heat them through but don't let them cook too long or they may start to fall apart.

◆

Classic Spaghetti and Meatballs

THIS STREAMLINED RECIPE CAN BE ON THE TABLE IN UNDER AN HOUR. SEE ILLUSTRATIONS 1 THROUGH 3 ON PAGE 209 FOR HELPFUL TIPS. SEE PAGE 222 FOR A VARIATION ON THIS RECIPE USING GROUND CHICKEN. SERVES 4 TO 6.

MEATBALLS
2 slices white sandwich bread (crusts discarded), torn into small bits
½ cup buttermilk or 6 tablespoons plain yogurt thinned with 2 tablespoons sweet milk
¾ pound ground chuck mixed with ¼ pound ground pork or 1 pound ground chuck
¼ cup grated Parmesan cheese
2 tablespoons minced fresh flat-leaf parsley leaves
1 large egg yolk
1 small garlic clove, minced
¾ teaspoon salt
Ground black pepper

Vegetable oil for pan-frying (about 1¼ cups)

SIMPLE TOMATO SAUCE
2 tablespoons extra-virgin olive oil
1 teaspoon minced garlic
1 28-ounce can crushed tomatoes
1 tablespoon minced fresh basil leaves
Salt and ground black pepper

1 pound spaghetti
Freshly grated Parmesan cheese

1. For the meatballs, combine the bread and buttermilk in a small bowl, mashing occasionally with a fork, until a smooth paste forms, about 10 minutes (see illustration 1, page 209).

2. Mix all the meatball ingredients, including the bread mixture and pepper to taste, in a medium bowl (see illustration 2, page 209).

3. Lightly form 3 tablespoons of the mixture into a 1½-inch round meatball; repeat with the remaining mixture to form approximately 14 meatballs. (Compacting can make the meatballs dense and hard. They can be placed on a large plate, covered loosely with plastic wrap, and refrigerated for several hours.)

4. Heat ¼ inch of vegetable oil over medium-high heat in a 10- or 11-inch sauté pan. When the edge of the meatball dipped in oil sizzles, add the meatballs in a single layer. Fry, turning several times, until cooked through and nicely browned on all sides, about 10 minutes, regulating the heat as needed to keep the oil sizzling but not smoking (see illustration 3, page 209). Transfer the browned meatballs to a paper towel–lined plate; set aside. Repeat, if necessary, with the remaining meatballs.

5. For the sauce, discard the oil in the pan, leaving behind any browned bits. Add the olive oil along with the garlic; sauté, scraping up any browned bits, just until the garlic is golden, about 30 seconds. Add the tomatoes, bring to a boil, and simmer gently until the sauce thickens, about 10 minutes. Stir in the basil; add salt and pepper to taste. Add the meatballs and simmer, turning them occasionally, until heated through, about 5 minutes. Keep warm over low heat.

6. Meanwhile, bring 4 quarts of water to a boil in a large pot for cooking pasta. Add 1 tablespoon salt and the pasta to the boiling water. Cook until al dente, drain, and return to the pot. Ladle several large spoonfuls of tomato sauce (without meatballs) over the spaghetti and toss until the noodles are well coated. Divide the pasta among individual bowls and top each with a little more tomato sauce and 2 or 3 meatballs. Serve immediately with grated cheese passed separately.

Sauces with Ribs and Chops

MANY THRIFTY ITALIAN cooks throw a stray piece of meat into a pot of simmering tomato sauce and let it cook until tender. The meat is taken off the bone and shredded and then returned to the sauce. The bone is discarded, but it has added depth of flavor to a humble tomato sauce.

We experimented with this idea using an array of cuts, including beef ribs (short ribs and back ribs), various beef roasts from the chuck and sirloin, pork ribs (spareribs, baby back ribs, and country-style ribs), as well as lamb riblets and lamb chops from the shoulder.

In all cases, we found that the fattier cuts work best with this technique. Fattier cuts won't dry out during the long simmering process and they are more flavorful than leaner cuts. For instance, small beef roasts from the chuck or shoulder dried out and were not especially tender when cooked this way. Beef short ribs are fattier (and more flavorful) than beef back ribs and worked best in this recipe. Pork spareribs were slightly better than leaner country-style or baby ribs in our tests. Lamb presented some challenges since riblets are so hard to find. Loin and rib chops are much too expensive to cook this way; however, sinewy shoulder chops worked well.

In our testing, we found that there can be such a thing as too much fat. It's the internal fat that lubricates the meat as it cooks and keeps it from drying out, so trim away excess external fat. Also, if there is a lot of fat in the pan after the meat has been browned, drain it. This is especially important when cooking spareribs.

Once the meat has been browned, add the tomatoes, reduce the heat, and simmer until the meat is falling off the bone. Shred the meat by hand and add it back to the sauce for a satisfying, rich meat sauce.

Ziti with Beef Ribs

SERVES 4

SHORT RIBS ARE AMONG the most flavorful cuts of beef; cooked in tomato sauce and served with pasta, they make a truly robust meal. Look for the meatiest ribs and trim as much external fat from them before cooking as you can, for a meaty but not overly greasy sauce.

1 tablespoon olive oil
1 1/2 pounds meaty beef short ribs, trimmed of excess fat
Salt and ground black pepper
1 28-ounce can whole tomatoes packed in juice, finely chopped, with juice reserved
2 medium garlic cloves, minced
1 teaspoon minced fresh thyme leaves
1 pound ziti or other short, tubular pasta

1. Heat the oil in a Dutch oven or large, heavy saucepan over medium-high heat; season the meat with salt and pepper and add to the pan. Brown on all sides, about 7 minutes.

2. Add the tomatoes and juice, garlic, and thyme and bring to a simmer. Reduce the heat to low and simmer, partly covered, until the meat is falling off the bone, about 1 1/2 hours. If the sauce looks like it is getting too dry, add 1/4 cup of water to moisten during cooking.

(continued on next page)

3. Remove the meat from the bones. Pull off any visible fat. Shred the meat and return to the sauce; discard the bones and excess fat. Season with salt and pepper to taste.

4. Meanwhile, bring 4 quarts of water to a boil in a large pot. Add 1 tablespoon salt and the pasta. Cook until al dente. Reserve ¼ cup of the cooking water; drain the pasta and return it to the cooking pot. Mix in the sauce and the reserved cooking water if necessary. Serve immediately.

◆

Ziti with Beef Ribs and Cinnamon

THE ADDITION OF GROUND CINNAMON AND CLOVES TO THE RECIPE FOR SHORT RIB SAUCE GIVES THIS DISH AN EASTERN MEDITERRANEAN FLAVOR. **SERVES 4.**

    1 tablespoon olive oil
    1½ pounds beef short ribs, trimmed of
       excess fat
    Salt and ground black pepper
    1 28-ounce can whole tomatoes packed in
       juice, finely chopped, with juice
       reserved
    2 medium garlic cloves, minced
    ½ teaspoon ground cinnamon
    Pinch ground cloves
    1 pound ziti or other short, tubular pasta

1. Heat the oil in a Dutch oven or large, heavy saucepan over medium-high heat; season the meat with salt and pepper and add to the pan. Brown on all sides, about 7 minutes.

2. Add the tomatoes and juice, garlic, cinnamon, and cloves and bring to a simmer. Reduce the heat to low and simmer, partly covered, until the meat is falling off the bone, about 1½ hours. If the sauce looks like it is getting too dry, add ¼ cup of water to moisten during cooking.

3. Remove the meat from the bones. Pull off any visible fat. Shred the meat and return to the sauce; discard the bones and excess fat. Season with salt and pepper to taste.

4. Meanwhile, bring 4 quarts of water to a boil in a large pot. Add 1 tablespoon salt and the pasta. Cook until al dente. Reserve ¼ cup of the cooking water; drain the pasta and return it to the cooking pot. Mix in the sauce and the reserved cooking water if necessary. Serve immediately.

Penne with Pork Ribs

SERVES 4

PORK RIBS ARE VERY FATTY, so drain the grease from the pan before adding the tomatoes. The rest of the excess fat is cut away from the cooked ribs before the meat is added back to the sauce.

    1 tablespoon vegetable oil
    3 pounds meaty spare ribs (6 to 8 ribs),
       separated into individual ribs
    Salt and ground black pepper
    1 medium onion, minced
    1 28-ounce can whole tomatoes packed in
       juice, finely chopped, with juice
       reserved
    1 pound penne or other short, tubular
       pasta

1. Heat the oil in a Dutch oven or large, heavy saucepan over medium heat. Sprinkle the ribs with salt and pepper. Add the ribs and brown on all sides, turning occasionally, 10 to 12 minutes.

2. Remove the ribs from the pot and drain away all but 1 tablespoon of the fat. Add the onion and cook until softened, 4 to 5 minutes. Return the ribs to the pot and add the tomatoes and juice; bring to a simmer. Reduce the heat to low and simmer, partly covered, until the meat is falling off the bone, about 1 hour. If the sauce looks like it is getting too dry, add ¼ cup of water to moisten during cooking.

3. Remove the meat from the bones. Pull off any visible fat. Shred the meat and return to the sauce; discard the bones and excess fat. Season with salt and pepper to taste.

4. Meanwhile, bring 4 quarts of water to a boil in a large pot. Add 1 tablespoon salt and the pasta. Cook until al dente. Reserve ¼ cup of the cooking water; drain the pasta and return it to the cooking pot. Mix in the sauce and the reserved cooking water if necessary. Serve immediately.

◆

Penne with Chili-Rubbed Pork Ribs

BROWNING THE CHILI POWDER AND CUMIN ALONG WITH THE RIBS BRINGS OUT THEIR FLAVORS IN THIS VIBRANT VARIATION ON BRAISED PORK RIB SAUCE. SERVES 4.

    4 medium garlic cloves, crushed
    1½ teaspoons chili powder
    ½ teaspoon ground cumin
    Salt
    3 pounds meaty spare ribs (6 to 8 ribs),
        separated into individual ribs
    1 tablespoon vegetable oil
    1 28-ounce can whole tomatoes packed in
        juice, finely chopped, with juice
        reserved
    10 large green olives, pitted and coarsely
        chopped (see illustrations 1–2, page
        62)
    Ground black pepper
    1 pound penne or other short, tubular
        pasta

1. Combine the garlic, chili powder, cumin, and ½ teaspoon salt in a small bowl and mash together with the back of a spoon to form a paste. Rub the paste into the ribs.

2. Heat the oil in a Dutch oven or large, heavy saucepan over medium heat. Add the ribs and brown on all sides, turning occasionally, 10 to 12 minutes.

3. Remove the ribs from the pot and drain away the fat. Return the ribs to the pot and add the tomatoes and juice; bring to a simmer. Reduce the heat to low and simmer, partly covered, until the meat is falling off the bone, about 1 hour. If the sauce looks like it is getting too dry, add ¼ cup of water to moisten during cooking.

4. Remove the meat from the bones. Pull off any visible fat. Shred the meat and return to the sauce; discard the bones. Stir in the olives. Season with salt and pepper to taste.

5. Meanwhile, bring 4 quarts of water to a boil in a large pot. Add 1 tablespoon salt and the pasta. Cook until al dente. Reserve ¼ cup of the cooking water; drain the pasta and return it to the cooking pot. Mix in the sauce and the reserved cooking water if necessary. Serve immediately.

Penne with Garlic- and Rosemary-Rubbed Pork Ribs

HERE, PORK RIBS ARE COVERED IN A FLAVORFUL ROSEMARY-GARLIC PASTE BEFORE THEY ARE BROWNED; THE PASTE GIVES THE FINISHED SAUCE A RICH, AROMATIC FLAVOR. SERVES 4.

    4 medium garlic cloves, crushed
    2 teaspoons minced fresh rosemary
    Salt
    3 pounds meaty spare ribs (6 to 8 ribs),
      separated into individual ribs
    1 tablespoon vegetable oil
    1 28-ounce can whole tomatoes packed in
      juice, finely chopped, with juice
      reserved
    Ground black pepper
    1 pound penne or other short, tubular
      pasta

1. Combine the garlic, rosemary, and ½ teaspoon salt in a small bowl and mash together with the back of a spoon to form a paste. Rub the paste into the ribs.

2. Heat the oil in a Dutch oven or large, heavy saucepan over medium heat. Add the ribs and brown on all sides, turning occasionally, 10 to 12 minutes.

3. Remove the ribs from the pot and drain away the fat. Return the ribs to the pot and add the tomatoes and juice; bring to a simmer. Reduce the heat to low and simmer, partly covered, until the meat is falling off the bone, about 1 hour. If the sauce looks like it is getting too dry, add ¼ cup of water to moisten during cooking.

4. Remove the meat from the bones. Pull off any visible fat. Shred the meat and return to the sauce; discard the bones and excess fat. Season with salt and pepper to taste.

5. Meanwhile, bring 4 quarts of water to a boil in a large pot. Add 1 tablespoon salt and the pasta. Cook until al dente. Reserve ¼ cup of the cooking water; drain the pasta and return it to the cooking pot. Mix in the sauce and the reserved cooking water if necessary. Serve immediately.

Ziti with Braised Lamb Sauce

INEXPENSIVE LAMB SHOULDER CHOPS MAKE A WONDERFUL MEAT SAUCE. THE TECHNIQUE HERE IS THE SAME AS THE ONE DESCRIBED IN THE MASTER RECIPE FOR PENNE WITH PORK RIBS ON PAGE 212. SERVES 4.

    1 tablespoon extra-virgin olive oil
    1½ pounds lamb shoulder chops
    Salt and ground black pepper
    1 medium onion, minced
    2 ounces pancetta, minced
    1 teaspoon minced fresh rosemary leaves
    1 28-ounce can whole tomatoes packed in
      juice, finely chopped, with juice
      reserved
    1 pound penne or other short, tubular
      pasta
    Grated pecorino Romano cheese

1. Heat the oil in a Dutch oven or large, heavy saucepan over medium-high heat. Sprinkle the chops with salt and pepper and add to the pan. Brown on all sides, 7 to 10 minutes.

2. Remove the chops from the pot and drain away all but 1 tablespoon of the fat. Add the onion, pancetta, and rosemary and cook until softened, 4 to 5 minutes. Return the chops to the pot and add the tomatoes and juice; bring to a simmer. Reduce the heat to low and simmer, partly covered, until the meat is falling off the bone, about 1 hour. If the sauce looks like it is getting too dry, add ¼ cup of water to moisten during cooking.

3. Remove the meat from the bones. Pull off any visible fat. Shred the meat and return to the sauce; discard the bones and excess fat. Season with salt and pepper to taste.

4. Meanwhile, bring 4 quarts of water to a boil in a large pot. Add 1 tablespoon salt and the pasta. Cook until al dente. Reserve ¼ cup of the cooking water; drain the pasta and return it to the cooking pot. Mix in the sauce and the reserved cooking water if necessary. Serve immediately with grated cheese passed separately.

SAUCES WITH POULTRY, GAME BIRDS, AND RABBIT

MAKING SAUCES WITH CHICKEN, DUCK, GAME BIRDS,

AND RABBIT PRESENTS SEVERAL COMMON CHAL-

LENGES. YOU WANT TO CAPTURE THE FULL FLAVOR OF

THE MEAT IN YOUR PASTA SAUCE, BUT YOU DON'T

want to end up with skin or bones in it. For the richest flavor, we found it best to use whole game birds or skin-on, bone-in parts. For example, we found that sauces made with braised chicken thighs have more flavor and character than those made with boneless, skinless breasts. Whole birds or skin-on parts require extra effort on the part of the cook. Once braised in the sauce, the skin and bones must be discarded and the meat returned to the sauce.

We realize that convenience must also count for something when making a pasta sauce, so we developed recipes using quicker-cooking poultry items such as boneless, skinless breasts and ground chicken. The methods for turning these "no-work" poultry products into pasta sauces takes into account their lower fat content and tendency to dry out.

To make this chapter as useful as possible, we have grouped sauces by the kind of poultry (chicken, duck, squab, etc.). Since there are so many chicken products, we have broken these sauces into three categories—sauces with boneless breast meat, sauces with braised thighs, and sauces with ground chicken. Note that rabbit is the one item covered in this chapter that does not belong to the poultry family. However, because rabbit presents the cook with many of the same problems as birds (i.e., dense meat attached to bones), we have included rabbit sauces in this chapter.

For more information on buying and preparing chicken, turkey, duck, and game birds, see *The Cook's Illustrated Complete Book of Poultry*.

Sauces with Boneless Chicken Breasts

BONELESS, SKINLESS CHICKEN breasts are the fastest way to turn chicken into a pasta sauce. Simply slice the chicken and you are ready to cook. The challenges with these sauces were keeping the chicken from drying out and becoming tough and making them as flavorful as possible.

When we tested cooking chicken in stock and tomatoes, we found that pieces were likely to become rubbery and did not meld well with the pasta. There were tough bits of dry chicken floating in a mass of tender pasta. We found that boneless breasts are so lean, they should be finished with some heavy cream to keep the pieces supple. Cream lubricates this lean cut and makes it tender enough to work as a pasta sauce. If you would rather not use cream in your cooking, try making sauces from much more forgiving chicken thighs. (See page 218 for more information.)

In addition to the dryness issue, boneless chicken makes a fairly bland pasta. Remember that pasta doesn't have all that much flavor, and neither does a skinless chicken breast. We had the best results when we added potent ingredients, like ham and porcini mushrooms, to these sauces.

Fusilli with Chicken and Cream

SERVES 4

IN THIS SIMPLE BUT luxurious dish, pieces of white-meat chicken are given a flavor boost with chopped ham and fresh tarragon. The sauce cooks in the same time as the pasta.

Salt
1 pound fusilli or other short, curly pasta
2 tablespoons unsalted butter
¼ pound ham, finely chopped
½ pound boneless, skinless chicken
   breasts, trimmed of fat and cut into
   1-inch-long by ¼-inch-thick strips
Ground black pepper
2 teaspoons minced fresh tarragon leaves
½ cup heavy cream
¼ cup grated Parmesan cheese

1. Bring 4 quarts of water to a boil in a large pot. Add 1 tablespoon salt and the pasta. Cook until al dente.

2. While the pasta is cooking, melt the butter over medium heat in a large sauté pan. Add the ham and cook for 2 or 3 minutes. Season the chicken with salt and pepper to taste. Turn the heat to medium-high and add the chicken to the pan. Sauté, stirring occasionally, until the chicken is opaque, 4 minutes. Add the tarragon and cream and cook until the sauce has thickened slightly, 1 to 2 minutes.

3. Reserve ½ cup of the cooking water; drain the pasta and return it to the cooking pot. Mix in ¼ cup of the reserved cooking water, the sauce, and the cheese; use the additional ¼ cup cooking water as needed to moisten the sauce. Season with salt and pepper to taste. Serve immediately.

◆

Penne with Chicken and Porcini Mushrooms

DRIED PORCINI MUSHROOMS LEND A MEATINESS TO THIS CHICKEN AND PASTA DISH. **SERVES 4.**

Salt
1 pound penne or other short, tubular
   pasta
2 tablespoons unsalted butter
1 ounce dried porcini mushrooms,
   rehydrated in 1 cup hot water for 20
   minutes and chopped coarse, liquid
   strained and reserved separately (see
   illustrations 1–2, page 169)
½ pound boneless, skinless chicken
   breasts, trimmed of fat and cut into
   1-inch-long by ¼-inch-thick strips
Ground black pepper
½ cup heavy cream
¼ cup grated Parmesan cheese

1. Bring 4 quarts of water to a boil in a large pot. Add 1 tablespoon salt and the pasta. Cook until al dente.

2. While the pasta is cooking, melt the butter over medium heat in a large sauté pan. Add the mushrooms and cook for 1 minute. Season the chicken with salt and pepper to taste. Turn to medium-high and add the chicken to the pan. Sauté, stirring occasionally, until the chicken is opaque, 4 minutes. Add the porcini soaking liquid and cream and cook until the sauce has thickened slightly, 2 to 3 minutes.

3. Drain the pasta and return it to the cooking pot. Toss with the sauce and cheese. Season with salt and pepper to taste. Serve immediately.

Fusilli with Chicken and Spinach

THE CREAM IS OPTIONAL HERE SINCE THE TOMATOES AND SPINACH DO A DECENT JOB OF KEEPING THE CHICKEN MOIST. HOWEVER, WE LIKE THE WAY THE CREAM ENRICHES THIS SIMPLE SAUCE AND RECOMMEND ADDING IT. SERVES 4.

> 2 tablespoons unsalted butter
> ½ pound boneless, skinless chicken
>   breasts, trimmed of fat and cut into
>   1-inch-long by ¼-inch-thick strips
> Salt and ground black pepper
> 1 pound spinach, stemmed and coarsely
>   chopped
> 1 cup canned crushed tomatoes
> ¼ cup heavy cream (optional)
> 1 pound fusilli or other short, curly pasta
> ¼ cup grated Parmesan cheese

1. Bring 4 quarts of water to a boil in a large pot for cooking the pasta.

2. Melt the butter over medium-high heat in a large sauté pan. Season the chicken with salt and pepper to taste. Add the chicken to the pan and sauté, stirring occasionally, until opaque, 4 minutes. Remove from the pan with a slotted spoon and set aside.

3. Add the spinach to the pan, season with salt and pepper to taste, and cook, stirring occasionally, until wilted, about 3 minutes. Add the tomatoes and cook, stirring occasionally, until heated through, another 2 minutes. Add the cream if desired and cook until the sauce has thickened slightly, 1 to 2 minutes. Return the chicken to the pan and adjust the seasonings.

4. Meanwhile, add 1 tablespoon salt and the pasta to the boiling water. Cook until al dente. Drain the pasta and return it to the cooking pot. Mix in the sauce and the cheese. Serve immediately.

Sauces with Chicken Thighs

WE CONSIDER THE THIGH to be the most flavorful part of the chicken. Thighs are unctuous and rich and have enough fat to keep the meat from drying out, even during prolonged cooking. That said, chicken thighs can be greasy.

We prefer to brown the chicken, drain off the fat, and then cook the chicken in a tomato sauce. When we tried this with boneless thighs, we found that the exterior layers of meat dry out and become stringy when browned.

We found that thighs must be covered with skin if they are going to be browned. We like to keep the skin on throughout the braising process as well. It imparts flavor and again cushions the meat from overcooking. Once the thighs are cooked through, they should be removed from the sauce, cooled, skinned, boned, and torn into bite-size chunks. Since chicken thighs have quite a lot of fat, be sure to skim the sauce of any excess before adding the meat back in. Just turn down the heat and you will see the fat pooling up in the pan. Simply spoon it off and discard.

Ziti with Braised Chicken Thighs in Tomato Sauce

SERVES 4

CHICKEN THIGHS SHOULD be slow-cooked in tomato sauce to soften the meat and release its flavor. Since chicken thighs have quite a lot of fat, be sure to skim the sauce of any excess before adding the meat back in. We like to pair chicken thighs with aggressive seasonings like olives and capers, but chicken is also delicious with a simpler tomato sauce.

2 pounds chicken thighs, rinsed and patted dry
Salt and ground black pepper
1 tablespoon unsalted butter
1 tablespoon extra-virgin olive oil
1 large onion, sliced thin
1 medium garlic clove, minced
1 28-ounce can whole tomatoes, drained, seeded, and coarsely chopped (see illustration, page 136)
3 tablespoons chopped fresh flat-leaf parsley leaves
3 tablespoons chopped fresh basil leaves
1/2 cup black olives (such as Kalamata), pitted and coarsely chopped (see illustrations 1–2, page 62)
2 teaspoons drained capers, rinsed
1/4 cup red wine
1 pound ziti or other short, tubular pasta

1. Sprinkle the chicken with salt and pepper. Heat the butter and oil in a 12-inch sauté pan or small Dutch oven over medium-high heat. When butter foaming subsides, add the chicken; sauté until browned on both sides, moving the pieces around to brown them evenly, 10 to 15 minutes. Remove the chicken pieces from the pan and set aside.

2. Discard all but a thin film of fat from the pan. Add the onion; sauté, stirring frequently to prevent scorching, until softened, 4 to 5 minutes. Stir in the garlic.

3. Return the chicken and accumulated juices to the pan. Add the tomatoes, parsley, basil, olives, capers, and wine; bring to a boil. Lower the heat, cover, and barely simmer until the chicken is cooked through, turning once, about 25 minutes. Remove the chicken from the pot with a slotted spoon and cool slightly. Skim the excess grease from the sauce. Remove the skin from the chicken and discard. Remove the meat from the bones and shred into bite-size pieces. Return the meat to the sauce. Taste for salt and pepper.

4. Bring 4 quarts of water to a boil in a large pot. Add 1 tablespoon salt and the pasta. Cook until al dente. Drain the pasta, return it to the cooking pot, and stir in the sauce. Serve immediately.

Fusilli with Braised Chicken, Tomatoes, and Peppers

DICED PEPPERS GIVE THIS BRAISED CHICKEN SAUCE A PLEASING SWEETNESS. YELLOW OR ORANGE PEPPERS MAY BE SUBSTITUTED FOR COLOR, BUT AVOID GREEN PEPPERS AS THEY CAN GIVE THE SAUCE A BITTER FLAVOR AS THEY COOK. SERVES 4.

- 2 pounds chicken thighs, rinsed and patted dry
- Salt and ground black pepper
- 1 tablespoon unsalted butter
- 1 tablespoon extra-virgin olive oil
- 1 large onion, sliced thin
- 1 medium garlic clove, minced
- 2 medium red bell peppers, stemmed, seeded, and cut into ½-inch dice
- 1 28-ounce can whole tomatoes, drained, seeded, and coarsely chopped (see illustration, page 136)
- ¼ cup chopped fresh flat-leaf parsley leaves
- ¼ cup dry white wine
- 1 pound fusilli or other short, curly pasta

1. Sprinkle the chicken with salt and pepper. Heat the butter and oil in a 12-inch sauté pan or small Dutch oven over medium-high heat. When butter foaming subsides, add the chicken; sauté until browned on both sides, moving the pieces around to brown them evenly, 10 to 15 minutes. Remove the chicken pieces from the pan and set aside.

2. Discard all but a thin film of fat from the pan. Add the onion; sauté, stirring frequently to prevent scorching, until softened, 4 to 5 minutes. Stir in the garlic and peppers. Sauté until the peppers are slightly softened, 3 to 4 minutes.

3. Return the chicken and accumulated juices to the pan. Add the tomatoes, parsley, and wine; stir well and bring to a boil. Lower the heat, cover, and barely simmer until the chicken is cooked through, turning once, about 25 minutes. Remove the chicken from the pot with a slotted spoon and cool slightly. Skim the excess grease from the sauce. Remove the skin from the chicken and discard. Remove the meat from the bones and shred into bite-size pieces. Return the meat to the sauce. Taste for salt and pepper.

4. Bring 4 quarts of water to a boil in a large pot. Add 1 tablespoon salt and the pasta. Cook until al dente. Drain the pasta, return it to the cooking pot, and stir in the sauce. Serve immediately.

◆

Penne with Chicken and Sausage

SAUSAGE ROUNDS ALONG WITH CHICKEN MEAT MAKE A PARTICULARLY HEARTY PASTA SAUCE. CHOOSE SWEET OR HOT ITALIAN SAUSAGE, ACCORDING TO TASTE, AND BE SURE TO DEGREASE THE SAUCE BEFORE SERVING. SERVES 4.

- 1½ pounds chicken thighs, rinsed and patted dry
- Salt and ground black pepper
- 1 tablespoon unsalted butter
- 1 tablespoon extra-virgin olive oil
- ¾ pound sweet or hot Italian sausage, cut into ¼-inch-thick rounds
- 1 medium garlic clove, minced
- 1 28-ounce can whole tomatoes, drained, seeded, and coarsely chopped (see illustration, page 136)
- ¼ cup chopped fresh flat-leaf parsley leaves
- ¼ cup dry white wine
- 1 pound penne or other short, tubular pasta

1. Sprinkle the chicken with salt and pepper. Heat the butter and oil in a 12-inch sauté pan or small Dutch oven over medium-high heat. When butter foaming subsides, add the chicken; sauté until browned on both sides, moving the pieces around to brown them evenly, 10 to 15 minutes. Remove the chicken pieces from the pan and set aside.

2. Discard all but a thin film of fat from the pan. Add the sausage and sauté, stirring frequently, until lightly browned, 4 to 5 minutes. Stir in the garlic.

3. Return the chicken and accumulated juices to the pan. Add the tomatoes, parsley, and wine; bring to a boil. Lower the heat, cover, and barely simmer until the chicken is cooked through, turning once, about 25 minutes. Remove the chicken from the pot with a slotted spoon and cool slightly. Skim the excess grease from the sauce. Remove the skin from the chicken and discard. Remove the meat from the bones and shred into bite-size pieces. Return the meat to the sauce. Taste for salt and pepper.

4. Bring 4 quarts of water to a boil in a large pot. Add 1 tablespoon salt and the pasta. Cook until al dente. Drain the pasta, return it to the cooking pot, and stir in the sauce. Serve immediately.

Sauces with Ground Chicken and Chicken Livers

GROUND CHICKEN CAN BE used in recipes originally designed for ground beef. It is especially appealing for people who are trying to cut fat from their diet. However, if this is your reason for choosing ground chicken, make sure to read labels: some ground chicken made with mostly dark meat and lots of skin actually has *more* fat than ground sirloin. It may taste good, but we don't quite see the logic of using high-fat ground chicken.

We have chosen two favorite meat sauces—bolognese sauce and meatballs—and used ground chicken instead. Ground chicken is fairly bland so we have added fresh mushrooms to our chicken bolognese-style sauce and used buttermilk to give our meatballs with ground chicken some tang.

We have also included a pasta sauce based on chicken livers for the more adventurous cook.

Fusilli with Chicken "Bolognese" Sauce

THIS IS A LIGHTENED VERSION OF A FAVORITE MEAT SAUCE FOR PASTA (SEE PAGE 198 FOR MORE INFORMATION). CHICKEN DOES NOT BENEFIT FROM SLOW SIMMERING FOR HOURS; WE PREFER TO USE IT FOR A QUICK SAUCE FLAVORED WITH MUSHROOMS AND TOMATOES. WE CHOOSE FUSILLI—LITTLE CORKSCREW SHAPES—BECAUSE THEY CATCH THE BITS OF GROUND CHICKEN AND MUSHROOM, BUT OTHER SHAPES WORK EQUALLY WELL—TRY ORECCHIETTE OR RIGATONI. SERVES 4.

> 1 tablespoon extra-virgin olive oil
> 1 pound ground chicken
> ½ pound fresh mushrooms, cleaned and
>   sliced thin
> Salt and ground black pepper
> 2 medium garlic cloves, finely chopped
> 1 tablespoon chopped fresh oregano *or*
>   ½ teaspoon dried oregano
> 3 cups canned crushed tomatoes
> 1 pound fusilli
> Grated Parmesan cheese

1. Heat the oil over medium-high heat in a large skillet. Add the chicken and cook, stirring frequently, until it loses its pink color, 3 to 4 minutes. Add the mushrooms and salt and pepper to taste and cook an additional 3 minutes. Add the garlic and oregano, and cook, stirring frequently, until the mushrooms release their juices, about 2 more minutes. Add the tomatoes and simmer, stirring occasionally, until the sauce thickens, about 15 minutes longer.

2. While the sauce is cooking, bring 4 quarts of water to a boil in a large pot. Add 1 tablespoon of salt and the fusilli and cook until al dente. Drain the pasta, return it to the cooking pot, and stir in the sauce. Serve immediately with grated Parmesan passed separately at the table.

Spaghetti and Chicken Meatballs

SEE PAGE 209 FOR MORE INFORMATION ON SPAGHETTI AND MEATBALLS. CHICKEN MEATBALLS ARE SOFTER THAN THOSE MADE FROM BEEF OR PORK, SO THEY SHOULD BE REFRIGERATED BEFORE FRYING TO PREVENT STICKING AND FALLING APART. **SERVES 4 TO 6.**

> 2 slices white sandwich bread, crusts removed and torn into small pieces
> ½ cup buttermilk
> 1 pound ground chicken
> ¼ cup grated Parmesan cheese, plus extra for the table
> 2 tablespoons finely minced fresh flat-leaf parsley leaves
> 1 large egg yolk
> 2 medium garlic cloves, finely chopped
> Salt and ground black pepper
> About 1¼ cups vegetable oil for pan-frying meatballs
> 2 tablespoons extra-virgin olive oil
> 1 28-ounce can crushed tomatoes
> 1 tablespoon finely chopped fresh basil leaves
> 1 pound spaghetti

1. Combine the bread and buttermilk in a small bowl, mashing with a fork until the buttermilk is absorbed and the mixture becomes a smooth paste (see illustration 1, page 209).

2. Place the ground chicken, cheese, parsley, egg yolk, half of the garlic, and salt and pepper to taste in a medium bowl. Add the bread-milk mixture and combine until evenly mixed. Shape 3 tablespoons of the mixture into 1½-inch round meatballs (you should get about 14 meatballs), cover with plastic wrap, and refrigerate until firm, about 1 hour.

3. Pour the vegetable oil into a 10- or 11-inch sauté pan. Turn the heat to medium-high. After several minutes, test the oil with the edge of a meatball. When the oil sizzles, add the meatballs in a single layer. Fry, turning several times, until nicely browned on all sides, about 10 minutes. Transfer the browned meatballs to a plate lined with paper towels.

4. Discard the oil in the pan but leave behind any browned bits. Add the olive oil along with the remaining garlic and sauté, scraping up any browned bits, just until the garlic is golden, about 30 seconds. Add the tomatoes, bring to a boil, then simmer gently until the sauce thickens, about 10 minutes. Stir in the basil and salt and pepper to taste. Add the meatballs and simmer, turning them occasionally, until heated through, about 5 minutes. Keep warm over low heat.

5. While the sauce is cooking, bring 4 quarts of water to a boil in a large pot. Add 1 tablespoon salt and the pasta. Cook until al dente, drain, and return to the pot. Ladle several large spoonfuls of tomato sauce (without meatballs) over the spaghetti and toss until the pasta is well coated. Divide the pasta among individual bowls and top each with a little more tomato sauce and several meatballs. Serve immediately with grated cheese passed separately.

◆

Spaghetti with Chicken Livers

CHICKEN LIVERS ARE SAUTEED, THEN BRAISED IN THIS RECIPE. DON'T LET THE LIVERS BROWN OR THEY WON'T ABSORB THE FLAVORS OF THE SAUCE AS WELL. WE FOUND IT BEST TO JUST COOK THE CHICKEN LIVERS UNTIL THEY NO LONGER LOOK RAW AND THEN ADD THE TOMATO PASTE AND WINE TO THE PAN. **SERVES 4.**

> 1 tablespoon unsalted butter
> 1 tablespoon extra-virgin olive oil
> 1 medium shallot, minced
> 1 medium garlic clove, minced
> 2 ounces pancetta, finely chopped
> 1 teaspoon minced fresh sage leaves
> ½ pound chicken livers, fat and membranes removed, cut into quarters
> Salt and ground black pepper
> 1 tablespoon tomato paste
> ¼ cup dry white wine
> 1 pound spaghetti
> ¼ cup grated Parmesan cheese

1. Heat the butter and oil in a large skillet over medium-high heat. Add the shallot and cook until softened, about 2 minutes. Add the garlic, pancetta, and sage and cook until the pancetta softens, 2 to 3 minutes. Add the chicken livers, season with salt and pepper to taste, and cook, stirring occasionally, until they have lost their raw color, 3 to 4 minutes.

2. Add the tomato paste and wine to the pan. Bring to a simmer and cook, stirring frequently, until most of the liquid has evaporated, 5 to 7 minutes. Season with salt and pepper.

3. Meanwhile, bring 4 quarts of water to a boil in a large pot. Add 1 tablespoon salt and the pasta to the boiling water. Cook until al dente. Reserve ½ cup cooking water; drain the pasta. Return the pasta to the cooking pot and stir in the sauce and cheese. Add as much reserved cooking water as needed to moisten the pasta and serve immediately.

Sauces with Game Birds

QUAIL AND SQUAB ARE commonly used in Italy to create pasta sauces. We find that these game birds are best in spare sauces that highlight the gaminess of the meat. If the game flavor does not come through in the sauce, you might as well use chicken.

We found that keeping the liquid in the sauce to a minimum helps bring out the flavor of the game. As with chicken thighs, we like to brown the birds and then braise them. However, we use far less tomato and wine. This way, the flavor of the meat—which must be stripped from the bones once the game birds are cooked through—remains intense.

Because there is so little tomato in these sauces, they are dry. Make sure to reserve some pasta cooking water for thinning the sauce to help it coat the noodles. These rich sauces are best with wide noodles such as fettuccine or pappardelle. They also work especially well with fresh pasta.

Fettuccine with Quail

ALTHOUGH THEY ARE TINY BIRDS, QUAIL YIELD A SUR-PRISING QUANTITY OF MEAT FOR THIS SAUCE. QUAIL MEAT IS DARK BUT DELICATE. JUST A SMALL AMOUNT OF CRUSHED TOMATO IS USED TO MOISTEN THE SAUCE —ANY MORE WOULD OVERWHELM THE FLAVOR OF THE QUAIL. THIS SAUCE IS ESPECIALLY GOOD WITH FRESH PASTA. SERVES 4.

> 4 whole quail (about 5 ounces each),
>   rinsed and patted dry
> Salt and ground black pepper
> 2 tablespoons extra-virgin olive oil
> 1 small onion, minced
> 1 small celery stalk, minced
> 1 small carrot, peeled and minced
> 1 teaspoon minced fresh rosemary leaves
> ½ cup dry white wine
> ¼ cup canned crushed tomatoes
> 1 pound Fresh Egg Pasta (page 21) cut
>   into fettuccine *or* dried fettuccine
> Grated Parmesan cheese

1. Sprinkle the quail with salt and pepper to taste. Heat the oil in a 12-inch sauté pan or small Dutch oven over medium-high heat. Add the quail; sauté until browned on both sides, moving them around to brown evenly, 10 to 15 minutes. Remove the quail from the pan and set aside.

2. Discard all but a thin film of fat from the pan. Add the onion, celery, carrot, and rosemary to the pan and sauté, stirring frequently, until softened, about 5 minutes. Return the quail to the pan. Add the wine and tomatoes and bring to a boil. Lower the heat, cover, and barely simmer until the quail are cooked through, basting 3 or 4 times, about 20 minutes. Remove the quail from the pot with a slotted spoon and cool slightly. Skim the excess grease from the sauce. Remove the skin from the quail and discard. Remove the meat from the bones and shred into bite-size pieces. Return the quail meat to the pot. Season with salt and pepper to taste.

(continued on next page)

3. Bring 4 quarts of water to a boil in a large pot. Add 1 tablespoon salt and the pasta to the boiling water. Cook until al dente. Reserve ½ cup of the cooking water; drain the pasta and return it to the cooking pot. Mix in ¼ cup of the reserved cooking water and the sauce; use the additional ¼ cup cooking water as needed to moisten the sauce. Serve immediately with cheese passed separately at the table.

◆

Pappardelle with Squab

SQUAB MEAT IS DARK AND GAMIER THAN EITHER CHICKEN THIGHS OR QUAIL MEAT. IT PAIRS WELL WITH STRONGLY FLAVORED INGREDIENTS LIKE PANCETTA AND SAGE. SQUAB, LIKE QUAIL, IS SO FLAVORFUL THAT WE LIKE TO LET IT SHINE ALMOST BY ITSELF. BE SURE TO RESERVE SOME OF THE COOKING LIQUID FROM THE PASTA TO MOISTEN THE SAUCE; THE DISH WILL BE TOO DRY OTHERWISE. SERVES 4.

> 2 squab (about 1 pound each), rinsed and patted dry
> Salt and ground black pepper
> 2 ¼-inch-thick slices pancetta (about 3 ounces)
> 2 tablespoons unsalted butter
> 2 tablespoons extra-virgin olive oil
> 1 tablespoon minced fresh sage leaves
> ½ cup dry white wine
> ¼ cup canned crushed tomatoes
> 1 pound Fresh Egg Pasta (page 21) cut into pappardelle *or* dried fettuccine
> Grated Parmesan cheese

1. Sprinkle the squab with salt and pepper to taste and place a piece of pancetta inside the cavity of each squab. Heat the butter and oil in a 12-inch sauté pan or small Dutch oven over medium-high heat. When butter foaming subsides, add the squab and sage; sauté until browned on all sides, moving around to brown evenly, 10 to 15 minutes.

2. Discard all but a thin film of fat from the pan. Add the wine and tomatoes and bring to a boil. Lower the heat, cover, and barely simmer until the squab are cooked through, basting and turning 3 or 4 times,

about 1 hour. Remove the squab from the pot with a slotted spoon and cool slightly. Skim the excess grease from the sauce. Remove the skin from the squab and discard. Remove the pancetta from the cavities and finely chop. Remove the meat from the bones and shred into bite-size pieces. Return the squab meat and pancetta to the pan. Taste for salt and pepper. Heat through.

3. Meanwhile, bring 4 quarts of water to a boil in a large pot. Add 1 tablespoon salt and the pasta to the boiling water. Cook until al dente. Reserve ½ cup of the cooking water; drain the pasta and return it to the cooking pot. Mix in ¼ cup of the reserved cooking water and the sauce; use the additional ¼ cup cooking water as needed to moisten the sauce. Serve immediately with cheese passed separately at the table.

Sauces with Duck

LIKE GAME BIRDS OR RABBIT, duck makes a rich sauce that is ideal with fresh pasta. The issue with duck, as always, is the fat. Since a whole duck is too large to fit into a braising pan, we started by cutting the duck into six pieces—two legs and thighs, two breasts, and two wings—and then following our recipe for chicken thighs. Unfortunately, even after thorough skimming the sauce was so greasy it was inedible.

Next we tried skinning the pieces before browning them. This was the key. The meat did not dry out because duck has so much internal fat that slowly renders during the browning and braising process. While we did cut down on the fat significantly, we still found it essential to degrease the sauce after the duck had been removed from the pan. Again, simply allow the sauce to cool slightly and wait for grease to pool up on top. It can then be spooned off and discarded.

The wings have so little meat on them that it is not worth cooking them in this recipe. Save the wings and back to make stock and rely on the legs and breasts for pasta sauces.

Fettuccine with Duck

SERVES 4

DUCK HAS MUCH MORE fat than chicken thighs, quail, or squab. Before braising, we remove as much of the fat and skin as possible. Plenty will still be rendered as the duck pieces cook, so it is important to skim the fat again from the finished sauce before serving. Ask your butcher to cut the prosciutto in one piece.

1 tablespoon extra-virgin olive oil
1 duck (about 4½ pounds), legs and
  breasts removed from the carcass and
  skinned (see illustrations 1–5, page
  226)
Salt and ground black pepper
1 medium onion, minced
1 thick slice prosciutto (about 4 ounces),
  cut into ¼-inch dice
3 medium garlic cloves, minced
4 large sage leaves, minced
1 cup dry white wine
1 cup canned crushed tomatoes
1 pound Fresh Egg Pasta (page 21) cut
  into fettuccine *or* dried fettuccine

1. Heat the oil in a 12-inch sauté pan or small Dutch oven over medium-high heat. Sprinkle the duck pieces with salt and pepper to taste. Add the duck pieces and brown quickly, about 3 minutes on each side. Remove the pieces and set aside.

2. Turn the heat down to medium. Add the onion and prosciutto to the pan and sauté, stirring frequently, until they soften, 1 to 2 minutes. Stir in the garlic and sage. Turn the heat back to high. Add the wine, and scrape the skillet bottom with a wooden spatula or spoon to loosen the browned bits. Add the tomatoes and bring to a boil. Return the duck and accumulated juices to the pan. Lower the heat, cover, and barely simmer, turning once, until the duck is cooked through, about 25 minutes. Remove the duck from the pot with a slotted spoon and cool slightly. Skim the excess grease from the pan. Remove the meat from the bones and shred into bite-size pieces. Return the meat to the pot and discard the bones. Taste for salt and pepper.

3. Meanwhile, bring 4 quarts of water to a boil in a large pot. Add 1 tablespoon salt and the pasta. Cook until al dente. Reserve ½ cup of the cooking water; drain the pasta and return it to the cooking pot. Mix in ¼ cup of the reserved cooking water and the sauce; use the additional ¼ cup cooking water as needed to moisten the sauce. Serve immediately.

CUTTING UP
A DUCK

We find that the legs and breast have all the meat on the duck and it's not worthwhile to braise the wings. Save them, along with the carcass, to make stock.

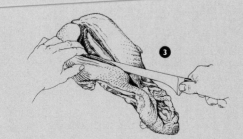

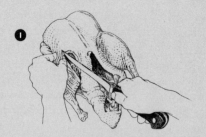

1. Start by slicing through the skin that attaches the leg to the breast with a boning knife. Continue cutting down through the meat until you feel the thigh joint with your knife. The thigh joint is much closer to the back than on a chicken.

2. When you feel the joint, pull back on the leg to pop it out. Continue cutting around the leg to free it from the carcass. Repeat with the other leg.

3. Slice down along the breastbone, peeling back the breast meat with your hand to separate it from the carcass.

4. Cut along the side of the duck where the ribs meet the back to free the breast half from the carcass. Repeat on the other side of the duck.

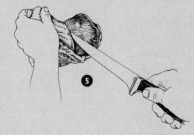

5. Using a boning knife, carefully separate the membrane and skin from each leg and breast piece. Pull away any visible pieces of fat as well.

Fettuccine with Duck and Olives

DUCK AND OLIVES ARE A CLASSIC COMBINATION. WE LIKE THE LOOK AND FLAVOR OF GREEN OLIVES WITH RED WINE, BUT BLACK OLIVES LIKE KALAMATA MAY BE SUBSTITUTED TO MAKE AN ATTRACTIVE DARK PURPLE SAUCE. SERVES 4.

1 tablespoon extra-virgin olive oil
1 duck (about 4½ pounds), legs and breasts removed from the carcass and skinned (see illustrations 1–5, page 226)
Salt and ground black pepper
1 medium garlic clove, minced
½ cup green olives, pitted and coarsely chopped (see illustrations 1–2, page 62)
1 cup red wine
½ cup water or chicken stock
¼ cup tomato paste
1 pound Fresh Egg Pasta (page 21) cut into fettuccine *or* dried fettuccine
1 tablespoon minced fresh flat-leaf parsley leaves

1. Heat the oil in a 12-inch sauté pan or small Dutch oven over medium-high heat. Sprinkle the duck pieces with salt and pepper to taste. Add the duck pieces and brown quickly, about 3 minutes on each side. Remove the pieces and set aside.

2. Turn the heat down to medium. Add the garlic and olives to the pan and sauté, stirring frequently, until the garlic just begins to color, about 30 seconds. Turn the heat back to high. Add the wine and scrape the skillet bottom with a wooden spatula or spoon to loosen the browned bits. Add the water and tomato paste and bring to a boil. Return the duck and accumulated juices to the pan. Lower the heat, cover, and barely simmer, turning once, until the duck is cooked through, about 25 minutes. Remove the duck from the pot with a slotted spoon and cool slightly. Skim the excess grease from the pan. Remove the meat from the bones and shred into bite-size pieces. Return the meat to the pot and discard the bones. Taste for salt and pepper.

3. Meanwhile, bring 4 quarts of water to a boil in a large pot. Add 1 tablespoon salt and the pasta. Cook until al dente. Reserve ½ cup of the cooking water; drain the pasta and return it to the cooking pot. Mix in ¼ cup of the reserved cooking water, the parsley, and the sauce; use the additional ¼ cup cooking water as needed to moisten the sauce. Serve immediately.

Sauces with Rabbit

LIKE QUAIL, SQUAB, and duck, rabbit makes a rich, intense sauce for pasta. We found it best to cut the rabbit into smaller pieces before browning and braising. Since the butcher removes the skin during the gutting process, we floured the rabbit pieces to keep the meat from drying out or scorching.

As with game birds, sauces made with rabbit are best when highly concentrated and not very liquidy. To spread the sauce over the pasta, make sure to reserve some of the cooking liquid. Again, rich rabbit sauces are especially well suited to wide fresh noodles such as pappardelle and fettuccine.

Pappardelle with Rabbit Sauce

SERVES 4

G AME SAUCES SUCH AS this one have been staples of Italian country cooking for centuries. We like to cook the rabbit on the bone for two reasons—bones give the sauce a wonderful flavor, and the meat is much easier to remove after cooking than before.

1 rabbit (about 1¾ pounds), cut up (see
   illustrations 1–4, page 229), rinsed and
   patted dry
Salt and ground black pepper
¼ cup all-purpose flour
3 tablespoons olive oil
2 fresh rosemary sprigs
1 small onion, minced
1 medium celery stalk, minced
1 medium garlic clove, minced
1 cup dry red wine
2 bay leaves
1 tablespoon tomato paste
1 pound Fresh Egg Pasta (page 21) cut
   into pappardelle *or* dried fettuccine
Grated Parmesan cheese

1. Sprinkle the rabbit pieces with salt and pepper to taste. Place the flour in a shallow bowl and dredge the rabbit pieces, shaking off any excess.

2. Heat the oil in a 12-inch sauté pan or small Dutch oven over medium-high heat. Add the rabbit and rosemary; sauté until browned on both sides, moving the pieces around to brown them evenly, 8 to 10 minutes. Remove the rabbit pieces from the pan and set aside.

3. Discard all but a thin film of fat from the pan but leave in the rosemary sprigs. Add the onion and celery; sauté, stirring frequently to prevent scorching, until softened, 4 to 5 minutes. Stir in the garlic.

4. Return the rabbit and accumulated juices to the pan. Add the wine, bay leaves, and tomato paste; bring to a boil. Lower the heat, cover, and barely simmer, basting 3 or 4 times, until the rabbit is tender, about 1½ hours. Remove the rabbit from the pot with a slotted spoon and cool slightly. Remove and discard the rosemary sprigs and bay leaves. Remove the meat from the bones. Shred the meat into bite-size pieces and return it to the pot; discard the bones. Taste for salt and pepper.

5. Meanwhile, bring 4 quarts of water to a boil in a large pot. Add 1 tablespoon salt and the pasta. Cook until al dente. Reserve ½ cup of the cooking water; drain the pasta and return it to the cooking pot. Mix in ¼ cup of the reserved cooking water and the sauce; use the additional ¼ cup cooking water as needed to moisten the sauce. Serve immediately with cheese passed separately at the table.

CUTTING UP A RABBIT

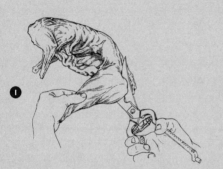

1. Cut each hindquarter away from the body using poultry shears or a cleaver. Each hindquarter is small enough to cook whole.

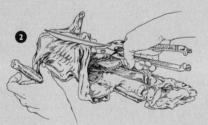

2. Cut through the rib cage along the breastbone. Open up the body of the rabbit and lay it flat like a book.

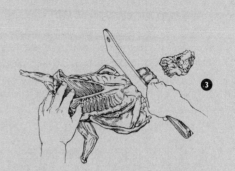

3. Starting at the tail end, use poultry shears or a cleaver to cut the body of the rabbit into 2-inch lengths.

4. When you reach the neck, separate each forequarter from the neck and discard the neck. As with the hindquarters, leave each forequarter whole.

Pappardelle with Rabbit and Shiitake Mushrooms

IN THIS SIMPLE VARIATION ON THE MASTER RECIPE, WOODSY MUSHROOMS COMPLEMENT THE GAMY FLAVOR OF THE MEAT. OTHER MUSHROOMS MAY BE SUBSTITUTED WITH EQUALLY GOOD RESULTS—TRY PORTOBELLOS OR MORELS. ASK YOUR BUTCHER TO CUT THE PANCETTA IN ONE PIECE. SERVES 4.

- 1 rabbit (about 1¾ pounds), cut up (see illustrations 1–4, page 229), rinsed, and patted dry
- Salt and ground black pepper
- ¼ cup all-purpose flour
- 3 tablespoons olive oil
- 1 thick slice pancetta (about ¼ pound), cut into ¼-inch dice
- 1 small onion, minced
- 4 medium garlic cloves, minced
- ¾ pound shiitake mushrooms, stemmed and halved if large
- 1 cup dry white wine
- 1 tablespoon tomato paste
- 2 tablespoons minced fresh flat-leaf parsley leaves
- 1 pound Fresh Egg Pasta (page 21) cut into pappardelle or dried fettuccine
- Grated Parmesan cheese

1. Sprinkle the rabbit pieces with salt and pepper to taste. Place the flour in a shallow bowl and dredge the rabbit pieces, shaking off any excess.

2. Heat the oil in a 12-inch sauté pan or small Dutch oven over medium-high heat. Add the rabbit; sauté until browned on both sides, moving the pieces around to brown them evenly, 8 to 10 minutes. Remove the rabbit pieces from the pan and set aside.

3. Discard all but a thin film of fat from the pan. Add the pancetta and cook until softened, 1 to 2 minutes. Add the onion; sauté, stirring frequently to prevent scorching, until softened, 4 to 5 minutes. Stir in the garlic.

4. Return the rabbit and accumulated juices to the pan. Add the mushrooms, wine, and tomato paste; bring to a boil. Lower the heat, cover, and barely simmer, basting 3 or 4 times, until the rabbit is tender, about 1½ hours. Remove the rabbit from the pot with a slotted spoon and cool slightly. Remove the meat from the bones. Shred the meat into bite-size pieces and return it to the pot; discard the bones. Stir in parsley and add salt and pepper to taste.

5. Meanwhile, bring 4 quarts of water to a boil in a large pot. Add 1 tablespoon salt and the pasta. Cook until al dente. Reserve ½ cup of the cooking water; drain the pasta and return it to the cooking pot. Mix in ¼ cup of the reserved cooking water and the sauce; use the additional ¼ cup cooking water as needed to moisten the sauce. Serve immediately with cheese passed separately at the table.

SAUCES WITH
SEAFOOD

/I\

THE MOST IMPORTANT THING TO REMEMBER WHEN

PREPARING SEAFOOD PASTA SAUCES IS TO KEEP THE

COOKING TIME TO A MINIMUM. YOU WANT TO RE-

TAIN AS MUCH AS POSSIBLE OF THE NATURAL JUICES

SHED BY THE COOKING SEAFOOD AND INCORPORATE

THEM INTO THE PASTA SAUCE. BESIDES, PROLONGED

COOKING WILL CAUSE MOST SEAFOOD (SQUID IS A

NOTABLE EXCEPTION) TO TOUGHEN OR DRY OUT.

Each kind of seafood presents its own challenge at the market when shopping, as well as at home when preparing and cooking it. The items from the sea that are most commonly used in pasta sauces are discussed in this chapter in alphabetical order.

Sauces with Anchovies

FOR MOST AMERICANS, anchovies are tiny, dark fillets packed in oil and sold in tiny cans. These anchovies are fine as long as the oil itself is of decent quality. We find that anchovies packed in olive oil are generally more flavorful than those packed in vegetable oil. However, for the best-quality anchovies,

look for fish that have been preserved with salt. Salt-packed anchovies, which are sold in cans in Italian markets and some gourmet shops, are larger and meatier than oil-packed fish. They also have a milder, less fishy flavor that we prefer.

When using salt-packed anchovies, rinse them to wash away excess salt. (You may want to rinse oil-packed anchovies as well, especially in recipes that call for more than three or four fillets.) Oil-packed anchovies are ready to be minced. Salt-packed anchovies must be filleted according to illustrations 1 and 2 and then minced.

◆

Spaghetti with Anchovies

SALT-PACKED ANCHOVIES ARE LARGER, MEATIER, AND HAVE A MILDER FLAVOR THAN THE MORE COMMON CANNED VARIETY PACKED IN OIL. THEY MAKE A DIFFERENCE IN A SAUCE LIKE THIS ONE, WHERE ANCHOVIES ARE THE MAIN INGREDIENT, NOT JUST A SUPPORTING ELEMENT. HOWEVER, THIS DISH IS STILL DELICIOUS WHEN MADE WITH OIL-PACKED ANCHOVIES. SERVES 4.

> Salt
> 1 pound spaghetti or other long, thin pasta
> ¼ cup extra-virgin olive oil
> 2 medium garlic cloves, minced
> 5 salt-packed anchovies, rinsed, bones removed (see illustrations 1–2), and minced, *or* 12 canned anchovy fillets, rinsed and minced
> ¼ cup lemon juice
> ¼ cup minced fresh flat-leaf parsley leaves
> Ground black pepper

1. Bring 4 quarts of water to a boil in a large pot. Add 1 tablespoon salt and the pasta and cook until al dente.

2. Meanwhile, heat the oil and garlic over medium heat in a small skillet; cook until fragrant, about 1 minute. Add the anchovies and cook, stirring, until dissolved, about 1 minute. Remove from the heat and stir in the lemon juice and parsley.

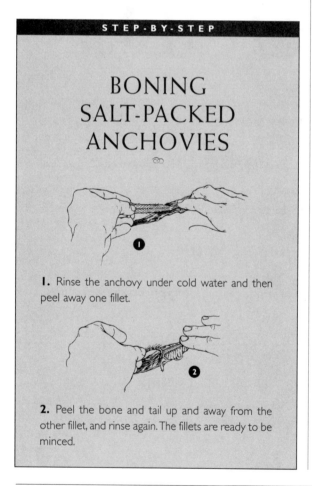

STEP-BY-STEP

BONING SALT-PACKED ANCHOVIES

1. Rinse the anchovy under cold water and then peel away one fillet.

2. Peel the bone and tail up and away from the other fillet, and rinse again. The fillets are ready to be minced.

3. Drain the pasta and return it to the cooking pot. Stir in the anchovy sauce and salt and pepper to taste. Divide among 4 warmed pasta bowls and serve immediately.

Sauces with Clams

LIKE MANY AMERICANS, we grew up eating spaghetti with clam sauce that was a soggy mess of canned clams tossed with some overcooked pasta. In our first go-round with the recipe, a number of years ago, we substituted fresh clams for canned, used extra-virgin olive oil, and added just a touch of white wine. We were pretty satisfied with these improvements, but we were determined to see if we could do better. Our memories of pasta and clam sauce eaten in Italy held this dish to an even higher standard.

First we decided to identify the best clams and to figure out the best way to cook them. We knew that the tiny clams of the Adriatic and other small seas adjacent to the Mediterranean were better than the littlenecks we'd been using, but we couldn't find those clams unless we begged them from chefs. So we began by buying the tiniest littlenecks we could find. This helped somewhat, but with clams selling for about $5 a dozen regardless of size, a simple pasta dish for four quickly became an extravagance.

At that point, we detoured to see whether we could make a credible dish using canned clams. In recent years, tiny canned clams have appeared on the supermarket shelves, and at about $1.50 a can, they seemed worth a try. Although using these tiny clams improved on the canned clam sauce of our childhood, it didn't measure up to even the worst pasta sauce with fresh clams we'd ever produced.

So we went back to finding a substitute for expensive littlenecks. First we tried the larger cherrystones and even giant quahogs (they're all the same species, just increasingly bigger specimens), lightly steamed and chopped into pieces. But no matter how long or short we cooked them, they were tough and they lacked the distinctive, fresh brininess of littlenecks. However, we did learn something: large, less palatable, and far less expensive clams gave us the same kind of delicious clam juice—the backbone of this dish—as small clams.

Then we found some cockles—baby clams that are almost as small as the kind you find in Italy. Because they're sold by the pound, not the dozen, and because they're small, these were less expensive and quite delicious. Unfortunately, they're not nearly as widely available as littlenecks. The alternative is littlenecks, the littler the better, and at least eight (preferably a dozen or more) per person.

Because we still favored using all littlenecks or cockles, this dish remained quite expensive. So we resolved that if we were going to pay a small fortune for the dish, we would make sure that it would be uniformly wonderful each time we cooked it. There were three problems with our original recipe. One was that the clam meat tended to become overcooked in the time it took to finish the sauce; the other was that there was often not enough clam juice; finally, we thought that the sauce itself could use another dimension of flavor.

Solving the first problem was easy: we cooked the clams first, just until they gave up their juices. Then we recombined the clams with the sauce at the last minute, just enough to reheat them.

Next we turned to the occasional dearth of clam juice. When we were too cheap to buy enough littlenecks, or couldn't find cockles, we combined a couple of dozen littlenecks with about six large quahogs, which we could often buy for just a couple of dollars. Because it's the juice we are after—not the clam meat—this worked out fine; we simply discarded the quahog meat after cooking it. In the end, we found that this cooking method worked well for all pasta sauces made with clams. Of course, the other choice is to buy enough littlenecks (we found that forty is a good number) to ensure that they produce enough juice.

We liked the flavor of white wine mixed with clam juice, but not more than 1/2 cup or so because its distinctive flavor was somewhat overwhelming. Cutting back on the wine, though, robbed the dish of needed acidity. We experimented with lemon juice, but felt that the flavor was too strong. Vinegar, of course, was even worse. Finally, we added just a little bit of diced plum tomato, barely enough to color the sauce. The benefits were immediate: not only was the flavor balanced but another welcome texture was added to the dish.

Satisfied at last, we pronounced this dish perfect. With the final recipe, you can steam the clams open while bringing the pasta water to a boil and preparing the other ingredients. Once the clams are done, begin browning the garlic; five minutes later, put in the pasta and finish the sauce. The timing is perfect, and perfectly easy.

We don't feel that it's worth the effort to remove the clams from their shells before serving. Simply put an empty bowl out on the table so each diner can pick out the meat and have a place to discard the empty shells.

Spaghetti with Clam Sauce

SERVES 4

YOU CAN SAVE A little money by substituting 6 large, inexpensive quahogs, which provide plenty of liquid for a briny, brothy dish, for about half the price of littlenecks or cockles. Because quahogs are so cheap, discard the steamed meat without guilt and dine on the sweet, tender littlenecks or cockles with the pasta.

40 littleneck clams (the smaller the better), *or* 3 pounds cockles, *or* 24 littleneck clams and 6 quahogs (the larger the better), all scrubbed thoroughly

½ cup dry white wine
Pinch cayenne pepper
¼ cup extra-virgin olive oil
2 medium garlic cloves, minced
1 large or 2 small plum tomatoes, peeled, seeded, and minced (see illustrations 1–3, page 112)
Salt
1 pound spaghetti or other long, thin pasta
¾ cup chopped fresh flat-leaf parsley leaves

1. Bring 4 quarts of water to a boil in a large pot for cooking the pasta.

2. Bring the clams, wine, and cayenne to a boil in a deep, 10- to 12-inch covered skillet over high heat. Boil, shaking the pan occasionally, until the littlenecks or cockles begin to open, 3 to 5 minutes. Transfer the littlenecks or cockles with a slotted spoon to a medium bowl; set aside. (If using quahogs, re-cover the pan and continue cooking until their liquid is released, about 5 minutes longer. Discard the quahogs.) Strain the liquid in the pan through a paper towel–lined sieve into a large measuring cup. Add enough water to make 1 cup; set aside.

3. Heat the oil and garlic in the cleaned skillet over medium-low heat until the garlic turns pale gold, 2 to 3 minutes. Add the tomatoes, raise the heat to high, and sauté until the tomatoes soften, about 2 minutes longer. Add the littlenecks or cockles and cover; cook until all the clams open fully, 1 to 2 minutes longer.

4. Meanwhile, add 1 tablespoon salt and the pasta to the boiling water. Cook until al dente. Drain the pasta, transfer to the skillet, and toss. Add the reserved clam liquid and cook until the flavors meld, about 30 seconds. Stir in the parsley and adjust the seasonings. Divide among 4 pasta bowls and serve immediately.

Cavatelli with White Beans and Clams

CLAMS HAVE A SURPRISING AFFINITY FOR WHITE BEANS;
THE BRINY, TENDER CLAMS CONTRAST BEAUTIFULLY
WITH CREAMY, MILD BEANS. THIS RECIPE COMES FROM
APULIA AND IS TRADITIONALLY MADE WITH TINY LOCAL
MUSSELS, ½ INCH TO ¾ INCH LONG. LARGER MUSSELS,
THE ONLY KIND AVAILABLE HERE, JUST WON'T DO, SO
WE HAVE SUBSTITUTED SMALL CLAMS WITH GREAT SUC-
CESS. IF YOU CAN FIND SMALL MUSSELS, HOWEVER, BY
ALL MEANS USE THEM. SEE PAGES 185–187 FOR MORE
INFORMATION ON COOKING BEANS. SERVES 4.

> ½ cup (about 3 ounces) dried cannellini
>   or great northern beans
> 1 bay leaf
> 4 medium garlic cloves, 2 peeled and
>   2 minced
> Salt
> 40 littleneck clams (the smaller the better),
>   *or* 3 pounds cockles, *or* 24 littleneck
>   clams and 6 quahogs (the larger the
>   better), all scrubbed thoroughly
> ⅓ cup extra-virgin olive oil
> 4 medium tomatoes, peeled, seeded, and
>   chopped (see illustrations, pages
>   111–112) *or* 2 cups diced canned
>   tomatoes
> ½ cup minced fresh flat-leaf parsley
>   leaves
> Ground black pepper
> 1 pound fresh Whole Wheat Pasta (page
>   25), shaped into cavatelli or small shells

1. Bring the beans, bay leaf, peeled garlic, ¾ teaspoon salt, and 4 cups of water to a boil in a large
saucepan. Simmer, partially covered, until the beans
are just tender, 30 to 45 minutes depending on the
type of bean and its age. Remove from the heat, cover,
and let the beans stand until completely tender, about
15 minutes. Discard the bay leaf and garlic. (The
beans in liquid can be cooled, covered, and refrigerated up to 5 days.) Reserve 1 cup of cooking liquid
and drain the beans when ready to use.

2. Bring the clams and ½ cup water to a boil in a
deep, 10- to 12-inch covered skillet over high heat.
Boil, shaking the pan occasionally, until the littlenecks
or cockles begin to open, 3 to 5 minutes. Transfer the
littlenecks or cockles with a slotted spoon to a
medium bowl; set aside. (If using quahogs, re-cover
the pan and continue cooking until their liquid is
released, about 5 minutes longer. Discard the quahogs.) Strain the liquid in the pan through a paper
towel–lined sieve into a large measuring cup. Add
enough bean cooking liquid to make 1 cup; set aside.
(Discard remaining bean cooking liquid.)

3. Heat the oil and minced garlic in the cleaned skillet over medium-low heat until fragrant, about 30 seconds. Stir in the drained beans and cook to blend the
flavors, about 5 minutes. Stir in the tomatoes, parsley,
clams, and ½ cup of the clam-bean liquid. Cover and
cook until all the clams open fully, 1 to 2 minutes
longer. Adjust the seasonings, adding salt and pepper
to taste.

4. Meanwhile, bring 4 quarts of water to a boil in a
large pot. Add 1 tablespoon salt and the pasta. Cook
until al dente. Drain the pasta, transfer to the skillet,
and toss. If the mixture seems dry, add more clam-
bean liquid. Adjust the seasonings. Divide among 4
pasta bowls and serve immediately.

Linguine with Clam Sauce with Tomatoes and Garlic

THIS IS OUR VERSION OF LINGUINE WITH RED CLAM SAUCE. IF YOU CAN, MAKE THIS SAUCE WITH TINY COCKLES, WHICH ARE PARTICULARLY TENDER AND SWEET. AS A SECOND CHOICE, BUY SMALL LITTLENECKS. SERVE WITH LINGUINE OR SPAGHETTI. SERVES 4.

    40 littleneck clams (the smaller the
        better), or 3 pounds cockles, or 24
        littleneck clams and 6 quahogs (the
        larger the better), all scrubbed
        thoroughly
    ¼ cup dry white wine
    1 bay leaf
    3 tablespoons extra-virgin olive oil
    3 medium garlic cloves, minced
    2 cups canned whole tomatoes, coarsely
        chopped, with liquid reserved
    1 tablespoon minced fresh oregano leaves
        or 1 teaspoon dried
    Salt and ground black pepper
    1 pound linguine or other long, thin pasta

1. Bring 4 quarts of water to a boil in a large pot for cooking the pasta.

2. Bring the clams, wine, and bay leaf to a boil in a deep 10- to 12-inch covered skillet over high heat. Boil, shaking the pan occasionally, until the littlenecks or cockles begin to open, 3 to 5 minutes. Transfer the littlenecks or cockles with a slotted spoon to a medium bowl; set aside. (If using quahogs, re-cover the pan and continue cooking until their liquid is released, about 5 minutes longer. Discard the quahogs.) Strain the liquid in the pan through a paper towel–lined sieve into a large measuring cup. Add enough water to make 1 cup; set aside.

3. Heat the oil and garlic in the cleaned skillet over medium-low heat until the garlic turns pale gold, 2 to 3 minutes. Add the tomatoes and oregano, raise the heat to high, and sauté until the sauce thickens slightly, about 2 minutes longer. Add the littlenecks or cockles and cover; cook until all the clams are open fully, 1 to 2 minutes longer. Season with salt and pepper.

4. Meanwhile, add 1 tablespoon salt and the pasta to the boiling water. Cook until al dente. Drain the pasta, transfer to the skillet, and toss. Add the reserved clam liquid and cook until the flavors meld, about 30 seconds. Divide among 4 pasta bowls and serve immediately.

◆

Linguine with Clams, Bacon, and Chiles

IN ADDITION TO THE SALTY LIQUID THAT THE CLAMS GIVE OFF AS THEY COOK, THIS SAUCE CONTAINS SALTY BACON, SO YOU MIGHT NOT NEED TO ADD SALT TO THE FINISHED DISH. THE FLAVOR OF THIS DISH CAN BE VARIED BY SUBSTITUTING PANCETTA FOR BACON. SERVES 4.

    40 littleneck clams (the smaller the
        better), or 3 pounds cockles, or 24
        littleneck clams and 6 quahogs (the
        larger the better), all scrubbed
        thoroughly
    ½ cup dry white wine
    ¼ pound sliced bacon, cut into ⅛-inch
        dice
    2 tablespoons extra-virgin olive oil
    4 medium garlic cloves, minced
    1 small fresh hot red chile, seeded and
        minced, or ½ teaspoon hot red pepper
        flakes or to taste
    2 teaspoons grated lemon zest (see
        illustration, page 42)
    Salt
    1 pound spaghetti or other long, thin
        pasta
    ¾ cup chopped fresh flat-leaf parsley
        leaves

1. Bring the clams and wine to a boil in a deep, 10- to 12-inch covered skillet over high heat. Boil, shaking the pan occasionally, until the littlenecks or cockles begin to open, 3 to 5 minutes. Transfer the littlenecks or cockles with a slotted spoon to a medium bowl; set aside. (If using quahogs, re-cover the pan and continue cooking until their liquid is released, about 5 minutes longer. Discard the quahogs.) Strain the liquid in the pan through a paper towel–lined sieve into a large measuring cup. Add enough water to make 1 cup; set aside.

2. Cook the bacon over medium-high heat in the cleaned skillet until crisp, 4 to 5 minutes. Spoon off all but 1 tablespoon bacon fat. Add the oil, garlic, and chile and cook until fragrant, about 1 minute. Stir in the zest and clam liquid. Add the littlenecks or cockles and cover; cook until all the clams open fully, 1 to 2 minutes longer.

3. Meanwhile, bring 4 quarts of water to a boil in a large pot. Add 1 tablespoon salt and the pasta. Cook until al dente. Drain the pasta, transfer to the skillet, and toss. Stir in the parsley and adjust the seasonings. Divide among 4 pasta bowls and serve immediately.

Sauces with Crab

THERE ARE DOZENS OF species of crabs, including stone crabs from Florida, king crabs from Alaska, and Dungeness crabs from the West Coast. The most widely available crab is the blue crab, which is found along the East Coast. Live blue crabs may be boiled and served as is, with a pair of crackers.

There's not much meat on a crab and getting to it is a messy proposition. For those who don't like a mess or to work for their dinner, fresh-picked crabmeat is a good, if expensive, alternative. Other forms of crabmeat just don't compare. A blind tasting of crabmeat found that canned crabmeat is horrible; like canned tuna it bears little resemblance to the fresh product. Fresh pasteurized crabmeat is watery and bland. Frozen crabmeat is stringy and wet. Fresh unpasteurized blue crab meat, preferably "jumbo lump"—which indicates the largest pieces and highest grade—has no substitutes.

Fresh lump crab meat is highly perishable and must be eaten soon after it has been purchased. For best flavor, don't rinse the crabmeat. Just pick over the meat to make sure all the cartilage and shell pieces have been removed. Add the crabmeat to the almost-finished pasta sauce—don't overcook the meat or it

will toughen. As soon as the crab is hot, take the sauce off the heat.

Perhaps the most popular way to consume blue crabs is when they are soft-shell crabs. Soft-shell crabs are blue crabs that have been taken out of the water just after they have shed their shells in the spring or summer. At this brief stage of its life, the whole crab, with its new, soft gray skin, is almost completely edible and especially delicious. They should be purchased live and cleaned at home for optimum flavor. Once cleaned, the crab should be cooked immediately.

To our mind, the whole point of soft-shells is that they must be crisp. The legs should crunch delicately, while the body should provide a contrast between its thin, crisp outer skin and the soft, rich interior that explodes juicily in the mouth. Deep-frying delivers these results, but this method is better suited to restaurants. Air pockets and water in the crab cause a lot of dangerous splattering. For optimum safety, crabs should be fried in a very large quantity of oil in a very deep pot, which is not practical at home.

We wanted to develop an alternative method for home cooks. We tried roasting but found it didn't get the crabs crisp enough. Pan-frying lightly floured crabs produces a satisfyingly crisp crust. As long as you slide a splatter screen over the pan, you can avoid the mess and danger of splattering hot fat. We tried various coatings, including cornmeal, bread crumbs, and even Cream of Wheat. We found that these coatings all detracted from the flavor of the crab. Flour produces a nice crisp crust with minimal flavor distractions.

We tried soaking the crabs in milk for two hours before applying the flour coating, a trick advocated by several sources to "sweeten" the meat. Again, we found that this method detracted from the fresh-from-the-water flavor of the crabs.

We tried various fats for pan-frying, including whole butter, clarified butter, vegetable and peanut oils, and a combination of whole butter and olive oil. We found that whole butter gives the crabs a nutty flavor and browns them well; it is our recommended all-purpose cooking fat. Peanut oil produces especially crisp crabs but does not add the rich flavor of butter.

We found that you need a tablespoon of fat for each crab and a large skillet that will accommodate four crabs in a single layer. Once the soft-shells have been cooked, drain them on paper towels while you build a quick pasta sauce in the now-empty pan.

When shopping for soft-shells, look for fresh rather than frozen crabs. Most stores will offer to clean the crabs for you. Refuse their offer if you can. Once you clean a live crab, it begins to lose its juices. In our tests, we found that a crab cooked immediately after cleaning is plumper and juicier than a crab cleaned several hours before cooking.

◆

Tagliatelle with Crabmeat and Cream Sauce

THIS ALFREDO-STYLE SAUCE DEMANDS THE DELICACY OF FRESH PASTA. SERVES 4.

> 1⅔ cups heavy cream, preferably not ultrapasteurized
> 5 tablespoons unsalted butter
> Salt
> 1 pound Fresh Egg Pasta (page 21) cut into fettuccine
> ½ pound fresh lump crabmeat, drained and picked over
> Pinch cayenne pepper

1. Combine 1⅓ cups cream and the butter in a sauté pan large enough to accommodate the cooked pasta. Heat over low until the butter is melted and the cream comes to a bare simmer. Turn off the heat and set aside.

2. Bring 4 quarts of water to a boil in a large pot. Add 1 tablespoon salt and the pasta to the boiling water. Cook until just al dente. Drain the pasta and add it to the sauté pan. Add the remaining ⅓ cup cream, crabmeat, ½ teaspoon salt, and cayenne. Cook over very low heat, tossing to combine ingredients, until the sauce is slightly thickened, 1 to 2 minutes. Divide among 4 warmed pasta bowls and serve immediately.

CLEANING A SOFT-SHELL CRAB

1. First cut off the soft-shell's mouth with a kitchen scissors. (The mouth is the first part of the shell to harden.) You can also cut off the eyes at the same time, but this is purely aesthetic; the eyes are edible.

2. Next lift the pointed sides of the crab, and cut out the spongy off-white gills underneath; the gills are fibrous and watery and unpleasant to eat.

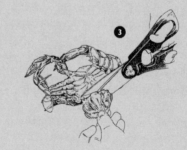

3. Finally, turn the crab on its back and cut off the triangular or T-shaped "apron" flap.

Linguine with Pan-Fried Soft-Shell Crabs

THE TIMING FOR THIS RECIPE IS A BIT TRICKY. START BY BRINGING THE WATER FOR THE PASTA TO A BOIL. WHILE WAITING FOR THE WATER TO COME TO A BOIL, READY THE INGREDIENTS FOR THE SAUCE. AS SOON AS THE PASTA GOES INTO THE BOILING WATER, START COOKING THE CRABS. IDEALLY, THE CRABS AND SAUCE WILL BE FINISHED JUST AS THE PASTA IS READY TO BE DRAINED. SERVES 4.

    Salt
    1 pound linguine or other long, thin pasta
    4 soft-shell crabs, cleaned (see
        illustrations 1–3, page 238) and patted
        dry with paper towels
    All-purpose flour for dredging
    8 tablespoons unsalted butter
    3 tablespoons lemon juice
    1 ½ teaspoons sherry vinegar
    1 ½ teaspoons capers, chopped
    2 tablespoons minced fresh flat-leaf
        parsley leaves
    2 teaspoons minced fresh tarragon
        leaves
    2 scallions, white and light green parts,
        minced
    Ground black pepper

1. Bring 4 quarts of water to a boil in a large pot. Add 1 tablespoon salt and the pasta. Cook until al dente.

2. Meanwhile, dredge the crabs in flour; pat off the excess. Heat an 11- or 12-inch heavy-bottomed frying pan over medium-high heat until the pan is quite hot. Add 4 tablespoons of butter to the pan, swirling the pan to keep the butter from burning as it melts. When the foam subsides, turn the heat to high and add the crabs, skin sides down, to the pan. Cover the pan with a splatter screen and cook, adjusting the heat as necessary to keep the butter from burning, until the crabs turn reddish brown, about 3 minutes. Turn the crabs with a spatula or tongs and cook until the second side is browned, about 3 minutes more. Drain the crabs on a paper towel–lined plate.

3. Pour off the butter from the pan and remove from the heat. Add the juice, sherry vinegar, capers, parsley, tarragon, scallions, and remaining 4 tablespoons butter to this still-warm pan. Swirl the pan to melt the butter. Scrape the bottom of the pan with a wooden spoon to loosen the browned bits.

4. Drain the pasta. Return to the cooking pot and toss with the butter sauce. Adjust the seasonings. Divide among 4 pasta bowls, place one crab on top of each bowl, and serve immediately.

Sauces with Fish

FISH FILLETS MAKE AN unusual but delicious addition to pasta sauces. In general, the fillets may be added directly to a sauce and flaked apart into tiny bits as they cook. The real danger when making these sauces is that the fish will overcook and become too dry. Therefore, it's important to limit the cooking time once the fish has been added to the sauce. Also, we found that flaked fish works best in relatively moist sauce, with tomatoes and/or cream. For instance, a simple olive oil and garlic sauce is too dry to keep swordfish or another fish steak or fillet moist enough to coat pasta evenly.

We have developed three recipes—one with swordfish, one with salmon, and a third with sole.

Penne with Swordfish, Sicilian Style

OTHER MEATY STEAK FISH, SUCH AS HALIBUT OR TUNA, MAY BE USED INSTEAD OF SWORDFISH. DON'T GARNISH THIS DISH WITH CHEESE, BUT USE ½ CUP FRESH TOASTED BREAD CRUMBS (PAGE 90) IF YOU'D LIKE. SERVES 4.

> ½ pound fresh swordfish steak, cut ½ inch thick
> Salt and ground black pepper
> ¼ cup extra-virgin olive oil
> 1 28-ounce can diced tomatoes or whole tomatoes packed in juice
> 2 medium garlic cloves, minced
> 1½ tablespoons pine nuts, toasted
> 1½ tablespoons golden raisins
> 2 tablespoons minced fresh flat-leaf parsley leaves
> 1 pound penne or other short, tubular pasta

1. Sprinkle the swordfish with salt and pepper. Heat 2 tablespoons oil in a small skillet and sauté the swordfish over high heat until browned but still rare inside, about 2 minutes per side. Cool slightly and flake into bite-size pieces with a fork, discarding skin if present; set fish aside.

2. If using diced tomatoes, go to step 3. If using whole tomatoes, drain and reserve the liquid. Dice the tomatoes by hand or in the work bowl of a food processor (use three or four ½-second pulses). The tomatoes should be coarse, with ¼-inch pieces visible. If necessary, add enough reserved liquid to the tomatoes to total 2⅔ cups.

3. Heat the remaining 2 tablespoons oil and the garlic in a medium sauté pan over medium heat until fragrant but not brown, about 2 minutes. Stir in the tomatoes; simmer until thickened slightly, about 10 minutes. Stir in the swordfish, pine nuts, raisins, parsley, and salt and pepper to taste.

4. Meanwhile, bring 4 quarts of water to a boil in a large pot. Add 1 tablespoon salt and the pasta. Cook until al dente. Reserve ¼ cup of the cooking water; drain the pasta and return it to the cooking pot. Toss with the sauce and reserved cooking water. Divide among 4 pasta bowls and serve immediately.

◆

Farfalle with Fresh Salmon and Tomatoes

BITS OF SALMON FILLET FLAKE APART AS THEY COOK IN A TOMATO SAUCE. THE SAUCE IS FINISHED WITH CREAM, WHICH COMPLEMENTS THE SILKY BITS OF FISH. SERVES 4.

> 1 28-ounce can diced tomatoes or whole tomatoes packed in juice
> 2 tablespoons extra-virgin olive oil
> 2 medium garlic cloves, minced
> ¼ teaspoon hot red pepper flakes, or to taste
> Salt
> ½ pound salmon fillet, skin removed and coarsely chopped
> ½ cup heavy cream
> Ground black pepper
> 2 tablespoons minced fresh basil leaves
> 1 pound farfalle

1. If using diced tomatoes, go to step 2. If using whole tomatoes, drain and reserve the liquid. Dice the tomatoes by hand or in the work bowl of a food processor (use three or four ½-second pulses). The tomatoes should be coarse, with ¼-inch pieces visible. If necessary, add enough reserved liquid to the tomatoes to total 2⅔ cups.

2. Heat 2 tablespoons oil, garlic, and hot red pepper flakes in a medium sauté pan over medium heat until fragrant but not brown, about 2 minutes. Stir in the tomatoes; simmer until thickened slightly, about 10 minutes. Stir in ½ teaspoon salt.

3. Add the salmon and cream to the tomato sauce and cook over medium-high heat, stirring occasionally, until the fish is cooked through and the cream has thickened slightly, about 5 minutes. Add pepper to taste and the basil. Adjust the seasonings.

4. Meanwhile, bring 4 quarts of water to a boil in a large pot. Add 1 tablespoon salt and the pasta. Cook until al dente. Reserve ¼ cup of the cooking water; drain the pasta and return it to the cooking pot. Toss with the sauce and reserved cooking water. Divide among 4 pasta bowls and serve immediately.

◆

Farfalle with Sole or Flounder

FILLETS OF SOLE OR FLOUNDER ARE BROWNED FIRST FOR FLAVOR, BROKEN INTO SMALLER PIECES, AND THEN BRIEFLY COOKED WITH TOMATOES. FLOUNDER AND SOLE ARE CATCH-ALL NAMES; ANY MILD FISH FILLETS CAN BE USED HERE—DOVER, LEMON, OR GRAY SOLE; FOUNDER; FLUKE; SAND DAB. CHOOSE WHATEVER LOOKS FRESHEST AT YOUR FISH MARKET. **SERVES 4.**

> 1 28-ounce can diced tomatoes or whole
>   tomatoes packed in juice
> 2 tablespoons extra-virgin olive oil
> 2 ounces thinly sliced pancetta, minced
> 1 medium shallot, minced
> ½ pound fillet of sole or flounder
> Salt and ground black pepper
> ½ cup dry white wine
> 2 tablespoons minced fresh flat-leaf
>   parsley leaves
> 1 pound farfalle

1. If using diced tomatoes, go to step 2. If using whole tomatoes, drain and reserve the liquid. Dice the tomatoes by hand or in the work bowl of a food processor (use three or four ½-second pulses). The tomatoes should be coarse, with ¼-inch pieces visible. If necessary, add enough reserved liquid to the tomatoes to total 2⅔ cups.

2. Heat the oil in a medium sauté pan over medium heat; add the pancetta and cook until softened, 1 to 2 minutes. Add the shallot and cook until softened, 3 to 4 minutes. Sprinkle the sole fillets with salt and pep-

per and add them to the pan. Sauté until just golden, turning once, 3 to 4 minutes. Stir in the tomatoes and wine and break up the fish with the back of the spoon; simmer until the tomatoes have thickened slightly, about 10 minutes. Stir in the parsley and season with salt and pepper to taste.

3. Meanwhile, bring 4 quarts of water to a boil in a large pot. Add 1 tablespoon salt and the pasta. Cook until al dente. Reserve ¼ cup of the cooking water; drain the pasta and return it to the cooking pot. Toss with the sauce and reserved cooking water. Divide among 4 pasta bowls and serve immediately.

Sauces with Lobster

WE HAVE COOKED LOBSTER every way imaginable—roasting, broiling, grilling, steaming, and boiling. Lobster meat is so delicate that we prefer to cook the lobster whole with moist heat. Splitting the lobster in half and cooking it on the grill, under the broiler, or in the oven tends to dry out the meat and doesn't make much sense when retrieving the meat for a pasta sauce is your end goal.

Our preference is steaming, not because it tastes better than boiling, but because the process is simpler, neater, and the finished product is less watery. Steaming the lobster on a rack or steamer basket keeps it from becoming waterlogged. (If you happen to live near the ocean, seaweed makes a natural rack.) In our tests, we found that neither beer nor wine in the pot improved the lobster's flavor, nor did any herbs, spices, or other seasonings.

In addition to cooking the lobster right, buying right is essential. Of course, the lobster should be alive and kicking, literally. However, you should also look for a hard-shell lobster if possible. Before working on this topic in the test kitchen, the terms hard-shell and soft-shell lobster meant nothing to us. Unlike crabs, there's certainly no distinction between the two at the retail level. Of course, we knew from past experience that some lobster claws rip open as easily as an aluminum flip-top can, while others require shop tools to crack. We also noticed the wimpy, limp claw meat of some lobsters and the full, packed meat of others. We attributed these differences to how long the lobsters had been stored in tanks. It seems we were wrong. These variations are caused by the particular stage of molting that the lobster was in at the time it was caught.

As it turns out, most of the lobsters we eat during the summer and fall are in some phase of molting. During the late spring as waters begin to warm, lobsters start to form the new shell tissue underneath their old shells. As early as June off the shores of New Jersey and in July or August in colder Maine and Canadian waters, the lobsters shed their hard exterior shell. Because the most difficult task in molting is pulling the claw muscle through the old shell, the lobster dehydrates its claw (hence the smaller, wimpier claw meat).

Once the lobster molts, it emerges with nothing but a wrinkled, soft covering, much like that on a soft-shell crab. Within fifteen minutes, the lobster inflates itself with water, increasing its length by 15 percent and its weight by 50 percent. This extra water expands the wrinkled, soft covering, allowing the lobster room to grow long after the shell starts to harden. The newly molted lobster immediately eats its old shell, digesting the crucial shell-hardening calcium.

Understanding the molt phase clarifies the deficiencies of soft-shell summer lobster. It explains why it is so waterlogged, why its claw meat is so shriveled and scrawny, and why its tail meat is so underdeveloped and chewy. There is also far less meat (as much as 25 percent less) in a soft-shell than a hard-shell lobster of the same weight.

During the fall, the lobster shell continues to harden and the meat expands to fill the new shell. By spring, lobsters are at their peak, packed with meat and relatively inexpensive since it is easier for fishermen to check their traps than it is during the winter. As the tail grows, it becomes firmer and meatier and will cook up tender, not tough. Better texture and more meat are two excellent reasons to give lobsters a squeeze at the market (see illustration, page 243) and buy only those with hard shells. As a rule of thumb, hard-shell lobsters are reasonably priced from Mother's Day through the Fourth of July.

Fusilli with Lobster and Saffron-Tomato Sauce

SAFFRON IS PARTICULARLY GOOD WITH LOBSTER AND TOMATOES. TO GET THE MOST OUT OF THE EXPENSIVE SEASONING, CRUSH THE SAFFRON THREADS BETWEEN YOUR FINGERTIPS AS YOU ADD THEM TO THE PAN. SERVES 4.

> 2 lobsters (each about 1 1/2 pounds)
> 1 28-ounce can diced tomatoes or whole tomatoes packed in juice
> 3 tablespoons extra-virgin olive oil
> 2 medium garlic cloves, minced
> 1/4 cup dry vermouth
> 1/2 teaspoon saffron threads
> 2 tablespoons coarsely chopped fresh basil leaves
> Salt
> 1 pound fusilli or other short, curly pasta

1. Bring 1 inch of water to a boil in a large soup kettle set up with a wire rack or pasta insert. Add the lobsters, cover, and return the water to a boil. Reduce the heat to medium-high; steam until the lobsters are done, 13 to 14 minutes for soft-shell lobsters, 15 to 16 minutes for hard-shell lobsters. Cool slightly, then remove the tail and claw meat (see illustrations 1–9, pages 244–245). Cut the lobster meat into bite-size pieces and set aside.

2. If using diced tomatoes, go to step 3. If using whole tomatoes, drain and reserve the liquid. Dice the tomatoes by hand or in the work bowl of a food processor (use three or four 1/2-second pulses). The tomatoes should be coarse, with 1/4-inch pieces visible. If necessary, add enough reserved liquid to the tomatoes to total 2 2/3 cups.

3. Heat 2 tablespoons oil and the garlic in a medium sauté pan over medium heat until fragrant but not brown, about 2 minutes. Stir in the tomatoes; simmer until thickened slightly, about 10 minutes. Add the vermouth and simmer until the alcohol evaporates, about 2 minutes. Crumble the saffron over the sauce and stir in the basil and 1/2 teaspoon salt. Adjust the seasonings.

4. Meanwhile, bring 4 quarts of water to a boil in a large pot. Add 1 tablespoon salt and the pasta. Cook until just al dente. Reserve ¼ cup of the cooking water; drain the pasta and transfer it back to the cooking pot. Mix in the lobster, reserved cooking water, tomato sauce, and remaining oil. Cook together over medium heat for 1 minute, stirring constantly. Divide among 4 pasta bowls and serve immediately.

◆

Spaghetti with Artichoke-Lobster Sauce

CRABMEAT MAKES A GOOD SUBSTITUTION FOR LOBSTER IN THIS DISH AND ALSO SAVES ON WORK. SERVES 4.

4 medium artichokes (about 2 pounds), rinsed, trimmed to the heart, and cut into ¼-inch-wide wedges (see illustrations 1–8, page 134)
Salt
2 fresh lobsters (each about 1½ pounds) *or* 2 cups fresh unpasteurized crabmeat
1 pound spaghetti
¼ cup extra-virgin olive oil
¼ teaspoon ground black pepper
6 tablespoons lemon juice
3 tablespoons minced fresh flat-leaf parsley leaves

1. Place a collapsible basket or bamboo steamer in the bottom of a large nonreactive pot with a tight-fitting lid. Add 1 inch of water, cover the pot, and bring the water to a boil.

2. Place the artichoke pieces in the steaming apparatus and sprinkle with ½ teaspoon salt. Cover the pot and steam over medium heat until the artichoke pieces are tender, 15 to 20 minutes. Carefully lift the steaming apparatus from the pot. Cool the artichoke pieces to room temperature and set them aside. (Steamed artichokes can be covered and refrigerated overnight. Bring to room temperature before proceeding).

3. Add more water (there should be an inch or so) to the empty pot used to steam the artichokes. Set a wire rack or pasta insert in the pot and bring the water to a boil. Add the lobsters, cover, and return the water to a boil. Reduce the heat to medium-high; steam until the lobsters are done, 13 to 14 minutes for soft-shell lobsters, 15 to 16 minutes for hard-shell lobsters. Cool slightly, then remove the tail and claw meat (see illustrations 1–9, pages 244–245). Cut the lobster meat into bite-size pieces and set it aside.

4. Bring 4 quarts of water to a boil in a large pot. Add 1 tablespoon salt and the pasta to the boiling water. Cook until just al dente.

5. Meanwhile, whisk together the oil, ½ teaspoon salt, the pepper, and lemon juice in a medium bowl.

6. Drain the pasta but do not shake dry; return it to the pot. Add the oil dressing; toss to coat. Add the lobster meat, artichokes, and parsley; toss gently. Divide among 4 pasta bowls and serve immediately.

STEP-BY-STEP

BUYING A LOBSTER

Hard-shell lobsters are much meatier than soft-shell lobsters, which have recently molted. To determine whether a lobster has a hard or soft shell, squeeze the side of the lobster's body. A soft-shell lobster will yield to pressure while a hard-shell lobster will feel hard, brittle, and tightly packed.

REMOVING MEAT FROM A COOKED LOBSTER

1. Twist the tail to separate it from the body.

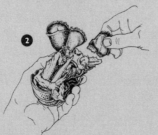

2. Twist off and discard the tail flippers.

3. Use a fork or your finger to push the tail meat up and out through the wide end of the tail. Pull the tail meat out the other end.

4. Twist a claw appendage off the body.

5. Twist the claw from the connecting joint.

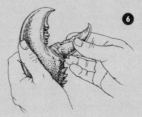

6. Remove the pincher portion of the claw. If you use a gentle motion, the meat will often stay attached to the rest of the claw; otherwise, you'll need a cocktail fork to pick out the meat from the shell.

7. If the lobster is a soft-shell, use your hands to break open the claw and remove the meat.

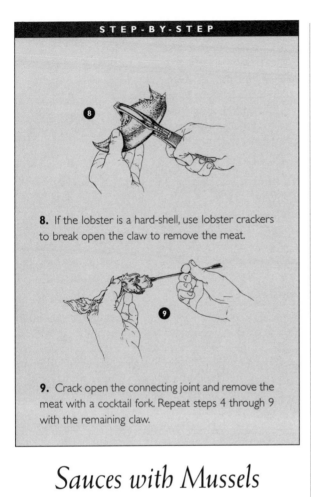

8. If the lobster is a hard-shell, use lobster crackers to break open the claw to remove the meat.

9. Crack open the connecting joint and remove the meat with a cocktail fork. Repeat steps 4 through 9 with the remaining claw.

Sauces with Mussels

LIKE CLAMS, MUSSELS are a common addition to pasta sauces. We wondered not only what kind of mussels to buy (there are now several choices based on how the mussels are raised) but also how to cook the mussels for pasta sauces. The most common choices are steaming in or over an aromatic broth (usually with some wine in it), roasting in the oven, or sautéing in some oil on the stove. In our tests, we found that mussels that were sautéed, roasted, or steamed over a broth tasted of pure shellfish. They cooked in their juices. In contrast, mussels that were steamed in a flavorful broth picked up flavors from the liquid. They became more complex tasting and, in our opinion, better.

With steaming as our preferred all-purpose cooking method, we started to test various amounts and types of liquids, including fish stock, water, wine, and beer. We found that white wine was the best choice. The bright acidity of white wine balances the briny flavor of clams and mussels. Fish stock and water (even when seasoned with garlic, herbs, and spices) were dull by comparison. Beer is delicious with mussels but makes an odd pairing with pasta.

It turns out, cooking mussels is relatively straightforward. As with clams, we found it best to cook mussels only until they give up their juices and start to open. We recombined the mussels with the sauce at the last minute, just enough to reheat them and allow stragglers to open fully. This two-step process ensures that the mussels will not overcook and toughen.

Other than not overcooking them, the real challenge in preparing mussels is the grit. It's a pain to strain any liquid after cooking. Besides being messy, solids such as shallots and garlic are removed. Worse still, careful straining, even through fine mesh, may not remove every trace of grit.

After much trial and error in the test kitchen, we concluded that it is impossible to remove all the sand from a dirty bivalve before cooking. We tried various soaking regimens—such as soaking in cold water for two hours, soaking in water with flour, soaking in water with cornmeal, and scrubbing and rinsing in five changes of water. None of these techniques worked. Dirty mussels must be rinsed and scrubbed before cooking and any cooking liquid must be strained after cooking.

During the course of this testing, we noticed that some varieties of mussels were extremely clean and free of grit. A quick scrub of the shell exterior and these bivalves were ready for the pot. After talking to seafood experts around the country we came to this conclusion: if you want to minimize your kitchen work and ensure that your mussels are free of grit, you must shop carefully.

Most mussels are now farmed either on ropes or along seabeds. (You may also see "wild" mussels at the market. These mussels are caught the old-fashioned way—by dredging along the sea floor. In our tests, we found them extremely muddy and basically inedible.) Rope-cultured mussels can cost twice as much as wild or bottom-cultured mussels, but we found them to be free of grit in our testing. Since mussels are generally inexpensive (no more than a few dollars a pound), we think clean mussels are worth the extra money.

Some mussels may also need debearding. Simply grab onto the weedy protrusion and pull it out from between the shells and discard. Don't debeard mussels until you are ready to cook them, as debearding can cause the mussel to die.

When shopping, look for tightly closed mussels (avoid any that are gaping). Don't store mussels in sealed plastic bags or under water or they will die. Keep them in a bowl in the refrigerator and use them within a day or two for best results.

As with clams, we don't feel that it's worth the effort to remove the mussels from their shells before serving. Put an empty bowl out on the table so each diner can pick out the meat and discard the empty shells.

Spaghetti with Mussels

SERVES 4

THIS IS OUR VERSION of the classic sauce made with mussels that have been steamed in white wine. This sauce is fairly soupy, so serve it with bread. Use linguine or spaghetti and feel free to substitute littleneck clams for the mussels.

1 ½ pounds black mussels (about 3 dozen),
   rinsed thoroughly, beards removed
½ cup dry white wine
¼ cup extra-virgin olive oil

2 medium garlic cloves, minced
½ teaspoon hot red pepper flakes
1 teaspoon grated lemon zest (see
   illustration, page 42)
2 tablespoons lemon juice
2 tablespoons minced fresh flat-leaf
   parsley leaves
Salt
1 pound spaghetti

1. Bring the mussels and wine to a boil in a deep, 10- to 12-inch covered skillet over high heat. Boil, shaking the pan occasionally, until the mussels begin to open, 3 to 5 minutes. Transfer the mussels with a slotted spoon to a medium bowl; set aside. Strain the liquid in the pan through a paper towel–lined sieve into a large measuring cup. Add enough water to make 1 cup; set aside.

2. Heat the oil over medium heat in the cleaned skillet. Add the garlic and pepper flakes; sauté over medium heat until the garlic is golden, about 1 minute. Add the strained mussel broth, zest, and juice; add the mussels and cover; cook until all the mussels open fully, 1 to 2 minutes longer. Stir in the parsley and add salt to taste.

3. Meanwhile, bring 4 quarts of water to a boil in a large pot. Add 1 tablespoon salt and the pasta. Cook until al dente. Drain the pasta, return it to the cooking pot, and toss with the sauce. Divide among 4 pasta bowls and serve immediately.

◆

Spaghetti with Mussels, Zucchini, and Spicy Sausage

SPICY SMOKED SAUSAGE MAY BE SUBSTITUTED FOR THE ITALIAN SAUSAGE HERE; TRY ANDOUILLE OR CHORIZO. SERVES 4.

1 ½ pounds black mussels (about 3 dozen),
   rinsed thoroughly, beards removed
½ cup dry white wine
¼ cup extra-virgin olive oil

1 medium zucchini, halved lengthwise and
   cut into ½-inch-thick pieces
1 medium onion, minced
2 medium garlic cloves, minced
½ pound hot Italian sausage, removed
   from casings and crumbled
6 plum tomatoes (about 1 pound), cored
   and cut into ¼-inch dice
2 tablespoons minced fresh flat-leaf
   parsley leaves
Salt
1 pound spaghetti or other long, thin
   pasta

1. Bring the mussels and wine to a boil in a deep, 10-
to 12-inch covered skillet over high heat. Boil, shaking the pan occasionally, until the mussels begin to
open, 3 to 5 minutes. Transfer the mussels with a slotted spoon to a medium bowl; set aside. Strain the liquid in the pan through a paper towel–lined sieve into
a large measuring cup. Add enough water to make 1
cup; set aside.

2. Heat the oil over medium heat in the cleaned skillet. Add the zucchini and sauté until softened and
golden, 5 to 7 minutes. Remove with a slotted spoon
and set aside. Add the onion and sauté until softened,
3 to 4 minutes. Add the garlic; sauté over medium heat
until the garlic is golden, about 1 minute. Add the
sausage and cook until it loses its pink color, stirring
occasionally, about 5 minutes. Add the tomatoes, zucchini, and strained mussel broth and bring to a boil.
Add the mussels and cover; cook until all the mussels
open fully, 1 to 2 minutes longer. Stir in the parsley
and add salt to taste.

3. Meanwhile, bring 4 quarts of water to a boil in a
large pot. Add 1 tablespoon salt and the pasta. Cook
until al dente. Drain the pasta, return it to the cooking
pot, and toss with the sauce. Divide among 4 pasta
bowls and serve immediately.

Linguine and Mussels with Saffron Cream Sauce

FOR A FLAVORFUL VARIATION, SUBSTITUTE 1 TEASPOON
CURRY POWDER AND 2 TABLESPOONS FINELY CHOPPED
FRESH CILANTRO FOR THE SAFFRON AND CHIVES.
SERVES 4.

   1½ pounds black mussels (about 3 dozen),
      rinsed thoroughly, beards removed
   ½ cup dry white wine
   2 tablespoons extra-virgin olive oil
   2 medium garlic cloves, minced
   ½ teaspoon saffron threads
   ½ cup heavy cream
   1 tablespoon minced fresh chives
   Salt
   1 pound linguine or other long, thin pasta

1. Bring the mussels and wine to a boil in a deep, 10-
to 12-inch covered skillet over high heat. Boil, shaking the pan occasionally, until the mussels begin to
open, 3 to 5 minutes. Transfer the mussels with a slotted spoon to a medium bowl; set aside. Strain the liquid in the pan through a paper towel–lined sieve into
a large measuring cup. If necessary, add enough water
to make ½ cup; set aside.

2. Heat the oil over medium heat in the cleaned skillet. Add the garlic and crumble the saffron over it;
sauté over medium heat until the garlic is golden,
about 1 minute. Add the strained mussel broth and
cream and bring to a boil. Add the mussels and cover;
cook until all the mussels open fully, 1 to 2 minutes
longer. Stir in the chives and add salt to taste.

3. Meanwhile, bring 4 quarts of water to a boil in a
large pot. Add 1 tablespoon salt and the pasta. Cook
until al dente. Drain the pasta, return it to the cooking
pot, and toss with the sauce. Divide among 4 pasta
bowls and serve immediately.

PREPARING FRESH SARDINES

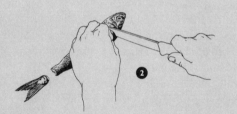

1. Working one at a time, slit each fish lengthwise through the stomach from the tail to the head with a paring knife. You should cut down to but not through skin on the back side of the fish.

2. Cut off the tail and the head, slicing right behind the gills.

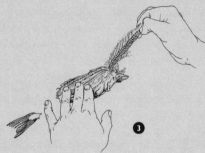

3. Open up the fish so that the skin side rests on the work surface. Carefully lift the spine from one end and pull to remove. Rinse the boned sardines under cold water to remove any remaining intestines or bones. Pat dry with paper towels.

Sauces with Sardines

LIKE ANCHOVIES, SARDINES are most commonly sold canned in oil. As long as the sardines are firm and the oil is of high quality, this product is fine. However, canned sardines cannot compare to fresh sardines that you fillet at home just before cooking. Filleting a fresh sardine is relatively easy (see illustrations 1–3) and the results are certainly worth the minimal effort.

◆

Perciatelli with Fresh Sardines

WILD FENNEL IS USED IN SICILY TO FLAVOR THIS TRADITIONAL DISH. IT IS UNAVAILABLE IN THIS COUNTRY, BUT DOMESTIC FENNEL, ALONG WITH ITS LEAFY TOP, IS AN ACCEPTABLE SUBSTITUTE. SERVES 4.

> 1/3 cup extra-virgin olive oil
> 1 medium fennel bulb (about 1 pound), stems and base trimmed; bulb cut vertically into 1/2-inch-thick strips and fronds chopped (see illustrations 1–5, page 154)
> 1 medium onion, minced
> 4 anchovy fillets, rinsed and minced
> 1 pound fresh sardines, cleaned (see illustrations 1–3) *or* two 3.75-ounce cans boneless oil-packed sardines, drained and rinsed
> 1/2 teaspoon saffron threads
> 3 tablespoons dried currants
> 3 tablespoons pine nuts
> Salt and ground black pepper
> 1 pound perciatelli or other long, thick pasta

1. Heat the oil in a large skillet. Add the fennel strips; toss to coat with oil. Cook over medium heat, stirring often, until the fennel has softened slightly, 8 to 10 minutes. Add the onion and cook until softened, 3 to 4 minutes. Add the anchovies and cook until they disintegrate, about 1 minute.

2. If using fresh sardines, push the fennel and onion to one side of the pan and place as many sardines as will fit on the cleared side in the pan. Sauté until just cooked, turning once, 2 to 3 minutes. When the first batch is cooked, shift to the side with the fennel and onion and sauté the remaining sardines. If using canned sardines, stir into the fennel and cook to heat through, about 1 minute. In either case, break up the sardines with the back of a spoon.

3. Crumble in the saffron; add the currants and pine nuts; and stir to combine. Cook for 3 to 4 minutes to combine flavors. Stir in the chopped fennel fronds. Season with salt and pepper.

4. Meanwhile, bring 4 quarts of water to a boil in a large pot. Add 1 tablespoon salt and the pasta. Cook until al dente. Reserve ¼ cup of the cooking water; drain the pasta and return it to the cooking pot. Toss with the sauce and the cooking water. Divide among 4 pasta bowls and serve immediately.

◆

Spaghetti with Sardines and Toasted Bread Crumbs

IN ITALY, GRATED CHEESE IS RARELY USED IN DISHES CONTAINING FISH; THE STRONG FLAVOR OF CHEESE IS THOUGHT TO CLASH WITH THE EQUALLY STRONG FLAVOR OF FISH. BREAD CRUMBS, RATHER THAN CHEESE, ADD TEXTURE AND MILD FLAVOR TO THIS SIMPLE DISH OF SPAGHETTI DRESSED IN A GARLICKY SAUCE OF SARDINES AND TOMATO PASTE. THIS DISH IS USUALLY MADE WITH CANNED SARDINES BUT MAY BE MADE WITH ½ POUND SARDINES (SEE ILLUSTRATIONS 1–3, PAGE 248, FOR PREPARATION INSTRUCTIONS) IF YOU LIKE. SERVES 4.

> 6 tablespoons extra-virgin olive oil
> 1 3.75-ounce can oil-packed sardines,
>   drained and rinsed
> 2 medium garlic cloves, minced
> 2 tablespoons tomato paste
> Salt
> 1 pound spaghetti or other long, thin
>   pasta
> 1 cup Toasted Bread Crumbs (page 90)
> Ground black pepper

1. Heat the oil, sardines, and garlic in a small skillet over medium heat, stirring and mashing with a wooden spoon until the sardines break up, about 2 minutes. Stir in the tomato paste and cook for 2 minutes. Remove the pan from the heat.

2. Meanwhile, bring 4 quarts of water to a boil in a large pot. Add 1 tablespoon salt and the pasta to the boiling water. Cook until al dente. Reserve ½ cup of the cooking water; drain the pasta and return it to the cooking pot. Mix in the bread crumbs, sardine mixture, and enough reserved water to keep the mixture moist. Adjust the salt and pepper. Divide among 4 pasta bowls and serve immediately.

Sauces with Scallops

SCALLOPS OFFER SEVERAL possible choices for the cook, when both shopping and cooking. There are three main varieties of scallops: sea, bay, and calico. Sea scallops are available year-round throughout the country and are the best choice in most instances. Like all scallops, the product sold at the market is the dense, disk-shaped muscle that propels the live scallop in its shell through the water. The guts and roe are usually jettisoned at sea because they are so perishable.

Small, cork-shaped bay scallops are harvested in a small area from Cape Cod to Long Island. Bay scallops are seasonal—available from late fall through early spring—and very expensive, up to $20 a pound. They are delicious but nearly impossible to find outside of top restaurants.

Calico scallops are a small species harvested in the waters of the southern United States and around the world. They are inexpensive (often priced at just a few dollars a pound) but generally not terribly good. Unlike sea and bay scallops, which are harvested by hand, calicos are shucked by machine-steaming. This steaming partially cooks them and gives them an opaque look. Note that calicos are often sold as "bays," but they are not the same thing. In our kitchen test, we found that calicos are easy to overcook and often end up with a rubbery, eraser-like texture. Our recommendation is to stick with sea scallops unless you have access to real bay scallops.

In addition to choosing the right species you should inquire about processing when purchasing scallops. Most scallops (by some estimates as much as 90 percent of the retail supply) are dipped in a phosphate-and-water mixture that may also contain citric and sorbic acids. Processing extends shelf-life but harms the flavor and texture of the scallop. The delicate, sweet scallop flavor can be masked by the bitter-tasting chemicals. Even worse, scallops absorb water during processing, which is thrown off when they are cooked.

By law, processed scallops must be identified at the wholesale level, so ask your fishmonger. Also, look at the scallops. Processing turns scallops, which are naturally ivory or pinkish tan, bright white. Processed scallops are slippery and swollen and usually sitting in milky white liquid at the store. Unsoaked scallops (also called dry scallops) are sticky and flabby. If they are surrounded by any liquid (and often they are not), the juices are clear, not white.

PREPARING SCALLOPS FOR COOKING

The small, rough-textured, crescent-shaped muscle that attaches the scallop to the shell is often not removed during processing. You can readily remove any muscles that are still attached. If you do not, they will toughen slightly during cooking.

Besides the obvious objections (why pay for water weight or processing that detracts from their natural flavor), processed scallops are more difficult to cook. You can't brown processed scallops—they shed so much liquid they steam. However, sautéing—so that the exterior caramelizes to a concentrated nutty-flavored, brown-and-tan crust—is one of the best ways to cook scallops. The caramelized exterior greatly enhances the natural sweetness of the scallop and provides a nice crisp contrast to the tender interior. Butter makes the best cooking medium when trying to brown scallops. It produced the thickest crust in our tests, and the nutty taste of butter complemented the sweetness of the scallop without compromising its delicate flavor.

For pasta sauces, scallops may also be cooked gently in olive oil to keep them from becoming tough. As soon as the scallops become opaque, remove the pan from the heat and toss the scallops with the pasta.

◆

Spaghetti with Scallops and Bread Crumbs

IF BAY SCALLOPS ARE AVAILABLE, THIS RECIPE SHOWS OFF THEIR DELICATE SWEETNESS EXTREMELY WELL. HOMEMADE BREAD CRUMBS ADD FLAVOR AND CRUNCH TO THIS DISH. OF COURSE, THIS DISH CAN BE MADE WITHOUT BREAD CRUMBS IF YOU PREFER, BUT DON'T USE COMMERCIAL BREAD CRUMBS IN THIS RECIPE. THEY WILL JUST MAKE THE SCALLOPS DRY AND POWDERY. SERVES 4.

Salt
1 pound spaghetti or other long, thin
    pasta
½ cup extra-virgin olive oil
2 medium garlic cloves, minced
½ teaspoon hot red pepper flakes, or to
    taste
1 pound sea scallops, small muscles
    removed (see illustration) and cut into
    ½-inch pieces
¼ cup minced fresh flat-leaf parsley leaves
½ cup Toasted Bread Crumbs (page 90)

1. Bring 4 quarts of water to a boil in a large pot. Add 1 tablespoon salt and the pasta and cook until al dente.

2. While the pasta is cooking, make the sauce. Heat the oil, garlic, and red pepper flakes in a large sauté pan over medium heat; cook until fragrant, about 1 minute. Add the scallops; cook, stirring occasionally, until the scallops are just opaque, about 3 minutes. Remove from the heat and stir in the parsley. Adjust the seasonings.

3. Drain the pasta but do not shake it completely dry, and return it to the cooking pot. Stir in the sauce and bread crumbs. Divide among 4 pasta bowls and serve immediately.

◆

Angel Hair Pasta with Seared Sea Scallops and Cream

IN THIS RECIPE, THE SCALLOPS ARE SEARED IN BUTTER TO FORM A NICELY CARAMELIZED CRUST THAT CONTRASTS WITH THE TENDER INTERIOR. IT'S CRITICAL FOR THE FORMATION OF A GOOD CRUST TO LEAVE THE SCALLOP ALONE ONCE IT HITS THE PAN. WE FOUND THE BEST METHOD FOR COOKING WAS TO PLACE THE SCALLOPS CAREFULLY IN THE PAN ONE AT A TIME, WITH ONE FLAT SIDE DOWN FOR MAXIMUM CONTACT WITH THE HOT PAN. WE TURNED THE SCALLOPS ONCE AND BROWNED THE SECOND FLAT SIDE. TONGS ARE THE BEST TOOL FOR TURNING SCALLOPS, ALTHOUGH A SPATULA CAN BE USED IN A PINCH. THE ONLY TRICKY PART OF THIS RECIPE IS ENSURING THAT THE PASTA AND SAUCE ARE DONE AT THE SAME TIME. START COOKING THE PASTA WHEN YOU ADD THE CREAM TO THE SAUTÉ PAN AND YOU'LL BE FINE. **SERVES 4.**

1½ pounds sea scallops, small muscles
    removed (see illustration, page 250)
Salt and ground black pepper
2 tablespoons unsalted butter
1 medium shallot, minced
2-inch-long piece fresh gingerroot,
    peeled, sliced thin, and julienned (see
    illustrations 1–3, page 43)

⅔ cup dry white wine
2 tablespoons white wine vinegar
1 cup heavy cream
¼ cup snipped fresh chives *or*
    ½ cup chopped scallion greens
1 pound angel hair pasta

1. Heat the oven to 200 degrees. Bring 4 quarts of water to a boil in a large pot for cooking the pasta.

2. Sprinkle the scallops on both sides with salt and pepper. Heat a large sauté pan over medium-high heat until hot. Add half the butter; swirl to coat the bottom. Continue to heat until the butter begins to turn golden brown. Add half the scallops, one at a time, flat side down; cook, adjusting the heat as necessary to prevent the butter from burning, until the scallops are well browned, 1½ to 2 minutes. Using tongs, turn the scallops, one at a time; cook until medium-rare (sides firmed up and all but the middle third of the scallop is opaque), 30 seconds to 1½ minutes longer, depending on size. Transfer scallops to warm platter. Cover the scallops with foil and keep warm in the oven with the door slightly ajar. Repeat the cooking process using the remaining half of the butter and scallops.

3. Return the scallop skillet to the burner; reduce the heat to low. Add the shallot and the ginger and cook until the shallot softens slightly, 1 to 2 minutes. Increase the heat to high; add the wine and vinegar and boil, scraping the pan bottom with a wooden spoon to loosen caramelized bits, until the liquid reduces to a glaze, 4 to 5 minutes. Add the cream, ½ teaspoon salt, and ⅛ teaspoon pepper; bring to a boil. Reduce the heat; simmer until the cream reduces very slightly, about 1 minute longer. Stir in the chives or scallions.

4. Meanwhile, add 1 tablespoon salt and the pasta to the boiling water. Cook until al dente. Drain the pasta and return it to the pot. Add the sauce; toss to coat. Divide the pasta among individual serving plates, arranging a portion of scallops around or on top of each. Serve immediately.

Sauces with Shrimp

COOKING SHRIMP IS A relatively straightforward process. As soon as the meat turns pink (which can happen in just two or three minutes over intense heat), the shrimp are done. We find it best to keep the heat down (medium is best) to keep the shrimp from cooking too quickly. Medium heat also helps keep some of the liquid the shrimp sheds in the pan. (At higher heat, this liquid will quickly evaporate.) Although shrimp require liquid (in the form of tomatoes or pasta cooking water) to make a sauce for pasta, there is no need to drive off all their natural juices.

Cooking shrimp is pretty easy. How the shrimp are handled before cooking actually generates more confusion. Should they be peeled? Should the vein that runs down the back of each shrimp be removed?

For pasta sauces, we think you should peel the shrimp before cooking, even if the shells do help retain moisture during cooking and add flavor. It's just too much hassle to serve pasta with shrimp shells. The issue of deveining is more complex. Although some people won't eat shrimp that has not been deveined, others believe that the "vein"—actually the animal's intestinal tract—contributes flavor and insist on leaving it in. In our tests, we could not detect an effect, positive or negative, on flavor when we left the vein in. The vein is generally so tiny in most medium-size shrimp that it virtually disappears with cooking. Out of laziness, we leave it alone. In larger shrimp, the vein may be noticeable and it is probably worth removing it.

A note about buying shrimp. There are more than three hundred species of shrimp grown around the world. (There is such a thing as "wild" shrimp, but most shrimp is farm-raised.) Black tiger shrimp from Asia is the most common variety sold in U.S. markets. It can be firm and tasty but the quality is inconsistent. In our taste-tests, we preferred Mexican whites from the Pacific Coast and Gulf whites. They were the firmest and had the strongest fresh-from-the-sea flavor. However, we didn't like all the white shrimp we tasted. Chinese white shrimp were decidedly inferior to the white shrimp we liked, as well as to tiger shrimp. Our advice is simple: if you have a choice, look for white shrimp from Mexico or the Gulf.

Linguine with Garlicky Shrimp

SERVES 4

REMOVE THE SHRIMP from the heat the instant they turn pink, so that they will be tender and not rubbery. Even when using small shrimp, we like to halve them so that the pieces are well distributed throughout the pasta. If you like heat, replace the black pepper with ½ teaspoon hot red pepper flakes.

Salt
1 pound linguine or other long, thin pasta
¼ cup extra-virgin olive oil
4 medium garlic cloves, minced
1 pound small shrimp, peeled, deveined (if desired), and halved
1 teaspoon grated lemon zest (see illustration, page 42)
¼ cup lemon juice
Ground black pepper
¼ cup minced fresh flat-leaf parsley leaves

1. Bring 4 quarts of water to a boil in a large pot. Add 1 tablespoon salt and the pasta and cook until al dente.

2. Meanwhile, place the oil and garlic in a large skillet over medium heat and cook until fragrant, about 2 minutes. Add the shrimp, zest, and juice; sauté until pink, stirring frequently, 3 to 4 minutes. Season to taste with salt and pepper.

3. Reserve ½ cup cooking liquid and drain the pasta. Return to the cooking pot and toss with the shrimp sauce, parsley, and enough cooking liquid to moisten the mixture. Divide among 4 pasta bowls and serve immediately.

◆

Linguine with Shrimp and Arugula

THERE IS NO NEED TO COOK THE ARUGULA HERE, BECAUSE IT WILTS AND BECOMES TENDER ON CONTACT WITH THE HOT PASTA AND SHRIMP. WATERCRESS MAY BE SUBSTITUTED SINCE IT REACTS THE SAME WAY. SERVES 4.

Salt
1 pound linguine or other long, thin pasta
¼ cup extra-virgin olive oil
2 medium garlic cloves, minced
1 pound small shrimp, peeled, deveined (if desired), and halved
1 teaspoon grated lemon zest (see illustration, page 42)
¼ cup dry white wine
Ground black pepper
1 large bunch arugula (about 2 cups), washed, stemmed, and coarsely chopped

1. Bring 4 quarts of water to a boil in a large pot. Add 1 tablespoon salt and the pasta and cook until al dente.

2. Meanwhile, place the oil and garlic in a large skillet over medium heat and cook until fragrant, about 1 minute. Add the shrimp, zest, and wine; sauté until pink, stirring frequently, 3 to 4 minutes. Season to taste with salt and pepper.

3. Reserve ½ cup cooking liquid and drain the pasta. Return to the cooking pot and toss with the shrimp sauce, arugula, and enough cooking liquid to moisten the mixture. Divide among 4 pasta bowls and serve immediately.

◆

Linguine with Shrimp, Tomatoes, and Capers

OREGANO GIVES THIS DISH A PARTICULARLY GREEK FLAVOR; ADD A SPRINKLING OF CRUMBLED FETA CHEESE TO EACH BOWL TO HEIGHTEN THIS EFFECT, IF YOU LIKE. SERVES 4.

Salt
1 pound linguine or other long, thin pasta
¼ cup extra-virgin olive oil
1 medium onion, minced
4 medium tomatoes, peeled, seeded, and chopped (see illustrations 1–3, pages 111–112) *or* 2 cups diced canned tomatoes
1 pound small shrimp, peeled, deveined (if desired), and halved
2 tablespoons capers
1 tablespoon minced fresh oregano leaves
Ground black pepper

1. Bring 4 quarts of water to a boil in a large pot. Add 1 tablespoon salt and the pasta and cook until al dente.

2. Meanwhile, place the oil and onion in a large skillet over medium-high heat and cook until softened, about 3 minutes. Add the tomatoes and cook until most of the liquid has evaporated, about 4 minutes. Add the shrimp, capers, and oregano and cook until pink, stirring frequently, 3 to 4 minutes. Season to taste with salt and pepper.

3. Drain the pasta. Return to the cooking pot and toss with the sauce. Divide among 4 pasta bowls and serve immediately.

Fettuccine with Shrimp and Asparagus

ASPARAGUS IS BRIEFLY STEAMED BEFORE BEING ADDED TO THE SAUCE TO MAKE SURE THAT IT IS COOKED ALL THE WAY THROUGH. FOR EXTRA FLAVOR, RESERVE SOME OF THE STEAMING LIQUID TO MOISTEN THE SAUCE. SERVES 4.

> ¾ pound medium asparagus, tough ends snapped off; spears halved lengthwise, then cut diagonally into 1-inch pieces (see illustrations 1–3, page 138)
> ¼ cup extra-virgin olive oil
> 3 medium garlic cloves, minced
> ¾ pound small shrimp, peeled, deveined (if desired), and halved
> Salt and ground black pepper
> 1 pound Fresh Egg Pasta (page 21) cut into fettuccine *or* dried fettuccine

1. Bring 1 inch of water to a boil in a large pot. Put the asparagus in a steamer basket, then carefully place the steamer basket in a pot. Cover and steam over medium-high heat until the asparagus is just tender, about 2 minutes. Remove the asparagus and set aside. Reserve ¾ cup of the asparagus steaming liquid.

2. Place the oil and garlic in a large skillet over medium heat and cook until fragrant, about 1 minute. Add the asparagus and ½ cup of the asparagus water and cook until the liquid has been reduced by half, about 3 minutes. Add the shrimp and cook until pink, stirring frequently, 3 to 4 minutes. Season to taste with salt and pepper.

3. Meanwhile, bring 4 quarts of water to a boil in a large pot. Add 1 tablespoon salt and the pasta to the boiling water. Cook until al dente. Drain the pasta and toss with the sauce, adding the remaining reserved cooking water as needed to moisten the pasta. Divide among 4 pasta bowls and serve immediately.

Linguine with Basil Sauce and Sautéed Shrimp

THIS SIMPLE BUT DELICIOUS SAUCE IS REALLY NOTHING MORE THAN SAUTEED SHRIMP TOSSED WITH A PESTO MADE WITHOUT CHEESE. SERVES 4.

> ¼ cup pine nuts, walnuts, or almonds
> 3 medium garlic cloves, threaded on a skewer
> 2 cups packed fresh basil leaves
> 2 tablespoons fresh flat-leaf parsley leaves (optional)
> 8 tablespoons extra-virgin olive oil
> Salt
> 1 pound small shrimp, peeled, deveined (if desired), and halved
> Ground black pepper
> 1 pound linguine or other long, thin pasta

1. Toast the nuts in a small, heavy skillet over medium heat, stirring frequently, until just golden and fragrant, 4 to 5 minutes.

2. Meanwhile, bring 4 quarts of water to a boil in a large pot. Lower the skewered garlic into the water (see illustration 1, page 56); boil for 45 seconds. Immediately run the garlic under cold water. Remove from the skewer; peel and mince. (Do not drain the water.)

3. Place the basil and parsley (if using) in a heavy-duty, quart-size, sealable plastic bag; pound with the flat side of a meat pounder until all the leaves are bruised (see illustration 2, page 56).

4. Place the nuts, garlic, herbs, 6 tablespoons oil, and ½ teaspoon salt in the work bowl of a food processor; process until smooth, stopping as necessary to scrape down the sides of the bowl. Transfer the mixture to a medium bowl and adjust the salt.

5. Heat the remaining 2 tablespoons oil in a large skillet. Add the shrimp and sauté over medium heat until pink, 3 to 4 minutes. Season to taste with salt and pepper. Transfer the shrimp to the bowl with the pesto and stir to coat.

6. Meanwhile, bring 4 quarts of water to a boil in a large pot. Add 1 tablespoon salt and the pasta and cook until al dente. Reserve ½ cup of the cooking water. Drain the pasta and return it to the cooking pot. Toss the pasta with the pesto and shrimp and enough cooking liquid to moisten the mixture. Divide among 4 pasta bowls and serve immediately.

Sauces with Squid

SQUID MAKES AN inexpensive and delicious addition to pasta sauces. However, it can become tough as rubber. The challenge for the cook is figuring out how to keep the squid tender and soft.

As it turns out, squid can be prepared two different ways. If quickly sautéed (just until it turns opaque), squid will be slightly chewy but still tender. It can be cooked in olive oil with seasonings like garlic and then sauced with pasta. In our tests, we found that squid gives off a fair amount of liquid. If the pasta is dripping wet, there should be no need for additional liquid or reserved pasta cooking water.

Once squid cooks for more than a minute or so, it begins to toughen; only after long, gentle cooking will it soften once again. Braising squid in tomato sauce keeps the squid moist as it cooks. We found that sliced squid requires at least 30 minutes of gentle braising.

You can clean your own squid if you like (see illustrations 1–6 on page 256), but there is no reason not to buy cleaned squid at the market. It may cost a little more, but cleaning is time-consuming. Squid loses about one-third of its weight when it is cleaned, so buy just 1 pound of cleaned squid for the recipes that follow if you don't want to clean the squid yourself. Squid cleaned by your fishmonger should still be rinsed, sliced, and dried.

Spaghetti with Sautéed Squid

BE SURE TO DRY THE SQUID WELL BEFORE SAUTEING TO PREVENT MESSY AND DANGEROUS SPLATTERING. BLAND SQUID TAKES WELL TO AGGRESSIVE SEASONINGS, HENCE THE USE OF GARLIC, GINGER, AND FRESH CHILE IN THIS RECIPE. SERVES 4.

Salt
1 pound spaghetti or other long, thin pasta
⅓ cup extra-virgin olive oil
4 medium garlic cloves, minced
½-inch piece gingerroot, peeled and finely chopped (see illustrations 1–3, page 43)
1 fresh hot red chile, seeded and minced (optional)
1½ pounds whole squid, cleaned, rinsed, cut up, and patted dry (see illustrations 1–6, page 256)
2 tablespoons minced fresh basil leaves

1. Bring 4 quarts of water to a boil in a large pot. Add 1 tablespoon salt and the pasta. Cook until al dente.

2. Meanwhile, heat the oil, garlic, ginger, chile (if using), and 1 teaspoon salt in a sauté pan large enough to hold the cooked pasta over medium-high heat until the garlic is just fragrant, about 1 minute. Turn the heat to high, add the squid and basil, and cook, stirring constantly, until the squid is just opaque, 1 to 1½ minutes. Remove from the heat.

3. Drain the pasta, allowing some of the cooking water to cling to the pasta. Toss with the squid. Season with salt to taste. Divide among 4 pasta bowls and serve immediately.

CLEANING SQUID

1. Pull the head of the squid from the body. Most of the entrails will still be attached to the head.

2. Remove the hard, plastic-like quill; it will come out easily once you find it with your fingers.

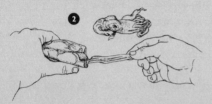

3. Cut the tentacles just below the squid's eyes. Be careful of the black ink, which does stain. Discard the innards.

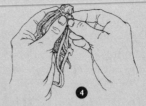

4. Check the tentacles for an inedible beak. Squeeze out and discard the beak if necessary. If the tentacles are large, cut them vertically in two.

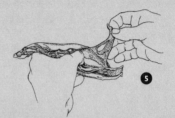

5. The thin, membrane-like skin on the squid body is edible, but it can be easily peeled off for a white appearance.

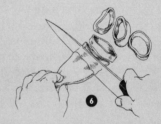

6. Rinse the interior of the squid body and then slice it crosswise into ¼-inch rings. Pat dry the squid with paper towels.

Spaghetti with Braised Squid and Spicy Tomato Sauce

IF NOT COOKED VERY QUICKLY, SQUID SHOULD BE BRAISED SLOWLY TO ENSURE TENDERNESS. HERE, THE SQUID IS COOKED FOR AT LEAST 30 MINUTES, UNTIL IT IS TENDER AND THE SPICY TOMATO SAUCE QUITE THICK AND CONCENTRATED. A LITTLE MORE TOMATO IS USED HERE THAN IN OUR STANDARD TOMATO SAUCE, TO MAKE SURE THAT THE SEAFOOD HAS ENOUGH COOKING LIQUID DURING ITS RELATIVELY LONG BRAISE. SERVES 4.

⅓ cup extra-virgin olive oil
4 medium garlic cloves, minced
¾ teaspoon hot red pepper flakes, or to taste
1 28-ounce and 1 14.5-ounce can whole tomatoes packed in juice, drained and chopped, with 1 cup juice reserved
1½ pounds whole squid, cleaned, rinsed, cut up, and patted dry (see illustrations 1–6, opposite)
¼ cup minced fresh flat-leaf parsley leaves
Salt
1 pound spaghetti or other long, thin pasta

1. Heat the oil, garlic, and red pepper flakes in a medium sauté pan over medium heat until fragrant but not brown, about 2 minutes. Stir in the tomatoes, the reserved tomato juice, and the squid. Simmer over medium-low heat until the squid is tender but not dry and almost all the liquid has evaporated from the pan, 30 to 40 minutes. Stir in the parsley and adjust the seasonings.

2. Meanwhile, bring 4 quarts of water to a boil in a large pot. Add 1 tablespoon salt and the pasta. Cook until just al dente. Reserve ¼ cup of the cooking water; drain the pasta and return it to the cooking pot. Mix in the reserved cooking water and squid sauce. Cook together over medium heat for 1 minute, stirring constantly, and serve immediately.

Sauces with Tuna

CANNED TUNA BULKS ANY basic tomato sauce and makes it a hearty topping for pasta. We tested a variety of canned tunas in a basic tomato sauce and found that tuna packed in olive oil is far superior to either tuna packed in water or tuna packed in vegetable oil. Tuna packed in water is too dry, while tuna packed in vegetable oil is moist but gets no flavor (just fat) from the oil.

Most brands of canned tuna packed in oil are actually swimming with oil that rarely tastes as good as the fresh olive oil you add yourself to a sauce. We found it best to drain off the oil and then simply flake the tuna with a fork before adding it to a pasta sauce.

MASTER RECIPE

Farfalle with Tuna and Green Olives

SERVES 4

THIS PANTRY SAUCE relies on canned tomatoes, green olives, and Italian-style canned tuna packed in olive oil. Serve it with farfalle, fusilli, or other shapes that will trap small bits of the sauce.

(continued on next page)

3 tablespoons extra-virgin olive oil
2 medium garlic cloves, minced
1 28-ounce can whole tomatoes, coarsely
   chopped, with ¾ cup juice reserved
1 6-ounce can tuna packed in olive oil,
   drained and flaked
12 large or 18 medium green olives,
   pitted and chopped (about ⅔ cup; see
   illustrations 1–2, page 62)
2 tablespoons minced fresh flat-leaf
   parsley leaves
Salt and ground black pepper
1 pound farfalle or other short, curly
   pasta

1. Heat the oil over medium heat in a large saucepan. Add the garlic; sauté until golden, about 1 minute. Add the tomatoes and juice; simmer until the tomatoes soften and the sauce thickens somewhat, about 15 minutes.

2. Add the tuna and olives to the sauce; simmer to blend the flavors, about 5 minutes longer. Stir in the parsley and season to taste with salt and pepper.

3. Meanwhile, bring 4 quarts of water to a boil in a large pot. Add 1 tablespoon salt and the pasta and cook until al dente. Drain the pasta and return it to the cooking pot. Stir in the sauce. Divide among 4 pasta bowls and serve immediately.

Farfalle with Tuna, Lemon, and Fennel

THE FLAVORS OF FENNEL AND LEMON COMPLEMENT THE RICHNESS OF THE TUNA AND MAKE THIS SAUCE ESPECIALLY LIGHT AND DELICIOUS. SERVES 4.

¼ cup extra-virgin olive oil
2 medium garlic cloves, minced
½ teaspoon hot red pepper flakes, or to
   taste
½ teaspoon fennel seeds
1 28-ounce can whole tomatoes,
   chopped, with ¾ cup juice reserved
1 6-ounce can tuna packed in olive oil,
   drained and flaked
1 teaspoon grated lemon zest (see
   illustration, page 42)
2 tablespoons minced fresh flat-leaf
   parsley leaves
Salt and ground black pepper
1 pound farfalle or other short, curly pasta

1. Heat the oil over medium heat in a large saucepan. Add the garlic, red pepper flakes, and fennel seeds; sauté until the garlic is golden, about 1 minute. Add the tomatoes and reserved juice; simmer until the tomatoes soften and the sauce thickens somewhat, about 10 minutes. Stir in the tuna, lemon zest, and parsley and simmer to blend flavors, about 2 minutes. Season to taste with salt and pepper.

2. Meanwhile, bring 4 quarts of water to a boil in a large pot. Add 1 tablespoon salt and the pasta and cook until al dente. Drain the pasta and return it to the cooking pot. Stir in the sauce. Divide among 4 pasta bowls and serve immediately.

Spaghetti with Tuna and Spinach

CANNED TUNA HAS A SPECIAL AFFINITY FOR TENDER GREENS LIKE SPINACH. SWISS CHARD OR BEET GREENS MAY BE SUBSTITUTED IF YOU LIKE. SHAKE THE WASHED GREENS TO REMOVE EXCESS WATER BUT DO NOT DRY THOROUGHLY—THEY NEED SOME MOISTURE TO WILT PROPERLY WHEN ADDED TO THE HOT OIL. SERVES 4.

- ¼ cup extra-virgin olive oil, plus more for drizzling
- 2 medium garlic cloves, minced
- 1 medium onion, minced
- 2 pounds spinach, washed, stemmed, and coarsely chopped
- Salt and ground black pepper
- 1 6-ounce can tuna packed in olive oil, drained and flaked
- 1 pound spaghetti
- 1 tablespoon red wine vinegar

1. Heat the oil with the garlic in a large sauté pan or Dutch oven over medium heat. When the garlic sizzles and starts to turn golden, about 1 minute, add the onion and cook until slightly softened, 3 to 4 minutes. Add the wet spinach. Cover and cook over medium-high heat, stirring occasionally, until the greens completely wilt but are still bright green, about 5 minutes. Uncover and season to taste with salt and pepper. Cook over high heat until the liquid evaporates, 2 to 3 minutes longer. Stir in the tuna and adjust the seasonings.

2. Meanwhile, bring 4 quarts of water to a boil in a large pot. Add 1 tablespoon salt and the pasta to the boiling water and cook until al dente. Reserve ½ cup cooking liquid. Drain the pasta and return it to the cooking pot. Stir in the tuna sauce and vinegar. If the pasta seems too dry, add the cooking liquid 1 tablespoon at a time until you reach the desired consistency. Divide among 4 pasta bowls and serve immediately with additional olive oil for drizzling on the side.

Farfalle with Seared Fresh Tuna

THIS SAUCE IS REALLY A SALAD NIÇOISE—SEARED, FLAKED TUNA, CHOPPED RIPE TOMATOES, GARLIC, OLIVES, CAPERS, AND HERBS. IF YOU PREFER, GRILL THE TUNA OVER A HOT FIRE. SERVES 4.

- ½ pound fresh tuna steak, cut ½ inch thick
- Salt and ground black pepper
- ¼ cup extra-virgin olive oil
- 1 pound farfalle or other short, curly pasta
- 3 medium, ripe tomatoes (about 1 pound), cored, seeded, and chopped (see illustrations 1–4, page 111)
- 1 medium garlic clove, minced
- 1 cup Niçoise olives, pitted and coarsely chopped (see illustrations 1–2, page 62)
- 1 tablespoon capers, rinsed
- 1 anchovy fillet, minced
- 2 tablespoons minced fresh oregano leaves
- 2 tablespoons minced fresh flat-leaf parsley leaves
- 1 teaspoon balsamic vinegar

1. Sprinkle the tuna with salt and pepper to taste. Heat 1 tablespoon oil in a small skillet over high heat. When the oil is quite hot, add the tuna and sauté, turning once, until browned on the exterior but still pink on the inside, about 4 minutes. Cool slightly and flake into bite-size pieces with a fork; set aside.

2. Bring 4 quarts of water to a boil in a large pot. Add 1 tablespoon salt and the pasta and cook until al dente.

3. While the pasta is cooking, combine the remaining 3 tablespoons oil, tomatoes, garlic, olives, capers, anchovy, oregano, parsley, and vinegar in a bowl large enough to hold the cooked pasta. Add the tuna.

4. Drain the pasta and toss it with the tomato mixture. Divide among 4 pasta bowls and serve immediately.

Sauces with Mixed Seafood

MIXED SEAFOOD PASTA SAUCES require precise timing to ensure that each kind of seafood is perfectly cooked. We found it best to start with squid that can braise for quite a long time in tomato sauce. Next, we cook clams and mussels sequentially in a separate pan with some wine. As soon as the bivalves open, they are removed from the pan and the steaming liquid is reserved to moisten the pasta. Finally, once the squid has become tender, the quick-cooking seafood (shrimp and scallops) is added to the sauce along with the cooked clams and mussels still in their shells. Everything is heated through (no more than a minute or two) and tossed with spaghetti and the reserved broth that was used to steam open the clams and mussels. The flavor of the sea is intense and each kind of seafood has been cooked to perfection. Put out empty bowls for the shells.

◆

Spaghetti with Mixed Seafood

THIS IS OUR VERSION OF THE CLASSIC SPAGHETTI WITH *FRUTTI DI MARE*, OR FRUITS OF THE SEA. ADJUST QUANTITIES AS NECESSARY TO TAKE ADVANTAGE OF THE SEAFOOD THAT LOOKS BEST AT YOUR MARKET. SERVES 4.

¼ cup extra-virgin olive oil
4 medium garlic cloves, minced
¼ teaspoon hot red pepper flakes, or to taste
1 28-ounce can whole tomatoes, drained and chopped, with ½ cup juice reserved
¾ pound whole squid, cleaned and sliced into ¼-inch rings, *or* ½ pound cleaned squid, sliced into ¼-inch rings (see illustrations 1–6, page 256)
12 littleneck clams, scrubbed thoroughly
½ cup dry white wine
12 mussels (about ½ pound), scrubbed thoroughly

Salt
1 pound spaghetti or other long, thin pasta
½ pound small shrimp, peeled, deveined (if desired), and halved
½ pound sea scallops, tendons discarded and cut into ½-inch pieces (see illustration, page 250)
¾ cup chopped fresh flat-leaf parsley leaves

1. Heat the oil, garlic, and red pepper flakes in a large sauté pan or Dutch oven over medium heat until fragrant but not brown, about 2 minutes. Stir in the tomatoes, juice, and squid. Simmer over medium-low heat until the squid is tender but not dry and almost all the liquid has evaporated from the pan, 30 to 40 minutes. Set aside.

2. While the squid and tomatoes are cooking, prepare the clams and mussels. Bring the clams and wine to a boil in a deep, 10- to 12-inch covered skillet over high heat. Boil, shaking the pan occasionally, until the clams begin to open, 3 to 5 minutes. Transfer the clams with a slotted spoon to a medium bowl. Add the mussels and bring to a boil again. Boil, shaking the pan occasionally, until the mussels begin to open, 3 to 5 minutes. Add the mussels to the bowl containing the clams. Strain the liquid in the pan through a paper towel–lined sieve into a large measuring cup. If necessary, add enough water to make ½ cup.

3. Bring 4 quarts of water to a boil in a large pot. Add 1 tablespoon salt and the pasta. Cook until just al dente.

4. Meanwhile, add the clams, mussels, shrimp, and scallops to the squid and tomatoes. Cook over high until all the clams and mussels open fully and the shrimp and scallops are opaque, 1 to 2 minutes.

5. Drain the pasta and return it to the cooking pot. Add the seafood and tomato mixture and toss. Add the reserved clam-mussel liquid and cook until the flavors meld, about 30 seconds. Stir in the parsley and adjust the seasonings. Divide among 4 pasta bowls and serve immediately.

PASTA

SALADS

/I\

THERE IS SOMETHING APPEALING ABOUT THE CON-

CEPT OF PASTA SALAD. ITALIANS MAY GASP AT

THE IDEA, BUT NO ONE WANTS TO EAT A BOWL OF

STEAMING HOT PASTA DURING THE DOG DAYS OF

SUMMER. A COOLING PASTA SALAD IS ANOTHER

MATTER. ◆ SINCE PASTA SALADS MAKE THE MOST

SENSE AS SIDE DISHES FOR A SUMMER MEAL, WE'VE

always found it odd that most recipes are so heavy and creamy. Mayonnaise is fine for potato salad, but it overwhelms the delicate texture of pasta. A good pasta salad should be light and refreshing, with a fair amount of vegetables. (We find little bits of salami a greasy and distressing addition to deli pasta salads.) The dressing should help convey flavors and keep the pasta moist, not weigh it down.

There are three styles of pasta salad that can taste good. One is dressed with a raw tomato sauce, one with a vinaigrette and some vegetables, and the last with pesto sauce and perhaps some vegetables, chicken, or shrimp.

Pasta with raw tomato sauce is covered in chapter 10. To turn these dishes into pasta salads, simply allow the sauced pasta to cool to room temperature. Because of the tomatoes, these salads should not be refrigerated and are best eaten within several hours of their preparation.

Of the remaining two styles of pasta salad—with vinaigrette and with pesto—each offers its own set of challenges, so we decided to consider each category separately.

Pasta Salads with Vinaigrette

ALMOST EVERY DELI IN America sells a pasta salad dressed with vinaigrette. Often made with fusilli (tricolor fusilli in trendier markets), this salad invariably looks unappetizing. The pasta is so mushy you can see it falling apart through the glass deli case. And the vegetables are tired and sad. The broccoli has faded to olive drab and the shredded carrots that most markets add (which always strikes us as a weird Americanization) have wilted. And as for the taste—well, these unattractive salads usually look better than they taste.

The problem with most of these pasta salads is that the acid causes the pasta to soften and dulls the color and flavor of many vegetables, especially green ones. But leave out the lemon juice or vinegar and the salad tastes flat. We wanted to develop a light, vinaigrette-dressed pasta salad that looked good and tasted even better.

We started our tests by making salads with four different vinaigrettes, each with a different acidic liquid, along with olive oil, salt, and pepper. Each was used to dress a simple pasta salad with blanched and cooled broccoli. The salads made with red wine vinegar and balsamic vinegar dyed the pasta and tasted too sharp. The salad made with white wine vinegar looked fine but tasted too acidic. The salad made with lemon juice was clearly the best. It had a nice bright flavor but was not puckery or sour. After half an hour, we noticed that the broccoli in the three salads with vinegar was turning olive green and starting to fall apart, but even after several hours, the broccoli in the salad with lemon juice was green and crunchy.

We were not quite ready to abandon vinegar. We were using a ratio of two parts oil to one part acid. Maybe this ratio was fine for lemon juice (with its acidity around 4 percent), but too high for vinegars with a 6 to 7 percent acidity. We added more oil to a white wine vinegar dressing, but now the salad tasted greasy and the broccoli still lost its fresh color. The lemon juice just tasted better and its lower acidity was helping to keep the vegetables green.

With lemon juice as our choice of acid, we focused on the sequence of events in assembling the pasta salad. Would hot vegetables absorb the dressing more and taste better? Or should we run the vegetables under cold water after cooking to set their color? Neither idea panned out. We found that green vegetables, like broccoli, are most susceptible to loss of color when they are hot. Letting the cooked vegetables cool to room temperature helps stem any color loss. Unfortunately you cannot speed up the process by running hot vegetables under cold water. The vegetables, no matter how well we drained them, tasted waterlogged when we rinsed them under cold water. The best method is to let them rest in the colander for at least twenty minutes, or until barely warm to the touch, before tossing them with the pasta and dressing.

At this point, we had a master recipe that we liked pretty well, but it needed some other flavors. An herb —we chose basil, but almost anything will work—

perked things up. Olives (or sun-dried tomatoes) made everything more lively because they add some acidity and saltiness to a dish that otherwise could be a bit bland, especially since the pasta is not eaten hot.

When we turned our attention to other vegetables, we wondered if cooking methods other than blanching might add even more flavor to our salad. As we suspected, a pasta salad made with roasted asparagus tasted better than one made with blanched asparagus. Grilling also gives the vegetables a lot of flavor and makes a better pasta salad. The chart on page 264 covers the vegetables we routinely add to salads. Grilling over a medium fire is our preferred cooking method, with the exceptions of broccoli and cauliflower, which are best blanched. Roasting is our second choice for most of the vegetables, with the exception of eggplant, which is better broiled. When cool, cut vegetables into bite-size pieces.

Pasta Salad with Vinaigrette

SERVES 6 TO 8

BROCCOLI AND OLIVES are used in this basic pasta salad. If you prefer, increase the hot red pepper flakes or replace them with a few grindings of black pepper.

3 pounds broccoli (about 2 small bunches), florets cut into bite-size pieces (about 7 cups; see illustrations 1–2, page 140)
½ teaspoon grated lemon zest (see illustration, page 42)
¼ cup lemon juice
Salt
1 medium garlic clove, minced
½ teaspoon hot red pepper flakes
½ cup extra-virgin olive oil
1 pound short, bite-size pasta, such as fusilli, farfalle, or orecchiette
20 large black olives, such as Kalamata or other brine-cured variety, pitted and chopped (see illustrations 1–2, page 62)
15 large fresh basil leaves, shredded

1. Bring 4 quarts of water to a boil in a large pot. Cook the broccoli until crisp-tender, about 2 minutes. Remove with a slotted spoon and set aside to cool for 20 minutes. Don't drain the water.

2. Whisk the lemon zest and juice, ¾ teaspoon salt, garlic, and red pepper flakes in a large bowl; whisk in the oil in a slow, steady stream until smooth.

3. Add 1 tablespoon salt and the pasta to the boiling water. Cook until the pasta is al dente and drain. Whisk the dressing again to blend; add the hot pasta, cooled broccoli, olives, and basil; toss to mix thoroughly. Cool to room temperature, adjust the seasonings, and serve. (Can be covered with plastic wrap and refrigerated for 1 day; return to room temperature before serving.)

PREPARING VEGETABLES FOR PASTA SALAD

VEGETABLE	PREPARATION	GRILLING METHOD	STOVETOP OR OVEN METHOD
ASPARAGUS	Trim tough ends; toss with olive oil and salt and pepper to taste.	Grill until tender and streaked with light grill marks, 5–7 minutes.	Roast in a 425-degree oven, shaking pan once, until lightly browned, 8–10 minutes.
BROCCOLI, CAULIFLOWER	Cut into bite-size pieces.	Not recommended.	Blanch in salted boiling water until crisp-tender, about 2 minutes.
EGGPLANT	Cut into ½-inch-thick rounds; brush lightly with olive oil and sprinkle with salt and pepper to taste.	Grill until marked with dark stripes on both sides, about 10 minutes.	Broil on baking sheet placed 4 inches from heating element, turning once, until tender and browned, about 7 minutes.
FENNEL	Cut off stalks and halve bulb through core; cut halves into ½-inch wedges; toss with olive oil and salt and pepper to taste.	Grill until tender and marked with dark stripes on both sides, about 15 minutes.	Roast in a 425-degree oven until tender and light brown on both sides, 15–20 minutes.
ONIONS	Peel and cut into ½-inch-thick rounds; toss with olive oil and salt and pepper to taste.	Grill until tender and marked with dark stripes on both sides, about 15 minutes.	Roast in a 425-degree oven until tender and light brown on both sides, 15–20 minutes.
PEPPERS	Core, seed, and cut into 1½-inch wedges; toss with olive oil and salt and pepper to taste.	Grill until tender and lightly charred, about 8 minutes.	Roast in a 425-degree oven until tender and lightly browned, 15–20 minutes.
TOMATOES	Core, seed, and cut into ½-inch chunks.	Do not cook.	Do not cook.
ZUCCHINI	Cut lengthwise into ½-inch-thick strips; toss with olive oil and salt and pepper to taste.	Grill until tender and marked with dark stripes on both sides, about 10 minutes.	Roast in a 425-degree oven until tender and lightly browned on both sides, about 15 minutes.

Pasta Salad with Fennel, Red Onions, and Sun-Dried Tomatoes

GRILLING GIVES THE FENNEL AND ONIONS AN ESPE-
CIALLY GOOD FLAVOR. HOWEVER, THE VEGETABLES CAN
BE ROASTED IN A 425-DEGREE OVEN UNTIL TENDER AND
LIGHT BROWN ON BOTH SIDES, 15 TO 20 MINUTES, IF
YOU PREFER. SERVES 6 TO 8.

- 2 large fennel bulbs, trimmed, halved, and cut into 1/2-inch wedges (see illustrations 1–5, page 154)
- 2 large red onions, peeled and cut into 1/2-inch-thick rounds
- 1/2 cup plus 1 tablespoon extra-virgin olive oil
- Salt and ground black pepper
- 1/2 teaspoon grated lemon zest (see illustration, page 42)
- 1/4 cup lemon juice
- 1 medium garlic clove, minced
- 1 pound short, bite-size pasta, such as fusilli, farfalle, or orecchiette
- 1/2 cup drained oil-packed sun-dried tomatoes, sliced thin
- 15 large fresh basil leaves, shredded

1. Light the grill. Toss the fennel and onions with 1 tablespoon oil and salt and pepper to taste. Grill until tender and marked with dark stripes on both sides, about 15 minutes.

2. Meanwhile, whisk the lemon zest and juice, 3/4 teaspoon salt, pepper to taste, and garlic in a large bowl; whisk in 1/2 cup oil in a slow, steady stream until smooth.

3. Bring 4 quarts of water to a boil in a large pot. Add 1 tablespoon salt and the pasta to the boiling water. Cook until the pasta is al dente and drain. Whisk the dressing again to blend; add the hot pasta, cooled vegetables, tomatoes, and basil; toss to mix thoroughly. Cool to room temperature, adjust the seasonings, and serve. (Can be covered with plastic wrap and refrigerated for 1 day; return to room temperature before serving.)

Pasta Salad with Eggplant, Tomatoes, and Basil

ZUCCHINI MAKES A GOOD SUBSTITUTE FOR EGGPLANT
IN THIS SUMMERY SALAD. SERVES 6 TO 8.

- 2 medium eggplants, cut into 1/2-inch-thick rounds
- 1/2 cup plus 1 tablespoon extra-virgin olive oil
- Salt and ground black pepper
- 1/2 teaspoon grated lemon zest (see illustration, page 42)
- 1/4 cup lemon juice
- 1 medium garlic clove, minced
- 1 pound short, bite-size pasta, such as fusilli, farfalle, or orecchiette
- 2 large ripe tomatoes, cored, seeded, and cut into 1/2-inch chunks (see illustrations 1–4, page 111)
- 20 large black olives, such as Kalamata or other brine-cured variety, pitted and chopped (see illustrations 1–2, page 62)
- 15 large fresh basil leaves, shredded

1. Light the grill. Toss the eggplant with 1 tablespoon oil and salt and pepper to taste. Grill until tender and marked with dark stripes on both sides, about 10 minutes. Or, heat the broiler and broil on a baking sheet placed 4 inches from the heating element, turning once, until tender and browned, about 7 minutes. Set aside to cool.

2. Meanwhile, whisk the zest and juice, 3/4 teaspoon salt, pepper to taste, and garlic in a large bowl; whisk in 1/2 cup oil in a slow, steady stream until smooth.

3. Bring 4 quarts of water to a boil in a large pot. Add 1 tablespoon salt and the pasta to the boiling water. Cook until the pasta is al dente and drain. Whisk the dressing again to blend; add the hot pasta, cooled eggplant, tomatoes, olives, and basil; toss to mix thoroughly. Cool to room temperature, adjust the seasonings, and serve. (Can be covered with plastic wrap and refrigerated for 1 day; return to room temperature before serving.)

Pasta Salad with Asparagus and Red Peppers

- 1 ½ pounds asparagus, tough ends
  trimmed (see illustrations 1–3, page
  138)
- 3 large red bell peppers, cored, seeded,
  and cut into 1 ½-inch wedges
- ½ cup plus 1 tablespoon extra-virgin
  olive oil
- Salt and ground black pepper
- ½ teaspoon grated lemon zest (see
  illustration, page 42)
- ¼ cup lemon juice
- 1 medium garlic clove, minced
- 1 pound short, bite-size pasta, such as
  fusilli, farfalle, or orecchiette
- 20 large black olives, such as Kalamata or
  other brine-cured variety, pitted and
  chopped (see illustrations 1–2, page
  62)
- 3 tablespoons snipped fresh chives
- ⅓ cup grated Parmesan cheese

1. Light the grill. Toss the asparagus and peppers with 1 tablespoon oil and salt and pepper to taste. Grill until tender and streaked with light grill marks, 5 to 7 minutes for the asparagus, 8 to 10 minutes for the peppers. Or, heat the oven to 425 degrees and roast until tender, about 10 minutes for the asparagus, 15 to 17 minutes for the peppers. Set aside to cool.

2. Meanwhile, whisk the lemon zest and juice, ¾ teaspoon salt, pepper to taste, and garlic in a large bowl; whisk in ½ cup oil in a slow, steady stream until smooth.

3. Bring 4 quarts of water to a boil in a large pot. Add 1 tablespoon salt and the pasta to the boiling water. Cook until the pasta is al dente and drain. Whisk the dressing again to blend; add the hot pasta, cooled asparagus and peppers, olives, chives, and cheese; toss

to mix thoroughly. Cool to room temperature, adjust the seasonings, and serve. (Can be covered with plastic wrap and refrigerated for 1 day; return to room temperature before serving.)

Pasta Salads with Pesto

PESTO IS A NATURAL sauce for pasta salad because of its concentrated flavor. But hot pasta can turn pesto sauce an unappealing greenish brown, a problem that becomes even more noticeable if the salad is set aside for some time before serving. With an excellent pesto sauce in hand (see chapter 6), we started cooking to see if we could remedy this problem.

Adding 2 tablespoons of parsley leaves to a batch of pesto, as the original pesto recipe suggested, helps retain the color but there still is some loss of brightness. We wondered how much more parsley could be added before the flavor of this herb was noticeable. After several tests, we decided that ¼ cup was the upper limit for parsley in pesto. At this level, the parsley delivers some color protection without interfering with the basil flavor. However, the pesto still loses much of its brightness on pasta, especially if the salad sits out for any length of time.

Next, we tried a trick we had seen in a chef cookbook for setting the color of pesto. We ground a vitamin C tablet with the other pesto ingredients. In theory, the ascorbic acid would keep the basil from turning brown. While we were unable to taste any difference in a sauce made with vitamin C, the trick was a bust, with the pesto losing its color within minutes.

At this point, we decided to see if we could delay adding the pesto to the pasta salad until serving time. We tossed the drained pasta with a little oil and some pasta cooking liquid to keep it from drying out. We then let the pasta come to room temperature. Right before serving we tossed the pesto with the pasta. The salad tasted delicious and kept its beautiful green color.

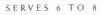
Pasta Salad with Pesto

SERVES 6 TO 8

To PREVENT DISCOLORATION, toss the cooked pasta with oil, let it cool to room temperature, and then toss with the pesto immediately before serving. If you like, add cooked and cooled vegetables to this recipe, along with the pesto. Broccoli florets are especially good, and so are tomatoes. About 3 cups of prepared vegetables (see chart on page 264) is enough for 1 pound of pasta.

¼ cup pine nuts, walnuts, or almonds
3 medium garlic cloves, threaded on a skewer
2 cups packed fresh basil leaves, rinsed thoroughly
¼ cup fresh flat-leaf parsley leaves
½ cup extra-virgin olive oil
Salt
¼ cup finely grated Parmesan cheese
1 pound fusilli or other short, curly pasta

1. Toast the nuts in a small, heavy skillet over medium heat, stirring frequently, until just golden and fragrant, 4 to 5 minutes.

2. Bring 4 quarts of water to a boil in a large pot. Lower the skewered garlic into the water (see illustration 1, page 56); boil until the garlic is partially blanched, about 45 seconds. Immediately run cold water over the garlic to stop the cooking. Remove from the skewer; peel and mince. Do not drain the water.

3. Place the basil and parsley in a heavy-duty, quart-size, sealable plastic bag; pound with the flat side of a meat pounder until all the leaves are bruised (see illustration 2, page 56).

4. Place the nuts, garlic, herbs, 7 tablespoons oil, and a pinch of salt in the bowl of a food processor fitted with a steel blade; process until smooth, stopping as necessary to scrape down the sides of the bowl. Transfer the mixture to a small bowl, stir in the cheese, and adjust salt. Cover with plastic wrap and set aside.

5. Add 1 tablespoon salt and the pasta to the boiling water. Cook until al dente. Reserve ¼ cup of the cooking water; drain the pasta and turn it into a serving bowl. Mix in the reserved cooking water and the remaining tablespoon oil. Cool to room temperature, toss with the pesto, and serve immediately.

◆

Pasta Salad with Cilantro Pesto and Shrimp

TO SAVE TIME, BUY SHRIMP THAT HAS BEEN PEELED AND COOKED. IF YOU WANT TO BOIL THE SHRIMP YOURSELF, BUY SLIGHTLY MORE THAN 1 POUND WITH THE SHELLS ON. SERVES 6 TO 8.

¼ cup walnuts
3 medium garlic cloves, threaded on a skewer
2 cups packed fresh cilantro leaves
½ cup extra-virgin olive oil
½ teaspoon grated lime zest (see illustration, page 42)
2 tablespoons lime juice
Salt
1 pound fusilli or other short, curly pasta
1 pound cooked medium shrimp

(continued on next page)

1. Toast the nuts in a small, heavy skillet over medium heat, stirring frequently, until just golden and fragrant, 4 to 5 minutes.

2. Meanwhile, bring 4 quarts of water to a boil in a large pot. Lower the skewered garlic into the water (see illustration 1, page 56); boil for 45 seconds. Immediately run the garlic under cold water. Remove from the skewer; peel and mince. Do not drain the water.

3. Place the nuts, garlic, cilantro, 7 tablespoons oil, zest, juice, and a pinch of salt in the work bowl of a food processor; process until smooth, stopping as necessary to scrape down the sides of the bowl. Transfer the mixture to a small bowl and adjust salt. Cover with plastic wrap and set aside.

4. Add 1 tablespoon salt and the pasta to the boiling water. Cook until al dente. Reserve ¼ cup of the cooking water; drain the pasta and turn it into a serving bowl. Mix in the reserved cooking water and the remaining tablespoon oil. Cool to room temperature, toss with the pesto and shrimp, and serve immediately.

◆

Pasta Salad with Mint Pesto and Chicken

BONE-IN CHICKEN BREASTS ROASTED IN THE OVEN ARE A SIMPLE AND FLAVORFUL ADDITION TO PASTA SALAD. SUBSTITUTE LEFTOVER COOKED CHICKEN IF YOU HAVE IT ON HAND. SERVES 6 TO 8.

> 2 large bone-in, skin-on chicken breasts (about 1½ pounds) *or* 12 ounces leftover cooked chicken meat
> 1 tablespoon vegetable oil
> Salt
> ¼ cup pine nuts, walnuts, or almonds
> 3 medium garlic cloves, threaded on a skewer
> 2 cups packed fresh mint leaves
> ½ cup extra-virgin olive oil
> ¼ cup finely grated Parmesan cheese
> 1 pound fusilli or other short, curly pasta

1. If cooking the chicken: Adjust the oven rack to the middle position and heat the oven to 400 degrees. Set the breasts on a small, foil-lined jelly roll pan. Brush with the vegetable oil and sprinkle generously with salt. Roast until a meat thermometer inserted into the thickest part of the breast registers 160 degrees, 35 to 40 minutes. Cool to room temperature, remove the skin, and shred the meat into bite-size pieces.

2. Toast the nuts in a small, heavy skillet over medium heat, stirring frequently, until just golden and fragrant, 4 to 5 minutes.

3. Meanwhile, bring 4 quarts of water to a boil in a large pot. Lower the skewered garlic into the water (see illustration 1, page 56); boil for 45 seconds. Immediately run the garlic under cold water. Remove from the skewer; peel and mince. Do not drain the water.

4. Place the mint in a heavy-duty, quart-size, sealable plastic bag; pound with the flat side of a meat pounder until all the leaves are bruised (see illustration 2, page 56).

5. Place the nuts, garlic, mint, 7 tablespoons oil, and a pinch of salt in the work bowl of a food processor; process until smooth, stopping as necessary to scrape down the sides of the bowl. Transfer the mixture to a small bowl, stir in the cheese, and adjust salt. Cover with plastic wrap and set aside.

6. Add 1 tablespoon salt and the pasta to the boiling water. Cook until al dente. Reserve ¼ cup of the cooking water; drain the pasta and turn it into a serving bowl. Mix in the reserved cooking water and the remaining tablespoon oil. Cool to room temperature, toss with the pesto and chicken, and serve immediately.

PASTA
SOUPS

/ꟾ\

THERE ARE A FEW GENERAL RULES TO REMEMBER

ABOUT PASTA SOUPS. FIRST, PASTA WORKS BEST IN

FAIRLY BROTHY SOUPS. IT NEEDS SOME LIQUID TO

HYDRATE AND SOFTEN, AND IF ADDED TO A THICK,

DENSE SOUP, THE PASTA MAY NOT COOK PROPERLY. ◆

ONCE THE PASTA IS ADDED, IT WILL SUCK UP LIQUID.

ALSO, AS THE PASTA COOKS, IT SHEDS STARCH AND

helps create body in brothy soups. We found that cooking the pasta right in the soup pot (as opposed to boiling it in a separate pot) gives soups a thick, creamy consistency. When it comes time to add the pasta, examine the soup and add more broth or water if it seems too thick.

Second, it is imperative to add pasta near the end of the cooking time. If added too early, the pasta will become too soft and fall apart. Once the soup is done, add the pasta and continue simmering until it is tender, then serve the soup. Pasta will continue to absorb liquid, so the soup may in fact become too thick if stored with the pasta already in it. If you want to save some soup for another day, ladle it into a container and then add the pasta to the pot with the remaining soup. When reheating the saved soup, you may add pasta at that time.

Third, we found that smaller pasta shapes work best in soups. Tiny orzo or elbows are preferable to large macaroni. Long, strand pasta, especially dried egg noodles, can be used, but we found it best to break this pasta into shorter lengths that can fit more easily onto a soup spoon when eaten.

This chapter covers four basic kinds of soup: pasta and bean soups, pasta soups made with chicken broth, pasta soups made with chicken broth and chicken meat, and pasta soups made with beef broth and meat.

Pasta Soups with Beans

WE FIND THAT CANNED beans are perfectly fine in pasta soups. (For information on buying canned beans, see page 186.) There are some cases (such as minestrone) where we like the texture of the beans to be relatively firm, so we add the beans after the pasta, just before serving the soup. In other cases, we like the beans to soften and break down a bit. To achieve this texture, we add the beans before the pasta. To use beans as a thickener, mash some of them before they go into the pot. This creates an especially creamy, thick texture.

Classic Minestrone with Pasta

SERVES 6 TO 8

THE RIND FROM A WEDGE of Parmesan cheese, preferably Parmigiano-Reggiano, adds complexity and depth to a soup made with water instead of stock. Remove the rind from a wedge of fresh Parmesan. (Rinds from which all the cheese has been grated can be stored in a sealable bag in the freezer to use as needed.) Adding pasta to Italian vegetable soup makes it hearty enough for dinner. If the soup seems too thick after adding the pasta, stir in a little water. Pasta does not hold up well when refrigerated or frozen, so serve this soup as soon as the pasta is tender, or refrigerate or freeze the soup before adding the pasta.

2 small leeks, white and light green parts
   only, sliced thin (see illustrations 1–6,
   page 165)
2 medium carrots, peeled and cut into
   small dice
2 small onions, cut into small dice
2 medium celery stalks, trimmed and cut
   into small dice
1 medium baking potato, peeled and cut
   into medium dice
1 medium zucchini, trimmed and cut into
   medium dice
3 cups stemmed spinach leaves, cut into
   thin strips
1 28-ounce can whole tomatoes packed in
   juice, drained and chopped
1 Parmesan cheese rind, about 5 inches
   long by 2 inches wide
Salt
½ cup small pasta such as elbows,
   ditalini, or orzo
1 15-ounce can cannellini or white beans,
   drained and rinsed (about 1½ cups)
¼ cup basil pesto (see page 55) *or*
   1 tablespoon minced fresh rosemary
   mixed with 1 teaspoon minced garlic
   and 1 tablespoon extra-virgin olive oil
Ground black pepper

1. Bring the vegetables, tomatoes, 8 cups water,
cheese rind, and 1 teaspoon salt to a boil in a soup kettle or pot. Reduce the heat to medium-low; simmer,
uncovered and stirring occasionally, until the vegetables are tender but still hold their shape, about 1 hour.
(Soup can be refrigerated in an airtight container for 3
days or frozen for 1 month. Defrost if necessary and
reheat before proceeding with the recipe.)

2. Add the pasta and continue cooking until almost al
dente, 8 to 12 minutes, depending on the shape.

3. Add the beans and cook until just heated through,
about 5 minutes. Remove the pot from the heat.
Remove and discard the cheese rind. Stir in the pesto
(or rosemary-garlic mixture). Adjust the seasonings,
adding pepper and more salt, if necessary. Ladle the
soup into bowls and serve immediately.

Penne and Chickpea Soup
with Tomatoes and Rosemary

THIS QUICK PASTA AND BEAN SOUP CAN BE READY IN
LESS THAN HALF AN HOUR. SERVES 6 TO 8.

   ¼ cup extra-virgin olive oil, plus more for
      drizzling if desired
   4 ounces lean salt pork, bacon, or
      pancetta, minced
   4 medium garlic cloves, bruised
   1 sprig fresh rosemary
   2 14.5-ounce cans diced tomatoes
   2 19-ounce cans chickpeas, drained and
      rinsed, and 2 cups of them mashed with
      a fork
   2 teaspoons salt
   8 ounces penne, elbow macaroni, or other
      short, tubular pasta
   1 tablespoon chopped fresh rosemary
   Ground black pepper
   Grated pecorino cheese

1. Heat the oil in a large soup kettle or stockpot over
medium heat. Add the salt pork; sauté until lightly
crisped, 4 to 5 minutes. Add the garlic and rosemary
sprig; sauté until fragrant, about 2 minutes longer. Add
the tomatoes and their juice, whole and mashed
chickpeas, 6 cups water, and salt; bring to a boil.
Reduce the heat and simmer to blend flavors, about 10
minutes.

2. Add the pasta and cook until tender. Remove the
garlic and rosemary sprig and add the chopped rosemary; season to taste with salt and ground black pepper. Ladle the soup into bowls and serve immediately,
passing grated cheese and more olive oil at the table.

Fettuccine and White Bean Soup with Prosciutto, Potato, and Sage

FETTUCCINE, WHITE BEANS, AND POTATOES MAY SOUND LIKE A RATHER HEAVY COMBINATION, BUT THIS SOUP IS FILLING WITHOUT BEING LEADEN. LIGHTEN UP THE MEAL WITH A GREEN SALAD DRESSED WITH OIL AND LEMON JUICE. **SERVES 6 TO 8.**

> ¼ cup extra-virgin olive oil
> 4 ounces prosciutto, diced fine
> 1 medium onion, diced fine
> 1 14.5-ounce can diced tomatoes
> 1 celery stalk, diced fine
> 1 medium baking potato, peeled and cut into ½-inch cubes
> 2 teaspoons salt
> 2 19-ounce cans white beans (such as cannellini, white kidney, or great northern), drained and rinsed
> 1½ tablespoons fresh sage leaves, minced
> 5 ounces dried fettuccine, broken into 2-inch pieces
> Ground black pepper

1. Heat the oil in a large soup kettle or stockpot over medium heat. Add the prosciutto and onion; sauté until the onion is translucent, 4 to 5 minutes. Add the tomatoes with their juice, celery, potato, salt, beans, sage, and 8 cups water; bring to a boil and cook until the potato is partially tender, about 5 minutes.

2. Add the fettuccine and cook, stirring occasionally, until the pasta is tender, 7 to 8 minutes. Off heat, season to taste with salt and pepper. Ladle the soup into bowls and serve immediately.

Orzo and Kidney Bean Soup with Leeks and Cabbage

WE LIKE THE CONTRASTING COLORS OF THE RED BEANS AND THE PALE PASTA AND VEGETABLES HERE, BUT WHITE BEANS MAY BE USED FOR A MONOCHROMATIC SOUP. **SERVES 6 TO 8.**

> Salt
> 1 pound (about ½ small head) green cabbage, cored and shredded (see illustrations 1–3, page 145)
> 3 tablespoons extra-virgin olive oil
> 1 medium onion, diced small
> 2 medium leeks, white part only, diced small (see illustrations 1–6, page 165)
> 1 small carrot, diced small
> 1 celery stalk, diced small
> 3 ounces lean salt pork, bacon, or pancetta, diced
> 1 medium baking potato, peeled and grated
> 1 19-ounce can red kidney beans, drained and rinsed
> ¼ teaspoon ground white pepper
> ¼ teaspoon ground cinnamon
> 6 ounces orzo (about 1 cup)
> Freshly grated Parmesan cheese

1. Bring 4 quarts of water to a boil in a large saucepan. Add 2 teaspoons salt and the cabbage; blanch until tender-crisp, about 5 minutes. Drain and rinse under cold water; set aside.

2. Heat the oil in a large soup kettle or Dutch oven over medium heat. Add the onion, leeks, carrot, celery, and salt pork; sauté until softened and golden, about 5 minutes. Add the cabbage, potato, beans, pepper, cinnamon, and 8 cups water; bring to a boil. Add the orzo, reduce the heat to low, and simmer until the orzo is tender, 7 to 8 minutes. Adjust the seasoning with additional salt, if necessary, and serve immediately, passing grated cheese at the table.

Macaroni and Pinto Bean Soup with Mussels and Rosemary

MUSSELS ADD A BRINY FLAVOR TO THIS SOUP, WHILE MACARONI AND PINTO BEANS GIVE IT MAIN-COURSE BULK. SERVE WITH CRUSTY BREAD AND SALAD FOR A COMPLETE MEAL. SERVES 6 TO 8.

  4 pounds mussels, scrubbed and debearded
  1 cup dry white wine
  ¼ cup extra-virgin olive oil
  3 large garlic cloves, slivered
  ½ teaspoon hot red pepper flakes
  1½ tablespoons chopped fresh rosemary
  Salt
  2 19-ounce cans pinto beans, drained and rinsed, 2 cups of them mashed with a fork
  1 14.5-ounce can diced tomatoes
  8 ounces elbow macaroni, penne, or other short, tubular pasta
  Ground black pepper

1. Bring the mussels and wine to a boil in a large covered soup kettle. Steam until the mussels open, 3 to 5 minutes. Transfer the mussels to a large bowl with a slotted spoon, allowing the liquid to drain back into the kettle; cool slightly. Separate the meat from the shells, reserving the meat in a small bowl and discarding the shells. Pour the mussel broth into a 1-quart Pyrex measuring cup. (Add water as necessary to make 2 cups.) Rinse and dry the kettle; return to the burner.

2. Heat the oil, garlic, red pepper flakes, and rosemary in the kettle over medium heat until the garlic is fragrant but not brown, 2 to 3 minutes. Add 6 cups water, 2 teaspoons salt, whole and mashed beans, tomatoes with their juice, and reserved mussel broth; bring to a boil.

3. Add the pasta and cook until the pasta is tender, 7 to 8 minutes. Add the reserved mussels; adjust the seasoning with salt and pepper to taste, and serve immediately.

Pasta and White Bean Soup with Clams and Sausage

KIELBASA AND CLAMS CAN BOTH BE RATHER SALTY, SO HOLD OFF ON SEASONING THIS SOUP UNTIL YOU ARE READY TO SERVE IT. SERVES 6 TO 8.

  4 pounds littleneck or cherrystone clams, scrubbed
  1 cup dry white wine
  1 tablespoon extra-virgin olive oil
  1 pound kielbasa, cut into ¼-inch rounds
  1 small onion, minced
  3 large garlic cloves, slivered
  ½ teaspoon hot red pepper flakes
  ½ teaspoon dried oregano
  1 19-ounce can white beans (such as cannellini, white kidney, or great northern), drained and rinsed
  6 ounces spaghetti, broken into 2-inch pieces
  ¼ cup minced fresh flat-leaf parsley leaves
  Salt and ground black pepper

1. Bring the clams and wine to a boil in a large covered soup kettle. Steam until the clams open, 3 to 5 minutes. Transfer the clams to a large bowl with a slotted spoon, allowing the liquid to drain back into the kettle; cool slightly. Separate the meat from the shells, coarsely chopping and reserving the meat in a small bowl and discarding the shells. Pour the clam broth into a 1-quart Pyrex measuring cup. (Add water as necessary to equal 2 cups.) Rinse and dry the kettle; return to the burner.

2. Heat the oil over medium-high heat. Add the sausage and cook until browned, about 5 minutes. Drain off all but 3 tablespoons of the fat. Stir in the onion and cook until softened, 3 to 4 minutes. Stir in the garlic, red pepper flakes, and oregano and cook until the garlic is fragrant but not brown, 2 to 3 minutes.

3. Add 8 cups water, the beans, and reserved clam broth; bring to a boil. Add the pasta and cook until the pasta is tender, 7 to 8 minutes. Add the reserved clam meat and parsley; adjust the seasoning with salt and pepper to taste, and serve immediately.

Minestrone with Pasta and Pancetta

PANCETTA CAN BE USED IN PLACE OF A CHEESE RIND TO BOOST THE FLAVOR OF MINESTRONE WITH PASTA. AMERICAN BACON CAN BE SUBSTITUTED, BUT ITS SMOKY FLAVOR CAN OVERWHELM THE VEGETABLES; TRY BLANCHING BACON STRIPS IN SIMMERING WATER FOR 1 MINUTE TO WASH AWAY SOME OF THE SMOKINESS. SERVES 6 TO 8.

Heat 1 tablespoon extra-virgin olive oil in a soup kettle or pot over medium heat. Add 2 ounces thinly sliced pancetta, minced, and sauté until crisp, 3 to 4 minutes. Follow the Master Recipe for Classic Minestrone with Pasta on page 270, adding the vegetables, tomatoes, water, and salt to the pot with the pancetta. Proceed as directed, omitting the cheese rind.

Pasta Soups with Chicken Stock

COOKING PASTA IN A chicken stock creates an especially rich flavor. In our testing of stock-making methods, we found that sautéing chicken parts that have been hacked into 2-inch pieces creates the richest flavor in the shortest amount of time. Once the chicken loses its raw color, cover the pot and cook until the chicken releases its flavorful juices. Add water and simmer the chicken until the broth is rich tasting. From start to finish, the process takes less than 1 hour.

Other stock-making methods, including simmering parts in water for hours, take much longer and often yield inferior results. In some recipes in this section, homemade stock is a must. For instance, a simple tortellini soup made with canned chicken broth is too salty and tastes of chemicals. In soups with more aggressive seasonings, such as tomatoes, it is possible to use canned chicken broth. Follow the recommendations in individual recipes.

Quick Chicken Stock

WE HAVE FOUND THAT BY BROWNING BEFORE BOILING, WE CAN EXTRACT ENOUGH FLAVOR FROM CHICKEN PIECES TO MAKE AN EXCELLENT STOCK IN LESS THAN AN HOUR. IF YOU'D LIKE CHICKEN MEAT AS WELL AS STOCK, SEE INDIVIDUAL RECIPES FOR CHICKEN NOODLE SOUPS (PAGES 276–279). ALSO, SEE *THE COOK'S ILLUSTRATED COMPLETE BOOK OF POULTRY* FOR MORE INFORMATION AND SOUP RECIPES. MAKES ABOUT 2 QUARTS.

> 1 tablespoon vegetable oil
> 1 medium onion, cut into medium dice
> 4 pounds chicken backs and wing tips or whole legs, cut into 2-inch pieces
> 2 quarts boiling water
> 2 teaspoons salt
> 2 bay leaves

1. Heat the oil in a large stockpot or soup kettle. Add the onion; sauté until colored and softened slightly, 2 to 3 minutes. Transfer the onion to a large bowl.

2. Add half of the chicken pieces to the pot; sauté until no longer pink, 4 to 5 minutes. Transfer the cooked chicken to the bowl with the onion. Sauté the remaining chicken pieces. Return the onion and chicken pieces to the pot. Reduce the heat to low, cover, and cook until the chicken releases its juices, about 20 minutes.

3. Increase the heat to high; add the boiling water, salt, and bay leaves. Return to a simmer, then cover and barely simmer until the broth is rich and flavorful, about 20 minutes.

4. Strain the broth; discard the solids. Skim the fat (reserve for later use, if desired). (The broth can be covered and refrigerated up to 2 days or frozen for several months.)

Chicken Soup with Tortellini and Watercress

THE STOCK MAY BE MADE AHEAD OF TIME, BUT COOK THE TORTELLINI AND WATERCRESS JUST BEFORE SERVING. SCRAPS OF FRESH EGG PASTA, SAVED FROM OTHER FRESH PASTA PROJECTS AND FROZEN, ARE ALSO GOOD WITH CHICKEN BROTH AND WATERCRESS. **SERVES 6 TO 8.**

1 recipe Quick Chicken Stock (page 274)
½ recipe Tortellini prepared through step
    1 (page 345) with any filling except
    shrimp or lamb
4 cups watercress, trimmed, washed, and
    coarsely chopped
Salt and ground black pepper

Bring the broth to a low boil in a wide, deep pot. Drop the tortellini and watercress into the pot. Cook until the tortellini are al dente, about 4 minutes. Add salt and pepper to taste. Ladle the soup and tortellini into bowls and serve immediately.

Tomato and Pasta Soup

CHICKEN STOCK GIVES THIS TOMATO SOUP A REAL RICHNESS, AND COOKED PASTA ADDS BULK, MAKING THIS SUITABLE AS A LUNCH ENTREE OR LIGHT MAIN COURSE. **SERVES 6.**

Salt
¾ cup small pasta such as elbows, ditalini,
    or orzo
2 tablespoons extra-virgin olive oil, plus
    extra for drizzling
2 medium garlic cloves, minced
3 pounds plum tomatoes, peeled, seeded,
    and coarsely chopped, *or* 1 28-ounce can
    whole tomatoes, drained and coarsely
    chopped (see illustrations, pages 112, 136)
4 cups Quick Chicken Stock (page 274)
    or low-sodium canned broth
2 tablespoons finely chopped fresh basil leaves
Ground black pepper
Freshly grated Parmesan cheese (optional)

1. Bring 3 quarts of water to a boil in a medium saucepan. Add 1 teaspoon salt and the pasta and cook until al dente.

2. While the pasta is cooking, heat 2 tablespoons oil and the garlic in a large saucepan over medium heat and cook until fragrant, 3 to 4 minutes. Add the tomatoes, bring to a boil, lower the heat, and simmer until the tomatoes are thickened, about 5 minutes. Add the stock, return to a boil, and boil for 2 minutes.

3. Drain the pasta and stir it into the soup along with the basil and salt and pepper to taste. Ladle the soup into bowls. Serve immediately with additional oil for drizzling and grated Parmesan cheese if desired.

Passatelli

PASSATELLI IS THE ITALIAN VERSION OF MATZOH BALL SOUP, WITH DUMPLINGS MADE OF CHEESE AND BREAD CRUMBS. TRADITIONALLY, THE CHEESE AND DUMPLING MIXTURE IS PUSHED THROUGH A POTATO RICER TO MAKE PASTALIKE THREADS, BUT WE LIKE TO SHAPE THE MIXTURE INTO SMALL DUMPLINGS BECAUSE THERE IS LESS DANGER THAT THE DUMPLINGS WILL DISINTE-GRATE IN THE SIMMERING SOUP. HOMEMADE BREAD CRUMBS ARE ESSENTIAL HERE AS IS THE BEST CHEESE, PREFERABLY PARMIGIANO-REGGIANO. FOR THE BREAD CRUMBS, GRIND TWO SLICES OF WHITE BREAD IN THE FOOD PROCESSOR AND THEN DRY OUT THE CRUMBS FOR 5 MINUTES IN A 300-DEGREE OVEN. **SERVES 6 TO 8.**

½ cup homemade bread crumbs (see
    headnote)
2 large eggs
1 cup freshly grated Parmesan cheese,
    plus more for the table
Pinch freshly grated nutmeg
Salt and ground black pepper
1 recipe Quick Chicken Stock (page 274)
2 tablespoons chopped fresh flat-leaf
    parsley leaves (optional)

1. Combine the bread crumbs, eggs, cheese, nutmeg, and salt and pepper to taste in a medium bowl. Refrigerate for 15 minutes to firm up the batter.

(continued on next page)

2. Bring the stock to a simmer in a wide, deep pot over medium heat.

3. With moistened hands, roll the dumpling mixture into grape-size balls. Drop the dumplings into the gently simmering broth and cook the dumplings until they float to the surface, 3 to 4 minutes. Stir in the parsley (if using) and ladle into soup bowls. Serve immediately with extra cheese.

◆

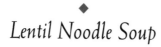

Lentil Noodle Soup

CRUSHED GARLIC STIRRED INTO THE SOUP JUST BEFORE SERVING IS FRESH-TASTING BUT NOT OVERPOWERING. THIS SOUP GETS QUITE THICK WHEN THE EGG NOODLES ARE FULLY COOKED. ADD BOILING WATER TO THIN IT, IF DESIRED. DRIED MINT, AVAILABLE AT MIDDLE EASTERN MARKETS, GIVES THIS SIMPLE SOUP A DISTINCTIVE FLAVOR, BUT IT IS ALSO DELICIOUS WITHOUT IT. SERVES 6 TO 8.

> 2 tablespoons extra-virgin olive oil
> 1 medium onion, minced
> 2 cups lentils
> 1 recipe Quick Chicken Stock (page 274)
> *or* 2 quarts low-sodium canned broth
> 6 ounces dried egg noodles, broken into 2-inch lengths
> 1 medium garlic clove, peeled (see illustration, page 39)
> ¼ cup minced fresh cilantro leaves
> 1 tablespoon dried mint (optional)
> Salt and ground black pepper

1. Heat the oil in a large soup kettle or stockpot over medium heat. Add the onion; sauté until translucent, 4 to 5 minutes.

2. Add the lentils and stock; bring to a boil. Reduce the heat and simmer until the lentils are tender, 15 to 20 minutes. Add the pasta; cook until the pasta is tender, about 10 minutes.

3. Process the garlic through a garlic press into the pot. Stir in the cilantro and mint (if using). Simmer for 1 minute. If necessary, add some boiling water to thin the soup. Season with salt and pepper. Serve immediately.

Pasta Soups with Chicken Meat

WHEN WE WANT CHICKEN meat in our pasta soups, we prefer to make homemade stock with a whole chicken. The breast is removed and split into two pieces. The remaining chicken is hacked into 2-inch pieces and then sautéed and sweated as for regular chicken stock. (The split breast is sautéed but not sweated to keep it from becoming overcooked and dry.) Once the water is added to make stock, the breast halves are returned to the pot and cooked through. The breast halves can now be skinned and shredded. The stock is strained (the hacked chicken pieces are discarded) and you are ready to make soup.

MASTER RECIPE

Chicken Noodle Soup

SERVES 6 TO 8

ATHER THAN INEDIBLE chicken backs and wings, this recipe calls for sautéing chicken pieces and split breasts with an onion and then cooking covered until they release their juices. Only then is water added. At this time, the chicken has let go of so much of its flavor that it only has to simmer for 20 minutes to create a remarkably flavorful broth with an abundance of perfectly cooked breast meat. An infinite variety of vegetables and noodles can then be added to create the chicken noodle soup of your desire.

1 tablespoon vegetable oil
1 whole chicken (about 4 pounds), breast removed, split, and reserved; remaining chicken cut into 2-inch pieces
2 medium onions, cut into medium dice
2 quarts boiling water
Salt
2 bay leaves
1 large carrot, sliced ¼ inch thick
1 celery stalk, sliced ¼ inch thick
½ teaspoon dried thyme
3 ounces dried egg noodles, broken into 2-inch pieces
¼ cup minced fresh flat-leaf parsley leaves
Ground black pepper

1. Heat the oil in a large soup kettle. When the oil shimmers and starts to smoke, add chicken breast halves; sauté until brown on both sides, about 5 minutes. Remove and set aside. Add half the chopped onions to the kettle; sauté until colored and softened slightly, 2 to 3 minutes. Transfer to a medium bowl. Add half of the chicken pieces; sauté until no longer pink, 4 to 5 minutes. Transfer to the bowl with the onions. Sauté the remaining chicken pieces. Return the sautéed onions and chicken pieces (excluding the breasts) to the kettle. Reduce the heat to low, cover, and cook until the chicken releases its juices, about 20 minutes. Increase the heat to high; add the boiling water along with both breast halves, 2 teaspoons salt, and bay leaves. Bring to a simmer, then cover and barely simmer until the chicken breasts are cooked and the broth is rich and flavorful, about 20 minutes.

2. Remove the chicken breasts from the kettle; set aside. When cool enough to handle, remove the skin from the breasts, then remove the meat from the bones and shred into bite-size pieces; discard the skin and bone. Strain the broth; discard the solids. Skim the fat from the broth, reserving 2 tablespoons. (Broth and meat can be covered and refrigerated up to 2 days.)

3. Return the soup kettle to medium-high heat. Add 2 tablespoons chicken fat (or use oil). Add the remaining onion, along with the carrot and celery; sauté until softened, about 5 minutes. Add the thyme, broth, and chicken; simmer until the vegetables are tender and the flavors meld, 10 to 15 minutes.

4. Add the noodles and cook until just tender, about 8 minutes. Stir in the parsley, add salt and pepper to taste, and serve immediately.

◆

Chicken Soup with Orzo and Spring Vegetables

LEEKS, ASPARAGUS, PEAS, AND TARRAGON MAKE FOR A FRESH-TASTING VARIATION ON CLASSIC CHICKEN NOODLE SOUP. SERVES 6 TO 8.

1 tablespoon vegetable oil
1 whole chicken (about 4 pounds), breast removed, split, and reserved; remaining chicken cut into 2-inch pieces
1 medium onion, cut into medium dice
1 medium leek, rinsed thoroughly, quartered lengthwise, then sliced thin crosswise (see illustrations 1–6, page 165)
2 quarts boiling water
Salt
2 bay leaves
1 large carrot, sliced ¼ inch thick
1 celery stalk, sliced ¼ inch thick
½ teaspoon dried thyme
½ cup orzo
¼ pound asparagus, tough ends snapped off and cut into 1-inch lengths (see illustrations 1–3, page 138)
¼ cup frozen peas
2 tablespoons minced fresh tarragon leaves
Ground black pepper

(continued on next page)

1. Heat the oil in a large soup kettle. When the oil shimmers and starts to smoke, add chicken breast halves; sauté until brown on both sides, about 5 minutes. Remove and set aside. Add half the onion and half the leek to the kettle; sauté until colored and softened slightly, 2 to 3 minutes. Transfer to a medium bowl. Add half of the chicken pieces; sauté until no longer pink, 4 to 5 minutes. Transfer to the bowl with the onion and leek. Sauté the remaining chicken pieces. Return the sautéed onion, leek, and chicken pieces (excluding the breasts) to the kettle. Reduce the heat to low, cover, and cook until the chicken releases its juices, about 20 minutes. Increase the heat to high; add the boiling water along with both breast halves, 2 teaspoons salt, and bay leaves. Bring to a simmer, then cover and barely simmer until the chicken breasts are cooked and the broth is rich and flavorful, about 20 minutes.

2. Remove the chicken breasts from the kettle; set aside. When cool enough to handle, remove the skin from the breasts, then remove the meat from the bones and shred into bite-size pieces; discard the skin and bone. Strain the broth; discard the solids. Skim the fat from the broth, reserving 2 tablespoons. (Broth and meat can be covered and refrigerated up to 2 days.)

3. Return the soup kettle to medium-high heat. Add 2 tablespoons chicken fat (or use oil). Add the remaining onion and leek, along with the carrot and celery; sauté until softened, about 5 minutes. Add the thyme, broth, and chicken; simmer until the vegetables are tender and the flavors meld, 10 to 15 minutes.

4. Add the orzo, asparagus, and peas and cook until the pasta is tender, about 7 minutes. Stir in the tarragon, add salt and pepper to taste, and serve immediately.

Chicken Soup with Pasta Shells, Tomatoes, and Zucchini

SERVE WITH GRATED PARMESAN CHEESE TO HIGHLIGHT THE ITALIAN FLAVORS OF THIS SOUP. **SERVES 6 TO 8.**

> 1 tablespoon vegetable oil
> 1 whole chicken (about 4 pounds), breast removed, split, and reserved; remaining chicken cut into 2-inch pieces
> 2 medium onions, cut into medium dice
> 2 quarts boiling water
> Salt
> 2 bay leaves
> 1 large carrot, sliced ¼ inch thick
> 1 celery stalk, sliced ¼ inch thick
> 1 medium zucchini, cut into medium dice
> ½ teaspoon dried thyme
> ½ cup chopped fresh or canned tomatoes
> 1 cup small shells or macaroni
> ¼ cup minced fresh basil leaves
> Ground black pepper

1. Heat the oil in a large soup kettle. When the oil shimmers and starts to smoke, add chicken breast halves; sauté until brown on both sides, about 5 minutes. Remove and set aside. Add half the chopped onions to the kettle; sauté until colored and softened slightly, 2 to 3 minutes. Transfer to a medium bowl. Add half of the chicken pieces; sauté until no longer pink, 4 to 5 minutes. Transfer to the bowl with the onion. Sauté the remaining chicken pieces. Return the sautéed onion and chicken pieces (excluding the breasts) to the kettle. Reduce the heat to low, cover, and cook until the chicken releases its juices, about 20 minutes. Increase the heat to high; add the boiling water along with both breast halves, 2 teaspoons salt, and bay leaves. Bring to a simmer, then cover and barely simmer until the chicken breasts are cooked and the broth is rich and flavorful, about 20 minutes.

2. Remove the chicken breasts from the kettle; set aside. When cool enough to handle, remove the skin from the breasts, then remove the meat from the bones and shred into bite-size pieces; discard the skin and bone. Strain the broth; discard the solids. Skim the fat from the broth, reserving 2 tablespoons. (Broth and meat can be covered and refrigerated up to 2 days.)

3. Return the soup kettle to medium-high heat. Add 2 tablespoons chicken fat (or use oil). Add the remaining onion, along with the carrot, celery, and zucchini; sauté until softened, 5 to 7 minutes. Add the thyme, broth, tomatoes, and chicken; simmer until the vegetables are tender and the flavors meld, 10 to 15 minutes.

4. Add the pasta and cook until just tender, about 10 minutes. Stir in the basil, add salt and pepper to taste, and serve.

◆

Curried Chicken and Couscous Soup

CURRY POWDER AND WINTER SQUASH GIVE THIS SOUP A VIBRANT FLAVOR AND BRIGHT ORANGE COLOR. FOR DETAILS ON COOKING COUSCOUS, SEE CHAPTER 24. SERVES 6 TO 8.

1 tablespoon vegetable oil
1 whole chicken (about 4 pounds), breast removed, split, and reserved; remaining chicken cut into 2-inch pieces
2 medium onions, cut into medium dice
2 quarts boiling water
Salt
2 bay leaves
1 medium baking potato, peeled and cut into ½-inch dice
1 small butternut squash (about 1 pound), peeled, seeded, and cut into ½-inch dice
3 cups stemmed spinach leaves, cut into thin strips
3 garlic cloves, minced
1 tablespoon curry powder
1 cup fresh or canned chopped tomatoes
½ cup couscous
¼ cup minced fresh cilantro leaves
Ground black pepper

1. Heat the oil in a large soup kettle. When the oil shimmers and starts to smoke, add chicken breast halves; sauté until brown on both sides, about 5 minutes. Remove and set aside. Add half the chopped onions to the kettle; sauté until colored and softened slightly, 2 to 3 minutes. Transfer to a medium bowl. Add half of the chicken pieces; sauté until no longer pink, 4 to 5 minutes. Transfer to the bowl with the onions. Sauté the remaining chicken pieces. Return the sautéed onions and chicken pieces (excluding the breasts) to the kettle. Reduce the heat to low, cover, and cook until the chicken releases its juices, about 20 minutes. Increase the heat to high; add the boiling water along with both breast halves, 2 teaspoons salt, and bay leaves. Bring to a simmer, then cover and barely simmer until the chicken breasts are cooked and the broth is rich and flavorful, about 20 minutes.

2. Remove the chicken breasts from the kettle; set aside. When cool enough to handle, remove the skin from the breasts, then remove the meat from the bones and shred into bite-size pieces; discard the skin and bone. Strain the broth; discard the solids. Skim the fat from the broth, reserving 2 tablespoons. (Broth and meat can be covered and refrigerated up to 2 days.)

3. Return the soup kettle to medium-high heat. Add 2 tablespoons chicken fat (or use oil). Add the remaining onions, along with the potato, squash, and spinach; sauté until the potato and squash begin to soften and the spinach is wilted, about 5 minutes. Add the garlic and curry powder and sauté another minute. Add the tomatoes, broth, and chicken; simmer until the vegetables are tender and the flavors meld, 10 to 15 minutes.

4. Add the couscous, remove from the heat, cover, and let stand 5 minutes. Stir in the cilantro, add salt and pepper to taste, and serve immediately.

Pasta Soups with Beef

MOST RECIPES FOR beef stock call for bones, vegetables, and an extraordinarily long simmering time. We followed these recipes (even going so far as to cook one stock for 8 hours) and were disappointed in every case. The stock tasted of bones, not beef.

We then tested various cuts of meat coupled with bones for their gelatin. We tested chuck, shank, round, arm-blade, oxtail, and short ribs. We browned the meat (adding small marrow bones to cuts without bones) and an onion. As with chicken stock, we covered the browned ingredients and let them sweat for 20 minutes. We added water and simmered the stock until it was rich and flavorful, about 2 hours, or a little less.

Our favorite stocks were made with shank followed by the marrow-enhanced chuck. These stocks were good but needed some enlivening. We tested tomato, vinegar, and red wine and found that adding a little

red wine once the meat has browned has the best effect on the stock.

In the end, good beef broth requires a tremendous amount of meat (6 pounds for just 2 quarts of stock). This may explain why canned beef broths have so little beef flavor—it's too expensive to use much meat in such a cheap product. In our tasting of ten canned beef broths, none was deemed acceptable. If you don't have the time to make beef broth for these soups, choose another recipe.

◆

Rich Beef Broth for Soup

IN ORDER TO PRODUCE A RICH-TASTING BEEF BROTH, YOU HAVE TO USE A LOT OF MEAT—MORE THAN YOU NEED FOR THE SOUP ITSELF. SAVE EXTRA BEEF FOR SANDWICHES OR COLD SALADS. MAKES SCANT 2 QUARTS.

2 tablespoons vegetable oil
6 pounds of shank, meat cut from bone in large chunks (see illustration), *or* 4 pounds chuck and 2 pounds of small marrow bones
1 large onion, halved
1/2 cup dry red wine
1/2 teaspoon salt

1. Heat 1 tablespoon oil in a large soup kettle or Dutch oven over medium-high heat; brown the meat, bones, and onion halves on all sides in batches, making sure not to overcrowd the pan, and adding the additional oil to the pan if necessary. Remove and set aside. Add the red wine to the empty kettle; cook until reduced to a syrup, 1 to 2 minutes. Return the browned bones, meat and juices given off, and onion to the kettle. Reduce the heat to low, then cover and sweat the meat and onions until they have released about 3/4 cup dark, very intensely flavored liquid, about 20 minutes. Increase the heat to medium-high, add 2 quarts water and the salt; bring to a simmer, reduce the heat to very low, partially cover, and barely simmer until the meat is tender, 1 1/2 to 2 hours.

2. Strain the broth, discard the bones and onions, and set the meat aside, reserving half of the meat for sandwiches or cold salads. (At this point the broth and

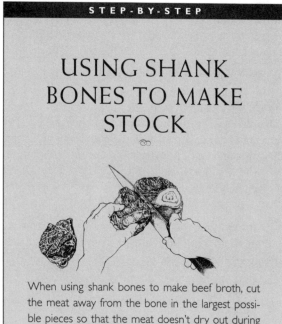

STEP-BY-STEP

USING SHANK BONES TO MAKE STOCK

When using shank bones to make beef broth, cut the meat away from the bone in the largest possible pieces so that the meat doesn't dry out during the long cooking time. Both the meat and bones contribute flavor to the final product.

meat can be cooled to room temperature and covered and refrigerated up to 5 days.) Let the broth stand until the fat rises to the top; skim and discard the fat. When the unreserved meat is cool enough to handle, shred into bite-size pieces.

Beef Noodle Soup

SERVES 6

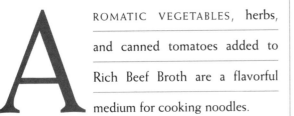

AROMATIC VEGETABLES, herbs, and canned tomatoes added to Rich Beef Broth are a flavorful medium for cooking noodles.

1 tablespoon vegetable oil
1 medium onion, cut into medium dice
2 medium carrots, cut into medium dice
1 celery stalk, cut into medium dice
½ teaspoon dried thyme *or* 1½ teaspoons minced fresh thyme leaves
½ cup canned tomatoes, cut into medium dice
1 recipe Rich Beef Broth (page 280), strained and skimmed of fat and 2 cups shredded meat
3 ounces dried egg noodles, broken into 2-inch pieces
¼ cup minced fresh flat-leaf parsley leaves
Salt and ground black pepper

1. Heat the oil over medium-high heat in a soup kettle or Dutch oven. Add the onion, carrots, and celery; sauté until softened, about 5 minutes. Add the thyme

and tomatoes, then the beef broth and meat; bring to a simmer. Reduce the heat to low; simmer until the vegetables are no longer crunchy and the flavors have blended, about 15 minutes.

2. Add the noodles; simmer until fully cooked, about 8 minutes longer. Stir in the parsley, adjust the seasonings, adding salt and pepper to taste, and serve immediately.

◆

Beef Noodle Soup with Mushrooms and Thyme

NOODLES, MUSHROOMS, AND THYME CONTRIBUTE TO THE EARTHY FLAVOR OF THIS BEEF SOUP. SERVES 6.

2 tablespoons vegetable oil
1 medium onion, cut into medium dice
2 medium carrots, cut into medium dice
12 ounces domestic or wild mushrooms, stems removed, wiped clean, and sliced thin
½ teaspoon dried thyme *or* 1½ teaspoons minced fresh thyme leaves
½ cup chopped canned tomatoes
1 recipe Rich Beef Broth (page 280), strained and skimmed of fat and 2 cups shredded meat
3 ounces dried egg noodles, broken into 2-inch pieces
¼ cup minced fresh flat-leaf parsley leaves
Salt and ground black pepper

1. Heat the oil over medium-high heat in a soup kettle or Dutch oven. Add the onion and carrots; sauté until almost soft, 3 to 4 minutes. Add the mushrooms; sauté until softened and the liquid almost evaporates, 4 to 5 minutes longer. Add the thyme and tomatoes, then beef broth and meat; bring to a simmer. Reduce the heat to low; simmer until the vegetables are no longer crunchy and the flavors have blended, about 15 minutes.

2. Add the noodles; simmer until fully cooked, about 8 minutes longer. Stir in the parsley, adjust the seasonings, adding salt and pepper to taste, and serve immediately.

BAKED

DRIED PASTA

/|\

THERE ARE TWO BASIC STYLES OF BAKED PASTA CAS-

SEROLES. THERE ARE DISHES THAT ALWAYS OR USUALLY

START WITH FRESH PASTA, INCLUDING LASAGNE, CAN-

NELLONI, AND CRESPELLE. THESE DISHES ARE USUALLY

QUITE DELICATE AND RICH. THEY REQUIRE A SIGNIFI-

CANT INVESTMENT OF TIME AND ENERGY AND ARE

GENERALLY CONSIDERED "SPECIAL OCCASION FOOD"

(FOR MORE INFORMATION, SEE CHAPTERS 21 AND 22).

A second type of baked pasta dishes starts with dried pasta and includes such popular favorites as macaroni and cheese, baked ziti, and noodle kugel. For the most part, these dishes are designed for weeknight cooking. They are hearty, relatively easy to prepare, and generally appeal to children as well as adults.

The recipes in this chapter are quite different from one another, although each dish starts with dried pasta that is boiled and then combined with other ingredients and cooked. (Most of these dishes are baked, but there are a few exceptions, as you will see.) This chapter covers seven types of pasta dishes, including macaroni and cheese; turkey tetrazzini and other casseroles bound with velouté (a sauce made with butter, flour, and stock); baked pasta dishes bound with béchamel (a sauce made with butter, flour, and milk); baked pasta dishes bound with cheese (usually mozzarella); stuffed and baked pasta dishes (shells and manicotti); pasta frittatas (open-faced Italian omelets made with cooked noodles, eggs, cheese, and seasonings); and kugel (baked Eastern European casseroles made with dried egg noodles).

Each type of baked pasta dish offers its own set of challenges and each is considered separately.

Macaroni and Cheese

OUR GOAL WHEN DEVELOPING a master recipe for macaroni and cheese was simple. Boxed versions, which is how most Americans eat this dish, have a thick, creamy sauce that oozes from inside each noodle. We like the texture of this sauce, but since it is made with orange "cheese" powder the flavor is awful. We wanted our macaroni to be enveloped in a rich, creamy sauce, but we also wanted every bite to deliver a good hit of real cheese flavor.

Our research uncovered two distinct styles of macaroni and cheese. The more common variety is béchamel based—the macaroni is blanketed with a cheese-flavored white sauce, usually topped with crumbs, and baked. The other variety is custard based—a mixture of eggs and milk is poured over layers of grated cheese and noodles. As the dish bakes,

the eggs, milk, and cheese set. This version is usually topped with bread crumbs as it bakes.

We prepared several versions of both styles of macaroni and cheese. Béchamel-based dishes were grainy and tasted like macaroni with cheese sauce. The cheese flavor was not penetrating deep into the pasta as we wanted. The sauce was simply too thick and the inside of each individual noodle was dry. The custard-based macaroni and cheese dishes that we prepared generally had a better cheese flavor, but these dishes set into a stiff "pudding." The sauce was not as creamy or smooth as we wanted.

Next, we stumbled upon an odd recipe in John Thorne's *Simple Cooking*. His recipe calls for a sauce made with evaporated milk, eggs, and a lot of cheese. Some of this sauce is tossed with cooked pasta, the rest is stirred into the noodles as they bake. Frequent stirring allows the eggs to thicken without setting and the result is an incredibly silky sauce.

We liked Thorne's recipe quite a lot but had some quibbles. His recipe was too rich and cheesy for our tastes, so we cut back the amount of cheese. We tried to use whole milk or half-and-half instead of evaporated milk, a product we don't often keep in our pantry. Less cheese made the dish less rich and easier to eat, but the versions made without evaporated milk curdled. The evaporation process stabilizes the milk, which in turn stabilizes the macaroni and cheese.

Next, we tested Vermont, New York, and Wisconsin cheddars. We preferred the less sharp Wisconsin variety. Our final tests focused on the frequent stirring in the oven that Thorne advocates. Opening the oven every few minutes causes the heat to dissipate, so the macaroni and cheese was taking at least twenty minutes to heat up. So we tried stirring the cooked pasta and sauce together on top of the stove and then pouring the macaroni and cheese into a baking dish, topping it with bread crumbs, and broiling for a few minutes to crisp up the crumbs. This worked beautifully and took far less time.

In the end, our version of macaroni and cheese is not really baked; it's stirred over low heat on top of the stove and then broiled. However, this method delivers the silkiest texture and best cheese flavor.

"Baked" Macaroni and Cheese

SERVES 4 AS A MAIN COURSE OR
6 TO 8 AS A SIDE DISH

O UR PREFERRED VERSION of

macaroni and cheese turned out

to be a simple stovetop recipe.

To finish the dish, we sprinkle it

with fresh bread crumbs and put it under the broiler

for a minute or two, for that baked casserole look with

golden-brown topping.

6 tablespoons unsalted butter
1 cup fresh bread crumbs (see page 89)
Salt
12 ounces sharp Wisconsin cheddar,
    American, or Monterey Jack cheese,
    shredded (about 3 cups)
2 large eggs, lightly beaten
1 can (12 ounces) evaporated milk
¼ teaspoon hot red pepper sauce
1 teaspoon dry mustard, dissolved in
    1 teaspoon water
12 ounces elbow macaroni
Ground black pepper

1. Heat 2 tablespoons butter in a large skillet over medium heat until the foam subsides. Add the bread crumbs and cook, tossing to coat with the butter, until the crumbs just begin to color. Season to taste with salt. Cool completely, toss with ¼ cup cheese, and set aside.

2. Adjust the oven rack 6 inches from the heating element and heat the broiler.

3. Mix the eggs, 1 cup evaporated milk, hot pepper sauce, and mustard mixture in a small bowl and set aside.

4. Meanwhile, bring 3 quarts of water to a boil in a large pot. Add 2 teaspoons salt and the macaroni and cook until almost tender but still a little firm to the bite. Drain and return the pasta to the pot over low heat. Add the remaining 4 tablespoons butter and toss to melt.

5. Pour the egg mixture over the pasta along with three-quarters of the remaining cheese. Stir until thoroughly combined and the cheese starts to melt. Gradually add the remaining milk and cheese, stirring constantly, until the mixture is hot and creamy, about 5 minutes. Season with salt and pepper to taste.

6. Pour the cooked macaroni and cheese into a 9-inch square baking dish. Spread the crumbs evenly over the top. Broil until the crumbs turn deep brown, 1 to 2 minutes. Let stand to set a bit, about 5 minutes, and serve.

Spicy Macaroni and Cheese

MACARONI AND CHEESE CAN BE VARIED ENDLESSLY WITH THE ADDITION OF NEW SEASONINGS AND SPICES. HERE, SOME CUMIN AND CHILI POWDER ALONG WITH A FRESH CHILE GIVE THE DISH A SOUTHWESTERN FLAVOR. SERVES 4 AS A MAIN COURSE OR 6 TO 8 AS A SIDE DISH.

> 6 tablespoons unsalted butter
> 1 cup fresh bread crumbs
> Salt
> 12 ounces Monterey Jack cheese, shredded (about 3 cups)
> 2 large eggs, lightly beaten
> 1 can (12 ounces) evaporated milk
> 1/2 teaspoon ground cumin
> 1/2 teaspoon chili powder
> 1 jalapeño chile, stemmed, seeded, and minced
> 12 ounces elbow macaroni
> Ground black pepper

1. Heat 2 tablespoons butter in a large skillet over medium heat until the foam subsides. Add the bread crumbs and cook, tossing to coat with the butter, until the crumbs just begin to color. Season to taste with salt. Cool completely, toss with 1/4 cup cheese, and set aside.

2. Adjust the oven rack 6 inches from the heating element and heat the broiler.

3. Mix the eggs, 1 cup evaporated milk, cumin, chili powder, and jalapeño in a small bowl and set aside.

4. Meanwhile, bring 3 quarts of water to a boil in a large pot. Add 2 teaspoons salt and the macaroni and cook until almost tender, but still a little firm to the bite. Drain and return the pasta to the pot over low heat. Add the remaining 4 tablespoons butter and toss to melt.

5. Pour the egg mixture over the pasta along with three-quarters of the remaining cheese. Stir until thoroughly combined and the cheese starts to melt. Gradually add the remaining milk and cheese, stirring constantly, until the mixture is hot and creamy, about 5 minutes. Season with salt and pepper to taste.

6. Pour the cooked macaroni and cheese into a 9-inch square baking dish. Spread the crumbs evenly over the top. Broil until the crumbs turn deep brown, 1 to 2 minutes. Let stand to set a bit, about 5 minutes, and serve.

◆

Macaroni with Spinach and Gorgonzola

MILD GORGONZOLA, SOMETIMES LABELED GORGONZOLA DOLCE, AND CHOPPED SPINACH GIVE CLASSIC MACARONI AND CHEESE AN ITALIAN FLAVOR. WE STILL LIKE TO USE A MILDER CHEESE ALONG WITH THE GORGONZOLA; GORGONZOLA ALONE PRODUCED AN OVERWHELMINGLY SHARP-TASTING DISH. SERVES 4 AS A MAIN COURSE OR 6 TO 8 AS A SIDE DISH.

> 6 tablespoons unsalted butter
> 1 cup fresh bread crumbs
> Salt
> 6 ounces sharp Wisconsin cheddar, American, or Monterey Jack cheese, shredded (about 1 1/2 cups)
> 10 ounces spinach, washed, stemmed, and coarsely chopped
> Ground black pepper
> 2 large eggs, lightly beaten
> 1 can (12 ounces) evaporated milk
> 12 ounces elbow macaroni
> 6 ounces mild Gorgonzola cheese, crumbled (about 1 1/2 cups)

1. Heat 2 tablespoons butter in a large skillet over medium heat until the foam subsides. Add the bread crumbs and cook, tossing to coat with the butter, until the crumbs just begin to color. Season to taste with salt. Cool completely, toss with 1/4 cup cheddar cheese, and set aside.

2. Heat 1 tablespoon butter in a large sauté pan. Add the wet spinach. Cover and cook over medium-high heat, stirring occasionally, until the greens completely wilt but are still bright green, about 5 minutes. Uncover and season to taste with salt and pepper. Cook over high heat until the liquid evaporates, 2 to 3 minutes longer; set aside.

3. Adjust the oven rack 6 inches from the heating element and heat the broiler.

4. Mix the eggs and 1 cup evaporated milk in a small bowl; set aside.

5. Meanwhile, bring 3 quarts of water to a boil in a large pot. Add 2 teaspoons salt and the macaroni and cook until almost tender but still a little firm to the bite. Drain and return the pasta to the pot over low heat. Add the remaining 3 tablespoons butter and toss to melt.

6. Pour the egg mixture over the pasta along with the remaining cheddar cheese; stir until thoroughly combined and the cheese starts to melt. Gradually add the remaining milk and the Gorgonzola, stirring constantly, until the mixture is hot and creamy, about 5 minutes. Stir in the spinach. Season with salt and pepper to taste.

7. Pour the cooked macaroni and cheese into a 9-inch square baking dish. Spread the crumbs evenly over the top. Broil until the crumbs turn deep brown, 1 to 2 minutes. Let stand to set a bit, about 5 minutes, and serve.

◆

Macaroni and Cheese with Tomato and Bacon

THE TOMATO MUST BE SEEDED HERE, SO IT DOESN'T MAKE THE MACARONI AND CHEESE TOO WATERY. SERVES 4 AS A MAIN COURSE OR 6 TO 8 AS A SIDE DISH.

> 6 tablespoons unsalted butter
> 1 cup fresh bread crumbs
> Salt
> 12 ounces sharp Wisconsin cheddar, American, or Monterey Jack cheese, shredded (about 3 cups)
> 4 ounces sliced bacon, cut into ½-inch pieces
> 2 large eggs, lightly beaten
> 1 can (12 ounces) evaporated milk
> ¼ teaspoon hot red pepper sauce

> 1 teaspoon dry mustard, dissolved in 1 teaspoon water
> 12 ounces elbow macaroni
> 1 large tomato (about 8 ounces), cored, peeled, seeded, and cut into ¼-inch dice (see illustrations 1–4, page 111)
> Ground black pepper

1. Heat 2 tablespoons butter in a large skillet over medium heat until the foam subsides. Add the bread crumbs and cook, tossing to coat with the butter, until the crumbs just begin to color. Season to taste with salt. Cool completely, toss with ¼ cup cheese, and set aside.

2. Cook the bacon in a small skillet over medium-high heat until crisp. Drain bacon on paper towels.

3. Adjust the oven rack 6 inches from the heating element and heat the broiler.

4. Mix the eggs, 1 cup evaporated milk, hot pepper sauce, and mustard mixture in a small bowl; set aside.

5. Meanwhile, bring 3 quarts of water to a boil in a large pot. Add 2 teaspoons salt and the macaroni and cook until almost tender, but still a little firm to the bite. Drain and return the pasta to the pot over low heat. Add the remaining 4 tablespoons butter; toss to melt.

6. Pour the egg mixture over the pasta along with three-quarters of the remaining cheese; stir until thoroughly combined and the cheese starts to melt. Gradually add the remaining milk and cheese, stirring constantly, until the mixture is hot and creamy, about 5 minutes. Stir in the bacon and tomato. Season with salt and pepper to taste.

7. Pour the cooked macaroni and cheese into a 9-inch square baking dish. Spread the crumbs evenly over the top. Broil until the crumbs turn deep brown, 1 to 2 minutes. Let stand to set a bit, about 5 minutes, and serve.

Macaroni and Cheese with Peas and Ham

GRUYERE ALL BY ITSELF IS TOO STRONG FOR MACARONI AND CHEESE; MIXED WITH MILDER PARMESAN, HOWEVER, IT ADDS A PLEASANT BITE TO THIS DISH. SERVES 4 AS A MAIN COURSE OR 6 TO 8 AS A SIDE DISH.

6 tablespoons unsalted butter
1 cup fresh bread crumbs
Salt
8 ounces Gruyère cheese, shredded (about 2 cups)
1 cup grated Parmesan cheese
2 large eggs, lightly beaten
1 can (12 ounces) evaporated milk
¼ teaspoon hot red pepper sauce
1 teaspoon dry mustard, dissolved in 1 teaspoon water
12 ounces elbow macaroni
4 ounces sliced ham, finely chopped
1 cup frozen peas, thawed
Ground black pepper

1. Heat 2 tablespoons butter in a large skillet over medium heat until the foam subsides. Add the bread crumbs and cook, tossing to coat with the butter, until the crumbs just begin to color. Season to taste with salt. Cool completely, toss with 2 tablespoons Gruyère and 2 tablespoons Parmesan, and set aside.

2. Adjust the oven rack 6 inches from the heating element and heat the broiler.

3. Mix the eggs, 1 cup evaporated milk, hot pepper sauce, and mustard mixture in a small bowl; set aside.

4. Meanwhile, bring 3 quarts of water to a boil in a large pot. Add 2 teaspoons salt and the macaroni and cook until almost tender but still a little firm to the bite. Drain and return the pasta to the pot over low heat. Add the remaining 4 tablespoons butter and toss to melt.

5. Pour the egg mixture over the pasta along with three-quarters of the remaining cheese; stir until thoroughly combined and the cheese starts to melt. Grad-ually add the remaining milk and cheese, stirring constantly, until the mixture is hot and creamy, about 5 minutes. Stir in the ham and peas. Season with salt and pepper to taste.

6. Pour the cooked macaroni and cheese into a 9-inch square baking dish pan. Spread the crumbs evenly over the top. Broil until the crumbs turn deep brown, 1 to 2 minutes. Let stand to set a bit, about 5 minutes, and serve.

Baked Pasta Casseroles with Velouté Sauce

A GOOD NOODLE CASSEROLE, such as turkey tetrazzini, should be an interesting blend of spaghetti, toasted bread crumbs, and turkey meat, all bound together by a silky sauce. However, when you put these ingredients together, the result is often a culinary train wreck in which the whole is less than the sum of its parts.

Often, the individual tastes and textures are fused and thereby diminished. The problem is that the ingredients are double-cooked: you cook the ingredients, mix them together, and then bake them in a casserole. By using a very shallow baking dish (rather than a deep casserole) and a very hot oven, we reduced the baking time to a mere fifteen minutes, a fraction of that suggested by most cookbooks. Tasted against longer baking times and slower ovens, this quick method won hands down; with its fresher-tasting vegetables, it easily avoided the wretched, overcooked dullness of cafeteria cuisine.

Next we adjusted the sauce. The traditional choice is béchamel, a sauce in which milk is added to a roux of butter and flour. We decided to use a sauce based on chicken stock (a velouté) instead. This brightened up both the texture and the flavor, since dairy tends to dampen other flavors. We also played around a bit with the amount of sauce, trying larger and smaller quantities, and found that more sauce overran the taste of the other ingredients. In this case, less was more. It still needed a burst of flavor, however, so we spruced it up with a shot of sherry and a little lemon juice and nutmeg; a bit of Parmesan cheese provided tang and bite; and a full 2 teaspoons of fresh thyme also helped freshen the overall impression.

Most recipes do not toast the bread crumbs before baking. This step does complicate the dish by adding an extra step (in a pinch, you can skip the toasting), but it is well worth it. Tossing the toasted bread crumbs with a bit of grated Parmesan also helps to boost the flavor.

With our turkey tetrazzini recipe in hand, we found that the same sauce could be used to re-create another all-American classic, the tuna noodle casserole. The vegetables are a bit different and tuna stands in for turkey, but otherwise the dishes are remarkably similar. Finally, we decided to apply the same formula to an orzo and cheese casserole. The results were delicious, with the cheese taking center stage as the only dairy component in this dish. While béchamel made this dish creamier, all that milk dulled the flavor of the cheese. We found that velouté let the strong, delicious flavor of the cheese shine through.

MASTER RECIPE

Turkey Tetrazzini

SERVES 6

TETRAZZINI IS GREAT with leftover chicken, as well. Using a shallow baking dish, no cover, and a very hot oven benefit both texture and flavor. This dish needs aggressive seasoning so don't be stingy with the salt and pepper. The recipe contains more onion and mushrooms than most similar casseroles for a stronger vegetable flavor.

TOPPING
1 cup fresh bread crumbs
Pinch salt
1 1/2 tablespoons unsalted butter, melted
1/4 cup grated Parmesan cheese

FILLING
Salt
3/4 pound spaghetti or other long, thin
    pasta
6 tablespoons unsalted butter
10 ounces white button mushrooms,
    wiped clean, stems trimmed, and sliced
    thin
2 medium onions, minced
Ground black pepper
1/4 cup all-purpose flour
2 cups chicken stock or canned low-
    sodium chicken broth
3 tablespoons dry sherry
1/2 cup grated Parmesan cheese
1/4 teaspoon grated nutmeg
2 teaspoons fresh lemon juice
2 teaspoons minced fresh thyme leaves
4 cups leftover turkey or chicken, cut into
    1/4-inch dice
2 cups frozen peas, thawed

1. For the topping: Set oven rack to middle position and heat oven to 350 degrees. Mix the bread crumbs, salt, and butter in a small baking dish; bake until golden brown and crisp, 15 to 20 minutes. Cool to room temperature, transfer to a bowl, and mix with 1/4 cup grated Parmesan.

2. For the filling: Increase oven temperature to 450 degrees. Butter a shallow casserole or baking dish that measures about 13 inches by 9 inches. Bring 4 quarts of water to a boil in a large pot. Add 1 tablespoon salt,

(continued on next page)

snap spaghetti in half and add; cook until almost al dente. Reserve ¼ cup of cooking water, drain spaghetti, and return to the pot with the reserved liquid. Set aside off heat.

3. Meanwhile, heat 2 tablespoons butter in a large skillet over medium heat until foaming subsides; add the mushrooms and onions and sauté, stirring frequently, until the onions soften and mushroom liquid evaporates, 7 to 10 minutes. Season to taste with salt and pepper; transfer to the pot with the spaghetti.

4. Melt the remaining 4 tablespoons butter in the now-cleaned skillet over medium heat. When foam subsides, whisk in the flour and cook, whisking constantly, until flour turns golden, 1 to 2 minutes. Whisking constantly, gradually add the chicken stock. Adjust heat to medium-high and simmer until the mixture thickens, 3 to 4 minutes. Off heat, whisk in the sherry, Parmesan, nutmeg, ½ teaspoon salt, the lemon juice, and thyme. Add sauce, turkey, and peas to the spaghetti and mix well, adjusting seasonings to taste.

5. Turn the mixture into a buttered baking dish, sprinkle evenly with the toasted bread crumbs, and bake until the mixture is bubbly, 13 to 15 minutes. Serve immediately.

◆

Tuna Noodle Casserole

WHEN WE SET OUT TO DEVELOP OUR VERSION OF THIS CLASSIC AMERICAN DISH, WE KNEW WHAT WE DIDN'T LIKE—AN OVERLY SOUPY, HEAVY MISHMASH CONTAINING EVERYTHING BUT THE KITCHEN SINK. AS WITH OUR STREAMLINED TURKEY TETRAZZINI, WE DECIDED TO FORGO THE CREAM AND CANNED SOUP IN FAVOR OF A SAUCE OF CHICKEN STOCK THICKENED WITH FLOUR. WE ALSO LIMITED OURSELVES TO MUSHROOMS AND PEPPERS AND ADDED A SQUIRT OF LEMON JUICE TO LIGHTEN THE TUNA FLAVOR. THE FINISHED DISH IS A COMFORTING, STRAIGHTFORWARD SUPPER SURE TO PLEASE THE WHOLE FAMILY. **SERVES 6.**

TOPPING
1 cup fresh bread crumbs
Pinch salt
1 ½ tablespoons unsalted butter, melted

FILLING
Salt
¾ pound dried fettuccine or egg noodles
6 tablespoons unsalted butter
10 ounces white button mushrooms, wiped clean, stems trimmed, sliced thin
2 medium onions, minced
1 medium red bell pepper, stemmed, seeded, and cut into ¼-inch dice
Ground black pepper
¼ cup all-purpose flour
2 cups chicken stock or canned low-sodium chicken broth
1 tablespoon lemon juice
¼ cup minced fresh flat-leaf parsley leaves
2 6-ounce cans oil-packed white tuna, drained and flaked with a fork
2 cups frozen peas, thawed

1. For the topping: Set oven rack to middle position and heat oven to 350 degrees. Mix the bread crumbs, salt, and butter in a small baking dish; bake until golden brown and crisp, 15 to 20 minutes. Cool to room temperature and transfer to a bowl.

2. For the filling: Increase oven temperature to 450 degrees. Butter a shallow casserole or baking dish that measures about 13 inches by 9 inches. Bring 4 quarts of water to a boil in a large pot. Add 1 tablespoon salt and the pasta and cook until almost al dente. Reserve ¼ cup of cooking water, drain the pasta, and return to the pot with the reserved liquid. Set aside off heat.

3. Meanwhile, heat 2 tablespoons butter in a large skillet over medium heat until foaming subsides; add the mushrooms, onions, and red pepper and sauté, stirring frequently, until the onions and pepper soften and the mushroom liquid evaporates, 7 to 10 minutes. Season to taste with salt and pepper; transfer to the pot with the spaghetti.

4. Melt the remaining 4 tablespoons butter in the now-cleaned skillet over medium heat. When foam subsides, whisk in the flour and cook, whisking constantly, until flour turns golden, 1 to 2 minutes. Whisking constantly, gradually add the chicken stock. Adjust heat to medium-high and simmer until the mixture thickens, 3 to 4 minutes. Off heat, whisk in ½ teaspoon salt, the lemon juice, and the parsley. Add the sauce, tuna, and peas to the pasta and mix well, adjusting seasonings to taste.

5. Turn the mixture into the buttered baking dish, sprinkle evenly with the toasted bread crumbs, and bake until the mixture is bubbly, 13 to 15 minutes. Serve immediately.

◆

Baked Orzo with Gruyère

ALTHOUGH THIS DISH IS MADE WITHOUT MEAT, IT IS AKIN TO TURKEY TETRAZZINI AND TUNA NOODLE CASSEROLE BECAUSE IT IS BOUND TOGETHER WITH VELOUTE. BAKED ORZO MAKES A WONDERFUL SIDE DISH TO ROAST TURKEY BREAST OR CHICKEN AS WELL AS LAMB. SERVES 6 TO 8 AS A SIDE DISH.

TOPPING
½ cup fresh bread crumbs
Pinch salt
1½ tablespoons unsalted butter, melted
¼ cup shredded Gruyère cheese

FILLING
Salt
1 pound orzo or other tiny pasta shape
6 tablespoons butter
2 medium shallots, minced
2 medium celery stalks, minced
Ground black pepper
¼ cup all-purpose flour
2 cups chicken stock or canned low-
    sodium chicken broth
2 teaspoons grated lemon zest (see
    illustration, page 42)
1 tablespoon minced fresh thyme leaves
5 ounces Gruyère cheese, shredded
    (about 1¼ cups)

1. For the topping: Set oven rack to middle position and heat oven to 350 degrees. Mix the bread crumbs, salt, and butter in a small baking dish; bake until golden brown and crisp, 15 to 20 minutes. Cool to room temperature, transfer to a bowl, and mix with ¼ cup Gruyère.

2. For the filling: Increase oven temperature to 450 degrees. Butter a shallow casserole or baking dish that measures about 13 inches by 9 inches. Bring 4 quarts of water to a boil in a large pot. Add 1 tablespoon salt and the pasta and cook until almost al dente. Reserve ¼ cup of cooking water, drain the pasta, and return it to the pot with the reserved liquid. Set aside off heat.

3. Meanwhile, heat 2 tablespoons butter in a large skillet over medium heat until foaming subsides; add the shallots and celery and sauté, stirring frequently, until softened, 5 to 7 minutes. Season to taste with salt and pepper; transfer to the pot with the pasta.

4. Melt the remaining 4 tablespoons butter in the now-cleaned skillet over medium heat. When foam subsides, whisk in the flour and cook, whisking constantly, until flour turns golden, 1 to 2 minutes. Whisking constantly, gradually add the chicken stock. Adjust heat to medium-high and simmer until the mixture thickens, 3 to 4 minutes. Off heat, whisk in ½ teaspoon salt, the zest, and thyme. Add the sauce and Gruyère to the pasta, adjusting seasonings to taste.

5. Turn the mixture into the buttered baking dish, sprinkle evenly with the toasted bread crumbs, and bake until the mixture is bubbly, 13 to 15 minutes. Serve immediately.

Baked Pasta Casseroles with Béchamel Sauce

ITALIAN BAKED PASTA DISHES are bound with either béchamel (a white sauce made with butter, flour, and milk) or cheese, usually mozzarella. Béchamel gives baked rigatoni and ziti a creamy but firm texture. The thick white sauce keeps the noodles moist and binds them together quite firmly. (For information on this sauce, see page 304.)

We experimented with various amounts of béchamel and found that 1½ cups of sauce was enough to bind a pound of pasta. More béchamel makes the pasta gluey when baked; less béchamel and the noodles do not stick together properly.

Although cheese is not the binder here, we find that these kinds of baked pasta casseroles are bland without some Parmesan. A flavorful "sauce," such as tomatoes and mushrooms or butter, leeks, and squash, is also essential for giving these dishes their individual character.

Since the pasta will be baked, it should be drained a minute or so before it is al dente. The pasta should be tender but still a little firm to the bite. The pasta will continue to soften as it is tossed with the other ingredients and baked. To help the sauce coat the drained pasta, we found it necessary to reserve a little of the cooking water and toss it with the drained pasta. As for pasta shapes, something that can hold bits of vegetables and sauce is best, such as rigatoni, ziti, penne, or shells.

Baked Rigatoni with Mushrooms

SERVES 4 TO 6

PASTA DISHES BOUND with béchamel sauce have a similar consistency to those bound with velouté, but are creamier since the sauce is made with milk, not stock. Béchamel sauce is especially good with tomato sauce. This dish tastes like lasagne but requires far less work.

- 2 tablespoons unsalted butter
- 2 tablespoons extra-virgin olive oil
- 1 medium onion, minced
- 10 ounces white button mushrooms, stemmed and thinly sliced
- 2 ounces dried porcini mushrooms, rehydrated in 2 cups hot water, strained, and chopped coarse; soaking liquid reserved (see illustrations 1–2, page 169)
- 1 14.5-ounce can whole tomatoes, drained, seeded, and chopped (see illustration, page 136)
- ¼ cup minced fresh flat-leaf parsley leaves
- Salt and ground black pepper
- 1½ cups Béchamel Sauce (page 306)
- 1 pound rigatoni or other short, tubular pasta
- ½ cup grated Parmesan cheese

1. Preheat the oven to 400 degrees. Butter a shallow casserole or baking dish that measures 13 by 9 inches.

2. Heat the butter and oil in a large skillet over medium heat. Add the onion and cook until softened, 5 to 7 minutes. Add the button mushrooms and sauté over medium-high heat until golden brown, about 8 minutes. Add the porcini, strained soaking liquid, and tomatoes, and cook, stirring occasionally, until almost all of the liquid has evaporated, 10 to 12 minutes. Stir in the parsley and season with salt and pepper to taste. Add the béchamel sauce and stir to combine.

3. While preparing the sauce, bring 4 quarts of water to a boil in a large pot. Add 1 tablespoon salt and the pasta. Cook until almost al dente, but still a little firm to the bite. Reserve ¼ cup of cooking water, drain the pasta, and return it to the pot with the reserved liquid.

4. Add the sauce and ¼ cup cheese to the pasta and stir to combine. Turn mixture into the buttered dish and sprinkle evenly with the remaining ¼ cup cheese.

5. Bake until the cheese is golden and the mixture is bubbly, 15 to 20 minutes. Remove the dish from the oven and let rest for 5 minutes before serving.

◆

Baked Shells with Butternut Squash

BAKED BUTTERNUT SQUASH, SMOOTH AND SLIGHTLY SWEET, CONTRIBUTES TO THE CREAMY CONSISTENCY OF THIS SATISFYING SIDE DISH. THIS PASTA CASSEROLE IS ESPECIALLY GOOD WITH ROAST PORK. **SERVES 8 AS A SIDE DISH.**

> 1 medium butternut squash (about 1½ pounds), halved lengthwise, strings and seeds discarded
> Pinch nutmeg
> Salt and ground black pepper
> 2 tablespoons unsalted butter
> 2 large leeks, white and light green parts, sliced thin (see illustrations 1–6, page 165)
> 1½ cups Béchamel Sauce (page 306)
> 1 pound small shells or penne
> ½ cup grated Parmesan cheese

1. Preheat the oven to 400 degrees. Butter a shallow casserole or baking dish that measures about 13 inches by 9 inches. Place the squash, cut side down, on an oiled baking sheet. Bake until soft, about 40 minutes. (Do not turn off the oven.) Cool, scrape the flesh into a medium bowl, and mash with a fork. Stir in the nutmeg. Season with salt and pepper to taste.

2. Meanwhile, heat the butter in a large skillet over medium heat. Add the leeks and cook until softened, 5 to 7 minutes. Transfer to the bowl with the squash. Add the béchamel sauce and stir to combine.

3. Bring 4 quarts of water to a boil in a large pot. Add 1 tablespoon salt and the pasta. Cook until almost al dente but still a little firm to the bite. Reserve ¼ cup of cooking water, drain the pasta, and return it to the pot with the reserved liquid.

4. Add the sauce and ¼ cup cheese to the pasta and stir to combine. Turn mixture into the buttered baking dish and sprinkle evenly with the remaining ¼ cup cheese.

5. Bake until the cheese is golden and the mixture is bubbly, 15 to 20 minutes. Remove the dish from the oven and let rest for 5 minutes before serving.

Baked Pasta Casseroles with Mozzarella

MOZZARELLA BINDS NOODLES together and makes these baked casseroles especially rich and gooey. Fresh mozzarella packed in water makes the texture of the finished dish especially moist and creamy and is recommended. While béchamel alone has enough moisture to keep the pasta from drying out as it bakes, mozzarella must be teamed with a tomato sauce. The mozzarella is really the binder; the tomatoes keep everything moist.

Mozzarella is a bit bland. We found that adding ¼ cup of Parmesan perks up the flavor. To ensure that the cheese is evenly distributed throughout the casserole, layer half the pasta into the baking dish, sprinkle with half the cheeses, then add the remaining pasta and cheeses.

As with casseroles bound with béchamel, the pasta for these dishes should be slightly undercooked (since it's going to soften further in the oven) and tossed with a little reserved cooking water to help spread the sauce.

Baked Ziti with Tomatoes and Mozzarella

SERVES 4 TO 6

IN THIS BAKED PASTA dish, melted mozzarella cheese provides the binding for the pasta and other ingredients. Use fresh mozzarella if possible—it will provide extra creaminess and moisture, which are important in this dish.

2 medium garlic cloves, peeled (see illustration, page 39)
3 tablespoons extra-virgin olive oil
1 28-ounce can crushed tomatoes
2 tablespoons coarsely chopped fresh basil leaves
Salt
1 pound ziti or other short, tubular pasta
8 ounces mozzarella cheese, shredded
¼ cup grated Parmesan cheese

1. Preheat the oven to 400 degrees. Process the garlic through a garlic press into a small bowl; stir in 1 teaspoon water (see illustrations 1–3, page 45). Heat 2 tablespoons oil and the garlic in a medium sauté pan over medium heat until fragrant but not brown, about 2 minutes. Stir in the tomatoes; simmer until thickened slightly, about 10 minutes. Stir in the basil and salt to taste.

2. Meanwhile, bring 4 quarts of water to a boil in a large pot. Add 1 tablespoon salt and the pasta. Cook until almost al dente but still a little firm to the bite. Reserve ¼ cup of cooking water, drain the pasta, and return it to the pot with the reserved liquid. Stir in the tomato sauce.

3. Brush a 13-by-9-inch baking dish with the remaining tablespoon oil. Pour half the pasta into the dish. Sprinkle with half the mozzarella and half the Parmesan. Pour the remaining pasta into the dish and sprinkle with the remaining mozzarella and Parmesan.

4. Bake until the cheeses turn golden brown, about 20 minutes. Remove the dish from the oven and let rest for 5 minutes before serving.

◆

Baked Ziti with Eggplant

EGGPLANT LENDS CLASSIC BAKED ZITI A SOUTHERN ITALIAN FLAVOR. SALTING THE EGGPLANT GIVES IT A CREAMY, MEATY TEXTURE AND PREVENTS IT FROM ABSORBING TOO MUCH OIL AS IT COOKS. SEE PAGE 148 FOR MORE INFORMATION. SERVES 6.

2 medium eggplants (about 2 pounds), ends trimmed and cut into ¾-inch cubes
Kosher salt
4 tablespoons extra-virgin olive oil
2 medium garlic cloves, minced
½ teaspoon hot red pepper flakes
1 28-ounce can crushed tomatoes
2 tablespoons coarsely chopped fresh basil leaves
1 pound ziti or other short, tubular pasta
8 ounces mozzarella cheese, shredded
¼ cup grated Parmesan cheese

1. Place the eggplant in a large colander and sprinkle with 1 tablespoon salt. Let stand 30 minutes. Using paper towels or a large kitchen towel, wipe the salt off and pat the excess moisture from the eggplant.

2. Heat 3 tablespoons oil in a large, heavy-bottomed skillet over medium-high heat until it shimmers and becomes fragrant. Add the eggplant; sauté until it begins to brown, about 4 minutes. Reduce the heat to medium-low and cook, stirring occasionally, until the eggplant is fully tender and lightly browned, 10 to 15 minutes. Stir in the garlic and red pepper flakes; cook to blend flavors, about 2 minutes. Stir in the tomatoes; simmer until thickened slightly, about 10 minutes. Stir in the basil and salt to taste.

3. Bring 4 quarts of water to a boil in a large pot. Add 1 tablespoon salt and the pasta. Cook until almost al dente but still a little firm to the bite. Reserve ¼ cup of cooking water, drain the pasta, and return it to the pot with the reserved liquid. Stir in the tomato sauce.

4. Brush a 13-by-9-inch baking dish with the remaining tablespoon of oil. Pour half the pasta into the dish. Sprinkle with half the mozzarella and half the Parmesan. Pour the remaining pasta into the dish and sprinkle with the remaining mozzarella and Parmesan.

5. Bake until the cheeses turn golden brown, about 20 minutes. Remove the dish from the oven and let rest for 5 minutes before serving.

◆

Baked Ziti with Meatballs

MEATBALLS MAKE A WONDERFUL ADDITION TO BAKED ZITI. FOR A QUICKER BUT STILL MEATY VERSION OF THIS DISH, SAUTE 1 POUND ITALIAN SAUSAGE REMOVED FROM ITS CASINGS, AND THEN PROCEED WITH THE RECIPE, ADDING THE GARLIC, AND THEN THE TOMATOES, TO THE SAUCEPAN WITH THE SAUSAGES. SERVES 6.

Vegetable oil for pan-frying (about
1¼ cups)
1 recipe Meatballs, prepared through step
2 (see page 210)
3 tablespoons extra-virgin olive oil

2 medium garlic cloves, minced
1 28-ounce can crushed tomatoes
2 tablespoons coarsely chopped fresh
basil leaves
Salt
1 pound ziti or other short, tubular pasta
8 ounces mozzarella cheese, shredded
¼ cup grated Parmesan cheese

1. Heat about ¼ inch of vegetable oil in a large skillet. Take a handful of the meat mixture, and working directly over the skillet, pinch off pieces no larger than a small grape and flatten them slightly (see illustration, page 313). Cooking in batches to avoid overcrowding, carefully drop them into the hot oil. Fry, turning once, until evenly browned, 3 to 4 minutes. Use a slotted spoon to transfer the meatballs to a paper towel on a platter.

2. Preheat the oven to 400 degrees. Heat 2 tablespoons olive oil and the garlic in a medium sauté pan over medium heat until fragrant but not brown, about 2 minutes. Stir in the tomatoes; simmer until thickened slightly, about 10 minutes. Stir in the basil and salt to taste.

3. Bring 4 quarts of water to a boil in a large pot. Add 1 tablespoon salt and the pasta. Cook until almost al dente but still a little firm to the bite. Reserve ¼ cup of cooking water, drain the pasta, and return it to the pot with the reserved liquid. Stir in the tomato sauce and meatballs.

4. Brush a 13-by-9-inch baking dish with the remaining tablespoon oil. Pour half the pasta into the dish. Sprinkle with half the mozzarella and half the Parmesan. Pour the remaining pasta into the dish and sprinkle with the remaining mozzarella and Parmesan.

5. Bake until the cheeses turn golden brown, about 20 minutes. Remove the dish from the oven and let rest for 5 minutes before serving.

Baked Shells and Manicotti

OVERSIZED PASTA SHAPES, such as jumbo shells and manicotti, can be stuffed, sauced, and baked. There are two challenges when making these dishes. First, the filling needs to remain thick when baked (in many recipes, the filling becomes watery and makes the pasta mushy). The second challenge is keeping the pasta from drying out in the oven. Since the filling is raw, these dishes require a fair lengthy baking time.

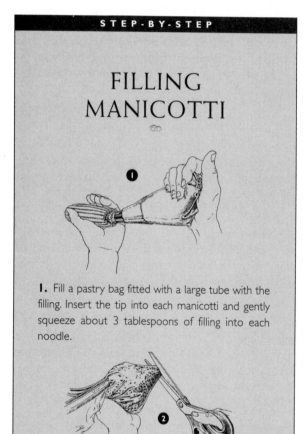

STEP-BY-STEP

FILLING MANICOTTI

1. Fill a pastry bag fitted with a large tube with the filling. Insert the tip into each manicotti and gently squeeze about 3 tablespoons of filling into each noodle.

2. If you don't own a pastry bag, you can use a large sealable plastic bag instead. Fill the bag with the filling, snip a hole in one corner with a pair of scissors, and press on the bag to fill the manicotti.

By the time the filling is hot and bubbling, the pasta can be crisp and browned.

We decided to tackle the filling first and then perfect the baking technique. Cheese is an essential filling ingredient—it adds flavor and keeps the filling moist. Ricotta cheese is the standard choice in baked shells and manicotti. Since ricotta is so bland, we found it essential to add some Parmesan as well. Although ricotta makes the filling creamy, it can be watery, especially the store-bought variety. We found that adding a whole egg to the filling helped to keep mass-market ricotta from shedding too much water and making the pasta soggy. It also gave the cheese filling a nice, firm texture.

If you can find creamy homestyle ricotta (the kind sold in real Italian delis and good cheese shops), buy it. Even though this firmer ricotta is less likely to make a watery filling, add the egg—it will make the filling taste richer.

Filling shells is easy. Simply spoon the filling in. Long tubular manicotti requires the use of a pastry bag or a makeshift pastry bag made from a large plastic bag. With either shape, it's important to use a light hand with the filling. Too much filling will simply ooze out and water down the tomato sauce.

With the filling issues settled, we turned to the problem of dried out or crisp pasta. The filling requires quite a while in the oven to heat through. Coating the filled shells or manicotti with tomato sauce helps keep them moist, but that is not enough. Covering the baking dish with foil is the key to keeping the pasta pliable and moist. The downside is no browning. However, browning is easily accomplished after the filling has been cooked by removing the foil and turning the broiler on for several minutes.

Baked Stuffed Shells with Spinach and Ricotta

BECAUSE THE FILLING CONTAINS UNCOOKED EGG, THESE STUFFED SHELLS ARE COOKED COVERED AT A LOWER TEMPERATURE FOR A LONGER TIME THAN BAKED ZITI OR LASAGNE. SERVES 6.

1 pound spinach, washed and stemmed
3 tablespoons unsalted butter
1 small onion, minced
Salt
1⅓ cups ricotta cheese (about 12 ounces)
1¼ cups grated Parmesan cheese
1 large egg, lightly beaten
2 medium garlic cloves, peeled (see illustration, page 39)
3 tablespoons extra-virgin olive oil
1 28-ounce can crushed tomatoes
2 tablespoons coarsely chopped fresh basil leaves
12 ounces jumbo pasta shells
8 ounces mozzarella cheese, shredded

1. Place the spinach leaves and any water that clings to them in a large soup kettle. Cover and cook over medium heat, stirring several times, until the spinach wilts, about 5 minutes. Cool the spinach slightly, squeeze out the excess liquid, and chop fine; set aside.

2. Heat the butter in a small skillet over medium heat. Add the onion and sauté until translucent, about 5 minutes. Stir in the chopped spinach and salt to taste; cook for 1 minute.

3. Transfer the spinach mixture to a medium bowl. Stir in the ricotta, 1 cup Parmesan, and the egg; adjust the seasonings and set aside. (Can be covered and refrigerated overnight.)

4. Process the garlic through a garlic press into a small bowl; stir in 1 teaspoon water (see illustrations 1–3, page 45). Heat 2 tablespoons oil and the garlic in a medium sauté pan over medium heat until fragrant but not brown, about 2 minutes. Stir in the tomatoes; simmer until thickened slightly, about 10 minutes. Stir in the basil and salt to taste.

5. Preheat the oven to 350 degrees. Bring 4 quarts of water to a boil in a large pot. Add 1 tablespoon salt and the pasta. Cook until almost al dente but still a little firm to the bite. Drain and set aside to cool slightly.

6. Brush a 13-by-9-inch baking dish with the remaining tablespoon of oil. Spoon about 1 tablespoon filling into each shell and place the filled shells in the dish open side up. Spoon the tomato sauce over the shells and sprinkle with mozzarella and the remaining ¼ cup Parmesan. Cover the dish with a piece of lightly oiled foil.

7. Bake until the filling is piping hot and bubbling, about 40 minutes. Uncover and broil until the cheese on top is golden brown, 2 to 3 minutes. Remove the dish from the oven and let rest for 5 minutes before serving.

◆

Baked Manicotti with Ground Pork Stuffing

THE SIMPLEST WAY TO FILL MANICOTTI IS WITH A PASTRY BAG (SEE ILLUSTRATION 1, PAGE 296) OR A LARGE SEALABLE PLASTIC BAG THAT HAS BEEN TURNED INTO A PASTRY BAG BY SNIPPING OFF A TINY BIT OF ONE CORNER (SEE ILLUSTRATION 2). DO NOT OVERFILL THE PASTA—ABOUT 3 TABLESPOONS SHOULD BE ENOUGH FOR EACH MANICOTTI. SERVES 6.

4½ tablespoons olive oil
4 medium garlic cloves, minced
12 ounces ground pork
1⅓ cups ricotta cheese (about 12 ounces)
⅔ cup grated Parmesan cheese
1 large egg, lightly beaten
½ cup minced fresh basil leaves
1 28-ounce can crushed tomatoes
Salt
½ pound manicotti (12 shells)

1. Heat 1½ tablespoons oil in a medium skillet. Add 2 minced garlic cloves and sauté until lightly colored, about 1 minute. Add the pork; cook over medium-high heat, stirring to break up the larger pieces, until

(continued on next page)

the liquid evaporates and the meat browns, 3 to 4 minutes. Drain off the fat; transfer the meat mixture to a medium bowl. Stir in the ricotta, ⅓ cup Parmesan, the egg, and 6 tablespoons basil and set the filling aside. (It can be covered and refrigerated overnight.)

2. Heat 2 tablespoons oil and the remaining garlic in a medium sauté pan over medium heat until fragrant but not brown, about 2 minutes. Stir in the tomatoes; simmer until thickened slightly, about 10 minutes. Stir in the remaining 2 tablespoons basil and salt to taste.

3. Preheat the oven to 350 degrees. Bring 4 quarts of water to a boil in a large pot. Add 1 tablespoon salt and the pasta. Cook until almost al dente, but still a little firm to the bite. Drain and set aside to cool slightly.

4. Brush a 13-by-9-inch baking dish with the remaining tablespoon of oil. Fill each manicotti with 3 tablespoons of cheese mixture using a pastry bag or sealable plastic bag, and place the filled manicotti in the dish. Spoon the tomato sauce over the manicotti and sprinkle with the remaining ⅓ cup Parmesan. Cover the dish with foil.

5. Bake until the filling is piping hot and bubbling, about 40 minutes. Uncover and broil until the cheese on top is golden brown, 1 to 2 minutes. Remove the dish from the oven and let rest for 5 minutes before serving.

Frittatas with Pasta

A FRITTATA IS AN ITALIAN open-faced omelet. Unlike omelets, which require complicated turning and flipping, frittatas are made by pouring the ingredients (eggs, cheese, and seasonings, plus vegetables, pastas, seafood, or meat) into a hot pan and cooking until the bottom is set. The pan is then slid under the broiler to firm up the top. The resulting dish is tender but firm, with the "filling" ingredients evenly incorporated throughout the eggs.

In Italy, pasta is often added to frittatas to make them especially hearty. We found that long strand pasta, such as spaghetti, works best in these dishes. Some sources suggest breaking the pasta in half but we found this step unnecessary. The long strands of pasta will be broken into smaller bits once the frittata is sliced into wedges. Some recipes dump hot pasta right into the egg mixture. However, this can cause the eggs to cook. We had better results adding room-temperature pasta to the eggs, cheese, and herbs. To keep the pasta from sticking together as it cools, toss the drained spaghetti with 2 tablespoons of oil.

As for making the frittata itself, a nonstick pan is essential. Conventional skillets require so much oil to prevent sticking that the eggs become greasy when cooked. Since the pan will go under the broiler, make sure the handle is ovenproof.

To ensure that the eggs will release from the pan, occasionally slide a spatula under the frittata to loosen it from the pan as it cooks on top of the stove. Also, we found it best to cook a frittata over medium-low heat. The eggs are less likely to overbrown on the bottom and will set nice and soft when cooked gently. At higher temperatures, the frittata became a bit tough.

MASTER RECIPE

Pasta Frittata

SERVES 4

SOME COOKS LIKE TO flip their frittatas over and brown both sides right in the pan, but after too many accidents, we settled on browning the top side under the broiler instead. Keep a careful watch over the frittata at this stage to make sure it doesn't burn. Vegetables, herbs, and cheeses can be added to create an infinite number of pasta frittatas.

Salt

8 ounces spaghetti or other long, thin pasta

3 tablespoons extra-virgin olive oil

7 large eggs

¼ cup grated Parmesan cheese

2 tablespoons minced fresh basil leaves

2 tablespoons minced fresh flat-leaf parsley leaves

Salt and ground black pepper

1. Bring 4 quarts of water to a boil in a large pot. Add 1 tablespoon salt and the pasta to the boiling water. Cook until just al dente. Drain the pasta, transfer it to a large bowl, and stir in 2 tablespoons oil. Set aside to cool.

2. Adjust the oven rack to the top position and preheat the broiler. Lightly beat together the eggs, cheese, basil, parsley, ¾ teaspoon salt, and pepper to taste in a medium bowl. Pour the egg mixture over the spaghetti and mix well.

3. Heat the remaining tablespoon oil in a 10-inch nonstick skillet with an ovenproof handle over medium-high heat until the oil is quite hot. Add the pasta mixture and distribute evenly across the bottom of the pan. Cook over medium-low heat, occasionally sliding a spatula around the edges of the pan to loosen the frittata as it sets. Cook until the bottom is golden brown, about 8 minutes.

4. Transfer the pan to a rack under the broiler and cook until the top of the frittata is golden brown, 1 to 2 minutes. Invert the frittata onto a large plate, cut it into wedges, and serve immediately. (Or, cool the frittata to room temperature and then cut it into wedges and serve.)

Pasta Frittata with Spicy Salami and Red Bell Pepper

WE DON'T RECOMMEND MOST COMMERCIAL PEPPERONI FOR THIS OR ANY OTHER RECIPE—THEY ARE TOO GREASY AND ARTIFICIAL-TASTING. INSTEAD, USE THINLY SLICED SOPPRESSATA FROM AN ITALIAN DELI OR A GOOD SUPERMARKET. SERVES 4.

Salt

8 ounces spaghetti or other long, thin pasta

3 tablespoons extra-virgin olive oil

7 large eggs

2 ounces thinly sliced spicy salami, finely chopped

1 small red bell pepper, stemmed, seeded, and cut into ¼-inch dice

2 tablespoons minced fresh flat-leaf parsley leaves

Ground black pepper

1. Bring 4 quarts of water to a boil in a large pot. Add 1 tablespoon salt and the pasta to the boiling water. Cook until just al dente. Drain the pasta, transfer it to a large bowl, and stir in 2 tablespoons oil. Set aside to cool.

2. Adjust the oven rack to the top position and preheat the broiler. Lightly beat together the eggs, salami, red pepper, parsley, ¾ teaspoon salt, and pepper to taste in a medium bowl. Pour the egg mixture over the spaghetti and mix well.

3. Heat the remaining tablespoon oil in a 10-inch nonstick skillet with an ovenproof handle over medium-high heat until the oil is quite hot. Add the pasta mixture and distribute evenly across the bottom of the pan. Cook over medium-low heat, occasionally sliding a spatula around the edges of the pan to loosen the frittata as it sets. Cook until the bottom is golden brown, about 8 minutes.

4. Transfer the pan to a rack under the broiler and cook until the top of the frittata is golden brown, 1 to 2 minutes. Invert the frittata onto a large plate, cut into wedges, and serve immediately. (Or, cool frittata to room temperature and then cut into wedges and serve.)

Pasta Frittata with Asparagus and Fontina

OTHER CHEESES (MOZZARELLA OR GRUYERE) AND OTHER VEGETABLES (BLANCHED ZUCCHINI, SPINACH) MAY BE ADDED TO PASTA FRITTATAS FOR VARIETY. SERVES 4.

Salt
1/2 pound asparagus, tough ends trimmed and cut into 1-inch pieces (see illustrations 1–3, page 138)
8 ounces spaghetti or other long, thin pasta
3 tablespoons extra-virgin olive oil
7 large eggs
1/2 cup shredded Fontina cheese
2 tablespoons minced fresh flat-leaf parsley leaves
Ground black pepper

1. Bring 4 quarts of water to a boil in a large pot. Add 1 tablespoon salt and the asparagus to the boiling water. Cook until tender, 1 to 2 minutes depending on thickness. Remove the asparagus with a slotted spoon and set aside in a large bowl.

2. Add 1 tablespoon salt and the pasta to the boiling water. Cook until just al dente. Drain the pasta, transfer it to the bowl with the asparagus, and stir in 2 tablespoons oil. Set aside to cool.

3. Adjust the oven rack to the top position and preheat the broiler. Lightly beat together the eggs, cheese, parsley, 3/4 teaspoon salt, and pepper to taste in a medium bowl. Pour the egg mixture over the spaghetti and mix well.

4. Heat the remaining tablespoon oil in a 10-inch nonstick skillet with an ovenproof handle over medium-high heat until the oil is quite hot. Add the pasta mixture and distribute evenly across the bottom of the pan. Cook over medium-low heat, occasionally sliding a spatula around the edges of the pan to loosen the frittata as it sets. Cook until the bottom is golden brown, about 8 minutes.

5. Transfer the pan to a rack under the broiler and cook until the top of the frittata is golden brown, 1 to 2 minutes. Invert the frittata onto a large plate, cut into wedges, and serve immediately. (Or, cool frittata to room temperature and then cut into wedges and serve.)

Noodle Kugel

EASTERN EUROPEAN JEWS combine eggs and pasta to make baked noodle puddings called kugels. (Kugels can also be made from eggs and potatoes.) Noodle kugels start with dried egg noodles, which are boiled, combined with eggs and seasonings, and then baked until crisp on the top and creamy on the inside.

There are two distinct styles of kugel popular in America. A savory noodle kugel rich with the flavor of onions is perfect as a side dish to meat. A second style of kugel is sweet and contains sugar, raisins, nuts, and cottage cheese. It is delicious hot or cold and can be eaten for dessert (our preference) or with a meal. Like rice pudding, it is creamy and sweet.

◆

Savory Noodle Kugel

WE TRIED MAKING SAVORY KUGELS WITH SOUR CREAM AND COTTAGE CHEESE, BUT THEY WERE TOO SWEET AND HEAVY. WE PREFER THIS CRISP, DAIRY-FREE KUGEL, WHICH HIGHLIGHTS ABUNDANT CARAMELIZED ONIONS. IF POSSIBLE, USE A GLASS BAKING DISH TO PROMOTE BROWNING ON THE UNDERSIDE OF THE KUGEL. THIS MAKES A GOOD SIDE DISH FOR POT ROAST OR BRISKET. SERVES 6 TO 8 AS A SIDE DISH.

Salt
1/2 pound dried egg noodles
6 tablespoons vegetable or canola oil
3 medium onions, minced
Ground black pepper
2 large eggs, lightly beaten

1. Preheat the oven to 350 degrees. Grease a 9-inch square baking dish. Bring 4 quarts of water to a boil in a large pot. Add 1 tablespoon salt and the noodles. Cook until almost tender but still a little firm to the bite. Drain the pasta, return it to the pot, and toss with 1 tablespoon oil. Cool the noodles to room temperature.

2. Heat the remaining 5 tablespoons oil in a large skillet. Add the onions and cook over medium-low heat until deep golden, 35 to 40 minutes. Stir in 1 teaspoon salt and pepper to taste.

3. Stir the onions and eggs into the noodles. Turn the mixture into the baking dish. Bake until the noodles on the surface are golden and crispy, about 35 minutes. Remove the dish from the oven and let rest for 5 minutes before serving.

Sweet Noodle Kugel

SOUR CREAM AND CREAM CHEESE GIVE SWEET KUGEL RICHNESS, BUT COTTAGE CHEESE IS ABSOLUTELY NECESSARY TO GIVE THE DISH ITS CHARACTERISTIC CURDY CONSISTENCY. OTHER CHOPPED DRIED FRUIT (APRICOTS, PRUNES, FIGS) MAY BE SUBSTITUTED FOR THE RAISINS HERE; OTHER NUTS (PECANS, SLICED ALMONDS) MAY BE USED IN PLACE OF WALNUTS. SERVE SWEET NOODLE KUGEL AS A SIDE DISH OR SAVE IT FOR DESSERT. IT IS GOOD HOT, WARM, OR CHILLED. **SERVES 6 TO 8 AS A DESSERT OR SIDE DISH.**

Salt
½ pound dried egg noodles
3 tablespoons unsalted butter
1 cup sour cream
1 cup cottage cheese
½ pound cream cheese
1 large egg plus 1 large yolk
¼ cup sugar
1 teaspoon vanilla extract
1 teaspoon grated lemon zest (see
   illustration, page 42)
½ cup golden raisins
¼ cup dark brown sugar
¼ cup chopped walnuts
½ teaspoon ground cinnamon

1. Preheat the oven to 350 degrees. Butter a 9-inch square baking dish. Bring 4 quarts of water to a boil in a large pot. Add 1 tablespoon salt and the noodles. Cook until almost tender but still a little firm to the bite. Drain the pasta, return it to the pot, and toss with 1 tablespoon butter. Cool the noodles to room temperature.

2. Combine the sour cream, cottage cheese, and cream cheese in the bowl of an electric mixer. Beat until smooth, about 1 minute. Add the egg and yolk, sugar, vanilla, and zest and mix until just combined, scraping down the sides of the bowl once or twice as necessary. Stir in the raisins.

3. Stir the mixture into the noodles. Turn the mixture into the buttered baking dish.

4. Combine the remaining 2 tablespoons butter, brown sugar, nuts, and cinnamon in a small bowl and mash together with a fork to distribute the butter. Sprinkle over the top of the noodles.

5. Bake until the noodles on the surface are golden and crispy, 40 to 45 minutes. Remove the dish from the oven and let rest for at least 5 minutes. Serve hot or warm; or refrigerate and serve cold.

CHAPTER 21

LASAGNE

/I\

THERE IS A SEEMINGLY ENDLESS NUMBER OF CHOICES

WHEN IT COMES TO LASAGNA NOODLES—DOMESTIC

AND IMPORTED DRIED NOODLES, DRIED NO-BOIL

NOODLES, FRESH NO-BOIL NOODLES, PURCHASED

FRESH PASTA SHEETS, AND HOMEMADE PASTA. AFTER

MAKING DOZENS OF LASAGNE RECIPES, WE HAVE

SOME CLEAR RECOMMENDATIONS. ◆ THERE IS NO

DOUBT THAT FRESH NOODLES (EITHER HOMEMADE OR

STORE-BOUGHT, WHICH WE FOUND TO BE EQUALLY

GOOD) MAKE THE BEST LASAGNE. SHEETS OF FRESH

pasta are now available in many Italian delicatessens, gourmet stores, and even some of the better supermarkets. (Check with the deli manager to see if fresh noodles must be ordered in advance.) While labels on some of these refrigerated noodles claim that cooking is not necessary, we found that uncooked noodles did not properly soften in the oven. We recommend that you treat them as you would homemade, and boil them first.

In our testing, we found that lasagne with béchamel sauce (a white sauce made with milk, butter, and flour) must be made with fresh pasta. Fresh noodles absorb the béchamel and produce a rich lasagne. Unfortunately, this sauce just sits on dried noodles and becomes gluey. We discovered that dried lasagna noodles are much starchier than fresh noodles, and when combined with the flour in béchamel the result is sticky and unpleasant. While we feel that fresh pasta is a must when using béchamel, it will improve any

lasagne, including those made with tomatoes and mozzarella.

Dried noodles work best with tomato-based lasagne. In these recipes, the layers of pasta are "glued" together by shredded cheese, usually mozzarella. Starting with dried noodles simplifies matters somewhat, but the process is still fairly time-consuming. If for reasons of convenience or availability you use dried noodles instead of fresh, be aware that their quality varies considerably. Some are quite good, others are wretched. The key is thinness. Every American brand we tested was too thick. Italian noodles are generally thinner and better approximate the delicate texture of fresh pasta. The best way to judge dried noodles is by counting the number of sheets per pound. Most domestic brands have eighteen or twenty noodles in a 1-pound box. In contrast, a box of DeCecco lasagna noodles has twenty-eight noodles in a pound. This brand, which is the most widely

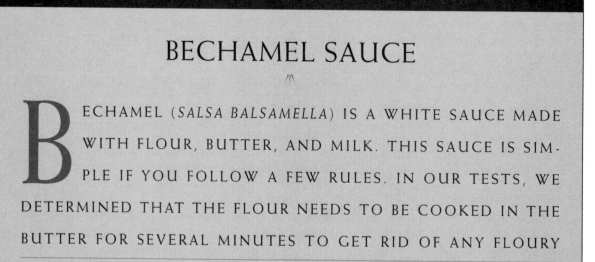

BECHAMEL SAUCE

/I\

B ECHAMEL (*SALSA BALSAMELLA*) IS A WHITE SAUCE MADE WITH FLOUR, BUTTER, AND MILK. THIS SAUCE IS SIMPLE IF YOU FOLLOW A FEW RULES. IN OUR TESTS, WE DETERMINED THAT THE FLOUR NEEDS TO BE COOKED IN THE BUTTER FOR SEVERAL MINUTES TO GET RID OF ANY FLOURY

flavor, but should never color or brown. Whisking the hot milk in gradually (rather than stirring it in with a wooden spoon as many sources suggest) prevents the formation of lumps. Add the first ½ cup or so of milk very slowly to the flour and butter and then add the remaining milk more

quickly once the mixture thins out. A whisk works better than a spoon in breaking up any lumps that do form. The finished sauce should be glossy and have the consistency of thick cream—too thin, and it will make your lasagne runny; too thick, and it will be hard to spread.

available imported Italian pasta, has shorter, wider noodles that fit just right when laid crosswise in a standard lasagne pan (see illustration on page 316). This makes for a much neater lasagne than longer noodles, which never seem quite long enough to fit a 13-by-9-inch pan.

In addition to fresh and dried lasagne, there is a relatively new product on the market—dried no-boil lasagna noodles. If you really want to reduce the prep time when making lasagne, these are the noodles to use. Here's how they work: First, the noodles are thinner than conventional dried lasagna noodles. Second, they are rippled; the accordion-like pleats relax as the pasta rehydrates in the oven, allowing the noodles to elongate. Lastly, the noodles are precooked at the factory; the extruded noodles are run through a water bath and then dried. The moisture from the sauce (as long as enough is used) will soften the noodles, especially if steam is trapped by covering the pan as it bakes.

No matter what kind of noodle you use, the layering procedure is pretty much the same. Use a 13-by-9-inch metal, glass, or ceramic dish with square corners that the pasta can easily rest against. We find it helpful to grease the baking pan with cooking spray. Spread a small amount of sauce without large chunks of meat or vegetables over the pan to moisten the bottom layer of pasta. Then lay down the first layer of noodles (choose large, whole noodles for this layer). Spread sauce evenly over the noodles and then cover with cheese. Build as many layers as directed in individual recipes by this same process, using any broken noodles in the middle where they won't be seen. The top layer should be covered with plenty of béchamel and/or cheese to give the top an attractive crust. Don't put sauce with bits of meat or vegetables on the top layer—they only dry out in the oven and are not very appealing.

Lasagne should be baked just until the top turns golden brown in spots and the sauce is bubbling. If you have any doubts about it being done, stick a knife into the center of the pan and hold it there for two seconds. When you remove it, the tip of the blade should be quite hot.

When the lasagne is cooked, remove it from the oven and let it rest for five minutes before serving.

This gives everything a chance to cool slightly and solidify a little. (Cover the pan with foil if you need to hold the baked lasagne for more than five minutes. It will stay warm for a good half hour.) To serve, use a sharp knife to cut squares of no more than 3 inches; larger pieces are almost impossible to extract intact from the pan. A flexible plastic spatula is the best way to dig underneath the lasagne and lift the pieces out.

If you want to prepare lasagne in advance, complete the layering process and then wrap the pan tightly with plastic wrap and refrigerate it for up to one day. To cook a chilled lasagne, take the dish directly from the refrigerator, unwrap it, and place it in a preheated oven. Uncooked lasagne can also be wrapped in plastic and then covered with aluminum foil and frozen for up to a month. Move the lasagne to the refrigerator at least twelve hours before baking. Allow it to defrost slowly, and then transfer it directly to a preheated oven.

Given that the type of noodle used will determine which kinds of lasagne you can make, we have divided the recipes in this chapter into three groups. The first section includes recipes that must be made with fresh pasta—the sauces are too delicate for dried pasta. The second group of recipes can be made with fresh or conventional dried noodles. The third group of recipes has been developed specifically for no-boil noodles.

Lasagne with Fresh Pasta

AMERICANS GENERALLY THINK of lasagne as a cheesy affair with plenty of gooey mozzarella cheese. However, in many regions of Italy, lasagne is made without tomatoes or mozzarella. These recipes call for béchamel sauce instead of cheese as the binder that holds the layers of pasta together. The only cheese most of these recipes call for is grated Parmesan.

The recipes in this section are delicate and often rich, not only because of the fresh pasta but also because of the béchamel and the sauce (such as bolognese sauce or pesto). In our tests, we found that 1 pound of fresh noodles (either purchased or made with 2 cups of flour and three large eggs) is enough for a standard six-layer lasagne. It is best to cook long sheets of fresh noodles in batches of three or four. When the noodles are almost al dente (after one to two minutes), gently retrieve them with a large slotted spoon and transfer them to a bowl of ice-cold water for thirty seconds. Then drain the noodles and lay them out on kitchen towels for up to one hour. Repeat the process with three or four more noodles and a fresh bowl of ice-cold water.

Béchamel Sauce

MAKES ABOUT 2 CUPS

BÉCHAMEL SAUCE IS used primarily as a binder for baked pasta dishes in Italian cooking. This recipe (and the variation that follows) makes about 2 cups, a little bit more than the 1½ cups called for in the lasagne recipes. It is better to have a little extra béchamel than to run short and risk a dry lasagne. Leftover sauce can be drizzled in the corners and around the edges for extra moisture and richness, if you like.

> 2 cups whole milk
> 4 tablespoons unsalted butter
> 3½ tablespoons all-purpose flour
> ¼ teaspoon salt

1. Heat the milk in a small saucepan over low until hot but not scalded or boiling.

2. Meanwhile, melt the butter in a medium saucepan over medium heat. When it is foamy, whisk in the flour. Whisk constantly for 2 minutes. Do not let the flour brown.

3. Remove the saucepan from the heat. Add 2 table-spoons of the hot milk and whisk vigorously. When the mixture is smooth, whisk in another 2 table-spoons, and then another. Return the pan to very low heat and slowly whisk in the remaining milk, at first in ¼-cup increments and then in ½-cup increments until it is all incorporated.

4. Raise the heat to medium-low. Add the salt and cook, whisking often, until the sauce thickens to the consistency of thick heavy cream, 7 to 10 minutes.

5. Remove the pan from the heat. Use immediately or cool to room temperature and whisk until smooth before using. (The sauce can be covered and refrigerated for up to 2 days. Before using, bring to room temperature and whisk until smooth.)

◆

Lower-Fat Béchamel Sauce

THIS LOWER-FAT BÉCHAMEL SAUCE IS AN ACCEPTABLE SUBSTITUTE WHEN FAT AND CALORIES ARE OF CONCERN. IF YOU WANT TO CUT DOWN ON SATURATED FAT, USE OLIVE OIL INSTEAD OF BUTTER, BUT BE AWARE THAT THE OLIVE OIL FLAVOR COMES THROUGH LOUD AND CLEAR. BECAUSE THERE IS LESS FAT (AND THEREFORE LESS FLOUR) IN THIS SAUCE, YOU CAN ADD ALL THE MILK AT ONCE WITHOUT THE DANGER OF LUMPS FORMING. MAKES ABOUT 2 CUPS.

> 2¼ cups low-fat milk
> 2½ tablespoons butter or extra-virgin olive oil
> 2½ tablespoons unbleached all-purpose flour
> ¼ teaspoon salt

1. Heat the milk in a small saucepan over low until hot but not scalded or boiling.

2. Meanwhile, heat the butter in a medium nonstick saucepan over medium heat. When it is foamy, whisk in the flour. Whisk constantly for 2 minutes. Do not let the flour brown.

3. Whisk in the hot milk all at once and continue to whisk to break up any lumps. Bring to a boil over medium-high heat and reduce the heat to a simmer. Whisk often as the sauce thickens, making sure it is not sticking to the bottom of the pan. Cook until the sauce has the consistency of light cream, about 5 minutes. Remove the pan from the heat and stir in the salt. Use immediately or cool to room temperature and whisk until smooth before using. (The sauce can be covered and refrigerated for up to 2 days. Before using, bring to room temperature and whisk until smooth.)

Lasagne with Bolognese Sauce

SERVES 6 TO 8

THE CLASSIC LASAGNE made with béchamel sauce is Lasagne Bolognese, a rich amalgam of slow-cooked meat sauce, Parmesan cheese, and creamy béchamel. Fresh egg pasta and spinach pasta are both good choices here.

Salt
1 pound Fresh Egg Pasta (page 21) or Spinach Pasta (page 22)
1 recipe Béchamel Sauce (page 306), warmed
1 recipe Bolognese Sauce (page 200), warmed
1 cup grated Parmesan cheese

1. Bring 6 quarts of water to a boil in a large soup kettle. Add 1 tablespoon salt and 3 or 4 noodles. Cook until almost al dente, then gently retrieve the noodles with a large slotted spoon and transfer them to a bowl of ice-cold water for 30 seconds. Then drain the noodles and lay them out on kitchen towels for up to 1 hour. Repeat the process with 3 or 4 more noodles and a fresh bowl of ice-cold water.

2. Grease a 13-by-9-inch pan with cooking spray. Smear several tablespoons of béchamel sauce across the bottom of the pan. Line the pan with a layer of pasta, making sure that noodles touch but do not overlap (see illustration, page 308). Spread a scant ⅔ cup bolognese sauce evenly over the pasta. Drizzle with 3 tablespoons béchamel and sprinkle with 2½ tablespoons Parmesan. Repeat the layering of the pasta, Bolognese sauce, béchamel sauce, and cheese 4 more times. For the sixth and final layer, coat the noodles with 6 tablespoons béchamel and sprinkle with the remaining 3½ tablespoons cheese. (The assembled lasagne can now be wrapped with plastic and refrigerated overnight or wrapped in plastic and aluminum foil and frozen for up to 1 month.)

3. Adjust the oven rack to the center position and heat the oven to 400 degrees. Bake until the cheese on top turns golden brown in spots and the sauce is bubbling, about 20 minutes (25 to 30 minutes with chilled lasagne). Remove the pan from the oven and let the lasagne rest for 5 minutes. Cut and serve.

Pesto Lasagne

PESTO LAYERED WITH FRESH EGG NOODLES AND BECHAMEL SAUCE MAKES A SPARE BUT RICH-TASTING LASAGNE. THE BECHAMEL SMOOTHS OUT THE SHARP EDGES IN THE PESTO AND MAKES THE FILLING ESPECIALLY CREAMY. RICOTTA CHEESE IS ADDED DIRECTLY TO THE PESTO FOR THE SAME REASON. BECAUSE THE FILLING IS RATHER THIN, YOU WILL NEED 1½ RECIPES OF EGG PASTA TO MAKE A SUBSTANTIAL LASAGNE. DELICIOUS AS A MAIN COURSE, THIS DISH ALSO WORKS WELL AS AN APPETIZER FOR 8 TO 10, AS PART OF A MORE ELABORATE ITALIAN MEAL. SERVES 6 TO 8.

> 6 tablespoons pine nuts, walnuts, or almonds
> 4 medium garlic cloves, threaded on a skewer
> 3 cups packed fresh basil leaves
> 3 tablespoons fresh parsley leaves (optional)
> 11 tablespoons extra-virgin olive oil
> Salt
> 1 cup grated Parmesan cheese
> ¼ cup ricotta cheese
> 1½ pounds Fresh Egg Pasta (page 21)
> 1 recipe Béchamel Sauce (page 306), warmed

1. Toast the nuts in a small, heavy skillet over medium heat, stirring frequently, until just golden and fragrant, 4 to 5 minutes.

2. Meanwhile, bring 6 quarts of water to a boil in a large soup kettle. Lower the skewered garlic into the water (see illustration 1, page 56); boil for 45 seconds. Immediately run the garlic under cold water. Remove from the skewer; peel and mince. Don't drain the water.

3. Place the basil and parsley (if using) in a heavy-duty, quart-size, sealable plastic bag; pound with the flat side of a meat pounder until all the leaves are bruised (see illustration 2, page 56).

4. Place the nuts, garlic, basil, parsley, oil, and salt in the work bowl of a food processor; process until smooth, stopping as necessary to scrape down the sides of the bowl. Transfer the mixture to a small bowl, stir in ¾ cup Parmesan and the ricotta, and adjust the salt.

5. Return the water to a boil. Add 1 tablespoon salt and 3 or 4 noodles. Cook until almost al dente, then gently retrieve the noodles with a large slotted spoon and transfer them to a bowl of ice-cold water for 30 seconds. Then drain the noodles and lay them out on kitchen towels for up to 1 hour. Repeat the process with 3 or 4 more noodles and a fresh bowl of ice-cold water. Reserve ¼ cup pasta cooking water and stir it into the pesto.

6. Grease a 13-by-9-inch pan with cooking spray. Smear several tablespoons of béchamel sauce across

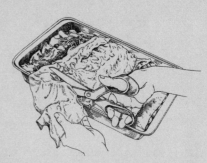

STEP-BY-STEP

CUTTING FRESH PASTA SHEETS FOR LASAGNE

We find it best to cook sheets of fresh pasta and then cut them to fit in the pan. (Pasta expands when boiled so you can't cut them before cooking.) Lay the cooked fresh noodle in the pan. Use sharp scissors to trim the edges to make it fit and make sure that pasta sheets touch but do not overlap. Save pasta scraps for patching or filling on subsequent layers.

the bottom of the pan. Line the pan with a layer of pasta, making sure that noodles touch but do not overlap (see illustration, page 308). Using a rubber spatula, spread ⅓ cup pesto evenly over the pasta. Cover with a second layer of noodles. Evenly spread ¼ cup béchamel sauce over this layer. Repeat the layering of pasta, pesto, pasta, béchamel 3 more times, using ⅓ cup béchamel sauce to coat the top. Sprinkle with the remaining ¼ cup Parmesan. (The assembled lasagne can now be wrapped with plastic and refrigerated overnight or wrapped in plastic and aluminum foil and frozen for up to 1 month.)

7. Adjust the oven rack to the center position and heat the oven to 400 degrees. Bake until the cheese on top turns golden brown in spots and the sauce is bubbling, about 15 minutes (20 to 25 minutes with chilled lasagne). Remove the pan from the oven and let the lasagne rest for 5 minutes. Cut and serve.

◆

Lasagne with Wild Mushrooms

A SMALL QUANTITY OF DRIED PORCINI ADDS DEPTH AND CHARACTER TO A SIMPLE MUSHROOM SAUCE. OTHER DRIED MUSHROOMS—TRY MORELS OR SHIITAKES—MAY BE SUBSTITUTED FOR THE PORCINI. **SERVES 6 TO 8.**

2 tablespoons extra-virgin olive oil
5 tablespoons unsalted butter
1 medium onion, minced
2½ pounds fresh button mushrooms, trimmed and sliced thin
¼ cup dry white wine
2 ounces dried porcini mushrooms, rehydrated in 2 cups hot water, strained, and chopped coarse; soaking liquid reserved (see illustrations 1–2, page 169)
1 tablespoon minced fresh oregano leaves
Salt and ground black pepper
1 pound Fresh Egg Pasta (page 21)
1 recipe Béchamel Sauce (page 306), warmed
1 cup grated Parmesan cheese

1. Heat the oil and 2 tablespoons butter in a Dutch oven. Add the onion and sauté over medium heat until softened, about 5 minutes. Add the fresh mushrooms and wine and stir. Cook until the mushrooms begin to give off their juices, about 5 minutes. Add the porcini, soaking liquid, and oregano; simmer briskly until the sauce thickens and most of the liquid has evaporated, 15 to 20 minutes. Swirl in the remaining 3 tablespoons butter and season with salt and pepper.

2. Bring 6 quarts of water to a boil in a large soup kettle. Add 1 tablespoon salt and 3 or 4 noodles. Cook until almost al dente, then gently retrieve the noodles with a large slotted spoon and transfer them to a bowl of ice-cold water for 30 seconds. Then drain the noodles and lay them out on kitchen towels for up to 1 hour. Repeat the process with 3 or 4 more noodles and a fresh bowl of ice-cold water.

3. Grease a 13-by-9-inch pan with cooking spray. Smear several tablespoons of béchamel sauce across the bottom of the pan. Line the pan with a layer of pasta, making sure that noodles touch but do not overlap (see illustration, page 308). Spread 1 cup of mushroom sauce evenly over the pasta. Drizzle with 3 tablespoons béchamel and sprinkle with 2½ tablespoons Parmesan. Repeat the layering of the pasta, mushroom sauce, béchamel sauce, and cheese 4 more times. For the sixth and final layer, coat the noodles with 6 tablespoons béchamel and sprinkle with the remaining 3½ tablespoons cheese. (The assembled lasagne can now be wrapped with plastic and refrigerated overnight or wrapped in plastic and aluminum foil and frozen for up to 1 month.)

4. Adjust the oven rack to the center position and heat the oven to 400 degrees. Bake until the cheese on top turns golden brown in spots and the sauce is bubbling, about 20 minutes (25 to 30 minutes with chilled lasagne). Remove the pan from the oven and let the lasagne rest for 5 minutes. Cut and serve.

Tricolor Vegetable Lasagne

THE VEGETABLES IN THIS PRETTY DISH MUST BE FINELY CHOPPED (NO LARGER THAN ¼-INCH CUBES) SO THAT THEY COOK QUICKLY AND ARE NOT TOO CHUNKY FOR THE DELICATE HOMEMADE NOODLES. THE CLARITY OF THE FLAVORS IS A RESULT OF COOKING EACH VEGETABLE SEPARATELY. EXTRA BÉCHAMEL SAUCE IS REQUIRED HERE TO KEEP THE VEGETABLES MOIST AND TENDER. SERVES 6 TO 8.

> 4 tablespoons unsalted butter
> 6 medium garlic cloves, peeled and crushed
> 1 pound carrots, finely chopped
> Salt
> 2 small red bell peppers (about ¾ pound), finely chopped
> 2 small heads broccoli (about 2½ pounds), stalks discarded; florets blanched for 2 minutes, drained, and finely chopped (see illustrations 1–2, page 140)
> 1 pound Fresh Egg Pasta (page 21)
> 1½ recipes Béchamel Sauce (page 306), warmed
> 1½ cups grated Parmesan cheese

1. Heat 1 tablespoon butter and 2 garlic cloves in a large skillet. Sauté over medium heat until golden, about 5 minutes. Remove and discard the garlic. Add the carrots and 2 tablespoons water and sauté, stirring occasionally, until softened, 10 to 12 minutes. Place the carrots in a medium bowl and season with salt to taste.

2. Add another tablespoon of butter and 2 more garlic cloves to the skillet. Sauté over medium heat until golden, about 5 minutes. Remove and discard the garlic. Add the peppers and sauté, stirring occasionally, until softened, about 4 minutes. Place the peppers in another medium bowl and season with salt to taste.

3. Add the remaining 2 tablespoons butter and the remaining 2 garlic cloves to the skillet. Sauté over medium heat until golden, about 5 minutes. Remove and discard the garlic. Add the broccoli and 2 table-spoons water and sauté, stirring occasionally, until softened, about 6 minutes. Place the broccoli in another medium bowl and season with salt to taste.

4. Bring 6 quarts of water to a boil in a large soup kettle. Add 1 tablespoon salt and 3 or 4 noodles. Cook until almost al dente, then gently retrieve the noodles with a large slotted spoon and transfer them to a bowl of ice-cold water for 30 seconds. Then drain the noodles and lay them out on kitchen towels for up to 1 hour. Repeat the process with 3 or 4 more noodles and a fresh bowl of ice-cold water.

5. Set ½ cup béchamel sauce aside. Add 1 cup béchamel sauce to the broccoli; stir to combine. Add 1 cup béchamel sauce to the carrots; stir to combine. Add ½ cup béchamel sauce to the peppers; stir to combine.

6. Grease a 13-by-9-inch pan with cooking spray. Smear 2 tablespoons of the reserved béchamel sauce across the bottom of the pan. Line the pan with a layer of pasta, making sure that noodles touch but do not overlap (see illustration, page 308). Spread half of the broccoli mixture over the noodles. Sprinkle with ¼ cup cheese and top with another layer of noodles. Spread half of the carrot mixture over the noodles. Sprinkle with ¼ cup cheese and another layer of noodles. Spread all of the pepper mixture over the noodles. Sprinkle with ¼ cup cheese and another layer of noodles. Use the remaining broccoli and carrot mixtures to form 2 more layers, sprinkling ¼ cup cheese over each layer. For the sixth and final layer, coat the noodles with the reserved 6 tablespoons béchamel and sprinkle with the remaining ¼ cup cheese. (The assembled lasagne can now be wrapped with plastic and refrigerated overnight or wrapped in plastic and aluminum foil and frozen for up to 1 month.)

7. Adjust the oven rack to the center position and heat the oven to 400 degrees. Bake until the cheese on top turns golden brown in spots and the sauce is bubbling, about 15 minutes (20 to 25 minutes with chilled lasagne). Remove the pan from the oven and let the lasagne rest for 5 minutes. Cut and serve.

Lasagne with
Shrimp and Scallops

CUT THE SEAFOOD INTO VERY SMALL PIECES SO THAT
IT CAN BE SPREAD EVENLY ACROSS THE HOMEMADE
NOODLES. TRANSFER THE SEAFOOD TO A BOWL AS
SOON AS IT IS FINISHED COOKING SO THAT IT REMAINS
TENDER. PARMESAN IS NOT USED HERE BECAUSE THE
STRONG FLAVOR OF CHEESE WOULD OVERWHELM THE
DELICATE SEAFOOD SAUCE. SERVES 6 TO 8.

> 3 tablespoons extra-virgin olive oil
> 1 small onion, minced
> 1 medium garlic clove, minced
> 2/3 pound sea scallops, muscles removed
>   (see illustration, page 250) and cut into
>   1/4-inch dice
> 2/3 pound medium shrimp, peeled,
>   deveined (if desired), and cut into
>   1/4-inch dice
> 2 tablespoons minced fresh flat-leaf
>   parsley leaves
> Salt and ground black pepper
> 1 pound Fresh Egg Pasta (page 21) or
>   Spinach Pasta (page 22)
> 1 recipe Béchamel Sauce (page 306),
>   warmed

1. Place the oil and onion in a large skillet and cook
over medium heat until softened, about 5 minutes.
Add the garlic and cook until fragrant, another minute
or so.

2. Turn the heat to medium-high and stir in the scallops and shrimp. Cook until just opaque, 1 to 2 minutes. Stir in the parsley and salt and pepper to taste.
Transfer the seafood to a bowl to stop the cooking.

3. Bring 6 quarts of water to a boil in a large soup kettle. Add 1 tablespoon salt and 3 or 4 noodles. Cook
until almost al dente, then gently retrieve the noodles
with a large slotted spoon and transfer them to a bowl
of ice-cold water for 30 seconds. Then drain the noodles and lay them out on kitchen towels for up to
1 hour. Repeat the process with 3 or 4 more noodles
and a fresh bowl of ice-cold water.

4. Grease a 13-by-9-inch pan with cooking spray.
Smear several tablespoons of béchamel sauce across
the bottom of the pan. Line the pan with a layer of
pasta, making sure that noodles touch but do not
overlap (see illustration, page 308). Spread about 1/2
cup of the seafood mixture evenly over the pasta.
Drizzle with 3 tablespoons béchamel. Repeat the layering of the pasta, seafood, and béchamel sauce 4
more times. For the sixth and final layer, coat the noodles with 6 tablespoons béchamel. (The assembled
lasagne can now be wrapped with plastic and refrigerated overnight or wrapped in plastic and aluminum
foil and frozen for up to 1 month.)

5. Adjust the oven rack to the center position and
heat the oven to 400 degrees. Bake until the béchamel
on top turns golden brown in spots and the sauce is
bubbling, about 15 minutes (20 to 25 minutes with
chilled lasagne). Remove the pan from the oven and
let the lasagne rest for 5 minutes. Cut and serve.

Lasagne with Conventional
Dried Noodles

THE RECIPES IN THIS section were designed to be
made with conventional dried noodles. They all can
be made with fresh pasta (they will taste even better),
but the sauces are sturdier than those in the preceding
pages and well suited to dried lasagna noodles. All the
recipes in this section contain tomatoes.

Most of these recipes are traditionally made with a
lot of cheese. Various recipes call for mozzarella,
ricotta (sometimes mixed with whole eggs or egg
yolks), and/or a hard grating cheese (usually Parmesan, but sometimes pecorino). After trying the various
combinations, we realized that ricotta was responsible
for what we call "lasagne meltdown"—the loss of
shape and distinct layering. Even with the addition of
whole eggs or yolks as a thickener, we found that
ricotta was too watery to use in lasagne and usually
leads to a sloppy mess.

Mozzarella provides more than enough creaminess, and its stringiness binds the layers to each other and helps keep them from slipping apart when served. After a few disastrous attempts with fresh mozzarella, we decided to stick with shrink-wrapped mozzarella in these recipes. Fresh mozzarella has too much moisture to be effective. When it melts, it releases so much liquid that the lasagne becomes mushy and watery. In addition, the delicate flavor of expensive fresh mozzarella is lost in the baking. We also found that a small amount of either Parmesan or pecorino provides a pleasantly sharp contrast to the somewhat bland mozzarella.

The cooking instructions for dried lasagna noodles are somewhat easier than fresh pasta. Eighteen sheets of dried Italian noodles (enough for a 6-layer lasagne) can be boiled at one time. Since it can be hard to taste whole lasagna sheets for doneness, throw in any scraps or broken pieces. You may also want to add a few extra noodles (remember, there are as many as 28 per package) in case some break as they cook. When the noodles are almost al dente, drain them, then soak them for 30 seconds in a bowl of ice-cold water, drain them again, and lay them out on kitchen towels for up to one hour.

Lasagne with Meatballs, Tomato Sauce, and Mozzarella

SERVES 6 TO 8

THIS IS OUR VERSION of the classic Italian-American lasagne with meatballs. Forming the meatballs into small, slightly flattened ovals as described below is quicker than rolling each meatball between the palms of your hands; less bulky meatballs are also a better shape for fitting between pasta layers.

Vegetable oil for pan-frying (about 1¼ cups)
1 recipe Meatballs, prepared through step 2 (page 210)

SIMPLE TOMATO SAUCE
3 tablespoons olive oil
2 medium garlic cloves, minced
1 28-ounce can crushed tomatoes

2 tablespoons minced fresh basil or flat-
leaf parsley leaves
Salt and ground black pepper

1 tablespoon salt
18 dried lasagna noodles *or* 1 pound
Fresh Egg Pasta (page 21)
4⅓ cups shredded mozzarella cheese
(about 1 pound)
1 cup grated Parmesan or pecorino cheese

1. Heat about ¼ inch of vegetable oil in a large skillet. Take a handful of the meat mixture, and working
directly over the skillet, pinch off pieces no larger
than a small grape and flatten them slightly. Cooking
in batches to avoid overcrowding, carefully drop them
into the hot oil (see illustration). Fry, turning once,
until evenly browned, 3 to 4 minutes. Use a slotted
spoon to transfer the meatballs to a paper towel on a
platter.

2. For the sauce: Heat the oil with the garlic in a
medium saucepan over medium heat. When the garlic
starts to sizzle, add the tomatoes, basil, and salt and
pepper to taste. Simmer until the sauce thickens
slightly, 15 to 20 minutes.

3. Add the meatballs to the tomato sauce and heat
through for several minutes; adjust the seasonings.
Keep the sauce warm while preparing the remaining
ingredients. (The sauce can be covered and refrigerated for 2 days; reheat before assembly.)

4. Meanwhile, bring 6 quarts of water to a boil in a
large soup kettle. Add the salt. If using dried pasta, add
all of the pasta. When the noodles are almost al dente,
drain them, then soak them for 30 seconds in a bowl
of ice-cold water, drain them again, and lay them out
on kitchen towels for up to 1 hour. If using fresh noodles, add in batches of 3 or 4, cook until almost al
dente, then gently retrieve them with a large slotted
spoon and transfer them to a bowl of ice-cold water
for 30 seconds. Drain the noodles and lay them out on
kitchen towels for up to 1 hour. Repeat the process
with 3 or 4 more noodles and a fresh bowl of ice-cold
water.

5. Grease a 13-by-9-inch pan with cooking spray.
Smear several tablespoons of tomato sauce (without

MAKING
FREE-FORM
MEATBALLS

Instead of large meatballs, this lasagne calls for free-
form mini-meatballs, which are easy to shape, cook
quickly, and fit well between pasta layers. Take a
handful of the meat mixture, and working directly
over the skillet, pinch off pieces no larger than a
small grape and flatten them slightly.

meatballs) across the pan bottom. Line the pan with a
layer of pasta, making sure that noodles touch but do
not overlap. Spread ¾ cup tomato sauce and meatballs evenly over the pasta. Sprinkle evenly with
⅔ cup mozzarella and 2½ tablespoons Parmesan.
Repeat the layering of the pasta, tomato sauce and
meatballs, and cheeses 4 more times. For the sixth and
final layer, cover the pasta with the remaining 1 cup
mozzarella and sprinkle with the remaining 3½ tablespoons Parmesan. (The assembled lasagne can now be
wrapped with plastic and refrigerated overnight or
wrapped in plastic and aluminum foil and frozen for
up to 1 month.)

6. Adjust the oven rack to the center position and
heat the oven to 400 degrees. Bake until the cheese on
top turns golden brown in spots and the sauce is bubbling, 20 to 25 minutes (25 to 35 minutes with chilled
lasagne). Remove the pan from the oven and let the
lasagne rest for 5 minutes. Cut and serve.

Lasagne with Chicken, Bell Peppers, and Tomato Sauce

THIS IS A LIGHTER MEAT LASAGNE. CHICKEN, UNLIKE MEATBALLS, TENDS TO BE BLAND, SO A HIGHLY SEASONED TOMATO SAUCE, ENLIVENED BY BELL PEPPERS AND MUSHROOMS, ADDS WELCOME FLAVOR. **SERVES 6 TO 8**.

4 tablespoons extra-virgin olive oil
¾ pound skinless, boneless chicken
  breasts, trimmed of fat
Salt and ground black pepper
2 medium onions, sliced thin
2 medium garlic cloves, minced
10 ounces button mushrooms, trimmed
  and sliced thin
1 large red bell pepper, stemmed, seeded,
  and cut into ½-inch dice
1 28-ounce can crushed tomatoes
2 tablespoons minced fresh flat-leaf
  parsley leaves
18 dried lasagna noodles *or* 1 pound
  Fresh Egg Pasta (page 21)
4⅓ cups shredded mozzarella cheese
  (about 1 pound)
1 cup grated Parmesan or pecorino cheese

1. Heat 2 tablespoons oil in a medium saucepan over medium-high heat. Sprinkle the chicken generously with salt and pepper to taste. Add the chicken to the pan and cook, turning once, until browned and cooked through, about 10 minutes. Remove the chicken from the pan, cool slightly, and shred into bite-size pieces.

2. Add the remaining 2 tablespoons oil and onions to the pan and cook the onions until softened, about 4 minutes. Add the garlic and mushrooms and cook until the mushrooms begin to give off their juices, about 5 minutes. Add the red pepper and cook for 2 minutes. Add the tomatoes, parsley, and salt and pepper to taste. Simmer over medium-low heat until the sauce thickens slightly, 15 to 20 minutes. Stir in the chicken pieces and keep the sauce warm while preparing the remaining ingredients. (The sauce can

be covered and refrigerated for 2 days; reheat before assembly.)

3. Meanwhile, bring 6 quarts of water to a boil in a large soup kettle. Add 1 tablespoon salt. If using dried pasta, add all of the pasta. When the noodles are almost al dente, drain them, then soak them for 30 seconds in a bowl of ice-cold water, drain them again, and lay them out on kitchen towels for up to 1 hour. If using fresh noodles, add in batches of 3 or 4, cook until almost al dente, then gently retrieve them with a large slotted spoon and transfer them to a bowl of ice-cold water for 30 seconds. Drain the noodles and lay them out on kitchen towels for up to 1 hour. Repeat the process with 3 or 4 more noodles and a fresh bowl of ice-cold water.

4. Grease a 13-by-9-inch pan with cooking spray. Smear several tablespoons of tomato sauce (without chicken pieces) across the pan bottom. Line the pan with a layer of pasta, making sure that noodles touch but do not overlap. Spread ¾ cup tomato sauce with chicken evenly over the pasta. Sprinkle evenly with ⅔ cup mozzarella and 2½ tablespoons Parmesan. Repeat the layering of the pasta, tomato sauce and chicken, and cheeses 4 more times. For the sixth and final layer, cover the pasta with the remaining 1 cup mozzarella and sprinkle with the remaining 3½ tablespoons Parmesan. (The assembled lasagne can now be wrapped with plastic and refrigerated overnight or wrapped in plastic and aluminum foil and frozen for up to 1 month.)

5. Adjust the oven rack to the center position and heat the oven to 400 degrees. Bake until the cheese on top turns golden brown in spots and the sauce is bubbling, 20 to 25 minutes (25 to 35 minutes with chilled lasagne). Remove the pan from the oven and let the lasagne rest for 5 minutes. Cut and serve.

Lasagne with Sausages, Broccoli Rabe, and Tomato Sauce

THIS HEARTY MEAT LASAGNE IS SIMPLER TO PREPARE THAN THE CLASSIC MEATBALL VERSION, BUT IT'S JUST AS SATISFYING. THE SLIGHTLY BITTER BROCCOLI RABE PROVIDES AN INTERESTING VEGETABLE CONTRAST TO THE SPICY SAUSAGE. CUT THE BROCCOLI RABE INTO SMALL PIECES BEFORE BLANCHING; LARGE PIECES SEEM STRINGY WHEN ENCOUNTERED IN THE FINISHED DISH, AND ARE MORE DIFFICULT TO EAT. SERVES 6 TO 8.

> Salt
> 1 pound broccoli rabe, washed, trimmed,
>   and cut into 1-inch pieces (see
>   illustrations 1–2, page 143)
> 2 tablespoons extra-virgin olive oil
> 1½ pounds hot Italian sausage, casing
>   removed
> 2 medium garlic cloves, minced
> 1 28-ounce can crushed tomatoes
> Ground black pepper
> 18 dried lasagna noodles *or* 1 pound
>   Fresh Egg Pasta (page 21)
> 4⅓ cups shredded mozzarella cheese
>   (about 1 pound)
> 1 cup grated Parmesan or pecorino cheese

1. Bring 1 quart of water to a boil in a large pot. Add salt to taste and the broccoli rabe. Return to a boil and cook until the broccoli rabe is bright green and almost tender, 2 to 3 minutes. Drain the broccoli rabe and plunge it into cold water to stop the cooking process. Drain well.

2. Heat the oil in a medium saucepan over medium-high heat. Crumble the sausage into the pan. Cook, breaking up the sausage meat with a wooden spoon, until the sausage has lost its pink color, about 5 minutes. Add the garlic and broccoli rabe and cook another 2 minutes.

3. Add the tomatoes and salt and pepper to taste. Simmer until the sauce thickens slightly, 15 to 20 minutes. Keep the sauce warm while preparing the remaining ingredients. (The sauce can be covered and refrigerated for 2 days; reheat before assembly.)

4. Meanwhile, bring 6 quarts of water to a boil in a large soup kettle. Add 1 tablespoon salt. If using dried pasta, add all of the pasta. When the noodles are almost al dente, drain them, then soak them for 30 seconds in a bowl of ice-cold water, drain them again, and lay them out on kitchen towels for up to 1 hour. If using fresh noodles, add in batches of 3 or 4, cook until almost al dente, then gently retrieve them with a large slotted spoon and transfer them to a bowl of ice-cold water for 30 seconds. Drain the noodles and lay them out on kitchen towels for up to 1 hour. Repeat the process with 3 or 4 more noodles and a fresh bowl of ice-cold water.

5. Grease a 13-by-9-inch pan with cooking spray. Smear several tablespoons of tomato sauce (without sausage) across the pan bottom. Line the pan with a layer of pasta, making sure that noodles touch but do not overlap. Spread ¾ cup tomato sauce with sausage evenly over the pasta. Sprinkle evenly with ⅔ cup mozzarella and 2½ tablespoons Parmesan. Repeat the layering of the pasta, tomato sauce and sausage, and cheeses 4 more times. For the sixth and final layer, cover the pasta with the remaining 1 cup mozzarella and sprinkle with the remaining 3½ tablespoons Parmesan. (The assembled lasagne can now be wrapped with plastic and refrigerated overnight or wrapped in plastic and aluminum foil and frozen for up to 1 month.)

6. Adjust the oven rack to the center position and heat the oven to 400 degrees. Bake until the cheese on top turns golden brown in spots and the sauce is bubbling, 20 to 25 minutes (25 to 35 minutes with chilled lasagne). Remove the pan from the oven and let the lasagne rest for 5 minutes. Cut and serve.

Lasagne with Cauliflower, Smoked Mozzarella, and Tomato Sauce

LARGE CHUNKS OF CAULIFLOWER ARE DIFFICULT TO WORK INTO A LASAGNE, BUT WHEN CHOPPED FINE MAKE A DELICIOUS AND UNUSUAL SAUCE. PLAIN MOZZARELLA MAY BE USED HERE, BUT WE LIKE THE WAY THAT SMOKED CHEESE PLAYS OFF OF THE SWEET FLAVOR OF THE SAUTEED CAULIFLOWER. SERVES 6 TO 8.

1 large head cauliflower (about
    2 pounds), cored and cut into florets
    (see illustrations 1–4, page 146)
4 tablespoons extra-virgin olive oil
2 tablespoons unsalted butter
2 medium onions, sliced thin
2 medium garlic cloves, minced
1 28-ounce can crushed tomatoes
½ teaspoon hot red pepper flakes, or to
    taste
2 tablespoons minced fresh flat-leaf
    parsley leaves
Salt and ground black pepper
18 dried lasagna noodles *or* 1 pound
    Fresh Egg Pasta (page 21)
4⅓ cups shredded smoked or plain
    mozzarella cheese (about 1 pound)
1 cup grated Parmesan or pecorino cheese

1. Finely chop the cauliflower florets. Heat 2 tablespoons oil and the butter in a medium saucepan over medium heat. Add the cauliflower and cook, stirring occasionally, until the cauliflower is tender and lightly browned, about 20 minutes. Remove the cauliflower from the pan with a slotted spoon and set aside.

2. Add the remaining 2 tablespoons oil to the pan and cook the onions until softened, 8 to 10 minutes. Add the garlic and cook until fragrant, about 1 minute. Add the tomatoes, red pepper flakes, parsley, and salt and pepper to taste. Simmer until the sauce thickens slightly, 15 to 20 minutes. Stir in the cauliflower and keep the sauce warm while preparing the remaining ingredients. (The sauce can be covered and refrigerated for 2 days; reheat before assembly.)

3. Meanwhile, bring 6 quarts of water to a boil in a large soup kettle. Add 1 tablespoon salt. If using dried pasta, add all of the pasta. When the noodles are almost al dente, drain them, then soak them for 30 seconds in a bowl of ice-cold water, drain them again, and lay them out on kitchen towels for up to 1 hour. If using fresh noodles, add in batches of 3 or 4, cook until almost al dente, then gently retrieve them with a large slotted spoon and transfer them to a bowl of ice-cold water for 30 seconds. Drain the noodles and lay them out on kitchen towels for up to 1 hour. Repeat the process with 3 or 4 more noodles and a fresh bowl of ice-cold water.

STEP-BY-STEP

FITTING DRIED LASAGNA NOODLES INTO A PAN

Italian dried lasagna noodles are generally thinner than American dried noodles and better approximate the delicate texture of fresh pasta. They are shorter and wider than American noodles and fit just right when laid crosswise in a 13-by-9-inch lasagne pan, 3 noodles per layer. The noodles can touch but they should not overlap.

4. Grease a 13-by-9-inch pan with cooking spray. Smear several tablespoons of tomato sauce across the pan bottom. Line the pan with a layer of pasta, making sure that noodles touch but do not overlap. Spread ¾ cup tomato sauce evenly over the pasta. Sprinkle evenly with ⅔ cup mozzarella and 2½ tablespoons Parmesan. Repeat the layering of the pasta, tomato sauce, and cheeses 4 more times. For the sixth and final layer, cover the pasta with the remaining 1 cup mozzarella and sprinkle with the remaining 3½ tablespoons Parmesan. (The assembled lasagne can now be wrapped with plastic and refrigerated overnight or wrapped in plastic and aluminum foil and frozen for up to 1 month.)

5. Adjust the oven rack to the center position and heat the oven to 400 degrees. Bake until the cheese on top turns golden brown in spots and the sauce is bubbling, 20 to 25 minutes (25 to 35 minutes with chilled lasagne). Remove the pan from the oven and let the lasagne rest for 5 minutes. Cut and serve.

◆

Lasagne with Mozzarella and Tomato-Cream Sauce

THIS SIMPLE BUT DECADENT DISH IS ESPECIALLY GOOD WITH FRESH PASTA. BECAUSE IT IS QUITE RICH, WE RECOMMEND THAT YOU SERVE SMALL PORTIONS AS AN APPETIZER RATHER THAN LARGE SQUARES AS A MAIN DISH. **SERVES 8 TO 10 AS A FIRST COURSE.**

2 tablespoons extra-virgin olive oil
2 medium garlic cloves, minced
1 28-ounce can crushed tomatoes
2 tablespoons minced fresh basil leaves
Salt and ground black pepper
2 cups heavy cream
18 dried lasagna noodles *or* 1 pound
    Fresh Egg Pasta (page 21)
4⅓ cups shredded mozzarella cheese
    (about 1 pound)
1 cup grated Parmesan or pecorino
    Romano cheese

1. Heat the oil with the garlic in a medium saucepan over medium heat. When the garlic starts to sizzle, add the tomatoes, basil, and salt and pepper to taste. Simmer until the sauce thickens slightly, 15 to 20 minutes. Stir in the cream and cook until slightly thickened, 3 to 4 minutes.

2. Meanwhile, bring 6 quarts of water to a boil in a large soup kettle. Add 1 tablespoon salt. If using dried pasta, add all of the pasta. When the noodles are almost al dente, drain them, then soak them for 30 seconds in a bowl of ice-cold water, drain them again, and lay them out on kitchen towels for up to 1 hour. If using fresh noodles, add in batches of 3 or 4, cook until almost al dente, then gently retrieve them with a large slotted spoon and transfer them to a bowl of ice-cold water for 30 seconds. Drain the noodles and lay them out on kitchen towels for up to 1 hour. Repeat the process with 3 or 4 more noodles and a fresh bowl of ice-cold water.

3. Grease a 13-by-9-inch pan with cooking spray. Smear several tablespoons of tomato sauce across the pan bottom. Line the pan with a layer of pasta, making sure that noodles touch but do not overlap. Spread ⅔ cup tomato sauce evenly over the pasta. Sprinkle evenly with ⅔ cup mozzarella and 2½ tablespoons Parmesan. Repeat the layering of the pasta, tomato sauce, and cheeses 4 more times. For the sixth and final layer, cover the pasta with the remaining 1 cup mozzarella and sprinkle with the remaining 3½ tablespoons Parmesan. (The assembled lasagne can now be wrapped with plastic and refrigerated overnight or wrapped in plastic and aluminum foil and frozen for up to 1 month.)

4. Adjust the oven rack to the center position and heat the oven to 400 degrees. Bake until the cheese on top turns golden brown in spots and the sauce is bubbling, 20 to 25 minutes (25 to 35 minutes with chilled lasagne). Remove the pan from the oven and let the lasagne rest for 5 minutes. Cut and serve.

Lasagne with No-Boil Noodles

THERE ARE TWO TYPES of no-boil lasagna noodles (see illustration, page 322). Most supermarkets stock American brands that are long and narrow. Three of these noodles, which measure 7 inches across and 3½ inches wide, will make a single layer in a conventional 13-by-9-inch lasagne pan when they swell in the oven.

We found two brands, Ronzoni and DeFino, in our local stores. They were equally thin (usually 14 noodles per pound, but inexplicably sometimes less) and both worked well. Ronzoni is made by Hershey Foods, which sells the same product under the American Beauty, Skinner, and San Giorgio labels in other parts of the country.

In terms of texture and flavor, our favorite brand was Delverde from Italy. However, these no-boil noodles have two serious drawbacks. First, they are hard to find. Italian specialty stores may stock them, but most supermarkets do not. Even more serious, these 7-inch square noodles are designed to fit into an 8-inch square pan. (The noodles are sold with two disposable pans.) Most Americans make lasagne for a crowd and will find this size inconvenient. To use these noodles in a 13-by-9-inch pan, they must be soaked in hot water until tender and then cut to fit with scissors. The slight advantage these noodles have in flavor and texture over domestic products is outweighed by their odd size. We recommend you stick with domestic brands.

So what's the best way to use no-boil noodles? Some recipes on boxes of no-boil noodles suggest soaking the noodles in either cold or hot tap water before layering them with the sauce and cheese. We found that this step made the pasta too soft after baking.

We then tried using no-boil noodles in a standard lasagne recipe and found that the noodles sucked all the moisture out of the sauce, leaving tiny bits of dried-out tomato pulp on them. As for the noodles, they were way too stiff, almost crunchy in places. The label on one brand suggested pouring stock over the lasagne just before it went into the oven. The result was a watery mess.

We found that it helped to use more sauce than we ordinarily use with boiled noodles. Also, leaving the tomato sauce fairly watery (we simmered it for just ten minutes and then added a little water) was a benefit. The no-boil noodles soaked up some of the excess liquid while baking, and the sauce reduced to the proper consistency.

In an attempt to keep the sauce from drying out, we wrapped the lasagne pan with foil and then baked it. This step was clearly an improvement. The noodles were tender, not crunchy, and the sauce was not overly reduced.

Covering the lasagne with foil as it bakes does present a couple of problems. First, the foil tends to stick to the top layer of cheese. Spraying the foil with cooking spray is an easy solution. The other issue was browning the top layer of cheese. When a conventional lasagne is baked uncovered in the oven, the top layer of cheese becomes golden and chewy in spots. We found that by removing the foil during the last fifteen minutes of baking we were able to achieve the color and texture we wanted.

Note that baking times for covered lasagne are longer than for uncovered conventional lasagne made with boiled noodles. A lasagne with no-boil noodles needs about forty minutes in the oven, as compared to twenty to twenty-five minutes for a conventional recipe.

In addition, we found that tomato sauce works much better than béchamel as a binder for no-boil noodles. The béchamel cooks down and becomes gluey. Even more important, béchamel, even when made with extra milk, has less available moisture (the starches in the flour hold on to any extra liquid) than tomato sauce and does not rehydrate no-boil noodles, especially those on the top layer, as well.

Quick Lasagne with Herbed Meatballs

SERVES 6 TO 8

O UR CLASSIC MEATBALL lasagne recipe (see page 312) can be adapted for use with no-boil noodles. Since more liquid is necessary to rehydrate the noodles, we have substituted a thinner tomato sauce. Because no-boil noodles come twelve to sixteen in a box, we suggest buying two boxes to ensure that you'll have the fifteen required for this lasagne, as well as those that follow.

Vegetable oil for pan-frying (about
  1 ¼ cups)
1 recipe Meatballs, prepared through step
  2 (see page 210)

THIN TOMATO SAUCE
2 tablespoons extra-virgin olive oil
2 medium garlic cloves, minced
1 28-ounce can crushed tomatoes
2 tablespoons chopped fresh basil or
  parsley leaves
Salt and ground black pepper

15 dried 7-by-3 ½-inch no-boil lasagna
  noodles
4 cups shredded mozzarella cheese
  (about 1 pound)
About 1 cup grated Parmesan or pecorino
  cheese

1. Heat about ¼ inch of vegetable oil in a large skillet. Take a handful of the meat mixture, and working directly over the skillet, pinch off pieces no larger than a small grape and flatten them slightly (see illustration, page 313). Cooking in batches to avoid overcrowding, carefully drop them into the hot oil. Fry, turning once, until evenly browned, 3 to 4 minutes. Use a slotted spoon to transfer the meatballs to a paper towel on a platter.

2. For the sauce: Heat the oil and garlic in a 10-inch skillet over medium heat until fragrant but not brown, about 2 minutes. Stir in the tomatoes; simmer until thickened slightly, about 10 minutes. Stir in the basil and salt and pepper to taste. Pour into a large measuring cup. Add enough water to make 3 ½ cups.

3. Spread ½ cup sauce evenly over the bottom of a greased 13-by-9-inch lasagne pan. Lay 3 noodles crosswise over the sauce, making sure they do not touch each other or the sides of the pan. Spread one-fourth of the meatballs evenly over the noodles, ½ cup sauce evenly over the meatballs, and ¾ cup mozzarella and 2 generous tablespoons of Parmesan evenly over the sauce. Repeat the layering of the noodles, meatballs, sauce, and cheese 3 more times. For the fifth and final layer, lay the final 3 noodles crosswise over the previous layer and top with the remaining 1 cup tomato sauce, 1 cup mozzarella, and 2 tablespoons Parmesan. (The lasagne can be wrapped with plastic and refrigerated overnight or wrapped in plastic and aluminum foil and frozen for up to 1 month. If frozen, defrost in the refrigerator.)

4. Adjust the oven rack to the middle position and heat the oven to 375 degrees. Cover the pan with a large sheet of foil greased with cooking spray. Bake for 25 minutes (30 minutes if chilled); remove foil and continue baking until the top turns golden brown in spots, about 15 minutes. Remove the pan from the oven and let the lasagne rest 5 minutes. Cut and serve.

PREPARING VEGETABLES FOR LASAGNE

THE MOISTURE CONTENT of the vegetable determines which cooking technique should be used when preparing it for the Master Recipe on page 321. For example, high-moisture mushrooms are best sautéed, but low-moisture broccoli must be blanched, chopped, and then sautéed.

While it is possible to combine two (or more) vegetables in one lasagne, choose vegetables that can be cooked in the same fashion to keep prep time to a minimum. For example, roasted zucchini and sautéed mushrooms are delicious together, but it would be easier to roast or sauté both the zucchini and mushrooms.

You need a total of 3 cups cooked and seasoned vegetables. Toss vegetables with olive oil before roasting or sauté them in olive oil. Season vegetables with salt and pepper as well as fresh herbs, garlic, or hot red pepper flakes, if desired.

VEGETABLE	PREPARATION AND COOKING METHOD
ASPARAGUS	Trim tough ends, slice in half lengthwise, and cut into ½-inch pieces; blanch until crisp tender, about 1 minute, drain well, and sauté until tender, about 3 minutes.
BROCCOLI/ CAULIFLOWER	Cut into florets; blanch until crisp-tender, about 2 minutes, drain well, chop into ¼-inch pieces, and sauté until tender, about 4 minutes.
EGGPLANT	Cut into ½-inch dice; roast until tender, about 35 minutes at 400 degrees.
FENNEL	Cut bulb into very thin strips; sauté or roast until tender, about 15 minutes for sautéing or 30 minutes at 400 degrees for roasting.
MUSHROOMS	Trim and slice or dice; sauté or roast until golden, 8 minutes for sautéing or 20 minutes at 400 degrees for roasting.
ONIONS	Peel and cut into thin slices; sauté or roast until soft and golden, 5 to 7 minutes for sautéing or 20 minutes at 400 degrees for roasting.
SPINACH/ SWISS CHARD	Wash, stem, and chop; sauté until wilted, about 5 minutes.
ZUCCHINI	Cut into ½-inch dice; sauté or roast until tender, about 7 minutes for sautéing or 35 minutes at 400 degrees for roasting.

Quick Vegetable Lasagne with Tomato Sauce

SERVES 6 TO 8

VEGETABLE LASAGNE SOUNDS wonderful but the reality is often quite disappointing. Too often, the dish is bland and watery, nothing like the rich, hearty version with meat. We found that precooking the vegetables was essential. (Lasagne made with raw vegetables is soggy.) Precooking the vegetables drives off excess liquid and gives the cook a chance to boost the flavor of the vegetables by caramelizing their natural sugars.

Smoked mozzarella, Gruyère, or Fontina can be substituted for the mozzarella and pecorino for the Parmesan. Also, 3½ cups of your favorite prepared tomato sauce can be substituted for the sauce in this recipe.

2 tablespoons extra-virgin olive oil
2 medium garlic cloves, minced
1 28-ounce can crushed tomatoes
2 tablespoons chopped fresh basil or parsley leaves
Salt and ground black pepper
15 dried 7-by-3½-inch no-boil lasagna noodles
3 cups cooked and seasoned vegetables (see "Preparing Vegetables for Lasagne," page 320, or the recipes that follow)
4 cups shredded mozzarella cheese (about 1 pound)
⅔ cup grated Parmesan cheese

1. Heat the oil and garlic in a 10-inch skillet over medium heat until fragrant but not brown, about 2 minutes. Stir in the tomatoes; simmer until thickened slightly, about 10 minutes. Stir in the basil and salt and pepper to taste. Pour into a large measuring cup. Add enough water to make 3½ cups.

2. Spread ½ cup sauce evenly over the bottom of a greased 13-by-9-inch lasagne pan. Lay 3 noodles crosswise over the sauce, making sure they do not touch each other or the sides of the pan. Spread ¾ cup prepared vegetables evenly over the noodles, ½ cup sauce evenly over the vegetables, and ¾ cup mozzarella and 2 generous tablespoons of Parmesan evenly over the sauce. Repeat the layering of the noodles, vegetables, sauce, and cheese 3 more times. For the fifth and final layer, lay the final 3 noodles crosswise over the previous layer and top with the remaining 1 cup tomato sauce, 1 cup mozzarella, and 2 tablespoons Parmesan. (The lasagne can be wrapped with plastic and refrigerated overnight or wrapped in plastic and aluminum foil and frozen for up to 1 month. If frozen, defrost in the refrigerator.)

3. Adjust the oven rack to the middle position and heat the oven to 375 degrees. Cover the pan with a large sheet of foil greased with cooking spray. Bake for 25 minutes (30 minutes if chilled); remove foil and continue baking until the top turns golden brown in spots, about 15 minutes. Remove the pan from the oven and let the lasagne rest 5 minutes. Cut and serve.

Roasted Zucchini and Eggplant Lasagne

CUBES OF ZUCCHINI AND EGGPLANT ARE ROASTED UNTIL GOLDEN BROWN, AND THEN INCORPORATED INTO A SIMPLE TOMATO SAUCE FOR THIS VERSION OF QUICK LASAGNE. SERVES 6 TO 8.

- 1 pound zucchini (about 3 medium), cut into 1/2-inch dice
- 1 pound eggplant (about 3 medium), cut into 1/2-inch dice
- 5 tablespoons extra-virgin olive oil
- 6 medium garlic cloves, minced
- Salt and ground black pepper
- 1 28-ounce can crushed tomatoes
- 2 tablespoons chopped fresh basil or flat-leaf parsley leaves
- 15 dried 7-by-3 1/2-inch no-boil lasagna noodles
- 4 cups shredded mozzarella cheese (about 1 pound)
- 2/3 cup grated Parmesan cheese

1. Adjust oven racks to upper- and lower-middle positions and heat the oven to 400 degrees. Toss the zucchini and eggplant with 3 tablespoons oil, 4 minced garlic cloves, and salt and pepper to taste. Spread out the vegetables on 2 greased baking sheets; roast, turning occasionally, until golden brown, about 35 minutes. Set the vegetables aside.

2. Heat the remaining 2 tablespoons oil and 2 minced garlic cloves in a 10-inch skillet over medium heat until fragrant but not brown, about 2 minutes. Stir in the tomatoes; simmer until thickened slightly, about 10 minutes. Stir in the basil and salt and pepper to taste. Pour into a large measuring cup. Add enough water to make 3 1/2 cups.

3. Spread 1/2 cup sauce evenly over the bottom of a greased 13-by-9-inch lasagne pan. Lay 3 noodles crosswise over the sauce, making sure they do not touch each other or the sides of the pan. Spread 3/4 cup prepared vegetables evenly over the noodles, 1/2 cup sauce evenly over the vegetables, and 3/4 cup mozzarella and 2 generous tablespoons of Parmesan evenly over the sauce. Repeat the layering of the noodles, vegetables, sauce, and cheese 3 more times. For the fifth and final layer, lay the final 3 noodles crosswise over the previous layer and top with the remaining 1 cup tomato sauce, 1 cup mozzarella, and 2 tablespoons Parmesan. (The lasagne can be wrapped with plastic and refrigerated overnight or wrapped in plastic and aluminum foil and frozen for up to 1 month. If frozen, defrost in the refrigerator.)

4. Adjust the oven rack to the middle position and heat the oven to 375 degrees. Cover the pan with a large sheet of foil greased with cooking spray. Bake for 25 minutes (30 minutes if chilled); remove foil and continue baking until the top turns golden brown in spots, about 15 minutes. Remove the pan from the oven and let the lasagne rest 5 minutes. Cut and serve.

STEP-BY-STEP

TWO TYPES OF NO-BOIL NOODLES

Italian no-boil noodles (right) have an inconvenient square shape. Domestic no-boil noodles (left) fit perfectly in a standard 13-by-9-inch lasagne pan.

Spinach and Mushroom Lasagne

CREMINI MUSHROOMS ARE PARTICULARLY GOOD IN THIS DISH, BUT ANY FRESH MUSHROOM IS FINE. SERVES 6 TO 8.

5 tablespoons extra-virgin olive oil
1 medium onion, minced
1 pound fresh mushrooms, trimmed and sliced
Salt and ground black pepper
10 ounces (12 cups) spinach, washed, stemmed, and chopped (see illustration 1, page 159)
2 medium garlic cloves, minced
1 28-ounce can crushed tomatoes
2 tablespoons chopped fresh basil or flat-leaf parsley leaves
Salt and ground black pepper
15 dried 7-by-3½-inch no-boil lasagna noodles
4 cups shredded mozzarella cheese (about 1 pound)
⅔ cup grated Parmesan cheese

1. Heat 2 tablespoons oil over medium heat in a deep soup kettle. Add the onion and sauté until translucent, about 5 minutes. Add the mushrooms; sauté until golden, about 8 minutes. Season with salt and pepper to taste. Remove the mushrooms and set aside.

2. In the same pan, heat 1 tablespoon oil over medium heat; add the spinach; cook, stirring often, until wilted, about 5 minutes. Season with salt and pepper to taste. Add to the mushrooms and stir to combine.

3. Heat the remaining 2 tablespoons oil and garlic in a 10-inch skillet over medium heat until fragrant but not brown, about 2 minutes. Stir in the tomatoes; simmer until thickened slightly, about 10 minutes. Stir in the basil and salt and pepper to taste. Pour into a large measuring cup. Add enough water to make 3½ cups.

4. Spread ½ cup sauce evenly over the bottom of a greased 13-by-9-inch lasagne pan. Lay 3 noodles crosswise over the sauce, making sure they do not touch each other or the sides of the pan. Spread ¾ cup prepared vegetables evenly over the noodles, ½ cup sauce evenly over the vegetables, and ¾ cup mozzarella and 2 generous tablespoons of Parmesan evenly over the sauce. Repeat the layering of the noodles, vegetables, sauce, and cheese 3 more times. For the fifth and final layer, lay the final 3 noodles crosswise over the previous layer and top with the remaining 1 cup tomato sauce, 1 cup mozzarella, and 2 tablespoons Parmesan. (The lasagne can be wrapped with plastic and refrigerated overnight or wrapped in plastic and aluminum foil and frozen for up to 1 month. If frozen, defrost in the refrigerator.)

5. Adjust the oven rack to the middle position and heat the oven to 375 degrees. Cover the pan with a large sheet of foil greased with cooking spray. Bake for 25 minutes (30 minutes if chilled); remove foil and continue baking until the top turns golden brown in spots, about 15 minutes. Remove the pan from the oven and let the lasagne rest 5 minutes. Cut and serve.

Asparagus and Gruyère Lasagne

OTHER VEGETABLES WORK WITH GRUYERE CHEESE, BUT WE ESPECIALLY LIKE THE COMBINATION WITH ASPARAGUS. SERVES 6 TO 8.

- 2 pounds asparagus, tough ends trimmed, sliced in half lengthwise, and cut into 1/2-inch pieces (see illustrations 1–3, page 138)
- 4 tablespoons extra-virgin olive oil
- 2 medium garlic cloves, minced
- 1 28-ounce can crushed tomatoes
- 2 tablespoons chopped fresh basil or flat-leaf parsley leaves
- Salt and ground black pepper
- 15 dried 7-by-3 1/2-inch no-boil lasagna noodles
- 4 cups shredded Gruyère cheese (about 1 pound)
- 2/3 cup grated Parmesan cheese

1. Bring 4 quarts of water to a boil in a large pot. Add the asparagus and cook for 1 minute. Drain well. Heat 2 tablespoons oil in a large skillet; add the asparagus and sauté until tender, about 3 minutes. Set aside.

2. Heat the remaining 2 tablespoons oil and garlic in a 10-inch skillet over medium heat until fragrant but not brown, about 2 minutes. Stir in the tomatoes; simmer until thickened slightly, about 10 minutes. Stir in the basil and salt and pepper to taste. Pour into a large measuring cup. Add enough water to make 3 1/2 cups.

3. Spread 1/2 cup sauce evenly over the bottom of a greased 13-by-9-inch lasagne pan. Lay 3 noodles crosswise over the sauce, making sure they do not touch each other or the sides of the pan. Spread 3/4 cup prepared asparagus evenly over the noodles, 1/2 cup sauce evenly over the asparagus, and 3/4 cup Gruyère and 2 generous tablespoons of Parmesan evenly over the sauce. Repeat the layering of the noodles, vegetables, sauce, and cheese 3 more times. For the fifth and final layer, lay the final 3 noodles crosswise over the previous layer and top with the remaining 1 cup tomato sauce, 1 cup Gruyère, and 2 tablespoons Parmesan. (The lasagne can be wrapped with plastic and refrigerated overnight or wrapped in plastic and aluminum foil and frozen for up to 1 month. If frozen, defrost in the refrigerator.)

4. Adjust the oven rack to the middle position and heat the oven to 375 degrees. Cover the pan with a large sheet of foil greased with cooking spray. Bake for 25 minutes (30 minutes if chilled); remove foil and continue baking until the top turns golden brown in spots, about 15 minutes. Remove the pan from the oven and let the lasagne rest 5 minutes. Cut and serve.

◆

Spicy Broccoli Lasagne

FOR THIS RECIPE, THE BROCCOLI MUST BE BLANCHED AND THEN CHOPPED FINE BEFORE BEING SAUTEED IN GARLICKY OLIVE OIL. CAULIFLOWER CAN BE PREPARED IN THE SAME FASHION. SERVES 8.

- 2 medium heads broccoli (about 2 pounds), stems removed and broken into florets (see illustrations 1–2, page 140)
- Salt
- 3 tablespoons extra-virgin olive oil
- 4 medium garlic cloves, minced
- 1 teaspoon hot red pepper flakes
- 1 28-ounce can crushed tomatoes
- 2 tablespoons chopped fresh basil or flat-leaf parsley leaves
- Ground black pepper
- 15 dried 7-by-3 1/2-inch no-boil lasagna noodles
- 4 cups shredded mozzarella cheese (about 1 pound)
- 2/3 cup grated Parmesan cheese

1. Bring several quarts of water to a boil in a large pot. Add the broccoli and salt to taste and cook until crisp-tender, about 2 minutes. Drain and cool slightly. Chop the broccoli fine.

2. Heat 2 tablespoons oil in a large skillet. Add 2 garlic cloves and sauté over medium heat until golden, about 1 minute. Add broccoli and cook until tender, about 3 minutes. Add red pepper flakes and salt to taste. Transfer the broccoli to a medium bowl.

3. Heat the remaining tablespoon oil and the remaining 2 garlic cloves in the now-empty skillet. Cook until fragrant, about 1 minute. Stir in the tomatoes; simmer until thickened slightly, about 10 minutes. Stir in the basil and salt and pepper to taste. Pour into a large measuring cup. Add enough water to make 3½ cups.

4. Spread ½ cup sauce evenly over the bottom of a greased 13-by-9-inch lasagne pan. Lay 3 noodles crosswise over the sauce, making sure they do not touch each other or the sides of the pan. Spread ¾ cup broccoli evenly over the noodles, ½ cup sauce evenly over the broccoli, and ¾ cup mozzarella and

2 generous tablespoons of Parmesan evenly over the sauce. Repeat the layering of the noodles, broccoli, sauce, and cheese 3 more times. For the fifth and final layer, lay the final 3 noodles crosswise over the previous layer and top with the remaining 1 cup tomato sauce, 1 cup mozzarella, and 2 tablespoons Parmesan. (The lasagne can be wrapped with plastic and refrigerated overnight or wrapped in plastic and aluminum foil and frozen for up to 1 month. If frozen, defrost in the refrigerator.)

5. Adjust the oven rack to the middle position and heat the oven to 375 degrees. Cover the pan with a large sheet of foil greased with cooking spray. Bake for 25 minutes (30 minutes if chilled); remove foil and continue baking until the top turns golden brown in spots, about 15 minutes. Remove the pan from the oven and let the lasagne rest 5 minutes. Cut and serve.

CRESPELLE,
CANNELLONI, AND
MISCELLANEOUS
BAKED FRESH
PASTA DISHES

/!\

FRESH PASTA IS MOST COMMONLY USED TO MAKE

LASAGNE AND FILLED PASTA SHAPES SUCH AS RAVIOLI

OR TORTELLINI. HOWEVER, THERE ARE A NUMBER OF

UNUSUAL BAKED DISHES THAT ALSO START WITH

fresh egg pasta. These include cannelloni (small squares of fresh pasta that are smeared with sauce and rolled up jelly-roll style and baked) as well as some regional specialties such as buckwheat pasta baked with potatoes, greens, and cheese, and a light soufflé made with fresh fettuccine.

In addition to these dishes, all of which start with sheets of fresh egg pasta, Italians fill and bake crepes, called *crespelle*. In many ways, crespelle are simpler to prepare than the other recipes in this chapter, since they do not require you to make fresh pasta. Rather, a simple batter is spooned into a hot pan to make individual crepes, which are then filled, rolled, sauced, and briefly baked.

All of the recipes in this chapter are prepared in a casserole dish and baked. They are relatively labor-intensive, but the results are worth the effort.

Crespelle

CRESPELLE ARE THIN, eggy pancakes that are similar to French crepes. They are used to make a filled pasta dish (also called crespelle) that is similar to manicotti (see chapter 20). Manicotti starts with dried pasta tubes, which are filled, placed in a single layer in a casserole dish, sauced, and baked. Crespelle are similar, except that the pasta is actually a crepe.

Unlike manicotti, which is a hearty, rugged dish, crespelle should be light and delicate. However, the pancakes must be sturdy enough to be filled, rolled, and baked. The standard batter is simple enough—flour, salt, milk, eggs, and often butter.

We experimented with various ratios of ingredients and found that a relatively lean batter without butter ensures that the crespelle will be sturdy enough to handle. (By comparison, a traditional French crepe batter contains 2 or 3 tablespoons of melted butter or oil, plus fat for cooking the crepes.)

We found the other important factor when developing a recipe for the batter was the amount of flour. Add too much flour and the batter is thick and does not spread quickly and evenly in the pan. The crespelle come out thick and doughy and the finished dish is not nearly as appealing. Baked crespelle must be delicate—this requires the thinnest crepe possible. A thin batter, with just ¾ cup of flour for every cup of milk and two eggs, worked best in our tests.

We found that a nonstick skillet is almost essential when cooking the batter. You could use a regular pan, but you have to add more butter and the risk of some sticking is quite high. With a nonstick skillet, we found that just a tablespoon of melted butter was enough to keep the pan greased when making sixteen crepes.

We found that the ideal crepe measures about 8 inches across and hence we prefer to use a 7- or 8-inch skillet. In order to get the necessary batter for each crepe into the pan at one time, we measure out 2 tablespoons of batter into a ¼-cup measure and then pour it into the pan all at once. Adding the first tablespoon, then the second, with a regular tablespoon measure was too slow. The first spoonful began to set, leaving the crepe too thick in the middle and the batter unevenly coating the pan.

Once the crespelle cool, they can be filled right away or refrigerated overnight. To keep them from sticking together, we found it best to separate each one with a piece of waxed paper and then refrigerate the stack in an airtight container.

Once crespelle are filled, they are rolled and snugly fitted into a buttered casserole dish. There are three possible options for "saucing" the crespelle before they go into the oven. The lightest choice (and the one that allows the filling flavors to dominate) is to dot the crespelle with butter and sprinkle with cheese. Each crespelle remains distinct though, and this dish does not really meld together to form a casserole.

Béchamel is a much more effective binder, gluing together the crespelle in a pleasant fashion. Béchamel also adds more richness to the dish. Finally, crespelle can be topped with a thick tomato sauce (a watery sauce will make the crepes soggy). The tomato sauce adds another distinct layer of flavor that complements the filling.

In some respects, the choice of sauce is open to change based on personal preference. Béchamel highlights the richness and silkiness of the filling but is quite heavy. Tomato sauce makes a more rustic dish, but it can overwhelm or clash with some delicate fillings. Butter and cheese are best when you want to keep the focus clearly on the crepes and the filling.

Crespelle

MAKES ABOUT 16 CRESPELLE

CRESPELLE ARE THIN pancakes, similar to French crepes. In Italian cooking, they are filled with savory stuffings, drizzled with béchamel or sprinkled with cheese, and then baked until golden. More delicate than manicotti or cannelloni, they pair well with light fillings like seafood, mushrooms, or a little cheese. Use a nonstick skillet and you won't have a problem flipping them.

¾ cup all-purpose flour
¼ teaspoon salt
2 large eggs
1 cup milk
1 tablespoon unsalted butter, melted

1. Whisk together the flour and salt in a medium bowl. Lightly beat the eggs in another bowl and beat in the milk. Slowly pour the liquid into the flour, whisking until the batter is smooth.

2. Place a 7- or 8-inch nonstick skillet over medium heat. When the pan is hot, brush with a little melted butter. Spoon 2 tablespoons of the batter into the pan and swirl to coat the bottom of the pan evenly (see illustration 1). Cook until the bottom is light golden, about 1 minute. Carefully flip with a spatula (see illustration 2) and cook until it is light golden in spots on the second side, about 45 seconds.

3. Transfer the crespelle to a platter. Brush the pan with a little more butter. Repeat until all the batter has been used, placing all the cooked crespelle in a single stack. Use the crespelle immediately or layer them with sheets of waxed paper when cooled. (The crespelle can be refrigerated in an airtight container for up to 2 days.)

MAKING CRESPELLE

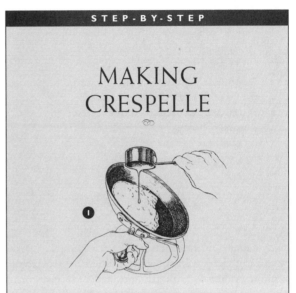

1. To ensure thin crespelle, spoon 2 tablespoons of batter into a hot nonstick skillet as quickly as possible and use the handle to swirl the batter over the bottom of the pan. We find it helpful to pour the 2 tablespoons of batter directly into the pan from a ¼-cup measure.

2. When the bottom of the crespelle is covered with light golden spots, use a spatula to turn it over carefully.

Mushroom Crespelle

THIS IS A RELATIVELY LIGHT DISH, FILLED WITH SOME SAUTEED MUSHROOMS AND TOPPED ONLY WITH A LITTLE BUTTER AND A SPRINKLING OF PARMESAN. SERVES 4.

> 5 tablespoons unsalted butter
> 1 medium onion, minced
> 1¼ pounds white button mushrooms, wiped clean, stems trimmed, and chopped
> Salt and ground black pepper
> ½ cup dry white wine
> 2 tablespoons minced fresh flat-leaf parsley leaves
> ¼ cup heavy cream
> ¾ cup grated Parmesan cheese
> 1 recipe Crespelle (page 329)

1. Heat 2 tablespoons butter in a large skillet. Add the onion and cook until softened, 3 to 4 minutes. Add the mushrooms and turn the heat to medium-high. Cook, stirring often, until the liquid has evaporated and the mushrooms are golden brown, about 8 minutes. Season with salt and pepper to taste. Add the wine and simmer until the alcohol has cooked off, about 2 minutes.

2. Stir in the parsley and cream. Simmer until the cream thickens slightly, 1 to 2 minutes. Transfer to a medium bowl and stir in ¼ cup cheese. Adjust the seasonings.

3. Preheat the oven to 450 degrees. Use 1 tablespoon of butter to grease a 13-by-9-inch baking dish. Lay one crespelle on a work surface and spread 2 tablespoons of the mushroom filling in a 1-inch-wide line going almost from the top to the bottom, about 2 inches from the left edge (illustration 1, page 331). Fold the left edge over the filling and roll up the crespelle (illustrations 2 and 3, page 331). Place it, seam side down, in the baking dish. Repeat with the remaining crespelle and filling. The crespelle should fit in a single layer (illustration 4, page 331).

4. Sprinkle the remaining ½ cup cheese over the crespelle. Dot with the remaining 2 tablespoons butter.

5. Bake until golden, about 12 minutes. Serve immediately.

◆

Squash Crespelle

SAGE-SCENTED SQUASH PUREE MAKES A COLORFUL AND FLAVORFUL FILLING FOR AN AUTUMN PASTA DISH. FRESH PUMPKIN, BUTTERNUT SQUASH, OR EVEN SWEET POTATOES MAY BE SUBSTITUTED FOR THE ACORN SQUASH HERE. SERVES 4.

> 2 small acorn squash (about 1½ pounds), halved and seeded
> ¼ pound prosciutto, minced fine
> 1 large egg yolk
> 1¼ cups grated Parmesan cheese
> 1 tablespoon minced fresh sage leaves
> ⅛ teaspoon grated nutmeg
> ¼ teaspoon salt
> 1 tablespoon unsalted butter
> 1 recipe Crespelle (page 329)
> ½ cup Béchamel Sauce (page 306)

1. Heat the oven to 400 degrees. Place the squash, cut sides down, on a small baking sheet; bake until tender, about 35 minutes. Cool the squash, then scoop out the flesh.

2. Mash the squash with the prosciutto, egg yolk, 1 cup cheese, the sage, nutmeg, and salt.

3. Preheat the oven to 450 degrees. Use the butter to grease a 13-by-9-inch baking dish. Follow instructions for "Filling Crespelle" on page 331, using 2 tablespoons of the squash filling for each crespelle.

4. Spoon the béchamel sauce over the crespelle. Sprinkle with the remaining ¼ cup cheese.

5. Bake until golden, about 12 minutes. Serve immediately.

FILLING CRESPELLE

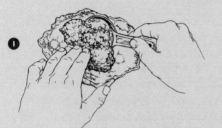

1. Spoon as much filling as indicated in individual recipes in a 1-inch-wide line going almost from the top to the bottom of a crespelle, about 2 inches from the left edge.

2. Fold the left edge of the crespelle over the line of filling and tuck around the filling to enclose.

3. Gently roll the filled crespelle to the right, making sure that filling stays securely in the crepe.

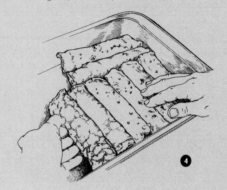

4. Place the rolled crespelle seam side down in the prepared pan. Fit the crespelle snugly into the pan so that they are all in a single layer.

Goat Cheese and Basil Crespelle

PIQUANT GOAT CHEESE GIVES THIS FILLING A STRONG FLAVOR, SO EACH CREPE REQUIRES JUST A TABLESPOON. THE RICH CHEESE FILLING IS NICELY OFFSET BY A QUICK TOMATO SAUCE. SERVES 4.

> 4½ ounces (about 1 cup) fresh goat cheese, crumbled
> 1 cup grated Parmesan cheese
> 1 large egg yolk
> ½ cup minced fresh basil leaves
> Salt
> 1 medium garlic clove, peeled (see illustration, page 39)
> 1 tablespoon extra-virgin olive oil
> ¼ teaspoon hot red pepper flakes (optional)
> 1 cup canned crushed tomatoes
> 1 tablespoon unsalted butter
> 1 recipe Crespelle (page 329)

1. Combine the goat cheese, ¾ cup Parmesan, egg yolk, basil, and ¼ teaspoon salt in a medium bowl; set aside.

2. Process the garlic through a garlic press into a small bowl; stir in 1 teaspoon water (see illustrations 1–3, page 45). Heat the oil, garlic, and red pepper flakes (if using) in a medium sauté pan over medium heat until fragrant but not brown, about 2 minutes. Stir in the tomatoes; simmer until thickened slightly, about 10 minutes. Season with salt to taste.

3. Preheat the oven to 450 degrees. Use the butter to grease a 13-by-9-inch baking dish. Follow instructions for "Filling Crespelle" on page 331, using 1 tablespoon of the cheese filling for each crespelle.

4. Spoon the tomato sauce over the crespelle. Sprinkle with the remaining ¼ cup cheese.

5. Bake until golden, about 12 minutes. Serve immediately.

Crespelle with Asparagus

BE SURE TO FINELY CHOP THE ASPARAGUS HERE—DELICATE CRESPELLE WON'T ACCOMMODATE AN OVERLY CHUNKY FILLING. SERVES 4.

> Salt
> 1½ pounds asparagus, tough ends snapped off and cut into 1-inch pieces (see illustrations 1–3, page 138)
> ¼ pound boiled ham, finely chopped
> ½ cup grated Parmesan cheese
> 1 cup Béchamel Sauce (page 306)
> Ground black pepper
> 1 tablespoon unsalted butter
> 1 recipe Crespelle (page 329)

1. Bring several quarts of water to a boil in a medium saucepan. Add 1 tablespoon salt and the asparagus to the boiling water. Cook until tender, 1 to 2 minutes depending on thickness. Drain, cool slightly, and finely chop.

2. Combine the asparagus, ham, ¼ cup cheese, and ½ cup béchamel sauce in a medium bowl. Season with salt and pepper to taste.

3. Preheat the oven to 450 degrees. Use the butter to grease a 13-by-9-inch baking dish. Follow instructions for "Filling Crespelle" on page 331, using 2 tablespoons of the filling for each crespelle.

4. Spoon the remaining ½ cup béchamel sauce over the crespelle. Sprinkle with the remaining ¼ cup cheese.

5. Bake until golden, about 12 minutes. Serve immediately.

Crespelle with Provolone and Ham

PROVOLONE, HAM, AND BÉCHAMEL SAUCE COMBINE TO MAKE A SILKEN, RICH CRESPELLE FILLING. AN EXTRA ½ CUP OF BÉCHAMEL SAUCE MAY BE SUBSTITUTED FOR THE TOMATO SAUCE IF YOU DESIRE EXTRA RICHNESS. SERVES 4.

½ pound sliced provolone, finely chopped
¼ pound boiled ham, finely chopped
½ cup grated Parmesan cheese
1 cup Béchamel Sauce (page 306)
Salt and ground black pepper
1 medium garlic clove, peeled (see illustration, page 39)
1 tablespoon extra-virgin olive oil
1 cup canned crushed tomatoes
1 tablespoon unsalted butter
1 recipe Crespelle (page 329)

1. Combine the provolone, ham, ¼ cup Parmesan, béchamel, and salt and pepper to taste in a medium bowl.

2. Process the garlic through a garlic press into a small bowl; stir in 1 teaspoon water (see illustrations 1–3, page 45). Heat the oil and garlic in a medium sauté pan over medium heat until fragrant but not brown, about 2 minutes. Stir in the tomatoes; simmer until thickened slightly, about 10 minutes. Season with salt to taste.

3. Preheat the oven to 450 degrees. Use the butter to grease a 13-by-9-inch baking dish. Follow instructions for "Filling Crespelle" on page 331, using 1½ tablespoons of the filling for each crespelle.

4. Spoon the tomato sauce over the crespelle. Sprinkle with the remaining ¼ cup Parmesan.

5. Bake until golden, about 12 minutes. Serve immediately.

Shrimp Crespelle

WE LIKE TO BIND TOGETHER THE SHRIMP WITH A LITTLE BÉCHAMEL SAUCE, BUT WE TOP THE DISH WITH SOME TARRAGON-SCENTED TOMATO SAUCE SO THAT IT'S NOT TOO HEAVY. AN EQUAL AMOUNT OF COOKED LOBSTER MEAT MAY BE SUBSTITUTED FOR THE SHRIMP HERE. YOU MAY BUY COOKED SHRIMP OR BOIL SHRIMP UNTIL BRIGHT PINK, 2 TO 3 MINUTES. SERVES 4.

1 pound shrimp, peeled, deveined (if desired), cooked, and coarsely chopped (see headnote)
2 teaspoons minced fresh tarragon leaves
½ cup Béchamel Sauce (page 306)
Salt and ground black pepper
1 medium garlic clove, peeled (see illustration, page 39)
1 tablespoon extra-virgin olive oil
1 cup canned crushed tomatoes
Salt
1 tablespoon unsalted butter
1 recipe Crespelle (page 329)

1. Combine the shrimp, 1 teaspoon tarragon, the béchamel, and salt and pepper to taste in a medium bowl.

2. Process the garlic through a garlic press into a small bowl; stir in 1 teaspoon water (see illustrations 1–3, page 45). Heat the oil and garlic in a medium sauté pan over medium heat until fragrant but not brown, about 2 minutes. Stir in the tomatoes; simmer until thickened slightly, about 10 minutes. Stir in the remaining 1 teaspoon tarragon. Season with salt to taste.

3. Preheat the oven to 450 degrees. Use the butter to grease a 13-by-9-inch baking dish. Follow instructions for "Filling Crespelle" on page 331, using 1½ tablespoons of the filling for each crespelle.

4. Spoon the tomato sauce over the crespelle. Bake until golden, about 12 minutes. Serve immediately.

Cannelloni

CANNELLONI ARE SMALL squares or rectangles of pasta that are smeared with sauce, rolled up, and baked. In our testing, we found that the key to this dish is making the pasta as thin as possible. If it is too thick, the cannelloni will be gummy, doughy, and heavy. We had the best success when we rolled the pasta out using the thinnest setting on our manual pasta machine. You should be able to see the outline of your hand through the dough. If you can't, the dough is too thick.

We tested various shapes and decided that we preferred to use pasta rectangles that could be rolled into small bundles. Rectangles are easy to roll up and make a substantial presentation on the plate. We also tried various sizes and saw that really large rectangles are hard to roll up. Each piece of pasta requires a lot of filling, which tends to leak out after rolling a long sheet into a tight bundle. On the other hand, small rectangles are not big enough to roll several times. The result is a loose bundle that tends to fall apart when placed in or taken out of the baking dish.

We found that 3-by-5-inch rectangles were ideal. They offer a good contrast between layers of pasta and sauce. These pieces are easy enough to roll but still require several complete revolutions during the rolling process so that the bundles will stay together. A note of caution: Spread the sauce very lightly over the pasta sheets. If you add too much sauce, it will leak out the sides of the pasta bundles. As further protection, leave a ¼-inch border unsauced around the edges of each rectangle of pasta.

Mozzarella and Tomato Cannelloni

IT'S IMPORTANT TO SQUEEZE OUT AS MUCH MOISTURE FROM THE TOMATOES AS POSSIBLE SO THAT YOUR FINISHED DISH WON'T BE WATERY. IF YOUR MOZZARELLA IS VERY WATERY, SQUEEZE THE SHREDDED CHEESE BETWEEN PAPER TOWELS BEFORE MIXING IT WITH THE REST OF THE FILLING INGREDIENTS. SERVES 4.

Salt
½ pound Fresh Egg Pasta (page 21), rolled thinly and cut into 20 3-by-5-inch rectangles (see illustration 1, page 337)
1 pound fresh mozzarella cheese packed in water, drained and shredded
2 pounds ripe fresh tomatoes, cored, seeded, cut into ¼-inch dice, and well drained (see headnote; see also illustrations 1–4, page 111)
¼ cup minced fresh basil leaves
1 large garlic clove, minced
¾ cup grated Parmesan cheese
1 tablespoon olive oil
Ground black pepper
1 tablespoon unsalted butter

1. Bring 6 quarts of water to a boil in a large soup kettle. Add salt to taste and 3 or 4 noodles. Cook until almost al dente, then gently retrieve the noodles with a large slotted spoon and transfer them to a bowl of ice water for 30 seconds. Drain the noodles and lay them out on kitchen towels. Repeat the process with 3 or 4 more noodles at a time and a fresh bowl of ice water. The pasta can stay out for up to 1 hour.

2. Combine three-quarters of the mozzarella with the tomatoes, basil, garlic, ½ cup Parmesan, oil, and salt and pepper to taste in a medium bowl.

3. Preheat the oven to 450 degrees. Use the butter to grease a 13-by-9-inch baking dish. Lay noodles on a work surface and spread 1½ tablespoons of the filling over each noodle, leaving a ¼-inch border on all sides (illustration 2, page 337). Starting at a shorter end, roll up the cannelloni jelly-roll style (illustration 3, page

337). Place it, seam side down, in the baking dish. Repeat with the remaining cannelloni and filling. The cannelloni should fit in a single layer (illustration 4, page 337).

4. Sprinkle the remaining mozzarella and Parmesan over the cannelloni. Bake until golden, about 12 minutes. Serve immediately.

◆

Eggplant and Pepper Cannelloni

THERE ARE A LOT OF STEPS INVOLVED IN THIS DISH— SALTING AND COOKING THE EGGPLANT, ROASTING AND PEELING THE PEPPERS, MAKING THE TOMATO SAUCE—BUT THE RESULTS ARE WORTH THE EFFORT. FOR MORE INFORMATION ON CORING, SEEDING, AND ROASTING PEPPERS, SEE THE ILLUSTRATIONS ON PAGE 175. SERVES 4.

> 2 pounds eggplant (about 2 medium), ends trimmed and cut into ¾-inch cubes
> Kosher salt
> 5 tablespoons extra-virgin olive oil
> 4 medium garlic cloves, minced
> ¼ cup minced fresh flat-leaf parsley or basil leaves
> 2 red bell peppers, cored and seeded
> 1 cup grated Parmesan cheese
> Ground black pepper
> ½ pound Fresh Egg Pasta (page 21), rolled thinly and cut into 20 3-by-5-inch rectangles (see illustration 1, page 337)
> 1 cup canned crushed tomatoes
> 1 tablespoon unsalted butter

1. Place the eggplant in a large colander and sprinkle with 1 tablespoon salt. Let stand 30 minutes. Using paper towels or a large kitchen towel, wipe the salt off and pat the excess moisture from the eggplant.

2. Heat 4 tablespoons oil in a large, heavy-bottomed skillet over medium-high heat until it shimmers and becomes fragrant. Add the eggplant; sauté until it begins to brown, about 4 minutes. Reduce the heat to medium-low and cook, stirring occasionally, until the eggplant is fully tender and lightly browned, 10 to

15 minutes. Stir in 3 garlic cloves and the parsley or basil; cook to blend flavors, about 2 minutes.

3. Adjust the oven rack to the top position. Turn the broiler on. With the oven door closed, let the oven heat for 5 minutes. The oven rack should be 2½ to 3½ inches from the heating element. If not, set a jelly-roll pan, turned upside down, on the oven rack to elevate the pan. Place the prepared peppers on a foil-lined baking sheet and flatten the peppers with the palm of your hand. Broil the peppers, with the oven door closed, until spotty brown, about 5 minutes. Reverse the pan in the oven; roast until the skin is charred and puffed but the flesh is still firm, 3 to 5 minutes longer.

4. Remove the pan from the oven; let the peppers sit until cool enough to handle; peel and discard the skin from each piece. For those who prefer, the peppers can be transferred to a large heat-resistant bowl, covered with plastic wrap, and steamed for 15 minutes before peeling the skin. Finely chop the peppers.

5. Mix the peppers with the eggplant and ¾ cup Parmesan. Season with salt and pepper to taste.

6. Bring 6 quarts of water to a boil in a large soup kettle. Add salt to taste and 3 or 4 noodles. Cook until almost al dente, then gently retrieve the noodles with a large slotted spoon and transfer them to a bowl of ice water for 30 seconds. Drain the noodles and lay them out on kitchen towels. Repeat the process with 3 or 4 more noodles at a time and a fresh bowl of ice water. (The pasta can stay out for up to 1 hour.)

7. Heat the remaining tablespoon oil and remaining garlic clove in a medium sauté pan over medium heat until fragrant but not brown, about 2 minutes. Stir in the tomatoes; simmer until thickened slightly, about 10 minutes. Season with salt to taste.

8. Preheat the oven to 450 degrees. Use the butter to grease a 13-by-9-inch baking dish. Follow instructions for "Making Cannelloni" on page 337.

9. Spoon the tomato sauce over the cannelloni. Sprinkle with the remaining ¼ cup Parmesan.

10. Bake until golden, about 12 minutes. Serve immediately.

Meat Cannelloni

BEEF, PORK, VEAL, OR ANY COMBINATION OF THESE MAY BE USED TO FILL CANNELLONI. IF USING ONLY PORK, YOU MIGHT WANT TO CUT DOWN THE QUANTITY OF MORTADELLA TO 1 OUNCE. SERVES 4.

Salt
½ pound Fresh Egg Pasta (page 21),
   rolled thinly and cut into 20 3-by-
   5-inch rectangles
2 tablespoons extra-virgin olive oil
3 medium garlic cloves, 2 minced, 1 peeled
½ pound ground meat (see headnote)
2 ounces mortadella, finely chopped
   (see headnote)
1 cup grated Parmesan cheese
1 large egg yolk
¼ teaspoon ground black pepper
1 cup canned crushed tomatoes
1 tablespoon unsalted butter

1. Bring 6 quarts of water to a boil in a large soup kettle. Add salt to taste and 3 or 4 noodles. Cook until almost al dente, then gently retrieve the noodles with a large slotted spoon and transfer them to a bowl of ice water for 30 seconds. Drain the noodles and lay them out on kitchen towels. Repeat the process with 3 or 4 more noodles at a time and a fresh bowl of ice water. The pasta can stay out for up to 1 hour.

2. Heat 1 tablespoon oil in a medium skillet. Add the minced garlic and sauté until lightly colored, about 1 minute. Add the meat; cook over medium-high heat, stirring to break up larger pieces, until the liquid evaporates and the meat browns, 3 to 4 minutes. Drain off the fat; transfer the meat mixture to a medium bowl. Stir in the mortadella, ¾ cup Parmesan, egg yolk, ½ teaspoon salt, and the pepper. Set aside.

3. Process the whole garlic through a garlic press into a small bowl; stir in 1 teaspoon water (see illustrations 1–3, page 45). Heat the remaining 1 tablespoon oil and the garlic in a medium sauté pan over medium heat until fragrant but not brown, about 2 minutes. Stir in the tomatoes; simmer until thickened slightly, about 10 minutes. Season with salt to taste.

4. Preheat the oven to 450 degrees. Use the butter to grease a 13-by-9-inch baking dish. Follow instructions for "Making Cannelloni" on page 337.

5. Spoon the tomato sauce over the cannelloni. Sprinkle with the remaining ¼ cup Parmesan.

6. Bake until golden, about 12 minutes. Serve immediately.

◆

Swiss Chard and Fontina Cannelloni

DO NOT SKIP THE STEP OF SQUEEZING THE WATER FROM THE COOKED CHARD—THIS WILL ENSURE THAT YOUR CANNELLONI ARE NOT WATERY. OTHER GREENS MAY BE SUBSTITUTED FOR THE CHARD; TRY SPINACH OR BEET GREENS. SERVES 4.

Salt
½ pound Fresh Egg Pasta (page 21),
   rolled thinly and cut into 20 3-by-
   5-inch rectangles
1 pound Swiss chard, stemmed and
   washed (see illustration 2, page 159)
½ pound Fontina cheese, shredded
1 large egg yolk
¼ teaspoon ground black pepper
1 medium garlic clove, peeled (see
   illustration, page 39)
2 tablespoons extra-virgin olive oil
1 cup canned crushed tomatoes
1 tablespoon unsalted butter
¼ cup grated Parmesan cheese

1. Bring 6 quarts of water to a boil in a large soup kettle. Add salt to taste and 3 or 4 noodles. Cook until almost al dente, then gently retrieve the noodles with a large slotted spoon and transfer them to a bowl of ice water for 30 seconds. Drain the noodles and lay them out on kitchen towels. Repeat the process with 3 or 4 more noodles at a time and a fresh bowl of ice water. (The pasta can stay out for up to 1 hour.) Keep the water at a boil.

2. Add the Swiss chard to the boiling water; stir until wilted. Cover and cook until the greens are tender,

MAKING CANNELLONI

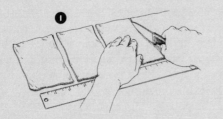

1. Cannelloni are simply small rectangles of fresh egg pasta that are coated with sauce and rolled into small bundles. To make the pasta for this dish, roll large sheets of pasta as thin as possible. Place the sheets on a work surface and use a sharp knife or pizza wheel to cut the dough into rectangles that measure 3 by 5 inches.

2. Spread 1 ½ tablespoons of the filling over the noodle, leaving a ¼-inch border on all sides.

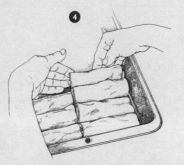

3. Starting at a shorter end, roll up the cannelloni jelly-roll style.

4. Place the cannelloni seam side down in the baking dish. They all should fit snugly in a single layer in the pan.

---

about 7 minutes; drain in a colander and rinse under cold water to stop the cooking process. Squeeze as much excess water as possible from the greens and coarsely chop them.

3. Combine the Swiss chard, Fontina cheese, egg yolk, ½ teaspoon salt, and the pepper in a medium bowl. Set aside.

4. Process the garlic through a garlic press into a small bowl; stir in 1 teaspoon water (see illustrations 1–3, page 45). Heat the oil and garlic in a medium sauté pan over medium heat until fragrant but not

brown, about 2 minutes. Stir in the tomatoes; simmer until thickened slightly, about 10 minutes. Season with salt to taste.

5. Preheat the oven to 450 degrees. Use the butter to grease a 13-by-9-inch baking dish. Follow the instructions for "Making Cannelloni," above.

6. Spoon the tomato sauce over the cannelloni. Sprinkle with the Parmesan.

7. Bake until golden, about 12 minutes. Serve immediately.

Miscellaneous Baked Fresh Pasta Dishes

THE TWO DISHES that follow are unique. The first starts with rectangles of buckwheat pasta, which are boiled, combined with spinach, cheese, and potatoes, and then baked in a casserole dish. The result is a hearty winter casserole. The second dish is much lighter. It starts with fresh egg fettuccine and adds the basic soufflé ingredients.

◆

Buckwheat Pasta with Spinach, Potato, and Taleggio

THERE ARE MANY VARIATIONS OF THIS TRADITIONAL NORTHERN ITALIAN DISH, KNOWN AS *PIZZOCCHERI DELLA VALTELLINA*. FONTINA OR BEL PAESE MAY BE SUBSTITUTED FOR THE CREAMY TALEGGIO CHEESE. SWISS CHARD OR CABBAGE MAY BE SUBSTITUTED FOR THE SPINACH. THE POTATOES MAY BE OMITTED IF A LIGHTER DISH IS DESIRED. THE ONE CONSTANT IS THE SPECIALLY CUT BUCKWHEAT PASTA. **SERVES 4**.

> 4 tablespoons unsalted butter
> Salt
> 1/2 pound baking potatoes, peeled and cut into 1/2-inch dice
> 1 medium garlic clove, minced
> 6 minced fresh sage leaves
> 1 pound fresh spinach leaves, washed, dried, and coarsely chopped
> Ground black pepper
> 1 pound Buckwheat Pasta (page 25) cut into pizzoccheri
> 1/4 pound taleggio cheese, cut into 1/4-inch dice

1. Preheat the oven to 450 degrees. Use 1 tablespoon butter to grease a 13-by-9-inch baking dish. Bring 4 quarts of water to a boil in a large pot. Add 1 tablespoon salt and the potatoes. Cook until tender but not mushy, 3 to 4 minutes. Remove with a slotted spoon and set aside. Do not discard the water.

2. Heat the remaining 3 tablespoons butter in a large saucepan over medium heat. Add the garlic and sage and cook until fragrant, about 1 minute. Add the spinach and cook, stirring frequently, until wilted, about 5 minutes. Turn the heat to medium-high and cook until the liquid is evaporated, about 2 minutes. Stir in the potatoes and cook another minute to combine flavors. Season with salt and pepper to taste.

3. Bring the water in the large pot back to a boil. Add the pasta to the boiling water and cook until al dente. Drain, return to the cooking pot, and toss with the spinach and potatoes. Turn the pasta mixture into the prepared baking dish and top with the taleggio.

4. Bake until the cheese is melted and bubbling, 5 to 7 minutes. Serve immediately.

Fresh Pasta Soufflé

THE LIGHTNESS OF THIS DISH DEPENDS NOT ONLY ON THE WHIPPED EGG WHITES BUT ALSO ON THINLY ROLLED FRESH PASTA. THE RESULT WILL NOT BE AS DELICATE WITH DRIED PASTA. THIS PASTA DISH MAKES A GOOD FIRST COURSE OR SIDE DISH ALONG WITH AN EQUALLY REFINED MAIN COURSE OF VEAL OR SALMON. IT IS ALSO AN EXCELLENT LUNCHEON OR BRUNCH MAIN COURSE, PERHAPS WITH A SALAD OR VEGETABLE DISH. SERVES 6 AS A LIGHT MAIN COURSE, 8 TO 10 AS A SIDE DISH OR FIRST COURSE.

3 tablespoons unsalted butter
Salt
1 pound Fresh Egg Pasta (page 21) cut into fettuccine
1 shallot, minced
2 ounces boiled ham, finely chopped
¾ cup grated Parmesan cheese
1 cup Béchamel Sauce (page 306)
5 large eggs, separated

1. Use 1 tablespoon butter to grease a 3½-quart soufflé dish. Preheat the oven to 375 degrees. Bring 4 quarts of water to a boil in a large pot. Add 1 tablespoon salt and the pasta to the boiling water. Cook until al dente. Drain and turn into a large bowl. Stir in 1 tablespoon butter and set aside to cool slightly.

2. Heat the remaining 1 tablespoon butter in a small skillet over medium heat. Add the shallot and cook until softened, 2 to 3 minutes. Add the ham and cook until the ham is softened, another 2 minutes. Scrape into a bowl and stir in the Parmesan, béchamel, and egg yolks. Stir the mixture into the cooled pasta.

3. Place the whites in the bowl of an electric mixer and whip until they hold stiff peaks. Gently fold the whites into the pasta mixture. Scrape the pasta mixture into the greased soufflé dish.

4. Bake until the pasta soufflé has puffed and is light golden, about 40 minutes. Serve immediately.

RAVIOLI
AND OTHER
FILLED PASTAS

/|\

FILLED PASTAS ARE ONE OF THOSE RARE TREATS THAT

THE HOME COOK IS BEST EQUIPPED TO EXECUTE

PROPERLY. COMMERCIAL FILLED PASTA ARE TOUGH

AND DOUGHY, NOT SUPPLE AND TENDER LIKE HOME-

MADE RAVIOLI AND TORTELLINI. SOME RESTAURANTS

MAY DO A GOOD JOB WITH FILLED PASTA, BUT THESE

pastas are best suited to small production and serving as soon as they are cooked, two things that most restaurants don't do well.

Of course, making filled pasta strikes fear into the hearts of many home cooks—it will be impossibly difficult and time-consuming. After testing dozens of shapes, we can honestly say that filled pastas are not difficult. However, they are time-consuming. Consider making filled pastas on a lazy weekend afternoon, ideally when there are several people in the kitchen to help out with the laborious hand-shaping of each piece.

The gimmicks we tried for making filled pastas don't really work. We began with the attachments that can be fitted onto a manual pasta machine to turn out ravioli. Unfortunately, we had problems with the pasta sticking together and can't recommend these attachments.

Likewise, we were disappointed with the metal molds sometimes used by pasta shops. They seemed more trouble than they are worth, since the pasta sheets must be cut precisely to fit in the molds. (The other choice is to waste a lot of fresh pasta.) We found that cutting and shaping the pasta dough by hand is the most straightforward and foolproof way to make filled pasta.

Because most filled pastas have doubled edges where the pasta has been folded over the filling and sealed together, it is essential that you roll the pasta sheets as thin as possible. Otherwise, the edges may remain too chewy when the rest of the pasta is already cooked through. Use the last setting on a manual pasta machine for the best results.

The biggest problem most home cooks encounter when making filled pastas is that the pastas sometimes open up when they are boiled. There's nothing worse than seeing all the filling floating around the pot, so it's imperative to seal the edges on each piece of filled pasta properly. We tried brushing the edges of the dough with water and with lightly beaten egg, but they both made the dough sticky and harder to handle. We had the best results when we used the pasta sheet as quickly as possible, when it was still moist and pliable. Pasta sheets that have been left out to dry (even for just twenty or thirty minutes) will be too brittle to manipulate. If your dough has become dry, brushing the edges lightly with water is best. (Eggs just make a sticky mess.) Just be careful to brush the edges lightly or the dough will become very tacky.

To guarantee that the pasta does not dry out, we recommend that you roll one sheet of dough at a time, then fill and shape it. Once the first batch of ravioli or tortellini is done, start over again with another piece of pasta dough, running it through the pasta machine and then cutting and filling it as directed.

Don't overload the pasta with too much filling, which could cause the pasta shape to burst in the boiling water. As an added precaution, cook the pasta in water that is at a low boil. Highly agitated water may actually rip open delicate pasta shapes.

To prevent them from sticking together in the pot, we cook the pasta in two batches. While the second batch is in the pot, you can sauce the first batch and bring it to the table. Warmed pasta bowls will keep the pasta hot while you finish cooking the remaining pasta. If you prefer, brings two pots of water to a boil and divide the pasta between them to cook all of it at one time.

Each of the recipes in this chapter will serve eight people as a first course. Filled pasta can also be a main course, with each recipe serving four to six.

◆

Ravioli

THIS RECIPE PRODUCES 2-INCH-SQUARE RAVIOLI WITH THREE CUT EDGES AND ONE FOLDED EDGE. THE FOLDED EDGE MAY BE TRIMMED WITH A FLUTED PASTRY WHEEL IF YOU LIKE. MAKES ABOUT 60.

> 1 pound Fresh Egg Pasta (page 21)
> 1 recipe any filling for pasta (pages 348–353)
> 1 tablespoon salt
> 1 recipe any sauce for filled pasta (pages 353–354)

1. Follow illustrations 1 through 4 on page 343 to form and fill the ravioli.

2. Bring 4 quarts of water to a boil in a large pot. Add the salt and half the pasta. Cook, lowering the heat if necessary to keep the water at a gentle boil, until the doubled edges are al dente, 4 to 5 minutes. With a slotted spoon, transfer the ravioli to warmed bowls or plates; add some sauce. Meanwhile, put the remaining ravioli in the boiling water and repeat the cooking and saucing process. Serve immediately.

MAKING RAVIOLI

1. Use a pizza wheel or sharp knife to cut pasta sheets into long rectangles measuring 4 inches across. Place small balls of filling (about 1 rounded teaspoon each) in a line 1 inch from the bottom of the pasta sheet. Leave 1¼ inches between each ball of filling.

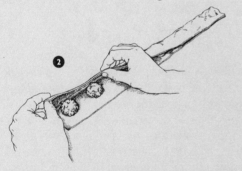

2. Fold over the top of the pasta and line it up with the bottom edge. Seal the bottom and the two open sides with your finger.

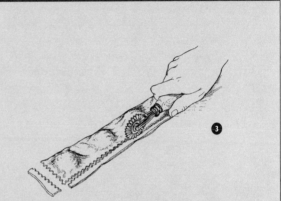

3. Use a fluted pastry wheel to cut along the two sides and bottom of the sealed pasta sheet.

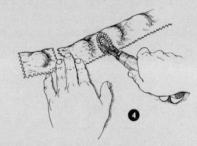

4. Run the pastry wheel between the balls of filling to cut out the ravioli.

MAKING RAVIOLINI

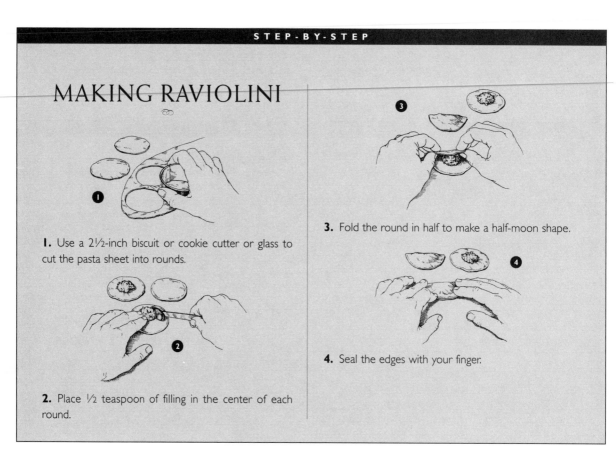

1. Use a 2½-inch biscuit or cookie cutter or glass to cut the pasta sheet into rounds.

2. Place ½ teaspoon of filling in the center of each round.

3. Fold the round in half to make a half-moon shape.

4. Seal the edges with your finger.

Raviolini

THESE SMALL, HALF-MOON–SHAPED PASTAS ARE ALSO KNOWN AS AGNOLINI OR AGNOLOTTI. **MAKES ABOUT 100.**

> 1 pound Fresh Egg Pasta (page 21)
> 1 recipe any filling for pasta (pages 348–353)
> 1 tablespoon salt
> 1 recipe any sauce for filled pasta (pages 353–354)

1. Follow illustrations 1 through 4 to form and fill the raviolini.

2. Bring 4 quarts of water to a boil in a large pot. Add the salt and half the pasta. Cook, lowering the heat if necessary to keep the water at a gentle boil, until the raviolini are al dente, about 4 minutes. With a slotted spoon, transfer the raviolini directly to warm bowls or plates; add some sauce. Meanwhile, put the remaining raviolini in the boiling water and repeat the cooking and saucing process. Serve immediately.

Tortellini

TORTELLINI'S ROUNDED SHAPE IS VERY LABOR INTEN-SIVE, MAKING IT A GOOD CHOICE WHEN THERE ARE SEVERAL PEOPLE WORKING IN THE KITCHEN. THIS RECIPE PRODUCES RELATIVELY LARGE TORTELLINI; TO MAKE TORTELLINI FOR SOUP, CUT THE PASTA INTO 1½- TO 2-INCH SQUARES. MAKES ABOUT 90.

1 pound Fresh Egg Pasta (page 21)
½ recipe any filling for pasta (pages 348–353)
1 tablespoon salt
1 recipe any sauce for filled pasta (pages 353–354)

1. Follow illustrations 1 through 4 to form and fill the tortellini.

2. Bring 4 quarts of water to a boil in a large pot. Add the salt and half the pasta. Cook, lowering the heat if necessary to keep the water at a gentle boil, until the tortellini are al dente, about 4 minutes. With a slotted spoon, transfer the tortellini directly to warm bowls or plates; add some sauce. Meanwhile, put the remaining tortellini in the boiling water and repeat the cooking and saucing process. Serve immediately.

STEP-BY-STEP

MAKING TORTELLINI

1. Use a pizza wheel or sharp knife to cut each pasta sheet into 2½-inch squares. Lift one square from the work surface (otherwise it may stick when stuffed) and place it on another clean part of the counter. Place ½ teaspoon of filling in the center of the square.

2. Fold the square diagonally in half to make a triangle. Make sure that the top piece of dough covers the filling but leaves a thin border of the bottom exposed. Seal the edges with your finger.

3. Lift the filled triangle from the counter and wrap the back of the triangle around the top of your index finger. Squeeze the two bottom corners of the triangle together.

4. As you pull back the top peak of the triangle, gently fold over the top ring of pasta so that the stuffing is completely enclosed. Slide the filled pasta off your finger.

Pansotti (Triangles)

TRIANGULAR PANSOTTI ARE LIKE TORTELLINI, ONLY SIMPLER, BECAUSE THE PASTA SQUARES ARE SIMPLY FOLDED OVER AND SEALED, BUT NOT TWISTED INTO "HAT" SHAPES. **MAKES ABOUT 90.**

> 1 pound Fresh Egg Pasta (page 21)
> 1 recipe any filling for pasta (pages 348–353)

STEP-BY-STEP

MAKING PANSOTTI (TRIANGLES)

I. Use a pizza wheel or sharp knife to cut each pasta sheet into 2½-inch squares. Lift one square from the work surface (otherwise it may stick when stuffed) and place it on another clean part of the counter. Place a scant teaspoon of filling in the center of the square.

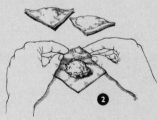

2. Fold the square diagonally in half to make 2 triangles. Seal the edges with your finger.

> 1 tablespoon salt
> 1 recipe any sauce for filled pasta (pages 353–354)

1. Follow illustrations 1 and 2 to form and fill the pansotti.

2. Bring 4 quarts of water to a boil in a large pot. Add the salt and half the pasta. Cook, lowering the heat if necessary to keep the water at a gentle boil, until the pansotti are al dente, about 4 minutes. With a slotted spoon, transfer the pansotti directly to warm bowls or plates; add some sauce. Meanwhile, put the remaining pansotti in the boiling water and repeat the cooking and saucing process. Serve immediately.

◆

Twisted Tortelli

MANY AMERICANS ARE NOT FAMILIAR WITH THIS PASTA FROM NORTHERN ITALY. THE SHAPE IS EXTREMELY EASY TO PREPARE AND TAKES LITTLE TIME TO EXECUTE. ITS TWISTED FORM RESEMBLES CANDY WRAPPERS. **MAKES ABOUT 36.**

> 1 pound Fresh Egg Pasta (page 21)
> 1 recipe any filling for pasta (pages 348–353)
> 1 tablespoon salt
> 1 recipe any sauce for filled pasta (pages 353–354)

1. Follow illustrations 1 through 4 on page 347 to form and fill the tortelli.

2. Bring 4 quarts of water to a boil in a large pot. Add the salt and half the pasta. Cook, lowering the heat if necessary to keep the water at a gentle boil, until the twisted ends are al dente, about 6 minutes. With a slotted spoon, transfer the tortelli to warmed bowls or pasta plates; add some sauce. Meanwhile, put the remaining tortelli in the boiling water and repeat the cooking and saucing process. Serve immediately.

MAKING TWISTED TORTELLI

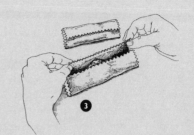

1. Use a fluted pastry wheel to cut each pasta sheet into rectangles measuring 4 inches by 5 inches. Lift one rectangle from the work surface (otherwise it may stick when stuffed) and place it on another clean part of the counter. Place a rounded tablespoon of filling in the center of the rectangle.

3. Fold the top third over the filling so that it just barely overlaps with the folded piece from the bottom. Seal the edges with your finger.

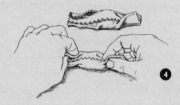

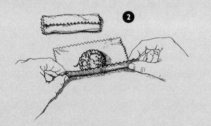

4. Place your hands at either end of the pasta and twist in opposite directions to form the candy-wrapper shape.

2. With a long side facing you, fold the bottom third of the rectangle over the filling.

Fillings for Pasta

MOST ANY FINELY chopped or ground meat, seafood, poultry, or vegetable can be turned into a filling for pasta, but there are a couple of guidelines. Most fillings have cheese to add flavor and a creamy texture. Fillings also contain an egg yolk, which helps bind the ingredients. When we tested fillings without an egg yolk, they tended to be runny and thin. We found it best to add just the yolk, which has most of the egg's thickening powers, and omit the watery white.

A liquidy filling will become even runnier when the pasta is cooked, so juices from vegetables should be cooked off. Some very loose ingredients, such as tomatoes, are best not included in fillings. Most of the following fillings are fairly stiff, even dry.

Each filled pasta recipe specifies how much filling is needed per pasta. In some cases, you may have extra filling. We feel it is better to end up with a couple of extra tablespoons of filling than to run short and have to throw out some homemade pasta.

In terms of choosing a sauce for filled pasta, we think the filling (not the pasta shape) should be the determining factor. We have suggested sauces that will complement the flavors in each filling.

◆

Parsley and Ricotta Filling

THE SIMPLEST PASTA FILLING, SINCE IT REQUIRES NO COOKING. OTHER HERBS—TRY BASIL OR MINT—MAY BE SUBSTITUTED. SERVE WITH GARDEN TOMATO SAUCE (PAGE 354). MAKES ABOUT 2½ CUPS.

> 1 cup ricotta cheese
> ¾ cup grated Parmesan cheese
> 1 large egg yolk
> ½ cup minced fresh flat-leaf parsley leaves
> ½ teaspoon salt
> Ground black pepper

Combine the ricotta, Parmesan, egg, parsley, salt, and pepper to taste in a medium bowl. (The filling can be covered and refrigerated overnight.)

◆

Spinach and Ricotta Filling

THIS FILLING WORKS WELL WITH EITHER THE GARDEN TOMATO SAUCE (PAGE 354) OR THE BROWN BUTTER AND PINE NUT SAUCE (PAGE 353). OTHER LEAFY VEGETABLES SUCH AS KALE AND SWISS CHARD MAY BE SUBSTITUTED FOR THE SPINACH. THREE-QUARTERS CUP CHOPPED FROZEN SPINACH MAY BE USED IF DESIRED; DEFROST THE SPINACH AND SQUEEZE OUT EXCESS LIQUID BEFORE COOKING IT WITH THE ONION. MAKES ABOUT 2½ CUPS.

> ¾ pound spinach leaves, stemmed and washed
> 2 tablespoons unsalted butter
> ½ small onion, minced (about ¼ cup)
> Salt
> 1 cup ricotta cheese
> ¾ cup grated Parmesan cheese
> 1 large egg yolk

1. Place cleaned spinach leaves and any water that clings to them in a nonreactive soup kettle. Cover and cook over medium heat until the spinach wilts, about 5 minutes. Cool the spinach slightly, squeeze out the excess liquid (see illustration, page 22), and chop fine; set aside.

2. Heat the butter in a small skillet. Add the onion and sauté until translucent, about 5 minutes. Stir in the chopped spinach and salt to taste; cook for 1 minute.

3. Transfer the spinach mixture to a medium bowl and cool slightly. Stir in the remaining ingredients. (The filling can be covered and refrigerated overnight.)

Pesto and Ricotta Filling

WE HAVE ADAPTED OUR RECIPE FOR RICOTTA PESTO TO TRANSFORM IT FROM A PASTA SAUCE TO A PASTA FILLING. INCREASING THE RICOTTA MAKES IT CREAMIER AND LESS PUNGENT; ADDING THE EGG YOLK BINDS THE FILLING. SERVE WITH BROWN BUTTER AND PINE NUT SAUCE (PAGE 353), OR SIMPLY TOSS WITH A LITTLE BUTTER AND SPRINKLE WITH GRATED PARMESAN. MAKES ABOUT 2½ CUPS.

¼ cup pine nuts, walnuts, or almonds
3 medium garlic cloves, threaded on a skewer
2 cups packed fresh basil leaves
2 tablespoons fresh flat-leaf parsley leaves (optional)
7 tablespoons extra-virgin olive oil
Pinch salt
¼ cup finely grated Parmesan cheese
2 cups ricotta cheese
1 large egg yolk

1. Toast the nuts in a small, heavy skillet over medium heat, stirring frequently, until just golden and fragrant, 4 to 5 minutes.

2. Meanwhile, bring a small saucepan of water to a boil. Lower the skewered garlic into the water (see illustration 1, page 56); boil for 45 seconds. Immediately run the garlic under cold water. Remove from the skewer; peel and mince.

3. Place the basil and parsley (if using) in a heavy-duty, quart-size, sealable plastic bag; pound with the flat side of a meat pounder until all the leaves are bruised (see illustration 2, page 56).

4. Place the nuts, garlic, basil, parsley, oil, and salt in the work bowl of a food processor; process until smooth, stopping as necessary to scrape down the sides of the bowl. Transfer the mixture to a small bowl, stir in the cheeses and egg yolk, and adjust the salt. (The filling can be covered and refrigerated overnight.)

STORING FILLED PASTA

O NCE THE PASTA HAS BEEN FILLED OR SHAPED, WE FOUND IT BEST TO TRANSFER IT TO A LIGHTLY FLOURED BAKING SHEET. (THE FLOUR HELPS PREVENT STICKING.) IF YOU ARE NOT GOING TO COOK THE PASTA RIGHT AWAY, STASH THE BAKING SHEETS IN THE REFRIGERATOR FOR UP TO TWO HOURS. FOR

longer storage, place the sheets in the freezer until the pasta shapes are frozen solid, about two hours. Transfer the frozen pastas to a large sealable plastic bag and freeze them for up to a month. Don't defrost frozen pasta. Simply drop it into boiling water and add a minute or two to the cooking time.

Meat and Ricotta with Basil Filling

THIS FILLING IS ESPECIALLY DELICIOUS WITH BEEF, VEAL, OR PORK. USE ANY COMBINATION OF THESE MEATS AND PAIR THIS HEARTY FILLING WITH GARDEN TOMATO SAUCE (PAGE 354). **MAKES ABOUT 2½ CUPS.**

    1 tablespoon extra-virgin olive oil
    2 medium garlic cloves, minced
    ½ pound ground meat (see headnote)
    1 cup ricotta cheese
    ¼ cup grated Parmesan cheese
    1 large egg yolk
    ¼ cup minced fresh basil leaves
    ½ teaspoon salt
    Ground black pepper

1. Heat the oil in a medium skillet. Add the garlic and sauté until lightly colored, about 1 minute. Add the meat; cook over medium-high heat, stirring to break up larger pieces, until the liquid evaporates and the meat browns, 3 to 4 minutes. Drain off the fat; transfer the meat mixture to a medium bowl. Cool the meat slightly.

2. Stir in the remaining ingredients, including pepper to taste. (The filling can be covered and refrigerated overnight.)

Squash, Prosciutto, and Parmesan Filling

FRESH SAGE PERFUMES THIS AUTUMNAL STUFFING THAT IS BEST PAIRED WITH THE BROWN BUTTER AND PINE NUT SAUCE (PAGE 353). OTHER HARD SQUASH OR PUMPKIN ALSO WORK WELL IN THIS FILLING. YOU CAN ALSO SUBSTITUTE FROZEN PUREED SQUASH FOR THE FRESH SQUASH. TWO 12-OUNCE PACKAGES OF FROZEN SQUASH COOKED OVER MEDIUM HEAT FOR 10 MINUTES (TO THICKEN THE SQUASH PUREE) YIELDS ABOUT 2 CUPS, MORE THAN THE 1½ CUPS YOU'LL NEED IN THIS RECIPE. **MAKES ABOUT 2½ CUPS.**

    2 small acorn squash (about 1½ pounds),
        halved and seeded
    ¼ pound thinly sliced prosciutto, minced
        fine
    1 large egg yolk
    1 cup grated Parmesan cheese
    1 tablespoon minced fresh sage leaves
    ½ teaspoon salt
    ⅛ teaspoon grated nutmeg

1. Heat the oven to 400 degrees. Place the squash, cut sides down, on a small baking sheet. Bake until tender, about 35 minutes. Cool the squash, then scoop out the flesh (about 1½ cups) and place it in a medium bowl.

2. Mix the squash with the remaining ingredients until very smooth. (The filling can be covered and refrigerated overnight.)

Wild Mushroom Filling

THIS EARTHY FILLING CAN BE SERVED WITH EITHER BUTTER AND SAGE SAUCE (PAGE 354) OR GARDEN TOMATO SAUCE (PAGE 354). RESERVE THE PORCINI SOAKING LIQUID FOR SOUPS OR RICE DISHES. **MAKES ABOUT 2½ CUPS.**

> 2 tablespoons extra-virgin olive oil
> 2 medium garlic cloves, minced
> 10 ounces fresh wild or domestic mushrooms, stems trimmed and minced
> 1 ounce dried porcini mushrooms, rehydrated in 1 cup hot water, strained, and minced (see illustrations 1–2, page 169)
> ¼ cup minced fresh flat-leaf parsley leaves
> Salt and ground black pepper
> 1 cup ricotta cheese
> ⅓ cup grated Parmesan cheese
> 1 large egg yolk

1. Heat the oil in a medium skillet. Add the garlic and sauté over medium heat until golden, about 2 minutes. Add the fresh mushrooms and cook until wilted, about 4 minutes. Stir in the porcini, parsley, and salt and pepper to taste. Cook until the liquid evaporates, about 2 minutes. Remove the pan from the heat and transfer the contents to a medium bowl. Cool slightly.

2. Stir in the remaining ingredients. (The filling can be covered and refrigerated overnight.)

Leek Filling

LEEKS ARE COOKED COVERED UNTIL SOFT, AND THEN BROWNED UNCOVERED FOR FLAVOR. FOR A FRESH-TASTING, LIGHT MAIN DISH, SERVE WITH GARDEN TOMATO SAUCE (PAGE 354); FOR A LUXURIOUS APPE-TIZER, SERVE WITH CREAM SAUCE (PAGE 354). **MAKES ABOUT 2½ CUPS.**

> 8 large leeks, white and light green parts, trimmed, washed, and cut into ¼-inch rounds (see illustrations 1–6, page 165)
> 3 tablespoons unsalted butter
> ½ cup grated Parmesan cheese
> 1 large egg yolk
> ½ teaspoon salt
> Ground black pepper

1. Combine the leeks, butter, and ½ cup water in a large sauté pan. Cook, covered, over medium heat until the leeks are very soft, about 30 minutes. Uncover, turn the heat to medium-high, and cook until the leeks are golden brown and all of the liquid has evaporated, about 5 minutes. Remove the pan from the heat and transfer the contents to a medium bowl. Cool slightly.

2. Stir in the remaining ingredients, including pepper to taste. (The filling can be covered and refrigerated overnight.)

Chicken and Mortadella Filling

GROUND CHICKEN GIVES THIS MEAT STUFFING A DELI-CATE TEXTURE; MORTADELLA, AN ITALIAN-STYLE BOLOGNA, ADDS MELLOW FLAVOR. THIS FILLING IS ESPECIALLY GOOD WITH THE BUTTER AND SAGE SAUCE (PAGE 354). MAKES ABOUT 2½ CUPS.

1 tablespoon extra-virgin olive oil
½ pound ground chicken
¼ pound mortadella, finely chopped
½ cup ricotta cheese
½ cup grated Parmesan cheese
1 large egg yolk
Pinch grated nutmeg
½ teaspoon salt
Ground black pepper

1. Heat the oil in a medium skillet. Add the chicken and cook over medium-high heat, stirring to break up larger pieces, until the liquid evaporates and the meat loses its pink color, 3 to 4 minutes. Transfer the chicken to a medium bowl and cool slightly.

2. Stir in the remaining ingredients, including pepper to taste. (The filling can be covered and refrigerated overnight.)

Shrimp Filling

SHRIMP MAKES AN EXCELLENT PASTA STUFFING. TO OBTAIN THE PROPER CONSISTENCY, IT MUST BE CHOPPED IN THE FOOD PROCESSOR UNTIL VERY FINE, BUT NOT PUREED OR LIQUEFIED. THIS FILLING IS DELI-CIOUS WITH BUTTER AND SAGE SAUCE (PAGE 354) OR CREAM SAUCE (PAGE 354). BECAUSE THERE IS NO CHEESE IN THE FILLING, WE FOUND WE NEEDED TWO EGG YOLKS TO BIND THE SHRIMP. MAKES ABOUT 2½ CUPS.

2 tablespoons unsalted butter
2 shallots, minced
2 pounds shrimp, peeled, deveined (if desired), and patted dry
2 large egg yolks
2 tablespoons minced fresh flat-leaf parsley leaves
½ teaspoon salt
Ground black pepper

1. Heat the butter in a large skillet over medium-high heat. Add the shallots and cook until softened, 3 to 4 minutes. Add the shrimp and cook, stirring occa-sionally, until just pink, 3 to 4 minutes.

2. Transfer the shrimp mixture to the work bowl of a food processor. Process until finely chopped but not entirely smooth. Transfer the shrimp to a medium bowl. Stir in the yolks, parsley, salt, and pepper to taste. (The filling can be covered and refrigerated overnight.)

Lamb Filling

GROUND LAMB PERFUMED WITH ROSEMARY MAKES A MORE ASSERTIVELY FLAVORED FILLING THAN OUR RECIPE USING GROUND MEAT AND RICOTTA. MELTED BUTTER AND GRATED CHEESE OR THE GARDEN TOMATO SAUCE (PAGE 354) WOULD BE EQUALLY GOOD CHOICES TO ACCOMPANY THE PASTA. MAKES ABOUT 2½ CUPS.

    1 tablespoon extra-virgin olive oil
    1 medium onion, minced
    1 medium garlic clove, minced
    1 pound ground lamb
    ½ teaspoon minced fresh rosemary leaves
    Pinch nutmeg
    ½ cup grated Parmesan cheese
    1 large egg yolk
    ½ teaspoon salt
    Ground black pepper

1. Heat the oil in a medium skillet. Add the onion and sauté over medium heat until softened, 3 to 4 minutes. Add the garlic and sauté until lightly colored, about 1 minute. Add the lamb and rosemary; cook over medium-high heat, stirring occasionally and using the back of a wooden spoon to break up larger pieces, until the liquid evaporates and the meat browns, 5 to 7 minutes. Drain off the fat; transfer the meat mixture to a medium bowl and cool slightly.

2. Stir in the remaining ingredients, including pepper to taste. (The filling can be covered and refrigerated overnight.)

Sauces for Filled Pasta

WE FIND THAT SIMPLE sauces are best with filled pastas. You don't want to overwhelm the filling, which you have worked hard to make and should be the focal point for your taste buds. Any filled pasta is delicious with melted butter and a sprinkling of grated Parmesan cheese. When you want to sauce the pasta a bit more elaborately, we offer the following four recipes.

    Note that all sauces for filled pasta should be fairly smooth. You don't want large chunks of vegetables to overwhelm or slide off the pasta. Filled pasta coated with any of these sauces can be served with grated Parmesan cheese at the table, if you like.

◆

Brown Butter and Pine Nut Sauce

THIS SIMPLE, ELEGANT SAUCE IS THE PERFECT MATCH FOR VEGETABLE AND CHEESE FILLINGS. MAKES ABOUT 1 CUP.

    ½ cup pine nuts
    8 tablespoons unsalted butter
    ½ teaspoon salt
    ¼ cup minced fresh flat-leaf parsley leaves

1. Toast the nuts in a small, heavy skillet over medium heat, stirring frequently, until just golden and fragrant, 4 to 5 minutes. Set the nuts aside.

2. Melt the butter in the empty skillet; cook over medium heat, swirling the pan, until the butter turns golden brown, about 5 minutes. Stir in the reserved nuts, salt, and parsley. Keep the sauce warm until ready to use it.

Butter and Sage Sauce

A SPRINKLING OF FRESH SAGE FLAVORS THE BUTTER HERE. IT IS SLIGHTLY MORE WORK THAN PLAIN MELTED BUTTER BUT MUCH MORE DELICIOUS. THIS SAUCE WORKS ESPECIALLY WELL WITH VEGETABLE, SEAFOOD, AND CHICKEN FILLINGS. **MAKES ABOUT 1 CUP.**

> 8 tablespoons unsalted butter
> 2 tablespoons minced fresh sage leaves
> 1/2 teaspoon salt

1. Melt the butter in a medium skillet; cook over medium heat, swirling the pan, until the butter just begins to color, about 3 minutes.

2. Add the sage and cook until golden brown, about 1 minute. Stir in the salt. Keep the sauce warm until ready to use it.

◆

Garden Tomato Sauce

CARROTS AND ONIONS GIVE THIS SAUCE A SWEETNESS THAT CONTRASTS NICELY WITH EITHER THE SPINACH OR THE MEAT FILLINGS. THE BUTTER WORKS WELL WITH FRESH EGG PASTA. FOR A SMOOTH, MORE REFINED SAUCE, PUREE THE MIXTURE IN A FOOD PROCESSOR OR BLENDER. RETURN THE PUREED SAUCE TO THE PAN AND STIR IN 1/2 CUP HEAVY CREAM. COOK, STIRRING CONSTANTLY, 1 TO 2 MINUTES. THIS SAUCE WILL WORK WITH MOST ANY FILLING, ESPECIALLY THOSE WITH A LOT OF CHEESE OR WITH MEAT. **MAKES ABOUT 2 1/2 CUPS.**

> 1 28-ounce can diced tomatoes or whole
>   tomatoes packed in juice
> 3 tablespoons unsalted butter
> 1 small onion, minced
> 1 medium carrot, peeled and minced
> Salt
> 2 tablespoons minced fresh basil or flat-
>   leaf parsley leaves

1. If using diced tomatoes, go to step 2. If using whole tomatoes, drain and reserve the liquid. Dice the tomatoes by hand or in the work bowl of a food processor (use three or four 1/2-second pulses). The

tomatoes should be coarse, with 1/4-inch pieces visible. If necessary, add enough reserved liquid to the tomatoes to total 2 2/3 cups.

2. Melt the butter in a medium saucepan. Add the onion and carrot; cook over medium heat until the vegetables soften, but do not brown, about 10 minutes. Stir in the tomatoes and 1/2 teaspoon salt; simmer until thickened slightly, about 10 minutes. Stir in the basil and adjust the seasonings. (The sauce can be covered and refrigerated for 2 days. Reheat before using.)

◆

Cream Sauce

CREAM SAUCE ENHANCES THE LUXURIOUS FLAVORS OF PASTAS FILLED WITH VEGETABLES, SEAFOOD, CHICKEN, OR MEAT. IT IS TOO RICH FOR FILLINGS WITH A LOT OF CHEESE. WE PREFER TO SERVE FILLED PASTA WITH CREAM SAUCE AS AN APPETIZER RATHER THAN A MAIN COURSE. FOR OPTIMUM ABSORPTION, WE FIND IT BEST TO SIMMER THE COOKED PASTA RIGHT IN THE CREAM SAUCE FOR A MINUTE OR TWO. THUS, IT IS IMPORTANT NOT TO OVERCOOK THE PASTA WHEN IT IS BOILED. YOU CAN MAKE THIS RECIPE THROUGH STEP 1 UP TO AN HOUR BEFORE COOKING THE PASTA. **MAKES ABOUT 1 1/2 CUPS.**

> 1 1/3 cups heavy cream, preferably not
>   ultrapasteurized
> 4 tablespoons unsalted butter
> 3/4 cup grated Parmesan cheese
> 1/2 teaspoon salt
> Ground black pepper
> Pinch nutmeg

1. Combine 1 cup cream and the butter in a sauté pan large enough to accommodate the cooked pasta. Heat over low until the butter is melted and the cream comes to a bare simmer. Turn off the heat and set aside.

2. Add the cooked and drained pasta of choice to the sauté pan. Add the remaining 1/3 cup cream, cheese, salt, pepper to taste, and nutmeg. Cook over very low heat, gently tossing to combine ingredients, until the sauce is slightly thickened, 1 to 2 minutes. Serve immediately.

COUSCOUS

/!\

MANY COOKS THINK THAT COUSCOUS IS A GRAIN LIKE BARLEY OR BULGUR. ACTUALLY, IT IS MADE FROM SEMOLINA AND WATER, JUST LIKE SPAGHETTI OR LINGUINE. COUSCOUS IS A PASTA COMMONLY PREPARED IN NORTH AFRICA AND PARTS OF SOUTHERN ITALY. THE GRAINS ARE TINY AND COOK IN JUST MINUTES. THEY CAN BE USED TO MAKE SIDE DISHES, ROOM-TEMPERATURE SALADS, OR EVEN ADDED TO SOUPS LIKE OTHER TINY PASTA. ◆ IN ADDITION TO COUSCOUS THE PASTA, THERE IS COUSCOUS THE DISH, A STEW MADE IN MOROCCO, TUNISIA, AND ALGERIA. IN these countries, couscous granules are steamed over a simmering stew, and the two are then served together. Since it has meat and vegetables as well as starch, couscous stew is a complete main course.

When shopping for couscous, ignore labels that say "instant" or "quick-cooking." All couscous is precooked and dried at the factory and can be ready in just five minutes. The job of the home cook is to rehydrate the tiny pellets and make them swell and soften. Cooked couscous should be light and fluffy.

The directions on most couscous boxes produce adequate couscous. The couscous is stirred into boiling liquid, covered, allowed to rest off heat for five minutes, then fluffed with a fork. We found that a ratio of three parts liquid to one part couscous works best. Depending on how the couscous is going to be used, it should be seasoned with butter, oil, or stew broth.

Traditionally, couscous is prepared differently in North Africa. The granules are steamed over simmering liquid, not cooked right in the liquid. The result is lighter couscous that swells much more than quick-cooked couscous. For instance, we found that 2 cups of couscous will swell to about 5 cups when cooked right in a hot liquid. However, if the couscous is steamed over the liquid, it will swell to 9 or 10 cups.

You may choose either method for any couscous dish. We find that steamed couscous may be worth the extra effort if making stew. For simple couscous side dishes and salads, we don't think that steamed couscous is worth the bother. The standard quick-cook method is fine for these dishes.

Couscous Stew

NORTH AFRICAN COOKS usually steam couscous directly above the simmering stew to conserve fuel and minimize the number of pots needed. They use a special pot called a couscoussier that is usually earthenware but sometimes made from metal. Since most American cooks do not have a couscoussier, we attempted to devise a method that could use the equipment most home cooks are likely to own.

Paula Wolfert, America's leading expert on couscous and the cuisines of North Africa, suggested using a conventional flat-bottomed steamer insert and a deep pot. As long as the steamer basket is at least 4 inches above the simmering liquid, we found that this setup works well. Since we like to cook stew in the oven (the gentle oven heat is less prone to overcooking, a common problem on stovetop burners that generally run too hot), we steam the couscous over water and then moisten it just before serving with liquid from the stew pot for additional flavor.

If you don't own a steamer, you can rig one up with a deep pot and a metal colander with small holes. Simply put water in the pot and suspend the metal colander above it. Ideally, the colander should fit snugly against the sides of the pot and sit no closer than 4 inches above the water. Once the water comes to a rolling boil, the couscous can be put into the colander and steamed. Even if the holes on the colander are fairly large, the couscous will not slip through as long as there is enough steam pressure to hold it in place. For this reason, it's imperative that the steam rise through the holes in the colander, not around the edges. If your colander does not fit tightly in the pot and steam comes up through the gap between them, wrap a piece of damp cheesecloth around the rim of the pot to seal this space (see illustration 2, page 357).

Ideally, couscous should be served in a wide, flat bowl with sloping sides. The couscous can be arranged in a ring on the bowl and the stew can be placed in the center. At the table, each person may take some of the couscous as well as the stew. The stew can be varied infinitely. We have offered a lamb, a chicken, and a vegetable stew, but feel free to use your own stews. As long as they are fairly brothy, they will work well with couscous.

Steamed Couscous

STEAMED COUSCOUS IS LIGHTER AND FLUFFIER THAN QUICK-COOKED COUSCOUS, BUT TAKES CONSIDERABLY MORE TIME. BOTH ARE MADE FROM THE SAME PRECOOKED AND THEN DRIED SEMOLINA PASTA, BUT THE TECHNIQUE IS DIFFERENT. QUICK-COOKED COUSCOUS IS QUICKLY REHYDRATED WHEN STIRRED INTO BOILING WATER. STEAMED COUSCOUS IS REHYDRATED MORE SLOWLY, BEING TWICE-STEAMED OVER A POT OF BOILING WATER FOR THE BEST RESULTS. **MAKES ABOUT 12 CUPS.**

2 cups couscous
1 teaspoon salt

1. Place the couscous in a fine-mesh strainer and rinse under cold running water (see illustration 1). Dump the couscous into a large bowl and let stand until the grains swell, about 10 minutes. Break up the lumps with your fingers.

2. Fill a large steamer pot or stockpot with water. Set up a steamer (see illustration 2), making sure there is 4 inches between the simmering water and the steamer basket or colander. Carefully pour the couscous into the steamer basket or colander. Steam the couscous, uncovered, over simmering water for 15 minutes.

3. Pour the couscous onto a large, rimmed baking sheet. Sprinkle with 1 cup of cold water and the salt; use oiled hands to spread the couscous and break up any lumps (see illustration 3). Set aside for at least 5 minutes. (The couscous can be covered with paper towels and stored at room temperature for up to 8 hours.)

4. Add more water to the pot, making sure there is 4 inches between the simmering water and the steamer basket or colander. Carefully pour the couscous back into the steamer basket or colander; steam the couscous, uncovered, over simmering water for 20 minutes. Assemble as directed in the Master Recipe for Couscous with Stew (page 358).

STEAMING COUSCOUS

1. Rinse the couscous in a fine-mesh strainer.

2. If you do not have a traditional steamer or couscoussier, set a metal colander over a deep pot of water, leaving 4 inches between the water and the bottom of a colander. Use a long piece of damp cheesecloth to seal the gap around the rim of the pot to force steam through the colander holes.

3. Once the couscous has been steamed the first time, spread it over a large, rimmed baking sheet, sprinkle it with water, and loosely rub the couscous between your lightly oiled hands to break up any lumps.

Quick-Cooked Couscous

QUICK-COOKED COUSCOUS IS PERFECT AS AN ACCOM-
PANIMENT TO ANY LEFTOVER STEW, AS WELL AS A SIM-
PLE ALTERNATIVE TO STEAMED COUSCOUS IN THE STEW
RECIPES THAT FOLLOW. MAKES ABOUT 12 CUPS.

> 3 cups water
> 2 cups couscous

Bring the water to a boil in a medium saucepan. Add
the couscous, stir, remove from the heat, and cover.
Let stand for 5 minutes. Fluff with a fork. Assemble as
directed in the Master Recipe for Couscous with Stew,
below.

MASTER RECIPE

Couscous with Stew

SERVES 10

STEAMED OR QUICK-COOKED Couscous absorbs the abundant cooking
juices in any of the stews that follow.
Couscous with stew makes an attractive
and slightly exotic meal for a crowd. Any favorite
stew that is very juicy may be used instead of the
recipes provided here. If adapting a recipe, don't
thicken the stew with flour and add extra stock or
water if there is not enough broth when the stew has
cooked down.

1 recipe Steamed Couscous (page 357) or
    Quick-Cooked Couscous
2 tablespoons unsalted butter
1 recipe Lamb Stew, Chicken Stew, or
    Vegetable Stew (pages 358–360)

1. Pour the warm couscous onto a large, flat serving
dish with sloping sides and toss with the butter. Use a
fork to smooth out any lumps. Form the couscous into
a large ring, leaving the center open for the stew.

2. Ladle the broth from the stew (you should be able
to spoon off about 3 cups) over the couscous. Place
the meat or vegetables in the center opening. Serve
immediately.

◆

Lamb Stew

IN THIS NORTH AFRICAN STEW, CANNED TOMATOES
AND WATER ARE THE STEWING LIQUID. THE SPICES GIVE
THIS DISH A RICH, EARTHY FLAVOR THAT IS WARM BUT
NOT SPICY. WE FIND THAT THE GENTLE, EVEN HEAT OF
THE OVEN IS THE BEST PLACE TO COOK A STEW. ON
TOP OF THE STOVE, THE STEW MAY SIMMER TOO
BRISKLY, RESULTING IN TOUGH MEAT. SERVES 10.

3 pounds lamb shoulder, trimmed and cut
    into 1 ½-inch cubes
1 ½ teaspoons salt
1 teaspoon ground black pepper
3 tablespoons vegetable oil
2 medium-large onions, coarsely chopped
    (about 2 cups)
4 medium garlic cloves, minced
1 14.5-ounce can diced tomatoes with
    juice
2 bay leaves
1 ½ teaspoons ground coriander
1 teaspoon ground cumin
¾ teaspoon ground cinnamon
½ teaspoon ground ginger
2 15-ounce cans chickpeas, rinsed and
    drained
¼ cup minced fresh cilantro leaves

1. Preheat the oven to 250 degrees. Place the lamb cubes in a large bowl. Sprinkle with the salt and pepper; toss to coat. Heat 2 tablespoons oil over medium-high heat in a large ovenproof Dutch oven. Add half of the lamb and brown on all sides, about 5 minutes. Remove the meat and set aside on a plate. Repeat the process with the remaining oil and lamb.

2. Add the onions to the empty Dutch oven and sauté until softened, 4 to 5 minutes. Add the garlic and continue to cook for 30 seconds. Add 3 cups water, scraping up any browned bits that may have stuck to the pot. Add the tomatoes, bay leaves, coriander, cumin, cinnamon, and ginger and bring to a simmer. Add the meat and return the liquid to a simmer. Cover and place the pot in the oven. Cook just until the meat is almost tender, 1½ to 2 hours.

3. Remove the pot from the oven and add the chickpeas. Cover and return the pot to the oven and cook until the meat is tender and the chickpeas are heated through, about 15 minutes. (The stew can be cooled, covered, and refrigerated up to 3 days. Reheat on top of the stove.)

4. Stir in the cilantro, discard the bay leaves, and adjust the seasonings. Assemble as directed in the Master Recipe for Couscous with Stew (page 358).

◆

Chicken Stew

WE RECOMMEND USING REGULAR CHICKEN THIGHS IN THIS RECIPE. AS A SECOND OPTION, YOU MAY USE BONELESS, SKINLESS CHICKEN THIGHS, ALTHOUGH THE OUTER LAYER OF MEAT WILL TOUGHEN DURING THE COOKING PROCESS. SUBSTITUTE ABOUT 12 BONELESS, SKINLESS THIGHS AND SAUTE THEM IN BATCHES, ADDING A FEW MORE TABLESPOONS OF VEGETABLE OIL DURING THE PROCESS TO KEEP THEM FROM STICKING. YOU MAY NEED TO USE A METAL SPATULA TO LOOSEN BROWNED SKINLESS THIGHS FROM THE PAN. SERVES 10.

> 10 bone-in, skin-on chicken thighs
>   (about 3¾ pounds)
> Salt and ground black pepper
> 2 tablespoons vegetable oil
> 3 large onions, coarsely chopped

> 2 medium garlic cloves, minced
> 2 cups chicken stock or low-sodium
>   canned broth
> 1 bay leaf
> ½ teaspoon dried thyme
> ½ teaspoon ground ginger
> 1½ teaspoons ground cinnamon
> 1 cup raisins
> 4 large carrots, peeled and sliced
>   ¼ inch thick
> 1½ pounds medium turnips, scrubbed
>   and quartered
> ¼ cup minced fresh flat-leaf parsley leaves

1. Preheat the oven to 300 degrees. Sprinkle the chicken with ½ teaspoon salt and ¼ teaspoon pepper. Heat the oil over medium-high heat in a large ovenproof Dutch oven. Add half of the chicken, skin side down, and brown, about 4 minutes. Turn the chicken and brown on the other side, about 4 minutes. Remove the chicken and set aside on a plate. Repeat the process with the remaining chicken. Drain and discard all but 1 tablespoon fat from the pot. When the chicken has cooled, remove and discard the skin.

2. Add the onions to the empty Dutch oven and sauté until softened, 4 to 5 minutes. Add the garlic and continue to cook for 30 seconds. Add the stock, 2½ cups water, bay leaf, thyme, ginger, cinnamon, 1½ teaspoons pepper, and the raisins, and bring the liquid to a simmer. Add the carrots and turnips and simmer for 10 minutes. Add the chicken, submerging it in the liquid, and return to a simmer. Cover and place the pot in the oven. Cook for 25 minutes. Remove the pot from the oven. (The stew can be cooled, covered, and refrigerated up to 3 days. Reheat on top of the stove.)

3. Stir in parsley, discard the bay leaf, and adjust the seasonings. Assemble as directed in the Master Recipe for Couscous with Stew (page 358).

Vegetable Stew

THIS SUMMER STEW HIGHLIGHTS THE FLAVORS OF A TRADITIONAL RATATOUILLE. IT WORKS ESPECIALLY WELL WITH COUSCOUS. SERVES 10.

- 3½ tablespoons olive oil
- 1 medium onion, minced
- 1 large red bell pepper, stemmed, seeded, and cut into ½-inch dice
- 2 medium garlic cloves, minced
- 1 teaspoon minced fresh rosemary
- 2 medium zucchini (about ¾ pound), quartered lengthwise and cut into ½-inch chunks
- 1 large eggplant (about 1 pound), cut into ½-inch dice
- ½ cup white wine
- 2 cups vegetable stock
- 1 14.5-ounce can diced tomatoes with juice
- 1 bay leaf
- 4 medium carrots, peeled and cut into ½-inch lengths
- 4 medium boiling potatoes, cut into ½-inch cubes
- 1 15-ounce can cooked chickpeas, drained and rinsed
- ¼ cup minced fresh mint leaves

1. Heat 2 tablespoons oil over medium-high heat in a large ovenproof Dutch oven. Add the onion and sauté until it begins to brown, about 10 minutes. Add the red pepper, garlic, and rosemary to the Dutch oven and cook for 30 seconds. Scrape the vegetables into a bowl.

2. Add ½ tablespoon oil and the zucchini to the empty Dutch oven and sauté until softened, about 7 minutes. Scrape the zucchini into the bowl with the other vegetables. Add the remaining tablespoon oil and the eggplant to the Dutch oven and sauté until softened, about 5 minutes. Add the vegetables in the bowl back to the pot.

3. Add the wine, scraping up any browned bits that may have stuck to the pot. Add the stock, tomatoes, bay leaf, carrots, and potatoes, and bring to a simmer. Simmer, partially covered, until the vegetables are tender, about 15 minutes.

4. Turn off the heat, stir in the chickpeas, cover, and allow to stand for 5 minutes. Stir in the mint, discard the bay leaf, and adjust the seasonings. Assemble as directed in the Master Recipe for Couscous with Stew (page 358).

Couscous Side Dishes

THERE IS NO QUICKER or simpler side dish than couscous. Quick-cooking couscous can be flavored in infinite ways with herbs, spices, fruit zest, stock or broth, and the addition of ingredients like dried fruits and nuts.

Side-dish couscous should be fluffy but moist and tender. We found that adding a little fat to the cooking liquid helped keep the couscous from seeming too dry. It also keeps the granules separate and prevents the couscous from clumping together when served. Depending on the dish the couscous will be served with, use either butter or olive oil.

You may also want to think about using stock instead of water as the cooking liquid. For instance, couscous cooked in chicken stock makes a full-flavored partner for a roast chicken. However, couscous cooked in water with a little fat is delicious, so don't hesitate to make this dish when stock is not on hand.

Couscous with Lemon and Herbs

SERVES 4 AS A SIDE DISH

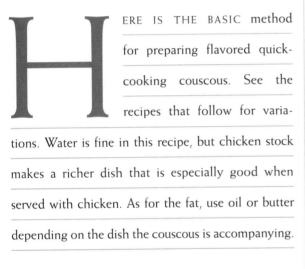

HERE IS THE BASIC method for preparing flavored quick-cooking couscous. See the recipes that follow for variations. Water is fine in this recipe, but chicken stock makes a richer dish that is especially good when served with chicken. As for the fat, use oil or butter depending on the dish the couscous is accompanying.

    1 1/2 cups chicken stock or water
    2 tablespoons extra-virgin olive oil or
        butter
    1/2 teaspoon grated lemon zest
        (optional; see illustration, page 42)
    1 cup couscous
    1/4 cup minced fresh basil, parsley, or mint
        leaves
    1 tablespoon lemon juice
    Salt and ground black pepper

Combine the stock, olive oil, and lemon zest (if using) in a medium saucepan. Bring to a boil. Stir in the couscous and remove from the heat. Cover and let stand 5 minutes. Fluff with a fork and stir in the herbs, juice, and salt and pepper to taste.

Couscous with Sautéed Squash

ZUCCHINI AND YELLOW SQUASH ARE SAUTEED TO GIVE THEM SOME GOOD CARAMELIZED FLAVOR, AND THEN ADDED TO THE REHYDRATED COUSCOUS BEFORE SERVING. OTHER VEGETABLES CAN BE SAUTEED AND STIRRED INTO COUSCOUS; TRY LEEKS, MUSHROOMS, OR SPINACH. SERVES 4.

    2 tablespoons extra-virgin olive oil
    1 shallot, minced
    1 small zucchini (about 6 ounces),
        quartered lengthwise and cut into 1/4-
        inch chunks
    1 small yellow squash (about 6 ounces),
        quartered lengthwise and cut into 1/4-
        inch chunks
    1 cup couscous
    1/4 cup minced fresh basil leaves
    1 tablespoon lemon juice
    Salt and ground black pepper

1. Heat the oil in a medium saucepan over medium-high heat. Add the shallot and cook until softened, 2 to 3 minutes. Add the zucchini and squash and cook, stirring occasionally, until golden, about 7 minutes. Scrape the vegetables into a bowl and set aside.

2. Add 1 1/2 cups water to the pan and bring to a boil. Stir in the couscous and remove from the heat. Cover and let stand 5 minutes. Fluff with a fork and stir in the vegetables, basil, juice, and salt and pepper to taste.

Curried Couscous with Raisins

HERE, CURRY POWDER AND RAISINS GIVE THE GRAIN A POWERFUL FLAVOR BOOST. SERVE WITH YOGURT-MARINATED CHICKEN OR LAMB KEBABS. **SERVES 4.**

2 tablespoons extra-virgin olive oil
¼ cup minced onion
1 medium garlic clove, minced
1 teaspoon curry powder
1½ cups chicken stock or water
6 tablespoons raisins
1 cup couscous
¼ cup minced fresh mint leaves
1 tablespoon lime juice
Salt and ground black pepper

Heat the oil and onion in a medium saucepan over medium-high heat. Cook until softened, about 5 minutes. Add the garlic and curry powder and cook another 30 seconds. Add the stock and raisins and bring to a boil. Stir in the couscous and remove from the heat. Cover and let stand 5 minutes. Fluff with a fork and stir in the herbs, juice, and salt and pepper to taste.

◆

Couscous with Cashews and Scallions

THIS DISH IS AN EXCELLENT ALTERNATIVE TO WHITE RICE WHEN SERVING SOY-MARINATED CHICKEN PARTS OR FLANK STEAK. PEANUT OIL MAKES A NICE SUBSTITUTE FOR OLIVE OIL, ESPECIALLY WITH ASIAN-FLAVORED MEALS. **SERVES 4.**

2 tablespoons extra-virgin olive oil or
   peanut oil
1 cup couscous
½ cup unsalted cashews, chopped
4 scallions, white and light green parts,
   minced
¼ cup minced fresh cilantro leaves
Salt and ground black pepper

Combine 1½ cups water and the oil in a medium saucepan. Bring to a boil. Stir in the couscous and remove from the heat. Cover and let stand 5 minutes. Fluff with a fork and stir in the cashews, scallions, cilantro, and salt and pepper to taste.

◆

Couscous with Carrots

GRATING THE CARROTS IN A FOOD PROCESSOR OR ON THE LARGE HOLES OF A BOX GRATER MAKES THEM ESPECIALLY QUICK TO COOK, SO THEY MELT INTO FINE-GRAINED COUSCOUS. THIS MILD, SLIGHTLY SWEET SIDE DISH COMPLEMENTS MORE STRONGLY FLAVORED MAIN DISHES LIKE GARLICKY ROAST CHICKEN. **SERVES 4.**

2 tablespoons unsalted butter
2 carrots, peeled and coarsely grated
1½ cups chicken stock or water
1 cup couscous
1 teaspoon minced fresh thyme leaves
1 tablespoon lemon juice
Salt and ground black pepper

Heat the butter in a medium saucepan over medium-high heat. Add the carrots and cook until softened, about 2 minutes. Add the stock to the pot and bring to a boil. Stir in the couscous and remove from the heat. Cover and let stand 5 minutes. Fluff with a fork and stir in the thyme, lemon juice, and salt and pepper to taste.

Couscous Salads

COUSCOUS DESTINED FOR side dishes and salads should be light, dry, and fluffy. We found it best to cook the couscous in plain water (without fat) and then dress it with oil once the vegetables and protein have been added. In general, we find that mild-tasting chicken and shrimp are the best additions to a couscous salad. Fresh, diced vegetables also add some crunch. We prefer light dressings made with olive oil and lemon juice.

Couscous Salad

SERVES 4

COUSCOUS MAKES AN excellent base for all kinds of salads served at room temperature or chilled. The addition of cooked shrimp or chicken turns the salad into a light one-dish meal.

1 cup couscous
1½ cups any combination peeled, seeded, and diced cucumber, quartered cherry tomatoes, diced bell peppers, peeled and diced carrots, diced celery
2 tablespoons minced red onion (optional)
1½ cups cooked and chopped shrimp or shredded cooked chicken (optional)
¼ cup extra-virgin olive oil
3 tablespoons lemon juice
2 tablespoons minced fresh parsley, basil, mint, or cilantro
Salt and ground black pepper

Bring 1½ cups water to a boil in a medium saucepan. Stir in the couscous and remove from the heat. Cover and let stand 5 minutes. Turn into a large serving bowl and fluff with a fork. Stir in the vegetables, onion if desired, shrimp or chicken if desired, oil, juice, herbs, and salt and pepper to taste. Serve at room temperature or refrigerate up to 6 hours and serve cold.

◆

Dilled Couscous Salad with Shrimp

TO MAKE THIS DISH EXTRA SIMPLE, BUY COOKED SHRIMP AND SIMPLY CHOP IT WHILE THE COUSCOUS IS COOKING. MINT MAY BE SUBSTITUTED FOR DILL WITH EQUALLY GOOD RESULTS. SERVES 4.

1 cup couscous
1 small cucumber, peeled, seeded, and diced
10 ounces peeled and cooked shrimp, chopped (about 1½ cups)
¼ cup extra-virgin olive oil
3 tablespoons lemon juice
2 tablespoons minced fresh dill
Salt and ground black pepper

Bring 1½ cups water to a boil in a medium saucepan. Stir in the couscous and remove from the heat. Cover and let stand 5 minutes. Turn into a large serving bowl and fluff with a fork. Stir in the cucumber, shrimp, oil, juice, dill, and salt and pepper to taste. Serve at room temperature or refrigerate up to 6 hours and serve cold.

Couscous Salad with Chicken, Almonds, and Apricots

OTHER NUTS (TRY PISTACHIOS OR PECANS) AND DRIED FRUITS MAY BE SUBSTITUTED ACCORDING TO TASTE OR CONVENIENCE. EITHER GREEN OR BLACK OLIVES MAKE A GOOD ACCENT. SAUTE OR POACH CHICKEN BREASTS ESPECIALLY FOR THIS DISH, OR USE THE MEAT FROM A LEFTOVER ROAST CHICKEN. **SERVES 4**.

- ½ cup sliced almonds
- 1 cup couscous
- 8 ounces skinless, boneless chicken breasts, cooked and chopped (about 1½ cups)
- ½ cup chopped dried apricots
- ¼ cup pitted and chopped olives (see illustrations 1–2, page 62)
- ¼ cup extra-virgin olive oil
- 3 tablespoons lemon juice
- 2 tablespoons minced fresh flat-leaf parsley leaves
- ¼ teaspoon ground cumin
- Salt and ground black pepper

1. Toast the nuts in a small, heavy skillet over medium heat, stirring frequently, until just golden and fragrant, 4 to 5 minutes. Set the nuts aside.

2. Bring 1½ cups water to a boil in a medium saucepan. Stir in the couscous and remove from the heat. Cover and let stand 5 minutes. Turn into a large serving bowl and fluff with a fork. Stir in the chicken, apricots, olives, oil, juice, parsley, cumin, and salt and pepper to taste. Sprinkle with the toasted nuts. Serve at room temperature or refrigerate up to 6 hours and serve cold.

MASTER RECIPE

Toasted Israeli Couscous

SERVES 4 TO 6

A LITTLE ONION AND garlic may be sautéed in the oil before the couscous is toasted for a pilaf-type dish. Feel free to stir in any of the herbs and seasonings recommended for quick-cooking couscous, as either side dish or salad.

- 2 tablespoons extra-virgin olive oil
- 2 cups Israeli couscous
- ½ teaspoon salt

1. Heat the oil in a medium saucepan over medium heat. Add the couscous and toast, stirring occasionally, until golden, about 5 minutes.

2. Add 3¾ cups water and the salt and bring to a boil. Lower the heat and simmer, covered, until the couscous is tender and all the water has been absorbed, 15 to 17 minutes. Serve immediately as a side dish or let cool and use in salads.

ISRAELI COUSCOUS

ISRAELI COUSCOUS IS ANOTHER ROUND SEMOLINA PASTA, ALTHOUGH IT IS MUCH LARGER (BY ABOUT TEN TIMES) THAN NORTH AFRICAN COUSCOUS. IT IS SIMILAR IN SIZE TO PEARL BARLEY OR ARBORIO RICE BUT PERFECTLY ROUND. BECAUSE IT IS LARGER, IT TAKES MORE TIME TO COOK. RATHER than simply stirring it into boiling water and letting it stand for five minutes, we found that you must simmer Israeli couscous for about fifteen minutes before it becomes tender. This cooking method is similar to the way you make rice pilaf.

We like the nutty flavor that Israeli couscous develops when toasted in a little bit of olive oil before it is rehydrated. We also find that couscous toasted this way produces beautifully separated grains, unlike untoasted couscous, which tends to be starchy and sticky. Use plain Israeli couscous the same way you would use regular quick-cooking couscous in side dishes or salads, cooking it as directed on page 364 and adding any of the flavorings suggested in the recipes on the preceding pages.

GNOCCHI

GNOCCHI IN ONE FORM OR ANOTHER HAVE BEEN

EATEN SINCE ROMAN TIMES. AT ONE TIME, THE MOST

BASIC RECIPE FOR THIS ITALIAN DUMPLING CALLED

FOR JUST FLOUR AND WATER—IN EFFECT, SOFT PIECES

OF BOILED DOUGH. OTHER VERSIONS, WHICH ARE

STILL MADE TODAY, USE RICOTTA CHEESE AND

SPINACH OR A MIXTURE OF SEMOLINA, MILK, BUTTER,

EGGS, AND PARMESAN. (BOTH VERSIONS ARE CONSID-

ERED IN THIS CHAPTER.) HOWEVER, POTATO GNOC-

CHI BEGAN TO GAIN WIDE CULINARY ACCEPTANCE IN

THE EIGHTEENTH CENTURY AND HAVE SINCE BECOME

the dominant kind of Italian dumpling. While many potato dumplings, especially those from Germany and other Central European regions, are heavy, stick-to-your-ribs fare, gnocchi should be light, airy, and fluffy.

Our mission was simple—figure out what makes potato dumplings heavy and then develop a recipe that avoids these pitfalls. After conducting thirty-six tests, we concluded that the real culprit behind leaden gnocchi is flour, not the potatoes. While it is important to use the right kind of potato (see "Which Potato Is Best?" on page 369), even the right potato will make terrible gnocchi if too much flour is added. The trick, then, is to prepare the potatoes so they require the least possible amount of flour to form a coherent dough.

Before we started our kitchen work, we gathered about seventy-five gnocchi recipes and analyzed them for ingredients and cooking methods. The majority called for boiling the potatoes with skins on, peeling and mashing them, and then combining with flour and salt. A smaller number advocated peeling the potatoes before boiling, or steaming them either with or without skins. We also ran across a few recipes that suggested baking potatoes in their skins. After working with four kinds of potatoes (reds, Yukon Golds, Idaho baking, and russets), we concluded that all potatoes respond best to baking.

Boiled peeled potatoes made the worst gnocchi in our tests, followed by boiled unpeeled potatoes. Steamed potatoes (either with or without skin) made less doughy gnocchi, but they were no match for gnocchi formed from baked potatoes. We attributed these results to the presence or absence of moisture during cooking. Boiling and steaming are wet cooking methods that theoretically leave potatoes quite moist. Baking in a hot oven, however, dries out the potatoes. This theory was supported by our observation that dry baked potatoes needed far less flour to form a coherent dough.

To see if our hunch was correct, we weighed several kinds of potatoes before and after cooking. Boiling and steaming had a negligible effect—boiling increased weight by about 0.5 percent, while steaming decreased weight by about 2 percent. However, baked potatoes shed between 15 and 20 percent of their weight, depending on the variety, after fifty minutes in the oven. This weight loss was caused by the evapora-

tion of water. As an added benefit, gnocchi made with baked potatoes have a stronger potato flavor. The release of water during cooking not only makes the potatoes drier, it also concentrates the flavor so much that we could pick out gnocchi made with baked potatoes by taste alone.

After settling on baking, we then experimented with a number of methods for peeling and mashing potatoes. While it would be more convenient to peel cool potatoes, we found that the skin, which lifts and separates from the flesh during baking, reattaches fairly quickly. It is possible to peel cooled potatoes, but you lose more flesh than if you peel potatoes as soon as they come out of the oven. To prevent scorching your hand, wear an oven mitt and hold hot potatoes in your protected hand. A swivel vegetable peeler can be used to lift the skin while fingers are best equipped to carefully peel and remove the skin.

Once the potatoes are peeled, they must be mashed. It quickly became clear that lumps caused the gnocchi to come apart when cooked and had to be avoided at all costs. The shredding disk on the food processor, a hand-held masher, and a fork all left lumps; the food processor also made the potatoes slightly gummy. We found that a $9 ricer was the best tool for mashing potatoes without lumps. This device gets its name from the tiny, rice-shaped pieces it produces. Simply place peeled potatoes in the round compartment fitted with the fine disk. Press down on the clamp and perfectly riced potatoes are extruded through the disk.

The next step is to add the salt and flour to make the dough. Again, working from the premise that less flour makes better gnocchi, we found it helpful to allow the steam from the riced potatoes to dissipate. By adding flour to room-temperature or only slightly warm potatoes we could prevent the gumminess that sometimes resulted when flour was sprinkled over steaming hot potatoes.

Kneading is the enemy of light gnocchi. When we combined the potatoes and flour in a standing mixer, the dough was incredibly tacky and the gnocchi cooked up like little "super balls" that bounced right off the plate. Working the dough by hand until it just comes together is the easiest and safest way to combine the flour and potatoes.

WHICH POTATO IS BEST?

/\\

SOME TRUSTED COOKBOOKS SWEAR THAT ONLY BOIL-
ING POTATOES CAN MAKE GOOD GNOCCHI, WHILE
OTHERS TOUT BAKING OR RUSSET POTATOES. AFTER A
NUMBER OF EXPERIMENTS WITH RED BOILING POTATOES,
YUKON GOLDS, RUSSETS, AND IDAHO BAKING POTATOES, WE

found that russet and baking potatoes consistently make the best gnocchi. So why the appar-
ent confusion and misinformation, even in some
usually reliable sources?

After some research, we have a tentative expla-
nation. Most everyone agrees that a relatively
dry, starchy potato makes the best gnocchi and
that a waxy potato should be avoided. We found
that red boiling potatoes (not tiny new potatoes
but those about the size of a tangerine) make
gummy, heavy gnocchi, as did freshly dug Yukon
Golds. Both potatoes seem to have too much
moisture in them.

In *The Essentials of Classic Italian Cooking* (Knopf,
1992), Marcella Hazan notes that knowledgeable
shoppers in Italy ask produce vendors for "old"
boiling potatoes when making gnocchi. She says
new potatoes should be avoided. Our theory is
that an "old" boiling potato simply doesn't exist in
this country. Given Americans' passion for potatoes, we think there is too much turnover in our
supermarkets. We also seem to remember from
our cooking experience in Italy that their boiling
potatoes are less waxy than ours.

Although we are fairly confident you could
make fine gnocchi from boiling potatoes that
were dug long ago, figuring out how long potatoes have been out of the ground is impossible
and storing them for the express purpose of some
day making gnocchi seems a waste of effort when
there is an easier option—starchy russet or baking potatoes.

As a side note, we felt compelled to try potato gnocchi made with an egg, a common addition to northern
European dumplings and a trick espoused by some Italian cookbook authors to bind the dough more tightly.
(Several usually reliable sources argued that eggs were
anathema to light gnocchi, so we had our doubts from
the start.) After trying whole eggs, whites, and yolks,
we concluded that while eggs make firmer gnocchi,
they also are gummier and heavier. We also felt that
the egg overwhelmed the delicate potato flavor.

Throughout most of our testing, we concentrated
on adding as little flour as possible to the potatoes.
However, when we began to roll and shape the gnocchi, we realized it was possible to add too little flour.
First of all, the potatoes need enough flour to make a
dough that is not sticky and that will roll easily. If the
dough comes apart (see illustration 3, page 373), you
must add more flour.

There also were times when we added enough flour,
just barely, to bind the dough and allow it to be rolled

HOW TO SHAPE POTATO GNOCCHI

A FAIR AMOUNT OF MYSTIQUE SURROUNDS THE CUT-TING AND SHAPING OF GNOCCHI. TRADITIONALLY, THE DOUGH IS ROLLED INTO LONG ROPES THAT ARE CUT INTO SMALL PIECES AND THEN IMPRINTED WITH RIDGES AS THE CENTER IS GENTLY INDENTED. THE FINAL RESULT should look like a slept-on pillow on one side with several thin grooves on the other side.

Rolling the dough into long ropes (we found a thickness of ¾ inch to be ideal) and then slicing the ropes into individual gnocchi seems unavoidable. In any case, the process is fairly quick. However, we wondered if the final shaping process—which can become tedious when one hundred gnocchi are involved—was necessary. The answer is yes.

We cooked traditionally formed gnocchi and compared them to gnocchi that were simply cut from the dough ropes and then dropped into the boiling water. The indentation in the center of the gnocchi has two purposes. First, it decreases the width of the gnocchi in the middle and allows the center to cook through more evenly. Gnocchi without this indentation often were a bit underdone in the center. Second, the indentation traps sauce on the otherwise smooth surface. As for the grooves, traditionally formed gnocchi did a better job of holding onto the sauce in our tests than gnocchi without creases or crevices.

Although we judged the traditional shape to be essential, we wanted to see if we could improve upon the process. Most sources use the tines of a fork to imprint ridges. We found that simply pressing the fork against the cut gnocchi, much like you press a fork against peanut butter cookie batter, squashes them and is not advised. Holding the tines of a fork parallel to a work surface and flipping little balls of dough off the tines imprints ridges and will give gnocchi their characteristic indentation if pressure is applied to the dough as it is flipped. The problem is that the dough tends to stick to the metal fork.

After looking around the kitchen for a better solution we noticed the ridges on a wooden mallet and wooden butter paddle. When we rolled and flipped gnocchi off these surfaces, we were pleasantly surprised. Not only was it easier because the surface we were working against was so much bigger, but the gnocchi did not stick. The bigger surface also meant the entire length of the gnocchi was covered by thin grooves, as opposed to fork-rolled gnocchi that had only a few crevices. More grooves translates into a more attractive appearance and better sauce retention.

and shaped. While the dough looked fine, the gnocchi cooked up a bit soft and mushy. We realized we were taking our obsession with flour too far and that our gnocchi would have been more resilient if we had added a few more tablespoons of flour after the dough seemed to first come together.

Since the moisture level of each potato varies according to how long it has been out of the ground and the variety, it is impossible to write a recipe with an exact ratio of potatoes to flour. We found that 2 pounds of baked potatoes could require as little as 1¼ cups of flour or as much as 1½ cups. As a general rule, we worked 1¼ cups of flour into the riced potatoes. In most cases, the dough seemed to be just barely bound so we added another 2 tablespoons of flour, as a kind of insurance policy. First-time gnocchi cooks may also want to boil a few quickly shaped gnocchi to evaluate their texture before shaping and rolling out dozens.

chi are too mushy, put the dough rope back into the potato mixture and add in another tablespoon or two of flour. It's better to take the time to test one or two gnocchi than to ruin the whole batch. Also, be careful not to overwork or overknead the dough; you simply want to incorporate the flour into the potatoes. Avoid cooking the gnocchi at a rolling boil since violently churning water makes it difficult to determine when the gnocchi are floating. Even gently boiling gnocchi may bob temporarily to the surface, but don't lift them out until they float.

Potato Gnocchi

MAKES ABOUT 100 GNOCCHI

TO ENSURE THAT GNOCCHI are the right texture, bring a small saucepan of water to a simmer while mixing the dough. Roll a small piece of the dough into the rope shape. Cut off a small piece or two from the rope, shape them into gnocchi, then drop them into the simmering water. If the gnoc-

2 pounds russet or baking potatoes, washed
1¼ cups all-purpose flour, plus more as needed
1 teaspoon salt, plus more for cooking

1. Heat the oven to 400 degrees. Bake the potatoes until a metal skewer slides easily through them, 45 minutes to 1 hour, depending on size.

2. Hold the potato with a pot holder or kitchen towel and peel it with a vegetable peeler or paring knife (see illustration 1, page 373); rice the peeled potato into a large bowl. Peel and rice the remaining potatoes. Cool until the potatoes are no longer hot, about 15 minutes.

3. Sprinkle 1¼ cups flour and 1 teaspoon salt over the warm potatoes. Using your hands, work the mixture into a soft, smooth dough. If the dough is sticky (which is often the case), add more flour as needed, up to 1½ cups total.

4. Roll about one-quarter of the dough into a long ¾-inch-thick rope (see illustration 2, page 373). If the

(continued on next page)

rope won't hold together (see illustration 3, page 373), return it to the bowl with the remaining dough and work in more flour as needed. Repeat until all the dough is rolled.

5. Cut the rope of dough into ¾-inch lengths (see illustration 4, page 373). Holding a butter paddle or fork in one hand, press each piece of cut dough against the ridged surface with your index finger to make an indentation in the center. Roll the dough down and off the ridges and allow it to drop to the work surface (see illustrations 5 and 6, page 373). (Gnocchi can be placed in a single layer on a baking sheet and refrigerated for several hours. Or, the baking sheet can be placed in the freezer for about 1 hour. Partially frozen gnocchi can be transferred to a plastic bag or container, sealed, and frozen for up to 1 month.)

6. Bring 4 quarts of water to a low boil in a large pot. Add 2 teaspoons salt or to taste. Add about one-third of the gnocchi and cook until they float, 1½ to 2 minutes (about 3 minutes for frozen gnocchi). Retrieve the gnocchi with a slotted spoon and transfer to a warm, shallow serving bowl or platter. Repeat the cooking process with the remaining gnocchi, following specific topping and tossing instructions in the recipes that follow.

◆

Potato Gnocchi with Tomato-Mint Sauce

TWO CUPS OF ANY SMOOTH TOMATO SAUCE CAN BE USED WITH A FULL RECIPE OF GNOCCHI. AN EQUAL AMOUNT OF BOLOGNESE SAUCE (SEE PAGE 200) IS ALSO APPROPRIATE. SERVES 8 AS A FIRST COURSE OR 4 TO 6 AS A MAIN COURSE.

> 3 tablespoons olive oil
> ½ small onion, chopped
> ½ small carrot, peeled and chopped
> ½ small celery stalk, chopped
> 1 14.5-ounce can crushed tomatoes
> 8 fresh mint or basil leaves
> Salt

> 1 recipe Potato Gnocchi (page 371), prepared through step 5
> Grated Parmesan cheese for passing at the table

1. Heat the oil in a medium saucepan. Add the onion, carrot, and celery; cook over medium heat until the vegetables soften slightly, about 5 minutes. Add the tomatoes and mint. Simmer until the sauce thickens and the vegetables soften completely, about 30 minutes. Puree the sauce in a food processor or blender. Adjust the seasonings, adding salt if necessary, and keep the sauce warm.

2. Cook the gnocchi according to step 6 of the Master Recipe and transfer them to a warm serving platter. Top each batch with a portion of the tomato sauce. When the last batch has been sauced, gently toss the gnocchi and serve immediately with cheese passed separately at the table.

◆

Potato Gnocchi with Butter, Sage, and Parmesan Cheese

ALTHOUGH SAGE IS THE CLASSIC HERB CHOICE IN THIS PREPARATION, OTHER FRESH HERBS SUCH AS OREGANO, THYME, CHIVES, OR MARJORAM CAN BE SUBSTITUTED. SERVES 8 AS A FIRST COURSE OR 4 TO 6 AS A MAIN COURSE.

> 6 tablespoons unsalted butter
> 12 fresh sage leaves, cut into thin strips
> 1 recipe Potato Gnocchi (page 371), prepared through step 5
> ½ cup grated Parmesan cheese, plus extra for passing at the table

1. Melt the butter in a small skillet. When the butter foams, add the sage. Remove the pan from the heat and set aside. Cover to keep warm.

2. Cook the gnocchi according to step 6 of the Master Recipe and transfer them to a warm platter. Top each batch with a portion of herbed butter and cheese. When the last batch has been sauced, gently toss the gnocchi and serve immediately with more cheese passed separately.

MAKING POTATO GNOCCHI

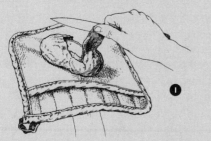

1. Hold the hot potato with a pot holder and use a vegetable peeler or paring knife to remove the skin.

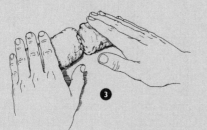

2. Break off a portion of the dough and roll it into a rough rope. Glide your hands over the dough to thin the rope evenly until about ¾ inch thick.

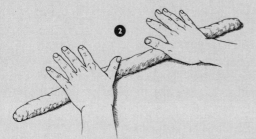

3. If the rope won't hold together when it's rolled, there is not enough flour in the dough. Return the rope to the bowl with the remaining dough and work in more flour as needed.

4. Use a sharp knife to cut the dough rope into ¾-inch-long pieces.

5. Hold a wooden butter paddle in one hand and press each piece of dough against its ridged surface with your finger to make an indentation in the center. Roll the dough down and off the ridges and let it drop to the work surface.

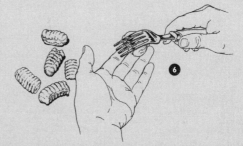

6. If you would rather shape the gnocchi with a fork, hold the fork so that the tines are parallel to the work surface. Place the gnocchi under the tines of the fork. Flip the gnocchi off the ends of the fork to imprint the ridges, applying some pressure as you do this in order to make a shallow indentation in the center.

Potato Gnocchi with Pesto

FEEL FREE TO USE AN EQUAL AMOUNT OF ANY FAVORITE TYPE OF PESTO (SEE CHAPTER 6) AS A SAUCE FOR A FULL RECIPE OF GNOCCHI. SERVES 8 AS A FIRST COURSE OR 4 TO 6 AS A MAIN COURSE.

> 1 recipe Pesto (page 55), prepared
>   through step 4
> 1 recipe Potato Gnocchi (page 371),
>   prepared through step 5

Return the water used for the pesto to a boil. Cook the gnocchi according to step 6 of the Master Recipe and transfer them to a warm platter. Top each batch with a portion of the pesto. When the last batch has been sauced, gently toss the gnocchi and serve immediately.

◆

Potato Gnocchi Gratinéed with Fontina Cheese

ONE CUP OF FRESHLY GRATED PARMESAN CHEESE CAN BE SUBSTITUTED FOR THE FONTINA CHEESE IN THIS RECIPE. SERVES 8 AS A FIRST COURSE OR 4 TO 6 AS A MAIN COURSE.

> 5 tablespoons unsalted butter
> 1 recipe Potato Gnocchi (page 371),
>   prepared through step 5
> 4 ounces Fontina cheese, shredded

1. Adjust the oven rack to the highest position and heat the broiler. Smear 2 tablespoons butter on a gratin dish large enough to hold the gnocchi in a single layer. Melt the remaining butter in a small skillet and set aside. Cover to keep warm.

2. Cook the gnocchi according to step 6 of the Master Recipe and transfer them to the buttered dish. When the last batch has been cooked, toss the gnocchi with melted butter and sprinkle evenly with cheese.

3. Broil the gnocchi until the cheese melts and just begins to brown, no more than 3 or 4 minutes. Serve immediately.

Gnocchi without Potatoes

ALTHOUGH POTATO GNOCCHI are the most common type of gnocchi made in Italy (and the most versatile), there are two other kinds of gnocchi worth discussing. Ricotta-based gnocchi, almost always flavored with spinach, are fluffier than potato gnocchi. Although the dough contains different ingredients, these gnocchi are boiled and sauced in the same fashion as potato gnocchi.

To ensure that ricotta gnocchi will be light, we found it essential to squeeze out all of the liquid from the cooked spinach (wet spinach will require more flour in the dough) and to mix the dough very lightly. In our testing, we found that fresh homestyle ricotta cheese (with a texture akin to goat cheese) made lighter gnocchi than moist commercial ricotta (which looks more like cottage cheese). If using supermarket ricotta, drain the cheese in a colander or mesh strainer lined with paper towels.

Unlike potato gnocchi, which are best made without eggs, ricotta needs the binding power of eggs. (Potatoes are naturally gluey and hold together with just flour to make a nice stiff dough. Ricotta falls apart with flour alone added to the dough.) Egg yolks deliver the real binding power, so rather than add unnecessary liquid we found it best to use yolks only. Four yolks keep the dough together in boiling water without making the gnocchi too heavy.

Ricotta gnocchi are really too soft to imprint with ridges. Simply roll the dough into ropes and then cut the ropes into ¾-inch pieces.

Gnocchi made from semolina and baked with butter and Parmesan are traditional in Rome. Baked semolina gnocchi are somewhat like baked polenta squares, but with a finer texture and sweeter flavor. The hot semolina is spread out onto a cutting board, cooled, and then cut into the characteristic round shape. These baked gnocchi are not sauced (a little cheese and butter may be sprinkled on top) like other gnocchi. They may be served as a first course (as is the case with other gnocchi) but also as a side dish with roasts or stews.

The delicacy of this dish depends on the thinness of the gnocchi—¼ inch is perfect. To spread the hot semolina, work quickly using a metal spatula, rinsed periodically in cold water. We tested both regular and instant semolina (sometimes labeled "ready to eat in five minutes" or "quick-cooking") and found the instant to be just as good as regular. Because it is easier to find (look in Italian delis and many supermarkets) and quicker to make, we recommend the instant.

Spinach and Ricotta Gnocchi

MAKES ABOUT 125 GNOCCHI

I F POSSIBLE, USE FRESH homestyle ricotta cheese, which is drier than commercial ricotta. If using supermarket ricotta, line a large colander or mesh strainer with paper towels and spread the cheese over the towels; let drain until thick, about 1 hour. Make sure to squeeze the spinach very dry after cooking.

2 10-ounce packages frozen spinach, thawed
4 tablespoons unsalted butter
2 tablespoons minced onion
1½ cups ricotta cheese (see headnote)
1⅓ cups all-purpose flour, plus more for your hands
4 large egg yolks
1 cup grated Parmesan cheese
Salt
¼ teaspoon nutmeg

1. Bring 2 quarts of water to a boil in a medium pot. Add the spinach and cook until tender, about 5 minutes. Drain and cool. Squeeze as much moisture as possible from the spinach (see illustration, page 22). Finely chop.

2. Melt the butter in a small skillet over medium heat. Add the onion and cook until softened, about 5 minutes. Add the spinach and cook until the butter is absorbed, about 5 minutes. Transfer to a large bowl.

3. Add the ricotta, flour, yolks, Parmesan, ½ teaspoon salt, and nutmeg to the bowl and mix until just combined.

4. Dust your hands with flour and roll small pieces of dough between your palms to shape ¾-inch-long pellets. (Gnocchi can be placed in a single layer on a baking sheet and refrigerated for several hours. Or, the baking sheet can be placed in the freezer for about 1 hour. Partially frozen gnocchi can be transferred to a plastic bag or container, sealed, and frozen for up to 1 month.)

5. Bring 4 quarts of water to a low boil in a large pot. Add 2 teaspoons salt or to taste. Add about one-third of the gnocchi and cook until they float, 1½ to 2 minutes (about 3 minutes for frozen gnocchi). Retrieve the gnocchi with a slotted spoon and transfer to a warm, shallow serving bowl or platter. Repeat the cooking process with the remaining gnocchi, following specific topping and tossing instructions in the recipes that follow.

Spinach and Ricotta Gnocchi with Gorgonzola Cream Sauce

AIRY SPINACH AND RICOTTA GNOCCHI MAKE A GOOD FOIL FOR RICH CREAM SAUCES, LIKE THIS ONE MADE FROM SWEET GORGONZOLA. THESE GNOCCHI SHOULD BE FINISHED RIGHT IN THE CREAM SAUCE FOR MAXIMUM ABSORPTION OF THE SAUCE. **SERVES 8 AS A FIRST COURSE OR 4 TO 6 AS A MAIN COURSE.**

> 1 ⅓ cups heavy cream, preferably not ultrapasteurized
> 4 tablespoons unsalted butter
> 1 recipe Spinach and Ricotta Gnocchi (page 375), prepared through step 4
> Salt
> 3 ounces sweet Gorgonzola, crumbled
> Ground black pepper

1. Combine 1 cup cream and the butter in a sauté pan large enough to accommodate the cooked gnocchi. Heat over low until the butter is melted and the cream comes to a bare simmer. Turn off the heat, cover to keep warm, and set aside.

2. Cook the gnocchi according to step 5 of the Master Recipe, transferring them to the pan with the cream sauce (not a platter) when they finish cooking. When all of the gnocchi are in the pan, add the remaining ⅓ cup cream, Gorgonzola, ½ teaspoon salt, and pepper to taste. Cook over very low heat, tossing to combine ingredients, until the sauce is slightly thickened, 1 to 2 minutes. Divide among warmed pasta bowls and serve immediately.

Spinach and Ricotta Gnocchi with Tomato-Cream Sauce

BRIGHT GREEN SPINACH AND RICOTTA GNOCCHI ARE ESPECIALLY ATTRACTIVE WITH SMOOTH TOMATO SAUCES. CREAM ADDS A TOUCH OF LUXURY, BUT IS OPTIONAL. **SERVES 8 AS A FIRST COURSE OR 4 TO 6 AS A MAIN COURSE.**

> 3 tablespoons olive oil
> ½ small onion, chopped
> ½ small carrot, peeled and chopped
> ½ small celery stalk, chopped
> 1 14.5-ounce can crushed tomatoes
> 8 minced fresh basil leaves
> ¼ cup heavy cream (optional)
> Salt
> 1 recipe Spinach and Ricotta Gnocchi (page 375), prepared through step 4
> Grated Parmesan cheese for passing at the table

1. Heat the oil in a medium saucepan. Add the onion, carrot, and celery; cook over medium heat until the vegetables soften slightly, about 5 minutes. Add the tomatoes and basil. Simmer until the sauce thickens and the vegetables soften completely, about 30 minutes. Stir in the cream if desired and heat through, 2 to 3 minutes. Puree the sauce in a food processor or blender. Adjust the seasonings, adding salt if necessary, and keep the sauce warm.

2. Cook the gnocchi according to step 5 of the Master Recipe and transfer to a warm serving platter. Top each batch with a portion of the tomato sauce. When the last batch has been sauced, gently toss the gnocchi and serve immediately with cheese passed separately at the table.

Baked Semolina Gnocchi

WE TESTED BOTH REGULAR AND INSTANT SEMOLINA
(SOMETIMES LABELED "READY TO EAT IN FIVE MINUTES"
OR "QUICK-COOKING") AND FOUND THE INSTANT TO
BE JUST AS GOOD AS REGULAR. LOOK FOR THIS PROD-
UCT IN ITALIAN DELIS AND MANY SUPERMARKETS.
SERVES 8 AS A FIRST COURSE OR SIDE DISH.

> 4 cups milk
> 1 1/2 cups instant semolina
> 2 large egg yolks
> 1 cup grated Parmesan cheese
> 6 tablespoons unsalted butter
> Salt

1. Heat the milk in a large saucepan over medium-
high heat until almost boiling. Turn the heat to low
and slowly whisk in the semolina, making sure that no
lumps form. Turn the heat to low and stir constantly
with a wooden spoon until the mixture pulls away easily from the side of the pan, 3 to 5 minutes.

2. Remove from the heat and beat in the yolks,
2/3 cup cheese, 2 tablespoons butter, and salt to taste,
stirring vigorously to prevent the eggs from cooking
before they are incorporated.

3. Moisten a large cutting board with water and
spread the semolina mixture on the board, smoothing it with a metal spatula dipped in cold water until
it is about 1/4 inch thick (see illustration 1). Cool
completely.

4. Preheat the oven to 450 degrees. Using a 2-inch
biscuit cutter or glass, cut the cooled semolina into
circles (see illustration 2). Grease a shallow 11-by-
9-inch ceramic or glass baking dish. Arrange the
scraps from the cut-out gnocchi in a single layer in the
dish. Make a second layer, placing the circles in overlapping rows (see illustration 3). Melt the remaining
4 tablespoons butter and drizzle over the gnocchi;
sprinkle with the remaining 1/3 cup cheese. Bake until
golden, 15 to 20 minutes. Serve immediately.

MAKING SEMOLINA GNOCCHI

1. Moisten a large cutting board with water. Spread
the hot semolina mixture on the board, smoothing
it with a metal spatula, occasionally dipped in cold
water, until the semolina is about 1/4 inch thick. Cool
completely.

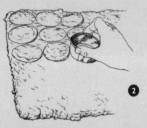

2. Using a 2-inch biscuit cutter or glass, cut the
cooled semolina into circles.

3. Arrange the scraps from the cut-out gnocchi in
a single layer in the bottom of a greased baking dish.
Make a second layer using the gnocchi rounds and
overlapping them in rows.

SPATZLE

/I\

SPATZLE ARE THIN, PASTALIKE DUMPLINGS COMMON

TO ALSACE, SOUTHERN GERMANY, AND SWITZERLAND.

THEY ARE BOILED, BUTTERED, AND SERVED AS A SIDE

DISH WITH ROASTS OR STEWS. THE NAME *SPATZLE*

COMES FROM THE GERMAN WORD FOR "LITTLE SPAR-

ROW" AND IS THOUGHT TO REFER TO THE ROUND

SHAPE OF THE NOODLES, WHICH LOOK SOMEWHAT

LIKE THE SMALL WORMS BIRDS EAT. ◆ THE BATTER

CONTAINS FLOUR, EGGS, SEASONINGS (USUALLY SALT,

PEPPER, AND NUTMEG), AS WELL AS SOME SORT OF

liquid. We tested cream, milk, buttermilk, and water. Cream made the spätzle too rich and heavy. Buttermilk gave them a tangy flavor that seemed out of place. Milk was our preferred liquid, although water made good, if somewhat less rich, spätzle.

The dough is relatively straightforward to assemble. Combine the liquid ingredients and seasonings and then stir in the flour. We found it best to let the dough rest for 10 minutes. The spätzle seemed a bit less gluey, no doubt because the glutens in the mixture had a chance to relax. However, we found no benefit to the longer rest or chilling some sources recommend. Also, we found mixing by hand to be the best technique; the flour and liquid must be well combined, but overbeaten dough will make tough spätzle.

The biggest issue when making spätzle is how to form the batter into the characteristic short, round "noodles." Not surprisingly, we found that a spätzle machine is the best tool for the job. To use the machine, set the grater over a pot of simmering salted water and pour the batter into the container on top. Slide the container back and forth, forcing small lengths of batter to drop through the holes in the grater and into the water. When the spätzle float (about two to three minutes), the noodles are done and should be retrieved with a slotted spoon. Spätzle can then be sautéed until crisp and used as a garnish for meat or game dishes, or baked au gratin and served as a hearty side dish or even a simple main course.

If you don't own a spätzle machine, a round potato ricer with interchangeable disks can be used instead. Simply fill the ricer (fitted with the large disk) with some batter and press it through until you have strands that are about ½ inch long. Then, slice the strands away from the ricer with a sharp knife and let them drop down into the boiling water. Spätzle made in a ricer sometimes stick together. If this happens, break up the noodles with a wooden spoon as they cook.

Some sources suggest pressing the batter through a metal colander if you don't own a spätzle machine. We found this method did not work. The holes are too large and widely spaced. Most of the batter ended up stuck to the inside of the colander; the rest clumped together in the pot. If you want to make spätzle, invest in a spätzle machine (which costs less than $10) or a ricer with interchangeable disks.

Buttered Spätzle

SERVES 4 AS A SIDE DISH

BOILED AND BUTTERED spätzle make a simple accompaniment to juicy main courses, such as pot roast or roast chicken with gravy.

2 large eggs, lightly beaten
⅓ cup milk or water
Salt
¼ teaspoon finely ground white pepper
⅛ teaspoon grated nutmeg
1½ cups all-purpose flour
4 tablespoons unsalted butter, cut into
    6 pieces and brought to room temperature

1. Beat the eggs, milk, ½ teaspoon salt, pepper, and nutmeg together in a medium bowl. Stir in the flour to form a smooth but thick batter; let the batter rest for 10 minutes.

2. Meanwhile, place 1 tablespoon butter into a bowl that has been rinsed in hot water (to heat the bowl) and dried. Bring 3 quarts of water to a boil in a 4- to 5-quart saucepan that is narrow enough so that the short ends of the spätzle machine can rest on top of the pan without falling into the water.

3. When the water comes to a boil, generously salt it. Spoon a portion of the batter into the square container that runs along the grater track. With the spätzle machine resting on the pan rim, move the metal container quickly back and forth along the grater until the dough is pressed through the grater into the boiling water (see illustration 1, page 382). Alternately, use a ricer to form the spätzle (see illustration 2, page 382).

4. With a slotted spoon, transfer the spätzle that have floated to the water's surface (this will take 2 to 3 minutes) to the warm bowl. Repeat cooking in batches with the remaining batter, adding butter to each batch of cooked spätzle. Toss and serve.

◆

Buttered Dill Spätzle

THE ADDITION OF FRESH DILL TO SPATZLE BATTER MAKES FOR FRESH-TASTING DUMPLINGS, PERFECT ON THE SIDE WITH HEARTY MEAT DISHES LIKE HUNGARIAN GOULASH OR POT ROAST. **SERVES 4 AS A SIDE DISH.**

Follow the Master Recipe for Buttered Spätzle (page 380), replacing the nutmeg with ⅓ cup minced fresh dill.

Sautéed Spätzle

SERVES 4 AS A SIDE DISH

BOILED AND BUTTERED spätzle have a doughy quality that some people like and others don't. However, toss the boiled spätzle into a hot skillet and sauté them until crisp and everyone will like them. Again, the spätzle are perfect with roasts.

2 large eggs, lightly beaten
⅓ cup milk or water
Salt
¼ teaspoon finely ground white pepper
⅛ teaspoon grated nutmeg
1½ cups all-purpose flour
4 tablespoons unsalted butter

1. Beat the eggs, milk, ½ teaspoon salt, pepper, and nutmeg together in a medium bowl. Stir in the flour to form a smooth but thick batter; let the batter rest for 10 minutes.

2. Meanwhile, bring 3 quarts of water to a boil in a 4- to 5-quart saucepan that is narrow enough so that the short ends of the spätzle machine can rest on top of the pan without falling into the water.

3. When the water comes to a boil, generously salt it. Spoon a portion of the batter into the square container that runs along the grater track. With the spätzle machine resting on the pan rim, move the metal container quickly back and forth along the grater until the dough is pressed through the grater into the boiling water (see illustration 1, page 382). Alternately, use a ricer to form the spätzle (see illustration 2, page 382).

4. With a slotted spoon, transfer the spätzle that have floated to the water's surface (this will take 2 to 3 minutes) to a bowl. Repeat cooking in batches with the remaining batter.

5. Heat the butter in a large skillet over medium-high heat. Add the drained spätzle and sauté, stirring occasionally, until golden and slightly crisp, 4 to 5 minutes. Serve immediately.

MAKING SPATZLE

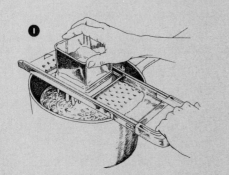

1. A spätzle machine makes the best spätzle with minimal effort. Simply set the machine over a pot of simmering water with the square metal container facing up. Spoon a portion of the batter into the box and run it back and forth along the grater to press the dough through the holes and into the boiling water.

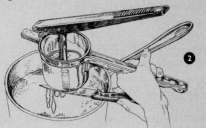

2. Although a spätzle machine cuts more precisely, spätzle batter may be formed by passing it through the large disk on a potato ricer. Put about a quarter of the dough into the ricer and press until you have strands about ½ inch long. Slice the strands away from the ricer with a sharp knife and directly into the boiling water. If the pieces stick together, break them up with a wooden spoon as they cook.

Sautéed Spätzle with Bread Crumbs

SPATZLE CRISPED IN A PAN WITH FRESH BREAD CRUMBS HAVE A DELICIOUS BROWN BUTTER FLAVOR AND SLIGHTLY CRUNCHY TEXTURE. (DON'T USE COMMERCIAL CRUMBS IN THIS RECIPE; THEY ARE TOO DRY AND POWDERY TO PROVIDE A PLEASANT CONTRAST TO THE SOFT SPATZLE.) IF THE BREAD CRUMBS ARE ADDED TO THE PAN BEFORE THE SPATZLE, THEY WILL QUICKLY SOAK UP ALL OF THE BUTTER, SO ADD THE TWO INGREDIENTS TOGETHER TO ENSURE EVEN DISTRIBUTION OF BUTTER. SEE CHAPTER 9 FOR IDEAS ON FLAVORING BREAD CRUMBS, IF YOU WOULD LIKE TO VARY THE FLAVORS OF THIS DISH. WE PARTICULARLY LIKE THIS DISH WITH ROAST CHICKEN. SERVES 4 AS A SIDE DISH.

> 2 large eggs, lightly beaten
> ⅓ cup milk or water
> Salt
> ¼ teaspoon finely ground white pepper
> ⅛ teaspoon grated nutmeg
> 1 ½ cups all-purpose flour
> 4 tablespoons unsalted butter
> ½ cup fresh bread crumbs

Follow the instructions for the Master Recipe for Sautéed Spätzle (page 381), adding the bread crumbs to the skillet at the same time as the boiled and drained spätzle.

◆

Sautéed Spätzle with Browned Onions

COOK THE ONIONS UNTIL THEY ARE WELL BROWNED; DEEPLY CARAMELIZED ONIONS ADD A RICH SWEETNESS TO THIS DISH. SERVES 4 AS A SIDE DISH.

> 4 tablespoons unsalted butter
> 1 medium onion, finely chopped
> 2 large eggs, lightly beaten
> ⅓ cup milk or water
> Salt
> ¼ teaspoon finely ground white pepper
> ⅛ teaspoon grated nutmeg
> 1 ½ cups all-purpose flour

1. Heat the butter in a skillet large enough to hold the cooked spätzle. Add the onion and sauté over medium heat until deep golden, about 15 minutes.

2. Meanwhile, follow steps 1 through 4 of the Master Recipe for Sautéed Spätzle (page 381).

3. Add the spätzle to the skillet with the onions. Cook over medium-high heat until heated through and a little bit crispy, about 5 minutes. Season with salt and pepper to taste. Serve immediately.

Spätzle Gratinéed with Cheese

SERVES 4 AS A SIDE DISH OR FIRST COURSE

BOILED SPATZLE CAN also be gratinéed with butter and cheese to make an excellent side dish for any main course you might serve with a potato gratin. They also could be served as a first course. Don't be alarmed by the abundant amount of butter bubbling around the spätzle as they brown under the broiler. The spätzle absorb the butter as soon as they are pulled from the oven.

2 large eggs, lightly beaten
⅓ cup milk or water
Salt
¼ teaspoon finely ground white pepper
⅛ teaspoon grated nutmeg
1½ cups all-purpose flour
4 tablespoons unsalted butter, cut into
  6 pieces and brought to room
  temperature
¼ cup grated Gruyère cheese

1. Beat the eggs, milk, ½ teaspoon salt, pepper, and nutmeg together in a medium bowl. Stir in the flour to form a smooth but thick batter; let the batter rest for 10 minutes.

2. Meanwhile, adjust the oven rack to the top position and preheat the broiler. Place 1 tablespoon butter into a bowl that has been rinsed in hot water (to heat the bowl) and dried. Bring 3 quarts of water to a boil in a 4- to 5-quart saucepan that is narrow enough so that the short ends of the spätzle machine can rest on top of the pan without falling into the water.

3. When the water comes to a boil, generously salt it. Spoon a portion of the batter into the square container that runs along the grater track. With the spätzle machine resting on the pan rim, move the metal container quickly back and forth along the grater until the dough is pressed through the grater into the boiling water (see illustration 1, page 382). Alternately, use a ricer to form the spätzle (see illustration 2, page 382).

4. With a slotted spoon, transfer the spätzle that have floated to the water's surface (this will take 2 to 3 minutes) to the warm bowl. Repeat cooking in batches with the remaining batter, adding butter to each batch of cooked spätzle. Toss and serve.

5. Transfer the spätzle to a shallow baking dish and sprinkle with the cheese. Slide the dish under the broiler and broil until the cheese is melted and golden, 1 to 2 minutes. Serve immediately.

CHINESE
WHEAT
NOODLES

/I\

WHEAT NOODLES ARE THE DOMINANT FORM OF PASTA

IN NORTHERN AND CENTRAL CHINA. (RICE NOODLES

ARE POPULAR IN SOUTHERN CHINA; FOR MORE INFOR-

MATION, SEE CHAPTER 29.) WHEAT NOODLES, BOTH

DRIED AND FRESH, ARE USED IN COUNTLESS DISHES,

including stir-fries (often called lo mein), crisp pan-fried noodle cakes, and cold noodle salads.

There are numerous kinds of dried and fresh wheat noodles in China, but American shoppers are likely to see only a few of them. The most common option is the round dried wheat noodle that is golden in color and about the width of spaghetti. Most supermarkets stock this item with other Chinese products like hoisin sauce and soy sauce.

For a greater selection of noodles, you will have to shop at an Asian market. There you will see thicker (but still round) fresh egg noodles as well as a variety of dried noodle shapes, some thicker, some flat. You may even see white (eggless) fresh noodles (sometimes called Shanghai noodles), as well as white dried noodles.

Figuring out the nomenclature on packages is nearly impossible. Most products are imported from

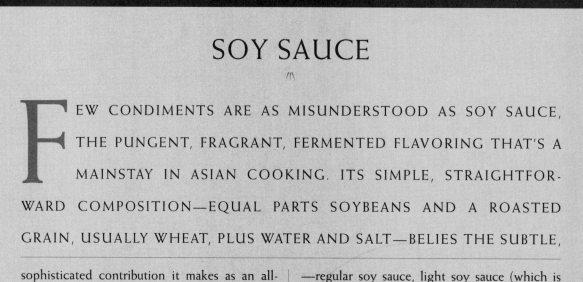

SOY SAUCE

FEW CONDIMENTS ARE AS MISUNDERSTOOD AS SOY SAUCE, THE PUNGENT, FRAGRANT, FERMENTED FLAVORING THAT'S A MAINSTAY IN ASIAN COOKING. ITS SIMPLE, STRAIGHTFORWARD COMPOSITION—EQUAL PARTS SOYBEANS AND A ROASTED GRAIN, USUALLY WHEAT, PLUS WATER AND SALT—BELIES THE SUBTLE,

sophisticated contribution it makes as an all-purpose seasoning, flavor enhancer, tabletop condiment, and dipping sauce.

Soy sauce evolved from *shih*, a fermented grain mixture first used as a preservative and flavoring in China more than 2,500 years ago. *Shih* was introduced in Japan during the seventh century by Buddhist monks. By 1700, commercial breweries across Japan began producing soy sauce and its wheat-free counterpart, tamari. Soy sauce is fermented for at least six months and often for several years (preferably in cedar casks for optimum flavor). Slow fermentation and aging create nearly 300 separate flavor compounds.

Today, soy sauce is made around the world, including in the United States. There are three products most consumers are likely to encounter

—regular soy sauce, light soy sauce (which is made with a higher percentage of water and hence contains less sodium), and tamari (made with just fermented soybeans, water, and salt).

Recipes in this book generally call for soy sauce, which means regular soy sauce. You may use tamari, which has a stronger flavor and thicker consistency, if you prefer. When using soy sauce to bulk up a sauce, we might call for light soy sauce so that the dish does not become too salty. If you don't have light soy sauce on hand, you may make your own by combining two parts regular soy sauce and one part water. This mixture will not have quite as strong a soy flavor, but at least you will have reduced the sodium in the sauce so the dish won't be inedible.

Asia and have little information in English. Even if you do read Chinese, the same noodle can have several names, depending on the region where it was manufactured. As for products with labels written in English, names such as Shanghai noodles, lo mein, and chow mein are not standardized the way names for Italian pasta shapes are.

Some noodles are made with durum wheat flour (just like Italian noodles) and have the same golden yellow color. Other noodles are made with other wheat flours (similar to all-purpose or bread flour) and are white in color. Despite all these differences, we found that flavor and texture differences were generally quite small among the dozen brands and types of noodles we tested. The one major distinction that American cooks must heed is the difference between dried and fresh noodles.

Dried Chinese wheat noodles are akin to Italian-style spaghetti. They cook up much the same and can be used interchangeably, although Chinese noodles tend to be a bit more absorbent and better in stir-fries.

Fresh egg noodles have a richer flavor and are more tender, although not nearly as delicate as Italian fresh pasta, which cannot be used in stir-fries and other dishes calling for fresh Chinese noodles. Fresh Chinese egg noodles do a better job of absorbing flavors and liquids, making them our first choice for stir-fries. They are so much better than dried noodles in crisp noodle cakes and cold salads that we recommend skipping these dishes if you can't get fresh noodles.

Whenever we are shopping at an Asian grocery, we pick up several bags of fresh egg noodles and store them in the freezer. They can be frozen for a couple of months and cooked, without defrosting, much like fresh noodles, adding an extra minute or two to the cooking time.

While we think it's worth the effort to get fresh Chinese wheat noodles made with egg (read labels; some inferior brands are made with dyes), dried wheat noodles are excellent. We found some flat white noodles (about the width of tagliatelle) at one market and became quite enamored of them in stir-fries. Note though that any dried Chinese noodle will work in the stir-fry recipes in this chapter.

Stir-Fried Noodles

COOKED DRIED AND FRESH noodles are both excellent in stir-fries. Fresh noodles are a bit softer and absorb flavors better, but either type of noodle can be used in the following recipes. Some sources suggest rinsing the cooked noodles to wash away excess starch, but we found that these noodles don't produce all that much starch, and the starch they do give up helps bind the stir-fry together and thicken the sauce. (There's no need to thicken these stir-fry sauces with cornstarch; the noodles take care of that.) To keep the cooked noodles from sticking together while you work on the rest of the stir-fry recipe, simply toss the drained noodles with a little sesame oil.

A large nonstick skillet is the best piece of equipment for stir-frying on American stoves. Woks are conical because in China they traditionally rest in cylindrical pits containing the fire. A wok was not designed for stovetop cooking, where heat comes only from the bottom. We think a horizontal heat source requires a horizontal pan.

American stoves require still other adjustments. In China, intense flames lick the bottom and sides of a wok, heating the whole surface to extremely high temperatures. Conventional stoves simply don't have enough British Thermal Units (BTUs) to heat any pan (a wok or flat skillet) as well. American cooks must accommodate the lower horsepower on their stoves. Throw everything into the pan at one time and the ingredients will steam and stew, not stir-fry.

Our solution is to add ingredients in batches and cut vegetables quite small. Another school of thought suggests blanching all vegetables so that they are merely heated through in the pan with the other stir-fry ingredients. We find this precooking to be burdensome and reserve it only for vegetables such as broccoli and cauliflower that require it.

We prefer to cut vegetables quite small and then add them in batches to the pan based on their cooking times. By adding a small volume of food at a time, the heat in the pan does not dissipate. Slow-cooking vegetables like carrots and onions go into the pan first, followed by quicker-cooking items like zucchini and bell pepper. Leafy greens and herbs go in last.

Most stir-fries start with some sort of protein, whether beef, chicken, pork, shrimp, scallops, squid, fish, or tofu. All protein must be cut into bite-size pieces. We find it best to freeze beef, chicken, and pork until firm (at least fifteen minutes or so) to make slicing easier. Once sliced, we marinate all protein in a mixture of soy sauce and dry sherry. Just make sure to drain thoroughly before stir-frying. If you add the liquid, the protein will stew rather than sear.

Many stir-fry recipes add the aromatics (scallions, garlic, and ginger) too early and they burn. After the vegetables have been cooked, we push them to the sides of the pan, add a little oil and the aromatics to the center of the pan, and cook briefly until fragrant but not colored, about ten seconds. The cooked protein, sauce, and noodles are then added to the pan,

everything is heated through, and the stir-fried noodles are ready to serve. (For more information on stir-fries, see *The Cook's Illustrated Complete Book of Poultry*.)

Stir-Fried Chinese Noodles

SERVES 4

Chinese noodles—whether dried or fresh—can be incorporated into almost any stir-fry recipe. Just make sure to add more liquid (we use chicken stock) than usual, so the noodles won't stick to the pan. Also, we find that thinner noodles (the width of spaghetti) work best. Really wide, fat noodles have a tendency to stick together when stir-fried. This recipe is a very basic outline—you can plug in whatever protein and vegetable you like. See the variations that follow for specific ideas as well as ways to vary this basic soy-garlic sauce.

JUDGING THE HEAT LEVEL WHEN STIR-FRYING

It's important to add ingredients to a stir-fry only when the pan is good and hot. To judge the heat level, hold your hand 1 inch over the pan. When the pan is so hot you can keep your hand there for only three seconds, add the oil and heat until it just starts to shimmer and smoke.

¾ pound meat, seafood, or tofu, cut into
   small, even pieces
1 tablespoon plus 2 teaspoons soy sauce
2 tablespoons plus 1 teaspoon dry sherry
12 ounces dried Chinese wheat or fresh
   egg noodles (the width of spaghetti)
1 tablespoon salt
1 teaspoon Asian sesame oil
3 tablespoons light soy sauce
½ cup chicken stock or low-sodium
   canned broth
½ teaspoon sugar
¼ teaspoon hot red pepper flakes
2 tablespoons very finely minced garlic
2–4 tablespoons peanut or vegetable oil
1½ pounds vegetables, trimmed and cut
   into small pieces (none bigger than a
   quarter) and divided into several
   batches based on cooking times
2 tablespoons minced scallions, white
   parts only
1 tablespoon minced fresh gingerroot (see
   illustrations 1–3, page 43)

1. Toss the meat, seafood, or tofu with 1 tablespoon soy sauce and 1 tablespoon sherry in a medium bowl; set aside and toss once or twice as you work on the rest of the recipe.

2. Bring 4 quarts of water to a boil in a large pot. Add the noodles and salt and boil until just tender, 3 to 4 minutes for fresh noodles and 7 to 9 minutes for dried. Drain thoroughly and toss with ½ teaspoon sesame oil.

3. Combine the remaining 2 teaspoons soy sauce, remaining 4 teaspoons sherry, remaining ½ teaspoon sesame oil, the light soy sauce, chicken stock, sugar, red pepper flakes, and 1 tablespoon garlic in a small bowl; set aside.

4. Heat a 12- or 14-inch nonstick skillet over high heat for 3 to 4 minutes. (The pan should be so hot you can hold an outstretched hand 1 inch over the pan for only 3 seconds; see illustration, page 388.) Add 1 tablespoon oil (2 tablespoons for fish) and swirl the oil so that it evenly coats the bottom of the pan. Heat the oil until it just starts to shimmer and smoke.

5. Drain the meat, seafood, or tofu and add to the pan. Stir-fry until seared and about three-quarters cooked, 40 to 60 seconds for fish and scallops; 1 minute for beef, shrimp, and squid; 2 minutes for pork; 2½ minutes for tofu; and 2½ to 3 minutes for chicken. Scrape the cooked meat, seafood, or tofu and all the liquid into a clean bowl. Cover and keep warm.

6. Let the pan come back up to temperature, 1 to 2 minutes. When hot, drizzle in 2 teaspoons oil. When the oil just starts to smoke, add the first batch of long-cooking vegetables. Stir-fry until the vegetables are just tender-crisp, 1 to 2 minutes. Leaving the first batch in the pan, repeat with the remaining vegetables, adding 1 teaspoon oil for each batch and cooking each set until tender-crisp, or wilted for leafy greens.

7. Clear the center of the pan and add the remaining tablespoon garlic and the scallions and ginger. Drizzle with 1 teaspoon oil. Mash into the pan with the back of a spatula. Cook until fragrant but not colored, about 10 seconds. Remove the pan from the heat and stir the garlic, scallions, and ginger into the vegetables for 20 seconds.

8. Return the pan to the heat and add the cooked meat, seafood, or tofu and noodles. Stir in the sauce and stir-fry until the ingredients are well coated with sauce and sizzling hot, about 1 minute. Serve immediately.

Stir-Fried Chinese Noodles with Chicken and Broccoli in Black Bean Sauce

FERMENTED BLACK BEANS IMPART A SLIGHTLY SMOKY, SALTY FLAVOR TO THIS STIR-FRY. THEY ARE AVAILABLE IN ASIAN GROCERIES AND SHOULD LOOK MOIST AND SOFT TO THE TOUCH. DON'T BUY BEANS THAT ARE DRIED OUT. FERMENTED BLACK BEANS CAN BE STORED IN AN AIRTIGHT CONTAINER IN THE REFRIGERATOR FOR SEVERAL WEEKS. SERVES 4.

- ¾ pound boneless, skinless chicken breasts, cut into uniform pieces (see illustrations 1–3, page 392)
- 2 tablespoons soy sauce
- 3 tablespoons dry sherry
- 1½ pounds broccoli, florets broken into bite-size pieces, stems peeled and cut into 3½-inch strips (see illustrations 1–2, page 140)
- 1 tablespoon salt
- 12 ounces dried Chinese wheat or fresh egg noodles (the width of spaghetti)
- 1 tablespoon plus ½ teaspoon Asian sesame oil
- ½ cup chicken stock or low-sodium canned broth
- ½ teaspoon sugar
- ¼ teaspoon ground black pepper
- 1 tablespoon Chinese fermented black beans
- 2 tablespoons peanut or vegetable oil
- 1 tablespoon minced garlic
- 2 tablespoons minced scallions, white parts only
- 1 tablespoon minced fresh gingerroot (see illustrations 1–3, page 43)

1. Toss the chicken with 1 tablespoon soy sauce and 1 tablespoon sherry in a medium bowl; set aside and toss once or twice as you work on the rest of the recipe.

2. Bring 4 quarts of water to a boil in a large pot. Add the broccoli and salt and cook until tender-crisp, about 2 minutes. Use a slotted spoon to transfer broccoli to a bowl. Add the noodles to the water and boil until just tender, 3 to 4 minutes for fresh noodles and 7 to 9 minutes for dried. Drain thoroughly and toss with ½ teaspoon sesame oil.

3. Combine the remaining tablespoon soy sauce, remaining 2 tablespoons sherry, remaining tablespoon sesame oil, the stock, sugar, pepper, and black beans in a small bowl; set aside.

4. Heat a 12- or 14-inch nonstick skillet over high heat for 3 to 4 minutes. (The pan should be so hot you can hold an outstretched hand 1 inch over the pan for only 3 seconds; see illustration, page 388.) Add 1 tablespoon oil and swirl the oil so that it evenly coats the bottom of the pan. Heat the oil until it just starts to shimmer and smoke.

5. Drain the chicken and add to the pan. Stir-fry until seared and about brown, 2½ to 3 minutes. Scrape the cooked chicken and all the liquid into a clean bowl. Cover and keep warm.

6. Let the pan come back up to temperature, 1 to 2 minutes. When hot, drizzle in 2 teaspoons oil. When the oil just starts to smoke, add the broccoli. Stir-fry until the just tender-crisp, 1 to 2 minutes.

7. Clear the center of the pan and add the garlic, scallions, and ginger. Drizzle with 1 teaspoon oil. Mash into the pan with the back of a spatula. Cook until fragrant but not colored, about 10 seconds. Remove the pan from the heat and stir the scallions, garlic, and ginger into the broccoli for 20 seconds.

8. Return the pan to the heat and add the cooked chicken and noodles. Stir in the sauce and stir-fry until the ingredients are well coated with sauce and sizzling hot, about 1 minute. Serve immediately.

Stir-Fried Chinese Noodles with Chicken in Szechwan Chile Sauce

SALTED OR NATURAL PEANUTS MAY BE USED IN THIS
RECIPE. SERVES 4 TO 6.

¾ pound boneless, skinless chicken
  breast, cut into uniform pieces (see
  illustrations 1–3, page 392)
2 tablespoons soy sauce
¼ cup dry sherry
12 ounces dried Chinese wheat or fresh
  egg noodles (the width of spaghetti)
1 tablespoon salt
1 tablespoon plus ½ teaspoon Asian
  sesame oil
½ cup chicken stock or low-sodium
  canned broth
2 tablespoons chili paste
¼ teaspoon toasted and ground
  Szechwan peppercorns (see headnote,
  page 395)
¼ teaspoon sugar
2 tablespoons plus 2 teaspoons peanut or
  vegetable oil
8 celery stalks, sliced thin on the bias
  (see illustration, page 399)
2 tablespoons minced scallions, white
  parts only
1 tablespoon minced garlic
1 tablespoon minced fresh gingerroot (see
  illustrations 1–3, page 43)
½ cup peanuts

1. Toss the chicken with 1 tablespoon soy sauce and 1 tablespoon sherry in a medium bowl; set aside and toss once or twice as you work on the rest of the recipe.

2. Bring 4 quarts of water to a boil in a large pot. Add the noodles and salt and boil until just tender, 3 to 4 minutes for fresh and 7 to 9 minutes for dried. Drain thoroughly and toss with ½ teaspoon sesame oil.

3. Combine the remaining 1 tablespoon soy sauce, remaining 3 tablespoons sherry, remaining 1 tablespoon sesame oil, the stock, chili paste, peppercorns, and sugar in a small bowl; set aside.

4. Heat a 12- or 14-inch nonstick skillet over high heat for 3 to 4 minutes. (The pan should be so hot you can hold an outstretched hand 1 inch over the pan for only 3 seconds; see illustration, page 388.) Add 1 tablespoon oil and swirl the oil so that it evenly coats the bottom of the pan. Heat the oil until it just starts to shimmer and smoke.

5. Drain the chicken and add to the pan. Stir-fry until slightly browned, 2½ to 3 minutes. Scrape the cooked chicken and all the liquid into a clean bowl. Cover and keep warm.

6. Let the pan come back up to temperature, 1 to 2 minutes. When hot, drizzle in 2 teaspoons oil. When the oil just starts to smoke, add half the celery. Stir-fry until just tender-crisp, 1½ to 2 minutes. Scrape into the bowl, drizzle 2 teaspoons oil into the pan, and cook the remaining celery. Return the first batch of celery to the pan.

7. Clear the center of the pan and add the scallions, garlic, and ginger. Drizzle with 1 teaspoon oil. Mash into the pan with the back of a spatula. Cook until fragrant but not colored, about 10 seconds. Remove the pan from the heat and stir the scallions, garlic, and ginger into the vegetables for 20 seconds.

8. Return the pan to the heat and add the cooked chicken and noodles. Stir in the sauce and peanuts, and stir-fry until the ingredients are well coated with sauce and sizzling hot, about 1 minute. Serve immediately.

SLICING CHICKEN FOR STIR-FRIES

Stir-Fried Chinese Noodles with Beef and Shiitakes in Hoisin Sauce

HOISIN SAUCE IS QUITE SWEET ON ITS OWN, SO WE OMIT THE SUGAR WHEN USING IT IN STIR-FRIES. SERVES 4.

> ¾ pound flank steak, sliced thin (see illustrations 1–2, page 393)
> 2 tablespoons soy sauce
> 3 tablespoons dry sherry
> 12 ounces dried Chinese wheat or fresh egg noodles (the width of spaghetti)
> 1 tablespoon salt
> 1 tablespoon plus ½ teaspoon Asian sesame oil
> ½ cup chicken stock or low-sodium canned broth
> 2 tablespoons hoisin sauce
> 2 tablespoons peanut or vegetable oil
> ½ pound shiitake mushrooms, stemmed and sliced thin
> ½ pound snow peas, stringed
> 1 tablespoon minced garlic
> 2 tablespoons minced scallions, white parts only
> 1 tablespoon minced fresh gingerroot (see illustrations 1–3, page 43)

1. To produce uniform pieces of chicken (that will cook at the same rate), separate the tenderloins from partially frozen skinless, boneless breasts.

2. Slice the breasts across the grain into ½-inch-wide strips. Cut the strips crosswise to yield pieces that are about 1 inch long.

3. Cut the tenderloins on the diagonal to produce pieces about the same size as the strips of breast meat.

1. Toss the flank steak with 1 tablespoon soy sauce and 1 tablespoon sherry in a medium bowl; set aside and toss once or twice as you work on the rest of the recipe.

2. Bring 4 quarts of water to a boil in a large pot. Add the noodles and salt and boil until just tender, 3 to 4 minutes for fresh noodles and 7 to 9 minutes for dried. Drain thoroughly and toss with ½ teaspoon sesame oil.

3. Combine the remaining tablespoon soy sauce, remaining 2 tablespoons sherry, remaining tablespoon sesame oil, the stock, and hoisin sauce in a small bowl; set aside.

4. Heat a 12- or 14-inch nonstick skillet over high heat for 3 to 4 minutes. (The pan should be so hot you can hold an outstretched hand 1 inch over the pan for only 3 seconds; see illustration, page 388.) Add 1 tablespoon oil and swirl the oil so that it evenly coats the bottom of the pan. Heat the oil until it just starts to shimmer and smoke.

5. Drain the flank steak and add to the pan. Stir-fry until seared, about 1 minute. Scrape the cooked steak and all the liquid into a clean bowl. Cover and keep warm.

6. Let the pan come back up to temperature, 1 to 2 minutes. When hot, drizzle in 2 teaspoons oil. When the oil just starts to smoke, add the mushrooms. Stir-fry until the mushrooms begin to soften, 1 minute. Add the snow peas and stir-fry until just tender-crisp, about 1 minute.

7. Clear the center of the pan and add the garlic, scallions, and ginger. Drizzle with 1 teaspoon oil. Mash into the pan with the back of a spatula. Cook until fragrant but not colored, about 10 seconds. Remove the pan from the heat and stir the scallions, garlic, and ginger into the vegetables for 20 seconds.

8. Return the pan to the heat and add the cooked flank steak and noodles. Stir in the sauce and stir-fry until the ingredients are well coated with sauce and sizzling hot, about 1 minute. Serve immediately.

SLICING FLANK STEAK FOR STIR-FRIES

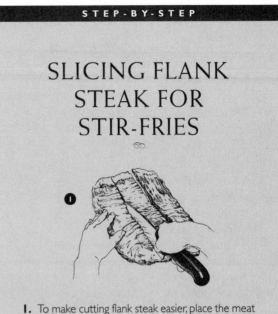

1. To make cutting flank steak easier, place the meat in the freezer for 15 minutes. Once the meat is firm, slice partially frozen flank steak into 2-inch-wide pieces. For most flank steaks, this means cutting the steak lengthwise into three pieces.

2. Cut each piece of flank steak against the grain into very thin slices, no more than ¼ inch thick.

Stir-Fried Chinese Noodles with Beef and Eggplant in Oyster Sauce

THE EGGPLANT MUST BE COOKED IN TWO BATCHES TO KEEP THE PAN FROM LOSING HEAT. IF YOU LIKE, ADD 1 TEASPOON MINCED FRESH HOT PEPPER WITH THE GARLIC AND GINGER. SERVES 4.

12 ounces flank steak, sliced thin (see illustrations 1–2, page 393)

2 tablespoons soy sauce

¼ cup dry sherry

12 ounces dried Chinese wheat or fresh egg noodles (the width of spaghetti)

1 tablespoon salt

1 tablespoon plus ½ teaspoon Asian sesame oil

2 tablespoons oyster sauce

½ cup chicken stock or low-sodium canned broth

½ teaspoon sugar

¼ teaspoon ground black pepper

3 tablespoons plus 1 teaspoon peanut or vegetable oil

1 medium eggplant (about 1 pound), cut into ¾-inch cubes

1 red bell pepper, stemmed, seeded, and cut into 3-by-½-inch strips

3 medium scallions, green parts cut into ¼-inch lengths and white parts minced

2 tablespoons minced garlic

1 tablespoon minced fresh gingerroot (see illustrations 1–3, page 43)

1. Toss the flank steak with 1 tablespoon soy sauce and 1 tablespoon sherry in a medium bowl; set aside and toss once or twice as you work on the rest of the recipe.

2. Bring 4 quarts of water to a boil in a large pot. Add the noodles and salt and boil until just tender, 3 to 4 minutes for fresh noodles and 7 to 9 minutes for dried. Drain thoroughly and toss with ½ teaspoon sesame oil.

3. Combine the remaining 1 tablespoon soy sauce, remaining 3 tablespoons sherry, remaining 1 tablespoon sesame oil, the oyster sauce, stock, sugar, and pepper in a small bowl; set aside.

4. Heat a 12- or 14-inch nonstick skillet over high heat for 3 to 4 minutes. (The pan should be so hot you can hold an outstretched hand 1 inch over the pan for only 3 seconds; see illustration, page 388.) Add 1 tablespoon oil and swirl the oil so that it evenly coats the bottom of the pan. Heat the oil until it just starts to shimmer and smoke.

5. Drain the flank steak and add to the pan. Stir-fry until seared, about 1 minute. Scrape the cooked flank steak and all the liquid into a clean bowl. Cover and keep warm.

6. Let the pan come back up to temperature, 1 to 2 minutes. When hot, drizzle in 1 tablespoon oil. When the oil just starts to smoke, add half the eggplant. Stir-fry until just tender-crisp, 1 to 2 minutes. Scrape into the bowl, drizzle in another tablespoon oil, and cook the remaining eggplant. Return the first batch of eggplant to the pan, add the bell pepper, and stir-fry 1 minute. Add the scallion greens and cook 15 to 30 seconds.

7. Clear the center of the pan and add the garlic, scallion whites, and ginger. Drizzle with 1 teaspoon oil. Mash into the pan with the back of a spatula. Cook until fragrant but not colored, about 10 seconds. Remove the pan from the heat and stir the garlic and ginger into the vegetables for 20 seconds.

8. Return the pan to the heat and add the cooked flank steak and noodles. Stir in the sauce and stir-fry until the ingredients are well coated with sauce and sizzling hot, about 1 minute. Serve immediately.

Stir-Fried Chinese Noodles with Pork and Spinach in Szechwan Chile Sauce

CHILI PASTE AND SZECHWAN PEPPERCORNS GIVE THIS STIR-FRY QUITE A LOT OF HEAT. TOAST THE PEPPERCORNS IN A SMALL SKILLET OVER MEDIUM-HIGH HEAT FOR 1 TO 2 MINUTES BEFORE GRINDING THEM IN A SPICE MILL OR COFFEE GRINDER FOR MAXIMUM FLAVOR. SERVES 4.

¾ pound pork tenderloin, trimmed of fat and shredded (see illustrations 1–2, page 397)
2 tablespoons soy sauce
¼ cup dry sherry
12 ounces dried Chinese wheat or fresh egg noodles (the width of spaghetti)
1 tablespoon salt
1 tablespoon plus ½ teaspoon Asian sesame oil
½ cup chicken stock or low-sodium canned broth
2 teaspoons chili paste
¼ teaspoon toasted and ground Szechwan peppercorns (see headnote)
¼ teaspoon sugar
4 tablespoons peanut or vegetable oil
2 pounds stemmed spinach leaves, washed and thoroughly dried
1 tablespoon minced garlic
2 tablespoons minced scallions, white parts only
1 tablespoon minced fresh gingerroot (see illustrations 1–3, page 43)

1. Toss the pork tenderloin with 1 tablespoon soy sauce and 1 tablespoon sherry in a medium bowl; set aside and toss once or twice as you work on the rest of the recipe.

2. Bring 4 quarts of water to a boil in a large pot. Add the noodles and salt and boil until just tender, 3 to 4 minutes for fresh noodles and 7 to 9 minutes for dried. Drain thoroughly and toss with ½ teaspoon sesame oil.

3. Combine the remaining 1 tablespoon soy sauce, remaining 3 tablespoons sherry, remaining 1 tablespoon sesame oil, the stock, chili paste, Szechwan peppercorns, and sugar in a small bowl; set aside.

4. Heat a 12- or 14-inch nonstick skillet over high heat for 3 to 4 minutes. (The pan should be so hot you can hold an outstretched hand 1 inch over the pan for only 3 seconds; see illustration, page 388.) Add 1 tablespoon oil and swirl the oil so that it evenly coats the bottom of the pan. Heat the oil until it just starts to shimmer and smoke.

5. Drain the pork tenderloin and add to the pan. Stir-fry until seared, about 2 minutes. Scrape the cooked pork and all the liquid into a clean bowl. Cover and keep warm.

6. Let the pan come back up to temperature, 1 to 2 minutes. When hot, drizzle in 2 teaspoons oil. When the oil just starts to smoke, add one-quarter of the spinach. Stir-fry until just wilted, 45 to 60 seconds. Scrape into the bowl with the pork and repeat with the remaining 3 batches of spinach, drizzling 2 teaspoons oil into the pan before adding the spinach.

7. Remove the last batch of spinach, and add the garlic, scallions, and ginger to the pan. Drizzle with 1 teaspoon oil. Mash into the pan with the back of a spatula. Cook until fragrant but not colored, about 10 seconds.

8. Add the cooked flank steak, spinach, and noodles. Stir in the sauce and stir-fry until the ingredients are well coated with sauce and sizzling hot, about 1 minute. Serve immediately.

PREPARING BOK CHOY

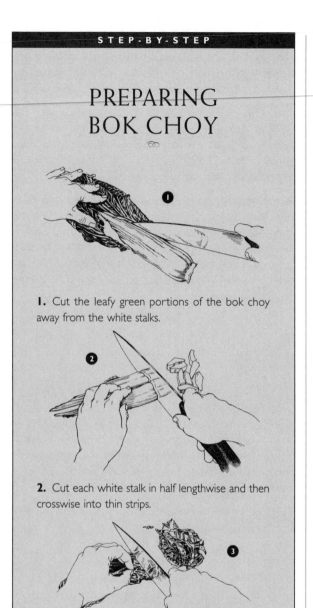

1. Cut the leafy green portions of the bok choy away from the white stalks.

2. Cut each white stalk in half lengthwise and then crosswise into thin strips.

3. Stack and loosely roll the leafy greens. Slice them crosswise into thin strips. Keep the sliced stalks and leaves separate.

Stir-Fried Chinese Noodles with Pork, Bok Choy, Mushrooms, and Sprouts

BOK CHOY STALKS TAKE MUCH LONGER TO SOFTEN THAN THE TENDER GREENS, SO SEPARATE THEM WHILE SLICING THE BOK CHOY (SEE ILLUSTRATIONS 1–3) AND ADD EACH PART TO THE PAN AT THE APPROPRIATE TIME. THE DRIED MUSHROOMS WILL NEED TO SOAK FOR ABOUT 20 MINUTES, SO PLAN ACCORDINGLY. SERVES 4.

- ¾ pound pork tenderloin, trimmed of fat and shredded (see illustrations 1–2, page 397)
- 1 tablespoon plus 2 teaspoons soy sauce
- 2 tablespoons plus 1 teaspoon dry sherry
- 12 ounces dried Chinese wheat or fresh egg noodles (the width of spaghetti)
- 1 tablespoon salt
- 1 teaspoon Asian sesame oil
- 3 tablespoons light soy sauce
- ½ cup chicken stock or low-sodium canned broth
- ½ teaspoon sugar
- ¼ teaspoon hot red pepper flakes
- 2 tablespoons very finely minced garlic
- 2 tablespoons peanut or vegetable oil
- 1 pound bok choy, stalks and greens separated and sliced thin (see illustrations 1–3)
- 5 dried Chinese black mushrooms or dried shiitake mushrooms, rehydrated in 2 cups hot water until softened, strained, and finely chopped
- 2 cups mung bean sprouts
- 2 tablespoons minced scallions, white parts only
- 1 tablespoon minced fresh gingerroot (see illustrations 1–3, page 43)

1. Toss the pork with 1 tablespoon soy sauce and 1 tablespoon sherry in a medium bowl; set aside and toss once or twice as you work on the rest of the recipe.

2. Bring 4 quarts of water to a boil in a large pot. Add the noodles and salt and boil until just tender, 3 to 4 minutes for fresh noodles and 7 to 9 minutes for dried. Drain thoroughly and toss with ½ teaspoon sesame oil.

3. Combine the remaining 2 teaspoons soy sauce, remaining 4 teaspoons sherry, remaining ½ teaspoon sesame oil, the light soy sauce, stock, sugar, red pepper flakes, and 1 tablespoon garlic in a small bowl; set aside.

4. Heat a 12- or 14-inch nonstick skillet over high heat for 3 to 4 minutes. (The pan should be so hot you can hold an outstretched hand 1 inch over the pan for only 3 seconds; see illustration, page 388.) Add 1 tablespoon oil and swirl the oil so that it evenly coats the bottom of the pan. Heat the oil until it just starts to shimmer and smoke.

5. Drain the pork and add to the pan. Stir-fry until seared, about 2 minutes. Scrape the cooked pork and all the liquid into a clean bowl. Cover and keep warm.

6. Let the pan come back up to temperature, 1 to 2 minutes. When hot, drizzle in 2 teaspoons oil. When the oil just starts to smoke, add the bok choy stalks. Stir-fry until just tender-crisp, 1 to 2 minutes. Add the bok choy greens, mushrooms, and bean sprouts and stir-fry an additional 30 seconds.

7. Clear the center of the pan and add the scallions, remaining tablespoon garlic, and ginger. Drizzle with 1 teaspoon oil. Mash into the pan with the back of a spatula. Cook until fragrant but not colored, about 10 seconds. Remove the pan from the heat and stir the scallions, garlic, and ginger into the vegetables for 20 seconds.

8. Return the pan to the heat and add the cooked pork and noodles. Stir in the sauce and stir-fry until the ingredients are well coated with sauce and sizzling hot, about 1 minute. Serve immediately.

SHREDDING PORK FOR STIR-FRIES

1. We find that the tenderloin is the best pork cut for stir-fries because it is tender and cooks so quickly. To shred the pork, freeze the tenderloin until firm, 15 to 30 minutes. Cut the partially frozen tenderloin crosswise into ¼-inch-thick medallions.

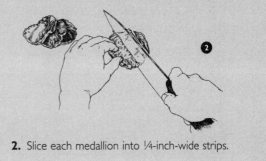

2. Slice each medallion into ¼-inch-wide strips.

Stir-Fried Chinese Noodles with Shrimp, Scallions, and Peppers

SCALLIONS ARE USED AS A VEGETABLE IN THIS RECIPE. YOU WILL NEED FOUR OR FIVE BUNCHES, ABOUT ¾ POUND. SERVES 4.

- ¾ pound medium shrimp, peeled and deveined if desired
- 1 tablespoon plus 2 teaspoons soy sauce
- 2 tablespoons plus 1 teaspoon dry sherry
- 12 ounces dried Chinese wheat or fresh egg noodles (the width of spaghetti)
- 1 tablespoon salt
- 1 teaspoon Asian sesame oil
- 3 tablespoons light soy sauce
- ½ cup chicken stock or low-sodium canned broth
- ½ teaspoon sugar
- ¼ teaspoon hot red pepper flakes
- 2 tablespoons very finely minced garlic
- 2 tablespoons peanut or vegetable oil
- 1 cup scallion whites, sliced into 1-inch pieces
- 2 medium red bell peppers, stemmed, seeded, and cut into 1-inch cubes
- 1½ cups scallion greens, sliced into ½-inch pieces
- 2 tablespoons minced scallions, white parts only
- 1 tablespoon minced fresh gingerroot (see illustrations 1–3, page 43)

1. Toss the shrimp with 1 tablespoon soy sauce and 1 tablespoon sherry in a medium bowl; set aside and toss once or twice as you work on the rest of the recipe.

2. Bring 4 quarts of water to a boil in a large pot. Add the noodles and salt and boil until just tender, 3 to 4 minutes for fresh noodles and 7 to 9 minutes for dried. Drain thoroughly and toss with ½ teaspoon sesame oil.

3. Combine the remaining 2 teaspoons soy sauce, remaining 4 teaspoons sherry, remaining ½ teaspoon sesame oil, the light soy sauce, stock, sugar, red pepper flakes, and 1 tablespoon garlic in a small bowl; set aside.

4. Heat a 12- or 14-inch nonstick skillet over high heat for 3 to 4 minutes. (The pan should be so hot you can hold an outstretched hand 1 inch over the pan for only 3 seconds; see illustration, page 388.) Add 1 tablespoon oil and swirl the oil so that it evenly coats the bottom of the pan. Heat the oil until it just starts to shimmer and smoke.

5. Drain the shrimp and add to the pan. Stir-fry until seared, about 1 minute. Scrape the cooked shrimp and all the liquid into a clean bowl. Cover and keep warm.

6. Let the pan come back up to temperature, 1 to 2 minutes. When hot, drizzle in 2 teaspoons oil. When the oil just starts to smoke, add the sliced scallion whites and cook 1 to 2 minutes. Add the bell peppers and cook 1 minute. Add the scallion greens and cook 30 seconds.

7. Clear the center of the pan and add the minced scallions, remaining tablespoon garlic, and ginger. Drizzle with ½ teaspoon oil. Mash into the pan with the back of a spatula. Cook until fragrant but not colored, about 10 seconds. Remove the pan from the heat and stir the scallions, garlic, and ginger into the vegetables for 20 seconds.

8. Return the pan to the heat and add the shrimp and noodles. Stir in the sauce and stir-fry until the ingredients are well coated with sauce and sizzling hot, about 1 minute. Serve immediately.

Stir-Fried Chinese Noodles with Shrimp in Hot-and-Sour Sauce

CELERY AND WATER CHESTNUTS ADD CRUNCH TO THIS CLASSIC STIR-FRY. YOU MAY USE EITHER SALTED OR NATURAL CASHEWS. SERVES 4 TO 6.

- ¾ pound medium shrimp, peeled and deveined if desired
- 2 tablespoons soy sauce
- 1 tablespoon dry sherry
- 12 ounces dried Chinese wheat or fresh egg noodles (the width of spaghetti)
- 1 tablespoon salt
- ½ teaspoon Asian sesame oil
- 3 tablespoons cider vinegar
- ½ cup chicken stock or low-sodium canned broth
- 2 teaspoons sugar
- 1½ tablespoons minced jalapeño or other fresh chile
- 2 tablespoons plus ½ teaspoon peanut or vegetable oil
- 3 celery stalks, sliced thin on the bias (see illustration)
- 2 8-ounce cans whole water chestnuts, drained and halved crosswise
- 2 tablespoons minced scallions, white parts only
- 1 tablespoon minced garlic
- 1 tablespoon minced fresh gingerroot (see illustrations 1–3, page 43)
- ½ cup cashews

1. Toss the shrimp with 1 tablespoon soy sauce and the sherry in a medium bowl; set aside and toss once or twice as you work on the rest of the recipe.

2. Bring 4 quarts of water to a boil in a large pot. Add the noodles and salt and boil until just tender, 3 to 4 minutes for fresh noodles and 7 to 9 minutes for dried. Drain thoroughly and toss with the sesame oil.

3. Combine the remaining tablespoon soy sauce, the vinegar, stock, sugar, and jalapeño in a small bowl; set aside.

4. Heat a 12- or 14-inch nonstick skillet over high heat for 3 to 4 minutes. (The pan should be so hot you can hold an outstretched hand 1 inch over the pan for only 3 seconds; see illustration, page 388.) Add 1 tablespoon oil and swirl the oil so that it evenly coats the bottom of the pan. Heat the oil until it just starts to shimmer and smoke.

5. Drain the shrimp and add to the pan. Stir-fry until bright pink, about 1 minute. Scrape into a clean bowl. Drizzle 1 tablespoon oil into the pan. Add the celery and cook 1 minute. Add the water chestnuts and cook 1 minute.

6. Clear the center of the pan and add the scallions, garlic, and ginger. Drizzle with ½ teaspoon oil. Mash into the pan with the back of a spatula. Cook until fragrant but not colored, about 10 seconds. Remove the pan from the heat and stir the scallions, garlic, and ginger into the vegetables for 20 seconds.

7. Return the pan to the heat and add the cooked shrimp and noodles. Stir in the sauce and cashews and stir-fry until the ingredients are well coated with sauce and sizzling hot, about 1 minute. Serve immediately.

STEP-BY-STEP

SLICING CELERY

To cut long, thin vegetables such as celery on the bias, hold the knife at a 45-degree angle to the celery as you slice. This cutting technique maximizes the surface area of the vegetable and promotes fast cooking.

Stir-Fried Chinese Noodles with Squid in Black Bean Sauce

IF YOU CAN, BUY CLEANED SQUID AND SIMPLY CUT IT INTO ½-INCH RINGS. OTHERWISE, BUY 1¼ POUNDS UNCLEANED SQUID AND SEE PAGE 256 FOR INFORMATION ON CLEANING IT YOURSELF. SERVES 4 TO 6.

- ¾ pound cleaned squid, cut into ½-inch rings
- 2 tablespoons soy sauce
- 3 tablespoons dry sherry
- 12 ounces dried Chinese wheat or fresh egg noodles (the width of spaghetti)
- 1 tablespoon salt
- 1 tablespoon plus ½ teaspoon Asian sesame oil
- ½ cup chicken stock or low-sodium canned broth
- ½ teaspoon sugar
- ¼ teaspoon freshly ground black pepper
- 1 tablespoon Chinese fermented black beans
- 2 tablespoons plus ½ teaspoon peanut or vegetable oil
- 2 celery stalks, halved lengthwise and sliced thin on the bias (see illustration, page 399)
- ¼ pound small shiitake mushrooms, stemmed and left whole (about 2 cups)
- 1 medium summer squash, quartered lengthwise and cut crosswise into ½-inch-thick triangles
- ½ pound sugar snap peas, stringed (about 3 cups)
- 2 tablespoons minced scallions, white parts only
- 1 tablespoon minced garlic
- 1 tablespoon minced fresh gingerroot (see illustrations 1–3, page 43)

1. Toss the squid with 1 tablespoon soy sauce and 1 tablespoon sherry in a medium bowl; set aside and toss once or twice as you work on the rest of the recipe.

2. Bring 4 quarts of water to a boil in a large pot. Add the noodles and salt and boil until just tender, 3 to 4 minutes for fresh noodles and 7 to 9 minutes for dried. Drain thoroughly and toss with ½ teaspoon sesame oil.

3. Combine the remaining 1 tablespoon soy sauce, remaining 2 tablespoons sherry, remaining 1 tablespoon sesame oil, the stock, sugar, pepper, and black beans in a small bowl; set aside.

4. Heat a 12- or 14-inch nonstick skillet over high heat for 3 to 4 minutes. (The pan should be so hot you can hold an outstretched hand 1 inch over the pan for only 3 seconds; see illustration, page 388.) Add 1 tablespoon oil and swirl the oil so that it evenly coats the bottom of the pan. Heat the oil until it just starts to shimmer and smoke.

5. Drain the squid and add it to the pan. Stir-fry until opaque, about 1 minute. Scrape the cooked squid and all the liquid into a clean bowl. Drizzle 1 tablespoon oil into the pan. Add the celery and cook 1½ minutes. Add the mushrooms and cook 1 minute. Add the squash and stir-fry until seared, about 2 minutes. Add the peas and cook 30 to 60 seconds.

6. Clear the center of the pan and add the scallions, garlic, and ginger. Drizzle with ½ teaspoon oil. Mash into the pan with the back of a spatula. Cook until fragrant but not colored, about 10 seconds. Remove the pan from the heat and stir the scallions, garlic, and ginger into the vegetables for 20 seconds.

7. Return the pan to the heat and add the cooked squid and noodles. Stir in the sauce and stir-fry until the ingredients are well coated with sauce and sizzling hot, about 1 minute. Serve immediately.

Stir-Fried Chinese Noodles with Sea Bass and Vegetables in Spicy Tomato Sauce

FOR THIS RECIPE, CUT THE VEGETABLES INTO VERY THIN STRIPS THAT RESEMBLE MATCHSTICKS OR CONFETTI (SEE ILLUSTRATIONS 1 AND 2, PAGE 404). YOU CAN ASK YOUR FISHMONGER TO SKIN THE FISH. SERVES 4.

- ¾ pound skinned sea bass fillet, cut into 1-inch cubes
- 3 tablespoons soy sauce
- 3 tablespoons dry sherry
- 12 ounces dried Chinese wheat or fresh egg noodles (the width of spaghetti)
- 1 tablespoon salt
- 1 teaspoon Asian sesame oil
- ½ cup chicken stock or low-sodium canned broth
- 3 tablespoons tomato paste
- 2 teaspoons chili paste
- ½ teaspoon toasted and ground Szechwan peppercorns (see headnote, page 395)
- ½ teaspoon sugar
- ½ teaspoon hot red pepper flakes
- 4 tablespoons peanut or vegetable oil
- 2 medium carrots, peeled and julienned (see illustrations 1–2, page 404)
- 1 medium zucchini, julienned (see illustrations 1–2, page 404)
- 1 medium yellow summer squash, julienned (see illustrations 1–2, page 404)
- ½ medium napa cabbage (about ½ pound), shredded
- 2 tablespoons minced scallions, white parts only
- 1 tablespoon minced garlic
- 2 tablespoons minced fresh gingerroot (see illustrations 1–3, page 43)

1. Toss the sea bass with 1 tablespoon soy sauce and 1 tablespoon sherry in a bowl; set aside and toss once or twice as you work on the rest of the recipe.

2. Bring 4 quarts of water to a boil in a large pot. Add the noodles and salt to the water and boil until just tender, 3 to 4 minutes for fresh noodles and 7 to 9 minutes for dried. Drain thoroughly and toss with ½ teaspoon sesame oil.

3. Combine the remaining 2 tablespoons soy sauce, remaining 2 tablespoons sherry, remaining ½ teaspoon sesame oil, the stock, tomato paste, chili paste, Szechwan peppercorns, sugar, and red pepper flakes in a small bowl; set aside.

4. Heat a 12- or 14-inch nonstick skillet over high heat for 3 to 4 minutes. (The pan should be so hot you can hold an outstretched hand 1 inch over the pan for only 3 seconds; see illustration, page 388.) Add 2 tablespoons oil and swirl the oil so that it evenly coats the bottom of the pan. Heat the oil until it just starts to shimmer and smoke.

5. Drain the sea bass and add to the pan. Stir-fry until lightly browned, 40 to 60 seconds. Scrape the cooked sea bass and all the liquid into a clean bowl. Cover and keep warm.

6. Let the pan come back up to temperature, 1 to 2 minutes. When hot, drizzle in 2 teaspoons oil. When the oil just starts to smoke, add the carrots and cook 1 minute. Drizzle in another 2 teaspoons oil, add the zucchini and squash, and cook 15 seconds. Drizzle in another 1½ teaspoons oil, add the cabbage, and cook 15 seconds.

7. Clear the center of the pan and add the scallions, garlic, and ginger. Drizzle with ½ teaspoon oil. Mash into the pan with the back of a spatula. Cook until fragrant but not colored, about 10 seconds. Remove the pan from the heat and stir the scallions, garlic, and ginger into the vegetables for 20 seconds.

8. Return the pan to the heat and add the cooked sea bass and noodles. Stir in the sauce and stir-fry until the ingredients are well coated with sauce and sizzling hot, about 1 minute. Serve immediately.

Stir-Fried Chinese Noodles with Scallops and Asparagus in Lemon Sauce

USE WHOLE BAY SCALLOPS OR CUT SEA SCALLOPS INTO 1-INCH PIECES FOR THIS DISH, WHICH IS FAIRLY SUBTLE AND BENEFITS FROM THE ADDITION OF SALT AND PEPPER JUST BEFORE SERVING. ASPARAGUS BLANCHED FOR 2 MINUTES WILL COOK EVENLY IN A SINGLE BATCH IN THIS DISH. SERVES 4.

¾ pound scallops, tendons removed (see illustration, page 250) and cut if necessary
2 tablespoons soy sauce
1 tablespoon dry sherry
2 pounds asparagus, ends snapped off, sliced on the bias into 2-inch pieces (see illustrations 1–3, page 138)
Salt
12 ounces dried Chinese wheat or fresh egg noodles (the width of spaghetti)
½ teaspoon Asian sesame oil
3 tablespoons lemon juice
½ teaspoon lemon zest
½ cup chicken stock or low-sodium canned broth
2 teaspoons sugar
2 tablespoons peanut or vegetable oil
2 tablespoons minced scallions, white parts only
1 tablespoon minced garlic
1 tablespoon minced fresh gingerroot (see illustrations 1–3, page 43)
¼ cup chopped fresh cilantro leaves
Ground black pepper

1. Toss the scallops with 1 tablespoon soy sauce and the sherry in a medium bowl; set aside and toss once or twice as you work on the rest of the recipe.

2. Bring 4 quarts of water to a boil in a large pot. Add the asparagus and 1 tablespoon salt and cook until tender-crisp, about 2 minutes. Use a slotted spoon to transfer asparagus to a bowl. Add the noodles to the water and boil until just tender, 3 to 4 minutes for fresh noodles and 7 to 9 minutes for dried. Drain thoroughly and toss with the sesame oil.

3. Combine the remaining tablespoon soy sauce, the juice, zest, stock, and sugar in a small bowl; set aside.

4. Heat a 12- or 14-inch nonstick skillet over high heat for 3 to 4 minutes. (The pan should be so hot you can hold an outstretched hand 1 inch over the pan for only 3 seconds; see illustration, page 388.) Add 1 tablespoon oil and swirl the oil so that it evenly coats the bottom of the pan. Heat the oil until it just starts to shimmer and smoke.

5. Drain the scallops and add to the pan. Stir-fry until seared, 40 to 60 seconds. Scrape the cooked scallops and all the liquid into a clean bowl. Cover and keep warm.

6. Let the pan come back up to temperature, 1 to 2 minutes. When hot, drizzle in 2 teaspoons oil. When the oil just starts to smoke, add the asparagus. Stir-fry until just tender-crisp, 1 to 2 minutes.

7. Clear the center of the pan and add the scallions, garlic, and ginger. Drizzle with 1 teaspoon oil. Mash into the pan with the back of a spatula. Cook until fragrant but not colored, about 10 seconds. Remove the pan from the heat and stir the scallions, garlic, and ginger into the asparagus for 20 seconds.

8. Return the pan to the heat and add the cooked scallops and noodles. Stir in the sauce and cilantro and stir-fry until the ingredients are well coated with sauce and sizzling hot, about 1 minute. Add salt and pepper to taste. Serve immediately.

Stir-Fried Chinese Noodles with Green Beans and Ginger

THIS SIMPLE RECIPE GETS ITS FLAVOR FROM AN ABUN-
DANCE OF GINGER. OTHER GREEN VEGETABLES,
INCLUDING ASPARAGUS OR BROCCOLI, CAN BE USED IN
PLACE OF THE BEANS. CUT THE ASPARAGUS IN HALF
LENGTHWISE AND THEN INTO 1½-INCH PIECES; TRIM
THE BROCCOLI FLORETS INTO BITE-SIZE PIECES.
BLANCH EITHER OF THESE FOR 2 MINUTES. **SERVES 4**.

- 1 pound green beans, ends snapped off
  and cut into 1½-inch pieces
- 1 tablespoon salt
- 12 ounces dried Chinese wheat or fresh
  egg noodles (the width of spaghetti)
- 1 tablespoon plus ½ teaspoon Asian
  sesame oil
- ½ cup chicken stock or low-sodium
  canned broth
- 3 tablespoons soy sauce
- 2 tablespoons mirin (Japanese sweet rice
  wine) or sherry
- 1½ tablespoons peanut oil
- 4 medium garlic cloves, minced
- 3 tablespoons minced fresh gingerroot
  (see illustrations 1–3, page 43)
- ¼ cup snipped chives

1. Bring 4 quarts of water to a boil in a large pot. Add the green beans and salt and cook until tender-crisp, about 2 minutes. Use a slotted spoon to transfer beans to a bowl. Add the noodles to the water and boil until just tender, 3 to 4 minutes for fresh noodles and 7 to 9 minutes for dried. Drain thoroughly and toss with ½ teaspoon sesame oil.

2. Combine the remaining tablespoon sesame oil, the stock, soy sauce, and mirin in a small bowl; set aside.

3. Heat a 12- or 14-inch nonstick skillet over high heat for 3 to 4 minutes. (The pan should be so hot you can hold an outstretched hand 1 inch over the pan for only 3 seconds; see illustration, page 388.) Add 4 teaspoons oil and swirl the oil so that it evenly coats the bottom of the pan. Heat the oil until it just starts to shimmer and smoke.

4. When the oil just starts to smoke, add the green beans. Stir-fry until the vegetables are just tender-crisp, 1 to 2 minutes.

5. Clear the center of the pan and add the garlic and ginger. Drizzle with ½ teaspoon oil. Mash into the pan with the back of a spatula. Cook until fragrant but not colored, about 10 seconds. Remove the pan from the heat and stir the garlic and ginger into the green beans for 20 seconds.

6. Return the pan to the heat and add the noodles. Stir in the sauce and chives and stir-fry until the ingredients are well coated with sauce and sizzling hot, about 1 minute. Serve immediately.

Stir-Fried Chinese Noodles with Mixed Vegetables and Sweet-and-Sour Sauce

A QUICK SWEET-AND-SOUR SAUCE IS A NICE COUNTER-POINT TO STIR-FRIED BELL PEPPER, RED ONION, AND ZUCCHINI. IF YOU LIKE, USE PINEAPPLE JUICE IN PLACE OF THE ORANGE JUICE OR SUBSTITUTE EGGPLANT FOR THE ZUCCHINI. SERVES 4.

> 12 ounces dried Chinese wheat or fresh
>   egg noodles (the width of spaghetti)
> 1 tablespoon salt
> ½ teaspoon Asian sesame oil
> ½ cup chicken stock or low-sodium
>   canned broth
> ¼ cup orange juice
> 3 tablespoons red wine vinegar
> 2 tablespoons sugar
> 1 tablespoon soy sauce
> 2 tablespoons peanut oil
> 1 large red onion, halved and sliced thin
> 2 medium zucchini, julienned (see
>   illustrations 1–2)
> 1 yellow or orange bell pepper, stemmed,
>   seeded, and cut into thin strips
> 4 medium garlic cloves, minced
> 1 tablespoon minced fresh gingerroot (see
>   illustrations 1–3, page 43)
> 3 medium whole scallions, sliced thin

1. Bring 4 quarts of water to a boil in a large pot. Add the noodles and salt and boil until just tender, 3 to 4 minutes for fresh noodles and 7 to 9 minutes for dried. Drain thoroughly and toss with the sesame oil.

2. Combine the stock, juice, vinegar, sugar, and soy sauce in a small bowl; set aside.

3. Heat a 12- or 14-inch nonstick skillet over high heat for 3 to 4 minutes. (The pan should be so hot you can hold an outstretched hand 1 inch over the pan for only 3 seconds; see illustration, page 388.) Add 1 tablespoon oil and swirl the oil so that it evenly coats the bottom of the pan. Heat the oil until it just starts to shimmer and smoke.

4. When the oil just starts to smoke, add the onion and stir-fry until softened, about 1½ minutes. Add 1 teaspoon oil and the zucchini and stir-fry until tender, 2 to 3 minutes. Add 1 teaspoon oil and the bell pepper and stir-fry until slightly softened, about 1 minute.

STEP-BY-STEP

CUTTING VEGETABLES INTO JULIENNE

1. Long vegetables such as carrots, zucchini, and summer squash can be cut into thin julienne strips (also called matchsticks) that cook quickly. Start by slicing the vegetables on the bias into rounds.

2. Stack two or three vegetable rounds in a neat pile and cut them into strips that measure about 2 inches long and ¼ inch thick.

5. Clear the center of the pan and add the garlic, ginger, and scallions. Drizzle with 1 teaspoon oil. Mash into the pan with the back of a spatula. Cook until fragrant but not colored, about 10 seconds. Remove the pan from the heat and stir the scallions, garlic, and ginger into the vegetables for 20 seconds.

6. Return the pan to the heat and add the noodles. Stir in the sauce and stir-fry until the ingredients are well coated with sauce and sizzling hot, about 1 minute. Serve immediately.

◆

Stir-Fried Chinese Noodles with Baked Tofu and Hot-and-Sour Sauce

BAKED TOFU IS A QUICK WAY TO ADD FLAVOR AND NUTRITION TO A NOODLE DISH. LOOK FOR VARIOUS FLAVORS OF BAKED TOFU IN THE REFRIGERATOR CASE AT YOUR SUPERMARKET OR NATURAL FOODS STORE. FOR THIS DISH, WE PREFER A SIMPLY FLAVORED BRAND, WITH SOY, SESAME, AND OTHER ASIAN FLAVORINGS (BARBECUED BAKED TOFU MAY TASTE A BIT ODD IN THIS DISH). SERVES 4.

- 12 ounces dried Chinese wheat or fresh egg noodles (the width of spaghetti)
- 1 tablespoon salt
- 1 tablespoon plus ½ teaspoon Asian sesame oil
- ½ cup chicken stock or low-sodium canned broth
- 3 tablespoons rice wine vinegar
- 2 tablespoons soy sauce
- 2 teaspoons sugar
- 1 teaspoon hot red pepper flakes
- 2 tablespoons peanut or vegetable oil
- 8 ounces baked flavored tofu, cut into ½-inch cubes
- ½ pound snow peas, ends snapped off
- 4 medium garlic cloves, minced
- 4 medium whole scallions, sliced thin

1. Bring 4 quarts of water to a boil in a large pot. Add the noodles and salt and boil until just tender, 3 to 4 minutes for fresh noodles and 7 to 9 minutes for dried. Drain thoroughly and toss with ½ teaspoon sesame oil.

2. Combine the remaining tablespoon sesame oil, the stock, vinegar, soy sauce, sugar, and red pepper flakes in a small bowl; set aside.

3. Heat a 12- or 14-inch nonstick skillet over high heat for 3 to 4 minutes. (The pan should be so hot you can hold an outstretched hand 1 inch over the pan for only 3 seconds; see illustration, page 388.) Add 1 tablespoon oil and swirl the oil so that it evenly coats the bottom of the pan. Heat the oil until it just starts to shimmer and smoke.

4. When the oil just starts to smoke, add the tofu. Stir-fry until browned on all sides, about 2½ minutes. Add the snow peas and 2 teaspoons oil and stir-fry until tender-crisp, 30 to 60 seconds.

5. Clear the center of the pan and add the garlic and scallions. Drizzle with 1 teaspoon oil. Mash into the pan with the back of a spatula. Cook until fragrant but not colored, about 10 seconds. Remove the pan from the heat and stir the scallions and garlic into the tofu and peas for 20 seconds.

6. Return the pan to the heat and add the noodles. Stir in the sauce and stir-fry until the ingredients are well coated with sauce and sizzling hot, about 1 minute. Serve immediately.

Pan-Fried Noodle Cakes

COOKED NOODLES CAN be formed into rounds and browned on both sides to make crisp noodle cakes. In our testing, we found that dried wheat noodles don't hold up all that well when cooked this way—they dry out and become very brittle. Fresh egg noodles are softer, allowing the outside of the browned cake to become crisp while the inside is tender and soft. A crispy noodle cake can take the place of steamed white rice or stir-fried noodles as an accompaniment to any stir-fry.

◆

Crispy Noodle Cake

A NONSTICK SKILLET IS ESSENTIAL FOR EASY TURNING. RATHER THAN ATTEMPTING TO FLIP THE CAKE OVER IN ONE DIFFICULT MOVE, SLIDE IT ONTO A PLATE, INVERT IT ONTO ANOTHER, AND THEN SLIDE THE CAKE, BROWNED SIDE UP, BACK INTO THE PAN. FOR BEST RESULTS, MAKE THE CAKE ABOUT ¾ INCH THICK—ANY THINNER AND IT MAY DRY OUT OR BE DIFFICULT TO TURN. WE DON'T RECOMMEND ADDING OTHER INGREDIENTS LIKE SCALLIONS OR GARLIC TO THE CAKE, SINCE THEY WILL JUST BURN. SERVE THIS CAKE WITH ANY OF THE STIR-FRY RECIPES ON PAGES 388 THROUGH 405, OMITTING THE NOODLES AND CHICKEN STOCK FROM THE STIR-FRY RECIPES. SERVES 4 TO 6.

> 1 pound Chinese fresh egg noodles (the width of spaghetti)
> 1 tablespoon salt
> 1 tablespoon soy sauce
> 2 teaspoons Asian sesame oil
> 2 tablespoons peanut oil, plus more if necessary

1. Bring 6 quarts of water to a boil in a large pot. Add the noodles and salt and cook until the noodles are just tender, 3 to 4 minutes. Drain thoroughly and toss with the soy sauce and sesame oil.

2. Heat 1 tablespoon peanut oil in a 10-inch nonstick skillet over medium-high heat. Add the noodles and spread evenly across the bottom of the pan. Press down with a spatula to flatten (see illustration 1, page 407). Cook until golden brown on the bottom, 5 to 7 minutes.

3. Slide the noodle cake onto a plate (see illustration 2, page 407). Add the remaining tablespoon peanut oil to the pan. Invert the cake onto another plate and slide it, browned-side-up, back into the pan (see illustration 3, page 407). Cook until golden brown on the bottom, 4 to 5 minutes. Slide the noodle cake onto a plate. (It can be covered with foil and kept warm in a 200-degree oven for 15 minutes.) Cut the noodle cake into 4 wedges and serve with any stir-fry recipe.

COOKING A PAN-FRIED NOODLE CAKE

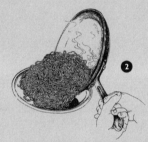

1. Spread the cooked noodles evenly across the bottom of a 10-inch nonstick skillet. Press down on the noodles with a spatula to flatten them.

2. When the bottom of the noodle cake has turned golden brown, slide the noodle cake onto a large plate.

3. Invert the noodle cake onto a second plate and then slide it, browned side up, back into the hot skillet. Brown on the second side and then slice and serve.

Cold Sesame Noodles

COLD SESAME NOODLES are a popular Chinese restaurant item and are easy to make at home as long as you have fresh egg noodles. The noodles are simply boiled, oiled, chilled, and then tossed with a smooth dressing.

Traditional recipes call for Chinese sesame paste, which is available only in Asian food stores. We tested both tahini (a Middle Eastern sesame paste sold in supermarkets) and peanut butter to see if either could be used as a substitute. We found that smooth peanut butter has a stronger nut flavor that comes closer to the flavor of Chinese sesame paste. Tahini has a nice creamy texture but the nut flavor is rather muted. Choose a smooth peanut butter made without sugar (look for a natural brand) for the best results.

We have found that mixing the pasta with the sauce and then refrigerating for any amount of time results in a rather dry and sticky mixture, no matter how much oil and water the sauce contains. It is best to mix the sauce with the chilled and oiled pasta just before serving to insure the creamiest result.

Cold Sesame Noodles

SERVES 4 TO 6

SMOOTH PEANUT BUTTER (a natural brand without added sugar) is actually a better substitute for difficult-to-find Chinese sesame paste than the some-what bland Middle Eastern–style tahini, which is why we use it here. If you can find real Chinese sesame paste, by all means use it. We like some heat in the sauce (it helps cut some of the richness), but you may omit the hot sauce if you prefer. Toasting the sesame seeds in a dry skillet until they achieve a rich golden color will boost their flavor.

- 1 pound fresh Chinese egg noodles (the width of spaghetti)
- 1 tablespoon salt
- 2 tablespoons Asian sesame oil
- 1/2 cup smooth natural peanut butter
- 3 tablespoons soy sauce
- 1 tablespoon sugar
- 1 tablespoon rice wine vinegar
- 1/2 teaspoon hot sauce, such as chili paste or Tabasco, or more to taste
- 1/2 cup hot water, or more

- 4 scallions, white and light green parts, finely chopped
- 2 tablespoons sesame seeds, toasted

1. Bring 6 quarts of water to a boil in a large pot. Add the noodles and salt and cook until the noodles are just tender, 3 to 4 minutes. Drain thoroughly and toss with the sesame oil. Refrigerate until ready to use, at least 2 hours and up to 1 day.

2. Place the peanut butter, soy sauce, sugar, vinegar, and hot sauce in the work bowl of a food processor. Process until smooth. With the motor running, add the water, 1 tablespoon at a time, until the sauce is the consistency of heavy cream. Scrape the sauce into a large bowl. (Can be covered and set aside for several hours.)

3. When ready to serve, toss the noodles with the peanut sauce and scallions. Sprinkle with sesame seeds and serve immediately.

◆

Cold Sesame Noodles with Chicken and Cucumber

THE ADDITION OF CHICKEN AND CUCUMBER MAKES THIS A GOOD MAIN DISH CHOICE IN WARM WEATHER. A LITTLE FRESH GINGER ENLIVENS THE INGREDIENTS. SERVES 4 TO 6.

- 1 pound fresh Chinese egg noodles (the width of spaghetti)
- Salt
- 2 tablespoons Asian sesame oil
- 2 large bone-in, skin-on chicken breasts (about 1 1/2 pounds)
- 1 tablespoon vegetable oil
- 1 tablespoon minced fresh gingerroot (see illustrations 1–3, page 43)
- 1/2 cup smooth natural peanut butter
- 3 tablespoons soy sauce
- 1 tablespoon sugar
- 1 tablespoon rice wine vinegar

½ teaspoon hot sauce, such as chili paste
or Tabasco, or more to taste

½ cup hot water, or more

1 medium cucumber, peeled, seeded, and
cut into ¼-inch dice (see page 458)

4 scallions, white and light green parts,
finely chopped

2 tablespoons sesame seeds, toasted

1. Bring 6 quarts of water to a boil in a large pot. Add the noodles and 1 tablespoon salt and cook until the noodles are just tender, 3 to 4 minutes. Drain thoroughly and toss with the sesame oil. Refrigerate until ready to use, at least 2 hours and up to 1 day.

2. Adjust the oven rack to the middle position and heat the oven to 400 degrees. Set the breast on a small, foil-lined jelly-roll pan. Brush with the vegetable oil and sprinkle generously with salt. Roast until a meat thermometer inserted into the thickest part of the breast registers 160 degrees, 35 to 40 minutes. Cool to room temperature, remove the skin, and shred the meat into bite-size pieces.

3. Place the ginger, peanut butter, soy sauce, sugar, vinegar, and hot sauce in the work bowl of a food processor. Process until smooth. With the motor running, add the water, 1 tablespoon at a time, until the sauce is the consistency of heavy cream. Scrape the sauce into a large bowl. (Can be covered and set aside for several hours.)

4. When ready to serve, toss the noodles with the chicken, cucumber, peanut sauce, and scallions. Sprinkle with sesame seeds and serve immediately.

Cold Sesame Noodles with Shrimp and Lime

THE ADDITION OF SOME FISH SAUCE, LIME JUICE, AND CHOPPED PEANUTS GIVES THIS DISH A THAI FLAVOR. BUY COOKED AND PEELED SHRIMP FOR EXTRA EASE. SERVES 4 TO 6.

1 pound fresh Chinese egg noodles
(the width of spaghetti)

1 tablespoon salt

2 tablespoons Asian sesame oil

1 small garlic clove, coarsely chopped

½ cup smooth natural peanut butter

2 tablespoons fish sauce

1 tablespoon soy sauce

1 tablespoon sugar

2 tablespoons lime juice

½ teaspoon hot sauce, such as chili paste
or Tabasco, or more to taste

½ cup hot water, or more

8 ounces cooked, peeled shrimp, coarsely
chopped

1 cup mung bean sprouts

4 scallions, white and light green parts,
finely chopped

¼ cup roasted unsalted peanuts, finely
chopped

1. Bring 6 quarts of water to a boil in a large pot. Add the noodles and salt and cook until the noodles are just tender, 3 to 4 minutes. Drain thoroughly and toss with the sesame oil. Refrigerate until ready to use, at least 2 hours and up to 1 day.

2. Place the garlic, peanut butter, fish sauce, soy sauce, sugar, lime juice, and hot sauce in the work bowl of a food processor. Process until smooth. With the motor running, add the water, 1 tablespoon at a time, until the sauce is the consistency of heavy cream. Scrape the sauce into a large bowl. (Can be covered and set aside for several hours.)

3. When ready to serve, toss the noodles with the shrimp, bean sprouts, peanut sauce, and scallions. Sprinkle with peanuts and serve immediately.

JAPANESE WHEAT NOODLES

NOODLES ARE AN IMPORTANT PART OF THE JAPANESE

DIET. MENTION JAPANESE CUISINE AND MOST AMERI-

CANS THINK SUSHI OR FISH, BUT NOODLES ARE EATEN

THROUGHOUT THE DAY AND ARE A VITAL SOURCE

OF NUTRITION AND CALORIES. ◆ JAPANESE NOODLES

are generally made from wheat or buckwheat (for information on the latter, which are called soba noodles, see chapter 31). There are three main types of Japanese wheat noodles—ramen, udon, and somen.

By far the most widely available in this country, ramen are traditionally long, thin, bright yellow noodles (many authentic recipes use eggs and the noodles are fresh), which are commonly used in brothy soups. Unless you shop at a Japanese market, you are unlikely to find this kind of ramen.

Americans (and many Japanese) are limited to experiencing ramen noodles in instant soup mixes. The noodles are dried into wavy bricks that will soften in just a few minutes in boiling water. Most packages of ramen noodles come with flavoring packets. Ramen noodles are also used in the instant soups sold in plastic cups.

While ramen noodles are available in most American supermarkets, udon and somen are much harder to find. Natural foods stores may carry these delicate, white-colored wheat noodles, but a decent Asian grocery store is your best bet.

Udon and somen made by American natural foods companies are generally not as good as the real thing from Japan. Japanese udon and somen are much more flavorful (unlike almost every other kind of noodle on the planet, the dough is made with a lot of salt), and the texture is superior. The American brands that we tested contained plenty of salt but were less wheaty tasting.

Udon are thick, flat noodles (almost as wide as fettuccine) with a slippery, starchy texture that works well in hearty soups. Somen are extremely thin (about the width of angel hair pasta) and can be used like ramen in brothy soups. They are also served iced—the Japanese equivalent of pasta salad.

All three kinds of noodles can be used interchangeably, with some difference in the final dish. We have developed recipes that are particularly well suited to each noodle. However, if you would like to use somen in any of the ramen soup recipes, go ahead. Just make sure to follow the cooking directions for somen (each noodle cooks a bit differently) and make sure to omit salt from the cooking water when preparing udon or somen.

Ramen Noodles

RAMEN ARE SOLD IN cellophane packages in most American supermarkets. They are called "instant" noodles because they cook so quickly, in just two minutes. They almost always come with a separate flavor packet, which we simply throw out. We prefer to make our own broth and add real meat, seafood, chicken, and vegetables.

In Japan, ramen noodles are available fresh and with egg in the dough. We are hard pressed to find fresh ramen in the United States and have to settle for the instant variety. Unlike fresh ramen, instant ramen never contain egg. Be wary of noodles with an unnaturally bright yellow color, which often comes from a list of chemicals and dyes. (Read labels and avoid those with ingredients other than flour, water, and salt.) If you prefer, you may substitute a long, thin Italian pasta shape (such as spaghettini) for instant ramen (increase the cooking time by a few minutes), but then you lose the distinctive wavy appearance and chewy texture of ramen.

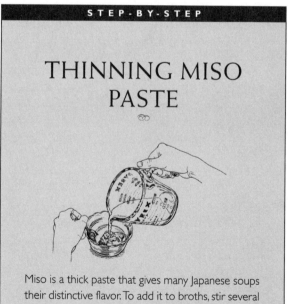

STEP-BY-STEP

THINNING MISO PASTE

Miso is a thick paste that gives many Japanese soups their distinctive flavor. To add it to broths, stir several tablespoons of hot stock into the miso and then add the thinned paste directly to the broth.

The Japanese eat these noodles in brothy soups. We offer two styles—one made with chicken stock, the other with dashi, the quick Japanese broth made from seaweed and dried bonito flakes. (See page 453 for more details about dashi.)

Ramen Noodles with Miso-Chicken Broth

SERVES 4

IN THIS RECIPE, chicken stock is enriched with red miso paste. The miso, which is derived from soybeans and grain, has so much flavor—it is earthy tasting with sweet, salty, and fermented notes—that canned broth is acceptable here, although homemade stock will yield superior results. Red miso paste is available in health food stores and Asian groceries. Miso loses some of its flavor when cooked, so add it at the last moment and don't let the soup boil.

2 large bone-in, skin-on chicken breasts (about 1 1/2 pounds)
1 tablespoon vegetable oil
Salt
5 cups Quick Chicken Stock (page 274) or canned low-sodium chicken broth
4 medium garlic cloves, peeled (see illustration, page 39)
1 2-inch piece fresh gingerroot, peeled, cut into 1/8-inch rounds, and smashed (see illustrations 1–3, page 43)
2 tablespoons soy sauce
1 tablespoon sugar
4 3-ounce packages instant ramen noodles, flavor packets discarded
3 tablespoons red miso (see headnote)
2 scallions, white and light green parts, sliced thin
1 tablespoon sesame seeds, toasted

1. Adjust the oven rack to the middle position and heat the oven to 400 degrees. Set the breasts, skin side up, on a small, foil-lined jelly-roll pan. Brush with the vegetable oil and sprinkle generously with salt. Roast until a meat thermometer inserted into the thickest part of the breast registers 160 degrees, 35 to 40 minutes. Cool to room temperature, remove the skin, and shred the meat into bite-size pieces. Divide the chicken pieces among 4 serving bowls.

2. Bring the stock, garlic, ginger, soy sauce, and sugar to a boil in a medium saucepan over medium-high heat. Reduce the heat to low; simmer, partially covered, to blend flavors, about 20 minutes. Remove the solids with a slotted spoon and discard. Cover and keep hot over low heat.

3. Bring 4 quarts of water to a boil in a large pot. Add the ramen noodles and 1 tablespoon salt and cook until just tender, about 2 minutes. Drain and divide the noodles among the bowls with the chicken.

4. Combine the miso and 2 tablespoons of the hot stock in a small bowl (see illustration, page 412). Stir until smooth. Stir the mixture back into the stock.

5. Pour the soup over the noodles and chicken. Sprinkle with scallions and sesame seeds. Serve immediately.

Hot-and-Sour Ramen Noodles with Beef

THE HOT-AND-SOUR SAUCE FROM A SIMPLE BEEF STIR-FRY FLAVORS A CHICKEN-STOCK-BASED SOUP. IF YOU WOULD LIKE A VEGETABLE COMPONENT, ADD 1 CUP OF OYSTER MUSHROOMS TO THE RECIPE, STIR-FRIED IN THE OIL THAT REMAINS AFTER THE FLANK STEAK HAS BEEN REMOVED FROM THE PAN. SERVES 4.

- 12 ounces flank steak, sliced thin (see illustrations 1–2, page 393)
- 4 tablespoons soy sauce
- 1 tablespoon dry sherry
- 5 cups Quick Chicken Stock (page 274) or canned low-sodium chicken broth
- 4 medium garlic cloves, peeled (see illustration, page 39)
- 1 2-inch piece fresh gingerroot, peeled, cut into ⅛-inch rounds, and smashed (see illustration, page 434)
- 1 tablespoon plus 2 teaspoons sugar
- 3 tablespoons cider vinegar
- 4 3-ounce packages instant ramen noodles, flavor packets discarded
- 1 tablespoon salt
- 1 tablespoon plus 1 teaspoon peanut or vegetable oil
- 1 tablespoon minced garlic
- 1 tablespoon minced fresh gingerroot (see illustrations 1–3, page 43)
- 1½ tablespoons minced jalapeño or other fresh chile
- 2 medium scallions, white and light green parts, minced

1. Toss the flank steak with 1 tablespoon soy sauce and 1 tablespoon sherry in a medium bowl; set aside and toss once or twice as you work on the rest of the recipe.

2. Bring the stock, peeled garlic, smashed ginger, 1 tablespoon sugar, and 2 tablespoons soy sauce to a boil in a medium saucepan over medium-high heat. Reduce the heat to low; simmer partially covered to blend flavors, about 20 minutes. Remove the solids with a slotted spoon and discard. Cover and keep hot over low heat.

3. Combine the remaining 1 tablespoon soy sauce, remaining 2 teaspoons sugar, the cider vinegar, and 1 tablespoon hot stock in a small bowl; set aside.

4. Bring 4 quarts of water to a boil in a large pot. Add the ramen noodles and salt and cook until just tender, about 2 minutes. Drain and divide the noodles among 4 serving bowls.

5. Heat a 12- or 14-inch nonstick skillet over high heat for 3 to 4 minutes. (The pan should be so hot you can hold an outstretched hand 1 inch over the pan for only 3 seconds; see illustration, page 388.) Add 1 tablespoon oil and swirl the oil so that it evenly coats the bottom of the pan. Heat the oil until it just starts to shimmer and smoke.

6. Drain the flank steak and add to the pan. Stir-fry until seared and about three-quarters cooked, about 1 minute. Scrape the cooked flank steak and all the liquid into a clean bowl. Cover and keep warm. Let the pan come back up to temperature, 1 to 2 minutes.

7. Add the minced garlic, minced ginger, and jalapeño. Drizzle with 1 teaspoon oil. Mash into the pan with the back of a spatula. Cook until fragrant but not colored, about 10 seconds. Add the cooked flank steak. Stir in the reserved sauce and stir-fry until the ingredients are well coated with sauce and sizzling hot, about 1 minute.

8. Scrape a portion of hot-and-sour beef and sauce onto each portion of noodles. Pour some broth into each bowl. Sprinkle with scallions. Serve immediately.

Ramen Noodles with Roast Pork and Spinach

A SMALL PIECE OF PORK TENDERLOIN, BRUSHED WITH A
SIMPLE HOISIN-BASED SAUCE AND ROASTED, MAKES A
GOOD ADDITION TO A RAMEN NOODLE SOUP. TO VARY
THE FLAVORS, SUBSTITUTE AN EQUAL AMOUNT OF
GROUND SZECHWAN PEPPERCORNS FOR THE FIVE-SPICE
POWDER. SERVES 4.

- 1 tablespoon hoisin sauce
- 2 tablespoons sugar
- 1½ teaspoons five-spice powder
- 5 tablespoons soy sauce
- ¾ pound pork tenderloin
- 5 cups Quick Chicken Stock (page 274)
  or canned low-sodium chicken broth
- 4 medium garlic cloves, peeled (see
  illustration, page 39)
- 1 2-inch piece fresh gingerroot, peeled,
  cut into ⅛-inch rounds, and smashed
  (see illustration, page 434)
- 4 3-ounce packages instant ramen
  noodles, flavor packets discarded
- 1 tablespoon salt
- 10 ounces spinach, washed and stemmed

1. Preheat the oven to 350 degrees. Combine the
hoisin sauce, 1 tablespoon sugar, five-spice powder,
and 1 tablespoon soy sauce in a small bowl. Brush the
pork with the mixture and roast until a thermometer
inserted into the center reads 160 degrees, about
30 minutes. Let stand on a cutting board 15 minutes.
Slice thin and halve the slices diagonally. Divide
among 4 serving bowls.

2. Bring the stock, garlic, ginger, remaining 1 tablespoon sugar, and remaining 4 tablespoons soy sauce to
a boil in a medium saucepan over medium-high heat.
Reduce the heat to low; simmer, partially covered, to
blend flavors, about 20 minutes. Remove the solids
with a slotted spoon and discard. Cover and keep hot
over low heat.

3. Bring 4 quarts of water to a boil in a large pot. Add
the ramen noodles and salt and cook until just tender,
about 2 minutes. Drain and divide the noodles among
the bowls with the pork.

4. Bring the hot stock back to a boil, stir in the
spinach, and simmer until wilted, 1 to 2 minutes.

5. Divide the spinach among the 4 bowls. Pour the
soup over the noodles and pork. Serve immediately.

Ramen Noodles with Dashi and Tofu

SERVES 4

D ASHI (DISCUSSED FURTHER in chapter 31) is the other broth choice besides chicken stock. Here, a flavorful stir-fry of tofu and cabbage seasoned with garlic complements our mild dashi and noodle combination. Mirin is a sweetened Japanese rice wine used for cooking rather than drinking. Look for small bottles of mirin near the soy sauce in supermarkets with a good supply of Asian ingredients.

4 3-ounce packages instant ramen, flavor
  packets discarded
Salt
1 ½ tablespoons peanut oil
8 ounces firm tofu, cut into ½-inch dice
  and patted dry with paper towels
2 medium garlic cloves, minced
2 cups shredded napa cabbage

6 cups (1 ½ recipes) Dashi (page 453)
¼ cup soy sauce
⅓ cup mirin (see headnote)
1 tablespoon sugar
2 tablespoons sesame seeds, toasted

1. Bring 4 quarts of water to a boil in a large pot. Add the noodles and 1 tablespoon salt and cook until just tender, about 2 minutes. Drain and divide among 4 serving bowls.

2. Heat a 12- or 14-inch nonstick skillet over high heat for 3 to 4 minutes. (The pan should be so hot you can hold an outstretched hand 1 inch over the pan for only 3 seconds; see illustration, page 388.) Add the oil and swirl so that it evenly coats the bottom of the pan. Heat the oil until it just starts to shimmer and smoke.

3. Add the tofu and cook, stirring occasionally, until golden on all sides, 2 to 3 minutes. Add the garlic and cook, stirring, for 30 seconds. Add the cabbage and cook, stirring occasionally, until it begins to wilt, about 2 minutes. Remove the pan from the heat and set the mixture aside.

4. Meanwhile, combine the dashi, soy sauce, mirin, and sugar in a large saucepan and bring it to a simmer. Stir in the tofu and cabbage and simmer until the cabbage is tender, about 2 minutes. Season with salt if necessary.

5. Pour the broth, tofu, and cabbage over the noodles, sprinkle with sesame seeds, and serve immediately.

◆

Ramen Noodles with Dashi and Shrimp

SUBSTITUTE SUGAR SNAP PEAS FOR THE SNOW PEAS IN THIS RECIPE IF YOU LIKE. **SERVES 4.**

4 3-ounce packages instant ramen, flavor
  packets discarded
Salt
6 cups (1 ½ recipes) Dashi (page 453)
2 tablespoons soy sauce

⅓ cup mirin (see headnote to Master Recipe)
1 tablespoon sugar
½ pound snow peas, ends snapped off
12 ounces medium shrimp, peeled
3 tablespoons red miso
2 tablespoons sesame seeds, toasted

1. Bring 4 quarts of water to a boil in a large pot. Add the noodles and 1 tablespoon salt and cook until just tender, about 2 minutes. Drain and divide among 4 serving bowls.

2. Combine the dashi, soy sauce, mirin, and sugar in a large saucepan and bring it to a simmer. Stir in the snow peas and shrimp and simmer until the shrimp turn pink, 1 to 2 minutes.

3. Combine the miso and 2 tablespoons of the hot stock in a small bowl and stir until smooth (see illustration, page 412). Stir the mixture back into the stock. Season with salt if necessary.

4. Pour the broth, peas, and shrimp over the noodles, sprinkle with sesame seeds, and serve immediately.

Somen

SOMEN ARE VERY LONG, very thin white noodles made from wheat flour, water, and salt. They may be used in soups (they would be good in any of the recipes on pages 413 through 416 that call for ramen). These delicate noodles are also used in a unique Japanese summer noodle dish—iced noodles. Note that somen, like udon, are quite salty—we purchased one brand with 6,000 milligrams of sodium in just 12 ounces of noodles—and should be cooked in plain water, without any salt. They are also quite starchy and should be rinsed after cooking.

Iced Somen Noodles

SERVES 4

THIS TRADITIONAL JAPANESE dish is exceedingly refreshing on a hot summer day. The noodles are served in ice water along with a bowl of dipping sauce and some pickled ginger, which is available in most natural foods stores as well as Asian groceries. Each person uses chopsticks (or a fork) to remove a few noodles and then dips them in the dashi-and-soy-flavored sauce. Although this may seem like an unusual way to serve and eat pasta, it is quite delicious. This dish looks best with thin slices of unpeeled cucumber, so buy an unwaxed cucumber.

2 cups Dashi (page 453)
½ cup soy sauce
¼ cup mirin (see headnote, page 416)
1 teaspoon sugar
12 ounces somen noodles
2 cups ice water
½ small cucumber, washed and sliced thin
1 tablespoon minced fresh cilantro leaves
¼ cup pickled ginger (see headnote)

(continued on next page)

1. Combine the dashi, soy sauce, mirin, and sugar in a small saucepan and bring to a boil. Remove from the heat, let cool to room temperature, then refrigerate until cold, up to 24 hours.

2. Bring 4 quarts of water to a boil in a large pot. Add the somen noodles and cook until al dente, about 2 minutes. Drain and rinse under cool, running water to remove excess starch.

3. Place a few ice cubes in a bowl of cold water and add the cooked noodles. Let chill for 2 to 3 minutes and drain.

4. Divide the noodles among 4 serving bowls. Cover each serving with ½ cup fresh ice water. Float some cucumber slices in each bowl and sprinkle with cilantro. Serve each bowl with a cup of chilled dipping sauce and some pickled ginger on the side.

◆

Iced Somen Noodles with Shrimp

COOKED, PEELED FROZEN SHRIMP ARE FINE IN THIS DISH. SIMPLY DEFROST THEM UNDER COOL, RUNNING WATER AND THEY WILL BE ICY COLD BUT THAWED—THE PERFECT TEMPERATURE FOR THIS DISH. **SERVES 4.**

Follow the Master Recipe on page 417, dividing ½ pound peeled and cooked small shrimp among the bowls along with the cucumber.

Udon

UDON ARE WHITE, slippery Japanese noodles that are especially thick and starchy. We like them best in hearty soups, which benefit from their starchiness. However, udon have so much starch, they should be rinsed after cooking. The following recipes have been designed with udon in mind but can be made with ramen or somen. The first two recipes are made with a dashi broth, the next two with chicken stock, and the last with water.

A note about udon. They are made with quite a bit of salt. Some brands (especially those imported from Japan) contain as much as 4,000 milligrams of sodium

per 12 ounces. Even domestic brands (a few natural foods companies sell udon) usually contain a lot of sodium. For this reason, there is no need to add salt to the cooking water when cooking the noodles and you should use salt sparingly in the soup broth.

Udon Noodles in Dashi with Silken Tofu and Toasted Nori

SERVES 4

WE LIKE THE CREAMY texture of silken tofu in this Japanese noodle dish. Make sure to use firm or extra-firm silken tofu; other varieties will be too soft and might fall apart in the broth. The toasted nori (also called sushi nori) garnish is optional but adds a delicious sea vegetable flavor. These thin seaweed wrappers are used to make sushi but can be added to soups as well. Use scissors to cut the crisp sheet of nori into thin strips. Keep in mind that udon noodles are quite salty when seasoning the broth in this and any of the following recipes.

12 ounces udon noodles
1 recipe Dashi (page 453)
¼ cup soy sauce
⅓ cup mirin (see headnote, page 416)
1 tablespoon sugar
4 medium scallions, sliced thin
12 ounces silken tofu, cut into
   ¾-inch cubes
Salt
1 sheet toasted nori, cut in half crosswise
   and then into thin strips (optional)

1. Bring 4 quarts of water to a boil in a large pot. Add the udon noodles and cook until al dente, 4 to 5 minutes. Drain and rinse under warm, running water to remove excess starch. Divide the noodles among 4 serving bowls.

2. Meanwhile, combine the dashi, soy sauce, mirin, and sugar in a large saucepan and bring almost to a boil. Add the scallions and tofu, cover, and remove from the heat. Let stand 3 minutes. Season with salt if necessary.

3. Pour some broth over each portion of noodles and sprinkle with the toasted nori. Serve immediately.

Udon Noodles in Mushroom-Dashi Broth

WHEATY, SLIPPERY UDON NOODLES MATCH UP WELL WITH THE INTENSE FLAVOR AND CHEWY TEXTURE OF DRIED AND FRESH MUSHROOMS. THE LIQUID USED TO REHYDRATE THE MUSHROOMS IS ADDED TO THE DASHI TO BOOST THE FLAVOR OF THE BROTH. SERVES 4.

12 ounces udon noodles
2 tablespoons peanut oil
1 medium onion, minced
12 ounces assorted fresh mushrooms, such
   as shiitakes, creminis, portobellos, and
   buttons, stems trimmed and sliced thin
6 Chinese black mushrooms or dried
   shiitake mushrooms, rehydrated in
   2 cups hot water until softened, strained
   (liquid reserved), and finely chopped
1 recipe Dashi (page 453)
¼ cup soy sauce
⅓ cup mirin (see headnote, page 416)
1 tablespoon sugar
Salt
3 medium whole scallions, sliced thin

1. Bring 4 quarts of water to a boil in a large pot. Add the udon noodles and cook until al dente, 4 to 5 minutes. Drain and rinse under warm, running water to remove excess starch. Divide the noodles among 4 serving bowls.

2. Meanwhile, heat the oil in a large saucepan. When the oil is quite hot, add the onion and stir-fry until lightly browned, about 1 minute. Add the fresh mushrooms and stir-fry until golden brown, about 4 minutes. Add the rehydrated shiitake mushrooms and stir-fry for 30 seconds to bring out their flavor.

3. Add the mushroom soaking liquid, dashi, soy sauce, mirin, and sugar to the onion and mushrooms and bring almost to a boil. Season with salt if necessary.

4. Pour some mushrooms, onion, and broth over each portion of noodles and sprinkle with scallions. Serve immediately.

Udon Noodles in Tomato Broth

SERVES 4

CHICKEN STOCK IS enriched with tomatoes here to create an intriguing fusion dish. The tomatoes are not cooked too long, so they retain as much of the flavor and texture as possible. Peeled fresh tomatoes, in season, can be substituted for canned. Scallion whites add flavor to this simple soup, while the greens are used as a colorful garnish.

12 ounces udon noodles
1 tablespoon peanut or vegetable oil
1 cup canned diced tomatoes
4 medium scallions, white parts minced, green parts coarsely chopped
¼ cup soy sauce
⅓ cup mirin (see headnote, page 416)
1 tablespoon sugar
1 quart Quick Chicken Stock (page 274) or low-sodium canned broth
Salt

1. Bring 4 quarts of water to a boil in a large pot. Add the udon noodles and cook until al dente, 4 to 5 minutes. Drain and rinse under warm, running water to remove excess starch. Divide the noodles among 4 serving bowls.

2. Heat the oil in a large saucepan. When the oil is quite hot, add the tomatoes and scallion whites and stir-fry until fragrant, about 30 seconds. Add the soy sauce, mirin, and sugar and cook, stirring, for 1 minute.

3. Add the stock and bring to a boil. Season with salt if necessary.

4. Pour some tomato broth over each portion of noodles and garnish with the scallion greens. Serve immediately.

◆

Moon-Viewing Noodles

A SINGLE POACHED EGG FLOATING IN A BOWL OF UDON NOODLES AND BROTH IS TRADITIONAL IN JAPAN, AND TRUE TO THE SPARE AESTHETIC OF JAPANESE CUISINE. (THE EGG LOOKS LIKE A FULL MOON, HENCE THE NAME COMMONLY GIVEN TO THIS DISH.) OUR METHOD FOR POACHING EGGS IS FOOLPROOF. TIPPING THE EGGS INTO THE WATER WITH A SMALL HANDLED CUP ENSURES THAT THEY WON'T BREAK; REMOVING THE PAN FROM THE HEAT MEANS THAT THEY WILL BE PERFECTLY COOKED. SERVES 4.

12 ounces udon noodles
1 quart Quick Chicken Stock (page 274)
¼ cup soy sauce
⅓ cup mirin (see headnote, page 416)
1 tablespoon sugar
Salt
2 tablespoons distilled white vinegar
4 large eggs, each cracked into a small handled cup

1. Bring 4 quarts of water to a boil in a large pot. Add the udon noodles and cook until al dente, 4 to 5 minutes. Drain and rinse under warm, running water to remove excess starch. Divide the noodles among 4 serving bowls.

2. Combine the stock, soy sauce, mirin, and sugar in a large saucepan and bring to a boil. Season with salt if necessary. Cover and keep warm.

3. Fill a 10-inch skillet nearly to the rim with water, add 1 teaspoon salt and the vinegar, and bring the mixture to a boil over high heat.

4. Lower the lips of each cup just into the water at once; tip the eggs into boiling water (see illustration), cover, and remove from the heat. Poach until yolks are medium-firm, exactly 4 minutes. For firmer yolks (or for extra large or jumbo eggs), poach 4½ minutes; for looser yolks (or for medium eggs), poach 3 minutes.

5. When the eggs are almost done, pour some hot broth over each portion of noodles. With a slotted spoon, carefully lift and drain each egg over the skillet and place on top of each bowl. Serve immediately.

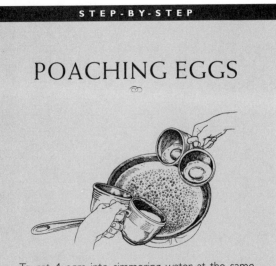

STEP-BY-STEP

POACHING EGGS

To get 4 eggs into simmering water at the same time, crack each into a small cup with a handle. Lower the lips of each cup just into the water at the same time and then tip the eggs into the pan.

Udon Noodles in Clam Broth

MIRIN, SWEET JAPANESE RICE WINE, IS AN EXCELLENT STEAMING LIQUID FOR CLAMS. ALONG WITH THE JUICE RELEASED BY THE CLAMS, THE MIRIN PROVIDES ENOUGH FLAVOR TO THIS WATER-BASED SOUP. **SERVES 4.**

> 12 ounces udon noodles
> 3 pounds fresh clams, scrubbed
> ¾ cup mirin (see headnote, page 416)
> 1 tablespoon peanut or vegetable oil
> 3 medium garlic cloves, minced
> ½ teaspoon crushed hot red pepper
>   flakes
> 2 tablespoons soy sauce
> ¼ cup minced fresh cilantro leaves
> Salt

1. Bring 4 quarts of water to a boil in a large pot. Add the udon noodles and cook until al dente, 4 to 5 minutes. Drain and rinse under warm, running water to remove excess starch. Divide the noodles among 4 serving bowls.

2. Bring the clams and mirin to a boil in a large covered soup kettle. Steam until the clams open, 3 to 5 minutes. Transfer the clams to a large bowl with a slotted spoon, allowing the liquid to drain back into the kettle; cool slightly. Separate the meat from the shells, coarsely chopping and reserving the meat in a small bowl and discarding the shells. Pour the clam broth into a 1-quart Pyrex measuring cup, holding back the last few tablespoons of broth in case of sediment; set aside. (You should have about 1 cup.) Add enough water to make 3 cups.

3. Heat the oil in a large saucepan. When the oil is quite hot, add the garlic and red pepper flakes and stir-fry until fragrant, about 30 seconds. Add the clam broth, soy sauce, and cilantro. Bring to a boil. Turn off the heat, add the clams, and season with salt if necessary.

4. Pour some clams and broth over each portion of noodles. Serve immediately.

RICE
NOODLES

/|\

IN SOUTHEAST ASIA, NOODLES GENERALLY MEANS

RICE NOODLES. THESE CHEWY WHITE NOODLES ARE

POPULAR IN VIETNAM, THAILAND, SINGAPORE, AND

PARTS OF CHINA. RICE NOODLES ARE MADE IN A VARI-

ETY OF THICKNESSES, FROM WIRY AND THINNER THAN

ANGEL HAIR PASTA TO ALMOST AN INCH WIDE. A VISIT

to an Asian grocery in New York's Chinatown revealed at least a dozen widths and as many different brands.

However, if you limit yourself to American supermarkets and natural foods stores (which often carry rice noodles), you are likely to see just two different styles: a thick, flat noodle that is somewhere between linguine and fettuccine and a very thin, threadlike noodle.

It's confusing to try to buy these noodles by name because they are marketed under different Asian names depending on where they were manufactured, including *pho, jantaboon,* and *chow fun.* The English names are no more helpful because they're not standardized; the term "vermicelli" generally applies to thin threadlike noodles, but we have seen the term "ricestick" on these thin noodles as well as on thicker, linguine-like noodles. To further confuse matters, thin cellophane noodles made from mung beans are also marketed as "vermicelli." (For more information on cellophane noodles, see chapter 30.) So don't bother with the names; just look for the shape of the noodle—all of the packages we've seen have been obligingly transparent.

The literature we have read indicates that rice noodles are made from rice flour and water. But some of the packages we've seen list cornstarch in the ingredient list as well as rice flour. In the fabrication of the noodles, rice flour may be stretched with or completely replaced by cornstarch, a cheaper ingredient. We found that noodles made with cornstarch break apart and stick together more readily than noodles made only with rice flour, so if you have a choice, buy noodles made without cornstarch.

Rice noodles are generally used in two kinds of dishes—stir-fries and soups. For soups, we found that either thin, wiry noodles or wider noodles are appropriate; it's really a matter of personal taste. For stir-fries, we disagree with much of the common wisdom found in Asian cookbooks. We find that thin rice noodles tend to stick together into a large, chewy ball when stir-fried. It's much too hard to pull apart these wiry noodles to get the sauce to coat each noodle evenly. We had much better luck with wider, thicker rice noodles in stir-fries.

Stir-Fried Rice Noodles

WIDER RICE NOODLES (at least as thick as linguine) are best for stir-frying since they are more easily pulled apart and coated with sauce. Many sources suggest soaking these noodles, draining them, and then adding them to the hot wok; we found that soaking left thick noodles too tough for stir-frying. Some sources suggest soaking and then boiling, but we tended to overcook the noodles when we followed this procedure. We had the best results by simply boiling the noodles until tender, which took between four and five minutes. This method is also the easiest for American cooks since it mimics the method for preparing durum semolina pasta.

Once the noodles have been cooked, they are drained and set aside until needed in the stir-fry. We found that rinsing the noodles to wash away the starch, as many sources suggest, was ineffective. The noodles still stuck together in one mass as they cooled, and they ended up a bit soggy. We found it better to skip the rinsing step and to toss the drained noodles with some oil to keep them nicely lubricated as they cool. (The noodles can be set aside for up to one hour at this point.)

We tested various oils, including vegetable, peanut, and sesame. All work equally well at greasing the noodles. However, for best flavor we prefer a roasted peanut oil that actually smells like peanuts. We like the Loriva brand, which is far less refined than neutral-tasting Planters peanut oil. We also like to use Loriva peanut oil when stir-frying.

Once the stir-fry sauce and ingredients are in the pan, it's simply a matter of adding the noodles and tossing to coat them with sauce. We found it helpful to pull apart the noodles with a pair of spring-loaded tongs or 2 forks to get them evenly coated with sauce, but we had no real problem with noodles sticking when we followed this procedure.

Stir-Fried Rice Noodles (Pad Thai)

SERVES 4

THE FOLLOWING stir-fried noodle recipes are based on the technique and timing used in this restaurant standard. Coating the noodles lightly with oil before stir-frying prevents too much sticking. Use a roasted peanut oil—which actually smells like peanuts when heated—if possible.

12 ounces thick rice noodles
Salt
¼ cup peanut oil
8 ounces shrimp, peeled and coarsely chopped
4 medium garlic cloves, minced
2 large eggs, lightly beaten
4 tablespoons fish sauce (see page 433)
1 tablespoon sugar
1½ cups mung bean sprouts
4 scallions, white and light green parts, finely chopped
¼ cup roasted unsalted peanuts, finely chopped
½ teaspoon hot red pepper flakes, or to taste
2 tablespoons minced fresh cilantro leaves
1 lime, quartered

1. Bring 4 quarts of water to a boil in a large pot. Add the noodles and 1 tablespoon salt and cook until the noodles are just tender but not mushy, 4 to 5 minutes. Drain thoroughly and toss with 2 tablespoons oil in a large bowl.

2. Heat a 12- or 14-inch nonstick skillet over high heat for 3 to 4 minutes. (The pan should be so hot you can hold an outstretched hand 1 inch over the pan for only 3 seconds; see illustration, page 388.) Add the remaining 2 tablespoons oil and swirl so that it evenly coats the bottom of the pan. Heat the oil until it just starts to shimmer and smoke.

3. Add the shrimp and cook, stirring, for 30 seconds. Add the garlic and cook, stirring, for another 30 seconds. Add the eggs and let sit until just beginning to set, another 15 seconds. Stir, breaking up the eggs with the spatula, until you have only small clumps.

4. Add the fish sauce and sugar and stir for 15 seconds to combine. Add the noodles and cook, pulling them apart with spring-loaded tongs or 2 forks and tossing to coat them with the sauce, until heated through (see illustration, page 427). Stir in 1 cup bean sprouts. Season with salt if necessary.

5. Divide the noodles among 4 serving plates. Garnish each plate with the remaining bean sprouts, scallions, peanuts, red pepper flakes, and cilantro. Squeeze ¼ lime over each plate. Serve immediately.

◆

Vegetarian Pad Thai

TOFU MAKES A GOOD VEGETARIAN SUBSTITUTE FOR SHRIMP IN THIS VARIATION. WE LIKE TO STIR-FRY IT BEFORE ADDING THE GARLIC, TO ALLOW TIME FOR THE TOFU TO DEVELOP A GOLDEN CRUST. SINCE THIS RECIPE CONTAINS FISH SAUCE, IT IS NOT STRICTLY VEGETARIAN. SOY SAUCE CAN BE USED INSTEAD. SERVES 4.

Follow the Master Recipe above, substituting 8 ounces firm tofu, cut into ½-inch dice and patted dry with paper towels, for the shrimp. Cook the tofu, stirring occasionally, until golden on all sides, 2 to 3 minutes. Add the garlic and proceed as directed.

Stir-Fried Rice Noodles with Red Curry Chicken

MOIST, THICK THAI RED CURRY PASTE IS AVAILABLE IN ASIAN GROCERIES AND IN THE ASIAN INGREDIENTS AISLE OF MANY SUPERMARKETS. FOR A FIERY, AUTHENTIC FLAVOR, DOUBLE THE CURRY PASTE. **SERVES 4.**

12 ounces thick rice noodles
Salt
¼ cup peanut oil
2 medium celery stalks, cut into ¼-inch dice
8 ounces boneless, skinless chicken breast, coarsely chopped
4 medium garlic cloves, minced
1 tablespoon red curry paste
2 tablespoons fish sauce (see page 433)
1 tablespoon soy sauce
1 tablespoon sugar
1 cup mung bean sprouts
2 tablespoons minced fresh cilantro leaves

1. Bring 4 quarts of water to a boil in a large pot. Add the noodles and 1 tablespoon salt and cook until the noodles are just tender but not mushy, 4 to 5 minutes. Drain thoroughly and toss with 2 tablespoons oil in a large bowl.

2. Heat a 12- or 14-inch nonstick skillet over high heat for 3 to 4 minutes. (The pan should be so hot you can hold an outstretched hand 1 inch over the pan for only 3 seconds; see illustration, page 388.) Add the remaining 2 tablespoons oil and swirl so that it evenly coats the bottom of the pan. Heat the oil until it just starts to shimmer and smoke.

3. Add the celery and cook, stirring constantly, until it begins to soften, 1 to 2 minutes. Add the chicken and cook, stirring constantly, until it loses its raw color, 2 to 3 minutes. Add the garlic and cook, stirring, until golden, about 30 seconds.

4. Add the curry paste, fish sauce, soy sauce, and sugar and stir for 15 seconds to combine. Add the noodles and cook, pulling them apart with spring-loaded tongs or 2 forks and tossing to coat them with

the sauce, until heated through. Stir in the bean sprouts and cilantro. Season with salt if necessary.

5. Divide the noodles among 4 serving plates. Serve immediately.

◆

Stir-Fried Rice Noodles with Chicken, Chiles, and Thai Basil

SWEET THAI BASIL (SOMETIMES CALLED HOLY BASIL) IS AVAILABLE IN ASIAN MARKETS AND SOME SUPERMARKETS. IF THAI BASIL IS UNAVAILABLE, MINT IS A BETTER SUBSTITUTE THAN REGULAR ITALIAN BASIL. **SERVES 4.**

12 ounces thick rice noodles
Salt
¼ cup peanut oil
8 ounces boneless, skinless chicken breast, coarsely chopped
4 medium garlic cloves, minced
1 medium jalapeño or small fresh hot chile, stemmed, seeded if desired, and minced
2 tablespoons fish sauce (see page 433)
1 tablespoon soy sauce
1 tablespoon sugar
¼ cup minced fresh Thai basil or mint leaves

1. Bring 4 quarts of water to a boil in a large pot. Add the noodles and 1 tablespoon salt and cook until the noodles are just tender but not mushy, 4 to 5 minutes. Drain thoroughly and toss with 2 tablespoons oil in a large bowl.

2. Heat a 12- or 14-inch nonstick skillet over high heat for 3 to 4 minutes. (The pan should be so hot you can hold an outstretched hand 1 inch over the pan for only 3 seconds; see illustration, page 388.) Add the remaining 2 tablespoons oil and swirl so that it evenly coats the bottom of the pan. Heat the oil until it just starts to shimmer and smoke.

3. Add the chicken and cook, stirring constantly, until it loses its raw color, 2 to 3 minutes. Add the garlic and chile and cook, stirring, until fragrant, about 30 seconds.

4. Add the fish sauce, soy sauce, and sugar and stir for 15 seconds to combine. Add the noodles and cook, pulling them apart with spring-loaded tongs or 2 forks and tossing to coat them with the sauce, until heated through. Stir in the basil. Season with salt if necessary.

5. Divide the noodles among 4 serving plates. Serve immediately.

◆

Stir-Fried Rice Noodles with Squid

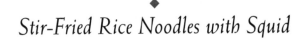

SQUID IS BEST WHEN COOKED VERY BRIEFLY, MAKING IT A PERFECT INGREDIENT IN THIS QUICK THAI-STYLE STIR-FRY. DON'T OVERCOOK THE SQUID OR IT WILL BECOME TOUGH. FOR MORE INFORMATION ON HANDLING AND COOKING SQUID, SEE PAGE 256. **SERVES 4.**

> 12 ounces thick rice noodles
> Salt
> ¼ cup peanut oil
> ¾ pound whole squid, cleaned, rinsed, cut up, and patted dry (see illustrations 1–6, page 256)
> 4 medium garlic cloves, minced
> 1 medium jalapeño or small fresh hot chile, stemmed, seeded if desired, and minced
> 1 tablespoon minced fresh gingerroot (see illustrations 1–3, page 43)
> 2 tablespoons fish sauce (see page 433)
> 1 tablespoon soy sauce
> 1 tablespoon sugar
> ¼ cup minced fresh Thai basil or mint leaves

1. Bring 4 quarts of water to a boil in a large pot. Add the noodles and 1 tablespoon salt and cook until the noodles are just tender but not mushy, 4 to 5 minutes. Drain thoroughly and toss with 2 tablespoons oil in a large bowl.

2. Heat a 12- or 14-inch nonstick skillet over high heat for 3 to 4 minutes. (The pan should be so hot you can hold an outstretched hand 1 inch over the pan for only 3 seconds; see illustration, page 388.) Add the remaining 2 tablespoons oil and swirl so that it evenly coats the bottom of the pan. Heat the oil until it just starts to shimmer and smoke.

3. Add the squid and cook, stirring constantly, until the squid is just opaque, 1 to 1½ minutes. Add the garlic, chile, and ginger and cook, stirring, until fragrant, about 30 seconds.

4. Add the fish sauce, soy sauce, and sugar and stir for 15 seconds to combine. Add the noodles and cook, pulling them apart with spring-loaded tongs or 2 forks and tossing to coat them with the sauce, until heated through. Stir in the basil. Season with salt if necessary.

5. Divide the noodles among 4 serving plates. Serve immediately.

STEP-BY-STEP

STIR-FRYING RICE NOODLES

Tossing the cooked rice noodles with some oil helps them separate when stir-fried later. However, to make sure that they absorb the sauce evenly, it's best to pull apart the noodles in the skillet by using spring-loaded tongs or 2 large forks.

Stir-Fried Rice Noodles with Beef and Broccoli

EGG IS TRADITIONAL IN THIS STANDARD THAI DISH, BUT MAY BE OMITTED, ALONG WITH THE FISH SAUCE (INCREASE THE SOY SAUCE TO 3 TABLESPOONS), IF YOU WANT A DISH WITH MORE OF A CHINESE FLAVOR. SERVES 4.

> 1 small head broccoli (about 1 pound), stems trimmed, and cut into small florets (see illustrations 1–2, page 140)
> 12 ounces thick rice noodles
> Salt
> ¼ cup peanut oil
> ½ pound flank steak, thinly sliced across the grain (see illustrations 1–2, page 393)
> 4 medium garlic cloves, minced
> 2 large eggs, lightly beaten
> 1 tablespoon fish sauce (see page 433)
> 2 tablespoons soy sauce
> 1 tablespoon sugar

1. Bring 4 quarts of water to a boil in a large pot. Add the broccoli and cook until just tender, 1 to 2 minutes. Remove the broccoli with a slotted spoon and set it aside in a bowl. Add the noodles and 1 tablespoon salt and cook until the noodles are just tender but not mushy, 4 to 5 minutes. Drain thoroughly and toss with 2 tablespoons oil in a large bowl.

2. Heat a 12- or 14-inch nonstick skillet over high heat for 3 to 4 minutes. (The pan should be so hot you can hold an outstretched hand 1 inch over the pan for only 3 seconds; see illustration, page 388.) Add the remaining 2 tablespoons oil and swirl so that it evenly coats the bottom of the pan. Heat the oil until it just starts to shimmer and smoke.

3. Add the flank steak and cook, stirring constantly, until it loses its raw color, about 2 minutes. Add the garlic and cook, stirring, for 30 seconds. Add the eggs and let sit until just beginning to set, another 15 seconds. Stir, breaking up the eggs with the spatula, until you have only small clumps.

4. Add the broccoli along with the fish sauce, soy sauce, and sugar and stir for 15 seconds to combine. Add the noodles and cook, pulling them apart with spring-loaded tongs or 2 forks and tossing to coat them with the sauce, until heated through. Season with salt if necessary.

5. Divide the noodles among 4 serving plates. Serve immediately.

◆

Stir-Fried Rice Noodles with Curried Pork

BEEF, CHICKEN, SHRIMP, OR EVEN TOFU MAY BE SUBSTITUTED FOR THE PORK HERE. EXTRA-WIDE RICESTICKS WORK WELL HERE, BUT REGULAR RICESTICKS ARE FINE. SERVES 4.

> 12 ounces thick rice noodles
> Salt
> ¼ cup peanut oil
> 8 ounces pork tenderloin, trimmed of fat and shredded (see illustrations 1–2, page 397)
> 4 medium garlic cloves, minced
> 1 tablespoon minced fresh gingerroot (see illustrations 1–3, page 43)
> 4 scallions, white and light green parts, finely chopped
> 3 tablespoons soy sauce
> 1 tablespoon sugar
> 1½ tablespoons curry powder
> 1 cup mung bean sprouts

1. Bring 4 quarts of water to a boil in a large pot. Add the noodles and 1 tablespoon salt and cook until the noodles are just tender but not mushy, 4 to 5 minutes. Drain thoroughly and toss with 2 tablespoons oil in a large bowl.

2. Heat a 12- or 14-inch nonstick skillet over high heat for 3 to 4 minutes. (The pan should be so hot you can hold an outstretched hand 1 inch over the pan for only 3 seconds; see illustration, page 388.) Add the remaining 2 tablespoons oil and swirl so that it evenly coats the bottom of the pan. Heat the oil until it just starts to shimmer and smoke.

3. Add the pork and cook, stirring, until it loses its pink color, about 2 minutes. Add the garlic, ginger, and scallions and cook, stirring, until fragrant, about 30 seconds.

4. Add the soy sauce, sugar, and curry powder and stir for 15 seconds to combine. Add the noodles and cook, pulling them apart with spring-loaded tongs or 2 forks and tossing to coat them with the sauce, until heated through. Stir in the bean sprouts. Season with salt if necessary.

5. Divide the noodles among 4 serving plates. Serve immediately.

◆

Stir-Fried Rice Noodles with Pork and String Beans

LONG BEANS, A VARIETY OF GREEN BEAN THAT GROWS AS LONG AS 3 FEET, ARE COMMON IN THAI COOKING. GREEN BEANS HAVE A SIMILAR FLAVOR AND ARE USED HERE. SERVES 4.

    ½ pound green beans, trimmed and cut
       into 1-inch lengths
    12 ounces thick rice noodles
    Salt
    ¼ cup peanut oil
    ½ pound pork tenderloin, trimmed of fat
       and shredded (see illustrations 1–2,
       page 397)
    4 medium garlic cloves, minced
    1 medium jalapeño or small fresh hot
       chile, stemmed, seeded if desired, and
       minced
    3 tablespoons fish sauce (see page 433)
    1 tablespoon sugar
    ¼ cup minced fresh cilantro leaves

1. Bring 4 quarts of water to a boil in a large pot. Add the beans and cook until just tender, 1 minute. Remove with a slotted spoon and set them aside in a bowl. Add the noodles and 1 tablespoon salt and cook until the noodles are just tender but not mushy, 4 to 5 minutes. Drain thoroughly and toss with 2 tablespoons oil in a large bowl.

2. Heat a 12- or 14-inch nonstick skillet over high heat for 3 to 4 minutes. (The pan should be so hot you can hold an outstretched hand 1 inch over the pan for only 3 seconds; see illustration, page 388.) Add the remaining 2 tablespoons oil and swirl so that it evenly coats the bottom of the pan. Heat the oil until it just starts to shimmer and smoke.

3. Add the pork tenderloin and cook, stirring constantly, until it loses its raw color, about 2 minutes. Add the garlic and chile and cook, stirring, until fragrant, about 30 seconds.

4. Add the beans along with the fish sauce and sugar and stir for 15 seconds to combine. Add the noodles and cook, pulling them apart with spring-loaded tongs or 2 forks and tossing to coat them with the sauce, until heated through. Stir in the cilantro. Season with salt if necessary.

5. Divide the noodles among 4 serving plates. Serve immediately.

CUTTING UP A PINEAPPLE

A pineapple can seem daunting to peel and core. We find the following method is easiest.

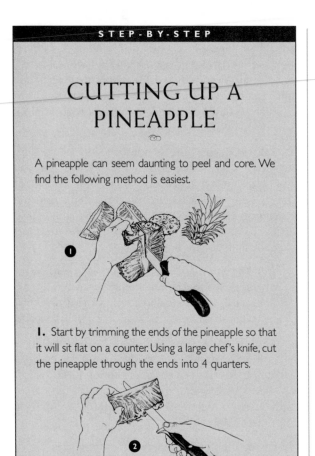

1. Start by trimming the ends of the pineapple so that it will sit flat on a counter. Using a large chef's knife, cut the pineapple through the ends into 4 quarters.

2. Lay each quarter cut side up on a work surface and slide a boning or carving knife between the skin and flesh to remove the skin. Most, if not all, of the brown "eyes" of the pineapple should come off with the skin. Cut out any remaining "eyes" with a paring knife.

3. Stand each peeled quarter on end and slice off the portion of the tough, light-colored core. The peeled and cored pineapple quarters can now be sliced or diced as desired.

Stir-Fried Rice Noodles with Shrimp, Pineapple, and Coconut Cream

FOR GUARANTEED SWEETNESS, LOOK FOR GOLDEN PINEAPPLES AT THE SUPERMARKET. THEIR YELLOW COLOR INDICATES SUPER-SWEET GOLDEN FRUIT UNDERNEATH THE SPINY SKIN. IN OUR TESTING, WE FOUND THAT REDUCED-FAT (OR LIGHT) COCONUT MILK WORKS JUST FINE IN STIR-FRIES LIKE THIS. **SERVES 4.**

> 12 ounces thick rice noodles
> Salt
> ¼ cup peanut oil
> 8 ounces shrimp, peeled and coarsely chopped
> 4 medium garlic cloves, minced
> 1 tablespoon minced fresh gingerroot (see illustrations 1–3, page 43)
> 1 medium jalapeño or small fresh hot chile, stemmed, seeded if desired, and minced
> 3 tablespoons fish sauce (see page 433)
> 1 tablespoon sugar
> ½ cup coconut milk (see headnote)
> 1½ cups fresh diced pineapple (see illustrations 1–3)

1. Bring 4 quarts of water to a boil in a large pot. Add the noodles and 1 tablespoon salt and cook until the noodles are just tender but not mushy, 4 to 5 minutes. Drain thoroughly and toss with 2 tablespoons oil in a large bowl.

2. Heat a 12- or 14-inch nonstick skillet over high heat for 3 to 4 minutes. (The pan should be so hot you can hold an outstretched hand 1 inch over the pan for only 3 seconds; see illustration, page 388.) Add the remaining 2 tablespoons oil and swirl so that it evenly coats the bottom of the pan. Heat the oil until it just starts to shimmer and smoke.

---

3. Add the shrimp and cook, stirring, until bright pink, about 1 minute. Add the garlic, ginger, and chile and cook, stirring, until fragrant, about 30 seconds.

4. Add the fish sauce, sugar, coconut milk, and pineapple and stir for 30 seconds to combine. Add the noodles and cook, pulling them apart with spring-loaded tongs or 2 forks and tossing to coat them with the sauce, until heated through. Season with salt if necessary.

5. Divide the noodles among 4 serving plates. Serve immediately.

◆

Stir-Fried Rice Noodles with Coconut Curry Sauce

RED PEPPER, SUGAR SNAP PEAS, AND NAPA CABBAGE GIVE THIS STIR-FRY COLOR AND FLAVOR, BUT EQUAL AMOUNTS OF OTHER VEGETABLES MAY BE SUBSTITUTED. SERVES 4.

12 ounces thick rice noodles
Salt
¼ cup peanut oil
1 medium red bell pepper, stemmed, seeded, and diced small
½ pound sugar snap peas, stringed
4 cups shredded napa cabbage
4 medium garlic cloves, minced
1 tablespoon minced fresh gingerroot (see illustrations 1–3, page 43)
2 tablespoons soy sauce
1 tablespoon fish sauce (see page 433)
1 tablespoon sugar
½ cup coconut milk (light preferred)
2 teaspoons curry powder

1. Bring 4 quarts of water to a boil in a large pot. Add the noodles and 1 tablespoon salt and cook until the noodles are just tender but not mushy, 4 to 5 minutes. Drain thoroughly and toss with 2 tablespoons oil in a large bowl.

2. Heat a 12- or 14-inch nonstick skillet over high heat for 3 to 4 minutes. (The pan should be so hot you can hold an outstretched hand 1 inch over the pan for only 3 seconds; see illustration, page 388.) Add the remaining 2 tablespoons oil and swirl so that it evenly coats the bottom of the pan. Heat the oil until it just starts to shimmer and smoke.

3. Add the bell pepper and stir-fry until slightly softened, about 30 seconds. Add the peas and stir-fry until tender, about 1 minute. Add the cabbage and stir-fry until wilted, about 1½ minutes. Add the garlic and ginger and cook, stirring, until fragrant, about 30 seconds.

4. Add the soy sauce, fish sauce, sugar, coconut milk, and curry powder and stir for 30 seconds to combine. Add the noodles and cook, pulling them apart with spring-loaded tongs or 2 forks and tossing to coat them with the sauce, until heated through. Season with salt if necessary.

5. Divide the noodles among 4 serving plates. Serve immediately.

Stir-Fried Rice Noodles with Fennel and Spicy Orange Sauce

FENNEL'S DENSE TEXTURE AND SWEET FLAVOR WORK ESPECIALLY WELL WHEN STIR-FRIED. TO REDUCE THE INTENSITY OF THE CHILES, REMOVE THE SEEDS BEFORE MINCING. SERVES 4.

> 12 ounces thick rice noodles
> Salt
> ¼ cup peanut oil
> 1 medium fennel bulb (about 1¼
>   pounds), stems, fronds, and tough outer
>   layer of bulb discarded, remaining bulb
>   diced (see illustrations 1–5, page 154)
> 4 medium garlic cloves, minced
> 1 to 2 fresh chiles, stemmed, seeded if
>   desired, and minced
> 5 tablespoons orange juice
> 2 tablespoons soy sauce
> 1 tablespoon sugar
> 1 teaspoon grated orange zest
> 1½ cups mung bean sprouts
> ¼ cup roasted unsalted peanuts, finely
>   chopped
> 2 tablespoons minced fresh cilantro leaves

1. Bring 4 quarts of water to a boil in a large pot. Add the noodles and 1 tablespoon salt and cook until the noodles are just tender but not mushy, 4 to 5 minutes. Drain thoroughly and toss with 2 tablespoons oil in a large bowl.

2. Heat a 12- or 14-inch nonstick skillet over high heat for 3 to 4 minutes. (The pan should be so hot you can hold an outstretched hand 1 inch over the pan for only 3 seconds; see illustration, page 388.) Add the remaining 2 tablespoons oil and swirl so that it evenly coats the bottom of the pan. Heat the oil until it just starts to shimmer and smoke.

3. Add the fennel and stir-fry until softened, about 3 minutes. Add the garlic and chiles and cook, stirring, until fragrant, about 30 seconds.

4. Add the juice, soy sauce, sugar, and zest and stir for 15 seconds to combine. Add the noodles and cook, pulling them apart with spring-loaded tongs or 2 forks and tossing to coat them with the sauce, until heated through. Stir in 1 cup bean sprouts. Season with salt if necessary.

5. Divide the noodles among 4 serving plates. Garnish each plate with the remaining bean sprouts, peanuts, and cilantro. Serve immediately.

Rice Noodle Soups

A GOOD SOUTHEAST ASIAN noodle soup (the kind you get in a Vietnamese or Thai restaurant) starts with a homemade broth flavored with Asian spices and sauces. The broth is richly flavored but not heavy and is filled with fettuccine-width rice noodles, maybe some paper-thin and barely cooked slices of beef, angled scallion slices, crisp bean sprouts, and lots of whole fresh mint and coriander leaves.

This kind of soup seems like such a terrific strategy for an everyday, home-cooked kind of one-pot meal that tastes anything but everyday. But we kept running into the inescapable fact that a broth of that caliber is impractical because it has to cook for several hours. Even a chicken stock would take at least an hour to make.

Faced with this dilemma in Western-style soups, we usually substitute canned broth, even though it doesn't taste homemade and we don't particularly like its taste. Because Western soups are typically set up something like a stew—sauté aromatics, add broth and whatever major ingredient, season with herbs, and simmer at least half an hour to cook the ingredients through and marry the flavors—by the time the soup is cooked, the flavor of the broth has been substantially transformed by the ingredients cooked in it.

Unfortunately, this model doesn't work for Southeast Asian soups. Asian soups are generally collections of raw and cooked ingredients combined at the last minute in the hot broth like a garnish, with little or no secondary cooking. So whereas the ingredients of a leek and potato soup are cooked until the edges of the flavors soften and merge (and are often pureed), Asian soups are structured in a way that allows the flavorings to remain distinct and separate, just as they do in a stir-fry.

It seemed to us that the Asian model might be well suited to the use of canned broth, but for entirely different reasons. What if we cooked strong flavorings, such as garlic and ginger, in the broth before it was ladled into bowls? Could we punch up and disguise the pallid flavor of the canned broth? It was time to put our research to the test in the kitchen.

From past tastings, we know that canned chicken broth is far superior to canned beef broth. Starting with chicken broth, we added chopped garlic and fresh ginger and simmered for 20 minutes. The flavor of the broth was immeasurably improved, but we wanted to do less work. So instead of chopping, we merely crushed medallions of ginger and whole garlic cloves with the side of a chef's knife before simmering in the canned stock; the resulting broth tasted equally good.

With this base to build on, we experimented with other ingredients to figure out how to get the taste we were looking for. We found that soy and fish sauces added much-needed body and depth of flavor to the broth; fish sauce, in particular, added just the right combination of salt and a musky sweetness. Other ingredients, such as cinnamon stick and star anise, were also appropriate with certain ingredients, especially beef.

We also experimented with lemongrass to determine how best to use it. (For more information on lemongrass, see page 436.) First we chopped it and cooked it in the broth from the beginning. Then we did the same with larger pieces of lemongrass, bruised with the flat of the knife. As a last test, we minced the lemongrass and added it fresh at the end of the process. We settled on bruising, which is both fast and efficient.

Satisfied with the broth, we turned our attention to the noodles. We found that boiled noodles, especially thin vermicelli, had a tendency to get mushy and, if left in the hot soup for any length of time, broke apart.

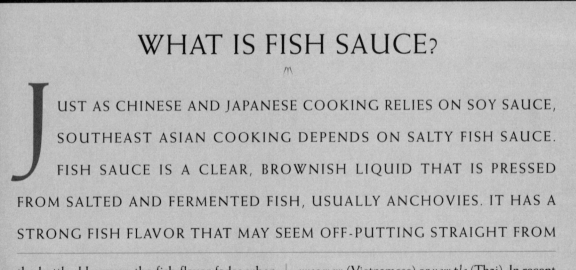

WHAT IS FISH SAUCE?

JUST AS CHINESE AND JAPANESE COOKING RELIES ON SOY SAUCE, SOUTHEAST ASIAN COOKING DEPENDS ON SALTY FISH SAUCE. FISH SAUCE IS A CLEAR, BROWNISH LIQUID THAT IS PRESSED FROM SALTED AND FERMENTED FISH, USUALLY ANCHOVIES. IT HAS A STRONG FISH FLAVOR THAT MAY SEEM OFF-PUTTING STRAIGHT FROM

the bottle. However, the fish flavor fades when cooked, and this sauce adds unusual (and irreplaceable) depth to countless dishes. If shopping in Asian food stores, look for products labeled *nuoc mam* (Vietnamese) or *nam pla* (Thai). In recent years, fish sauce has become a staple in most American supermarkets. It is also sold in natural foods stores.

Ultimately, we settled on soaking the noodles in very hot water—a simple process that did not overcook the noodles. We drained the noodles when they had softened to the point that they were tender but still had tooth. Thin rice vermicelli require just five or ten minutes of soaking. Thicker rice noodles (about the width of linguine or narrow fettuccine) take ten to fifteen minutes to soften up. (You may also boil thicker noodles as directed on page 424. They are sturdy enough to withstand some cooking before they go into hot soup.)

MASTER RECIPE

Quick Vietnamese-Style Broth

MAKES ABOUT 5 CUPS

THE SECRET TO MAKING superquick, Asian-style noodle soups is to enliven canned chicken broth with classic Vietnamese flavorings. Of course, you can use homemade Quick Chicken Stock (page 274) if you have it on hand. This Vietnamese-style broth is used in the Beef Noodle Soup recipe below and has been adapted, with a few small changes, for the other soup recipes in this chapter.

You can also use it in any number of Vietnamese-style soups of your own devising.

> 5 cups canned low-sodium chicken broth
> 4 medium garlic cloves, peeled (see illustration, page 39)
> 1 2-inch piece fresh gingerroot, peeled, cut into ⅛-inch rounds, and smashed (see illustration)
> 2 3-inch cinnamon sticks
> 2 star anise pods
> 2 tablespoons fish sauce (see page 433)
> 1 tablespoon soy sauce
> 1 tablespoon sugar

Bring all ingredients to a boil in a medium saucepan over medium-high heat. Reduce the heat to low; simmer partially covered to blend flavors, about 20 minutes. Remove the solids with a slotted spoon and discard. Cover and keep hot over low heat.

STEP-BY-STEP

SMASHING GINGER

Smash peeled ginger slices with the handle of a chef's knife to release their flavor.

Vietnamese-Style Beef and Rice Noodle Soup

SERVES 4

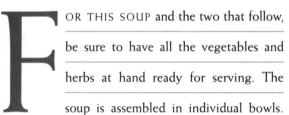

FOR THIS SOUP and the two that follow, be sure to have all the vegetables and herbs at hand ready for serving. The soup is assembled in individual bowls.

8 ounces thick rice noodles
12 ounces flank steak, sliced crosswise into ¼-inch strips (see illustrations 1–2, page 393)
Salt and ground black pepper
1 tablespoon vegetable oil
2 cups mung bean sprouts
1 recipe Quick Vietnamese-Style Broth (page 434)
1 medium jalapeño chile, stemmed, seeded, and sliced thin
2 scallions, white and green parts, sliced thin on an angle
⅓ cup loose-packed basil leaves, torn in half if large
½ cup loose-packed fresh mint leaves, torn in half if large
½ cup loose-packed fresh cilantro leaves

2 tablespoons chopped roasted unsalted peanuts
Lime wedges

1. Bring 4 quarts of water to a boil in a large pot. Off heat, add the rice noodles and let sit, stirring occasionally, until tender, 10 to 15 minutes. Drain and distribute among 4 bowls.

2. Season the steak slices with salt and pepper to taste. Heat the oil in a medium skillet over medium-high heat until shimmering. Add half of the steak slices in a single layer and sear until well browned, 1 to 2 minutes on each side; set aside. Repeat with the remaining slices.

3. Following illustrations 1–3 on page 438, assemble the soup in bowls and serve immediately, passing lime wedges separately.

FRESH LEMONGRASS IS
ALWAYS GREENER

/|\

VISUALLY AKIN TO A SCALLION BUT LONGER, PALE YELLOW-GREEN IN COLOR, AND EXTREMELY FIBROUS, LEMONGRASS IS AN INTEGRAL PART OF SOUTHEAST ASIAN COOKING. IT IMPARTS A RICH, ETHEREAL LEMONY ESSENCE NOT EASILY MIMICKED BY LEMON ZEST. ALTHOUGH EVEN THE WOODY UPPER PORTION OF

the stalk can be used, most often it is trimmed to the lower third, the tough outer leaves stripped away, and the soft inner core chopped or minced. If it is eventually to be removed from what is being cooked, as in a broth, the stalk—leaves and all—can simply be bruised and used as is (see illustration, page 437). This is the approach that we took, for example, in making the broth for Hot and Sour Rice Noodle Soup with Shrimp and Tomato (page 437).

Fresh lemongrass is a staple in many Asian grocery stores, but it is not always available everywhere. We did, however, find it in both dried and water-packed forms in our local grocery store. We thought that these varieties warranted investigation as preparation for those times when fresh lemongrass is unavailable. So we cooked them into broths and compared them with broths made

with fresh lemongrass and lemon zest. Here are our findings.

Fresh lemongrass was the most aromatic, infusing the broth with a delicate, lemony freshness that made it the clear favorite. The next best was the water-packed lemongrass. Although it lacked the crispness and clarity of fresh, this version still maintained lemongrass characteristics. Grated lemon zest finished a remote third. Better zest than dried lemongrass, though. While the broth made with lemon zest was flat and one-dimensional compared with those made with fresh or water-packed lemongrass, it was still, at the very least, lemony. Dried lemongrass was the dog, with a dull, "off" herbal quality; the broth made with it lacked not only freshness but also any lemon flavor.

Hot and Sour Rice Noodle Soup with Shrimp and Tomato

LEMONGRASS IS AN ESSENTIAL INGREDIENT IN SOUTH-
EAST ASIAN COOKING; IT LENDS A SUBTLE FRAGRANT
LEMON ESSENCE WITHOUT HARSH CITRUS NOTES. USE
FRESH LEMONGRASS IF YOU CAN FIND IT. OTHERWISE,
TWO PIECES OF WATER-PACKED LEMONGRASS, BRUISED,
OR ½ TEASPOON GRATED LEMON ZEST MAKE AN
ACCEPTABLE SUBSTITUTE. SERVES 4.

6 ounces thin rice noodles (rice vermicelli)
5 cups canned low-sodium chicken broth
4 medium garlic cloves, peeled (see
    illustration, page 39)
1 2-inch piece fresh gingerroot, peeled,
    cut into ⅛-inch rounds, and smashed
    (see illustration, page 434)
2 star anise pods
3 tablespoons fish sauce (see page 433)
1 tablespoon soy sauce
1 teaspoon sugar
1 stalk lemongrass, bruised (see
    illustration)
12 ounces shrimp, peeled, shells reserved
1 medium jalapeño chile, stemmed,
    seeded if desired, and sliced thin
¼ cup lime juice
Salt
2 cups mung bean sprouts
1 medium tomato, cut into 12 wedges
2 scallions, green and white parts, sliced
    thin on an angle
½ cup loose-packed fresh mint leaves,
    torn in half if large
½ cup loose-packed fresh cilantro leaves,
    torn in half if large

1. Bring 4 quarts of water to a boil in a large pot. Off heat, add the rice noodles and let sit, stirring occasionally, until tender, 5 to 10 minutes. Drain and distribute among 4 bowls.

2. Meanwhile, bring the broth, garlic, ginger, star anise, fish sauce, soy sauce, sugar, lemongrass, and shrimp shells to a boil in a medium saucepan over medium-high heat. Reduce the heat to low; simmer partially covered to blend flavors, about 15 minutes. Remove the solids with a slotted spoon and discard.

3. Add the shrimp and simmer until opaque and cooked through, about 2 minutes. Remove with a slotted spoon; set aside. Add the chile and lime juice, and season broth to taste with salt if necessary. Cover and keep hot over low heat.

4. Following illustrations 1–3 on page 438, assemble the soup in bowls and serve immediately.

STEP·BY·STEP

BRUISING LEMONGRASS

To bruise fresh lemongrass, press down on the stalk with the back of a large chef's knife.

ASSEMBLING AN ASIAN NOODLE SOUP

1. Once the noodles have been soaked in hot water and drained, divide them among individual bowls along with any sprouts or cabbage.

2. Add the meat, seafood, or chicken, then ladle in the hot broth.

3. Sprinkle the herbs and other flavorings of choice into each bowl and serve immediately.

Vietnamese-Style Noodle Soup with Chicken and Napa Cabbage

WE SLIGHTLY ALTERED THE BASIC BROTH HERE, OMIT-TING THE CINNAMON, INCREASING THE FISH SAUCE, AND DECREASING THE SUGAR, SO DIRECTIONS AND INGREDIENTS ARE INCLUDED BELOW. SERVES 4.

> 8 ounces thick rice noodles
> 5 cups canned low-sodium chicken broth
> 4 medium garlic cloves, peeled (see illustration, page 39)
> 1 2-inch piece fresh gingerroot, peeled, cut into 1/8-inch rounds, and smashed (see illustration, page 434)
> 2 star anise pods
> 3 tablespoons fish sauce (see page 433)
> 1 tablespoon soy sauce
> 2 teaspoons sugar
> 12 ounces boneless, skinless chicken thighs, trimmed of excess fat
> Salt
> 1/2 medium napa cabbage, rinsed and sliced thin crosswise (about 4 cups)
> 2 scallions, white and green parts, sliced thin on an angle
> 1/2 cup loose-packed fresh mint leaves, torn in half if large
> 1/2 cup loose-packed fresh cilantro leaves
> 2 tablespoons chopped roasted unsalted peanuts
> Lime wedges

1. Bring 4 quarts of water to a boil in a large pot. Off heat, add the rice noodles, and let sit, stirring occasionally, until tender, 10 to 15 minutes. Drain and distribute among 4 bowls.

2. Meanwhile, bring the broth, garlic, ginger, star anise, fish sauce, soy sauce, sugar, and chicken to a boil in a medium saucepan over medium-high heat. Reduce the heat to low; simmer until the chicken thighs are cooked through, about 10 minutes. Remove the chicken with a slotted spoon and set aside; when cool enough to handle, slice thin. Continue to simmer the broth 10 minutes longer to blend flavors. Strain the broth, return to the pot; season to taste with if necessary. Cover and keep hot over low heat.

3. Following illustrations 1–3 on page 438, assemble the soup in bowls and serve immediately, passing lime wedges separately.

SOUTHEAST ASIAN SPRING ROLLS

/I\

THE SAME RICE FLOUR AND WATER DOUGH USED TO MAKE RICE NOODLES IS ALSO TURNED INTO SHEER DISKS CALLED RICE PAPER WRAPPERS. THESE PAPER-THIN BRITTLE DISKS ARE USED IN VIETNAM AND THAILAND TO MAKE SPRING ROLLS. WE THINK THESE EASY-TO-USE WRAPPERS ARE THE BEST WAY

for home cooks to make any of the popular rolled and wrapped Asian appetizers.

We find that deep-fried egg rolls are better suited to restaurants than home cooking. Spring roll wrappers need only be moistened in warm water to become soft and pliable. They are wrapped around fillings—cooked items like pork or shrimp, thin rice or cellophane noodles, and fresh vegetables and herbs—and served as is without further cooking. Add a simple peanut dipping sauce (which is the traditional sauce in Vietnam) and you are done.

A couple of notes about buying and using rice paper wrappers. You will need to visit an Asian grocery store since most supermarkets do not stock them. Wrappers come in a variety of sizes. We find that really small wrappers are hard to

work with since they hold so little filling. You must make a lot of spring rolls for each serving and the filling tends to leak out of small wrappers. We find that medium-to-large wrappers (about 8 inches in diameter) work best.

Rice paper wrappers need to be softened in a bowl of warm tap water before filling. Ten seconds in the water is enough. An important warning: Leave the wrappers, which should be softened one at a time, in the water too long, and they will disintegrate. Once the wrapper comes out of the water, it should be placed on a kitchen towel. It will continue to soften. In about thirty seconds, it will be pliable enough to fill and fold. If the wrapper is still too brittle, you can always dip it again in the water.

MAKING
RICE PAPER
SPRING ROLLS

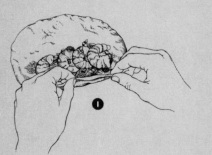

1. Fold up the bottom 2-inch border of a soaked and pliable rice paper wrapper over the filling.

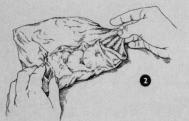

2. Fold in the left, then the right edge of the rice paper wrapper over the filling.

3. Roll the filling to the top edge of the rice paper wrapper to form a tight cylinder. Cover finished rolls with damp paper towels until serving.

Rice Paper Spring Rolls with Rice Noodles and Shrimp

COOKED SHRIMP, LETTUCE, CARROTS, AND HERBS MAKE A TASTY, LIGHT FILLING. THE CHILE GIVES THE FILLING SOME HEAT AND CAN BE OMITTED IF YOU PREFER MILDER DISHES. BUY COOKED SHRIMP OR BOIL SHRIMP IN THE SHELL UNTIL BRIGHT PINK, ABOUT 3 MINUTES, FOR THIS DISH. SERVES 4 AS AN APPETIZER.

2 ounces thin rice noodles (rice vermicelli)
Salt
1 large carrot, shredded
½ cup fresh Thai basil or mint leaves
½ cup fresh cilantro leaves
1 teaspoon sugar
1½ tablespoons fish sauce (see page 433)
1½ tablespoons lime juice
1 medium jalapeño or other small fresh chile, stemmed, seeded if desired, and minced
8 rice paper circles (each 8½ inches in diameter)
4 large Boston lettuce leaves, trimmed of tough ribs and halved
16 medium cooked shrimp, peeled and halved lengthwise
Peanut Dipping Sauce (page 442)

1. Bring several quarts of water to a boil in a medium saucepan. Add the noodles and 1 teaspoon salt to the water and boil until just tender but not mushy, 1 to 1½ minutes. Drain thoroughly and set aside to cool.

2. Combine the carrot, basil, cilantro, sugar, fish sauce, lime juice, and chile in a medium bowl and mix thoroughly.

3. Working with one wrapper at a time, immerse a rice paper wrapper in a large bowl of warm water for 10 seconds. Transfer to a work surface covered with a clean kitchen towel and let stand until softened, about 30 seconds. Center a lettuce leaf half on the bottom two-thirds of the rice paper, leaving a 2-inch border of paper around the bottom edge. Spread a little of the rice noodles along the bottom half of the lettuce leaf. Top the noodles with one-eighth of the carrot mixture and then top with 4 shrimp halves.

4. Follow the instructions for "Making Rice Paper Spring Rolls" on page 440. Serve within 1 hour with the dipping sauce.

◆

Rice Paper Spring Rolls with Rice Noodles and Pork

WHEN USED IN SOUPS, THIN RICE VERMICELLI NEED ONLY BE SOAKED, NOT COOKED, SINCE THEY WILL SUFFICIENTLY SOFTEN IN THE BROTH. BUT IN SPRING ROLLS, IT IS BEST TO BOIL THE NOODLES BRIEFLY (AND SKIP SOAKING) TO TENDERIZE THEM FULLY. IF YOU LIKE, USE THIN CELLOPHANE NOODLES INSTEAD; THEY GIVE SPRING ROLLS A PLEASANT CHEWINESS. WE FIND THAT TWO SPRING ROLLS MAKE A SUBSTANTIAL APPETIZER. IF YOU ARE SERVING OTHER APPETIZERS, ONE SPRING ROLL PER PERSON MAY BE ENOUGH. **SERVES 4 AS AN APPETIZER.**

> 1 tablespoon soy sauce
> 1 tablespoon honey
> 1 medium garlic clove, minced
> 8 ounces pork tenderloin
> 2 ounces thin rice noodles (rice vermicelli)
> Salt
> 1 large carrot, shredded
> 1 cup mung bean sprouts
> 1 teaspoon sugar
> ½ cup fresh Thai basil or mint leaves
> ½ cup fresh cilantro leaves
> 1½ tablespoons fish sauce (see page 433)
> 1½ tablespoons lime juice
> 8 rice paper circles (each 8½ inches in
>   diameter)
> 4 large Boston lettuce leaves, trimmed of
>   tough ribs and halved
> 16 fresh chives
> Peanut Dipping Sauce (page 442)

1. Preheat the oven to 350 degrees. Combine the soy sauce, honey, and garlic in a small bowl. Brush the pork with the mixture and roast until a thermometer inserted into the center reads 160 degrees, about 30 minutes. Let stand on a cutting board 15 minutes. Slice thin and cut each slice into thin strips. Set aside to cool.

2. Bring several quarts of water to a boil in a medium saucepan. Add the noodles and 1 teaspoon salt to the water and boil until just tender but not mushy, 1 to 1½ minutes. Drain thoroughly and set aside to cool.

3. Combine the carrot, bean sprouts, sugar, basil, cilantro, fish sauce, and lime juice in a medium bowl and mix thoroughly.

4. Working with one wrapper at a time, immerse a rice paper wrapper in a large bowl of warm water for 10 seconds. Transfer to a work surface covered with a clean kitchen towel and let stand until softened, about 30 seconds. Center a lettuce leaf half on the bottom two-thirds of the rice paper, leaving a 2-inch border of paper around the bottom edge. Spread a little of the rice noodles along the bottom half of the lettuce leaf. Top the noodles with one-eighth of the carrot mixture and then one-eighth of the pork. Place 2 chives on top of the filling.

5. Fold up the bottom 2-inch border of rice paper over the filling (see illustration 1, page 440). Fold upward again to just enclose the lettuce leaf. Fold in the left, then right edge of the rice paper over the filling (see illustration 2, page 440). Roll the paper-enclosed filling to the top edge of the rice paper, forming a tight cylinder (see illustration 3, page 440). Transfer to a platter, seam side down. Cover with a damp paper towel and repeat with the remaining wrappers and filling. Serve within 1 hour with the dipping sauce.

Peanut Dipping Sauce

THIS SMOOTH, CREAMY, FLAVORFUL SAUCE IS THE PER-
FECT FOIL FOR RICE PAPER SPRING ROLLS. VARY THE
AMOUNTS OF CHILI PASTE AND HOT RED PEPPER FLAKES
AS DESIRED. MAKES ABOUT ⅓ CUP.

½ teaspoon chili paste
1 tablespoon tomato paste
2 tablespoons smooth peanut butter
2 tablespoons hoisin sauce
1 teaspoon peanut or vegetable oil
1 medium garlic clove, minced
½ teaspoon hot red pepper flakes

1. Combine the chili paste, tomato paste, peanut butter, hoisin sauce, and ¼ cup water in a small bowl.

2. Heat the oil in a small saucepan over medium-high
heat. Add the garlic and red pepper flakes and sauté
until fragrant, about 30 seconds. Stir in the peanut
butter mixture and cook to combine flavors, 2 to
3 minutes. If the sauce is too thick (it should be the
consistency of ketchup), add more water, 1 teaspoon
at a time. Serve warm or at room temperature.

CHAPTER 30

CELLOPHANE

NOODLES

/|\

AT FIRST GLANCE, CELLOPHANE NOODLES LOOK LIKE

THIN WIRY RICE NOODLES. HOWEVER, CELLOPHANE

NOODLES (ALSO CALLED GLASS OR SLIPPERY NOODLES)

ARE MADE FROM MUNG BEAN STARCH, NOT RICE

FLOUR. WHILE RICE NOODLES REMAIN WHITE WHEN

COOKED, CELLOPHANE NOODLES BECOME TRANSPAR-

ENT WHEN COOKED (HENCE THE NAMES CELLOPHANE

OR GLASS). ◆ CELLOPHANE NOODLES HAVE ALMOST

no flavor of their own and are generally used in highly seasoned cold salads and soups. Their chewy, springy texture is the main attraction. Because they are so thin, cellophane noodles do not need to be cooked. In fact, when we cooked these noodles for just one minute, they became mushy.

Soaking in hot tap water is a far more reliable method of "cooking" these noodles. We tested various soaking times and found some variation among brands, due mostly to the fact that some noodles were slightly thicker than others. In general, cellophane noodles will soften in twenty to thirty minutes. When the noodles taste slippery and chewy (characteristics prized in Asian noodles), they are ready to be drained.

The drained noodles can then be added to soups (much like rice noodles) or tossed with a highly seasoned dressing to make a cold noodle salad. In either case, make sure to compensate for the blandness of the noodles by using potent dressings or broths.

Cellophane Noodle Salad

SERVES 4

CELLOPHANE NOODLES make an excellent base for warm-weather salads. In the master recipe, a simple dressing of lime juice, fish sauce, and peanut oil moistens the noodles; diced mango and red pepper add color and some tropical flavor. Use a firm, rather than very ripe, mango for the salad for a tart rather than sweet result. Eight ounces of diced cooked chicken or shrimp may be added to turn the salad into a main dish.

8 ounces cellophane noodles
¼ cup lime juice
3 tablespoons fish sauce (see page 433)
1½ tablespoons peanut oil
1 medium garlic clove, minced
1½ tablespoons minced fresh gingerroot (see illustrations 1–3, page 43)
1 tablespoon sugar
½ teaspoon hot red pepper flakes
Salt
1 medium mango, peeled, pitted, and cut into ¼-inch dice (see illustrations 1–4, page 446)
1 red bell pepper, stemmed, seeded, and cut into ¼-inch dice
2 scallions, white and light green parts, minced
2 tablespoons minced fresh cilantro leaves

1. Place the noodles in a medium bowl and cover with warm water. Soak until softened, 20 to 30 minutes. Drain well and set aside.

2. Whisk the lime juice, fish sauce, oil, garlic, ginger, sugar, and red pepper flakes together in a large bowl until the sugar has dissolved.

3. Add the noodles; toss to mix thoroughly. Season with salt if necessary. Sprinkle the mango, red bell pepper, scallions, and cilantro evenly over the noodles and serve. (Can be covered with plastic wrap and refrigerated for 1 day; return to room temperature before serving.)

Cellophane Noodle Salad with Cucumber and Sesame

HERE IS A COOLING VARIATION OF CELLOPHANE NOO-
DLE SALAD, EXCELLENT AS AN ACCOMPANIMENT TO
SIMPLY GRILLED SALMON OR TUNA. TOAST THE SESAME
SEEDS IN A DRY SKILLET OVER MEDIUM HEAT UNTIL
LIGHT GOLDEN IN COLOR. SERVES 4.

        8 ounces cellophane noodles
        2 tablespoons lime juice
        2 tablespoons rice vinegar
        2 tablespoons fish sauce (see page 433)
        1 1/2 tablespoons Asian sesame oil
        1 medium garlic clove, minced
        1 1/2 tablespoons minced fresh gingerroot
          (see illustrations 1–3, page 43)
        1 tablespoon sugar
    Salt
        1 medium cucumber, peeled, seeded, and
          cut into 1/4-inch dice (see illustrations
          1–4, page 458)
        2 scallions, white and light green parts,
          minced
        2 tablespoons minced fresh mint leaves
        3 tablespoons sesame seeds, toasted

1. Place the noodles in a medium bowl and cover
with warm water. Soak until softened, 20 to 30 minutes. Drain well and set aside.

2. Whisk the lime juice, vinegar, fish sauce, oil, garlic, ginger, and sugar together in a large bowl until the
sugar has dissolved.

3. Add the noodles; toss to coat. Season with salt if
necessary. Sprinkle the cucumber, scallions, and mint
evenly over the noodles. (Can be covered with plastic
wrap and refrigerated for 1 day; return to room temperature before serving.) Add the sesame seeds and
serve.

Cellophane Noodle Salad with Chicken and Pineapple

WE LIKE THE COMBINATION OF HOT CURRY POWDER
AND SWEET PINEAPPLE, BUT OTHER FRUITS—MANGO,
PAPAYA, ORANGE, OR GRAPEFRUIT—MAY BE SUBSTI-
TUTED WITH EQUALLY GOOD OUTCOME. SERVES 4.

        8 ounces cellophane noodles
        2 large bone-in, skin-on chicken breasts
          (about 1 1/2 pounds)
        2 1/2 tablespoons peanut oil
    Salt
        1/4 cup lime juice
        3 tablespoons fish sauce (see page 433)
        1 medium garlic clove, minced
        1 1/2 teaspoons curry powder
        1 tablespoon sugar
        1 1/2 cups fresh diced pineapple (see
          illustrations 1–3, page 430)
        2 scallions, white and light green parts,
          minced
        2 tablespoons minced fresh cilantro leaves

1. Place the noodles in a medium bowl and cover
with warm water. Soak until softened, 20 to 30 minutes. Drain well and set aside.

2. Meanwhile, adjust the oven rack to the middle position and heat the oven to 400 degrees. Set the chicken
breasts, skin side up, on a small, foil-lined jelly-roll pan.
Brush with 1 tablespoon oil and sprinkle generously
with salt. Roast until a meat thermometer inserted into
the thickest part of the breast registers 160 degrees, 35
to 40 minutes. Cool to room temperature, remove the
skin, and shred the meat into bite-size pieces.

3. Whisk the lime juice, fish sauce, remaining
1 1/2 tablespoons oil, the garlic, curry powder, and
sugar together in a large bowl until the sugar has
dissolved.

4. Add the noodles; toss to coat. Season with salt if
necessary. Sprinkle the chicken, pineapple, scallions,
and cilantro evenly over the noodles and serve. (Can
be covered with plastic wrap and refrigerated for
1 day; return to room temperature before serving.)

Cellophane Noodle Salad with Chicken and Coconut Dressing

COCONUT MILK ADDED TO THE DRESSING GIVES THIS SALAD A SILKY TEXTURE AND FLAVOR. BE SURE TO SHAKE YOUR CAN OF COCONUT MILK WELL BEFORE MEASURING OUT THE ½ CUP NEEDED IN THE RECIPE, IN ORDER TO GET THE RIGHT PROPORTION OF "CREAM," WHICH OTHERWISE WILL FLOAT TO THE TOP OF THE CAN. IF YOU LIKE, USE 2 TO 3 CUPS OF CHOPPED LEFT-OVER COOKED CHICKEN MEAT RATHER THAN COOKING THE TWO BREASTS SPECIFICALLY FOR THIS RECIPE. SERVES 4.

8 ounces cellophane noodles
2 large bone-in, skin-on chicken breasts
  (about 1½ pounds)
2½ tablespoons peanut oil
Salt
½ cup coconut milk (see headnote)
2 tablespoons lime juice
3 tablespoons fish sauce (see page 433)
1 medium garlic clove, minced
1½ tablespoons minced fresh gingerroot
  (see illustrations 1–3, page 43)
1 tablespoon sugar
½ teaspoon hot red pepper flakes

STEP-BY-STEP

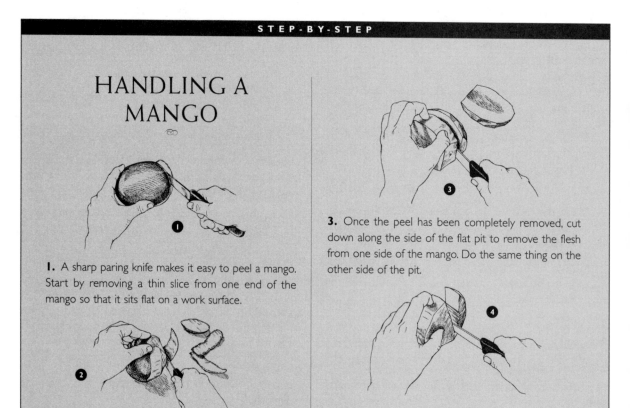

HANDLING A MANGO

1. A sharp paring knife makes it easy to peel a mango. Start by removing a thin slice from one end of the mango so that it sits flat on a work surface.

2. Hold the mango, cut side down, and remove the skin in thin strips with a paring knife, working from top to bottom.

3. Once the peel has been completely removed, cut down along the side of the flat pit to remove the flesh from one side of the mango. Do the same thing on the other side of the pit.

4. Trim around the pit to remove any remaining flesh. The flesh can be chopped as needed for recipes.

---

1 medium mango, peeled, pitted, and cut
   into ¼-inch dice (see illustrations 1–4,
   page 446)
¼ cup roasted unsalted peanuts, finely
   chopped
2 scallions, white and light green parts,
   minced
2 tablespoons minced fresh cilantro leaves

1. Place the noodles in a medium bowl and cover with warm water. Soak until softened, 20 to 30 minutes. Drain well and set aside.

2. Meanwhile, adjust the oven rack to the middle position and heat the oven to 400 degrees. Set the chicken breasts, skin side up, on a small, foil-lined jelly-roll pan. Brush with 1 tablespoon oil and sprinkle generously with salt. Roast until a meat thermometer inserted into the thickest part of the breast registers 160 degrees, 35 to 40 minutes. Cool to room temperature, remove the skin, and shred the meat into bite-size pieces.

3. Whisk the coconut milk, lime juice, fish sauce, remaining 1½ tablespoons oil, the garlic, ginger, sugar, and red pepper flakes together in a large bowl until the sugar has dissolved.

4. Add the noodles; toss to coat. Season with salt if necessary. Sprinkle the chicken, mango, peanuts, scallions, and cilantro evenly over the noodles and serve. (Can be covered with plastic wrap and refrigerated for 1 day; return to room temperature before serving.)

Cellophane Noodle Salad with Charred Beef and Snow Peas

THIS SALAD MAY BE CHILLED BEFORE SERVING, BUT IS ALSO GOOD WHEN STILL WARM FROM THE SLICED STEAK. SERVES 4.

8 ounces cellophane noodles
1½ cups snow peas, ends snapped off
2½ tablespoons peanut oil
8 ounces flank steak
Salt and ground black pepper
¼ cup lime juice
3 tablespoons fish sauce (see page 433)
1 medium garlic clove, minced
1½ tablespoons minced fresh gingerroot
   (see illustrations 1–3, page 43)
1 tablespoon sugar
½ teaspoon hot red pepper flakes
2 scallions, white and light green parts,
   minced
2 tablespoons minced fresh cilantro leaves

1. Place the noodles in a medium bowl and cover with warm water. Soak until softened, 20 to 30 minutes. Drain well and set aside.

2. Bring several cups of water to a boil in a small saucepan. Add the snow peas and cook until just tender, about 1 minute. Drain well and set aside.

3. Heat 1 tablespoon oil in a medium skillet over medium-high heat. Sprinkle the steak with salt and pepper to taste and sauté, turning once, until well browned on the outside and still rare on the inside, 8 to 10 minutes. Let stand 5 minutes and thinly slice.

4. Whisk the lime juice, fish sauce, remaining 1½ tablespoons oil, the garlic, ginger, sugar, and red pepper flakes together in a large bowl until the sugar has dissolved.

5. Add the noodles; toss to coat. Season with salt if necessary. Sprinkle the steak, snow peas, scallions, and cilantro evenly over the noodles and serve. (Can be covered with plastic wrap and refrigerated for 1 day; return to room temperature before serving.)

DICING A PAPAYA

Firm but ripe papayas, which will be sweet but not sugary, are best in savory salads.

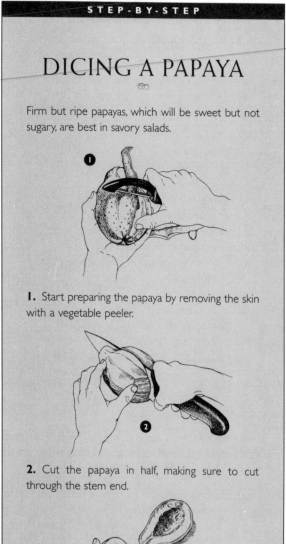

1. Start preparing the papaya by removing the skin with a vegetable peeler.

2. Cut the papaya in half, making sure to cut through the stem end.

3. Use a spoon to scoop out and discard the gelatinous black seeds from each half. Dice or slice as desired.

Cellophane Noodle Salad with Shrimp and Papaya

TO SAVE TIME, BUY PRECOOKED AND FROZEN SHRIMP AND SIMPLY RUN THEM UNDER COOL WATER. **SERVES 4.**

8 ounces cellophane noodles
¼ cup lime juice
3 tablespoons fish sauce (see page 433)
1 ½ tablespoons peanut oil
1 medium garlic clove, minced
1 ½ tablespoons minced fresh gingerroot
 (see illustrations 1–3, page 43)
1 tablespoon sugar
½ teaspoon hot red pepper flakes
Salt
½ pound cooked medium shrimp,
 coarsely chopped
1 small papaya, peeled, seeded, and cut
 into ¼-inch dice (see illustrations 1–3)
1 red bell pepper, stemmed, seeded, and
 cut into ¼-inch dice
6 peeled water chestnuts (fresh or
 canned), minced
2 scallions, white and light green parts,
 minced
2 tablespoons minced fresh cilantro leaves

1. Place the noodles in a medium bowl and cover with warm water. Soak until softened, 20 to 30 minutes. Drain well and set aside.

2. Whisk the lime juice, fish sauce, oil, garlic, ginger, sugar, and red pepper flakes together in a large bowl until the sugar has dissolved.

3. Add the noodles; toss to coat. Season with salt if necessary. Sprinkle the shrimp, papaya, bell pepper, water chestnuts, scallions, and cilantro evenly over the noodles and serve. (Can be covered with plastic wrap and refrigerated for 1 day; return to room temperature before serving.)

Cellophane Noodle Soup with Cabbage and Mushrooms

SERVES 4

L IKE RICE NOODLES, cellophane noodles are excellent in brothy soups. In fact, cellophane noodles may be used in any of the rice noodle soups on pages 435 through 438. They swell quite considerably, so use just 4 ounces of cellophane noodles in recipes that call for 6 or 8 ounces of rice noodles. Since cellophane noodles have almost no flavor of their own, we find that they work best in soups with flavorful ingredients, like cabbage and dried mushrooms. Also, make sure that the broth is highly seasoned to balance the very bland noodles.

4 ounces cellophane noodles
6 medium garlic cloves
5 cups canned low-sodium chicken broth
1 2-inch piece fresh gingerroot, peeled, cut into ⅛-inch rounds, and smashed (see illustration, page 434)
4 tablespoons soy sauce
1 tablespoon sugar
1 tablespoon peanut oil
1 small napa cabbage, shredded
10 dried Chinese black mushrooms or dried shiitake mushrooms, rehydrated in 2 cups hot water, strained, and finely chopped
¼ cup mirin (see headnote, page 416)
Salt

1. Place the noodles in a medium bowl and cover with warm water. Soak until softened, 20 to 30 minutes. Drain well and set aside.

2. Smash and peel 4 of the garlic cloves. Bring the broth, smashed garlic, ginger, soy sauce, and sugar to a boil in a medium saucepan over medium-high heat. Reduce the heat to low; simmer partially covered to blend flavors, about 20 minutes. Remove the solids with a slotted spoon and discard. Cover and keep hot over low heat.

3. Peel and mince the remaining 2 garlic cloves. Heat the oil in a large, deep pot over medium heat. Add the garlic, cabbage, and mushrooms and cook, stirring occasionally, until the cabbage begins to soften, 3 to 4 minutes. Add 1 cup broth and the mirin and bring to a simmer. Lower the heat, cover, and simmer until the cabbage is completely softened, about 5 minutes.

4. Add the remaining broth, bring to a boil, lower the heat, and simmer, uncovered, for 30 minutes. Add the noodles and simmer until heated through, about 2 minutes. Season with salt and serve immediately.

Cellophane Noodle Soup with Minced Pork

PORK TENDERLOIN, CHOPPED AND THEN STIR-FRIED, LENDS A MEATY FLAVOR TO THIS SOUP WITHOUT MUCH FAT. SERVES 4.

4 ounces cellophane noodles
6 medium garlic cloves
5 cups canned low-sodium chicken broth
1 2-inch piece fresh gingerroot, peeled, cut into ⅛-inch rounds, and smashed (see illustration, page 434)
2 tablespoons fish sauce (see page 433)
2 tablespoons soy sauce
1 tablespoon sugar
4 ounces pork tenderloin, sliced thin and then coarsely chopped
Salt and ground black pepper
1 tablespoon peanut oil
2 medium scallions, white and light green parts, minced
1 tablespoon minced fresh cilantro leaves

1. Place the noodles in a medium bowl and cover with warm water. Soak until softened, 20 to 30 minutes. Drain well and set aside.

2. Smash and peel 4 of the garlic cloves. Bring the broth, smashed garlic, ginger, fish sauce, 1 tablespoon soy sauce, and the sugar to a boil in a medium saucepan over medium-high heat. Reduce the heat to low; simmer partially covered to blend flavors, about 20 minutes. Remove the solids with a slotted spoon and discard. Cover and keep hot over low heat.

3. Mince the remaining 2 garlic cloves. Combine the minced garlic, pork, remaining tablespoon soy sauce, and salt and pepper in a medium bowl. Heat 1 tablespoon oil in a medium skillet over medium-high heat. Add the seasoned pork and cook until it loses its raw color.

4. Return the saucepan to a simmer and add the pork and noodles. Simmer until the noodles are heated through, about 2 minutes.

5. Ladle the soup into 4 serving bowls. Sprinkle with the scallions and cilantro and serve immediately.

SOBA

NOODLES

/\\

SOBA NOODLES ARE ONE OF THE FOUR MAIN PASTAS

IN JAPAN (SEE CHAPTER 28 FOR INFORMATION ON

RAMEN, UDON, AND SOMEN NOODLES, THE OTHER

THREE). UNLIKE RAMEN, UDON, AND SOMEN, SOBA

NOODLES ARE MADE FROM BUCKWHEAT. DESPITE ITS

NAME, BUCKWHEAT IS NOT RELATED TO WHEAT. IN

FACT, IT'S NOT EVEN A GRAIN, IT'S A GRASS. THE

whole kernels, which are called kasha, are familiar to anyone with roots in Eastern Europe.

Buckwheat flour has a robust, earthy flavor. Soba noodles are long and thin (like Italian linguine) but have a brownish-gray color. Their hearty flavor works well with strongly flavored ingredients.

There are several kinds of soba noodles. The first choice is between domestic or imported noodles. In our testing, we found that soba noodles imported from Japan are generally much darker in color and have a stronger buckwheat flavor. Many American brands, which are usually sold in natural foods stores, are quite light in color and don't have all that much flavor. No doubt the product has been adapted to suit American tastes.

Our tasters preferred the richer, deeper flavor of the imported noodles, which tasted earthier. If you want bland pasta, there are plenty of wheat-based choices. Soba noodles generally cost $3 to $4 per pound, so we think they should taste like buckwheat.

In addition to point of origin, make sure to read labels carefully. Some brands, especially those made in the United States, may not contain 100 percent buckwheat flour. Again, we preferred brands made with buckwheat and nothing else.

Buying soba noodles is fairly straightforward, but cooking seemed much more complex at the outset. Traditionally, the Japanese cook all noodles (including soba) by a process called *sashimizu*, or "add water." The idea is to add cold water to the pot occasionally to slow down the process. Some sources indicate that Japanese noodles, especially soba, cook through to the core without the outside layers becoming soggy when prepared this way.

We tested and dismissed this technique with wheat-based somen and udon (see chapter 28), finding that they responded best to the traditional boiling method for other kinds of wheat pasta. However, we wondered about soba.

We prepared several batches the traditional way, adding a little cold water every time the water came to a boil. The noodles took about eight minutes to cook after the first boil. We then prepared several batches of noodles cooked as is the custom in the West. The noodles were done in about four minutes and tasted the same.

The next issue was rinsing. Most Japanese recipes instruct the cook to rinse the noodles under hot, warm, or cold water to wash away the excess starch. In our research, we ran across recipes in American cookbooks that did not rinse the noodles at all.

We started by preparing noodles without rinsing, which turned out to be a disaster. While Italian pasta should never be rinsed (the starch on the noodles helps the sauce adhere), soba noodles give off much more starch. We found that unrinsed noodles congealed into a starchy, gluey mass.

When we rinsed the noodles under hot water, we found that they softened further and became mushy. This makes sense—the noodles were continuing to cook. Rinsing the noodles under cold water was fine, but the noodles sometimes cooled down too much and were too chilled when covered with broth. Warm water washed away the starch without further cooking. It also kept the noodles the right temperature when covered with hot broth for soups.

In addition to soups, soba noodles are traditionally used in saladlike dishes.

Soba Noodles in Broth

A FAVORITE USE FOR soba noodles is soup. The cooked and rinsed noodles are placed in a bowl, covered with hot broth, and served. In most cases, other ingredients—everything from scallions and bean sprouts to sliced cooked pork—are added to the broth. However, because each item can be added singly, its flavor remains fairly distinct. This method of soup assembly in the bowl also permits a fair amount of creative license on the part of the cook.

Dashi, a sweet, fishy broth, is the traditional choice for Japanese cooks. We offer a recipe for this quick broth (ready in just minutes). We also found that homemade chicken stock can be ladled over soba noodles to create a quick soup. Because the broth plays such an important role in soba noodle soups, we found that canned chicken broth was unacceptable. Use homemade chicken broth or take ten minutes to make dashi.

Dashi

MAKES 1 QUART

DASHI IS THE classic stock used in Japanese soba noodle soups. It starts with cold water, kombu (dried seaweed), and dried bonito flakes (bonito is a kind of fish). Kombu gives dashi some smokiness, while the bonito flakes give the broth its sweet, fishy flavor. Both products are readily available at natural foods stores and Asian groceries. Dashi is simple to make and best when fresh, so prepare it immediately before using, or refrigerate for several hours but no more. Dashi has a fairly strong, sweet flavor. Many traditional Japanese recipes use even more bonito flakes. However, we found more than ½ cup for every quart of water to be overpowering. You may adjust the amount of bonito flakes to suit your personal tastes.

1 4-inch piece kombu (kelp)
½ cup dried bonito flakes

1. Combine 1 quart water and the kombu in a 2-quart saucepan over medium-low heat. Heat just to a boil. Remove and discard the kombu.

2. Remove the pot from the heat, stir in the bonito flakes, and let stand 3 minutes. Strain the dashi, pressing the rehydrated bonito flakes against the strainer with the back of a spoon. Use immediately or refrigerate for several hours before use.

Soba Noodles in Dashi

SERVES 4

THIS IS THE simplest Japanese soup. Dashi is simply ladled over noodles that have been boiled and rinsed to remove excess starch. On its own, dashi is too plain. However, when enriched with soy sauce for saltiness as well as sugar and mirin (Japanese sweet rice wine) for sweetness, the flavors are quite satisfying and complex. A little ginger and scallions provide another layer of flavor. If you like hot foods, add the optional wasabi paste. If using, divide the paste among 4 small dishes and allow each person to dab his or her noodles with the paste before eating. Wasabi may be served with any of the noodles and broth variations that follow.

2 tablespoons wasabi powder (optional)
Salt
1 pound soba noodles
1 quart Dashi (page 453)
¼ cup soy sauce
⅓ cup mirin (see headnote, page 416)
1 tablespoon sugar
6 scallions, white, light, and dark green parts, trimmed and minced
1 tablespoon minced fresh gingerroot (see illustrations 1–3, page 43)

1. If using, combine the wasabi powder and 4 tablespoons water in a small bowl and stir until smooth. Divide the wasabi paste among 4 small plates and let stand for at least 10 minutes for flavors to develop.

2. Bring 4 quarts of water to a boil in a large pot. Add 1 tablespoon salt and the soba noodles and cook until al dente, 4 to 5 minutes. Drain and rinse under warm, running water to remove excess starch. Divide the noodles among 4 serving bowls.

3. While the noodles are cooking, combine the dashi, soy sauce, mirin, and sugar in a 2-quart saucepan over medium-high heat until almost boiling. Season with salt if necessary. Pour some broth over each portion of noodles and sprinkle with scallions and ginger. Serve immediately.

Soba Noodles in Dashi with Shiitake Mushrooms and Shrimp

SMOKY SHIITAKE MUSHROOMS AND SWEET, BRINY SHRIMP MAKE THE MASTER RECIPE A BIT MORE STURDY. TOAST THE SESAME SEEDS IN A SMALL SKILLET OVER MEDIUM HEAT UNTIL LIGHT GOLDEN IN COLOR. SAVE THE LIQUID USED TO REHYDRATE THE MUSHROOMS AND USE IN OTHER SOUPS, PASTA SAUCES, OR STIR-FRIES. SERVES 4.

Salt
1 pound soba noodles
1 quart Dashi (page 453)
¼ cup soy sauce
⅓ cup mirin (see headnote, page 416)
1 tablespoon sugar
6 Chinese black mushrooms or dried
   shiitake mushrooms, rehydrated in
   2 cups hot water until softened,
   strained, and finely chopped
½ pound shrimp, peeled, deveined if
   desired, coarsely chopped
1 tablespoon Asian sesame oil
¼ cup sesame seeds, lightly toasted

1. Bring 4 quarts of water to a boil in a large pot. Add 1 tablespoon salt and the soba noodles and cook until al dente, 4 to 5 minutes. Drain and rinse under warm, running water to remove excess starch. Divide the noodles among 4 serving bowls.

2. While the noodles are cooking, combine the dashi, soy sauce, mirin, sugar, and mushrooms in a 2-quart saucepan over medium-high heat until almost boiling. Stir in the shrimp and cook until the shrimp are just pink, 1 to 2 minutes. Season with salt if necessary. Pour some broth over each portion of noodles, drizzle with sesame oil, and sprinkle with sesame seeds. Serve immediately.

Soba Noodles in Chicken Stock with Pork and Bean Sprouts

WE LIKE TO SERVE SOBA NOODLES AND PORK WITH HOMEMADE CHICKEN STOCK. TO OUR WESTERN PALATES, RICHER CHICKEN STOCK WORKS BETTER WITH PORK THAN THE TRADITIONAL DASHI. HOWEVER, YOU MAY SUBSTITUTE AN EQUAL AMOUNT OF DASHI FOR A LIGHTER, MORE AUTHENTIC-TASTING DISH. SERVES 4.

2 tablespoons soy sauce
2 teaspoons honey
1 pork tenderloin (about ¾ pound)
Salt
1 pound soba noodles
1 quart Quick Chicken Stock (page 274)
1 tablespoon lemon juice
1 small jalapeño or other fresh chile,
   stemmed, seeded, and minced
1½ cups mung bean sprouts
6 scallions, white, light, and dark green
   parts, trimmed and minced
1 tablespoon minced pickled ginger
   (optional)

1. Preheat the broiler. Combine 1 tablespoon soy sauce and the honey in a small bowl. Brush the pork tenderloin with the mixture. Broil until the pork is just slightly pink at the center, 10 to 12 minutes, turning once. Set aside and let rest.

2. Bring 4 quarts of water to a boil in large pot. Add 1 tablespoon salt and the soba noodles and cook until al dente, 4 to 5 minutes. Drain and rinse under warm, running water to remove excess starch. Divide the noodles among 4 serving bowls.

3. While the noodles are cooking, combine the stock, remaining tablespoon soy sauce, lemon juice, and chile in a 2-quart saucepan over medium-high heat until almost boiling. Season with salt if necessary.

4. Divide the bean sprouts among the 4 serving bowls. Cut the tenderloin into ¼-inch slices and divide among the 4 serving bowls. Pour some broth over each portion of noodles and sprinkle with scallions and pickled ginger if using. Serve immediately.

Stir-Fried Soba Noodles

THIS DISH IS NOT at all authentic, but the hearty flavor of soba noodles works beautifully in a stir-fry with spicy leafy greens. Chinese wheat noodles can be used in place of the soba noodles here. If you really like soba noodles, try using them in any of the wheat noodle stir-fries on pages 388 through 405. We find that buckwheat noodles are a bit starchy for stir-fries, and with the exception of the following recipe, we prefer to use wheat noodles. But noodle stir-fries will certainly work with soba noodles.

◆

Soba Noodles with Spicy Greens

USE BROCCOLI RABE, CHINESE BROCCOLI, KALE, OR BOK CHOY, ADJUSTING THE COOKING TIME AS NECESSARY. DEPENDING ON HOW MUCH OF THE STEM IS ATTACHED, YOU WILL NEED BETWEEN 1 AND 1½ POUNDS OF GREENS TO YIELD THE NECESSARY 8 CUPS OF CHOPPED LEAVES. SERVES 4.

Salt
1 pound soba noodles
1 tablespoon peanut oil
1 tablespoon Asian sesame oil
4 medium garlic cloves, minced
1 teaspoon hot red pepper flakes
About 1¼ pounds leafy greens (see headnote), tough stems discarded and leaves cut into 1-inch pieces (about 8 cups)
¼ cup mirin (see headnote, page 416) or sherry
2 tablespoons soy sauce

1. Bring 4 quarts of water to a boil in a large pot. Add 1 tablespoon salt and the soba noodles and cook until al dente, 4 to 5 minutes. Drain and rinse under warm, running water to remove excess starch. Drain again well. Set the noodles aside.

2. Heat the oils in a large nonstick skillet. When the oils are quite hot, add the garlic and red pepper flakes and stir-fry until fragrant, about 20 seconds. Add the greens and cook, stirring to coat with oil, about 30 seconds. Add the mirin and ½ cup water, cover, and cook until the greens are tender, 2 to 4 minutes.

3. Uncover the pan and add the soba noodles and soy sauce. Stir-fry to combine ingredients and reheat noodles, about 1 minute. Serve immediately.

Soba Noodle Salads

COOKED AND RINSED soba noodles may be dressed with a simple but vibrantly flavored dressing and then served warm, at room temperature, or chilled. Any combination of vegetables, meat, and seafood may be added to the dressed noodles to vary the dish. We found it worked best to add these additional ingredients just before serving to prevent the noodles from losing their distinct texture and flavor.

MASTER RECIPE

Soba Noodle Salad

SERVES 4

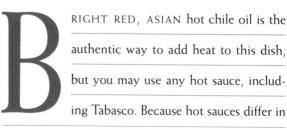

RIGHT RED, ASIAN hot chile oil is the authentic way to add heat to this dish, but you may use any hot sauce, including Tabasco. Because hot sauces differ in intensity, you may need to adjust the amount.

¼ cup vegetable oil

2 tablespoons lemon juice

1 tablespoon soy sauce

1 tablespoon Asian sesame oil

2 teaspoons Asian hot chile oil

1 small garlic clove, minced

1 teaspoon minced fresh gingerroot (see illustrations 1–3, page 43)

1 tablespoon minced pickled ginger

Salt

1 pound soba noodles

2 tablespoons minced fresh cilantro leaves

2 medium scallions, white and light green parts, cut into thin rings

1. Bring 4 quarts of water to a boil in a large pot for cooking the noodles.

2. Place the oil, lemon juice, soy sauce, sesame oil, chile oil, garlic, and both gingers in the work bowl of a small food processor or blender. Process until smooth. Adjust the seasonings, adding salt if necessary. (Can be refrigerated up to 4 hours.)

3. Add 1 tablespoon salt and the soba noodles to the boiling water and cook until al dente, 4 to 5 minutes. Drain and rinse under warm, running water to remove excess starch. Drain again well.

4. Toss the noodles, sauce, cilantro, and scallions in a large bowl. Mix well and adjust the seasonings. Serve immediately or refrigerate and serve chilled.

◆

Soba Noodle Salad with Stir-Fried Flank Steak

THE ADDITION OF STIR-FRIED FLANK STEAK TURNS SOBA NOODLE SALAD INTO A MAIN COURSE. AN EQUAL AMOUNT OF STIR-FRIED CHICKEN, PORK, OR SHRIMP MAY BE SUBSTITUTED FOR THE FLANK STEAK IF YOU LIKE. SERVES 4.

½ pound flank steak, sliced against the grain into thin strips (see illustrations 1–2, page 393)

2 tablespoons soy sauce

1 tablespoon dry sherry

5 tablespoons vegetable oil

2 tablespoons lime juice

1 tablespoon Asian sesame oil

2 teaspoons Asian hot chile oil

1 small garlic clove, minced

1 teaspoon minced fresh gingerroot (see illustrations 1–3, page 43)

Salt

1 pound soba noodles

2 tablespoons minced fresh cilantro leaves

2 medium scallions, white and light green parts, cut into thin rings

1. Toss the flank steak with 1 tablespoon soy sauce and the sherry in a medium bowl; set aside and toss once or twice as you work on the rest of the recipe.

2. Place 4 tablespoons oil, the lime juice, remaining 1 tablespoon soy sauce, sesame oil, chile oil, garlic, and ginger in the work bowl of a small food processor or blender. Process until smooth. Adjust the seasonings, adding salt if necessary. (Can be refrigerated up to 4 hours.)

3. Bring 4 quarts of water to a boil in a large pot. Add 1 tablespoon salt and the soba noodles and cook until al dente, 4 to 5 minutes. Drain and rinse under warm, running water to remove excess starch. Drain again well. Toss the noodles and sauce in a large bowl. Mix well; refrigerate if serving chilled.

4. Heat a 12-inch nonstick skillet over high heat for 3 to 4 minutes. Hold a hand 1 inch over the pan. When the pan is so hot you can keep your hand there for only 3 seconds (see illustration, page 388), add the remaining tablespoon of oil and heat until it just starts to shimmer and smoke.

5. Drain the meat and add to the hot pan. Cook, stirring constantly, until it has lost its pink color, about 2 minutes.

6. Divide the noodles among 4 serving bowls and top each with a portion of the flank steak. Sprinkle with the cilantro and scallions and serve immediately.

Soba and Spinach Salad with Chile-Lime Dressing

COOKING THE SOBA NOODLES AND SPINACH TO-
GETHER SAVES TIME AND EFFORT SINCE ONLY ONE POT
IS REQUIRED. AN EQUAL AMOUNT OF LINGUINE OR
SPAGHETTI MAY BE SUBSTITUTED FOR THE SOBA.
SERVES 4.

> 2 tablespoons lime juice
> 1 small garlic clove, peeled (see
>   illustration, page 39)
> 12 large fresh mint leaves, minced
> 1 jalapeño or other fresh chile, stemmed,
>   seeded if desired, and minced
> 1 teaspoon honey
> ¼ cup canola oil
> Salt
> 1 pound soba noodles
> 6 cups packed spinach leaves, stemmed
>   and roughly chopped
> 2 cups mung bean sprouts
> 1 red bell pepper, cored, seeded, and
>   minced

1. Bring 4 quarts of water to a boil in a large pot for cooking the noodles.

2. Place the lime juice, garlic, mint, chile, honey, and oil in the work bowl of a small food processor or blender. Process, scraping down the sides of the bowl as needed, until the dressing is smooth. Add salt to taste and set the dressing aside.

3. Add 1 tablespoon salt and the soba noodles to the boiling water. Cook until the soba noodles are almost al dente, about 4 minutes. Add the spinach and continue cooking until the soba noodles are al dente and the spinach is tender, about 1 minute. Drain and rinse under warm, running water to remove excess starch.

4. Toss the noodles and sauce in a large bowl. Mix well; refrigerate if serving chilled.

5. Divide the noodles among 4 serving bowls and top each with some sprouts and red bell pepper. Serve immediately.

SEEDING A CUCUMBER

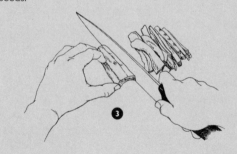

1. Peel and halve the cucumber lengthwise.

2. Use a small spoon to scoop out and discard the seeds.

3. Cut the seeded cucumber crosswise into 2-inch chunks and then into long, thin strips.

Soba Noodle Salad with Spicy Sesame Sauce

TAHINI TAKES THE PLACE OF VEGETABLE OIL IN THE DRESSING HERE TO GIVE THIS DISH A SESAME FLAVOR. CUCUMBER, BEAN SPROUTS, AND SCALLIONS ADD CRUNCH AND COLOR TO THIS SALAD, WHICH IS SERVED LIGHTLY CHILLED. **SERVES 4.**

¼ cup tahini (sesame paste)
2 tablespoons lemon juice
1 tablespoon soy sauce
1 tablespoon Asian sesame oil
2 teaspoons Asian hot chile oil
Salt
1 pound soba noodles
1 medium cucumber, peeled, seeded, and cut into thin 2-inch-long strips (see illustrations 1–3, page 458)
1 cup mung bean sprouts
2 medium scallions, white and light green parts, cut into thin rings

1. Bring 4 quarts of water to a boil in a large pot for cooking the noodles.

2. Place the tahini, juice, soy sauce, and both oils in the work bowl of a small food processor or blender. Process until smooth. Adjust the seasonings, adding salt if necessary. (Can be refrigerated up to 4 hours.)

3. Add 1 tablespoon salt and the soba noodles to the boiling water. Cook until al dente, 4 to 5 minutes. Drain and rinse under warm, running water to remove excess starch. Drain again well.

4. Toss the noodles and sauce in a large bowl. Mix well; refrigerate if serving chilled.

5. Divide the noodles among 4 serving bowls and top each with some cucumber, sprouts, and scallions. Serve immediately.

Soba Noodle Salad with Fusion Pesto

THIS LIGHT DISH TAKES ITS CUES FROM ITALIAN BASIL PESTO. ALTHOUGH THE TEXTURE OF THE SAUCE IS THICK AND CREAMY LIKE THE ORIGINAL, THE FLAVORS ARE DIFFERENT. THIS VERSION GETS SOME SWEETNESS FROM THE MIRIN AND SOME HEAT FROM THE GINGER AND HOT PEPPER FLAKES. THE PEANUT OIL, SOY SAUCE, AND CILANTRO ALSO ADD AN ASIAN TWIST. **SERVES 4.**

Salt
1 pound soba noodles
2 tablespoons pine nuts, walnuts, or almonds
1 small garlic clove, peeled (see illustration, page 39)
½-inch-square piece peeled fresh gingerroot, sliced
1 cup packed fresh basil leaves
1 cup packed fresh cilantro leaves
½ teaspoon hot red pepper flakes, or to taste
2 tablespoons peanut oil
2 tablespoons mirin or sherry
1 tablespoon soy sauce

1. Bring 4 quarts of water to a boil in a large pot. Add 1 tablespoon salt and the noodles and cook until al dente, 4 to 5 minutes. Drain and rinse under warm, running water to remove excess starch. Drain again well. Set the noodles aside in a large bowl.

2. Meanwhile, place the nuts, garlic, ginger, basil, cilantro, and red pepper flakes in a blender or food processor. Process, scraping down the sides of the bowl as necessary, until the ingredients are finely ground. Add the oil, mirin, and soy sauce and puree until smooth.

3. Scrape the pesto into the bowl with the noodles. Toss to coat the noodles with the pesto and serve immediately or refrigerate and serve chilled.

INDEX

/∖

T

tagliatelle
  with Crabmeat and Cream Sauce,
    238
  see also fettuccine, fresh
taglierini, 4, 29
tahini, 407
Taleggio, Buckwheat Pasta with
    Spinach, Potato, and, 338
tamari, 386
taste tests
  canned beans, 186
  canned tomatoes, 119–20, 124
  dried egg fettuccine, 182
  dried spaghetti, 10
  olive oils, 41
toasted bread crumbs
  adding to pasta, 89–90
  best ways to make, 88–89
  fusilli with
    Dried Figs, Orange, Sage, and,
      95
    Sun-Dried Tomatoes and, 96
  Master Recipe, 90
    with Cracked Black Pepper, 92
    with Herbs and Lemon Zest, 90
    with Orange and Sage, 91
    with White Whine and Butter,
      92
  Spaghetti with, 92–93
    and Asparagus, 139
    Capers, Olives, and Anchovies,
      94
    and Cracked Black Pepper, 94
    and Golden Raisins, 95
    Herbs, and Lemon Zest, 93
    Oil, and Garlic, 92–93
    and Sardines, 249
    and Scallops, 250–51
    White Wine, and Butter, 93
tofu
  Baked, and Hot-and-Sour Sauce,
    Stir-Fried Chinese Noodles
    with, 405
  Ramen Noodles with Dashi and,
    416
  Silken, Udon Noodles in Dashi
    with Toasted Nori and,
    418–19
  Vegetarian Pad Thai, 425

tomato(es)
  Baked Ziti with Mozzarella and,
    294
  Broth, Udon Noodles in, 420
  canned, seeding, *136*
  canned, types of, 124
  Chicken Soup with Pasta Shells,
    Zucchini, and, 278–79
  -Chipotle Sauce, Penne with
    Black Beans and, 192
  -Cream Sauce, Linguine with
    Leeks, 164
  -Cream Sauce, Spinach and
    Ricotta Gnocchi with, 376
  Farfalle with Fresh Salmon and,
    240–41
  Farfalle with Grilled Zucchini
    and, 180
  Farfalle with Sole or Flounder, 241
  for bolognese sauce, 198–99
  for chicken-based sauces, 218, 221
  for lasagne, 304, 311, 318
  for quick ground meat sauces, 203
  for ribs and chops sauces, 211
  for sauces with meatballs, 210
  for sausage-based sauces, 206
  fresh, peeling, *111, 112*
  fresh, seeding, *98, 110, 111, 112*
  Fusilli with Braised Chicken,
    Peppers, and, 220
  in casseroles with mozzarella,
    293–95
  Linguine with Asparagus and, 138
  Linguine with Clam Sauce with
    Garlic and, 236
  Linguine with Shrimp, Capers,
    and, 253
  Macaroni and Cheese with Bacon
    and, 287
  -Mint Sauce, Potato Gnocchi
    with, 372
  and Mozzarella Cannelloni,
    334–35
  Orecchiette with Fava Beans,
    Pancetta, and, 152
  Pasta, 28
  Pasta alla Norma, 149
  Pasta Salad with Eggplant, Basil,
    and, 265
  and Pasta Soup, 275

paste, 124
Paste, Spaghetti with Oil, Garlic,
    and, 50
peeling, 110
Penne with Lentils, Carrots, and,
    195
Penne with White Beans,
    Potatoes, and, 189
—Porcini Mushroom Sauce, Fusilli
    with, 168
preparing for salads, 264
Raw, Fusilli with Chopped
    Arugula and, 135
-Saffron Sauce, Fusilli with
    Lobster and, 242–43
Sauce, Fettuccine with Zucchini,
    Red Pepper, and, 178–79
Sauce, Garden, 353
Sauce, Spicy, Spaghetti with
    Braised Squid and, 257
Sauce, Ziti with Braised Chicken
    Thighs in, 219
Spaghetti with Braised Artichokes
    and, 132–33
Spaghetti with Tender Greens,
    Cumin, Cilantro, and, 161
see also sun-dried tomato(es);
    tomato sauce
tomato sauce (fresh)
  best pasta shapes for, 112
  best tomatoes for, 110–11
  best way to make, 111–12
  Farfalle with and Aromatic
    Vegetables, 114
  Fusilli with Bell Pepper and, 116
  Fusilli with Butter, Onions, and,
    114
  Fusilli with Cream and, 115
  Fusilli with Fontina and, 116
  Penne with, 113
  Penne with Mint and, 113–14
  Penne with Pancetta and, 115
tomato sauce (raw)
  added to pasta salads, 262
  best pasta shapes for, 99
  best tomatoes for, 97, 98
  best way to make, 98–99
  Fusilli with Avocado and, 107
  Fusilli with Corn and, 103
  Fusilli with Mozzarella and, 108